BATMAN
BIRTH OF THE DEMON

Mike W. Barr
Dennis O'Neil
Writers

Jerry Bingham
Tom Grindberg
Norm Breyfogle
Artists

Jerry Bingham
Eva Grindberg
Norm Breyfogle
Colorists

John Costanza
Gaspar Saladino
Ken Bruzenak
Letterers

Andy Kubert
Collection Cover Artist

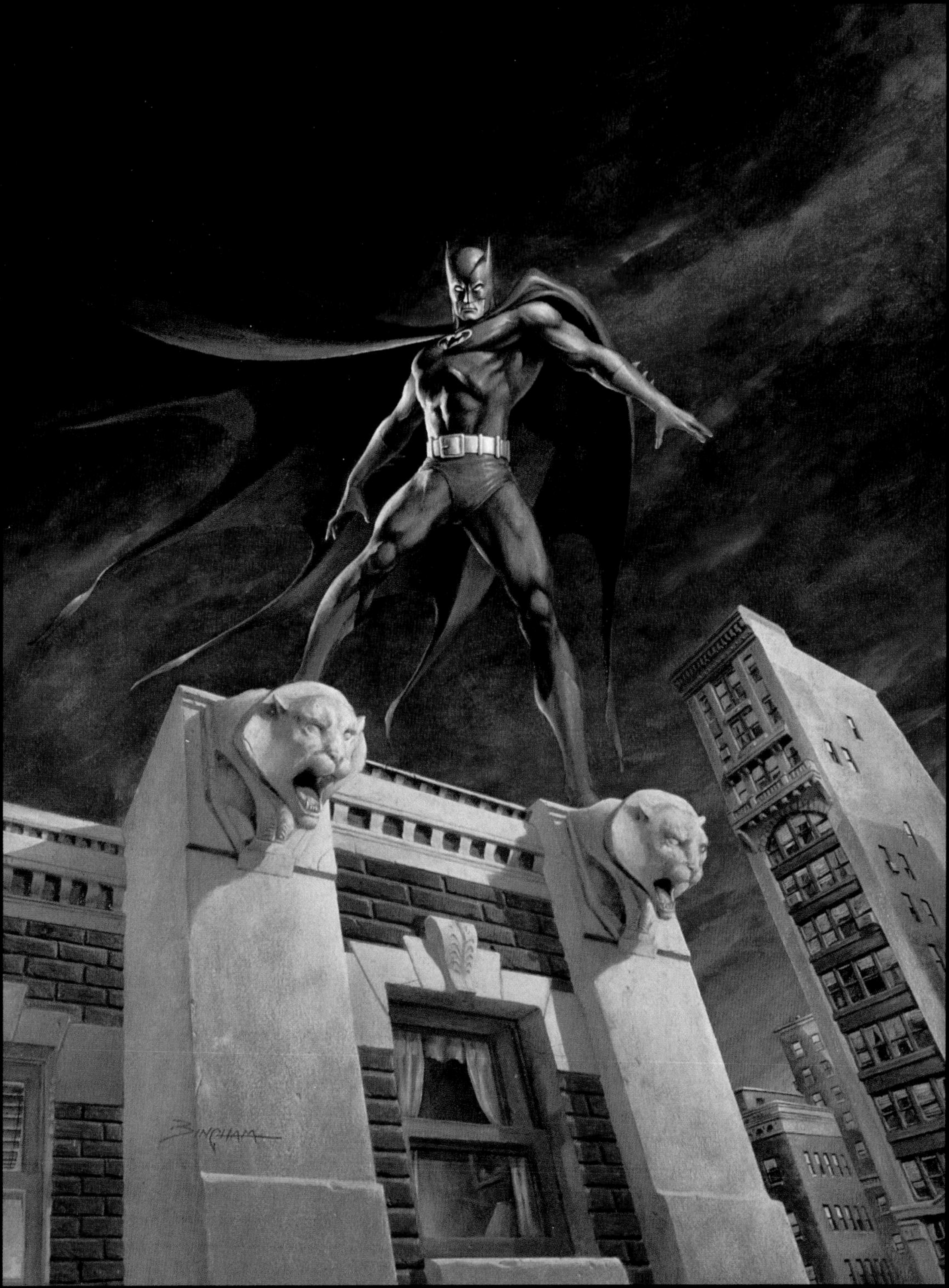
BINGHAM

BATMAN
SON OF THE DEMON

Mike W. Barr   *Writer*

Jerry Bingham   *Art, Colors & Cover*

John Costanza   *Letters*

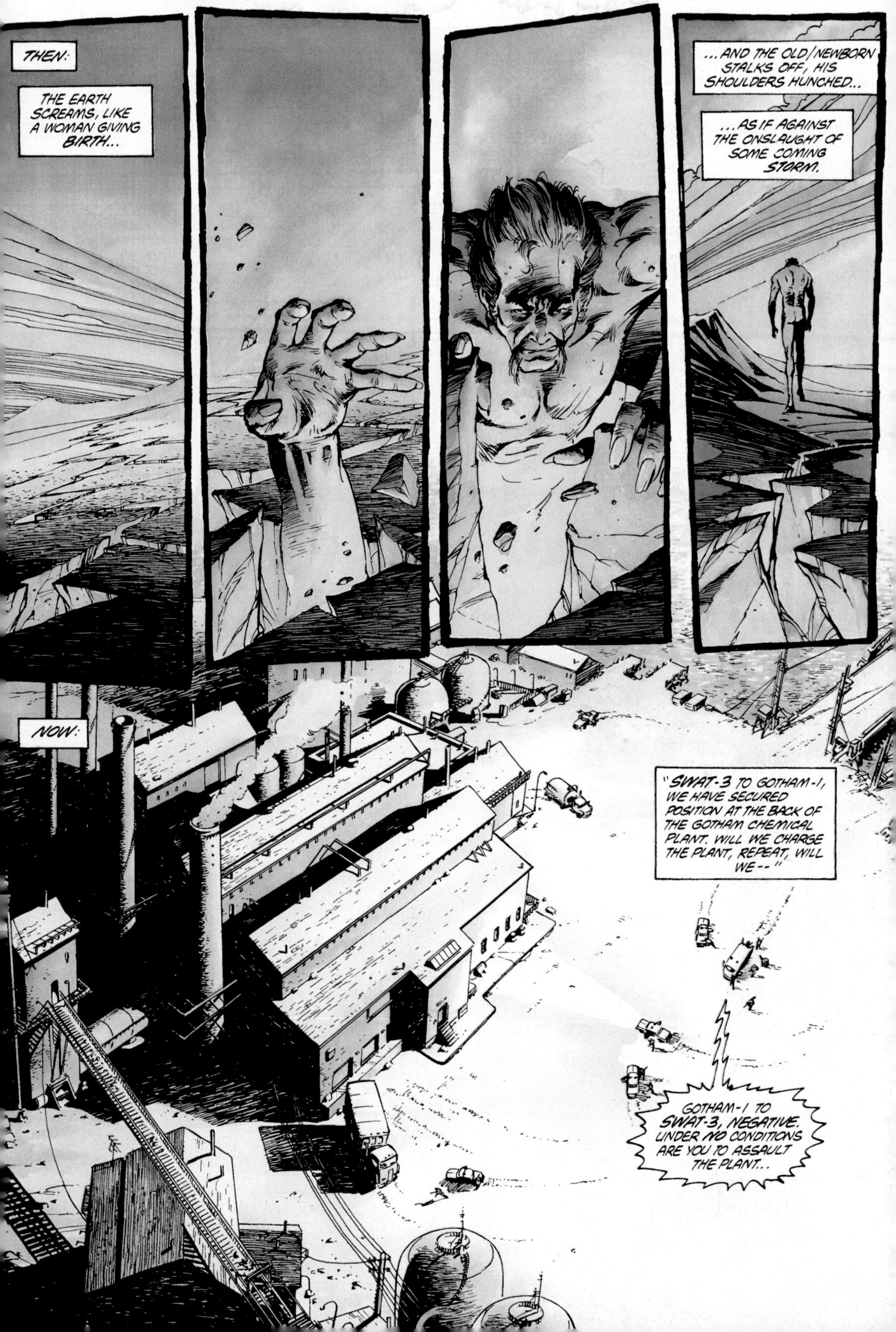
THEN:
THE EARTH SCREAMS, LIKE A WOMAN GIVING BIRTH...
...AND THE OLD/NEWBORN STALKS OFF, HIS SHOULDERS HUNCHED...
...AS IF AGAINST THE ONSLAUGHT OF SOME COMING STORM.
NOW:
"SWAT-3 TO GOTHAM-1, WE HAVE SECURED POSITION AT THE BACK OF THE GOTHAM CHEMICAL PLANT. WILL WE CHARGE THE PLANT, REPEAT, WILL WE--"
GOTHAM-1 TO SWAT-3, NEGATIVE. UNDER NO CONDITIONS ARE YOU TO ASSAULT THE PLANT...

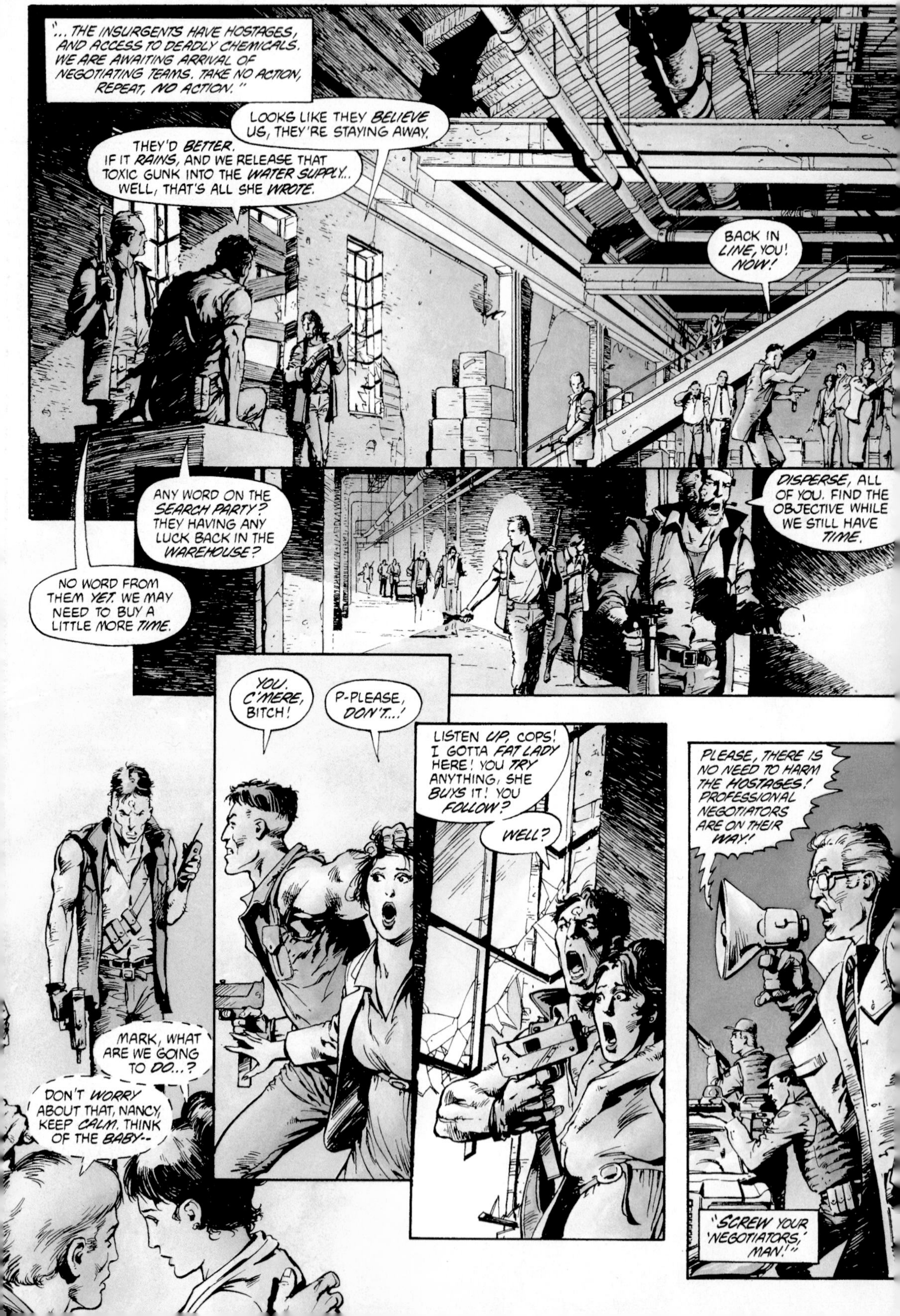
"...THE INSURGENTS HAVE HOSTAGES, AND ACCESS TO DEADLY CHEMICALS. WE ARE AWAITING ARRIVAL OF NEGOTIATING TEAMS. TAKE NO ACTION, REPEAT, NO ACTION."
LOOKS LIKE THEY BELIEVE US, THEY'RE STAYING AWAY.
THEY'D BETTER. IF IT RAINS, AND WE RELEASE THAT TOXIC GUNK INTO THE WATER SUPPLY... WELL, THAT'S ALL SHE WROTE.
BACK IN LINE, YOU! NOW!
ANY WORD ON THE SEARCH PARTY? THEY HAVING ANY LUCK BACK IN THE WAREHOUSE?
NO WORD FROM THEM YET. WE MAY NEED TO BUY A LITTLE MORE TIME.
DISPERSE, ALL OF YOU. FIND THE OBJECTIVE WHILE WE STILL HAVE TIME.
MARK, WHAT ARE WE GOING TO DO...?
DON'T WORRY ABOUT THAT, NANCY, KEEP CALM. THINK OF THE BABY--
YOU. C'MERE, BITCH!
P-PLEASE, DON'T...!
LISTEN UP, COPS! I GOTTA FAT LADY HERE! YOU TRY ANYTHING, SHE BUYS IT! YOU FOLLOW?
WELL?
PLEASE, THERE IS NO NEED TO HARM THE HOSTAGES! PROFESSIONAL NEGOTIATORS ARE ON THEIR WAY!
"SCREW YOUR 'NEGOTIATORS,' MAN."

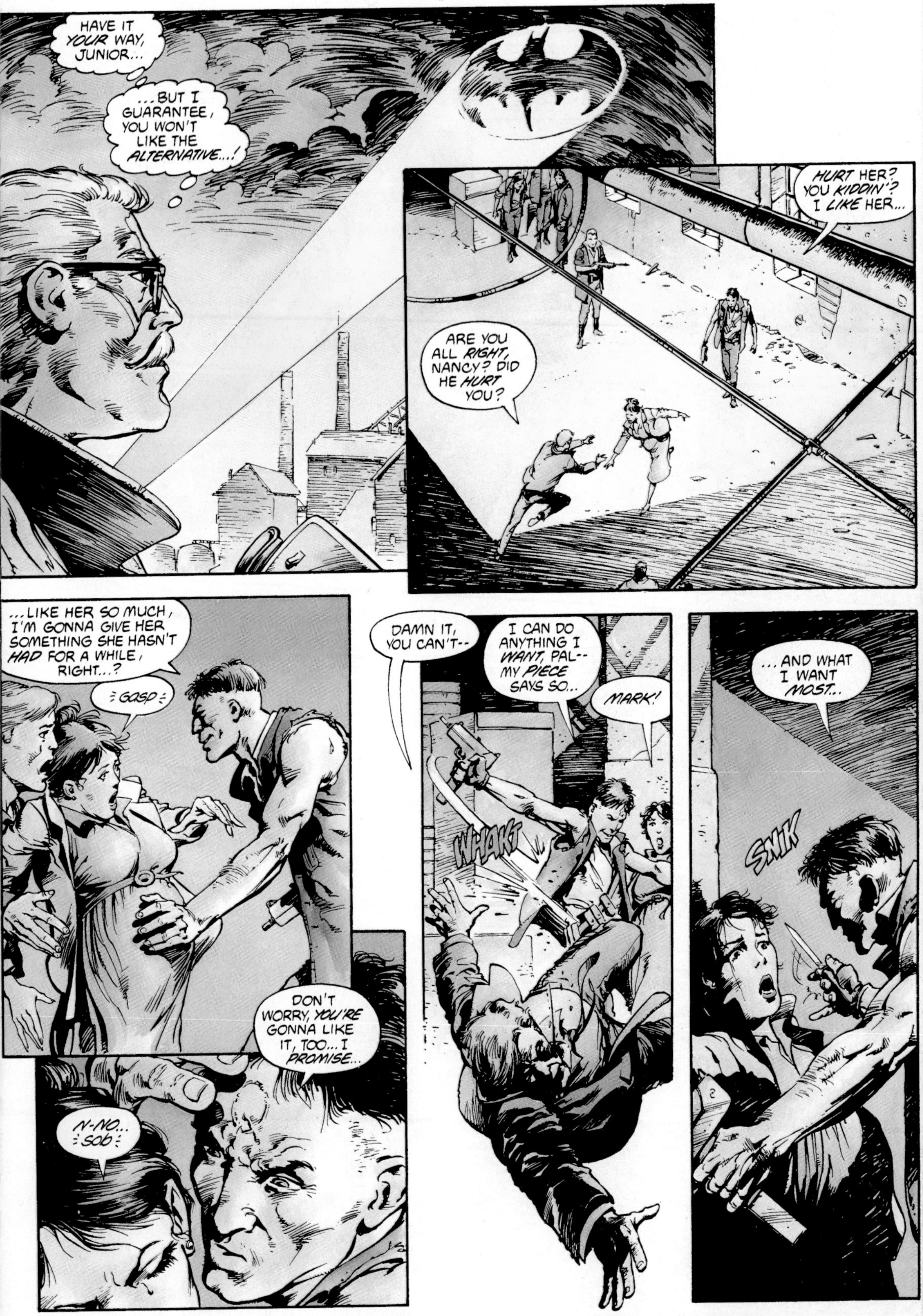
HAVE IT YOUR WAY, JUNIOR...
...BUT I GUARANTEE, YOU WON'T LIKE THE ALTERNATIVE...!
HURT HER? YOU KIDDIN'? I LIKE HER...
ARE YOU ALL RIGHT, NANCY? DID HE HURT YOU?
...LIKE HER SO MUCH, I'M GONNA GIVE HER SOMETHING SHE HASN'T HAD FOR A WHILE, RIGHT...?
GASP
DON'T WORRY, YOU'RE GONNA LIKE IT, TOO... I PROMISE...
N-NO... SOB
DAMN IT, YOU CAN'T--
I CAN DO ANYTHING I WANT, PAL-- MY PIECE SAYS SO...
MARK!
WHAKT
...AND WHAT I WANT MOST...
SNIK

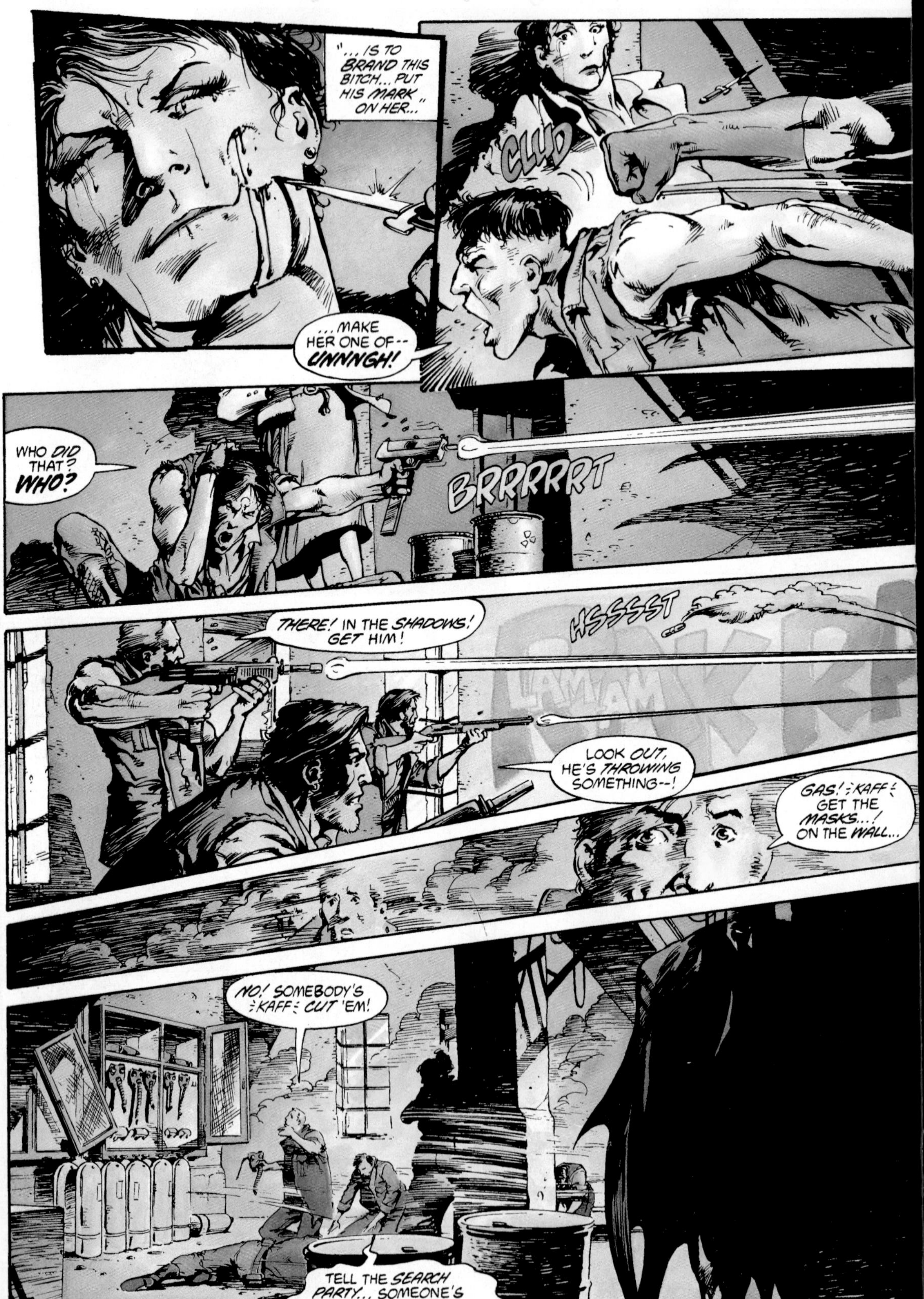
"...IS TO BRAND THIS BITCH... PUT HIS MARK ON HER..."
CLUD
...MAKE HER ONE OF-- UNNNGH!
WHO DID THAT? WHO?
BRRRRRT
THERE! IN THE SHADOWS! GET HIM!
HSSSST
LOOK OUT, HE'S THROWING SOMETHING--!
GAS! KAFF GET THE MASKS...! ON THE WALL...
NO! SOMEBODY'S KAFF CUT 'EM!
TELL THE SEARCH PARTY... SOMEONE'S AFTER KAFF AFTER USSSS...

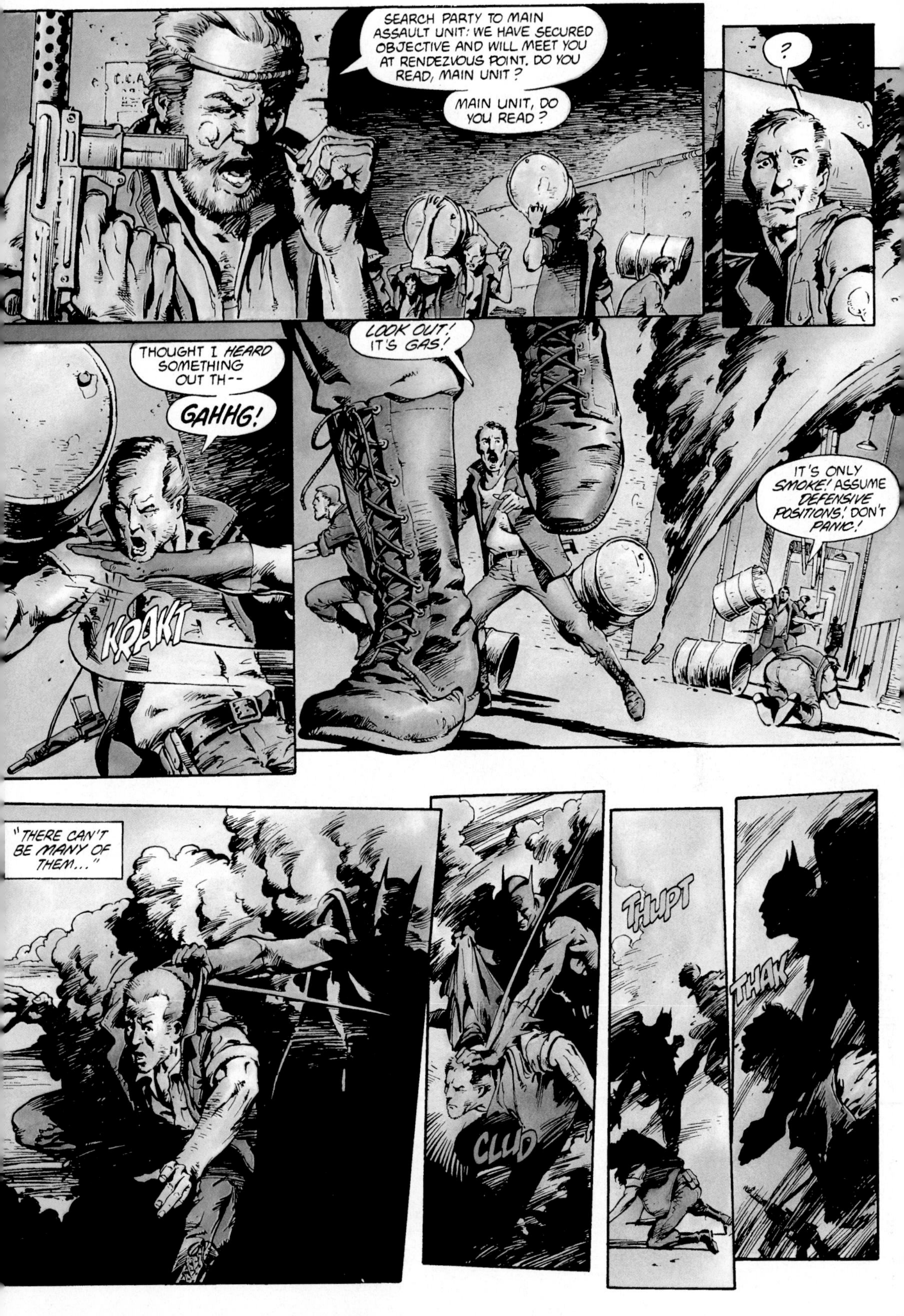
SEARCH PARTY TO MAIN ASSAULT UNIT: WE HAVE SECURED OBJECTIVE AND WILL MEET YOU AT RENDEZVOUS POINT. DO YOU READ, MAIN UNIT?
MAIN UNIT, DO YOU READ?
?
THOUGHT I HEARD SOMETHING OUT TH--
GAHHG!
KRAKT
LOOK OUT! IT'S GAS!
IT'S ONLY SMOKE! ASSUME DEFENSIVE POSITIONS! DON'T PANIC!
"THERE CAN'T BE MANY OF THEM..."
CLUD
THUPT
THAK

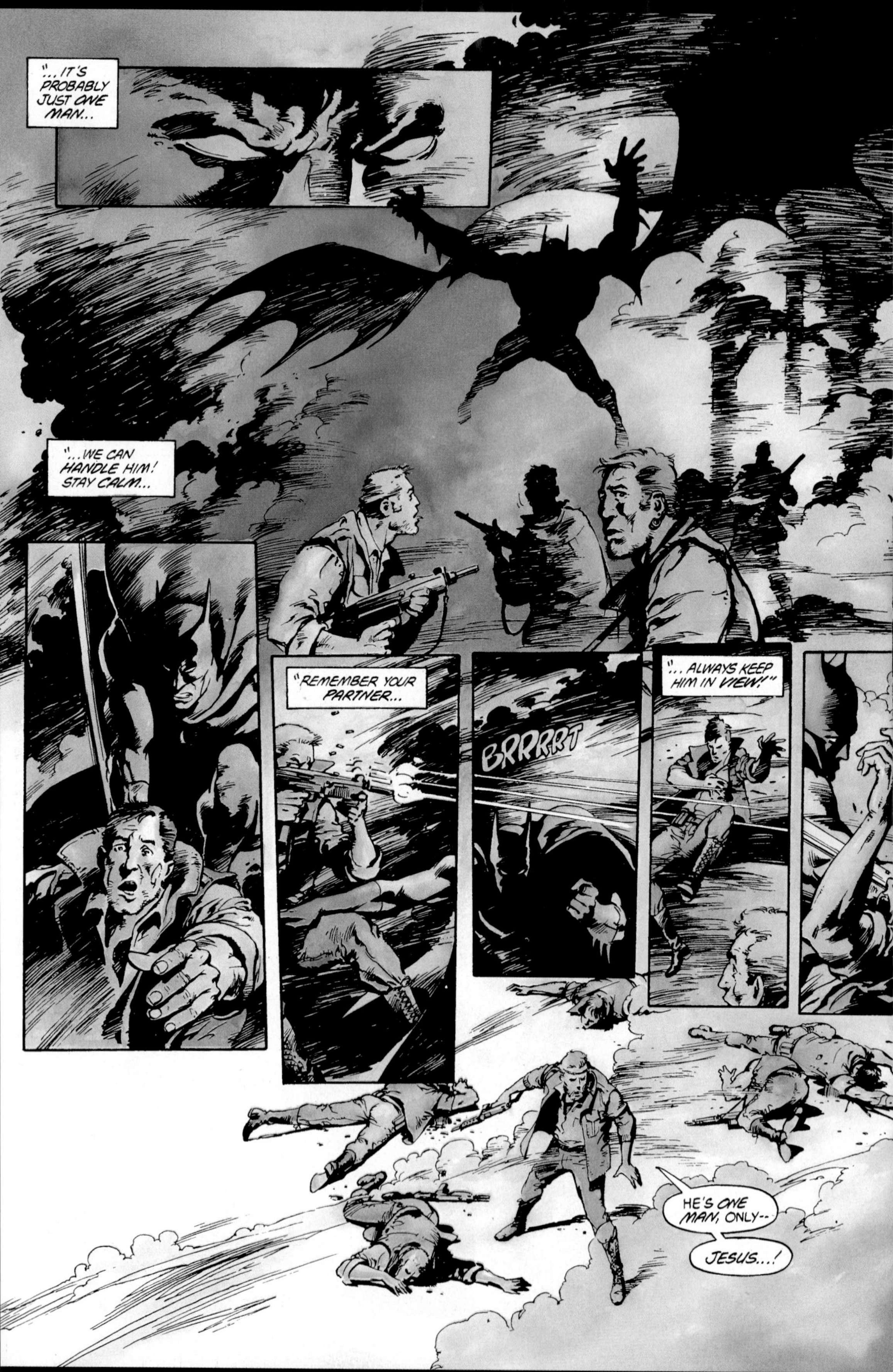
"...IT'S PROBABLY JUST ONE MAN...
"...WE CAN HANDLE HIM! STAY CALM...
"REMEMBER YOUR PARTNER...
BRRRRT
"...ALWAYS KEEP HIM IN VIEW!"
HE'S ONE MAN, ONLY--
JESUS...!

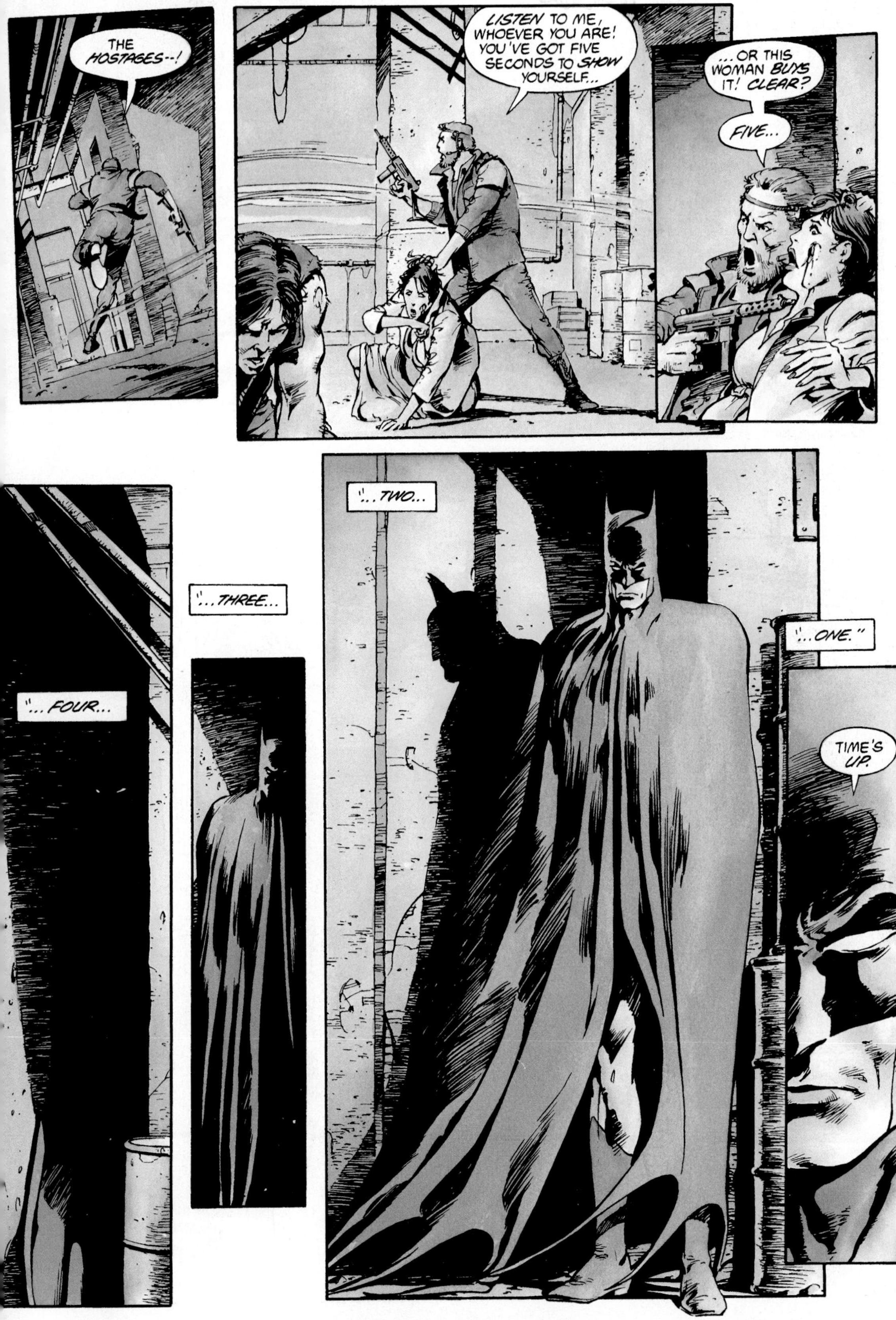

THE HOSTAGES--!
LISTEN TO ME, WHOEVER YOU ARE! YOU'VE GOT FIVE SECONDS TO SHOW YOURSELF...
...OR THIS WOMAN BUYS IT! CLEAR?
FIVE...
"...FOUR...
"...THREE...
"...TWO...
"...ONE."
TIME'S UP.

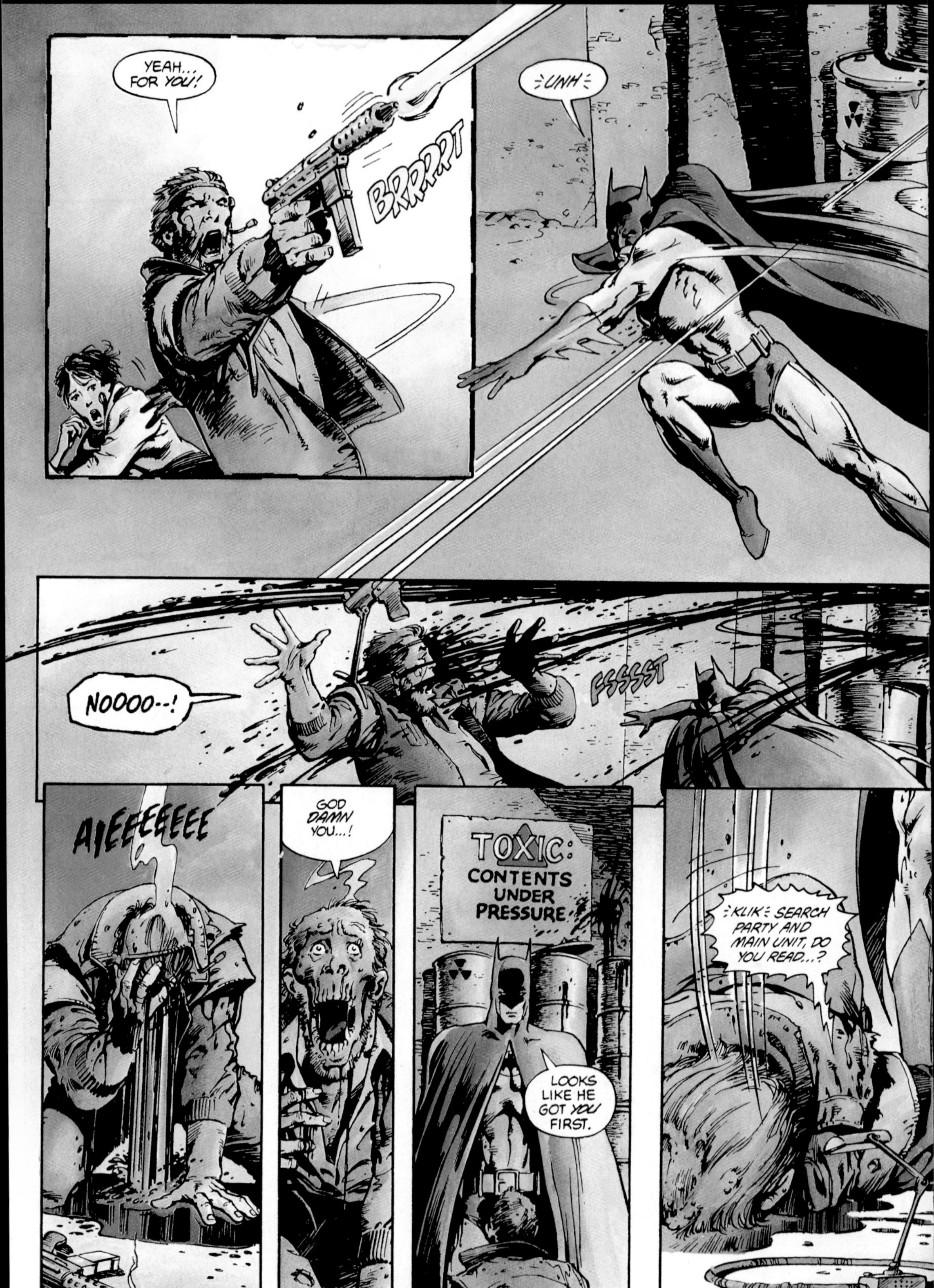
YEAH... FOR YOU!
BRRRRPT
UNH
NOOOO--!
FSSSST
AIEEEEEEE
GOD DAMN YOU...!
TOXIC: CONTENTS UNDER PRESSURE
LOOKS LIKE HE GOT YOU FIRST.
KLIK SEARCH PARTY AND MAIN UNIT, DO YOU READ...?

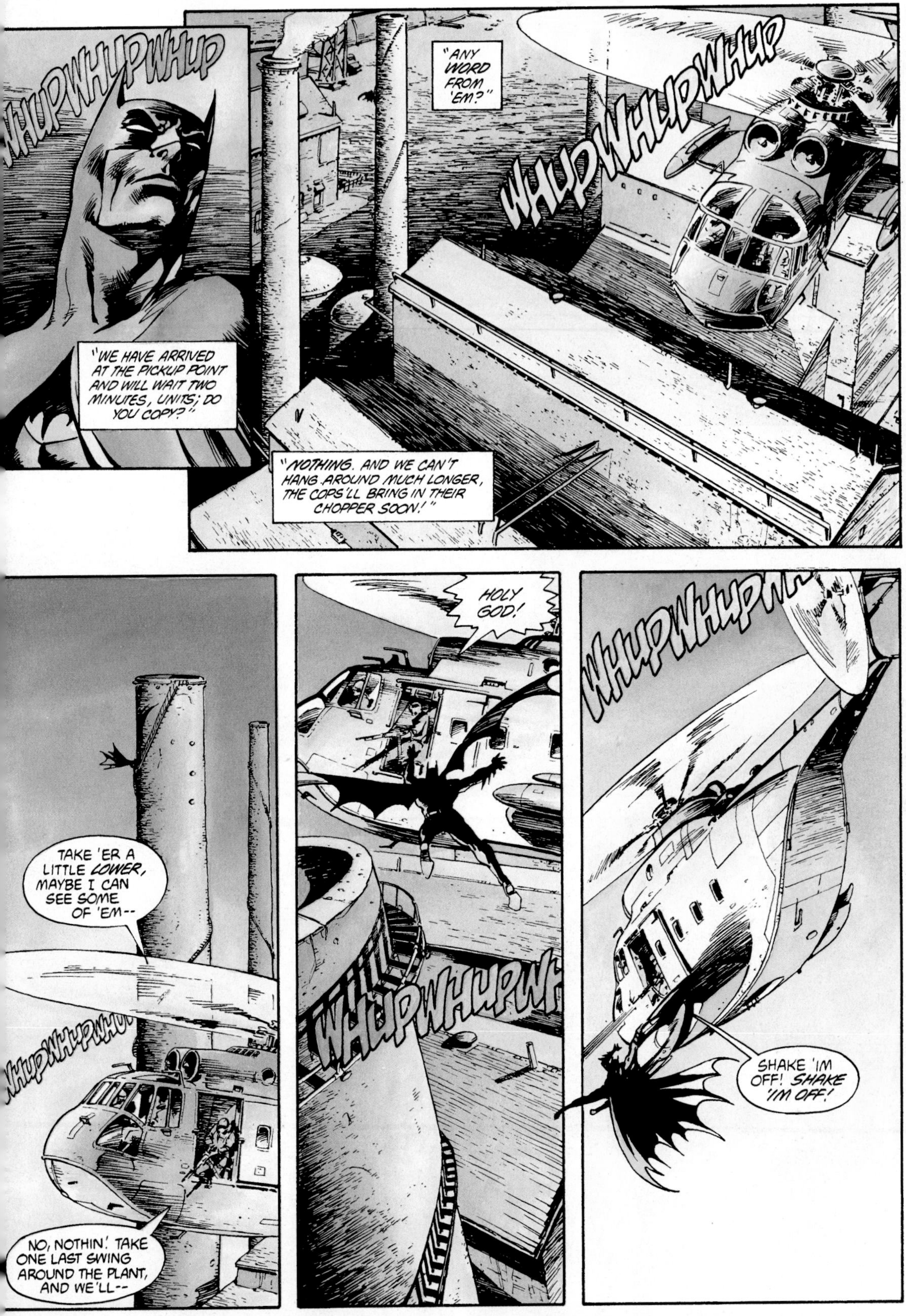
WHUPWHUPWHUP
"ANY WORD FROM 'EM?"
WHUPWHUPWHUP
"WE HAVE ARRIVED AT THE PICKUP POINT AND WILL WAIT TWO MINUTES, UNITS; DO YOU COPY?"
"NOTHING. AND WE CAN'T HANG AROUND MUCH LONGER, THE COPS'LL BRING IN THEIR CHOPPER SOON!"
TAKE 'ER A LITTLE LOWER, MAYBE I CAN SEE SOME OF 'EM--
WHUPWHUPWHUP
NO, NOTHIN'! TAKE ONE LAST SWING AROUND THE PLANT, AND WE'LL--
HOLY GOD!
WHUPWHUPWH
WHUPWHUPW
SHAKE 'IM OFF! SHAKE 'IM OFF!

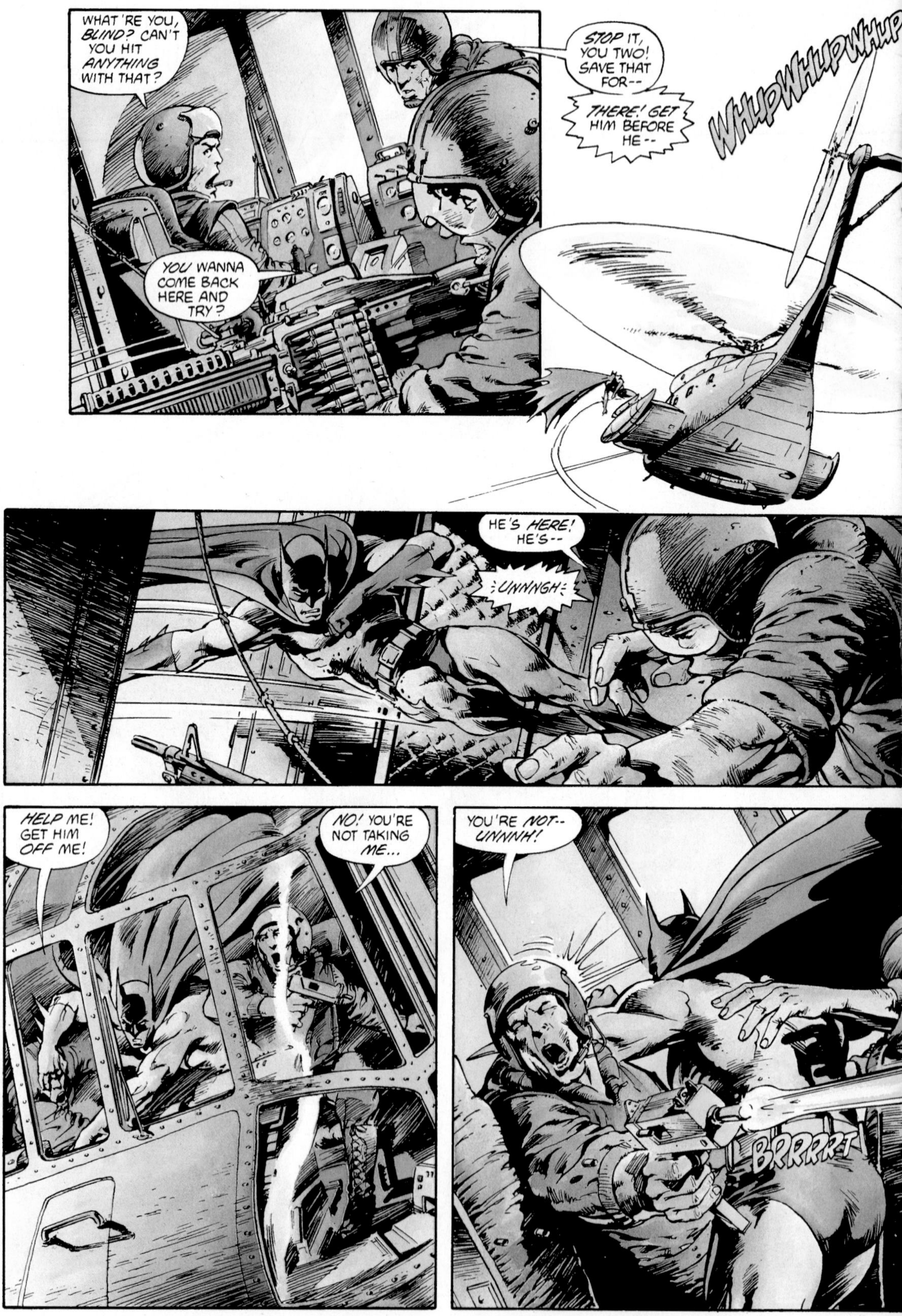
WHAT'RE YOU, BLIND? CAN'T YOU HIT ANYTHING WITH THAT?
STOP IT, YOU TWO! SAVE THAT FOR--
THERE! GET HIM BEFORE HE--
YOU WANNA COME BACK HERE AND TRY?
WHUPWHUPWHUP
HE'S HERE! HE'S--
UNNNGH
HELP ME! GET HIM OFF ME!
NO! YOU'RE NOT TAKING ME...
YOU'RE NOT-- UNNNH!
BRRRRT

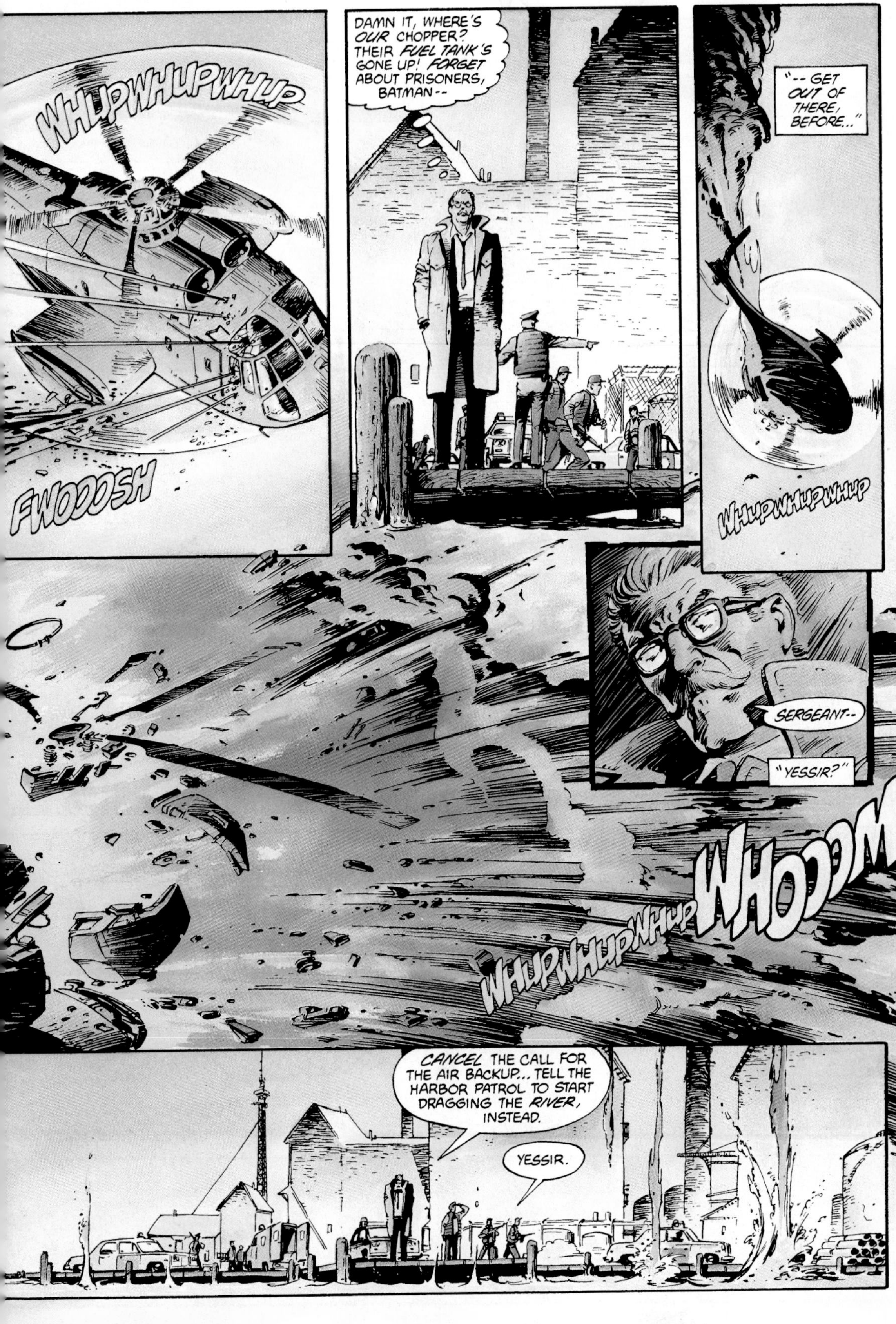
WHUPWHUPWHUP
FWOOOSH
DAMN IT, WHERE'S OUR CHOPPER? THEIR FUEL TANK'S GONE UP! FORGET ABOUT PRISONERS, BATMAN--
"--GET OUT OF THERE, BEFORE..."
WHUPWHUPWHUP
SERGEANT--
"YESSIR?"
WHUPWHUPWHUP
WHOOOM
CANCEL THE CALL FOR THE AIR BACKUP... TELL THE HARBOR PATROL TO START DRAGGING THE RIVER, INSTEAD.
YESSIR.

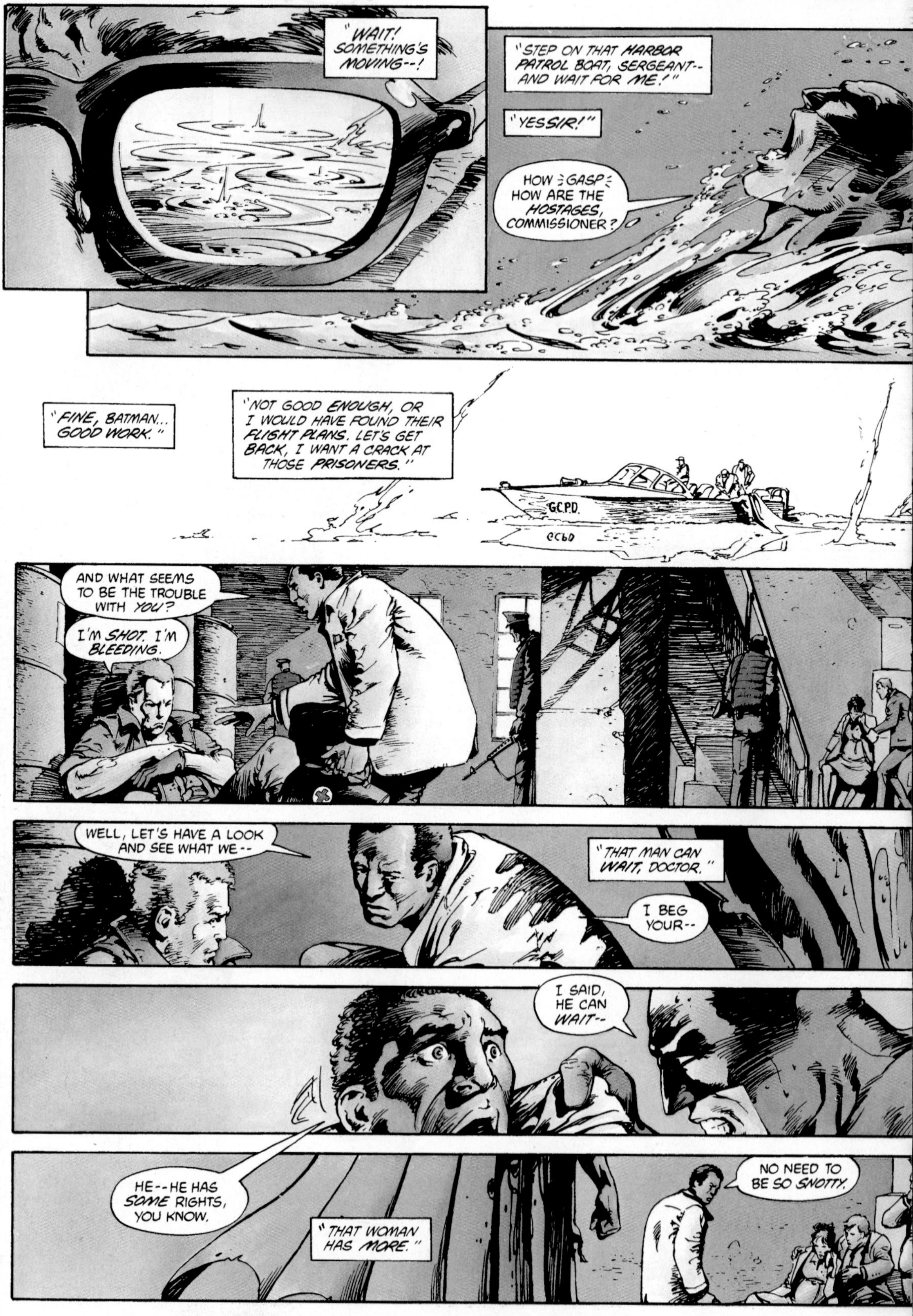

"WAIT! SOMETHING'S MOVING--!
"STEP ON THAT HARBOR PATROL BOAT, SERGEANT--AND WAIT FOR ME!"
"YESSIR!"
HOW ⫶GASP⫶ HOW ARE THE HOSTAGES, COMMISSIONER?
"FINE, BATMAN... GOOD WORK."
"NOT GOOD ENOUGH, OR I WOULD HAVE FOUND THEIR FLIGHT PLANS. LET'S GET BACK, I WANT A CRACK AT THOSE PRISONERS."
G.C.P.D.
AND WHAT SEEMS TO BE THE TROUBLE WITH YOU?
I'M SHOT. I'M BLEEDING.
WELL, LET'S HAVE A LOOK AND SEE WHAT WE--
"THAT MAN CAN WAIT, DOCTOR."
I BEG YOUR--
I SAID, HE CAN WAIT--
HE--HE HAS SOME RIGHTS, YOU KNOW.
"THAT WOMAN HAS MORE."
NO NEED TO BE SO SNOTTY.

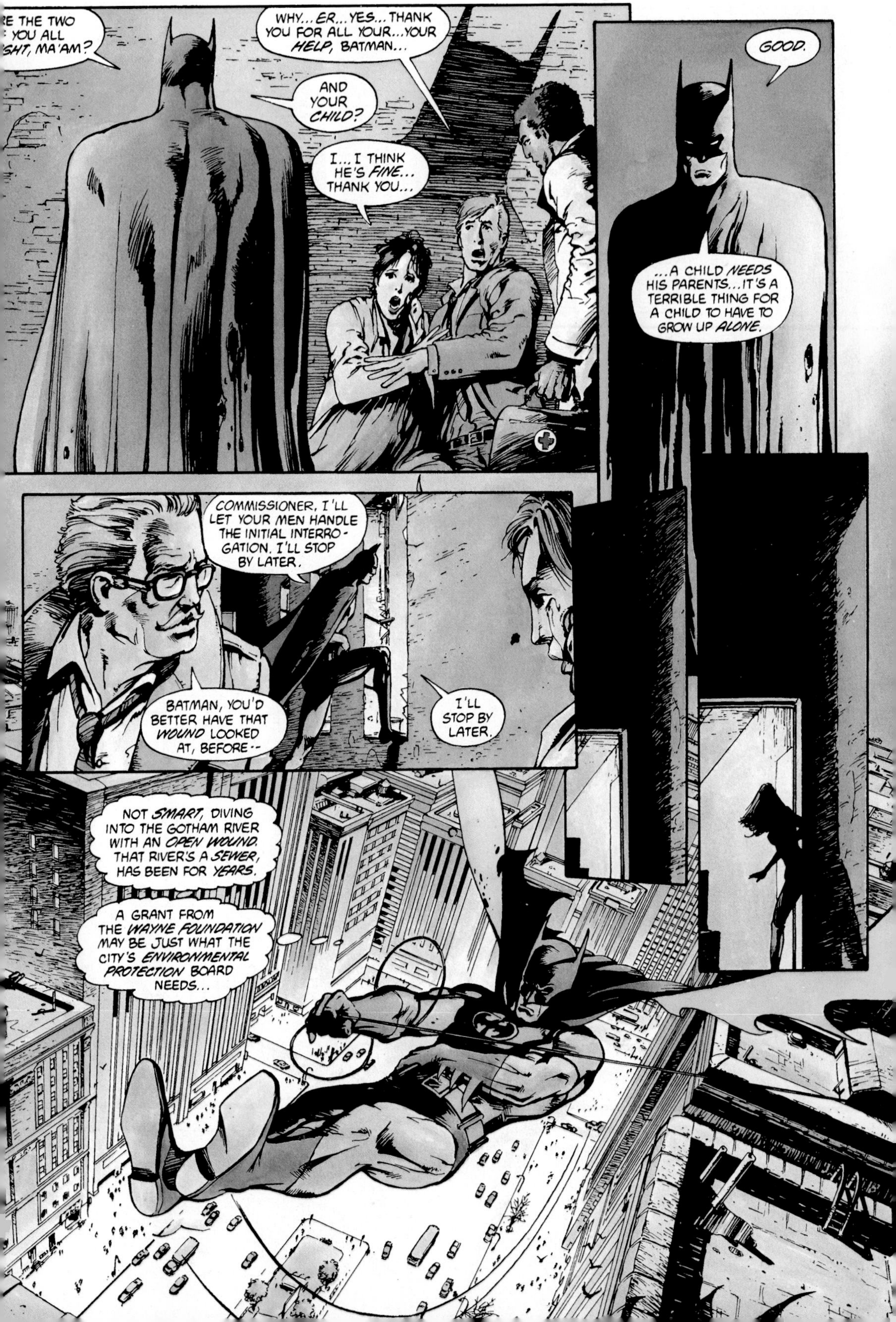
RE THE TWO
YOU ALL
SHT, MA'AM?
WHY... ER... YES... THANK YOU FOR ALL YOUR... YOUR HELP, BATMAN...
AND YOUR CHILD?
I... I THINK HE'S FINE... THANK YOU...
GOOD.
...A CHILD NEEDS HIS PARENTS... IT'S A TERRIBLE THING FOR A CHILD TO HAVE TO GROW UP ALONE.
COMMISSIONER, I'LL LET YOUR MEN HANDLE THE INITIAL INTERRO-GATION. I'LL STOP BY LATER.
BATMAN, YOU'D BETTER HAVE THAT WOUND LOOKED AT, BEFORE--
I'LL STOP BY LATER.
NOT SMART, DIVING INTO THE GOTHAM RIVER WITH AN OPEN WOUND. THAT RIVER'S A SEWER, HAS BEEN FOR YEARS.
A GRANT FROM THE WAYNE FOUNDATION MAY BE JUST WHAT THE CITY'S ENVIRONMENTAL PROTECTION BOARD NEEDS...

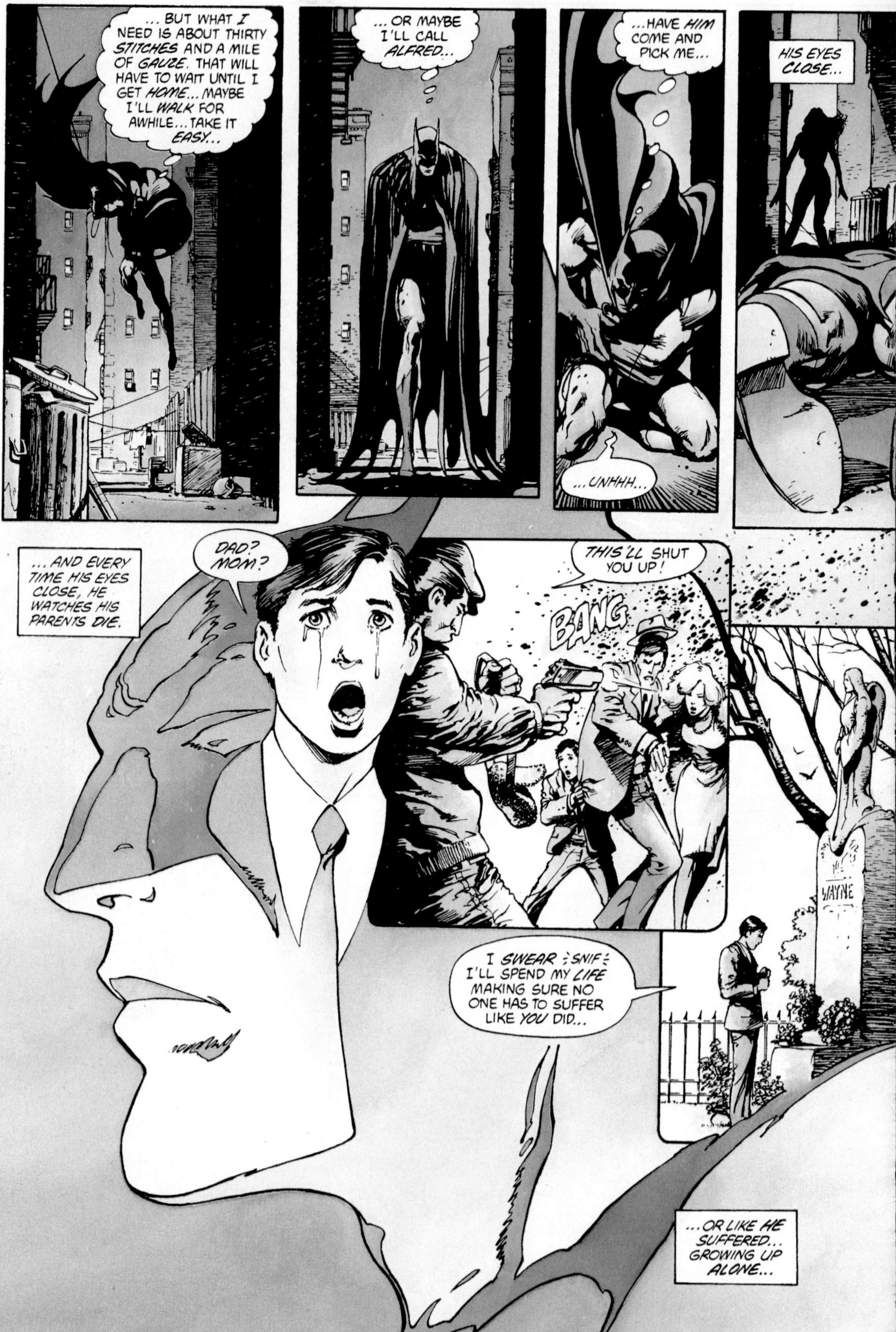
... BUT WHAT I NEED IS ABOUT THIRTY STITCHES AND A MILE OF GAUZE. THAT WILL HAVE TO WAIT UNTIL I GET HOME... MAYBE I'LL WALK FOR AWHILE... TAKE IT EASY...
... OR MAYBE I'LL CALL ALFRED...
...HAVE HIM COME AND PICK ME...
...UNHHH...
HIS EYES CLOSE...
... AND EVERY TIME HIS EYES CLOSE, HE WATCHES HIS PARENTS DIE.
DAD? MOM?
THIS'LL SHUT YOU UP!
BANG
I SWEAR -SNIF- I'LL SPEND MY LIFE MAKING SURE NO ONE HAS TO SUFFER LIKE YOU DID...
WAYNE
...OR LIKE HE SUFFERED... GROWING UP ALONE...

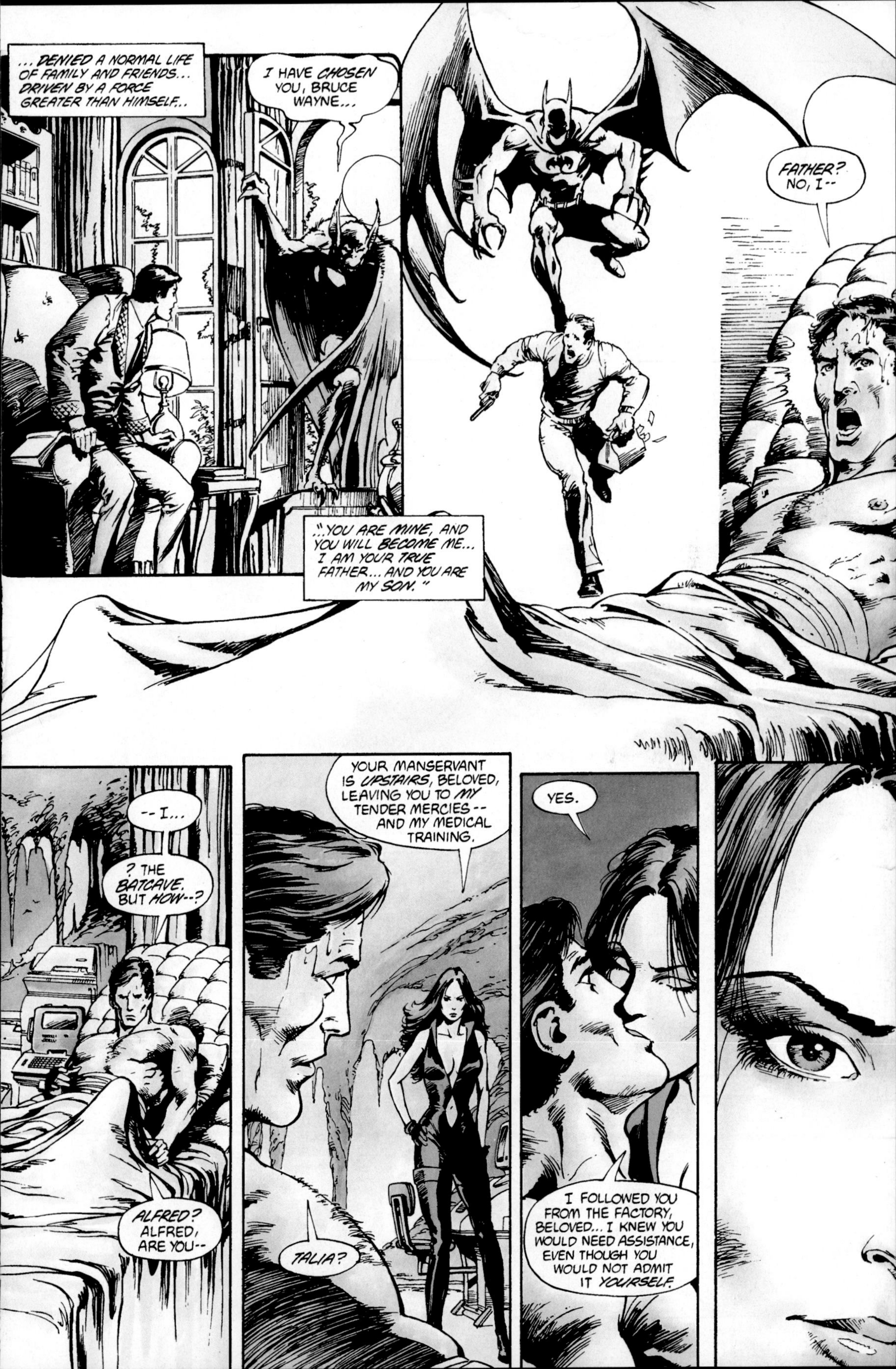
...DENIED A NORMAL LIFE OF FAMILY AND FRIENDS... DRIVEN BY A FORCE GREATER THAN HIMSELF...
I HAVE CHOSEN YOU, BRUCE WAYNE...
..."YOU ARE MINE, AND YOU WILL BECOME ME... I AM YOUR TRUE FATHER... AND YOU ARE MY SON."
FATHER? NO, I--
--I...
? THE BATCAVE. BUT HOW--?
ALFRED? ALFRED, ARE YOU--
YOUR MANSERVANT IS UPSTAIRS, BELOVED, LEAVING YOU TO MY TENDER MERCIES-- AND MY MEDICAL TRAINING.
TALIA?
YES.
I FOLLOWED YOU FROM THE FACTORY, BELOVED... I KNEW YOU WOULD NEED ASSISTANCE, EVEN THOUGH YOU WOULD NOT ADMIT IT YOURSELF.

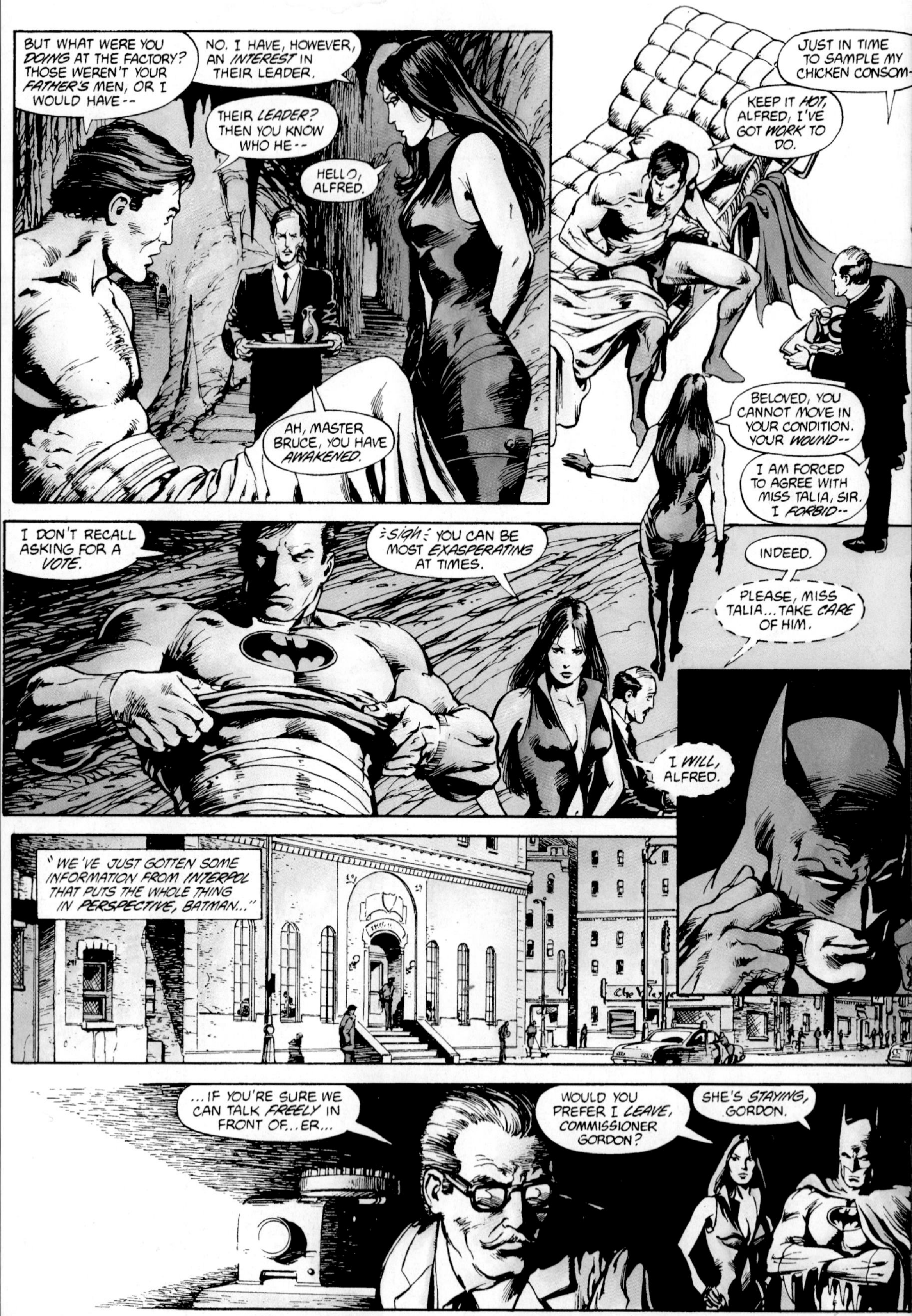

BUT WHAT WERE YOU DOING AT THE FACTORY? THOSE WEREN'T YOUR FATHER'S MEN, OR I WOULD HAVE--
NO. I HAVE, HOWEVER, AN INTEREST IN THEIR LEADER.
THEIR LEADER? THEN YOU KNOW WHO HE--
HELLO, ALFRED.
AH, MASTER BRUCE, YOU HAVE AWAKENED.
JUST IN TIME TO SAMPLE MY CHICKEN CONSOM-
KEEP IT HOT, ALFRED, I'VE GOT WORK TO DO.
BELOVED, YOU CANNOT MOVE IN YOUR CONDITION. YOUR WOUND--
I AM FORCED TO AGREE WITH MISS TALIA, SIR. I FORBID--
I DON'T RECALL ASKING FOR A VOTE.
=SIGH= YOU CAN BE MOST EXASPERATING AT TIMES.
INDEED.
PLEASE, MISS TALIA... TAKE CARE OF HIM.
I WILL, ALFRED.
"WE'VE JUST GOTTEN SOME INFORMATION FROM INTERPOL THAT PUTS THE WHOLE THING IN PERSPECTIVE, BATMAN..."
...IF YOU'RE SURE WE CAN TALK FREELY IN FRONT OF...ER...
WOULD YOU PREFER I LEAVE, COMMISSIONER GORDON?
SHE'S STAYING, GORDON.

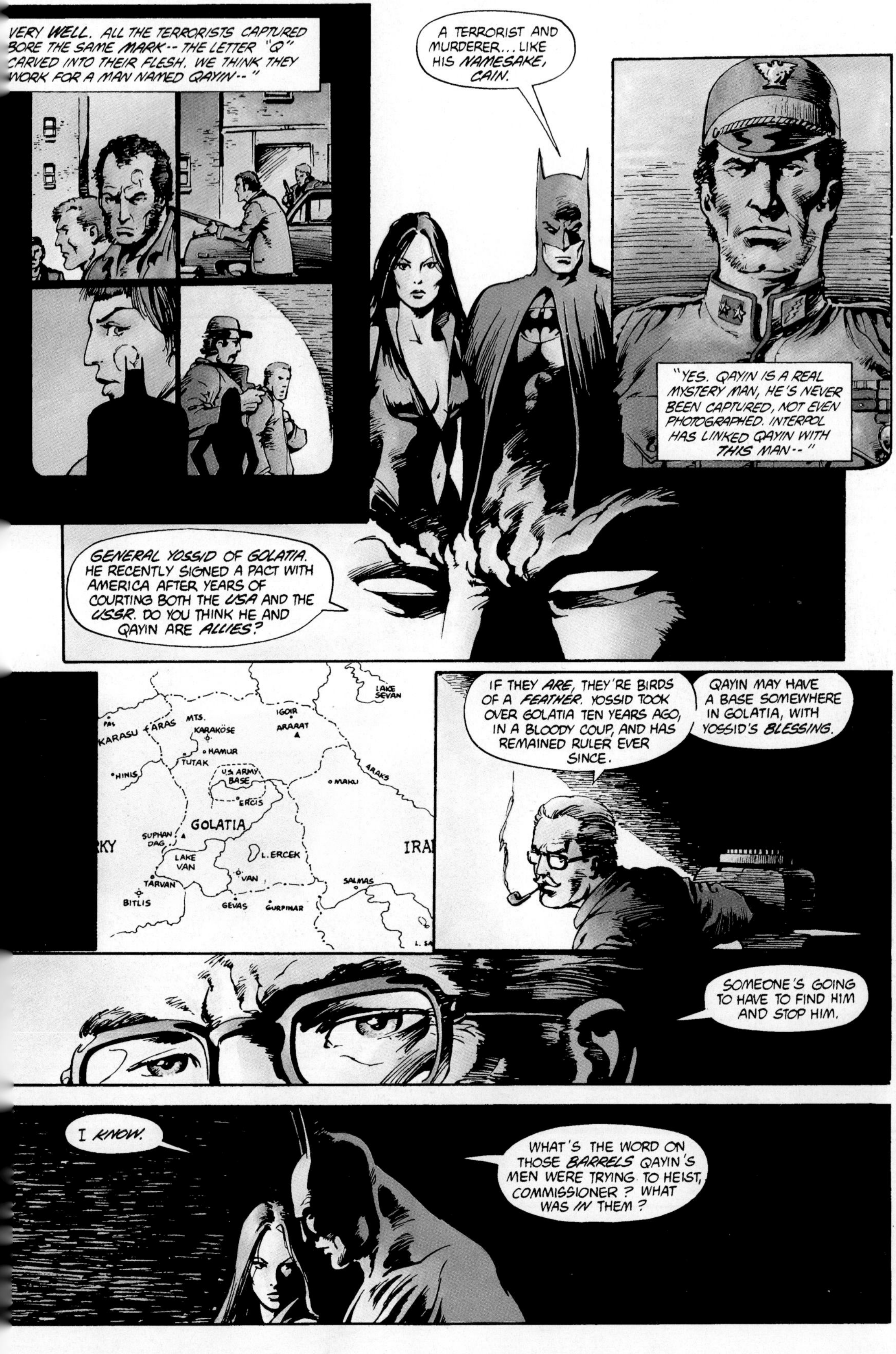

VERY WELL. ALL THE TERRORISTS CAPTURED BORE THE SAME MARK -- THE LETTER "Q" CARVED INTO THEIR FLESH. WE THINK THEY WORK FOR A MAN NAMED QAYIN --"
A TERRORIST AND MURDERER... LIKE HIS NAMESAKE, CAIN.
"YES. QAYIN IS A REAL MYSTERY MAN, HE'S NEVER BEEN CAPTURED, NOT EVEN PHOTOGRAPHED. INTERPOL HAS LINKED QAYIN WITH THIS MAN --"
GENERAL YOSSID OF GOLATIA. HE RECENTLY SIGNED A PACT WITH AMERICA AFTER YEARS OF COURTING BOTH THE USA AND THE USSR. DO YOU THINK HE AND QAYIN ARE ALLIES?
LAKE SEVAN
PAS
KARASU
ARAS
MTS.
KARAKÖSE
IGOIR
ARARAT
HAMUR
TUTAK
HINIS
U.S. ARMY BASE
ERCIS
MAKU
ARAKS
GOLATIA
SUPHAN DAG
LAKE VAN
L. ERCEK
VAN
TARVAN
BITLIS
GEVAS
GURPINAR
SALMAS
IF THEY ARE, THEY'RE BIRDS OF A FEATHER. YOSSID TOOK OVER GOLATIA TEN YEARS AGO, IN A BLOODY COUP, AND HAS REMAINED RULER EVER SINCE.
QAYIN MAY HAVE A BASE SOMEWHERE IN GOLATIA, WITH YOSSID'S BLESSING.
SOMEONE'S GOING TO HAVE TO FIND HIM AND STOP HIM.
I KNOW.
WHAT'S THE WORD ON THOSE BARRELS QAYIN'S MEN WERE TRYING TO HEIST, COMMISSIONER? WHAT WAS IN THEM?

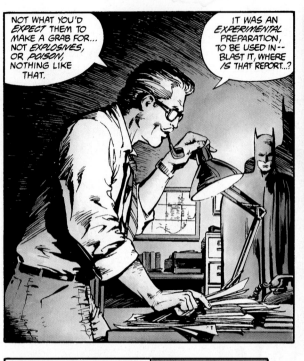

NOT WHAT YOU'D *EXPECT* THEM TO MAKE A GRAB FOR... NOT *EXPLOSIVES*, OR *POISON*, NOTHING LIKE THAT.

IT WAS AN *EXPERIMENTAL* PREPARATION, TO BE USED IN -- BLAST IT, WHERE *IS* THAT REPORT..?

HERE WE ARE. *PLUVICULTURE*, THAT'S WHAT THE CHEMICAL WAS TO BE USED FOR... WHATEVER *THAT* IS.

I SEE.

YOU *DO?*

PLUVICULTURE IS THE SCIENCE OF *RAINMAKING*, COMMISSIONER AND WHAT I DON'T *KNOW,* I CAN *LOOK UP.*

"*BLAINE-PEARSON RESEARCH. BELOVED, IS THAT DR. HARRIS BLAINE?*"

"*THAT'S RIGHT, TALIA. YOU WAIT HERE, I WON'T BE LONG.*"

BLAINE-PEARSON
RESEARCH
FACILITY

EXCELLENT SECURITY SYSTEM, IT TOOK ME ALMOST *30 SECONDS* TO BYPASS IT. AS I RECALL, THIS IS DR. BLAINE'S OFFICE--

DR. BLAINE?

DEAD. BUT ONLY *SECONDS* AGO. THE KILLER MAY STILL BE AROUND...

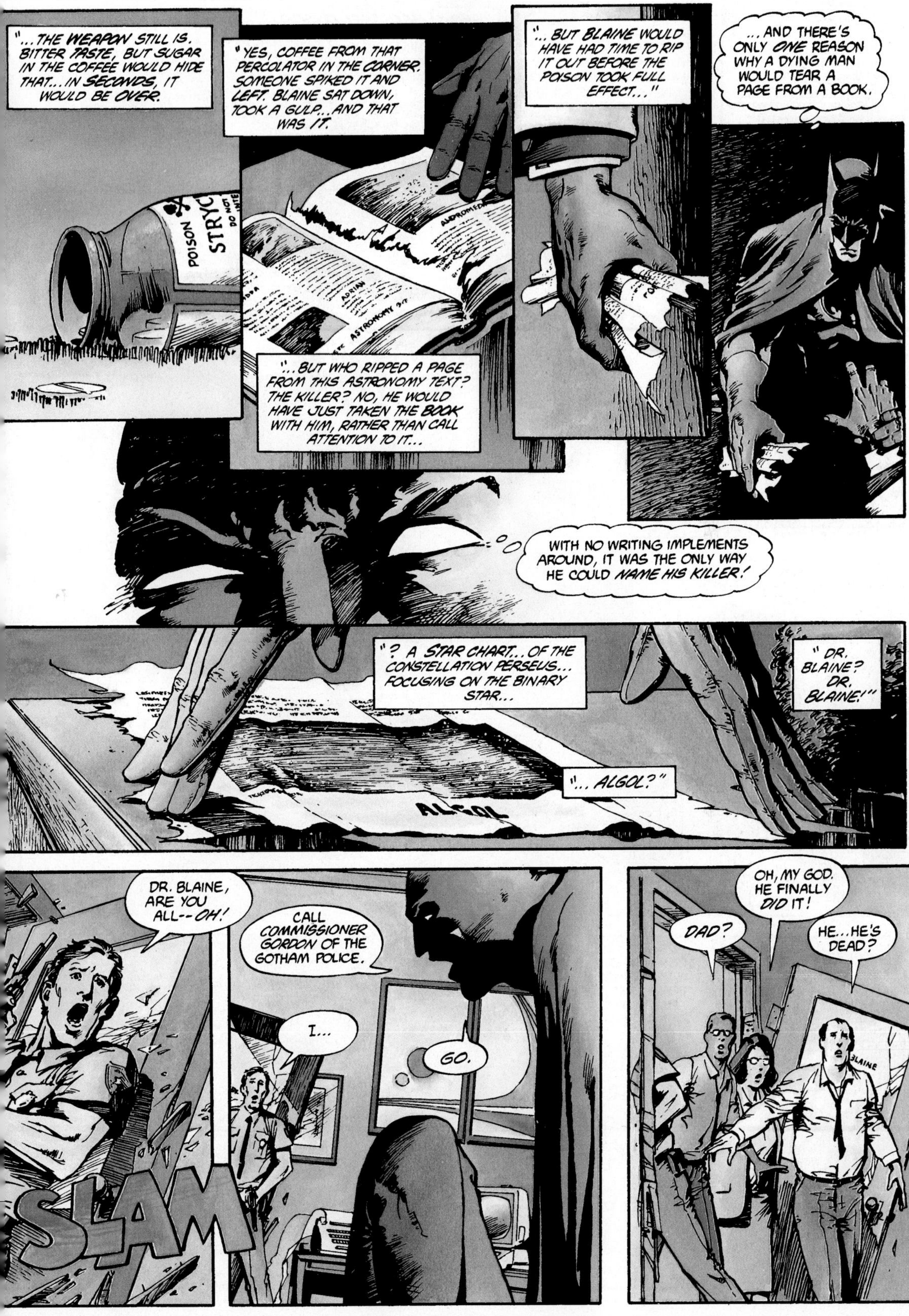
"...THE WEAPON STILL IS. BITTER TASTE, BUT SUGAR IN THE COFFEE WOULD HIDE THAT...IN SECONDS, IT WOULD BE OVER.
POISON
STRYC
DO NOT
"YES, COFFEE FROM THAT PERCOLATOR IN THE CORNER. SOMEONE SPIKED IT AND LEFT. BLAINE SAT DOWN, TOOK A GULP...AND THAT WAS IT.
ASTRONOMY
"...BUT WHO RIPPED A PAGE FROM THIS ASTRONOMY TEXT? THE KILLER? NO, HE WOULD HAVE JUST TAKEN THE BOOK WITH HIM, RATHER THAN CALL ATTENTION TO IT...
"...BUT BLAINE WOULD HAVE HAD TIME TO RIP IT OUT BEFORE THE POISON TOOK FULL EFFECT..."
...AND THERE'S ONLY ONE REASON WHY A DYING MAN WOULD TEAR A PAGE FROM A BOOK.
WITH NO WRITING IMPLEMENTS AROUND, IT WAS THE ONLY WAY HE COULD NAME HIS KILLER!
"? A STAR CHART...OF THE CONSTELLATION PERSEUS... FOCUSING ON THE BINARY STAR...
"... ALGOL?"
ALGOL
"DR. BLAINE? DR. BLAINE!"
DR. BLAINE, ARE YOU ALL--OH!
SLAM
CALL COMMISSIONER GORDON OF THE GOTHAM POLICE.
I...
GO.
DAD?
OH, MY GOD. HE FINALLY DID IT!
HE...HE'S DEAD?
BLAINE

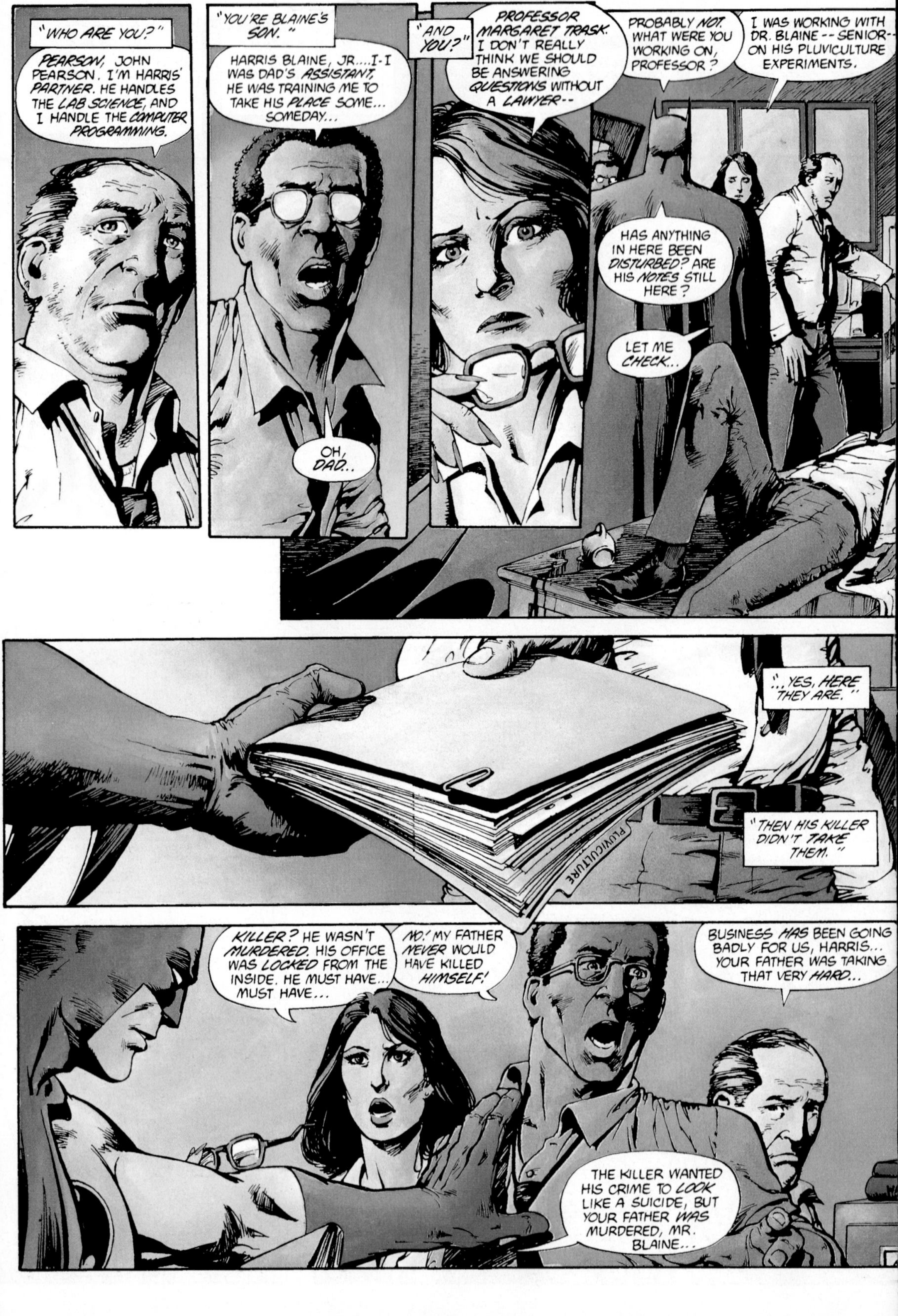
"WHO ARE YOU?"
PEARSON, JOHN PEARSON. I'M HARRIS' PARTNER. HE HANDLES THE LAB SCIENCE, AND I HANDLE THE COMPUTER PROGRAMMING.
"YOU'RE BLAINE'S SON."
HARRIS BLAINE, JR....I-I WAS DAD'S ASSISTANT, HE WAS TRAINING ME TO TAKE HIS PLACE SOME... SOMEDAY...
OH, DAD...
"AND YOU?"
PROFESSOR MARGARET TRASK. I DON'T REALLY THINK WE SHOULD BE ANSWERING QUESTIONS WITHOUT A LAWYER--
PROBABLY NOT. WHAT WERE YOU WORKING ON, PROFESSOR?
I WAS WORKING WITH DR. BLAINE--SENIOR--ON HIS PLUVICULTURE EXPERIMENTS.
HAS ANYTHING IN HERE BEEN DISTURBED? ARE HIS NOTES STILL HERE?
LET ME CHECK...
"...YES, HERE THEY ARE."
PLUVICULTURE
"THEN HIS KILLER DIDN'T TAKE THEM."
KILLER? HE WASN'T MURDERED. HIS OFFICE WAS LOCKED FROM THE INSIDE. HE MUST HAVE... MUST HAVE...
NO! MY FATHER NEVER WOULD HAVE KILLED HIMSELF!
BUSINESS HAS BEEN GOING BADLY FOR US, HARRIS... YOUR FATHER WAS TAKING THAT VERY HARD...
THE KILLER WANTED HIS CRIME TO LOOK LIKE A SUICIDE, BUT YOUR FATHER WAS MURDERED, MR. BLAINE...

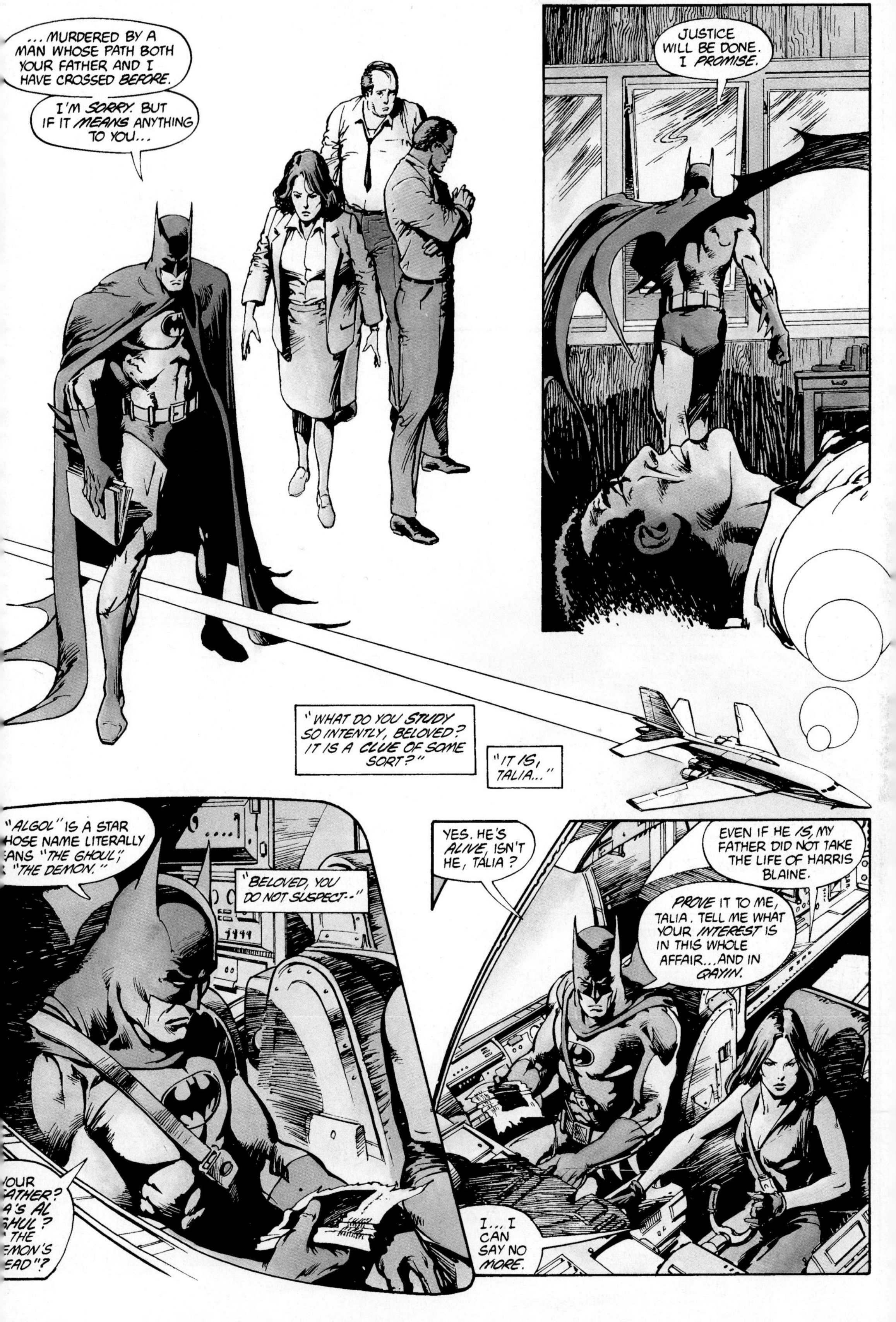

...MURDERED BY A MAN WHOSE PATH BOTH YOUR FATHER AND I HAVE CROSSED BEFORE.
I'M SORRY. BUT IF IT MEANS ANYTHING TO YOU...
JUSTICE WILL BE DONE. I PROMISE.
"WHAT DO YOU STUDY SO INTENTLY, BELOVED? IT IS A CLUE OF SOME SORT?"
"IT IS, TALIA..."
"ALGOL" IS A STAR
HOSE NAME LITERALLY
EANS "THE GHOUL,"
"THE DEMON."
"BELOVED, YOU DO NOT SUSPECT--"
YOUR
ATHER?
A'S AL
GHUL?
THE
EMON'S
EAD"?
YES. HE'S ALIVE, ISN'T HE, TALIA?
EVEN IF HE IS, MY FATHER DID NOT TAKE THE LIFE OF HARRIS BLAINE.
PROVE IT TO ME, TALIA. TELL ME WHAT YOUR INTEREST IS IN THIS WHOLE AFFAIR...AND IN QAYIN.
I...I CAN SAY NO MORE.

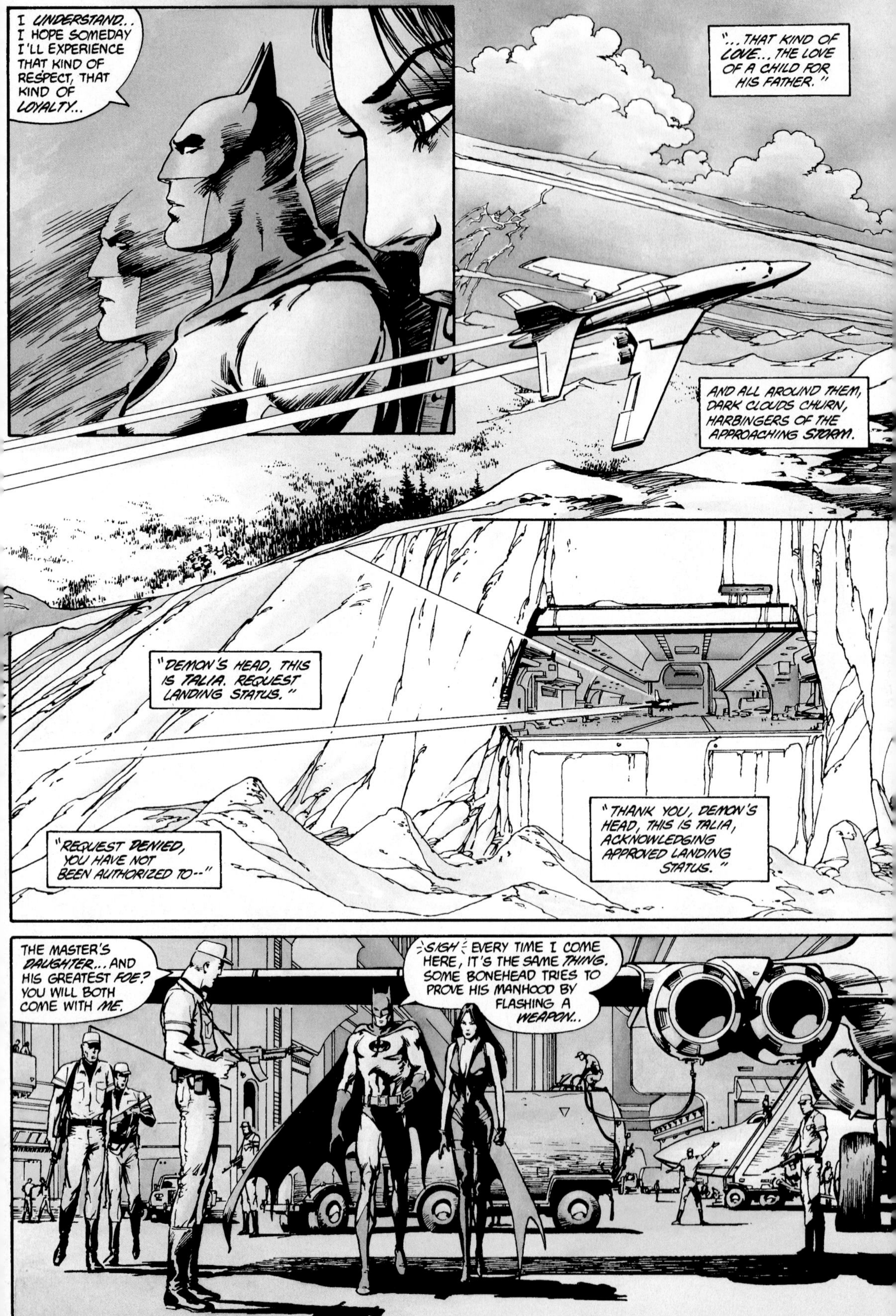
I *UNDERSTAND*... I HOPE SOMEDAY I'LL EXPERIENCE THAT KIND OF RESPECT, THAT KIND OF *LOYALTY*...
"...THAT KIND OF *LOVE*... THE LOVE OF A CHILD FOR HIS FATHER."
AND ALL AROUND THEM, DARK CLOUDS CHURN, HARBINGERS OF THE APPROACHING *STORM*.
"DEMON'S HEAD, THIS IS *TALIA*. REQUEST LANDING STATUS."
"REQUEST *DENIED*, YOU HAVE NOT BEEN AUTHORIZED TO--"
"THANK YOU, DEMON'S HEAD, THIS IS TALIA, ACKNOWLEDGING APPROVED LANDING STATUS."
THE MASTER'S *DAUGHTER*... AND HIS GREATEST *FOE*? YOU WILL BOTH COME WITH *ME*.
SIGH EVERY TIME I COME HERE, IT'S THE SAME *THING*. SOME BONEHEAD TRIES TO PROVE HIS MANHOOD BY FLASHING A *WEAPON*...

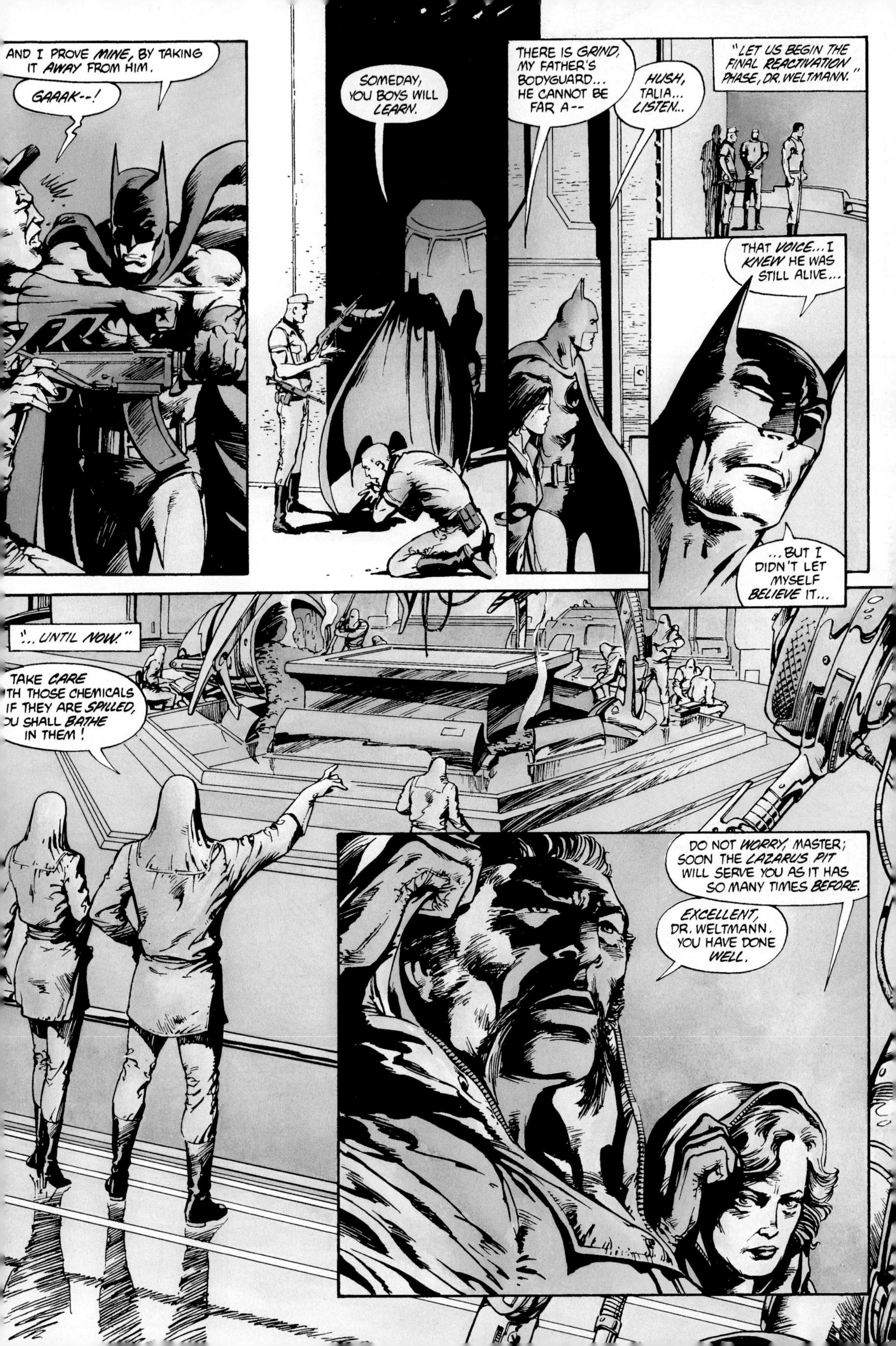
AND I PROVE MINE, BY TAKING IT AWAY FROM HIM.
GAAAK--!
SOMEDAY, YOU BOYS WILL LEARN.
THERE IS GRIND, MY FATHER'S BODYGUARD... HE CANNOT BE FAR A--
HUSH, TALIA... LISTEN...
"LET US BEGIN THE FINAL REACTIVATION PHASE, DR. WELTMANN."
THAT VOICE... I KNEW HE WAS STILL ALIVE...
...BUT I DIDN'T LET MYSELF BELIEVE IT...
"...UNTIL NOW."
TAKE CARE ITH THOSE CHEMICALS IF THEY ARE SPILLED, OU SHALL BATHE IN THEM!
DO NOT WORRY, MASTER; SOON THE LAZARUS PIT WILL SERVE YOU AS IT HAS SO MANY TIMES BEFORE.
EXCELLENT, DR. WELTMANN. YOU HAVE DONE WELL.

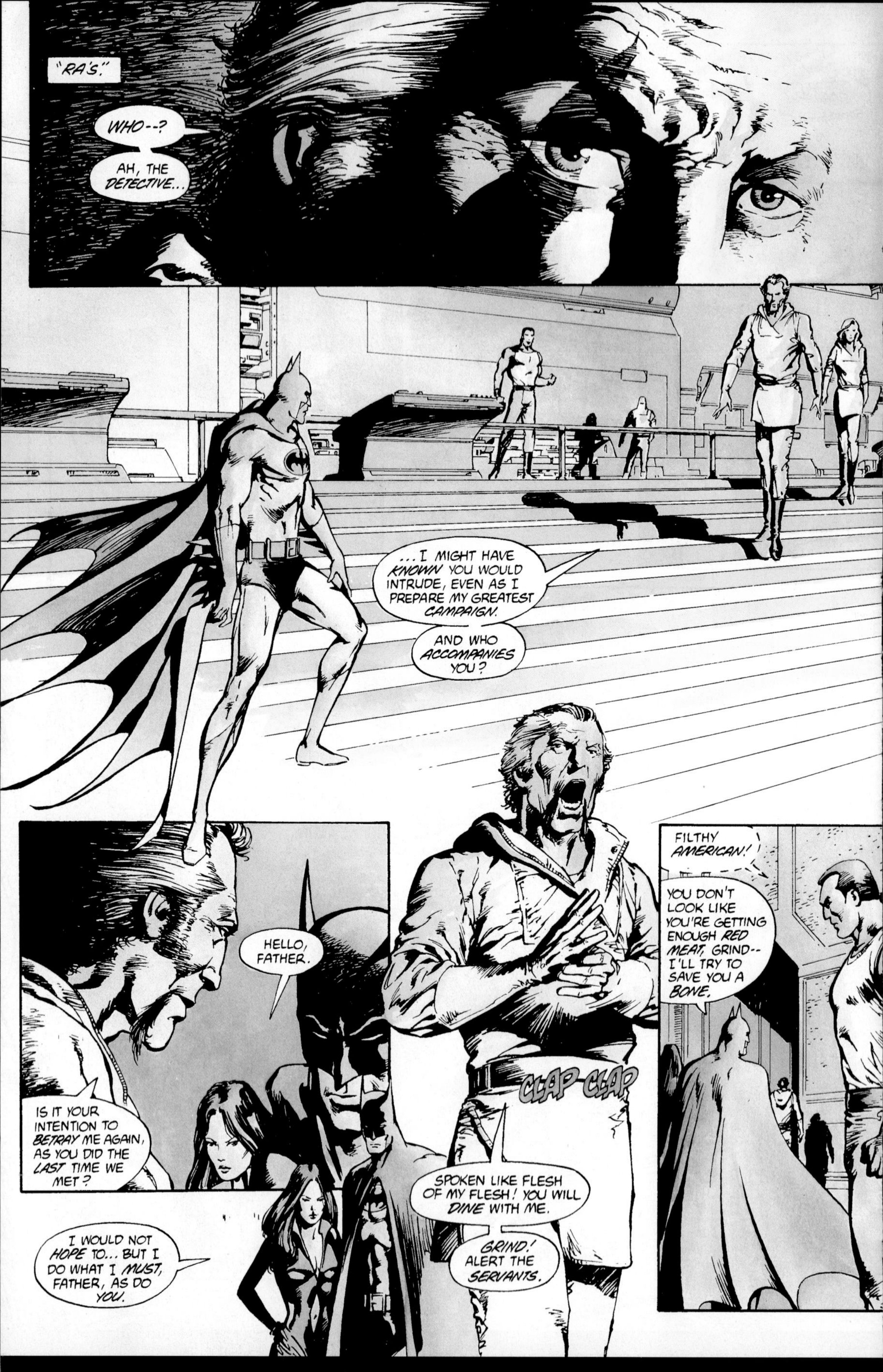
"RA'S."
WHO--?
AH, THE DETECTIVE...
...I MIGHT HAVE KNOWN YOU WOULD INTRUDE, EVEN AS I PREPARE MY GREATEST CAMPAIGN.
AND WHO ACCOMPANIES YOU?
HELLO, FATHER.
IS IT YOUR INTENTION TO BETRAY ME AGAIN, AS YOU DID THE LAST TIME WE MET?
I WOULD NOT HOPE TO... BUT I DO WHAT I MUST, FATHER, AS DO YOU.
CLAP CLAP
SPOKEN LIKE FLESH OF MY FLESH! YOU WILL DINE WITH ME.
GRIND! ALERT THE SERVANTS.
FILTHY AMERICAN!
YOU DON'T LOOK LIKE YOU'RE GETTING ENOUGH RED MEAT, GRIND-- I'LL TRY TO SAVE YOU A BONE.

YOU DO NOT *EAT*, DETECTIVE. IS THE MEAL *DISTASTEFUL* TO YOU?

I CAN'T ACCEPT A MAN'S *HOSPITALITY* UNDER *FALSE PRETENSES*, RA'S. YOU MENTIONED *"YOUR GREATEST CAMPAIGN."* I HAVE TO KNOW WHAT THAT *IS*.

I *SEE*. IT MAY BE A MISSION IN WHICH THE THREE OF US FIND OURSELVES AS *ALLIES*... AND IT MAY BE MY *LAST* MISSION, FOR SHOULD I PERISH IN THIS ENDEAVOR, THE LAZARUS PIT MAY NO LONGER BE ABLE TO RESTORE ME.

"AND SHOULD THAT BE THE CASE, ARE YOU SEEING THAT ALL YOUR OLD ENEMIES PRECEDE YOU?"

"YOU MAY SPEAK MORE CLEARLY THAN THAT, DETECTIVE."

"LIKE DR. HARRIS BLAINE."

"BLAINE. HE ONCE HAD THE PRESUMPTION TO JOIN YOUR FORCES AGAINST ME, DID HE NOT?"

HE *DID*. HE'S BEEN *MURDERED*, AND I HAVE REASON TO BELIEVE *YOU* WERE BEHIND IT.

"I ASSURE YOU, DETECTIVE, I WAS IN NO WAY INVOLVED IN BLAINE'S DEATH. INDEED, THE RENDERING USELESS OF SUCH AN INTELLECT IS DISTASTEFUL TO ME."

YOU'LL UNDERSTAND IF I NEED TO BE *CONVINCED*.

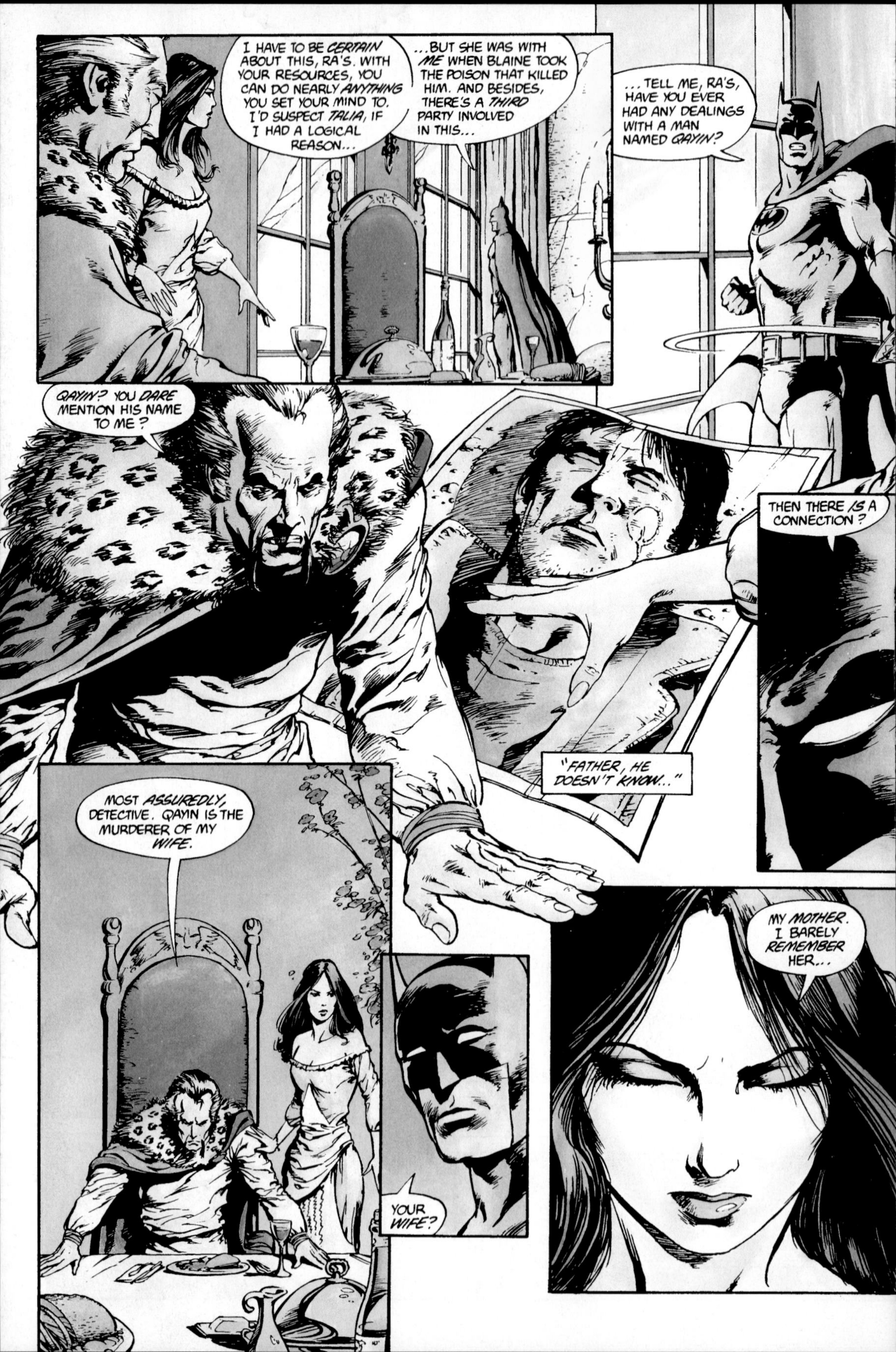
I HAVE TO BE CERTAIN ABOUT THIS, RA'S. WITH YOUR RESOURCES, YOU CAN DO NEARLY ANYTHING YOU SET YOUR MIND TO. I'D SUSPECT TALIA, IF I HAD A LOGICAL REASON...
...BUT SHE WAS WITH ME WHEN BLAINE TOOK THE POISON THAT KILLED HIM. AND BESIDES, THERE'S A THIRD PARTY INVOLVED IN THIS...
...TELL ME, RA'S, HAVE YOU EVER HAD ANY DEALINGS WITH A MAN NAMED QAYIN?
QAYIN? YOU DARE MENTION HIS NAME TO ME?
THEN THERE IS A CONNECTION?
"FATHER, HE DOESN'T KNOW..."
MOST ASSUREDLY, DETECTIVE. QAYIN IS THE MURDERER OF MY WIFE.
YOUR WIFE?
MY MOTHER. I BARELY REMEMBER HER...

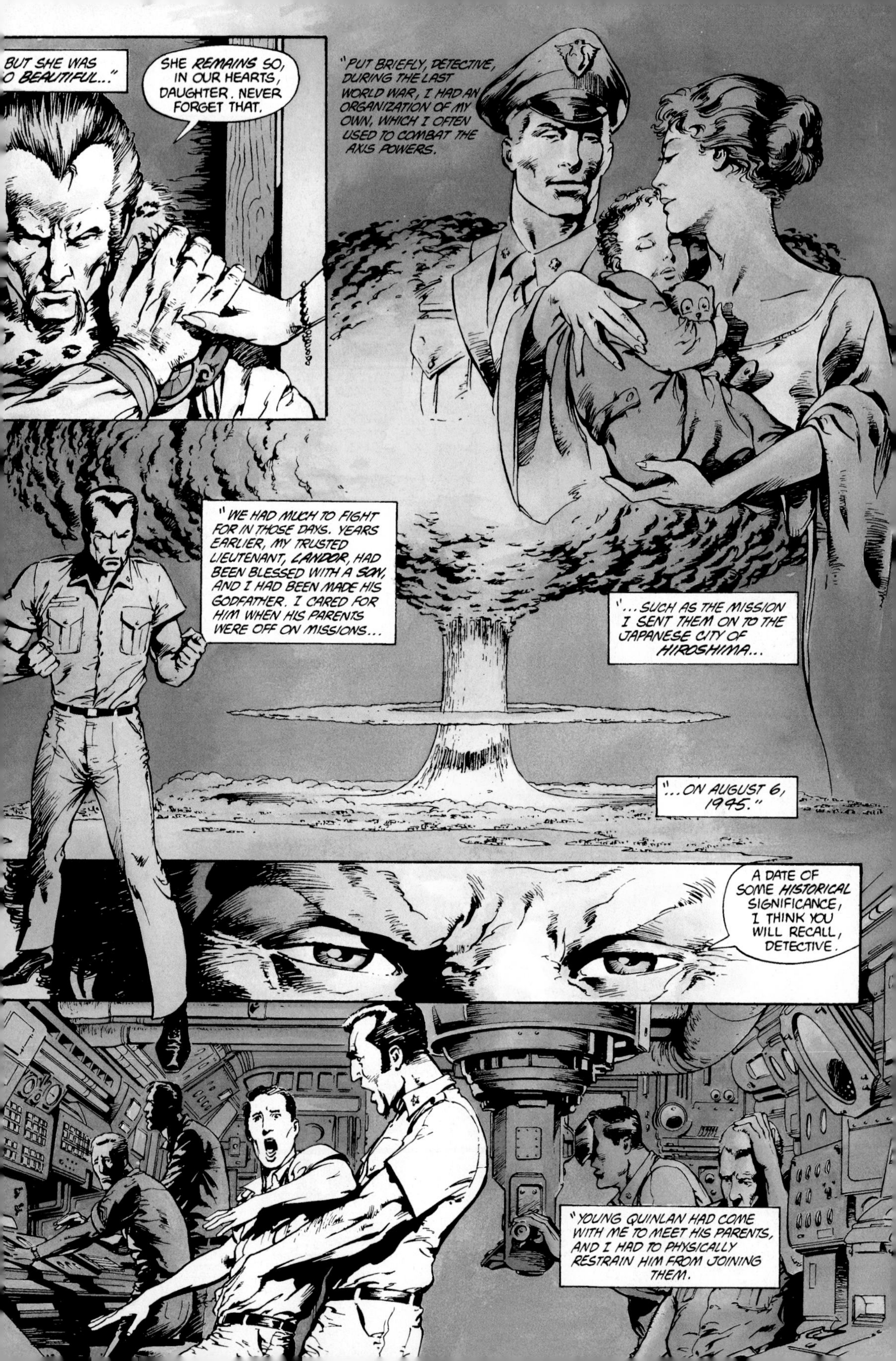

BUT SHE WAS O BEAUTIFUL..."
SHE REMAINS SO, IN OUR HEARTS, DAUGHTER. NEVER FORGET THAT.
"PUT BRIEFLY, DETECTIVE, DURING THE LAST WORLD WAR, I HAD AN ORGANIZATION OF MY OWN, WHICH I OFTEN USED TO COMBAT THE AXIS POWERS.
"WE HAD MUCH TO FIGHT FOR IN THOSE DAYS. YEARS EARLIER, MY TRUSTED LIEUTENANT, LANDOR, HAD BEEN BLESSED WITH A SON, AND I HAD BEEN MADE HIS GODFATHER. I CARED FOR HIM WHEN HIS PARENTS WERE OFF ON MISSIONS...
"...SUCH AS THE MISSION I SENT THEM ON TO THE JAPANESE CITY OF HIROSHIMA...
"...ON AUGUST 6, 1945."
A DATE OF SOME HISTORICAL SIGNIFICANCE, I THINK YOU WILL RECALL, DETECTIVE.
"YOUNG QUINLAN HAD COME WITH ME TO MEET HIS PARENTS, AND I HAD TO PHYSICALLY RESTRAIN HIM FROM JOINING THEM.

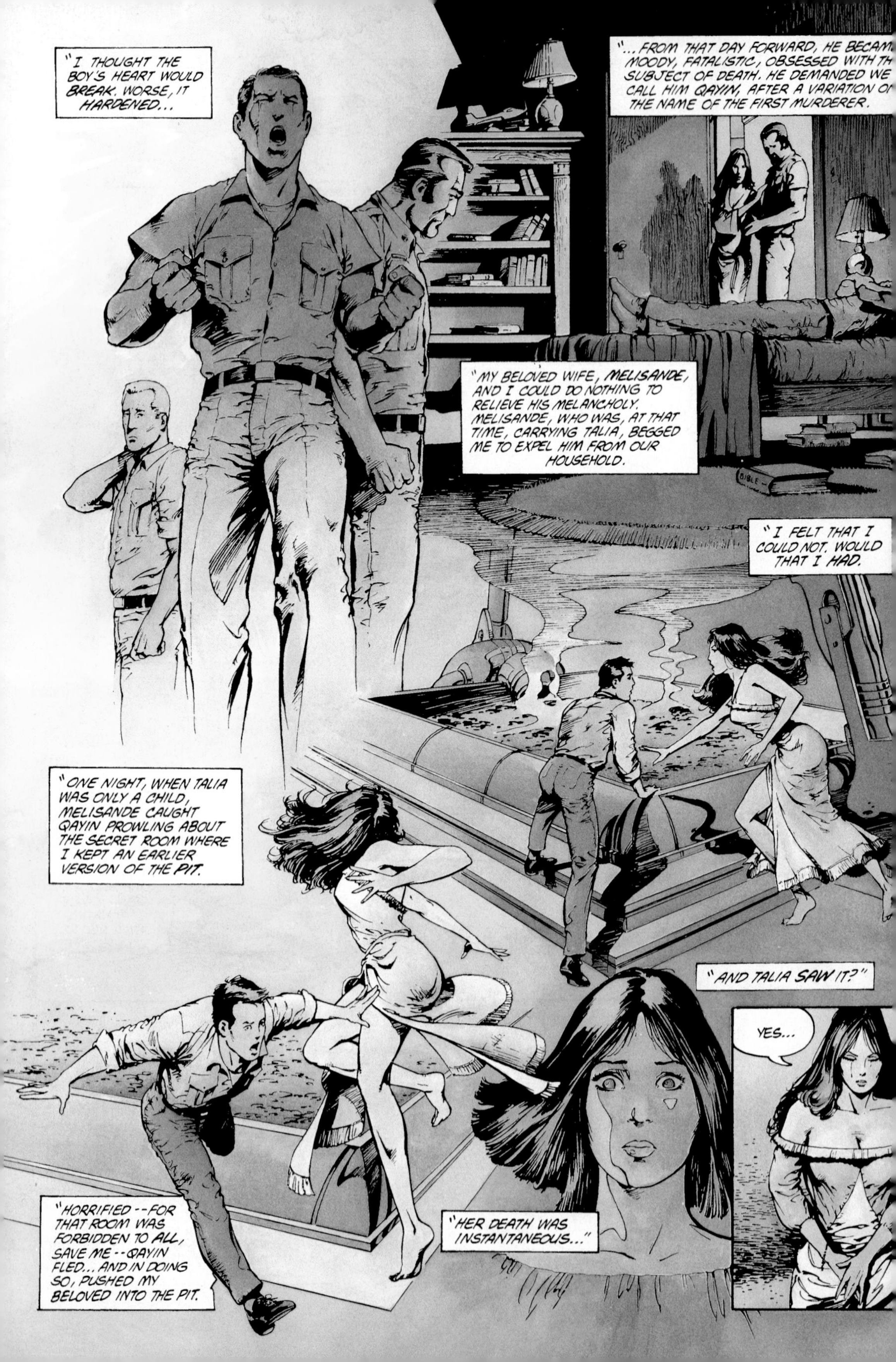
"I THOUGHT THE BOY'S HEART WOULD BREAK. WORSE, IT HARDENED...
"...FROM THAT DAY FORWARD, HE BECAM MOODY, FATALISTIC, OBSESSED WITH TH SUBJECT OF DEATH. HE DEMANDED WE CALL HIM QAYIN, AFTER A VARIATION OF THE NAME OF THE FIRST MURDERER.
"MY BELOVED WIFE, MELISANDE, AND I COULD DO NOTHING TO RELIEVE HIS MELANCHOLY. MELISANDE, WHO WAS, AT THAT TIME, CARRYING TALIA, BEGGED ME TO EXPEL HIM FROM OUR HOUSEHOLD.
BIBLE
"I FELT THAT I COULD NOT. WOULD THAT I HAD.
"ONE NIGHT, WHEN TALIA WAS ONLY A CHILD, MELISANDE CAUGHT QAYIN PROWLING ABOUT THE SECRET ROOM WHERE I KEPT AN EARLIER VERSION OF THE PIT.
"AND TALIA SAW IT?"
YES...
"HORRIFIED--FOR THAT ROOM WAS FORBIDDEN TO ALL, SAVE ME--QAYIN FLED... AND IN DOING SO, PUSHED MY BELOVED INTO THE PIT.
"HER DEATH WAS INSTANTANEOUS..."

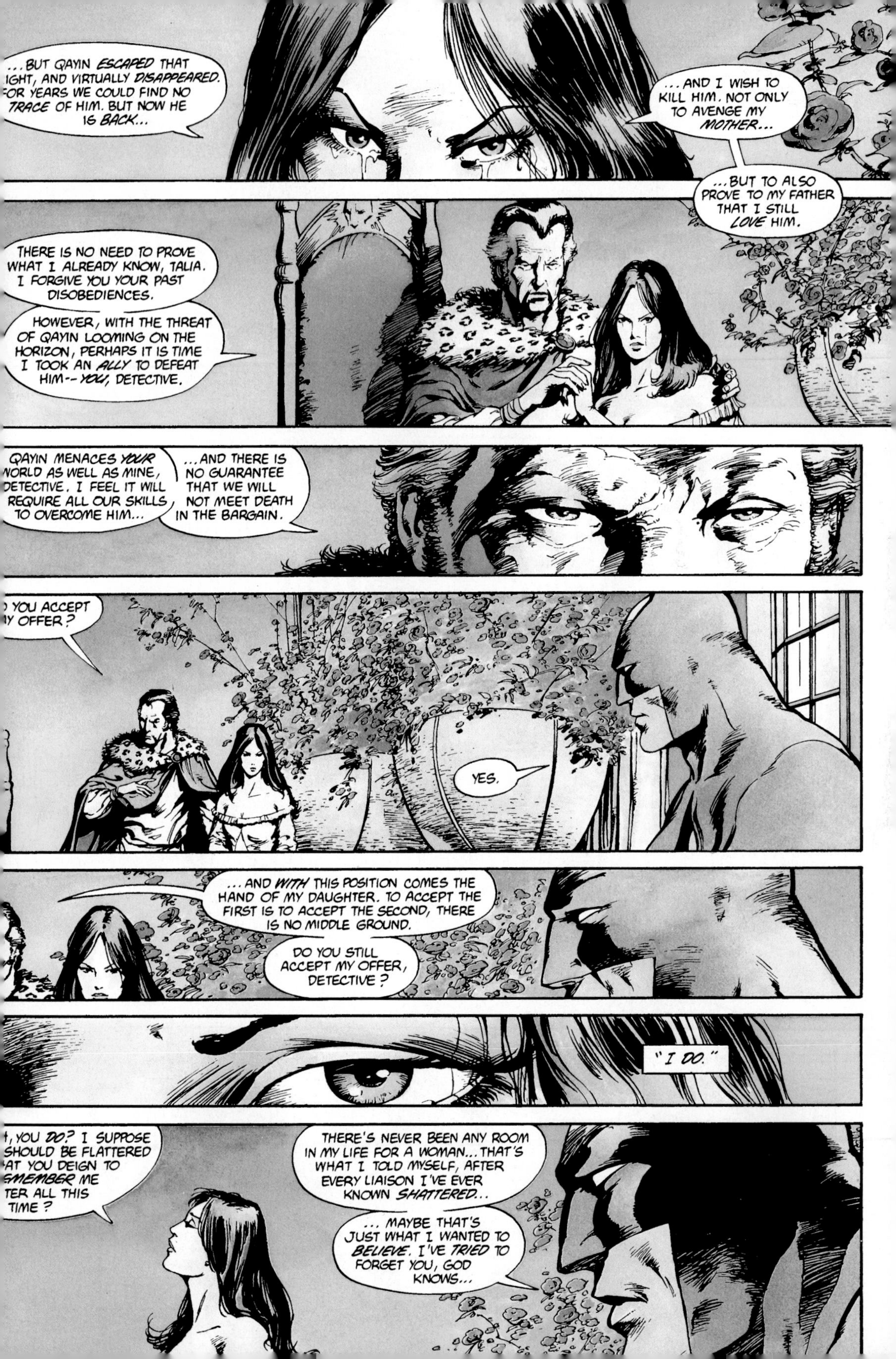
...BUT QAYIN ESCAPED THAT IGHT, AND VIRTUALLY DISAPPEARED. FOR YEARS WE COULD FIND NO TRACE OF HIM. BUT NOW HE IS BACK...
...AND I WISH TO KILL HIM. NOT ONLY TO AVENGE MY MOTHER...
...BUT TO ALSO PROVE TO MY FATHER THAT I STILL LOVE HIM.
THERE IS NO NEED TO PROVE WHAT I ALREADY KNOW, TALIA. I FORGIVE YOU YOUR PAST DISOBEDIENCES.
HOWEVER, WITH THE THREAT OF QAYIN LOOMING ON THE HORIZON, PERHAPS IT IS TIME I TOOK AN ALLY TO DEFEAT HIM-- YOU, DETECTIVE.
QAYIN MENACES YOUR WORLD AS WELL AS MINE, DETECTIVE. I FEEL IT WILL REQUIRE ALL OUR SKILLS TO OVERCOME HIM...
...AND THERE IS NO GUARANTEE THAT WE WILL NOT MEET DEATH IN THE BARGAIN.
YOU ACCEPT OFFER?
YES.
...AND WITH THIS POSITION COMES THE HAND OF MY DAUGHTER. TO ACCEPT THE FIRST IS TO ACCEPT THE SECOND, THERE IS NO MIDDLE GROUND.
DO YOU STILL ACCEPT MY OFFER, DETECTIVE?
"I DO."
, YOU DO? I SUPPOSE SHOULD BE FLATTERED AT YOU DEIGN TO EMEMBER ME TER ALL THIS TIME?
THERE'S NEVER BEEN ANY ROOM IN MY LIFE FOR A WOMAN... THAT'S WHAT I TOLD MYSELF, AFTER EVERY LIAISON I'VE EVER KNOWN SHATTERED...
... MAYBE THAT'S JUST WHAT I WANTED TO BELIEVE. I'VE TRIED TO FORGET YOU, GOD KNOWS...

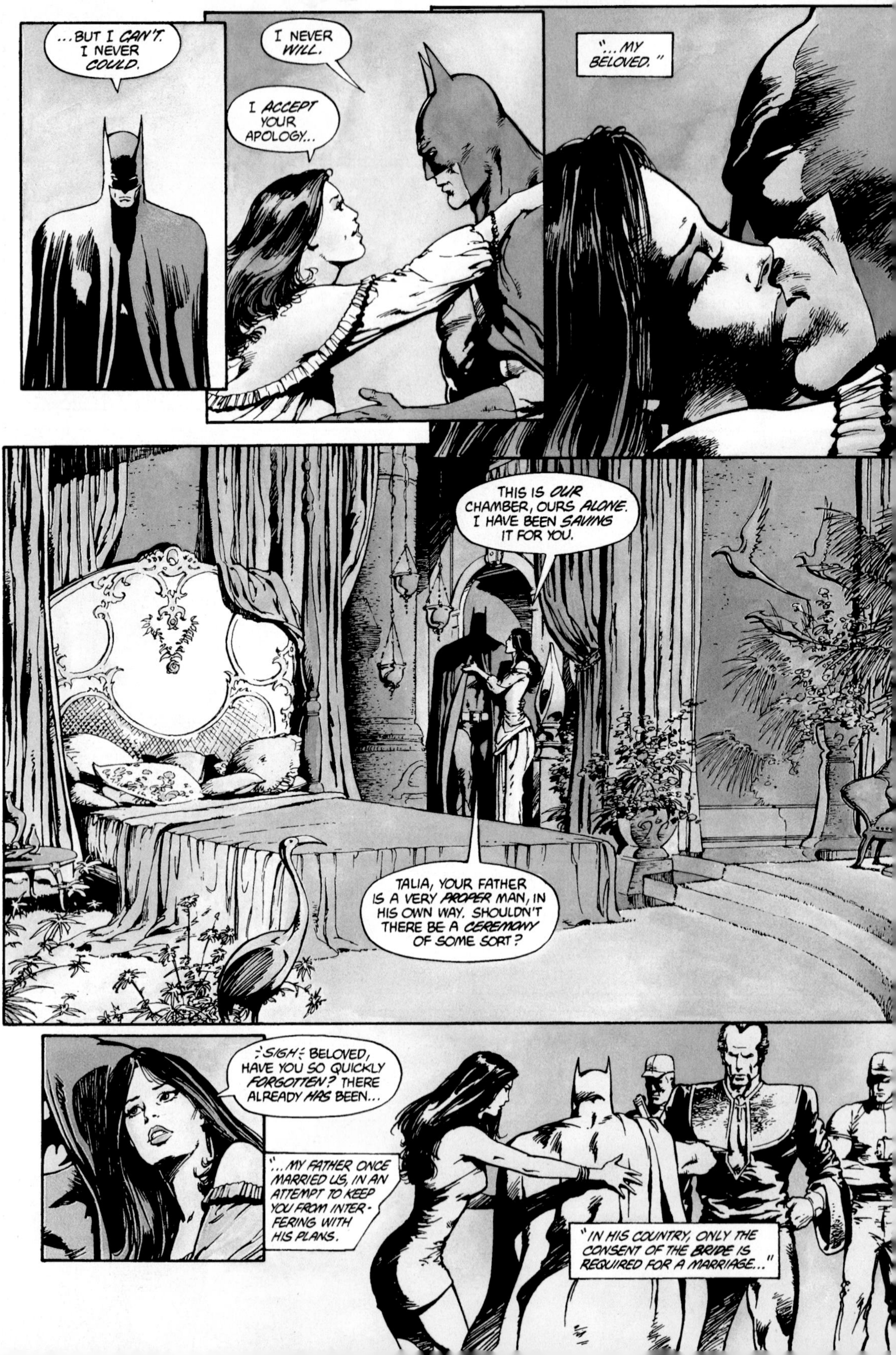
...BUT I CAN'T. I NEVER COULD.
I NEVER WILL.
I ACCEPT YOUR APOLOGY...
"...MY BELOVED."
THIS IS OUR CHAMBER, OURS ALONE. I HAVE BEEN SAVING IT FOR YOU.
TALIA, YOUR FATHER IS A VERY PROPER MAN, IN HIS OWN WAY. SHOULDN'T THERE BE A CEREMONY OF SOME SORT?
SIGH BELOVED, HAVE YOU SO QUICKLY FORGOTTEN? THERE ALREADY HAS BEEN...
"...MY FATHER ONCE MARRIED US, IN AN ATTEMPT TO KEEP YOU FROM INTERFERING WITH HIS PLANS.
"IN HIS COUNTRY, ONLY THE CONSENT OF THE BRIDE IS REQUIRED FOR A MARRIAGE..."

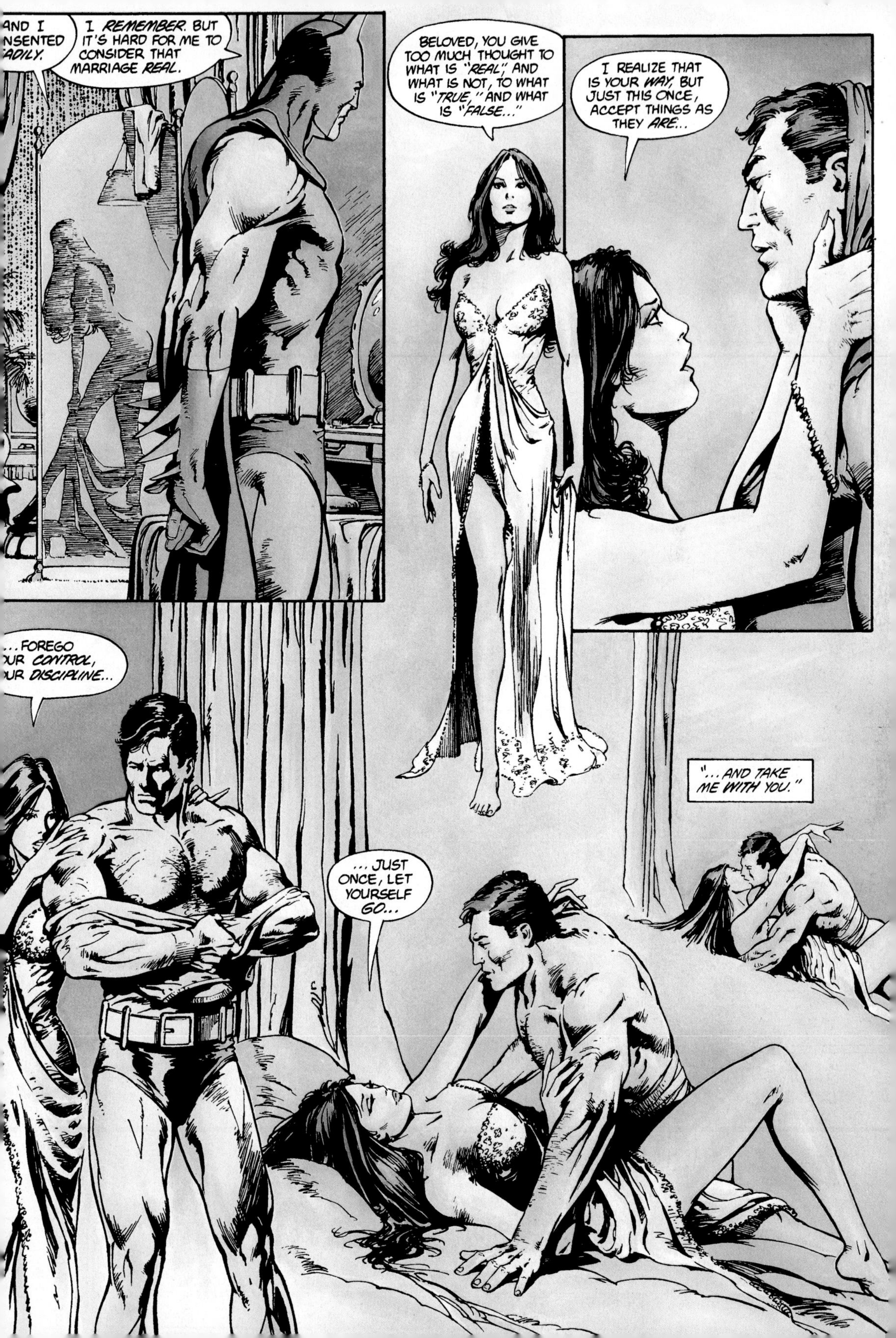
AND I NSENTED ADILY.
I REMEMBER. BUT IT'S HARD FOR ME TO CONSIDER THAT MARRIAGE REAL.
BELOVED, YOU GIVE TOO MUCH THOUGHT TO WHAT IS "REAL," AND WHAT IS NOT, TO WHAT IS "TRUE," AND WHAT IS "FALSE..."
I REALIZE THAT IS YOUR WAY, BUT JUST THIS ONCE, ACCEPT THINGS AS THEY ARE...
...FOREGO OUR CONTROL, OUR DISCIPLINE...
...JUST ONCE, LET YOURSELF GO...
"...AND TAKE ME WITH YOU."

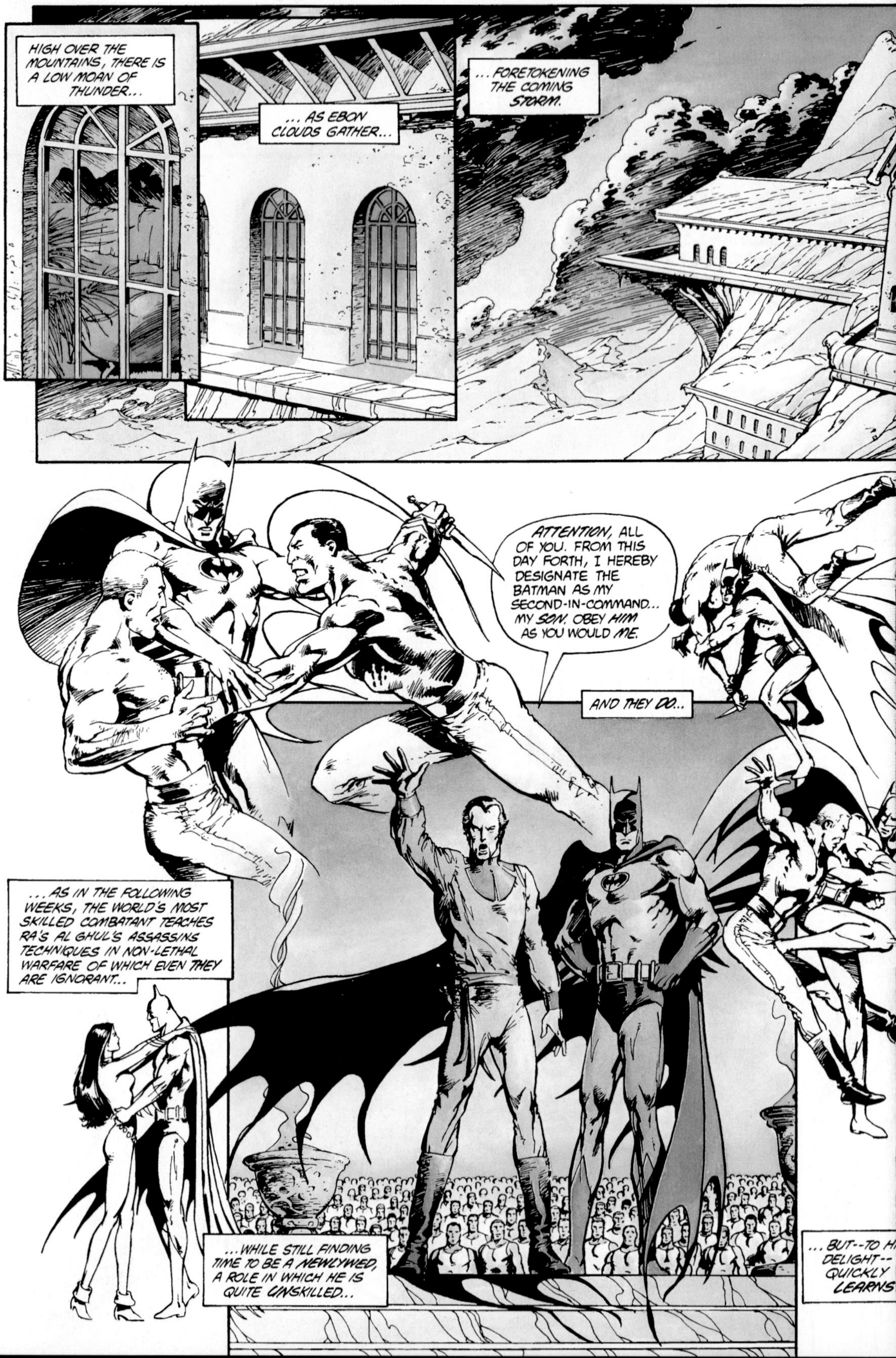
HIGH OVER THE MOUNTAINS, THERE IS A LOW MOAN OF THUNDER...
...AS EBON CLOUDS GATHER...
...FORETOKENING THE COMING STORM.
ATTENTION, ALL OF YOU. FROM THIS DAY FORTH, I HEREBY DESIGNATE THE BATMAN AS MY SECOND-IN-COMMAND... MY SON. OBEY HIM AS YOU WOULD ME.
AND THEY DO...
...AS IN THE FOLLOWING WEEKS, THE WORLD'S MOST SKILLED COMBATANT TEACHES RA'S AL GHUL'S ASSASSINS TECHNIQUES IN NON-LETHAL WARFARE OF WHICH EVEN THEY ARE IGNORANT...
...WHILE STILL FINDING TIME TO BE A NEWLYWED, A ROLE IN WHICH HE IS QUITE UNSKILLED...
...BUT--TO HI DELIGHT-- QUICKLY LEARNS

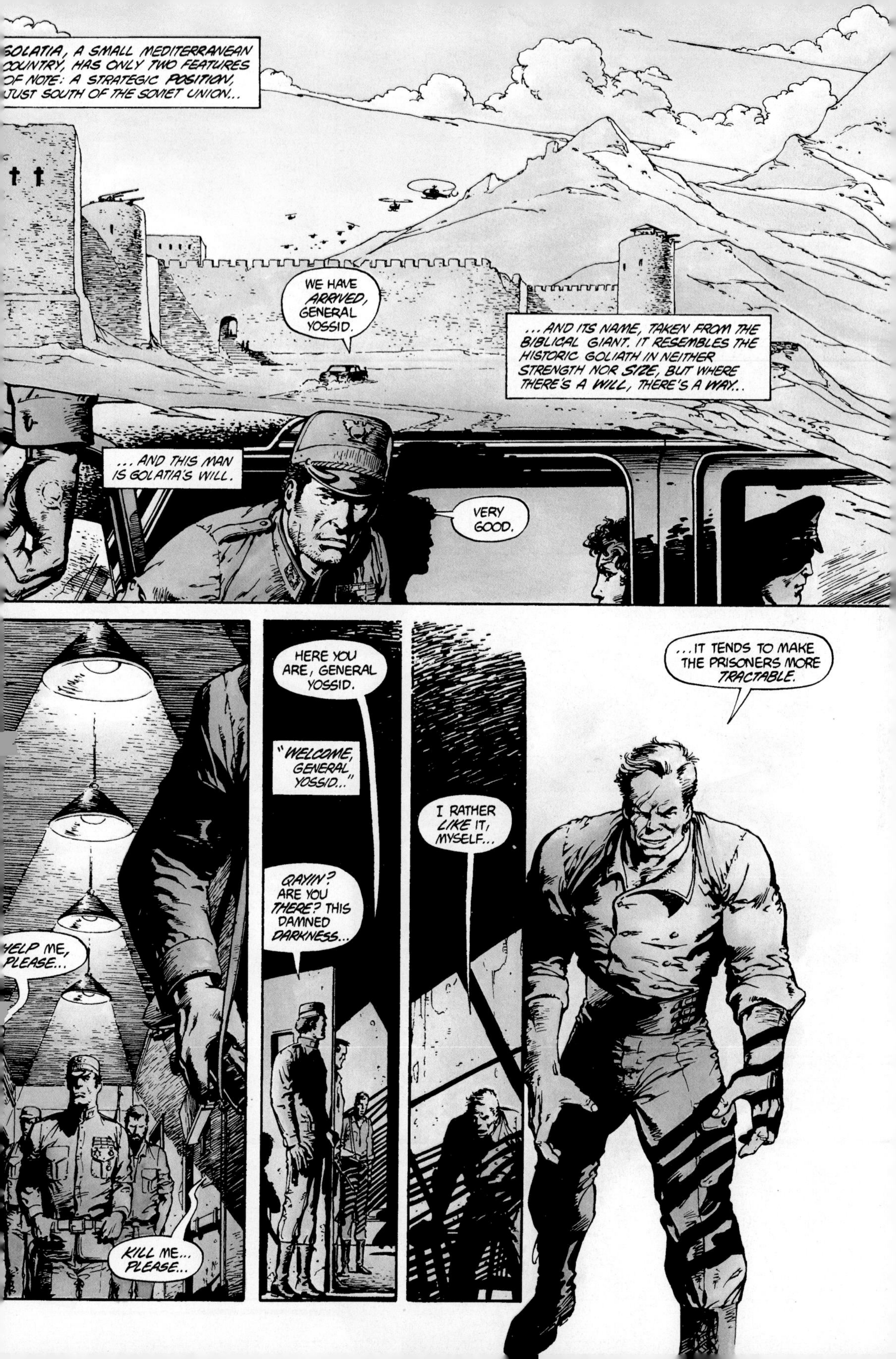
GOLATIA, A SMALL MEDITERRANEAN COUNTRY, HAS ONLY TWO FEATURES OF NOTE: A STRATEGIC POSITION, JUST SOUTH OF THE SOVIET UNION...
WE HAVE ARRIVED, GENERAL YOSSID.
...AND ITS NAME, TAKEN FROM THE BIBLICAL GIANT. IT RESEMBLES THE HISTORIC GOLIATH IN NEITHER STRENGTH NOR SIZE, BUT WHERE THERE'S A WILL, THERE'S A WAY...
...AND THIS MAN IS GOLATIA'S WILL.
VERY GOOD.
HELP ME, PLEASE...
KILL ME... PLEASE...
HERE YOU ARE, GENERAL YOSSID.
"WELCOME, GENERAL YOSSID..."
QAYIN? ARE YOU THERE? THIS DAMNED DARKNESS...
I RATHER LIKE IT, MYSELF...
...IT TENDS TO MAKE THE PRISONERS MORE TRACTABLE.

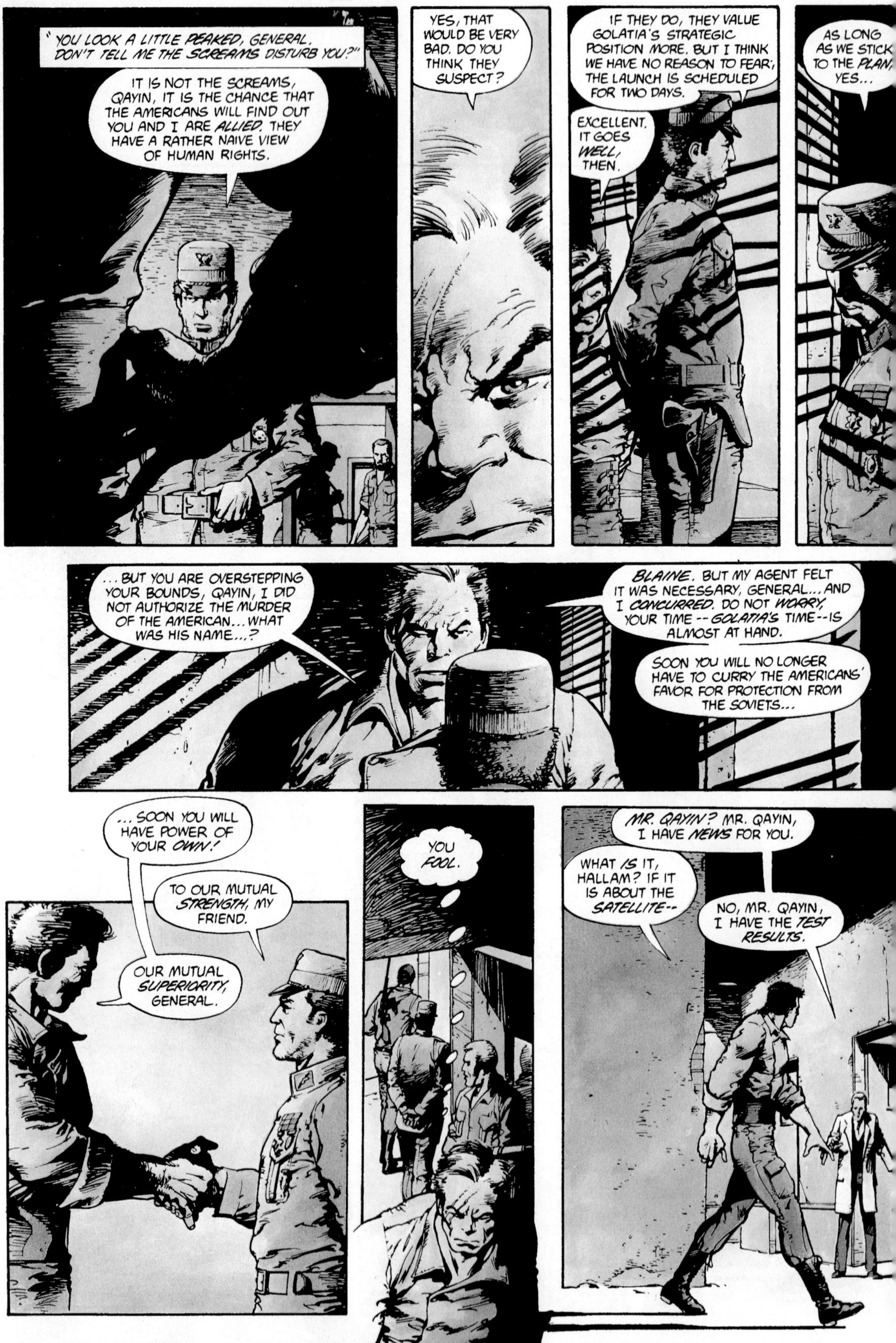
"YOU LOOK A LITTLE PEAKED, GENERAL. DON'T TELL ME THE SCREAMS DISTURB YOU?"
IT IS NOT THE SCREAMS, QAYIN, IT IS THE CHANCE THAT THE AMERICANS WILL FIND OUT YOU AND I ARE ALLIED. THEY HAVE A RATHER NAIVE VIEW OF HUMAN RIGHTS.
YES, THAT WOULD BE VERY BAD. DO YOU THINK THEY SUSPECT?
IF THEY DO, THEY VALUE GOLATIA'S STRATEGIC POSITION MORE. BUT I THINK WE HAVE NO REASON TO FEAR; THE LAUNCH IS SCHEDULED FOR TWO DAYS.
EXCELLENT. IT GOES WELL, THEN.
AS LONG AS WE STICK TO THE PLAN, YES...
...BUT YOU ARE OVERSTEPPING YOUR BOUNDS, QAYIN. I DID NOT AUTHORIZE THE MURDER OF THE AMERICAN... WHAT WAS HIS NAME...?
BLAINE. BUT MY AGENT FELT IT WAS NECESSARY, GENERAL... AND I CONCURRED. DO NOT WORRY, YOUR TIME -- GOLATIA'S TIME -- IS ALMOST AT HAND.
SOON YOU WILL NO LONGER HAVE TO CURRY THE AMERICANS' FAVOR FOR PROTECTION FROM THE SOVIETS...
...SOON YOU WILL HAVE POWER OF YOUR OWN!
TO OUR MUTUAL STRENGTH, MY FRIEND.
OUR MUTUAL SUPERIORITY, GENERAL.
YOU FOOL.
MR. QAYIN? MR. QAYIN, I HAVE NEWS FOR YOU.
WHAT IS IT, HALLAM? IF IT IS ABOUT THE SATELLITE--
NO, MR. QAYIN, I HAVE THE TEST RESULTS.

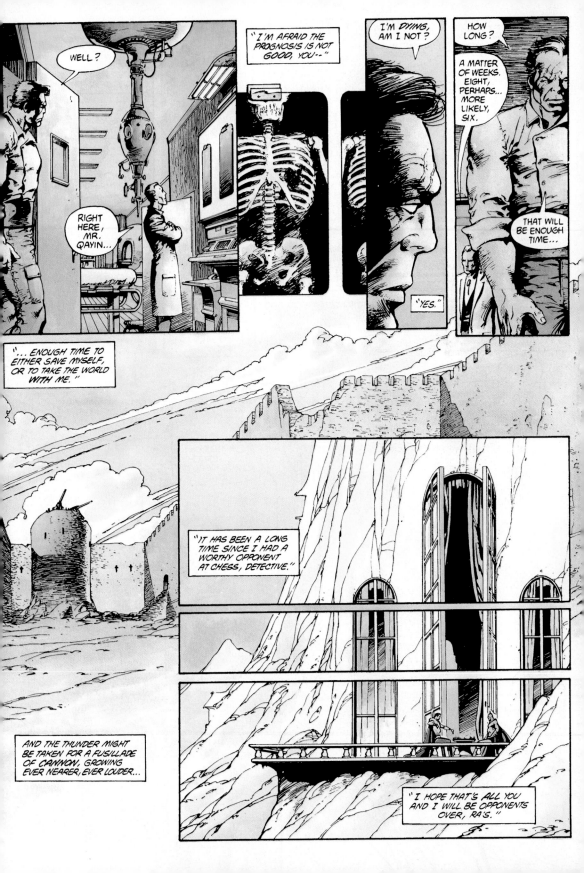

WELL?

RIGHT HERE, MR. QAYIN...

"I'M AFRAID THE PROGNOSIS IS NOT GOOD, YOU--"

I'M *DYING*, AM I NOT?

HOW LONG?

A MATTER OF WEEKS. EIGHT, PERHAPS... MORE LIKELY, SIX.

"YES."

THAT WILL BE ENOUGH TIME...

"... ENOUGH TIME TO EITHER SAVE MYSELF, OR TO TAKE THE WORLD WITH ME."

"IT HAS BEEN A LONG TIME SINCE I HAD A WORTHY OPPONENT AT CHESS, DETECTIVE."

AND THE THUNDER MIGHT BE TAKEN FOR A FUSILLADE OF CANNON, GROWING EVER NEARER, EVER LOUDER...

"I HOPE THAT'S ALL YOU AND I WILL BE OPPONENTS OVER, RA'S."

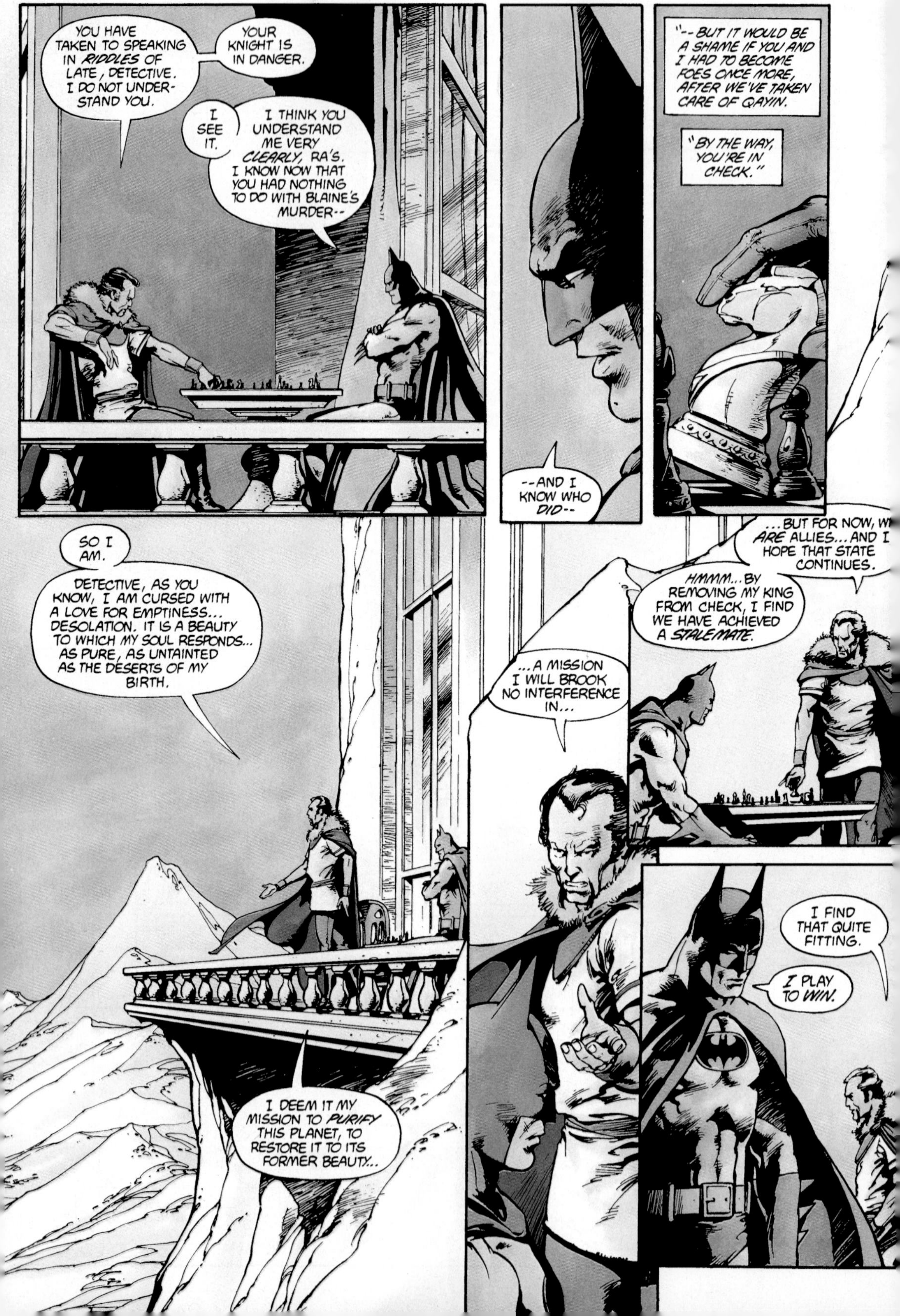

YOU HAVE TAKEN TO SPEAKING IN RIDDLES OF LATE, DETECTIVE. I DO NOT UNDERSTAND YOU.
YOUR KNIGHT IS IN DANGER.
I SEE IT.
I THINK YOU UNDERSTAND ME VERY CLEARLY, RA'S. I KNOW NOW THAT YOU HAD NOTHING TO DO WITH BLAINE'S MURDER--
--AND I KNOW WHO DID--
"--BUT IT WOULD BE A SHAME IF YOU AND I HAD TO BECOME FOES ONCE MORE, AFTER WE'VE TAKEN CARE OF QAYIN.
"BY THE WAY, YOU'RE IN CHECK."
SO I AM.
DETECTIVE, AS YOU KNOW, I AM CURSED WITH A LOVE FOR EMPTINESS... DESOLATION. IT IS A BEAUTY TO WHICH MY SOUL RESPONDS... AS PURE, AS UNTAINTED AS THE DESERTS OF MY BIRTH.
I DEEM IT MY MISSION TO PURIFY THIS PLANET, TO RESTORE IT TO ITS FORMER BEAUTY...
...A MISSION I WILL BROOK NO INTERFERENCE IN...
HMMM... BY REMOVING MY KING FROM CHECK, I FIND WE HAVE ACHIEVED A STALEMATE.
...BUT FOR NOW, WE ARE ALLIES... AND I HOPE THAT STATE CONTINUES.
I FIND THAT QUITE FITTING.
I PLAY TO WIN.

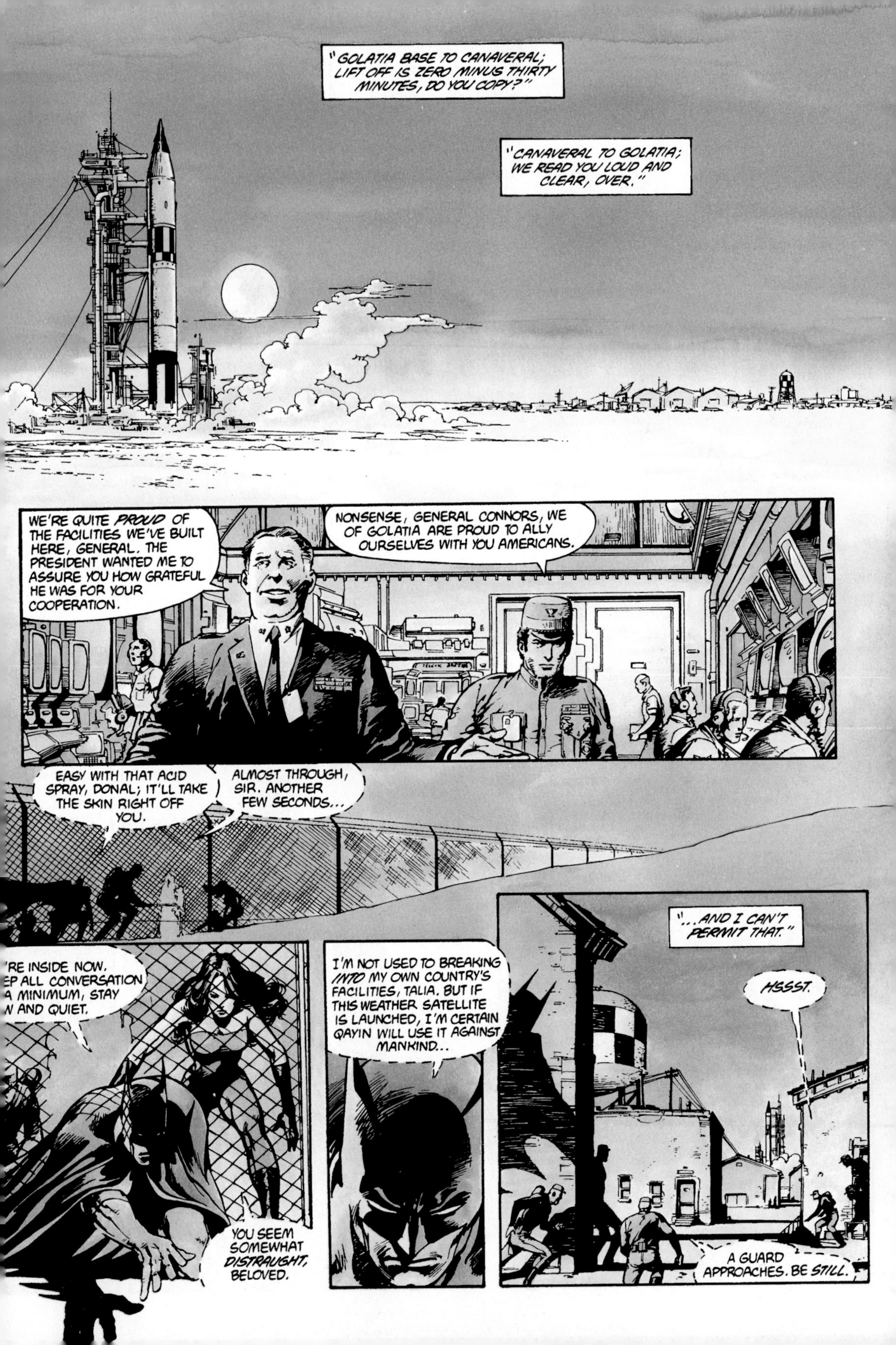
"GOLATIA BASE TO CANAVERAL; LIFT OFF IS ZERO MINUS THIRTY MINUTES, DO YOU COPY?"
"CANAVERAL TO GOLATIA; WE READ YOU LOUD AND CLEAR, OVER."
WE'RE QUITE PROUD OF THE FACILITIES WE'VE BUILT HERE, GENERAL. THE PRESIDENT WANTED ME TO ASSURE YOU HOW GRATEFUL HE WAS FOR YOUR COOPERATION.
NONSENSE, GENERAL CONNORS, WE OF GOLATIA ARE PROUD TO ALLY OURSELVES WITH YOU AMERICANS.
EASY WITH THAT ACID SPRAY, DONAL; IT'LL TAKE THE SKIN RIGHT OFF YOU.
ALMOST THROUGH, SIR. ANOTHER FEW SECONDS...
'RE INSIDE NOW. EP ALL CONVERSATION A MINIMUM, STAY N AND QUIET.
YOU SEEM SOMEWHAT DISTRAUGHT, BELOVED.
I'M NOT USED TO BREAKING INTO MY OWN COUNTRY'S FACILITIES, TALIA. BUT IF THIS WEATHER SATELLITE IS LAUNCHED, I'M CERTAIN QAYIN WILL USE IT AGAINST MANKIND...
"...AND I CAN'T PERMIT THAT."
HSSST.
A GUARD APPROACHES. BE STILL.

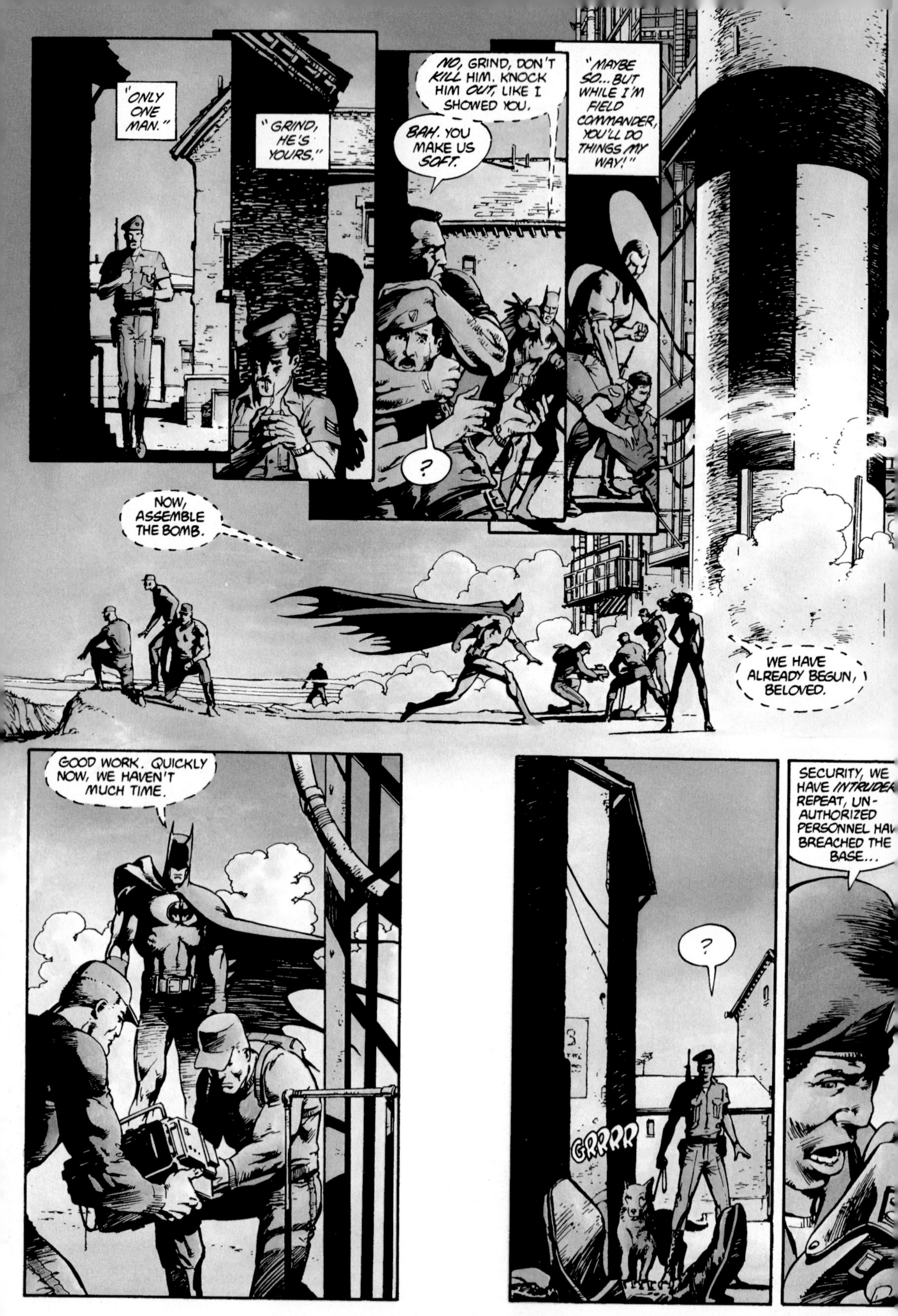
"ONLY ONE MAN."
"GRIND, HE'S YOURS."
NO, GRIND, DON'T KILL HIM. KNOCK HIM OUT, LIKE I SHOWED YOU.
BAH. YOU MAKE US SOFT.
"MAYBE SO... BUT WHILE I'M FIELD COMMANDER, YOU'LL DO THINGS MY WAY!"
?
NOW, ASSEMBLE THE BOMB.
WE HAVE ALREADY BEGUN, BELOVED.
GOOD WORK. QUICKLY NOW, WE HAVEN'T MUCH TIME.
?
GRRRR
SECURITY, WE HAVE INTRUDER REPEAT, UN-AUTHORIZED PERSONNEL HAV BREACHED THE BASE...

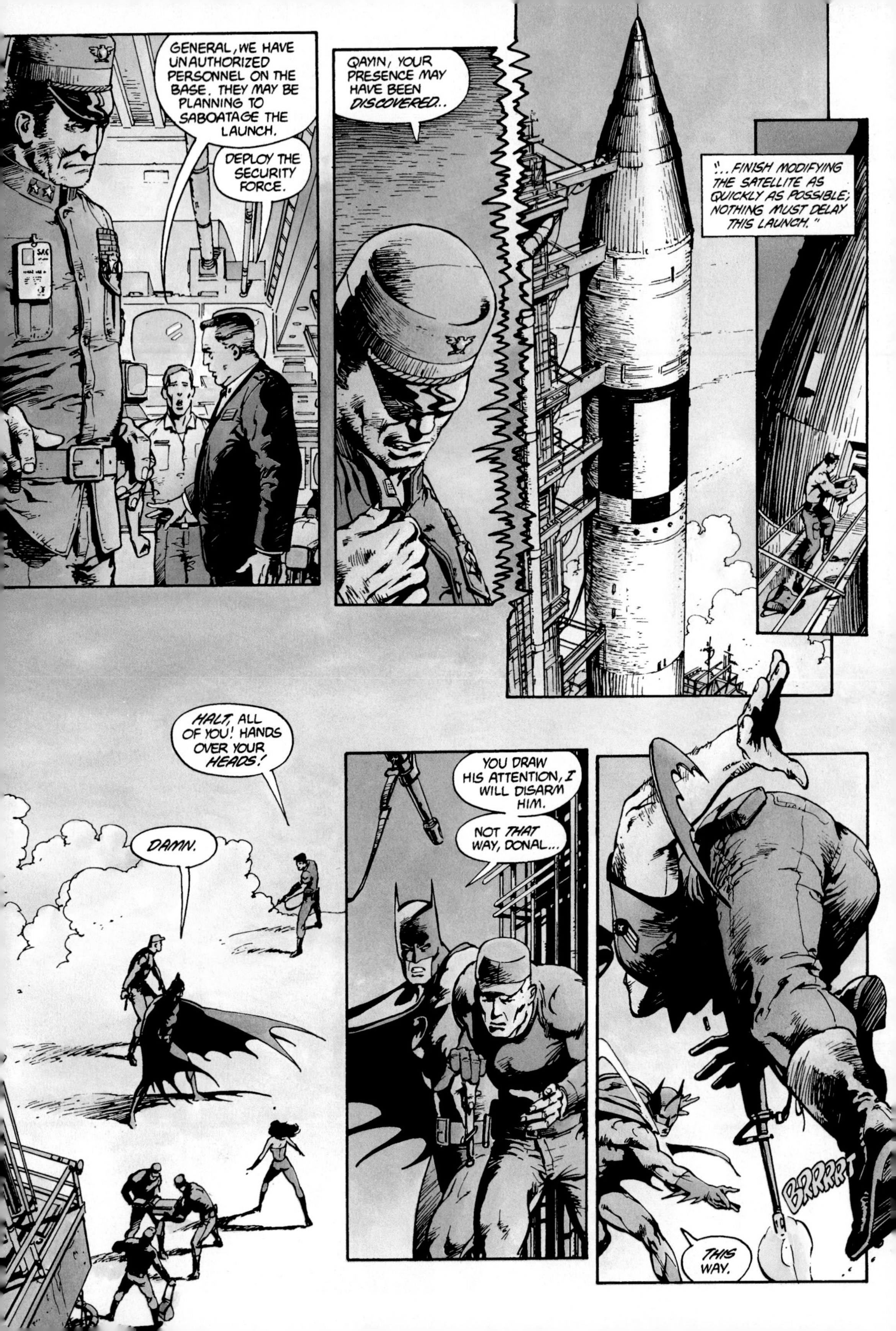
GENERAL, WE HAVE UNAUTHORIZED PERSONNEL ON THE BASE. THEY MAY BE PLANNING TO SABOATAGE THE LAUNCH.
DEPLOY THE SECURITY FORCE.
QAYIN, YOUR PRESENCE MAY HAVE BEEN DISCOVERED..
"...FINISH MODIFYING THE SATELLITE AS QUICKLY AS POSSIBLE; NOTHING MUST DELAY THIS LAUNCH."
HALT, ALL OF YOU! HANDS OVER YOUR HEADS!
DAMN.
YOU DRAW HIS ATTENTION, I WILL DISARM HIM.
NOT THAT WAY, DONAL...
BRRRRPT
THIS WAY.

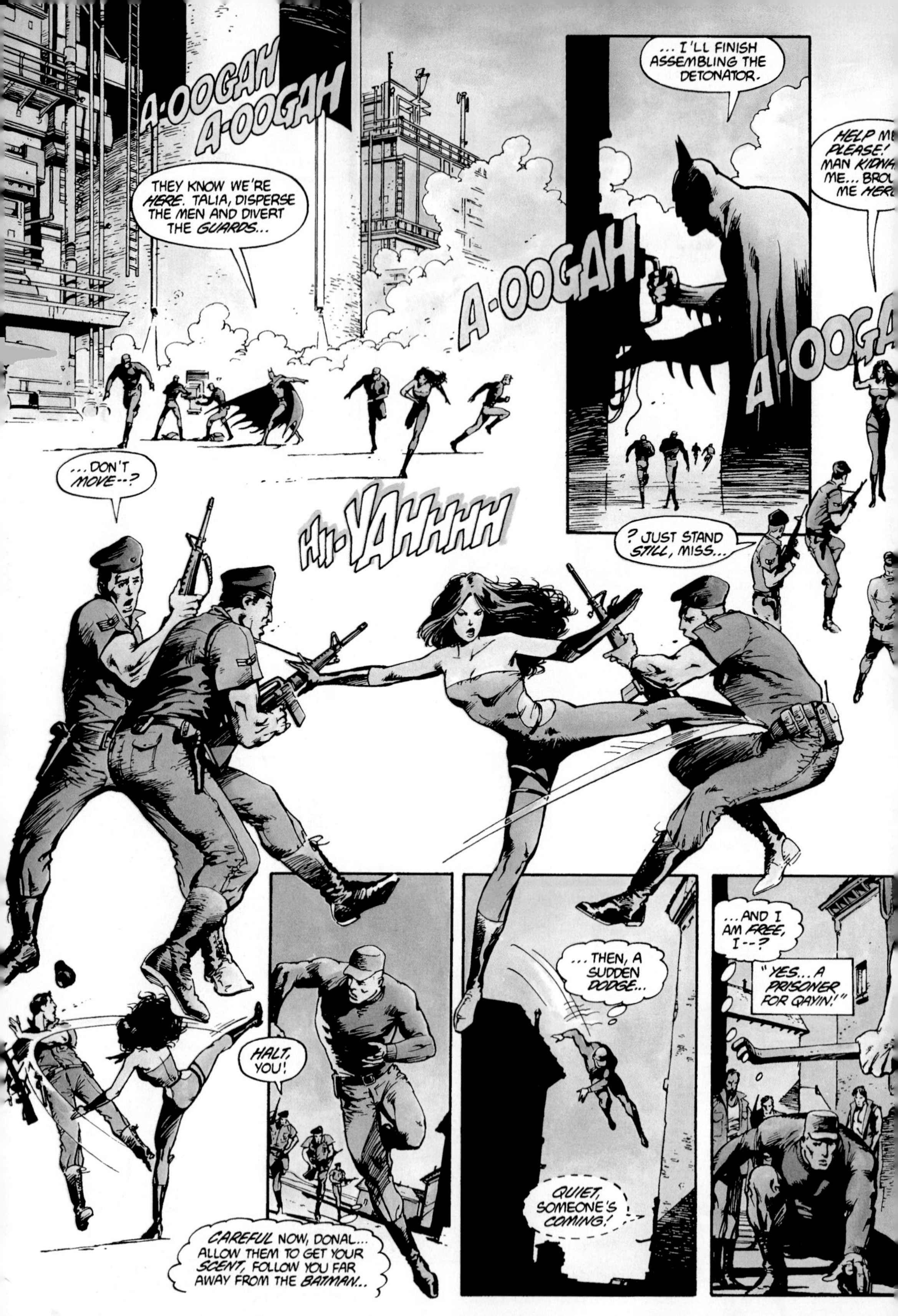

A-OOGAH
A-OOGAH
THEY KNOW WE'RE HERE. TALIA, DISPERSE THE MEN AND DIVERT THE GUARDS...
A-OOGAH
... I'LL FINISH ASSEMBLING THE DETONATOR.
A-OOGA
...DON'T MOVE--?
HI-YAHHHH
? JUST STAND STILL, MISS...
HALT, YOU!
CAREFUL NOW, DONAL... ALLOW THEM TO GET YOUR SCENT, FOLLOW YOU FAR AWAY FROM THE BATMAN...
...THEN, A SUDDEN DODGE...
QUIET, SOMEONE'S COMING!
...AND I AM FREE, I--?
"YES... A PRISONER FOR QAYIN!"

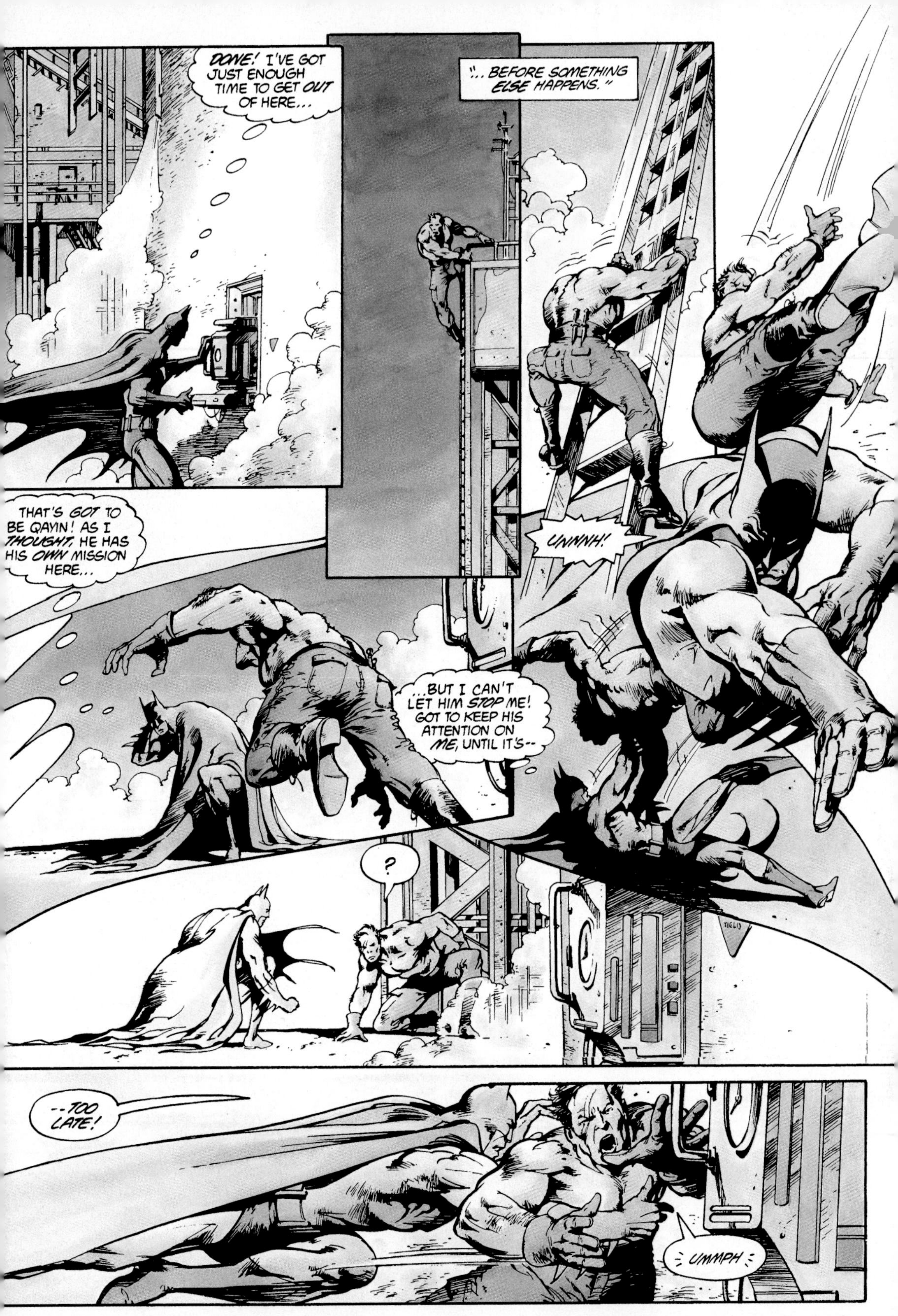
DONE! I'VE GOT JUST ENOUGH TIME TO GET OUT OF HERE...
"... BEFORE SOMETHING ELSE HAPPENS."
THAT'S GOT TO BE QAYIN! AS I THOUGHT, HE HAS HIS OWN MISSION HERE...
...BUT I CAN'T LET HIM STOP ME! GOT TO KEEP HIS ATTENTION ON ME, UNTIL IT'S--
UNNNH!
?
--TOO LATE!
UMMPH

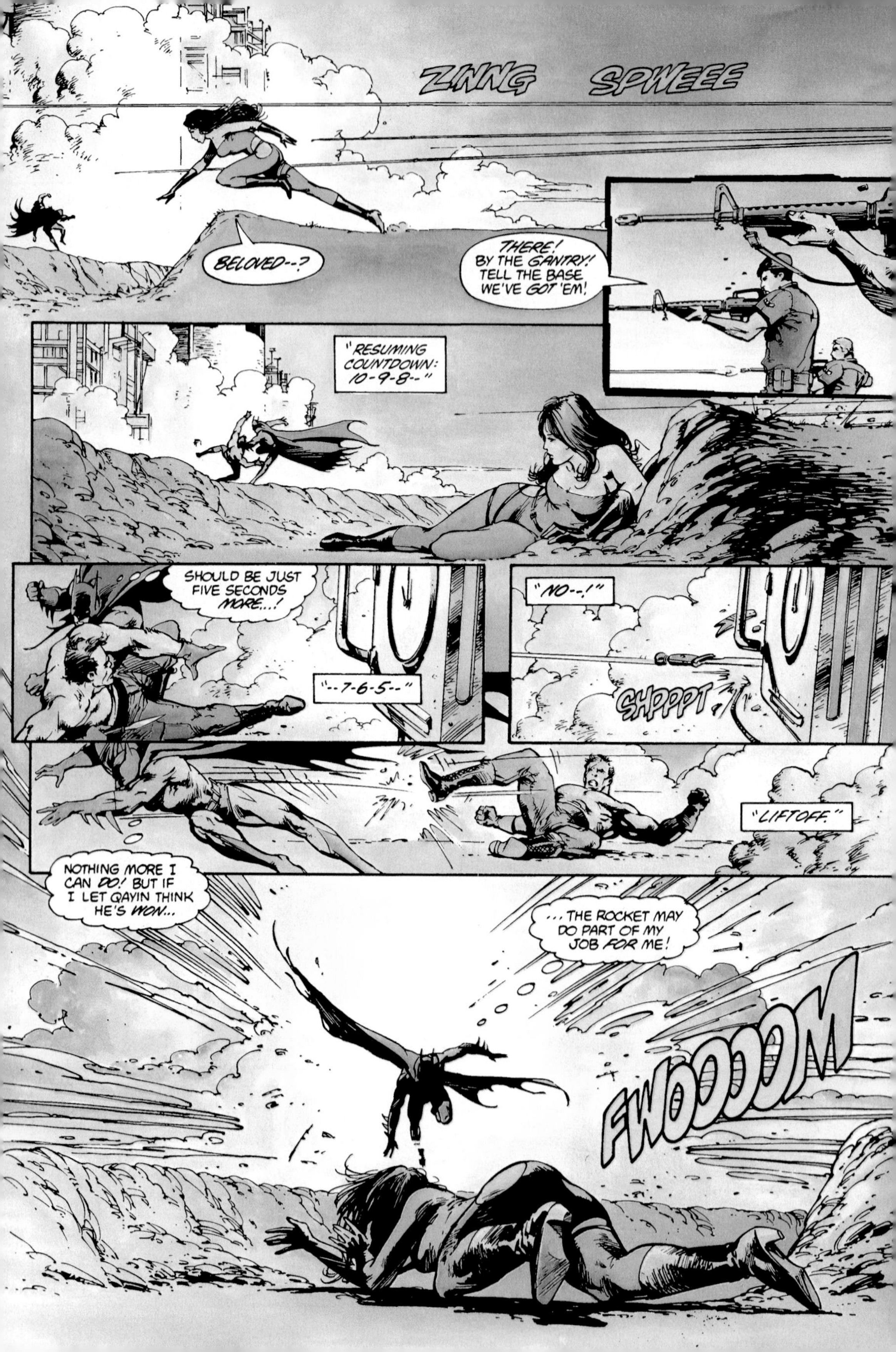
ZNNG
SPWEEE
BELOVED--?
THERE! BY THE GANTRY! TELL THE BASE WE'VE GOT 'EM!
"RESUMING COUNTDOWN: 10-9-8--"
SHOULD BE JUST FIVE SECONDS MORE...!
"--7-6-5--"
"NO--!"
SHPPPT
"LIFTOFF."
NOTHING MORE I CAN DO! BUT IF I LET QAYIN THINK HE'S WON...
...THE ROCKET MAY DO PART OF MY JOB FOR ME!
FWOOOOM

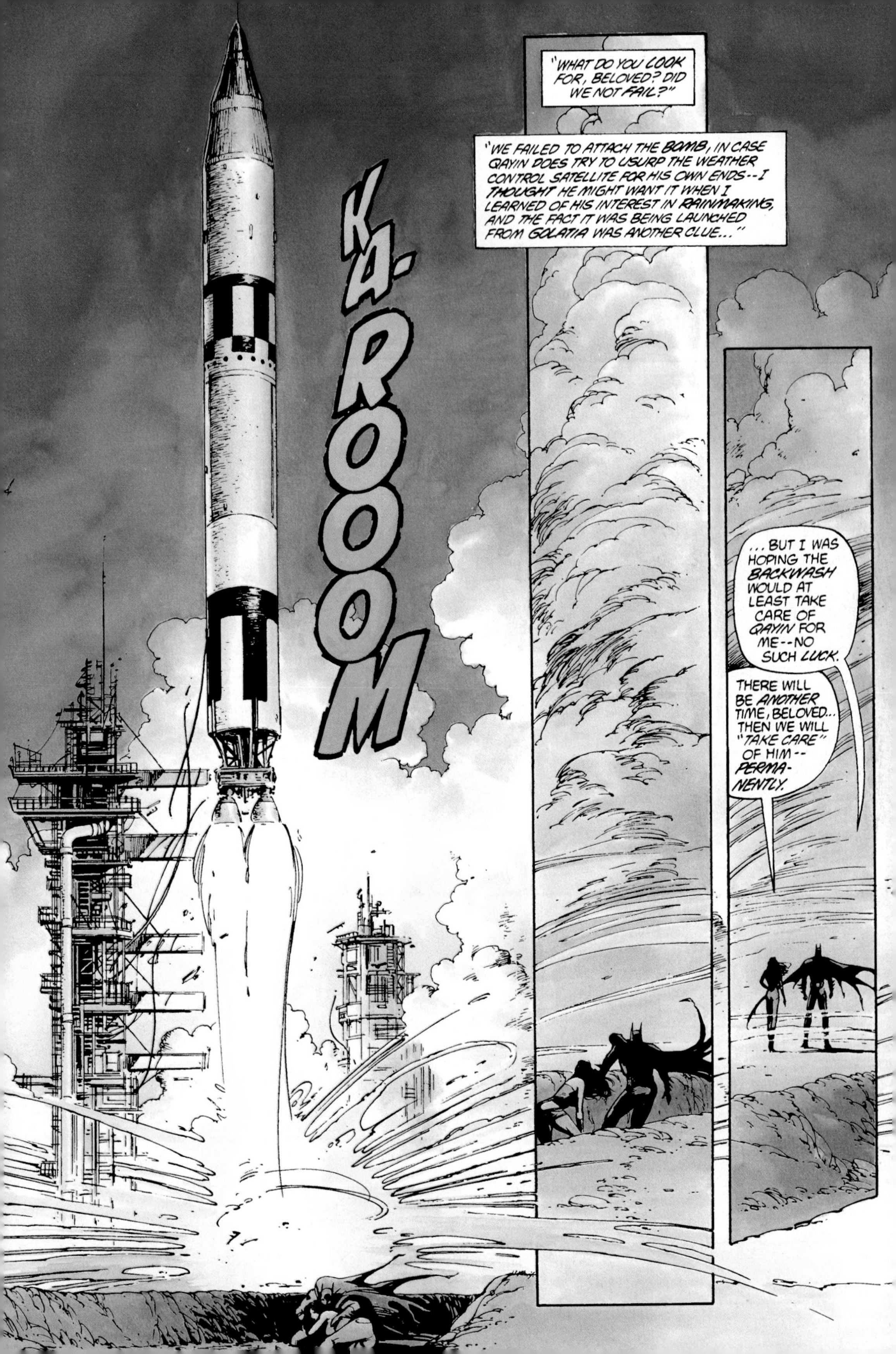
"WHAT DO YOU LOOK FOR, BELOVED? DID WE NOT FAIL?"
"WE FAILED TO ATTACH THE BOMB, IN CASE QAYIN DOES TRY TO USURP THE WEATHER CONTROL SATELLITE FOR HIS OWN ENDS--I THOUGHT HE MIGHT WANT IT WHEN I LEARNED OF HIS INTEREST IN RAINMAKING, AND THE FACT IT WAS BEING LAUNCHED FROM GOLATIA WAS ANOTHER CLUE..."
KA-ROOOOM
...BUT I WAS HOPING THE BACKWASH WOULD AT LEAST TAKE CARE OF QAYIN FOR ME--NO SUCH LUCK.
THERE WILL BE ANOTHER TIME, BELOVED... THEN WE WILL "TAKE CARE" OF HIM--PERMANENTLY.

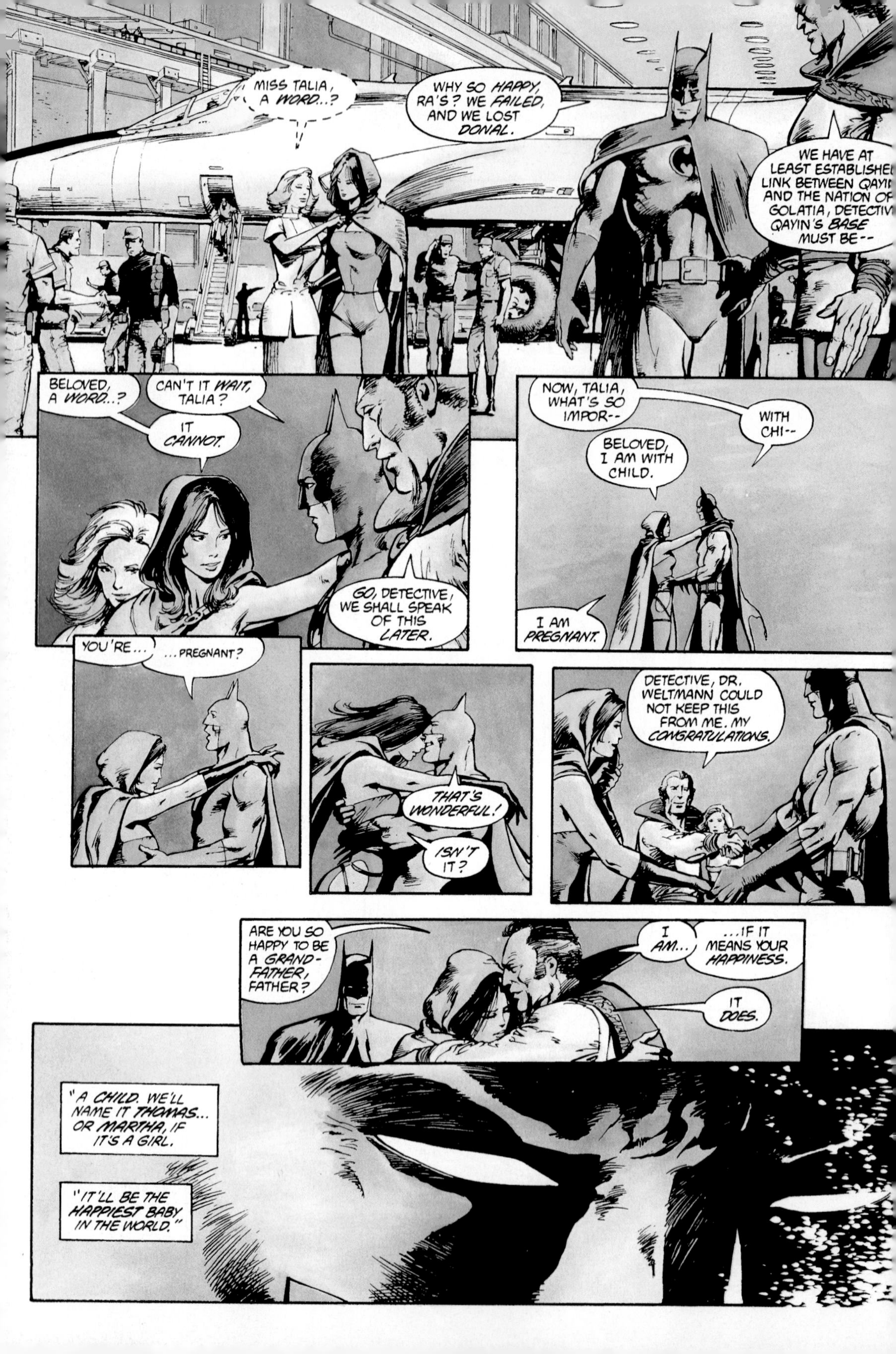
MISS TALIA, A WORD...?
WHY SO HAPPY, RA'S? WE FAILED, AND WE LOST DONAL.
WE HAVE AT LEAST ESTABLISHE LINK BETWEEN QAYI AND THE NATION OF GOLATIA, DETECTIV QAYIN'S BASE MUST BE--
BELOVED, A WORD...?
CAN'T IT WAIT, TALIA?
IT CANNOT.
GO, DETECTIVE, WE SHALL SPEAK OF THIS LATER.
NOW, TALIA, WHAT'S SO IMPOR--
BELOVED, I AM WITH CHILD.
WITH CHI--
I AM PREGNANT.
YOU'RE...
...PREGNANT?
THAT'S WONDERFUL!
ISN'T IT?
DETECTIVE, DR. WELTMANN COULD NOT KEEP THIS FROM ME. MY CONGRATULATIONS.
ARE YOU SO HAPPY TO BE A GRAND-FATHER, FATHER?
I AM...
...IF IT MEANS YOUR HAPPINESS.
IT DOES.
"A CHILD. WE'LL NAME IT THOMAS... OR MARTHA, IF IT'S A GIRL.
"IT'LL BE THE HAPPIEST BABY IN THE WORLD."

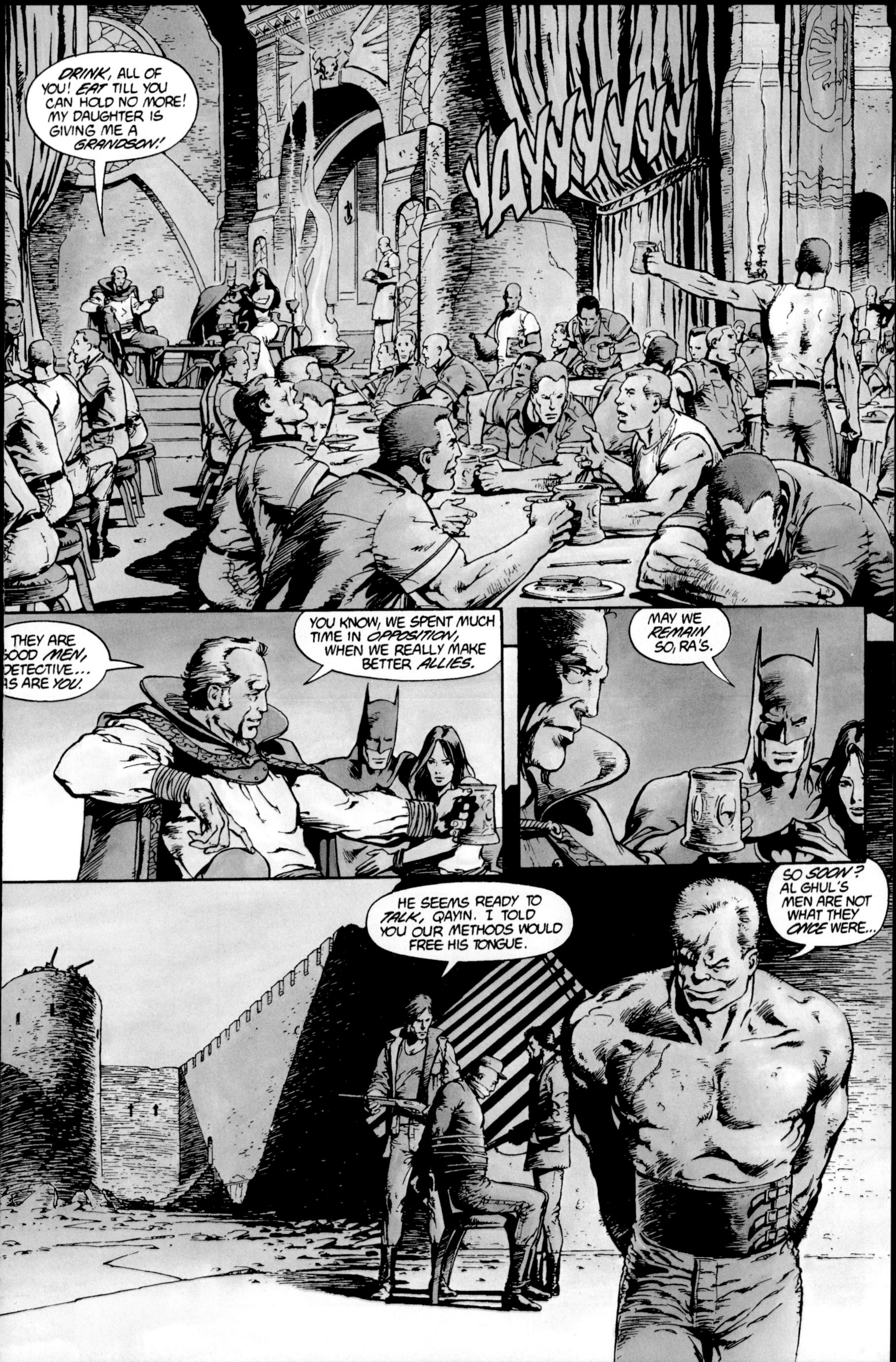
DRINK, ALL OF YOU! EAT TILL YOU CAN HOLD NO MORE! MY DAUGHTER IS GIVING ME A GRANDSON!
YAYYYYYYY
THEY ARE GOOD MEN, DETECTIVE... AS ARE YOU.
YOU KNOW, WE SPENT MUCH TIME IN OPPOSITION, WHEN WE REALLY MAKE BETTER ALLIES.
MAY WE REMAIN SO, RA'S.
HE SEEMS READY TO TALK, QAYIN. I TOLD YOU OUR METHODS WOULD FREE HIS TONGUE.
SO SOON? AL GHUL'S MEN ARE NOT WHAT THEY ONCE WERE...

...BUT ANY OLD PORT IN A STORM, I SUPPOSE.

RELEASE HIS GAG--LET HIM *SPEAK*.

YES, QAYIN.

...HIS ACQUIESCENCE WAS MERELY A *SHAM*...

MRRRG!

"HA! AS I SUSPECTED..."

...SO YOU WOULD REMOVE HIS *GAG*...

"... AND HE COULD RELEASE THE POISON IN THIS *FALSE TOOTH*..."

...THUS DEPRIVING *ME* OF DESIRED *INFORMATION*... AND YOU OF NO LITTLE *PLEASURE*, DR. HALLAM.

MOST DISCOURTEOUS.

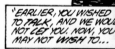

"EARLIER, YOU WISHED TO *TALK*, AND WE WOULD NOT LET YOU. NOW, YOU MAY NOT *WISH* TO..."

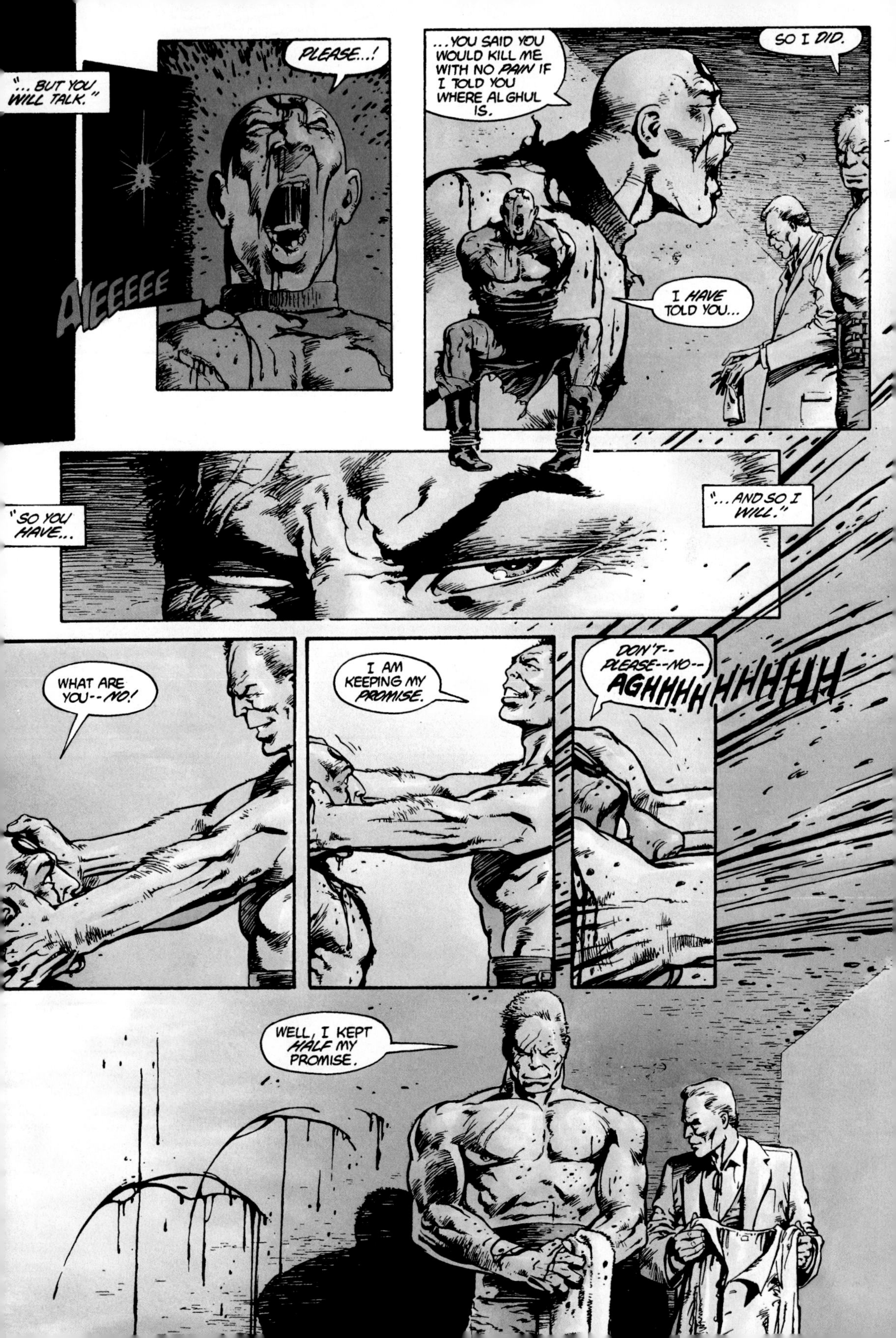
"...BUT YOU WILL TALK."
PLEASE...!
AIEEEEE
...YOU SAID YOU WOULD KILL ME WITH NO PAIN IF I TOLD YOU WHERE AL GHUL IS.
SO I DID.
I HAVE TOLD YOU...
"SO YOU HAVE...
"...AND SO I WILL."
WHAT ARE YOU--NO!
I AM KEEPING MY PROMISE.
DON'T--PLEASE--NO--AGHHHHHHHHHH
WELL, I KEPT HALF MY PROMISE.

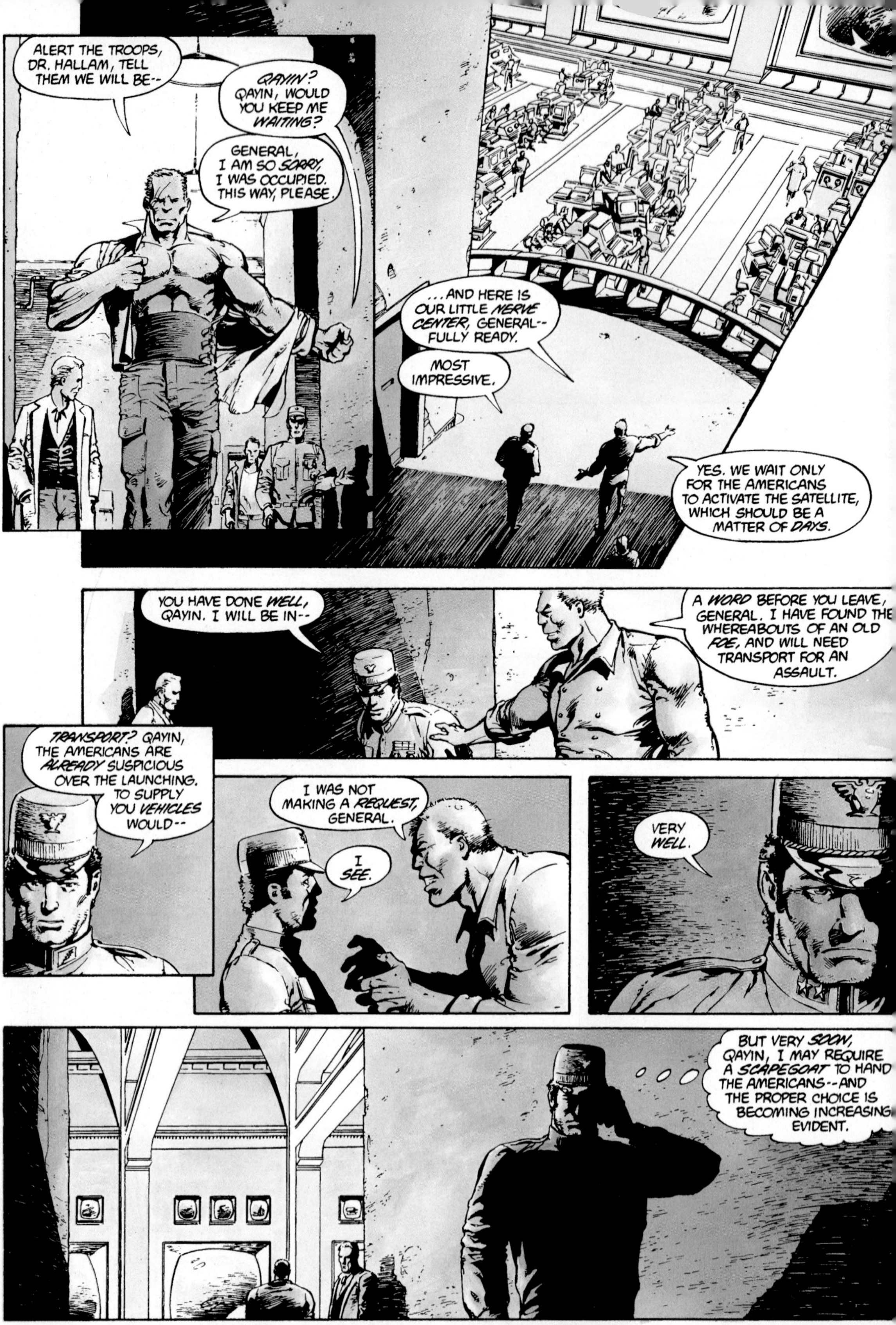
ALERT THE TROOPS, DR. HALLAM, TELL THEM WE WILL BE--
QAYIN? QAYIN, WOULD YOU KEEP ME WAITING?
GENERAL, I AM SO SORRY, I WAS OCCUPIED. THIS WAY, PLEASE.
...AND HERE IS OUR LITTLE NERVE CENTER, GENERAL--FULLY READY.
MOST IMPRESSIVE.
YES. WE WAIT ONLY FOR THE AMERICANS TO ACTIVATE THE SATELLITE, WHICH SHOULD BE A MATTER OF DAYS.
YOU HAVE DONE WELL, QAYIN. I WILL BE IN--
A WORD BEFORE YOU LEAVE, GENERAL. I HAVE FOUND THE WHEREABOUTS OF AN OLD FOE, AND WILL NEED TRANSPORT FOR AN ASSAULT.
TRANSPORT? QAYIN, THE AMERICANS ARE ALREADY SUSPICIOUS OVER THE LAUNCHING. TO SUPPLY YOU VEHICLES WOULD--
I WAS NOT MAKING A REQUEST, GENERAL.
I SEE.
VERY WELL.
BUT VERY SOON, QAYIN, I MAY REQUIRE A SCAPEGOAT TO HAND THE AMERICANS--AND THE PROPER CHOICE IS BECOMING INCREASING EVIDENT.

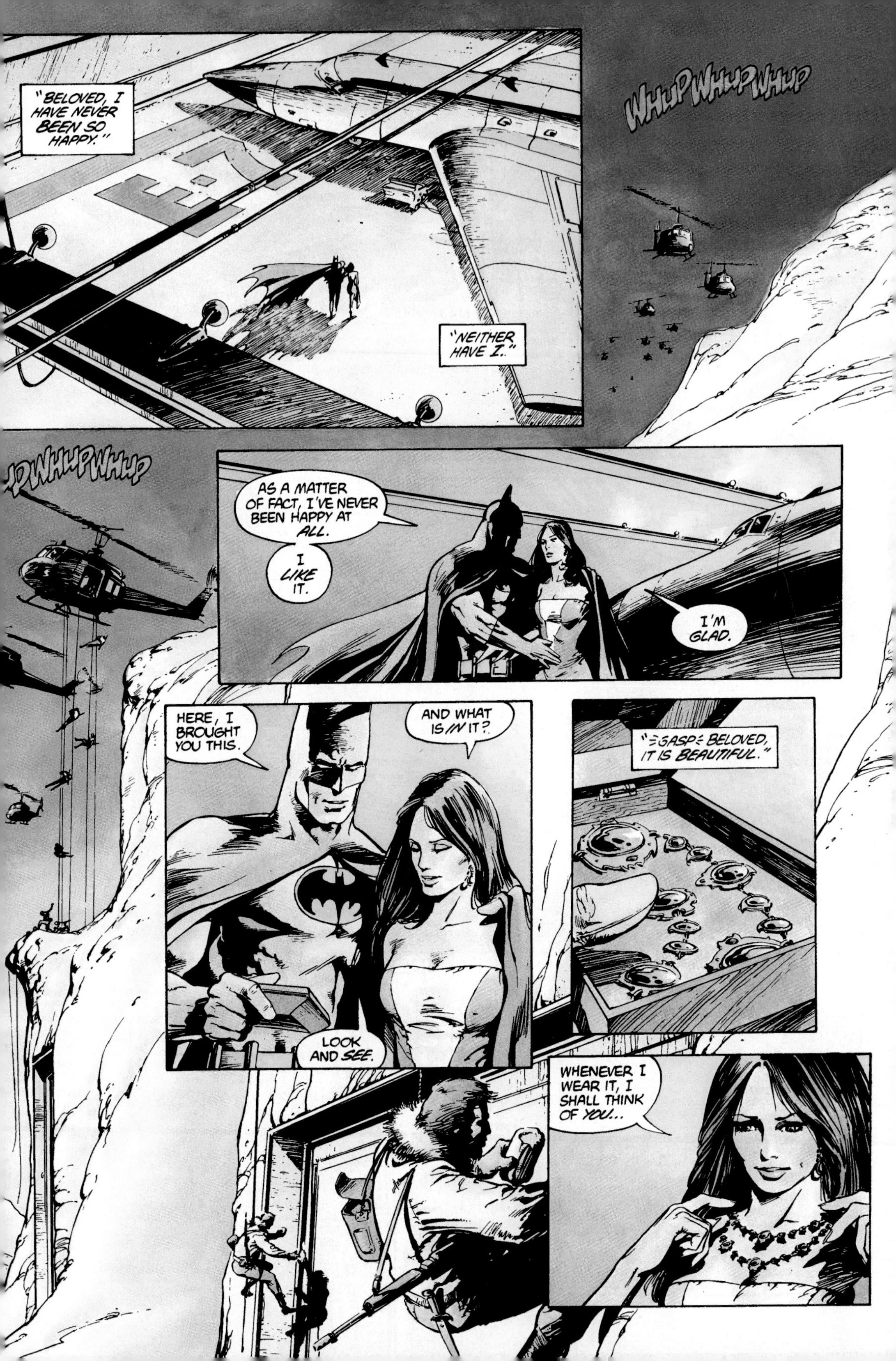
"BELOVED, I HAVE NEVER BEEN SO HAPPY."
WHUPWHUPWHUP
"NEITHER HAVE I."
DWHUPWHUP
AS A MATTER OF FACT, I'VE NEVER BEEN HAPPY AT ALL.
I LIKE IT.
I'M GLAD.
HERE, I BROUGHT YOU THIS.
AND WHAT IS IN IT?
LOOK AND SEE.
"=GASP= BELOVED, IT IS BEAUTIFUL."
WHENEVER I WEAR IT, I SHALL THINK OF YOU...

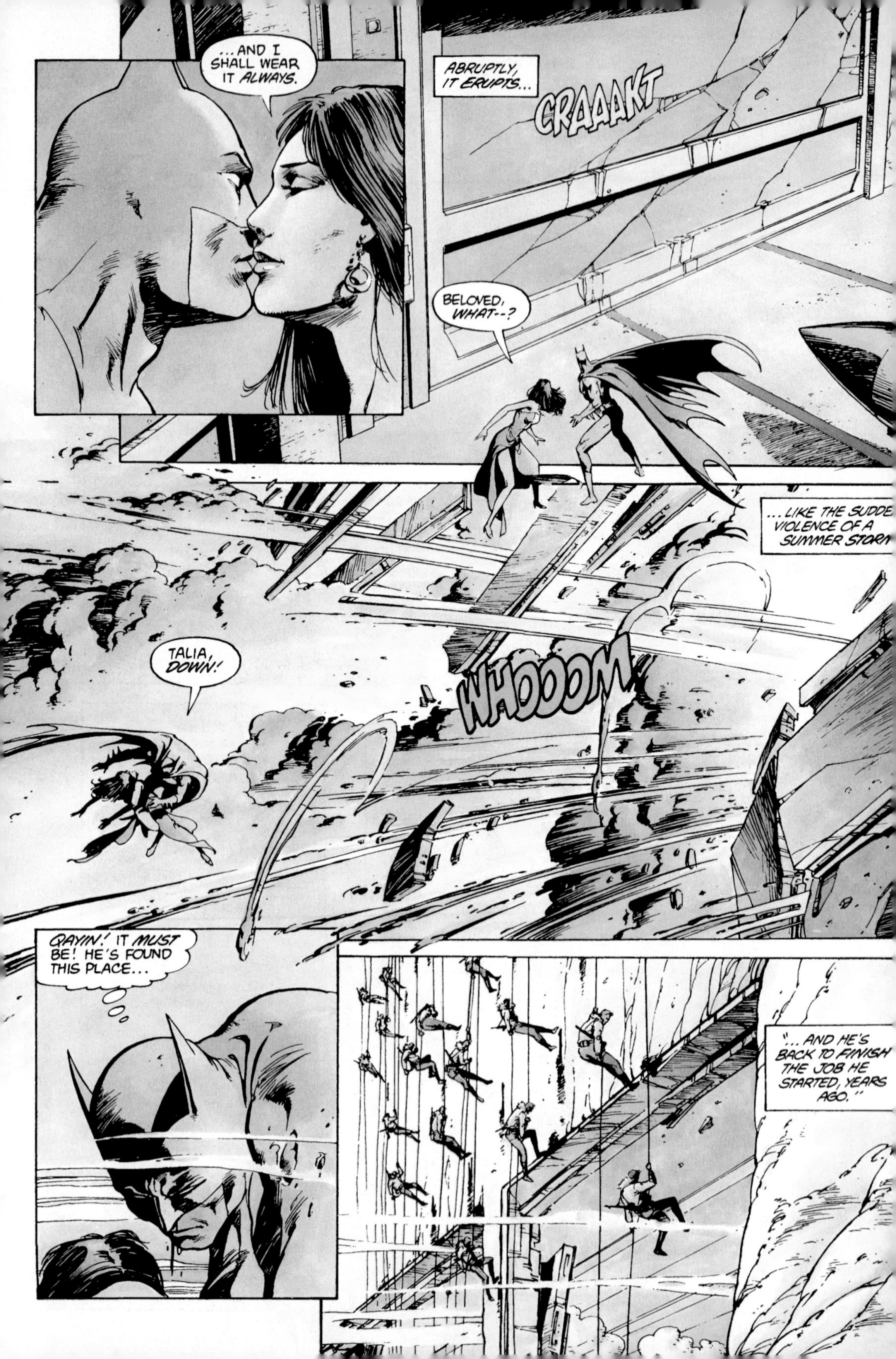
...AND I SHALL WEAR IT ALWAYS.
ABRUPTLY, IT ERUPTS...
CRAAAKT
BELOVED, WHAT--?
...LIKE THE SUDDEN VIOLENCE OF A SUMMER STORM
TALIA, DOWN!
WHOOOM
QAYIN! IT MUST BE! HE'S FOUND THIS PLACE...
"...AND HE'S BACK TO FINISH THE JOB HE STARTED, YEARS AGO."

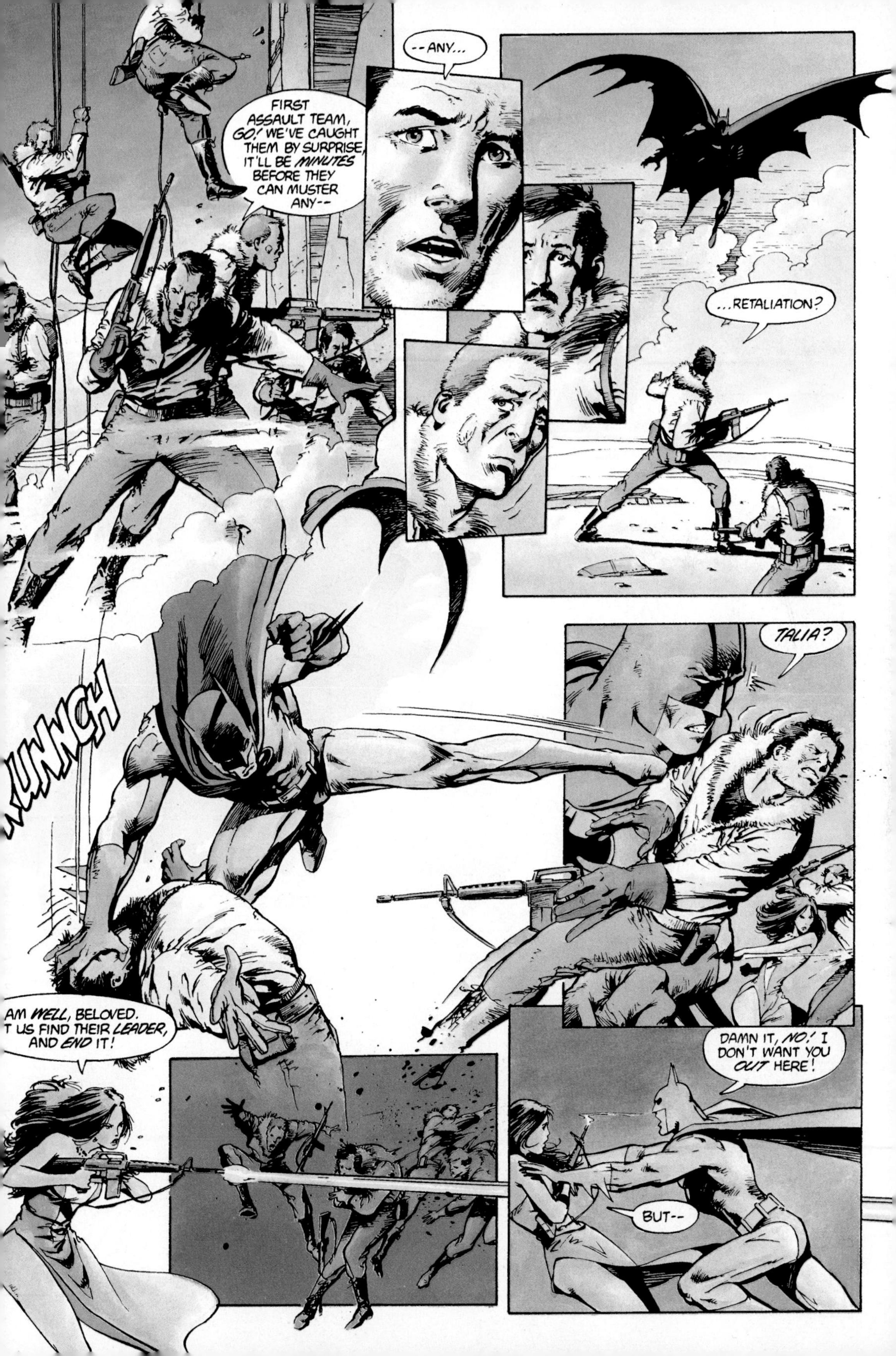
FIRST ASSAULT TEAM, GO! WE'VE CAUGHT THEM BY SURPRISE, IT'LL BE MINUTES BEFORE THEY CAN MUSTER ANY--
--ANY...
...RETALIATION?
UNNCH
TALIA?
AM WELL, BELOVED. T US FIND THEIR LEADER, AND END IT!
DAMN IT, NO! I DON'T WANT YOU OUT HERE!
BUT--

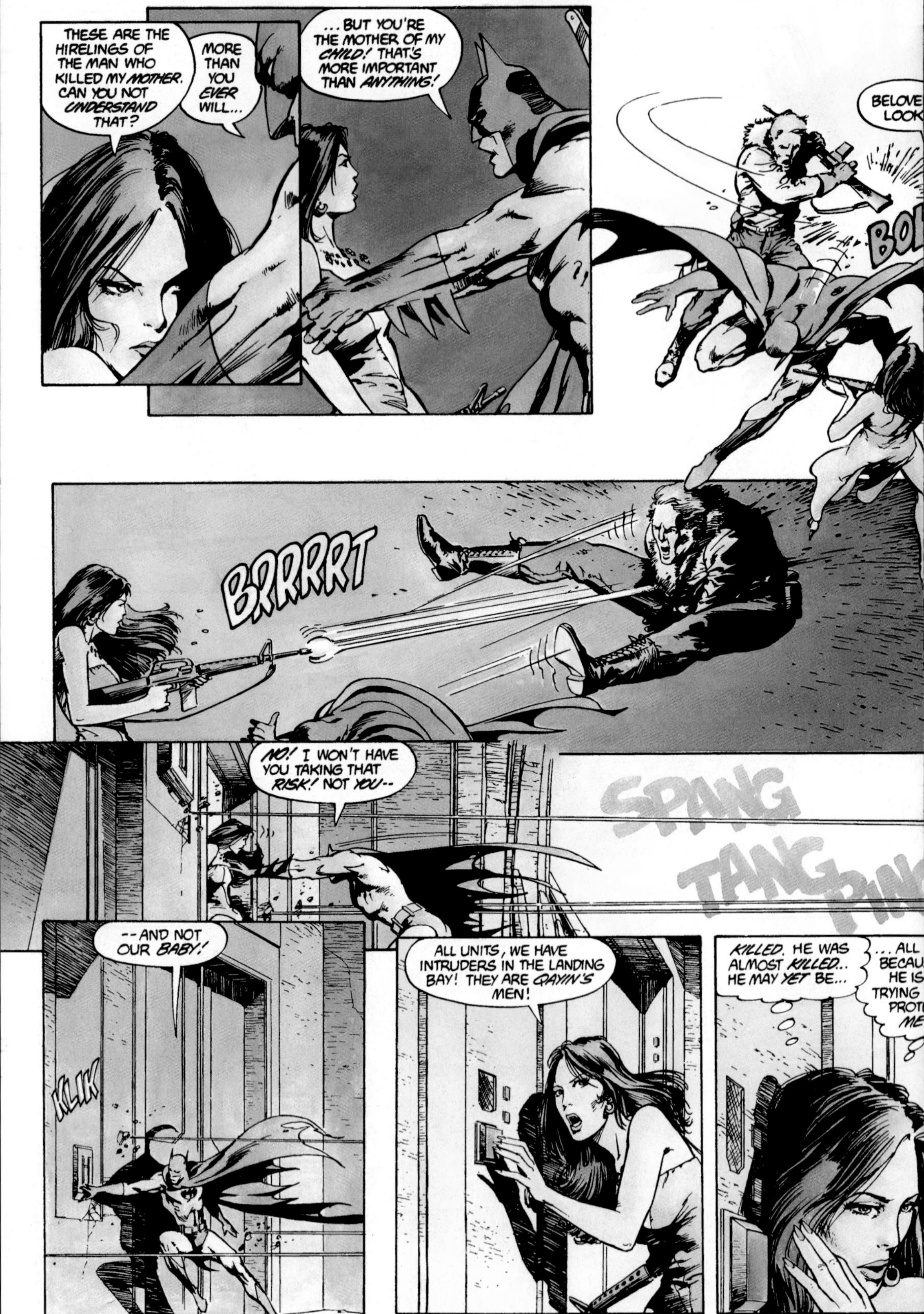

THESE ARE THE HIRELINGS OF THE MAN WHO KILLED MY MOTHER. CAN YOU NOT UNDERSTAND THAT?
MORE THAN YOU EVER WILL...
...BUT YOU'RE THE MOTHER OF MY CHILD! THAT'S MORE IMPORTANT THAN ANYTHING!
BELOVE LOOK
BOH
BRRRRT
NO! I WON'T HAVE YOU TAKING THAT RISK! NOT YOU--
SPANG
TANG
PIN
--AND NOT OUR BABY!
KLIK
ALL UNITS, WE HAVE INTRUDERS IN THE LANDING BAY! THEY ARE QAYIN'S MEN!
KILLED. HE WAS ALMOST KILLED.. HE MAY YET BE...
...ALL BECAU HE IS TRYING PROT ME

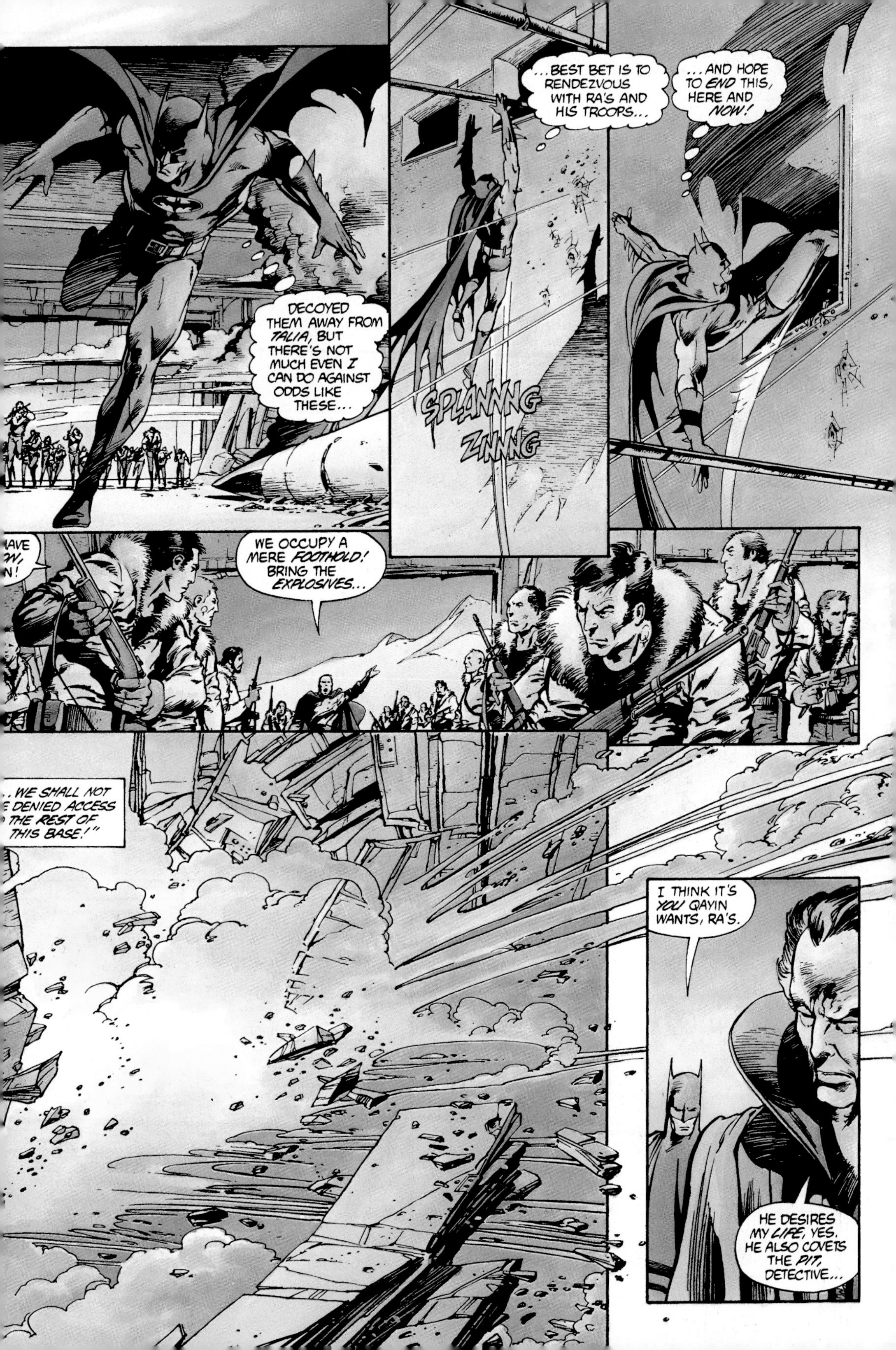
DECOYED THEM AWAY FROM *TALIA*, BUT THERE'S NOT MUCH EVEN *I* CAN DO AGAINST ODDS LIKE THESE...
...BEST BET IS TO RENDEZVOUS WITH RA'S AND HIS TROOPS...
SPLANNNG
ZINNNG
...AND HOPE TO *END* THIS, HERE AND *NOW!*
WE OCCUPY A MERE *FOOTHOLD!* BRING THE *EXPLOSIVES*...
..WE SHALL NOT E DENIED ACCESS THE *REST OF* THIS BASE!"
I THINK IT'S *YOU* QAYIN WANTS, RA'S.
HE DESIRES MY *LIFE*, YES. HE ALSO COVETS THE *PIT*, DETECTIVE...

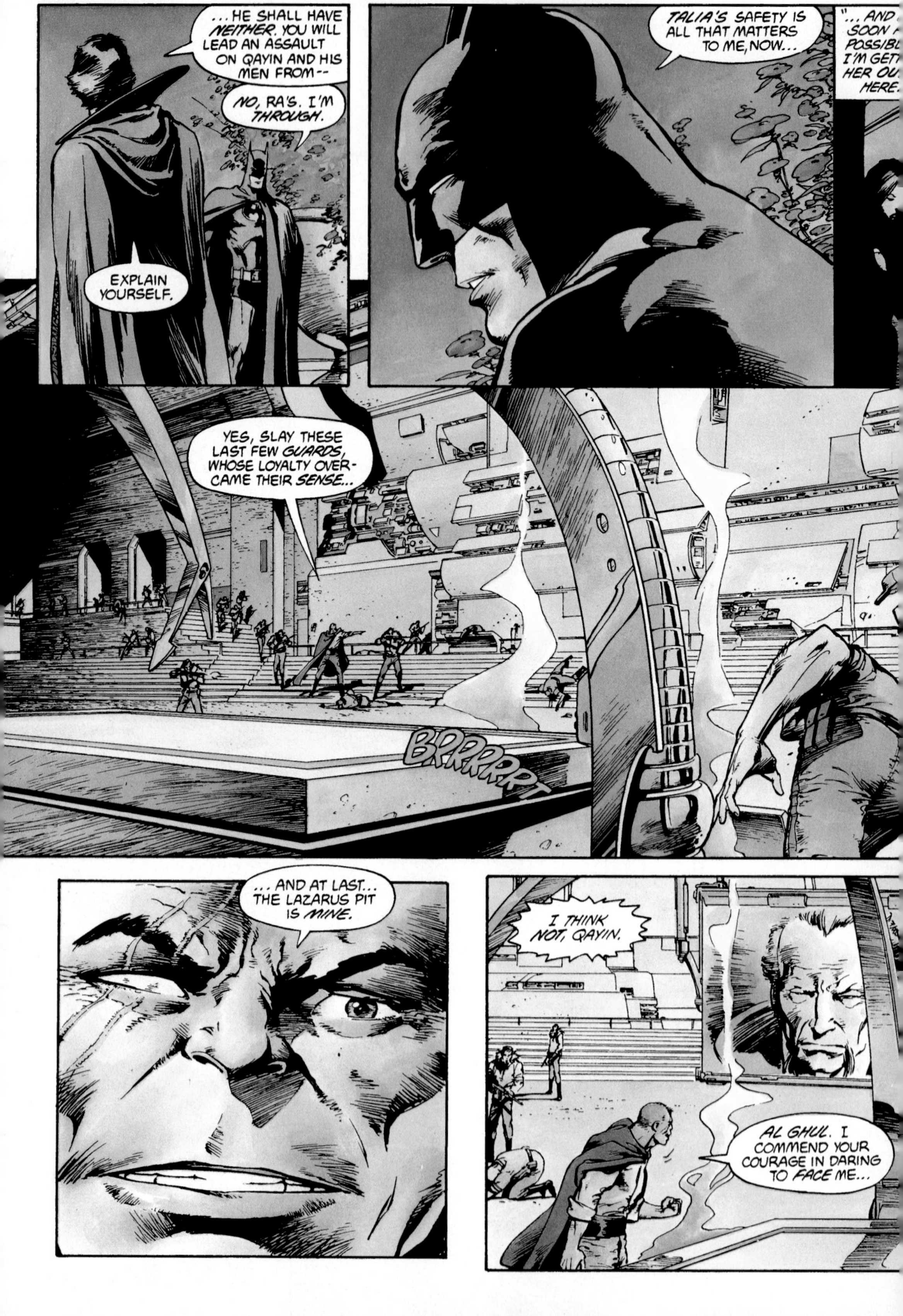
...HE SHALL HAVE NEITHER. YOU WILL LEAD AN ASSAULT ON QAYIN AND HIS MEN FROM--
NO, RA'S. I'M THROUGH.
EXPLAIN YOURSELF.
TALIA'S SAFETY IS ALL THAT MATTERS TO ME, NOW...
"...AND SOON POSSIBL I'M GETT HER OU HERE.
YES, SLAY THESE LAST FEW GUARDS, WHOSE LOYALTY OVER-CAME THEIR SENSE...
BRRRRRRT
...AND AT LAST... THE LAZARUS PIT IS MINE.
I THINK NOT, QAYIN.
AL GHUL. I COMMEND YOUR COURAGE IN DARING TO FACE ME...

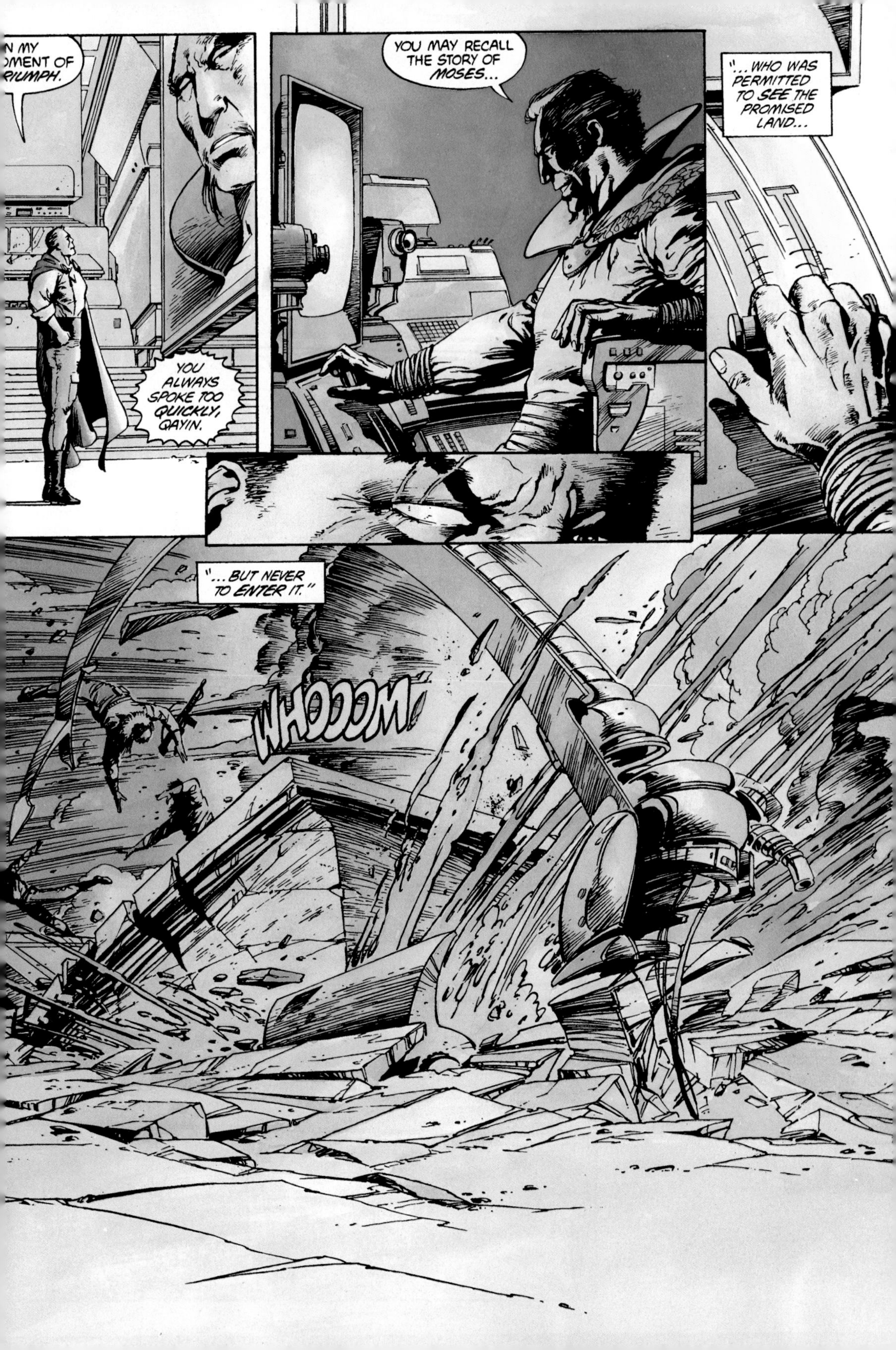
N MY
OMENT OF
RIUMPH.
YOU ALWAYS SPOKE TOO QUICKLY, QAYIN.
YOU MAY RECALL THE STORY OF MOSES...
"...WHO WAS PERMITTED TO SEE THE PROMISED LAND...
"...BUT NEVER TO ENTER IT."
WHOOOM

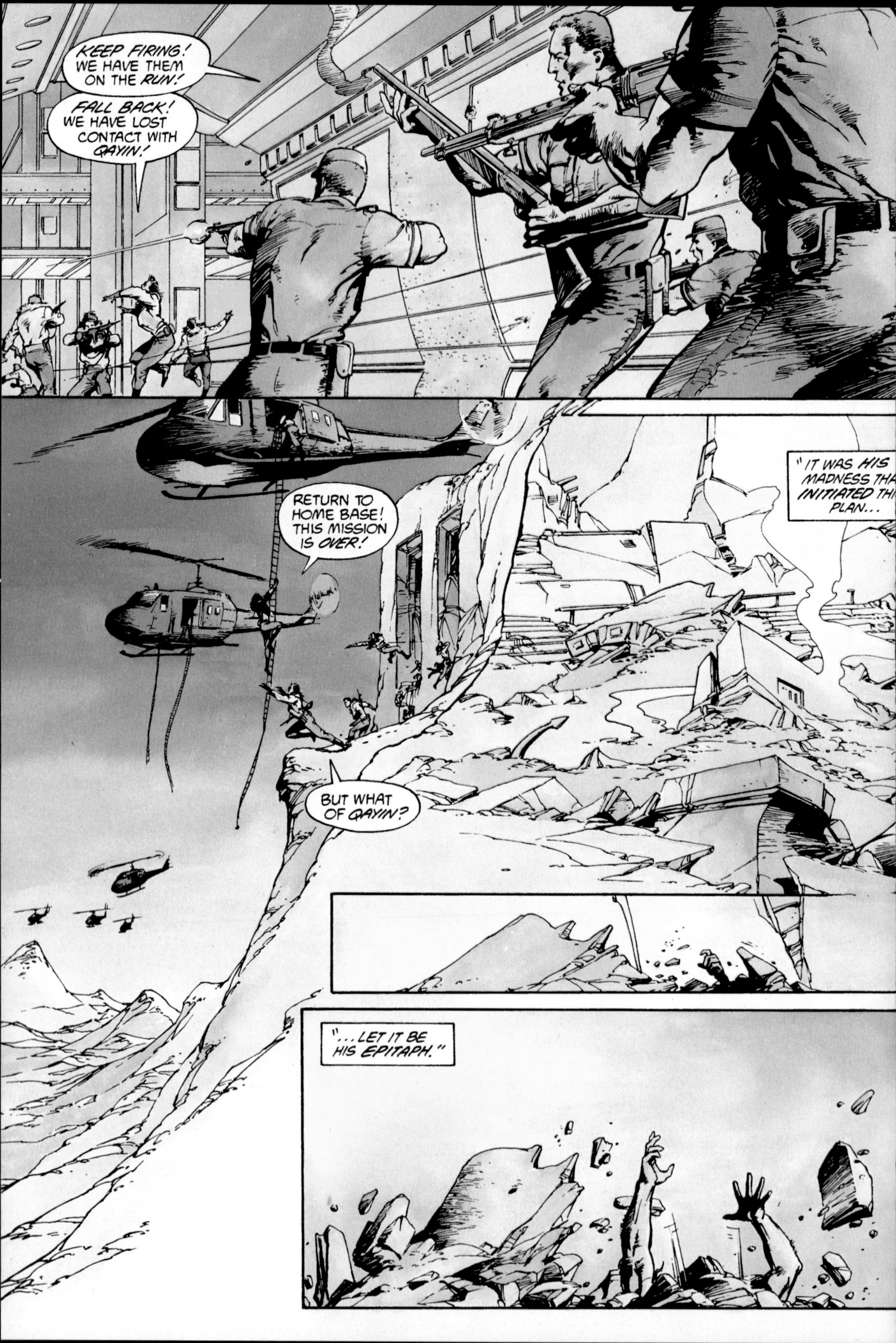
KEEP FIRING! WE HAVE THEM ON THE RUN!
FALL BACK! WE HAVE LOST CONTACT WITH QAYIN!
RETURN TO HOME BASE! THIS MISSION IS OVER!
"IT WAS HIS MADNESS THA INITIATED THI PLAN...
BUT WHAT OF QAYIN?
"...LET IT BE HIS EPITAPH."

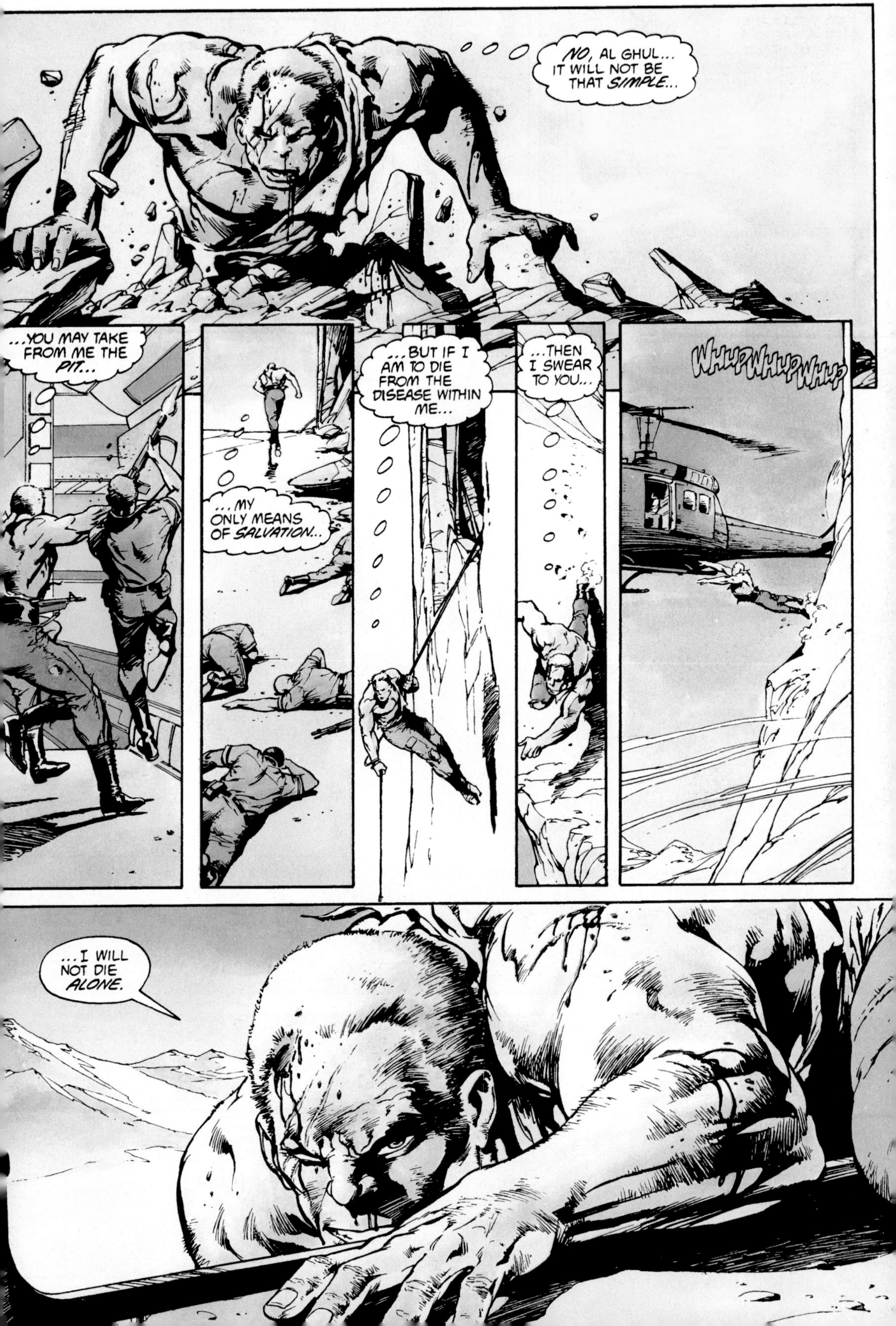
NO, AL GHUL... IT WILL NOT BE THAT SIMPLE...
...YOU MAY TAKE FROM ME THE PIT...
...MY ONLY MEANS OF SALVATION...
...BUT IF I AM TO DIE FROM THE DISEASE WITHIN ME...
...THEN I SWEAR TO YOU...
WHUPWHUPWHUP
...I WILL NOT DIE ALONE.

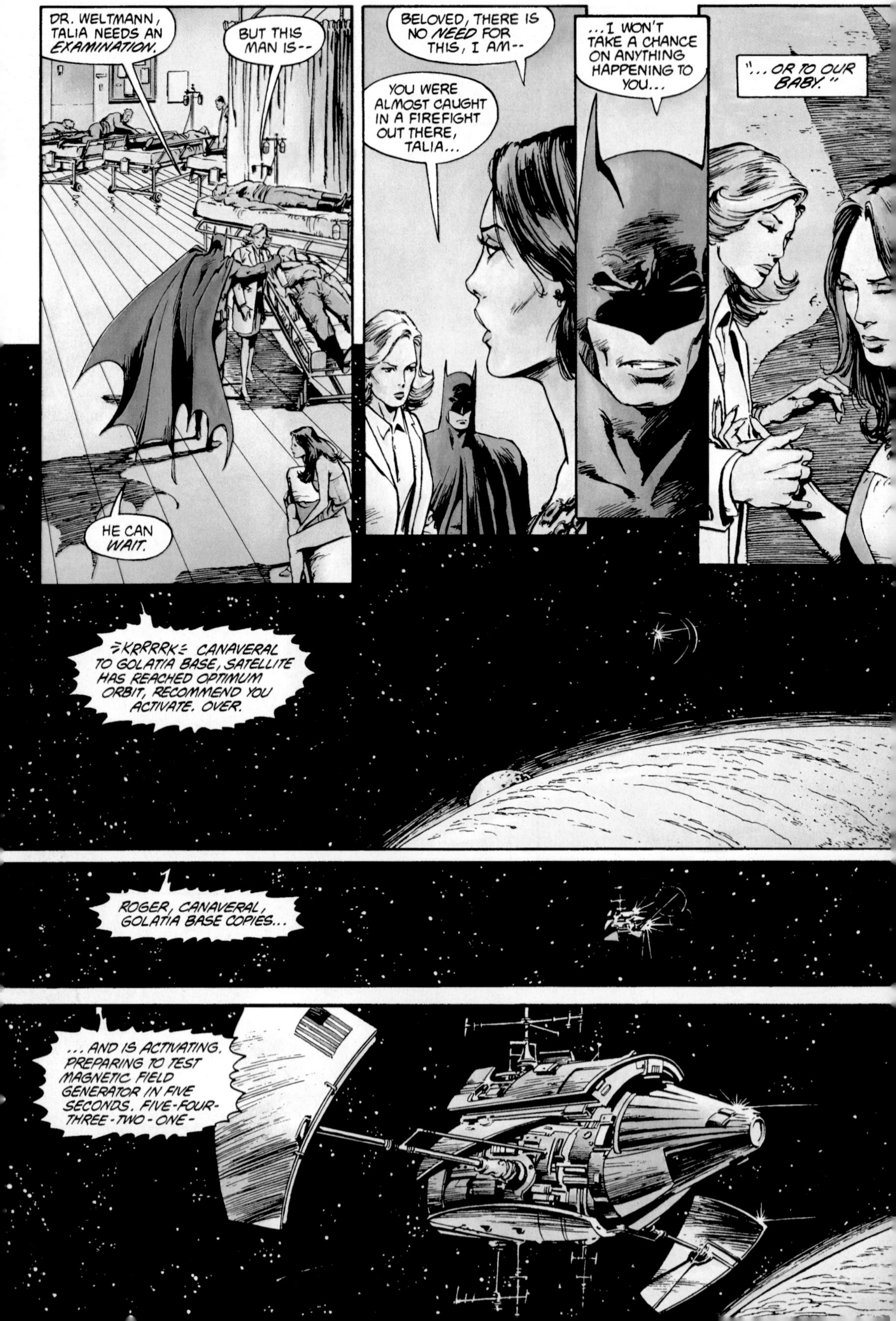
DR. WELTMANN, TALIA NEEDS AN EXAMINATION.
BUT THIS MAN IS--
HE CAN WAIT.
BELOVED, THERE IS NO NEED FOR THIS, I AM--
YOU WERE ALMOST CAUGHT IN A FIREFIGHT OUT THERE, TALIA...
...I WON'T TAKE A CHANCE ON ANYTHING HAPPENING TO YOU...
"...OR TO OUR BABY."
=KRRRRK= CANAVERAL TO GOLATIA BASE, SATELLITE HAS REACHED OPTIMUM ORBIT, RECOMMEND YOU ACTIVATE. OVER.
ROGER, CANAVERAL, GOLATIA BASE COPIES...
...AND IS ACTIVATING. PREPARING TO TEST MAGNETIC FIELD GENERATOR IN FIVE SECONDS. FIVE-FOUR-THREE-TWO-ONE-

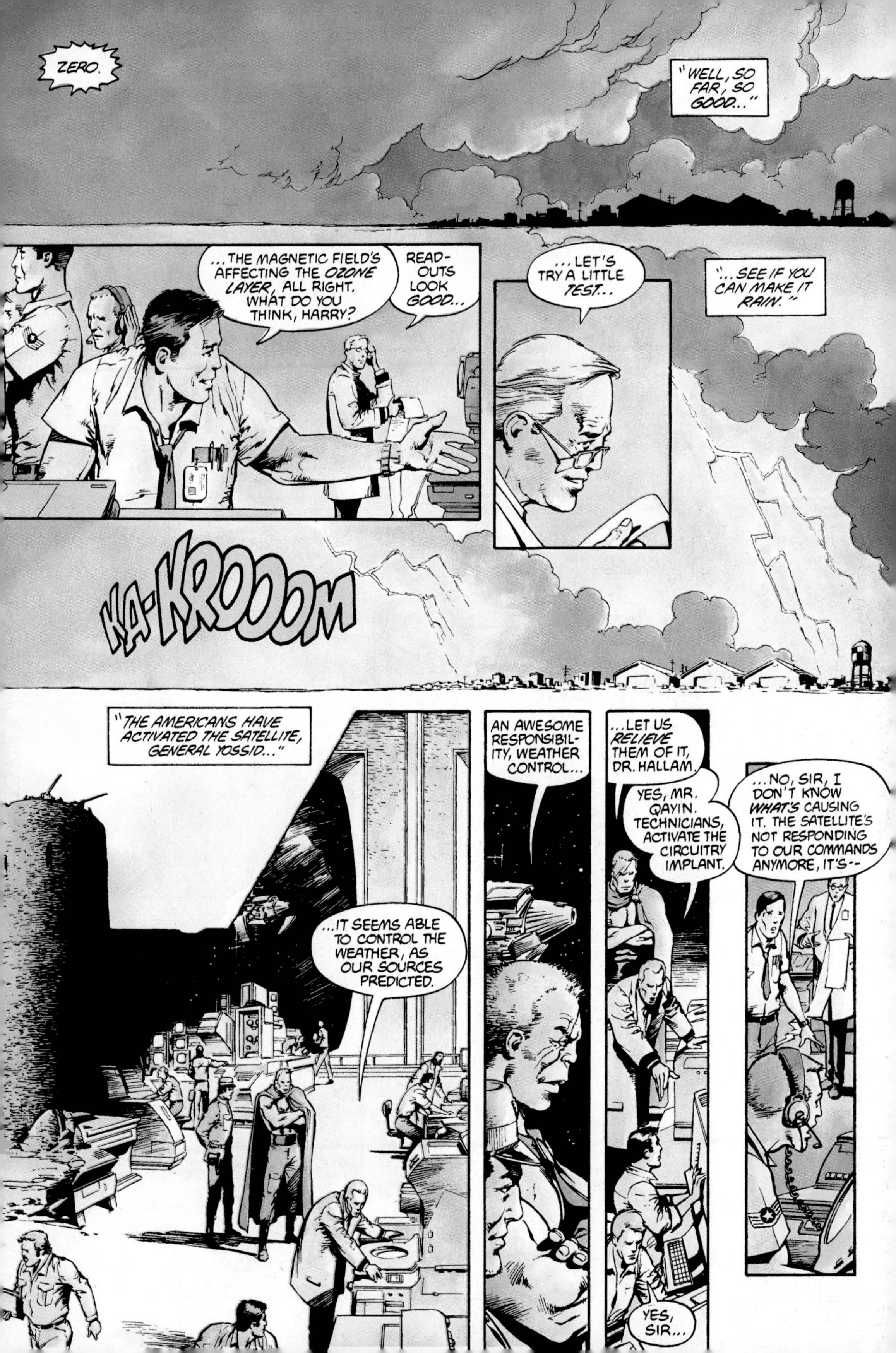
ZERO.
"WELL, SO FAR, SO GOOD..."
...THE MAGNETIC FIELD'S AFFECTING THE OZONE LAYER, ALL RIGHT. WHAT DO YOU THINK, HARRY?
READ-OUTS LOOK GOOD...
...LET'S TRY A LITTLE TEST...
"...SEE IF YOU CAN MAKE IT RAIN."
KA-KROOOOM
"THE AMERICANS HAVE ACTIVATED THE SATELLITE, GENERAL YOSSID..."
...IT SEEMS ABLE TO CONTROL THE WEATHER, AS OUR SOURCES PREDICTED.
AN AWESOME RESPONSIBIL-ITY, WEATHER CONTROL...
...LET US RELIEVE THEM OF IT, DR. HALLAM.
YES, MR. QAYIN. TECHNICIANS, ACTIVATE THE CIRCUITRY IMPLANT.
YES, SIR...
...NO, SIR, I DON'T KNOW WHAT'S CAUSING IT. THE SATELLITE'S NOT RESPONDING TO OUR COMMANDS ANYMORE, IT'S--

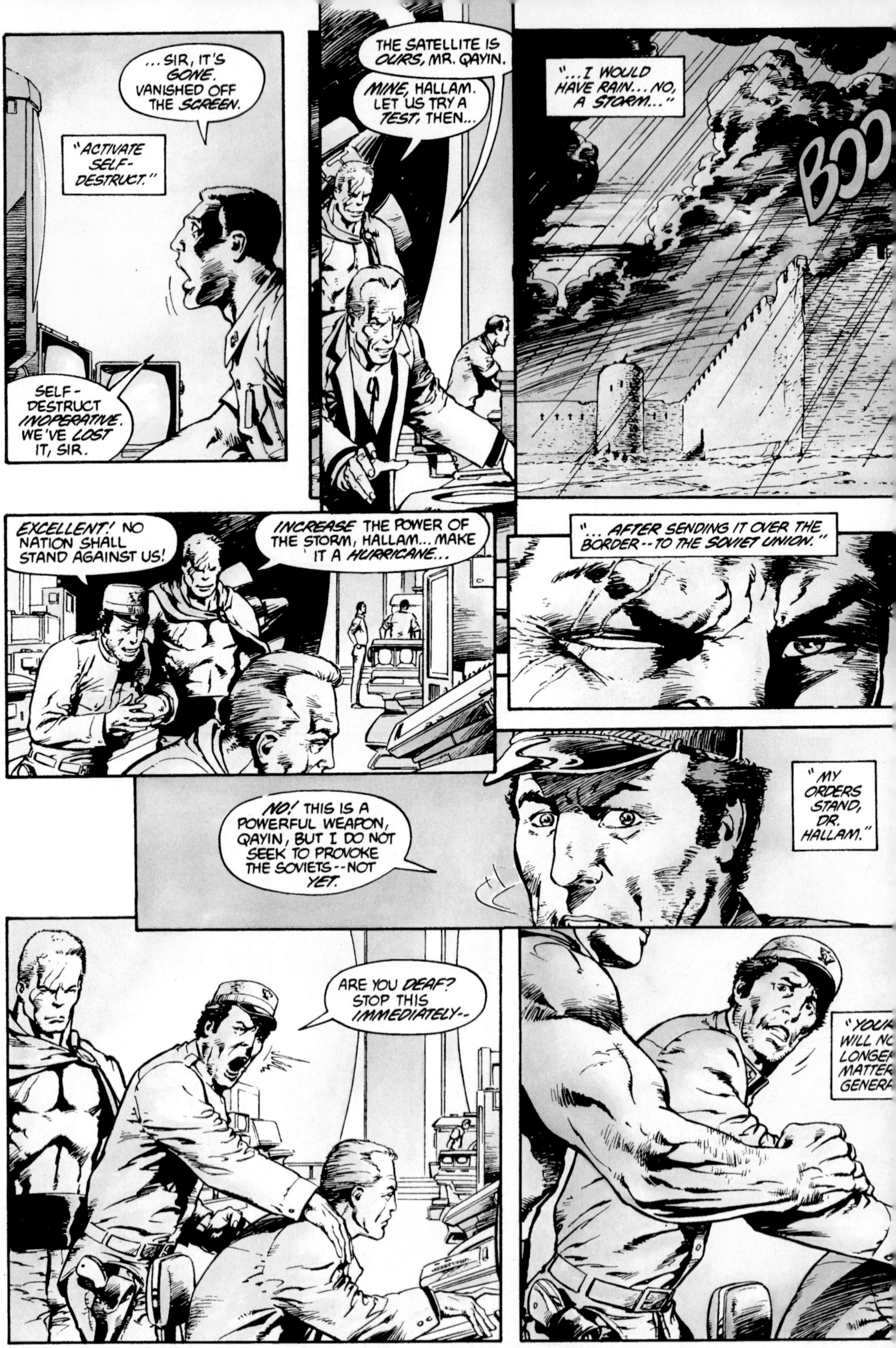
... SIR, IT'S GONE. VANISHED OFF THE SCREEN.
"ACTIVATE SELF-DESTRUCT."
SELF-DESTRUCT INOPERATIVE. WE'VE LOST IT, SIR.
THE SATELLITE IS OURS, MR. QAYIN.
MINE, HALLAM. LET US TRY A TEST, THEN...
"...I WOULD HAVE RAIN... NO, A STORM..."
BOO
EXCELLENT! NO NATION SHALL STAND AGAINST US!
INCREASE THE POWER OF THE STORM, HALLAM... MAKE IT A HURRICANE...
"... AFTER SENDING IT OVER THE BORDER--TO THE SOVIET UNION."
NO! THIS IS A POWERFUL WEAPON, QAYIN, BUT I DO NOT SEEK TO PROVOKE THE SOVIETS--NOT YET.
"MY ORDERS STAND, DR. HALLAM."
ARE YOU DEAF? STOP THIS IMMEDIATELY--

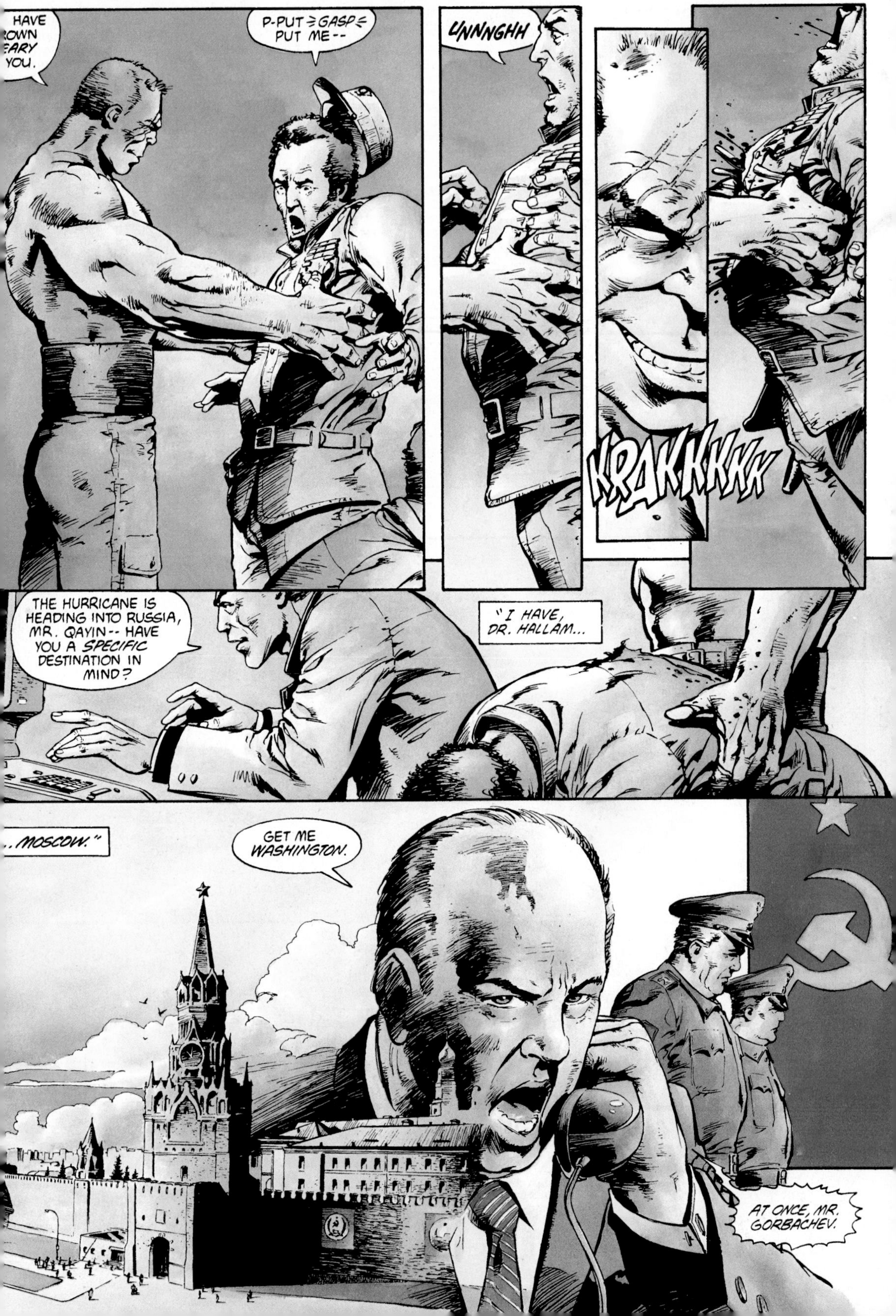

HAVE
ROWN
EARY
YOU.
P-PUT ≡GASP≡ PUT ME--
UNNNGHH
KRAKKKKKK
THE HURRICANE IS HEADING INTO RUSSIA, MR. QAYIN-- HAVE YOU A SPECIFIC DESTINATION IN MIND?
"I HAVE, DR. HALLAM...
..MOSCOW."
GET ME WASHINGTON.
AT ONCE, MR. GORBACHEV.

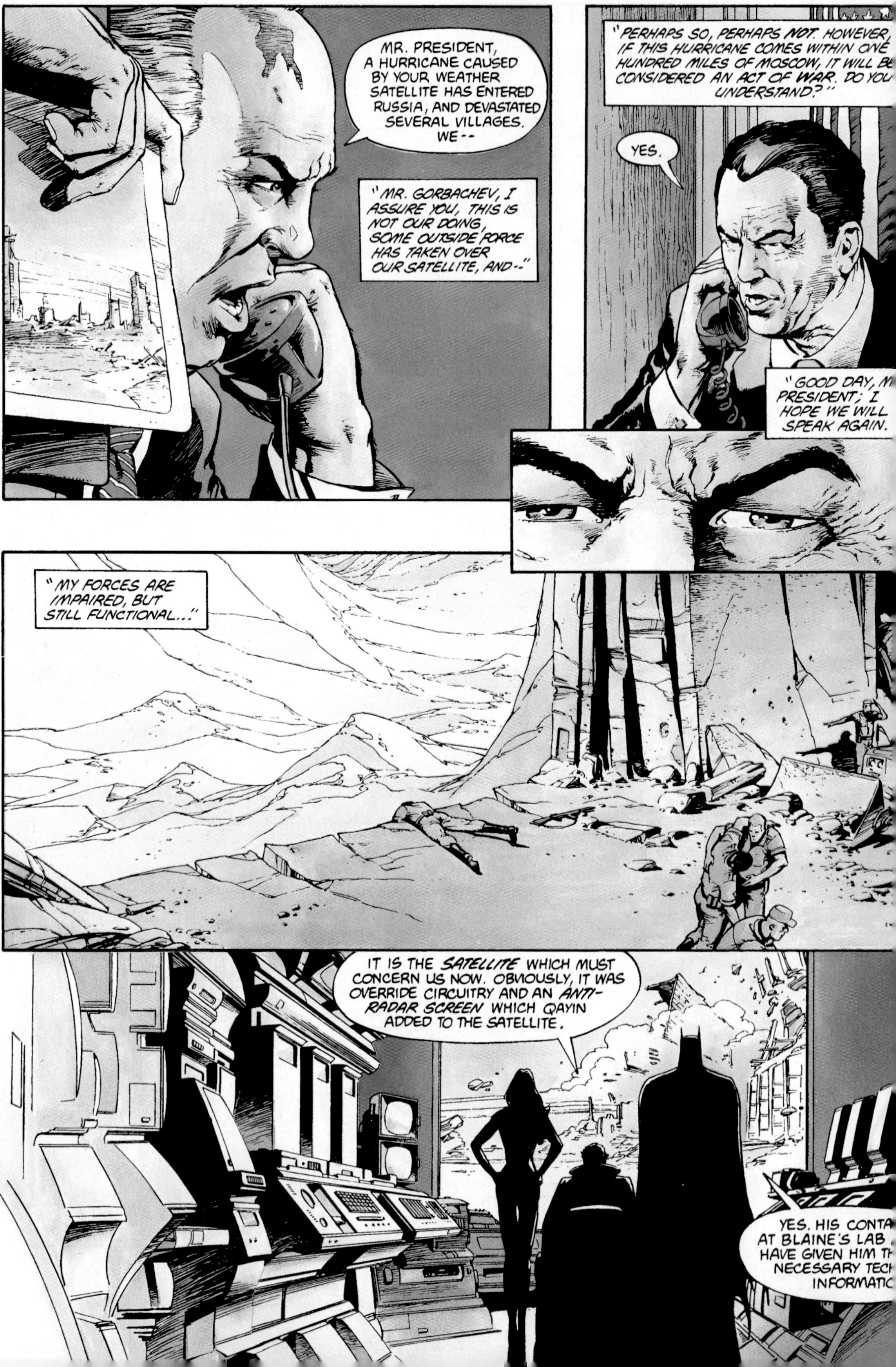

MR. PRESIDENT, A HURRICANE CAUSED BY YOUR WEATHER SATELLITE HAS ENTERED RUSSIA, AND DEVASTATED SEVERAL VILLAGES. WE--
"MR. GORBACHEV, I ASSURE YOU, THIS IS NOT OUR DOING, SOME OUTSIDE FORCE HAS TAKEN OVER OUR SATELLITE, AND--"
"PERHAPS SO, PERHAPS NOT. HOWEVER, IF THIS HURRICANE COMES WITHIN ONE HUNDRED MILES OF MOSCOW, IT WILL BE CONSIDERED AN ACT OF WAR. DO YOU UNDERSTAND?"
YES.
"GOOD DAY, M PRESIDENT; I HOPE WE WILL SPEAK AGAIN.
"MY FORCES ARE IMPAIRED, BUT STILL FUNCTIONAL..."
IT IS THE SATELLITE WHICH MUST CONCERN US NOW. OBVIOUSLY, IT WAS OVERRIDE CIRCUITRY AND AN ANTI-RADAR SCREEN WHICH QAYIN ADDED TO THE SATELLITE.
YES. HIS CONTA AT BLAINE'S LAB HAVE GIVEN HIM TH NECESSARY TECH INFORMATIO

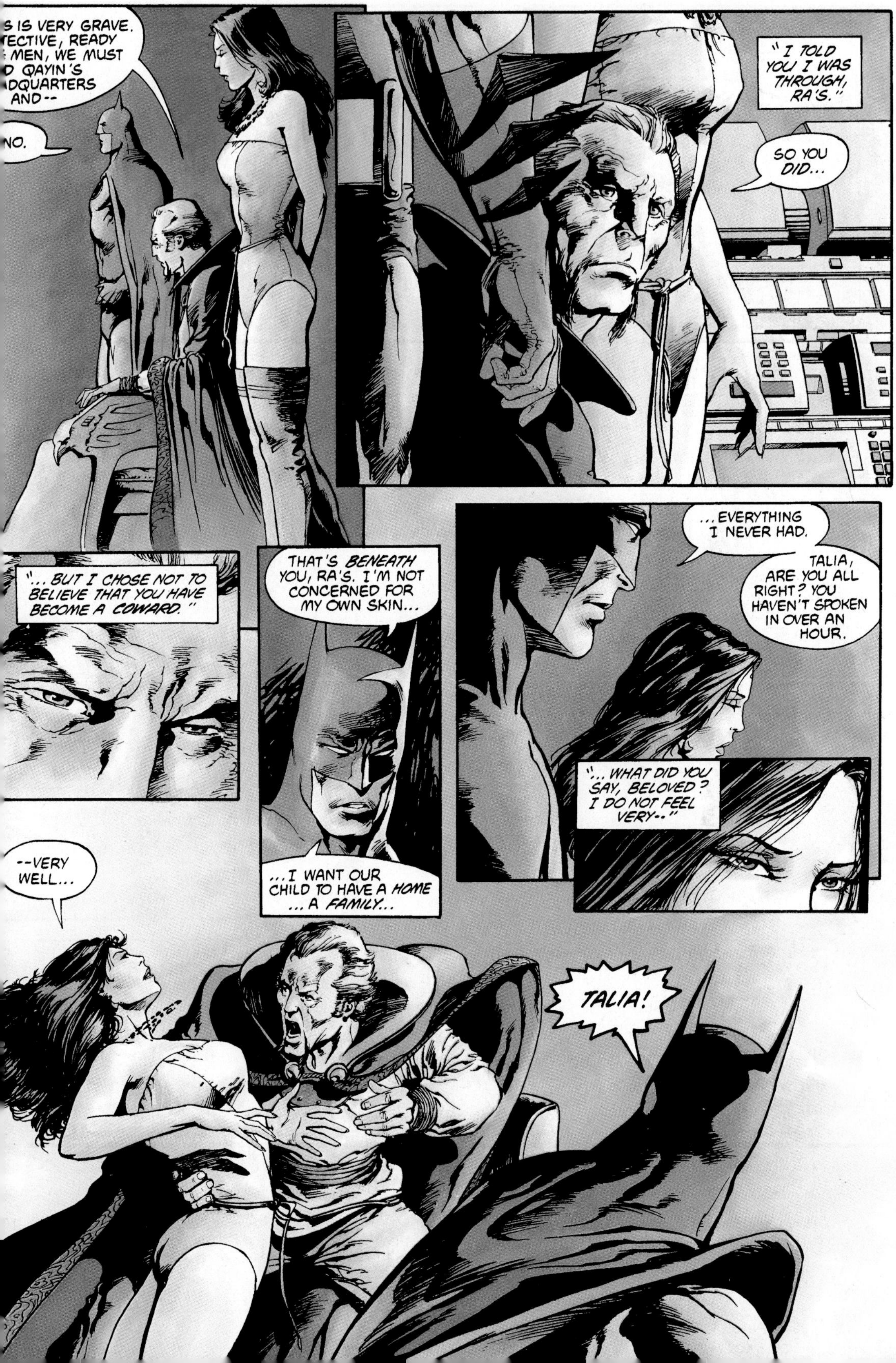

S IS VERY GRAVE. TECTIVE, READY MEN, WE MUST D QAYIN'S DQUARTERS AND--
NO.
"I TOLD YOU I WAS THROUGH, RA'S."
SO YOU DID...
"...BUT I CHOSE NOT TO BELIEVE THAT YOU HAVE BECOME A COWARD."
THAT'S BENEATH YOU, RA'S. I'M NOT CONCERNED FOR MY OWN SKIN...
...I WANT OUR CHILD TO HAVE A HOME ...A FAMILY...
...EVERYTHING I NEVER HAD.
TALIA, ARE YOU ALL RIGHT? YOU HAVEN'T SPOKEN IN OVER AN HOUR.
"...WHAT DID YOU SAY, BELOVED? I DO NOT FEEL VERY--"
--VERY WELL...
TALIA!

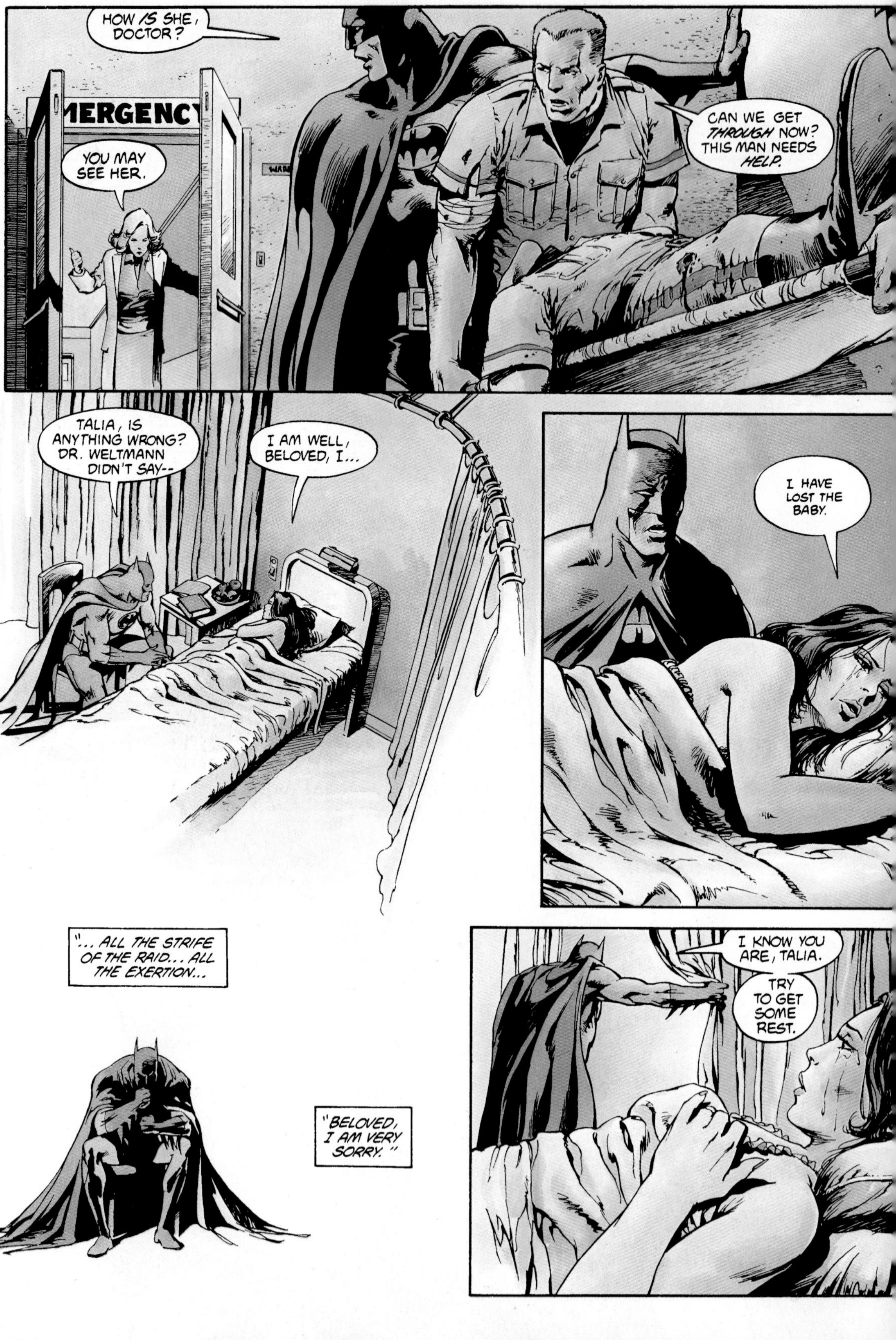
HOW IS SHE, DOCTOR?
MERGENCY
YOU MAY SEE HER.
CAN WE GET THROUGH NOW? THIS MAN NEEDS HELP.
TALIA, IS ANYTHING WRONG? DR. WELTMANN DIDN'T SAY--
I AM WELL, BELOVED, I...
I HAVE LOST THE BABY.
"... ALL THE STRIFE OF THE RAID... ALL THE EXERTION...
"BELOVED, I AM VERY SORRY."
I KNOW YOU ARE, TALIA.
TRY TO GET SOME REST.

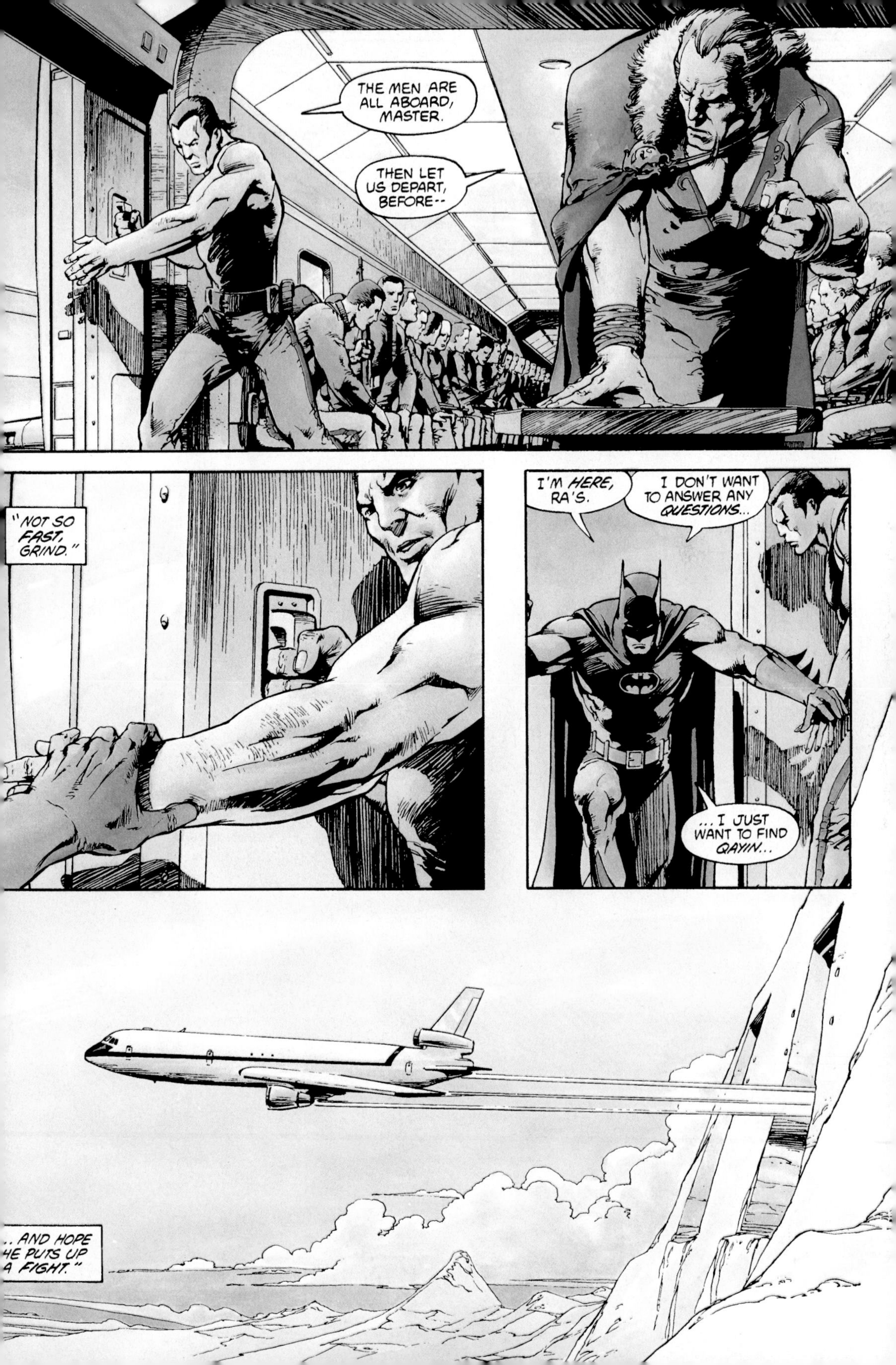
THE MEN ARE ALL ABOARD, MASTER.
THEN LET US DEPART, BEFORE--
"NOT SO FAST, GRIND."
I'M HERE, RA'S.
I DON'T WANT TO ANSWER ANY QUESTIONS...
...I JUST WANT TO FIND QAYIN...
..AND HOPE HE PUTS UP A FIGHT."

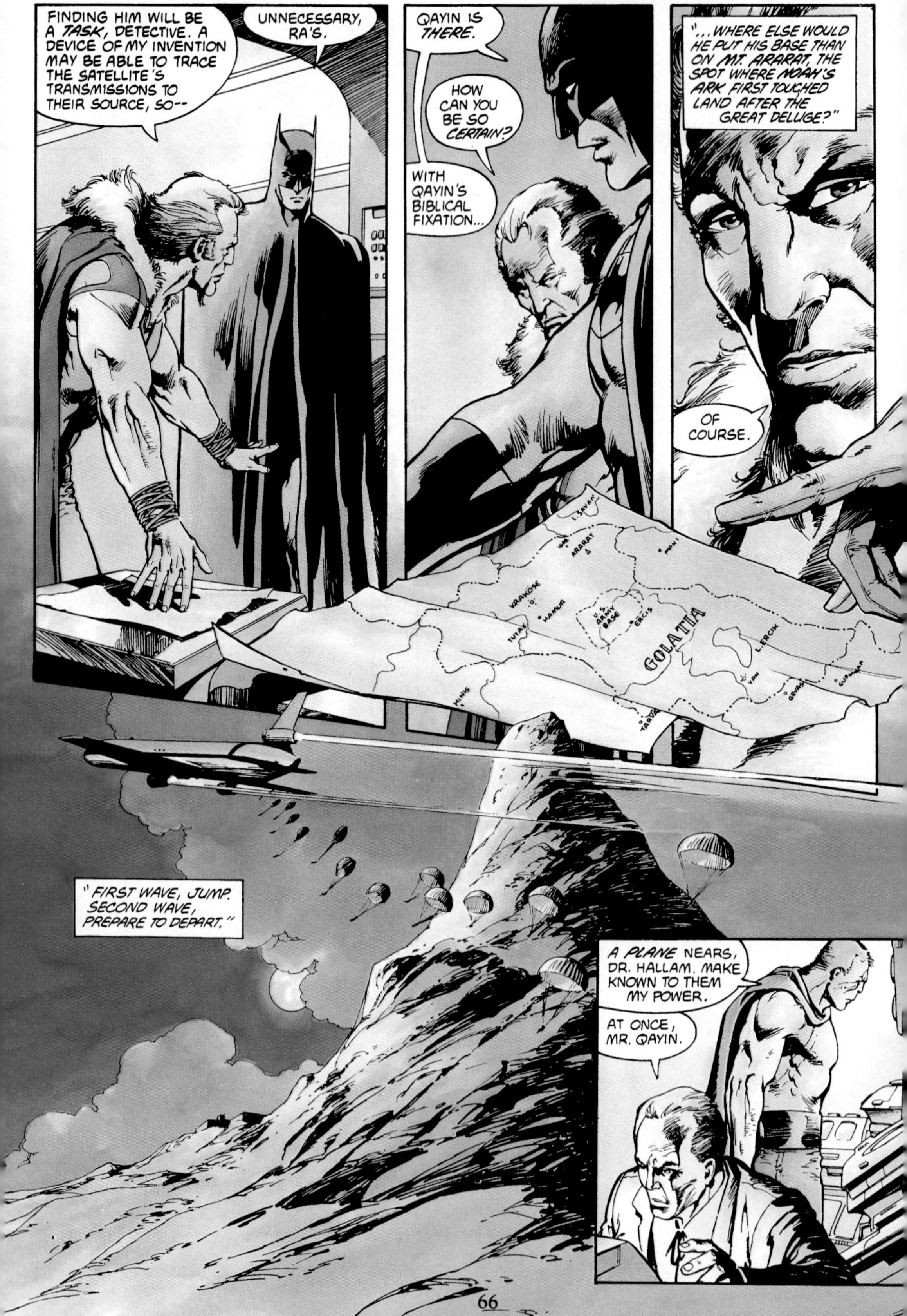
FINDING HIM WILL BE A TASK, DETECTIVE. A DEVICE OF MY INVENTION MAY BE ABLE TO TRACE THE SATELLITE'S TRANSMISSIONS TO THEIR SOURCE, SO--
UNNECESSARY, RA'S.
QAYIN IS THERE.
HOW CAN YOU BE SO CERTAIN?
WITH QAYIN'S BIBLICAL FIXATION...
"...WHERE ELSE WOULD HE PUT HIS BASE THAN ON MT. ARARAT, THE SPOT WHERE NOAH'S ARK FIRST TOUCHED LAND AFTER THE GREAT DELUGE?"
OF COURSE.
ARARAT
GOLATIA
U.S. ARMY BASE
"FIRST WAVE, JUMP. SECOND WAVE, PREPARE TO DEPART."
A PLANE NEARS, DR. HALLAM. MAKE KNOWN TO THEM MY POWER.
AT ONCE, MR. QAYIN.

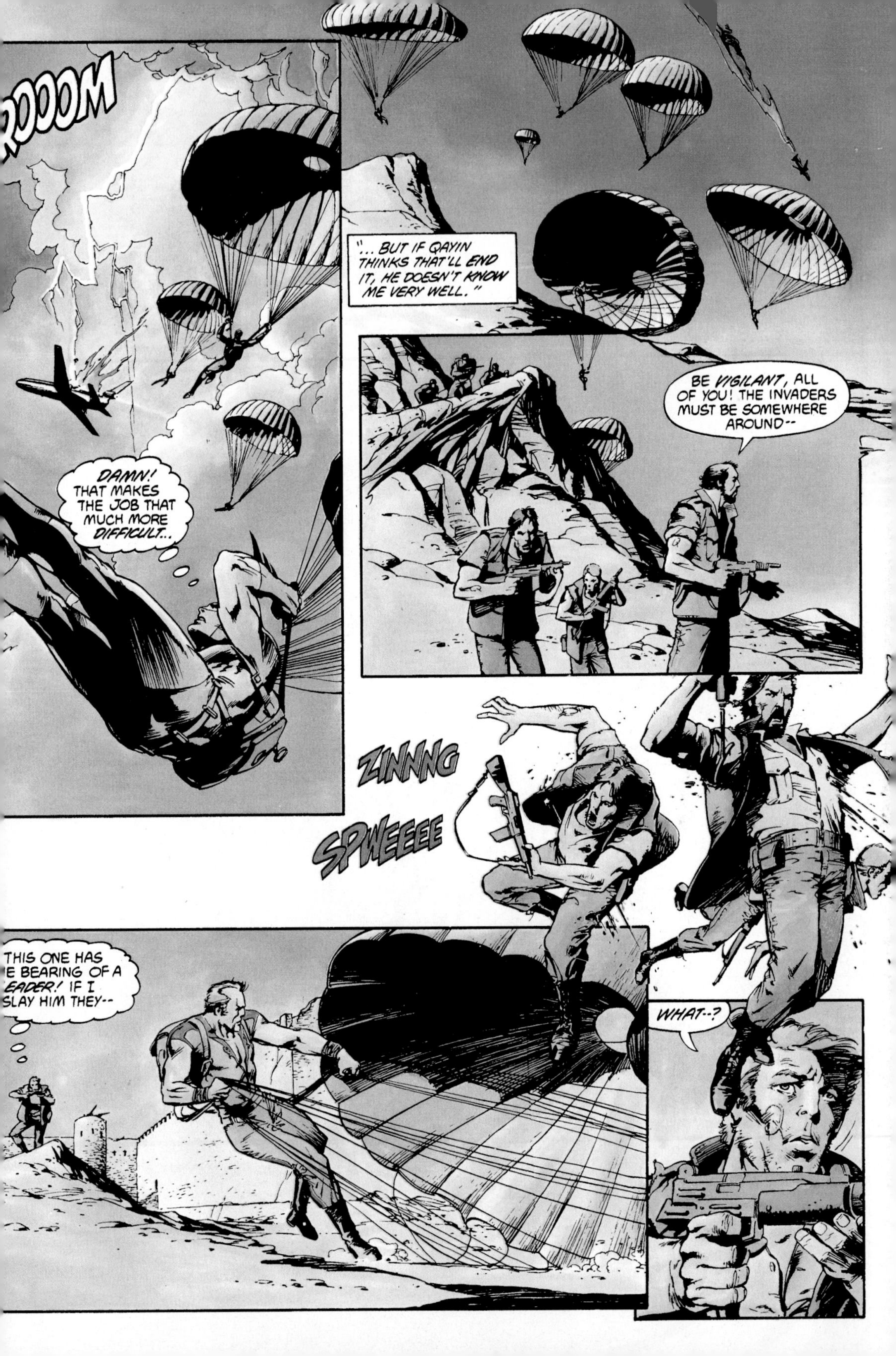
ROOOM
DAMN! THAT MAKES THE JOB THAT MUCH MORE DIFFICULT...
"... BUT IF QAYIN THINKS THAT'LL END IT, HE DOESN'T KNOW ME VERY WELL."
BE VIGILANT, ALL OF YOU! THE INVADERS MUST BE SOMEWHERE AROUND--
ZINNNG
SPWEEEE
THIS ONE HAS E BEARING OF A EADER! IF I SLAY HIM THEY--
WHAT--?

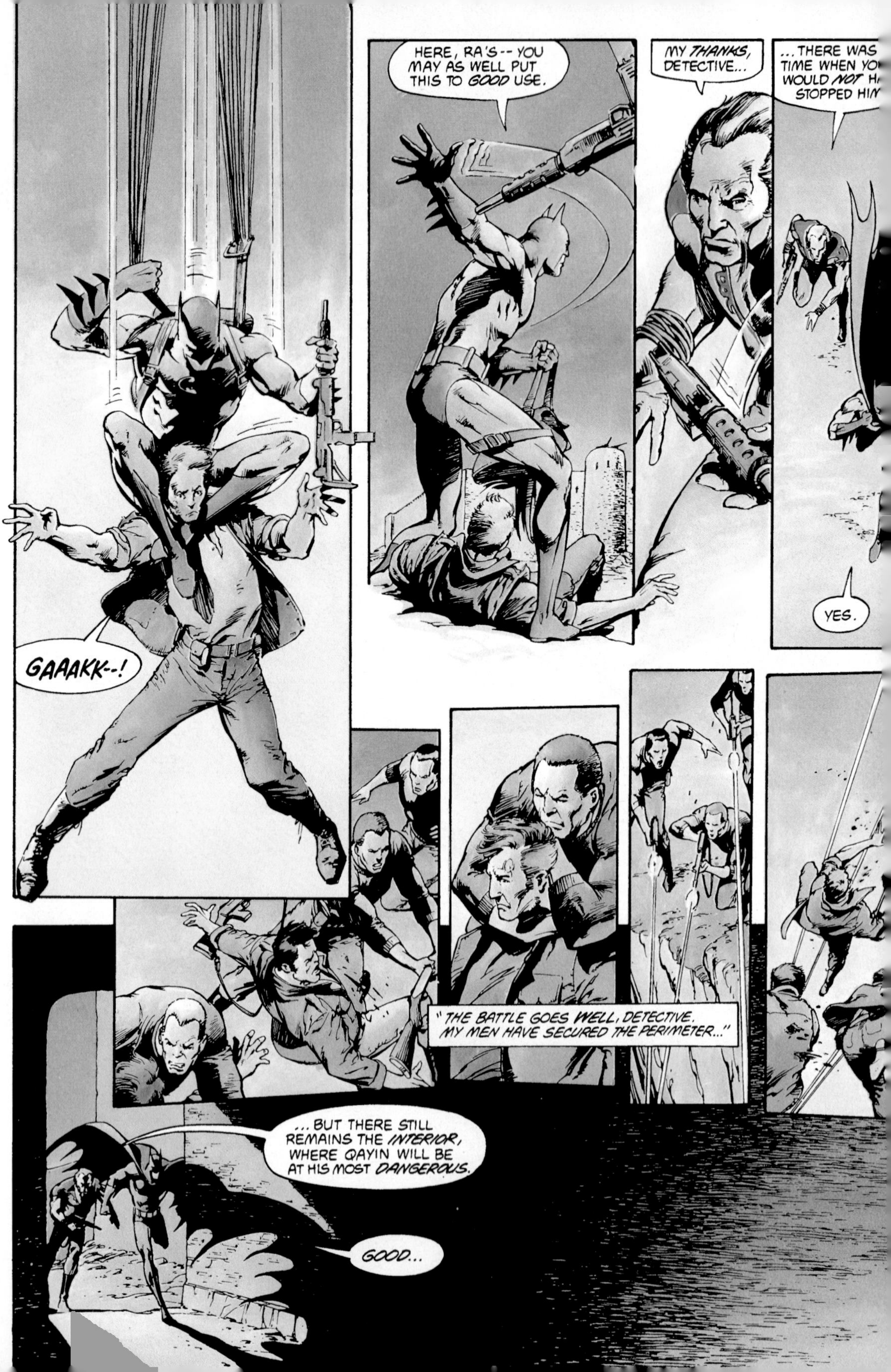
GAAAKK--!
HERE, RA'S-- YOU MAY AS WELL PUT THIS TO GOOD USE.
MY THANKS, DETECTIVE...
...THERE WAS TIME WHEN YO WOULD NOT H STOPPED HIM
YES.
"THE BATTLE GOES WELL, DETECTIVE. MY MEN HAVE SECURED THE PERIMETER..."
...BUT THERE STILL REMAINS THE INTERIOR, WHERE QAYIN WILL BE AT HIS MOST DANGEROUS.
GOOD...

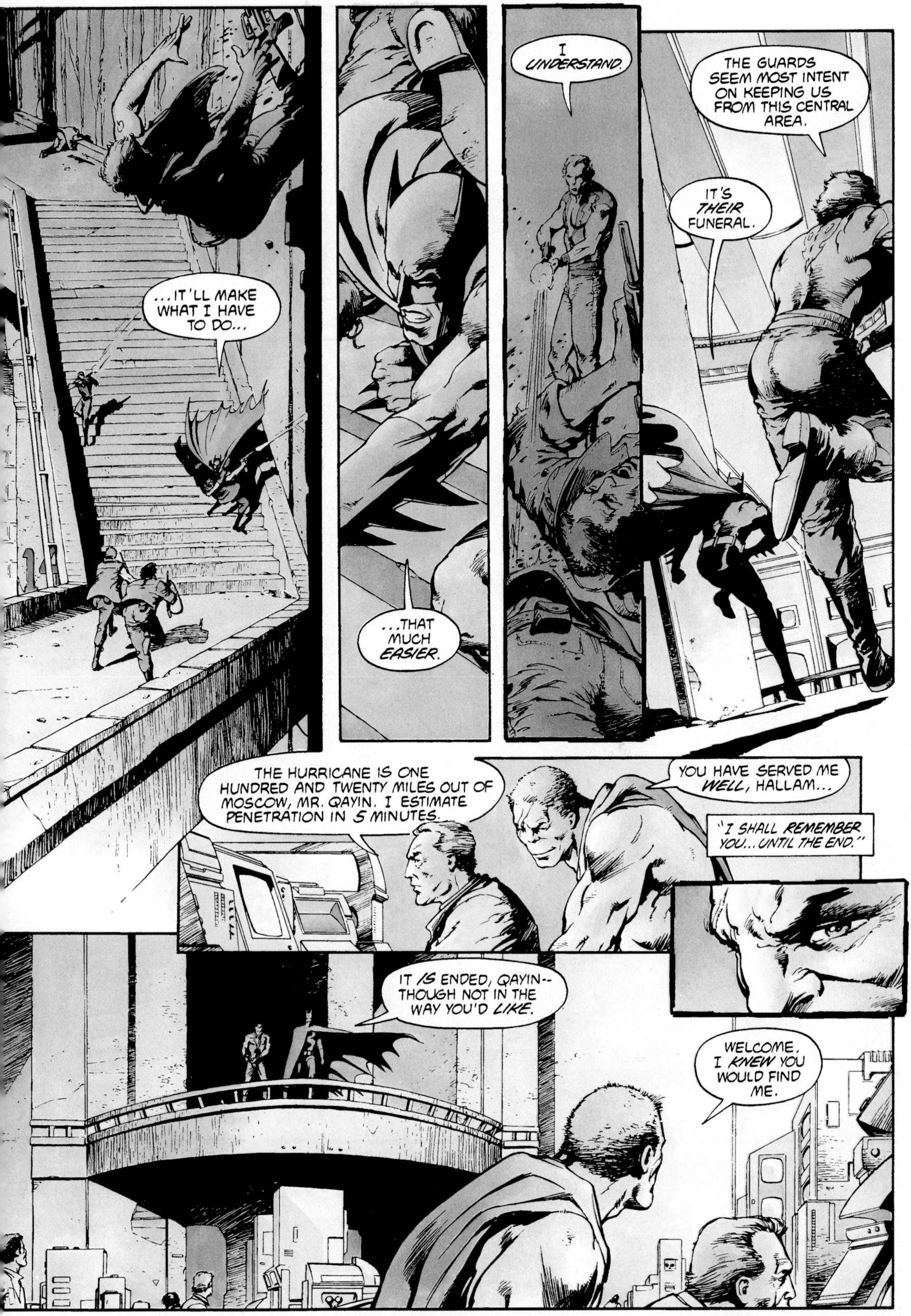
...IT'LL MAKE WHAT I HAVE TO DO...
...THAT MUCH EASIER.
I UNDERSTAND.
THE GUARDS SEEM MOST INTENT ON KEEPING US FROM THIS CENTRAL AREA.
IT'S THEIR FUNERAL.
THE HURRICANE IS ONE HUNDRED AND TWENTY MILES OUT OF MOSCOW, MR. QAYIN. I ESTIMATE PENETRATION IN 5 MINUTES.
YOU HAVE SERVED ME WELL, HALLAM...
"I SHALL REMEMBER YOU... UNTIL THE END."
IT IS ENDED, QAYIN-- THOUGH NOT IN THE WAY YOU'D LIKE.
WELCOME. I KNEW YOU WOULD FIND ME.

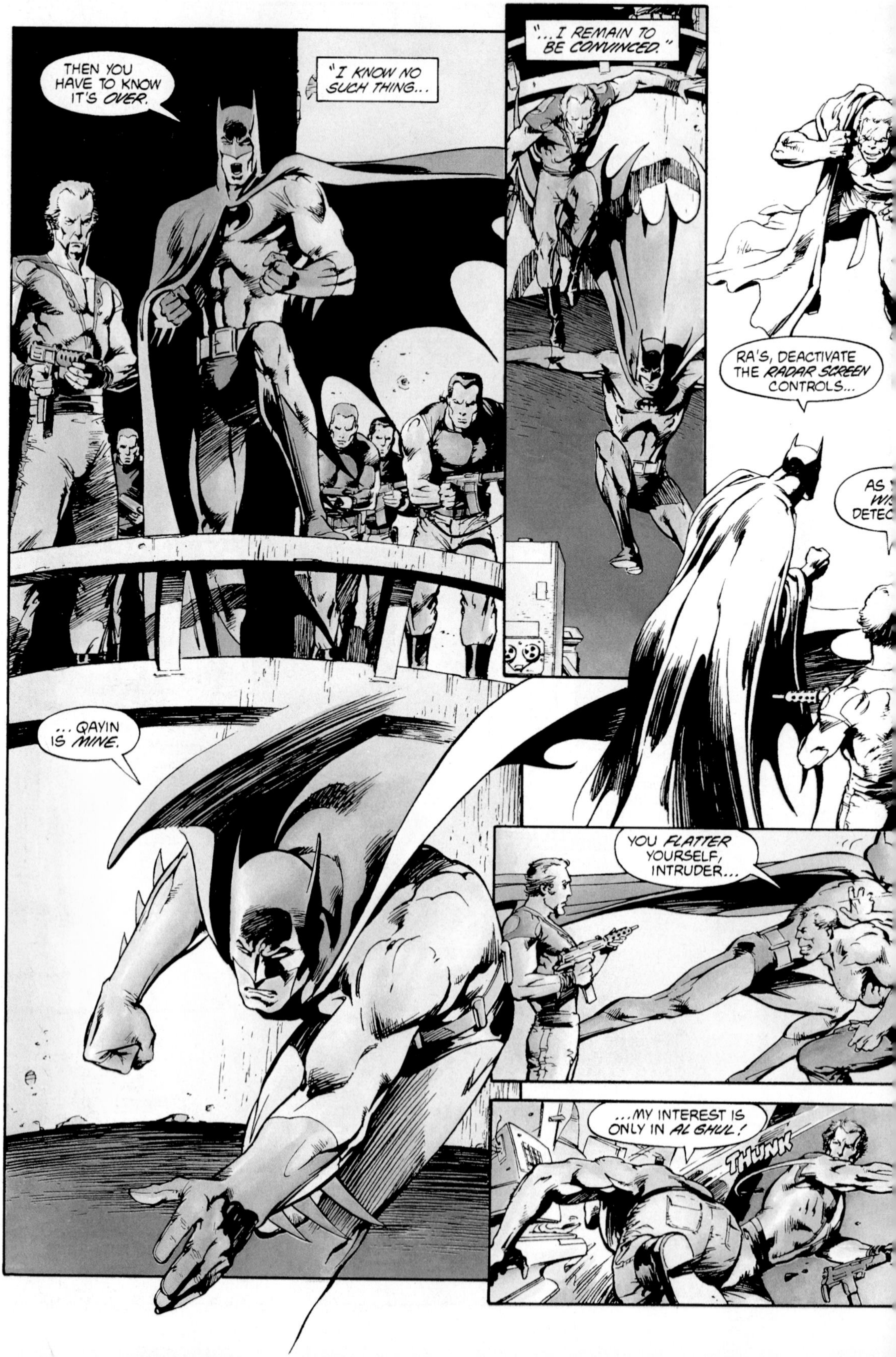

THEN YOU HAVE TO KNOW IT'S *OVER.*
"I KNOW NO SUCH THING...
"...I REMAIN TO BE CONVINCED."
RA'S, DEACTIVATE THE *RADAR SCREEN* CONTROLS...
... QAYIN IS *MINE.*
YOU *FLATTER* YOURSELF, INTRUDER...
...MY INTEREST IS ONLY IN *AL GHUL!*
THUNK

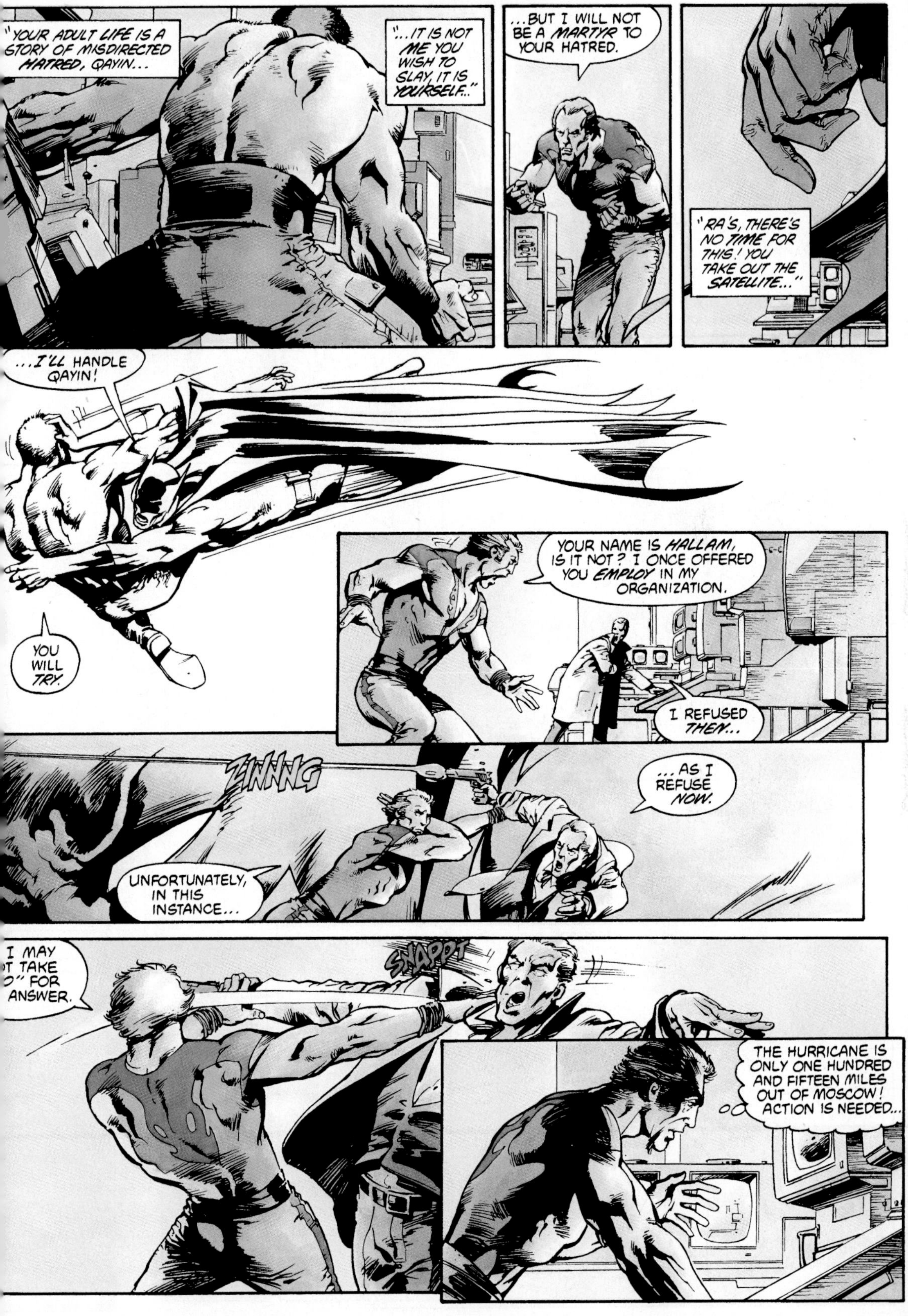
"YOUR ADULT LIFE IS A STORY OF MISDIRECTED HATRED, QAYIN...
"...IT IS NOT ME YOU WISH TO SLAY, IT IS YOURSELF..."
...BUT I WILL NOT BE A MARTYR TO YOUR HATRED.
"RA'S, THERE'S NO TIME FOR THIS! YOU TAKE OUT THE SATELLITE..."
...I'LL HANDLE QAYIN!
YOU WILL TRY.
YOUR NAME IS HALLAM, IS IT NOT? I ONCE OFFERED YOU EMPLOY IN MY ORGANIZATION.
I REFUSED THEN...
ZINNNG
...AS I REFUSE NOW.
UNFORTUNATELY, IN THIS INSTANCE...
I MAY
T TAKE
O" FOR
ANSWER.
SHAPPT
THE HURRICANE IS ONLY ONE HUNDRED AND FIFTEEN MILES OUT OF MOSCOW! ACTION IS NEEDED...

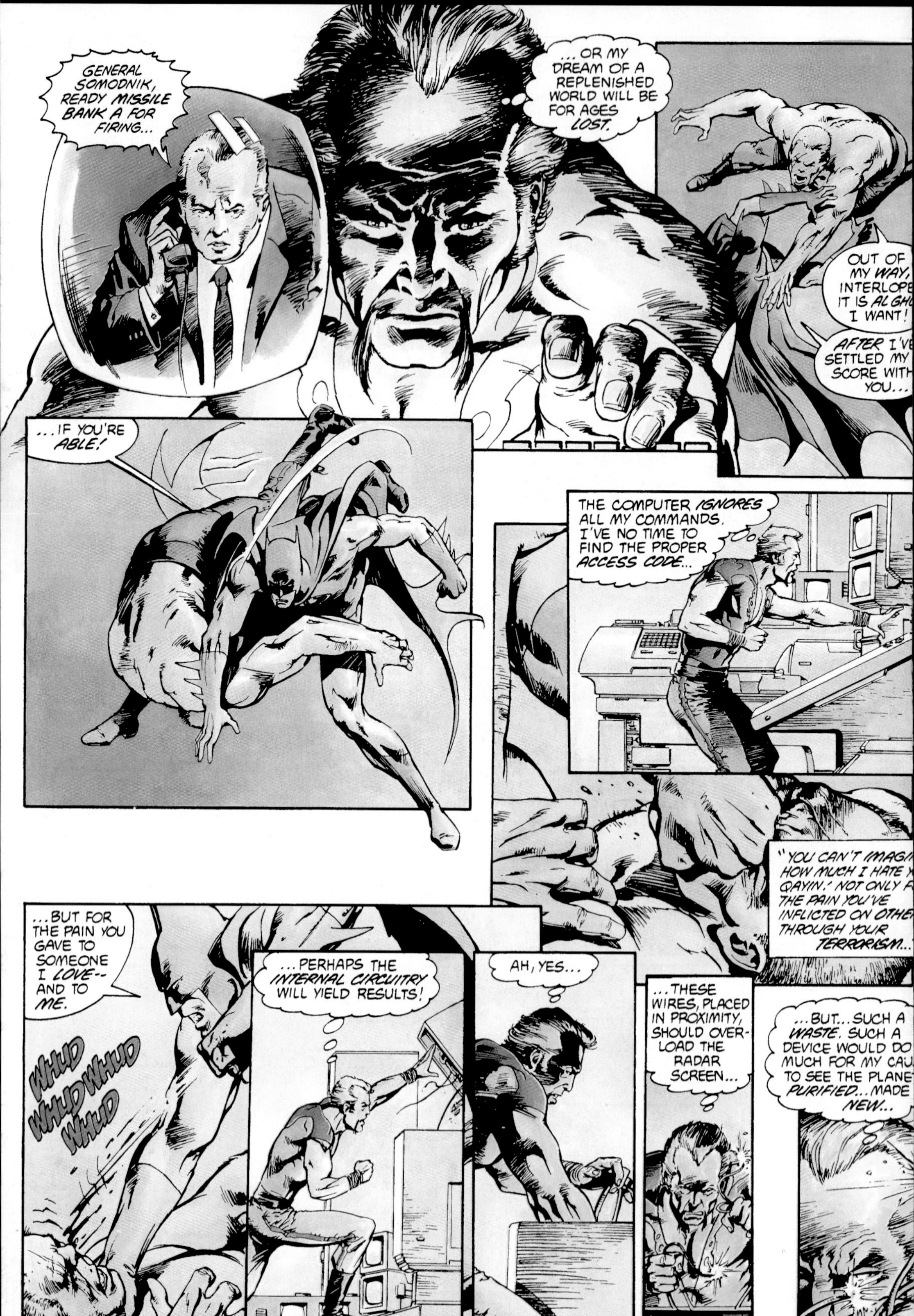
GENERAL SOMODNIK, READY MISSILE BANK A FOR FIRING...
...OR MY DREAM OF A REPLENISHED WORLD WILL BE FOR AGES LOST.
OUT OF MY WAY, INTERLOPE IT IS AL GHU I WANT!
AFTER I'VE SETTLED MY SCORE WITH YOU...
...IF YOU'RE ABLE!
THE COMPUTER IGNORES ALL MY COMMANDS. I'VE NO TIME TO FIND THE PROPER ACCESS CODE...
"YOU CAN'T IMAGI HOW MUCH I HATE Y QAYIN! NOT ONLY F THE PAIN YOU'VE INFLICTED ON OTHE THROUGH YOUR TERRORISM...
...BUT FOR THE PAIN YOU GAVE TO SOMEONE I LOVE-- AND TO ME.
WHUD WHUD WHUD WHUD WHUD
...PERHAPS THE INTERNAL CIRCUITRY WILL YIELD RESULTS!
AH, YES...
...THESE WIRES, PLACED IN PROXIMITY, SHOULD OVER-LOAD THE RADAR SCREEN...
...BUT...SUCH A WASTE. SUCH A DEVICE WOULD DO MUCH FOR MY CAU TO SEE THE PLANE PURIFIED...MADE NEW...

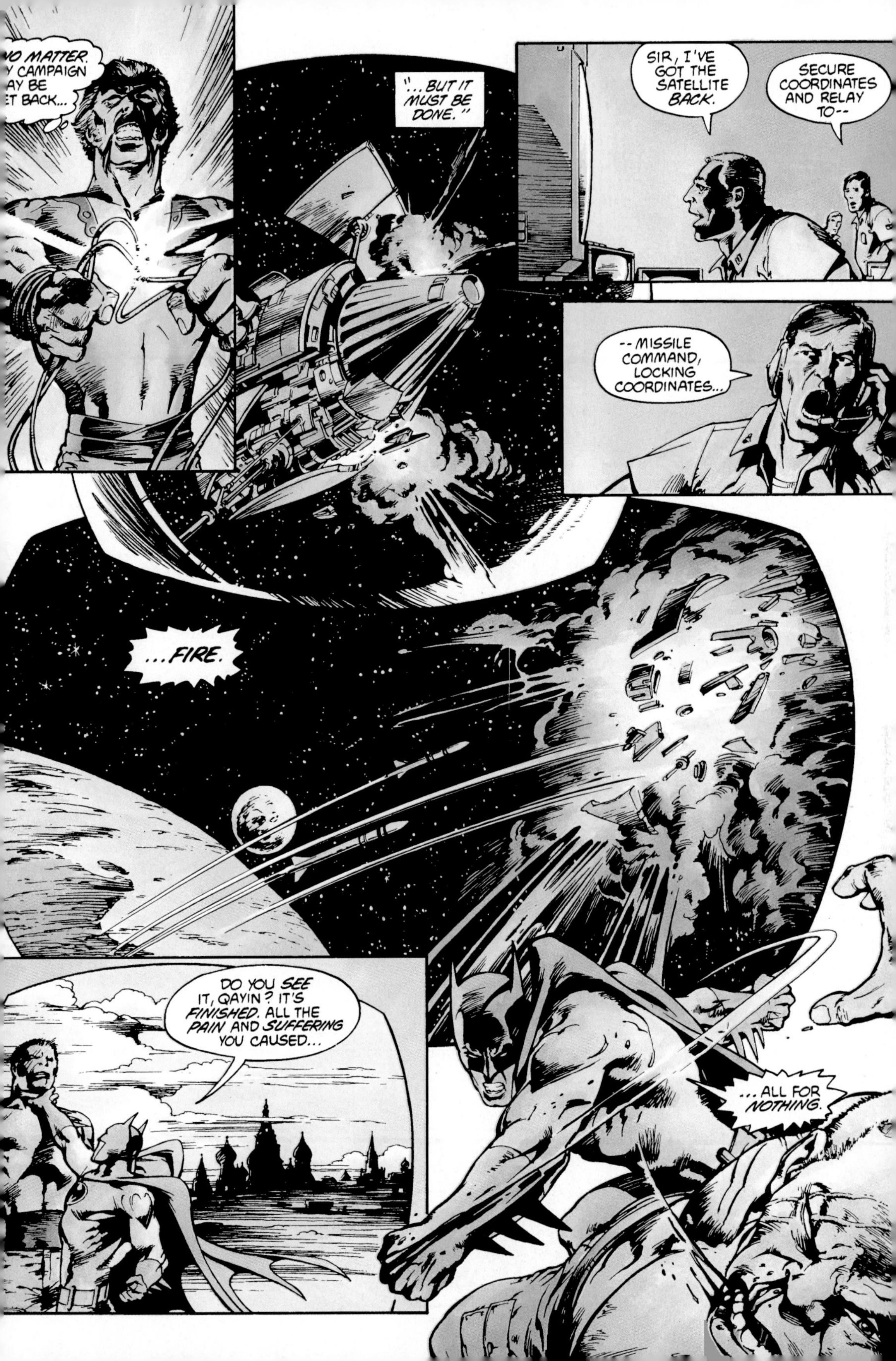
NO MATTER. MY CAMPAIGN MAY BE SET BACK...
"...BUT IT MUST BE DONE."
SIR, I'VE GOT THE SATELLITE BACK.
SECURE COORDINATES AND RELAY TO--
--MISSILE COMMAND, LOCKING COORDINATES...
...FIRE.
DO YOU SEE IT, QAYIN? IT'S FINISHED. ALL THE PAIN AND SUFFERING YOU CAUSED...
...ALL FOR NOTHING.

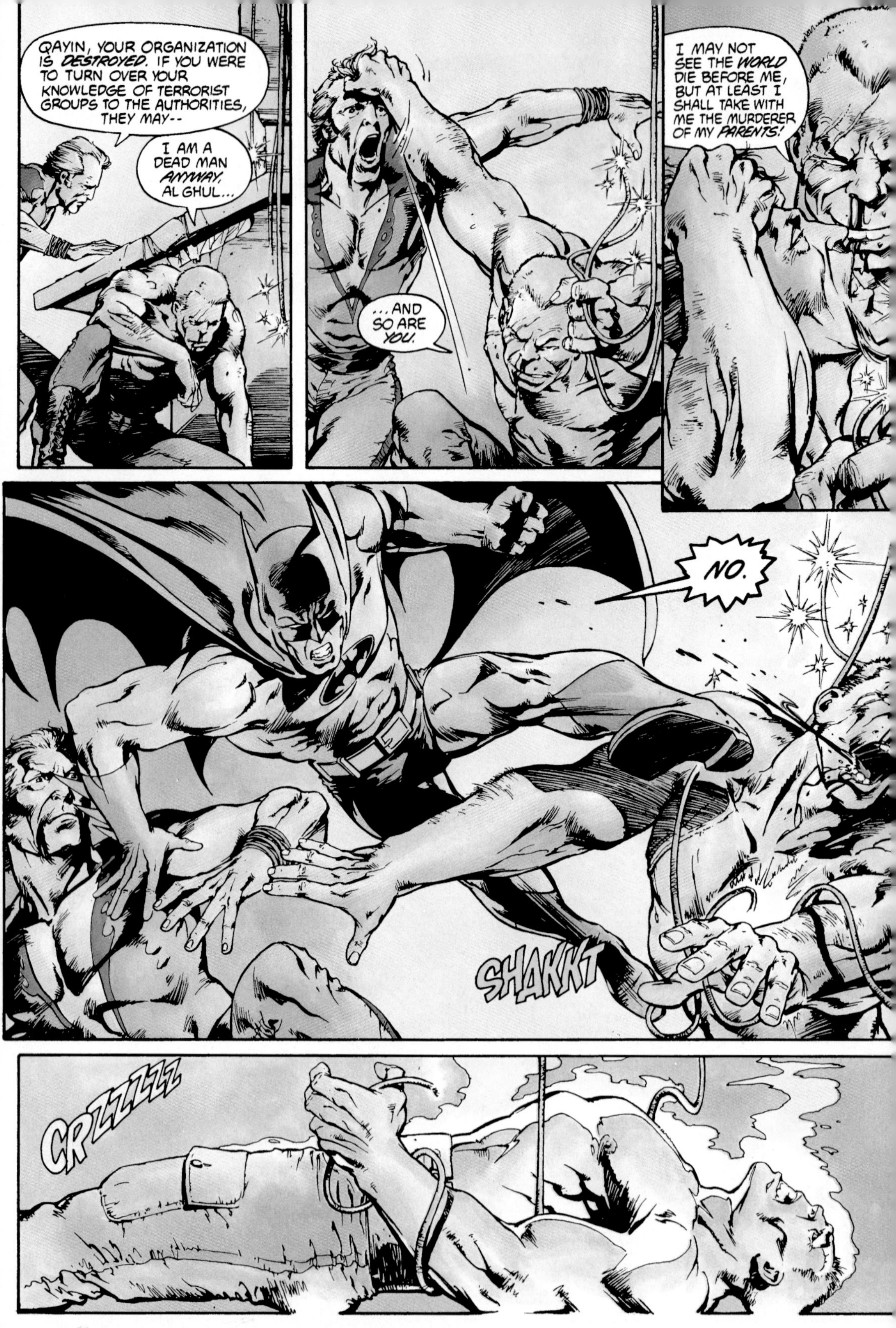
QAYIN, YOUR ORGANIZATION IS DESTROYED. IF YOU WERE TO TURN OVER YOUR KNOWLEDGE OF TERRORIST GROUPS TO THE AUTHORITIES, THEY MAY--
I AM A DEAD MAN ANYWAY, AL GHUL...
...AND SO ARE YOU.
I MAY NOT SEE THE WORLD DIE BEFORE ME, BUT AT LEAST I SHALL TAKE WITH ME THE MURDERER OF MY PARENTS!
NO.
SHAKKT
CRZZZZZ

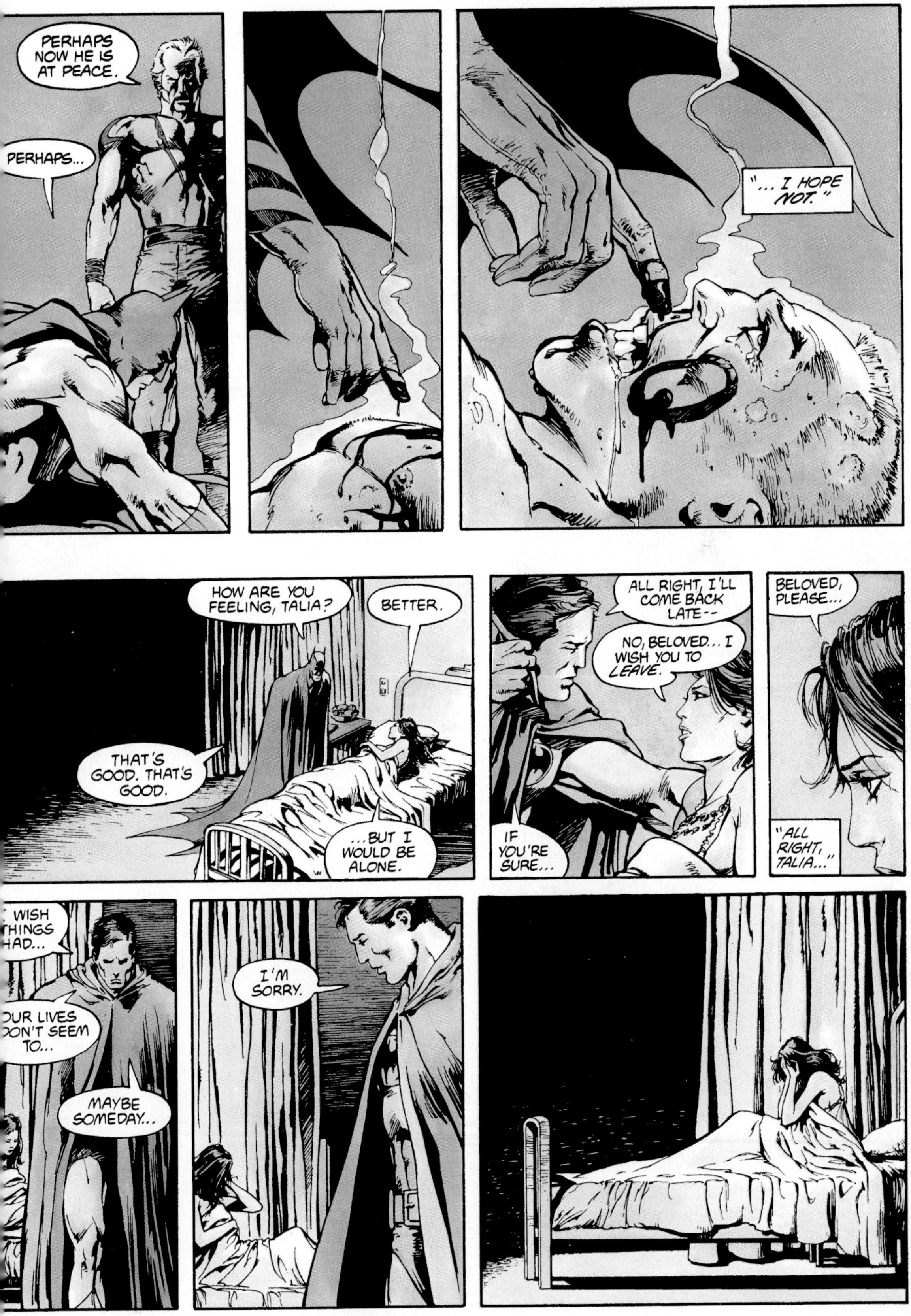
PERHAPS NOW HE IS AT PEACE.
PERHAPS...
"... I HOPE NOT."
HOW ARE YOU FEELING, TALIA?
BETTER.
THAT'S GOOD. THAT'S GOOD.
...BUT I WOULD BE ALONE.
ALL RIGHT, I'LL COME BACK LATE--
NO, BELOVED... I WISH YOU TO LEAVE.
IF YOU'RE SURE...
BELOVED, PLEASE...
"ALL RIGHT, TALIA..."
WISH THINGS HAD...
OUR LIVES ON'T SEEM TO...
MAYBE SOMEDAY...
I'M SORRY.

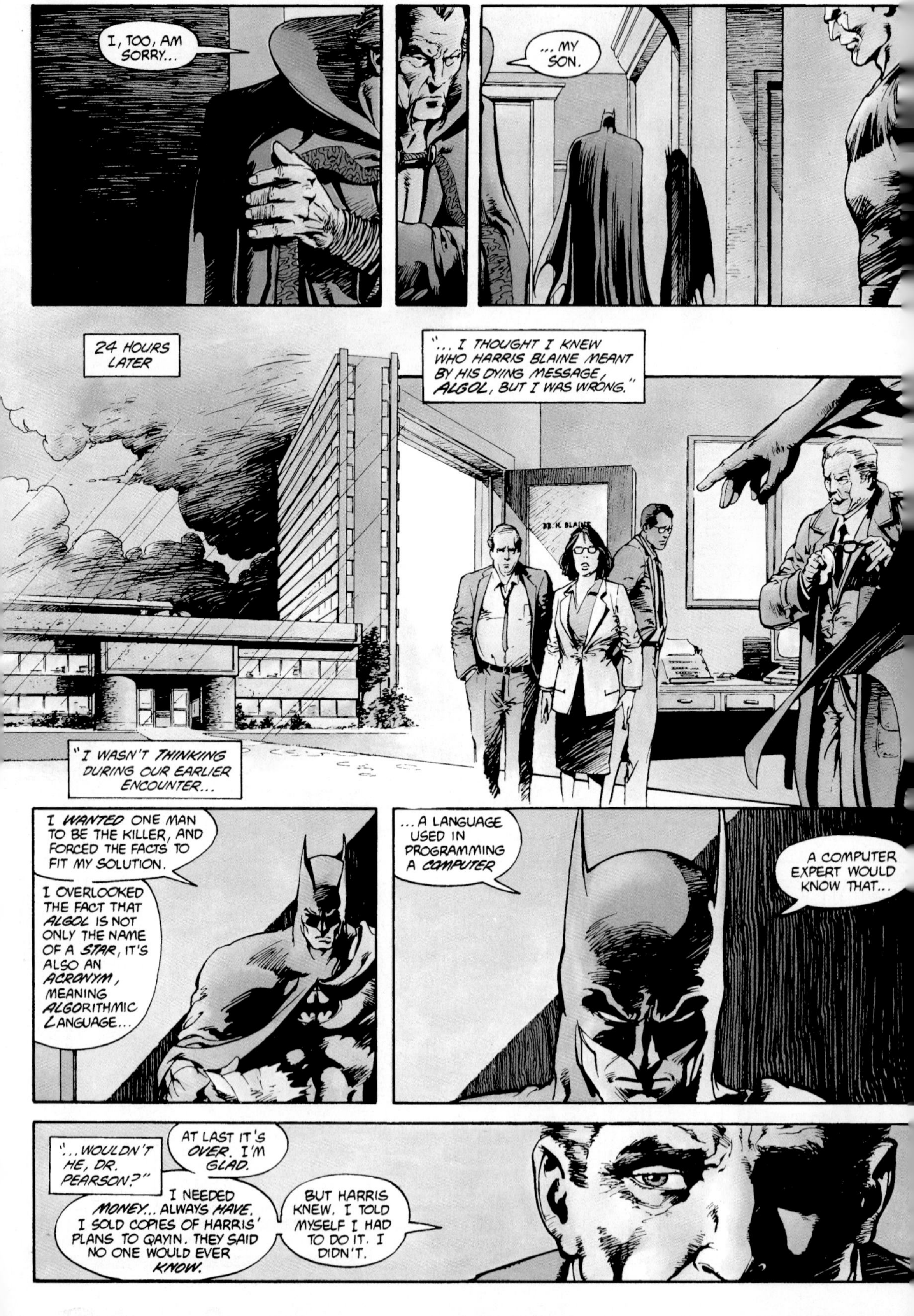

I, TOO, AM SORRY...
...MY SON.
24 HOURS LATER
"...I THOUGHT I KNEW WHO HARRIS BLAINE MEANT BY HIS DYING MESSAGE, ALGOL, BUT I WAS WRONG."
"I WASN'T THINKING DURING OUR EARLIER ENCOUNTER...
I WANTED ONE MAN TO BE THE KILLER, AND FORCED THE FACTS TO FIT MY SOLUTION.
I OVERLOOKED THE FACT THAT ALGOL IS NOT ONLY THE NAME OF A STAR, IT'S ALSO AN ACRONYM, MEANING ALGORITHMIC LANGUAGE...
...A LANGUAGE USED IN PROGRAMMING A COMPUTER
A COMPUTER EXPERT WOULD KNOW THAT...
"...WOULDN'T HE, DR. PEARSON?"
AT LAST IT'S OVER. I'M GLAD.
I NEEDED MONEY... ALWAYS HAVE. I SOLD COPIES OF HARRIS' PLANS TO QAYIN. THEY SAID NO ONE WOULD EVER KNOW.
BUT HARRIS KNEW. I TOLD MYSELF I HAD TO DO IT. I DIDN'T.

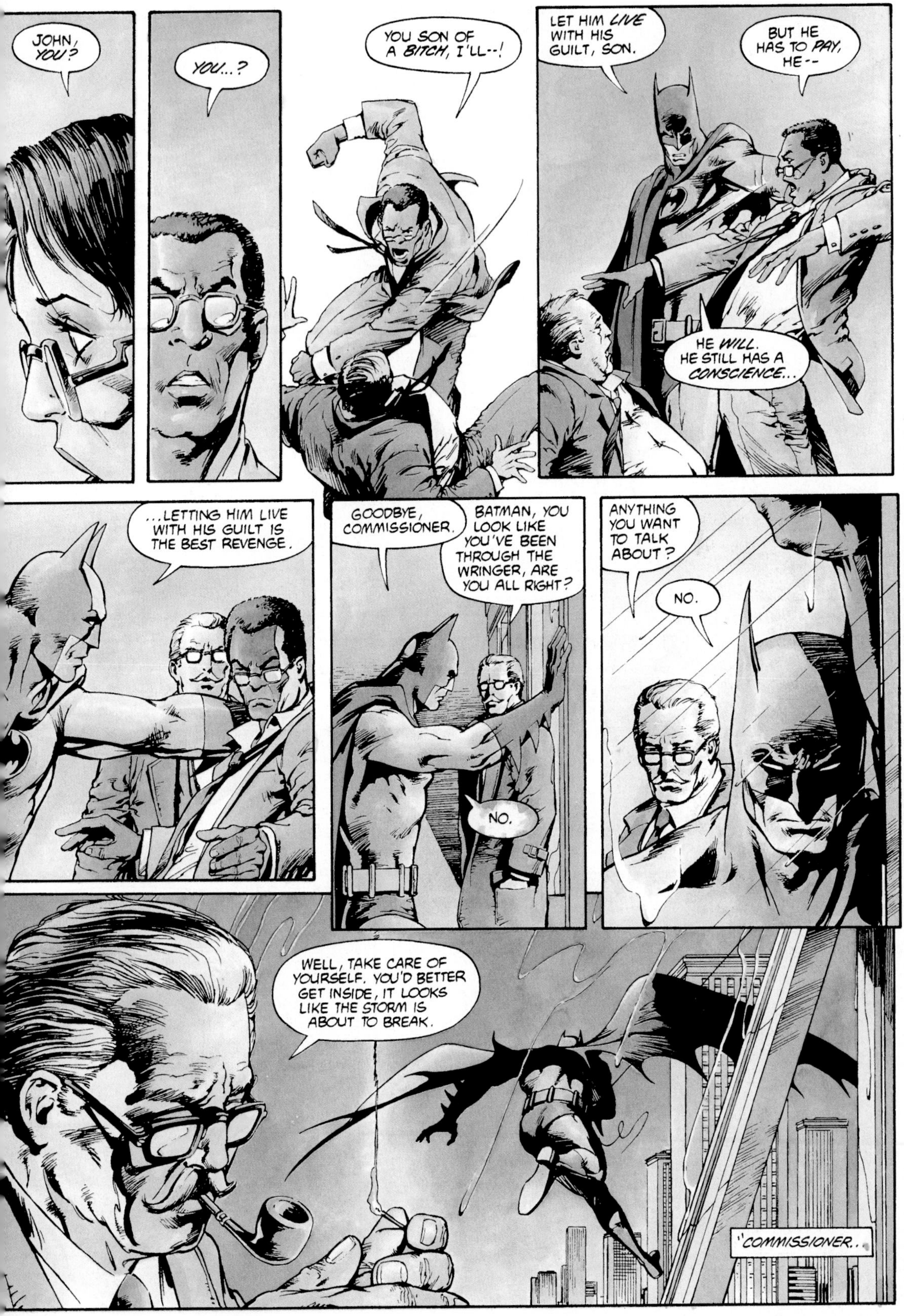
JOHN, YOU?
YOU...?
YOU SON OF A BITCH, I'LL--!
LET HIM LIVE WITH HIS GUILT, SON.
BUT HE HAS TO PAY, HE--
HE WILL. HE STILL HAS A CONSCIENCE...
...LETTING HIM LIVE WITH HIS GUILT IS THE BEST REVENGE.
GOODBYE, COMMISSIONER.
BATMAN, YOU LOOK LIKE YOU'VE BEEN THROUGH THE WRINGER, ARE YOU ALL RIGHT?
NO.
ANYTHING YOU WANT TO TALK ABOUT?
NO.
WELL, TAKE CARE OF YOURSELF. YOU'D BETTER GET INSIDE, IT LOOKS LIKE THE STORM IS ABOUT TO BREAK.
"COMMISSIONER..

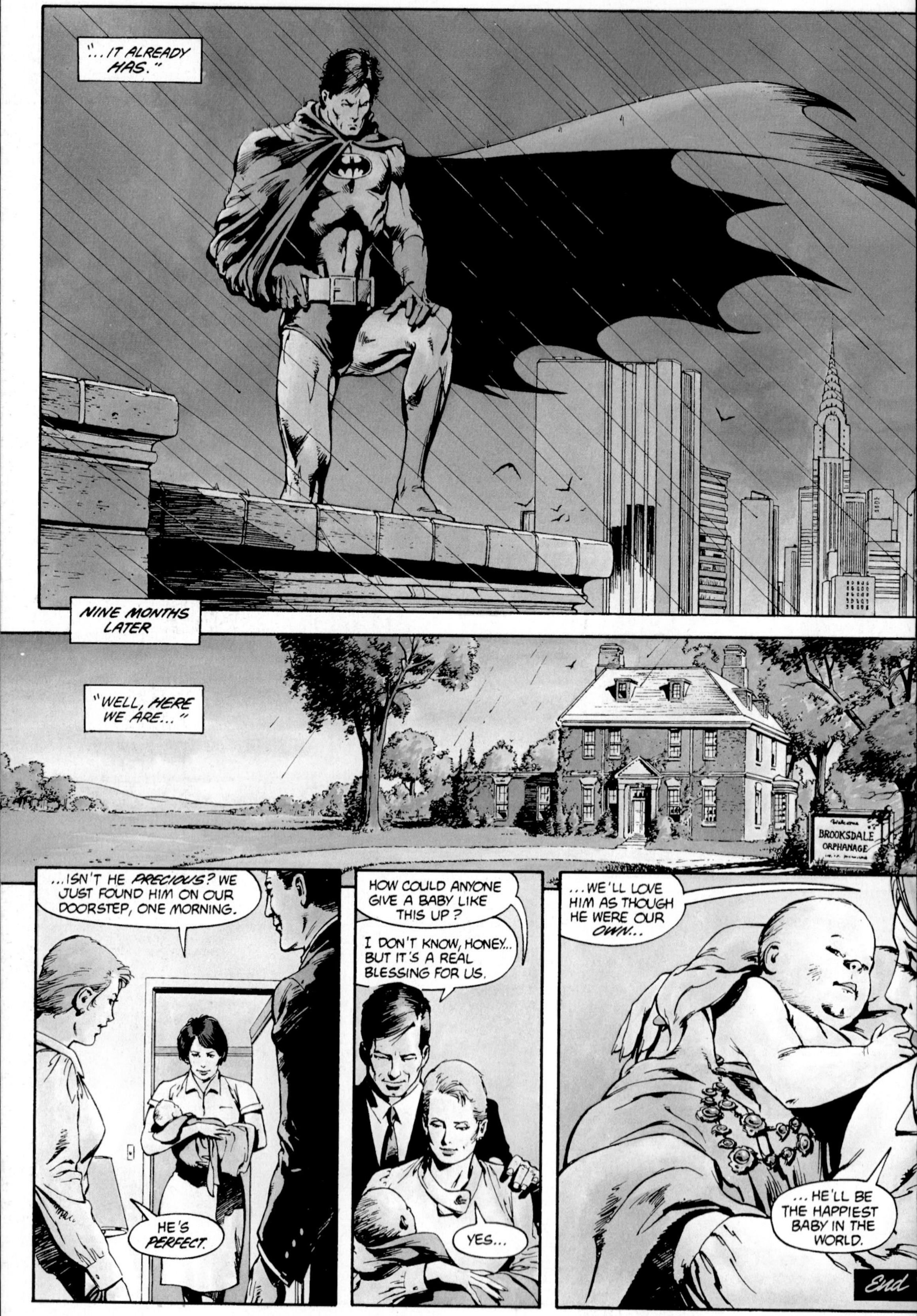
"...IT ALREADY HAS."
NINE MONTHS LATER
"WELL, HERE WE ARE..."
BROOKSDALE ORPHANAGE
...ISN'T HE PRECIOUS? WE JUST FOUND HIM ON OUR DOORSTEP, ONE MORNING.
HE'S PERFECT.
HOW COULD ANYONE GIVE A BABY LIKE THIS UP?
I DON'T KNOW, HONEY... BUT IT'S A REAL BLESSING FOR US.
YES...
...WE'LL LOVE HIM AS THOUGH HE WERE OUR OWN...
...HE'LL BE THE HAPPIEST BABY IN THE WORLD.
End

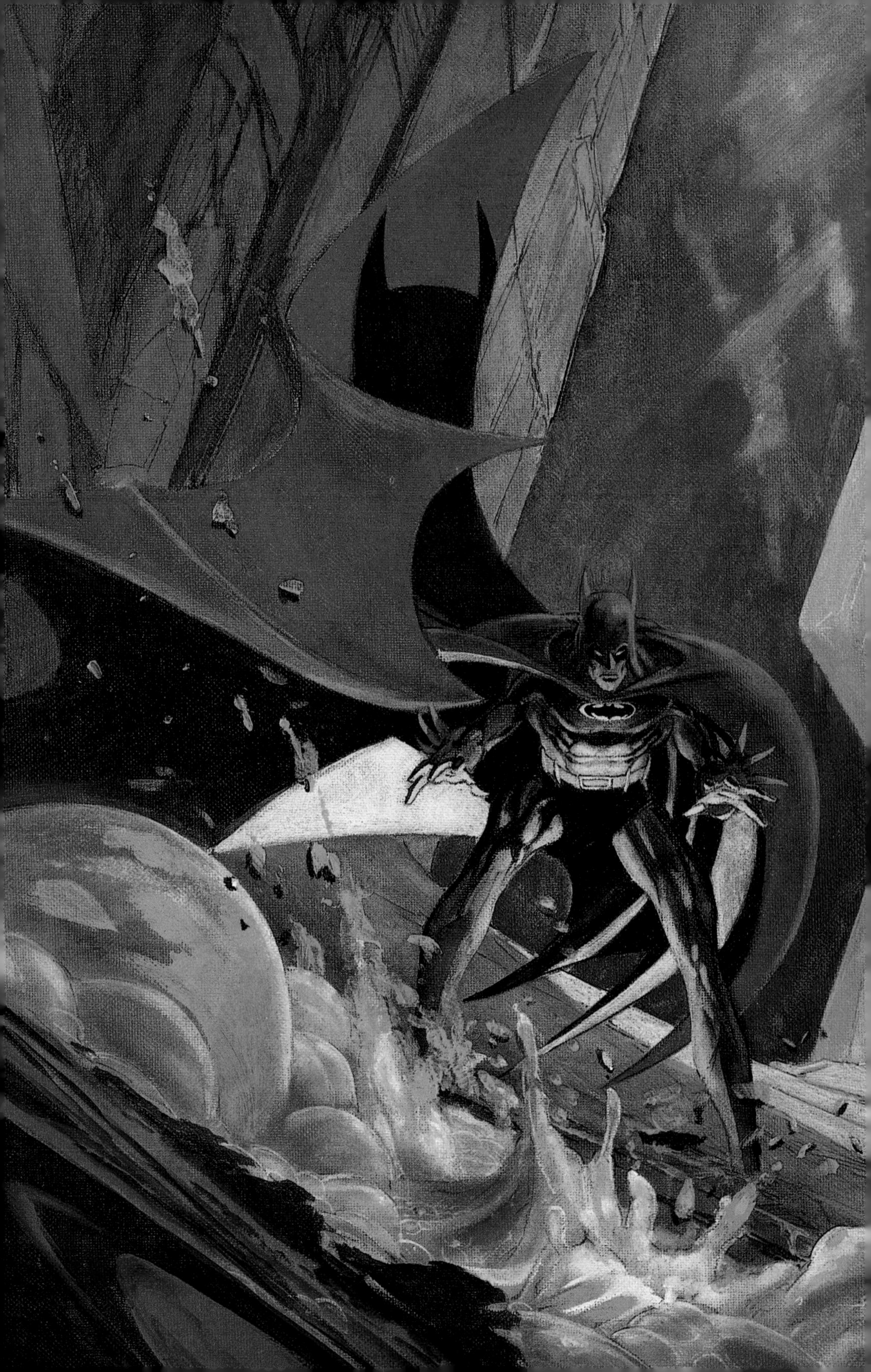

BATMAN
BRIDE OF THE DEMON

Mike W. Barr *Writer*

Tom Grindberg *Art & Cover*

Eva Grindberg *Colors*

Gaspar Saladino *Letters*

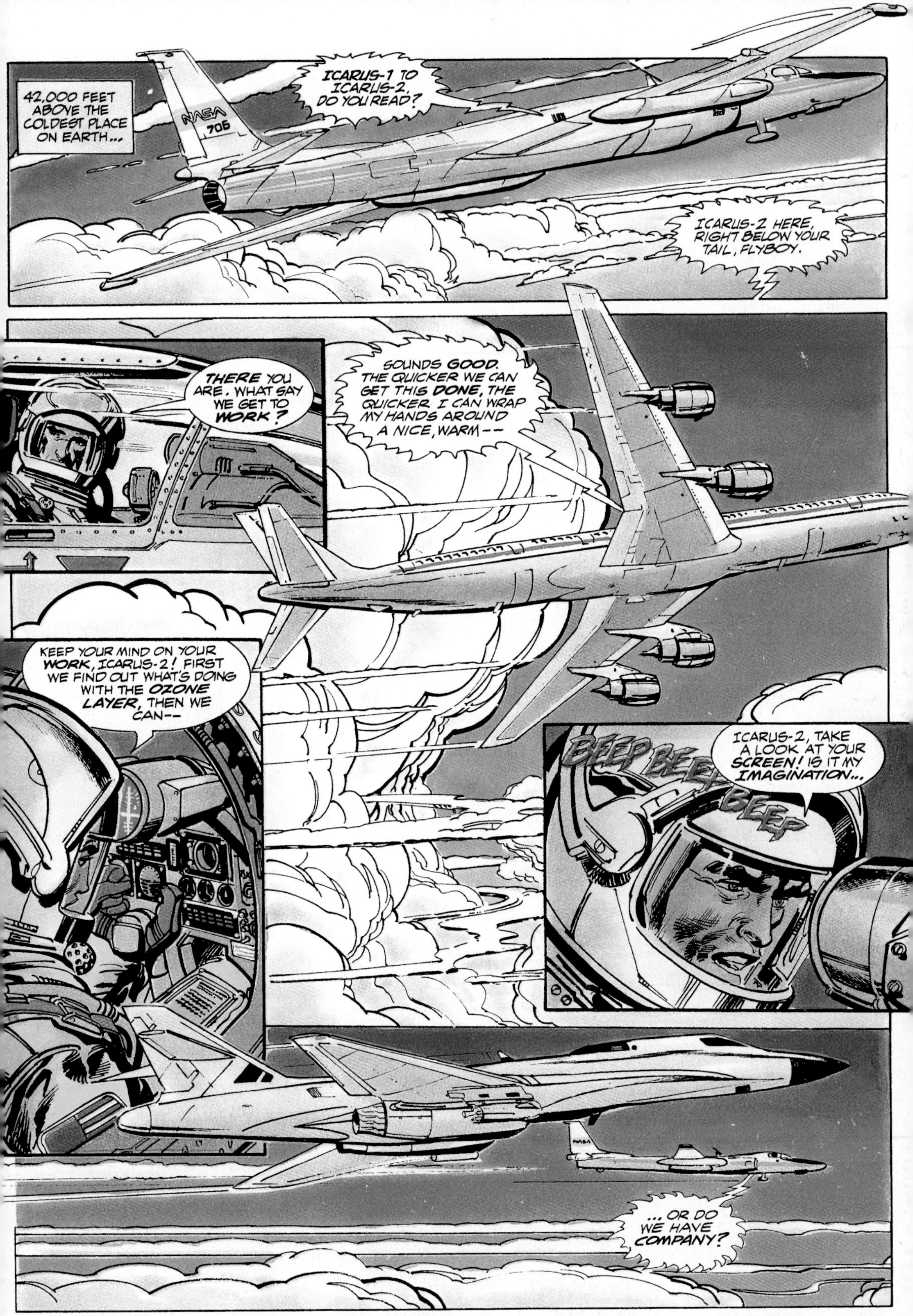
42,000 FEET ABOVE THE COLDEST PLACE ON EARTH...
ICARUS-1 TO ICARUS-2, DO YOU READ?
NASA 706
ICARUS-2 HERE, RIGHT BELOW YOUR TAIL, FLYBOY.
THERE YOU ARE. WHAT SAY WE GET TO WORK?
SOUNDS GOOD. THE QUICKER WE CAN GET THIS DONE, THE QUICKER I CAN WRAP MY HANDS AROUND A NICE, WARM--
KEEP YOUR MIND ON YOUR WORK, ICARUS-2! FIRST WE FIND OUT WHAT'S DOING WITH THE OZONE LAYER, THEN WE CAN--
BEEP BEEP BEEP
ICARUS-2, TAKE A LOOK AT YOUR SCREEN! IS IT MY IMAGINATION...
...OR DO WE HAVE COMPANY?

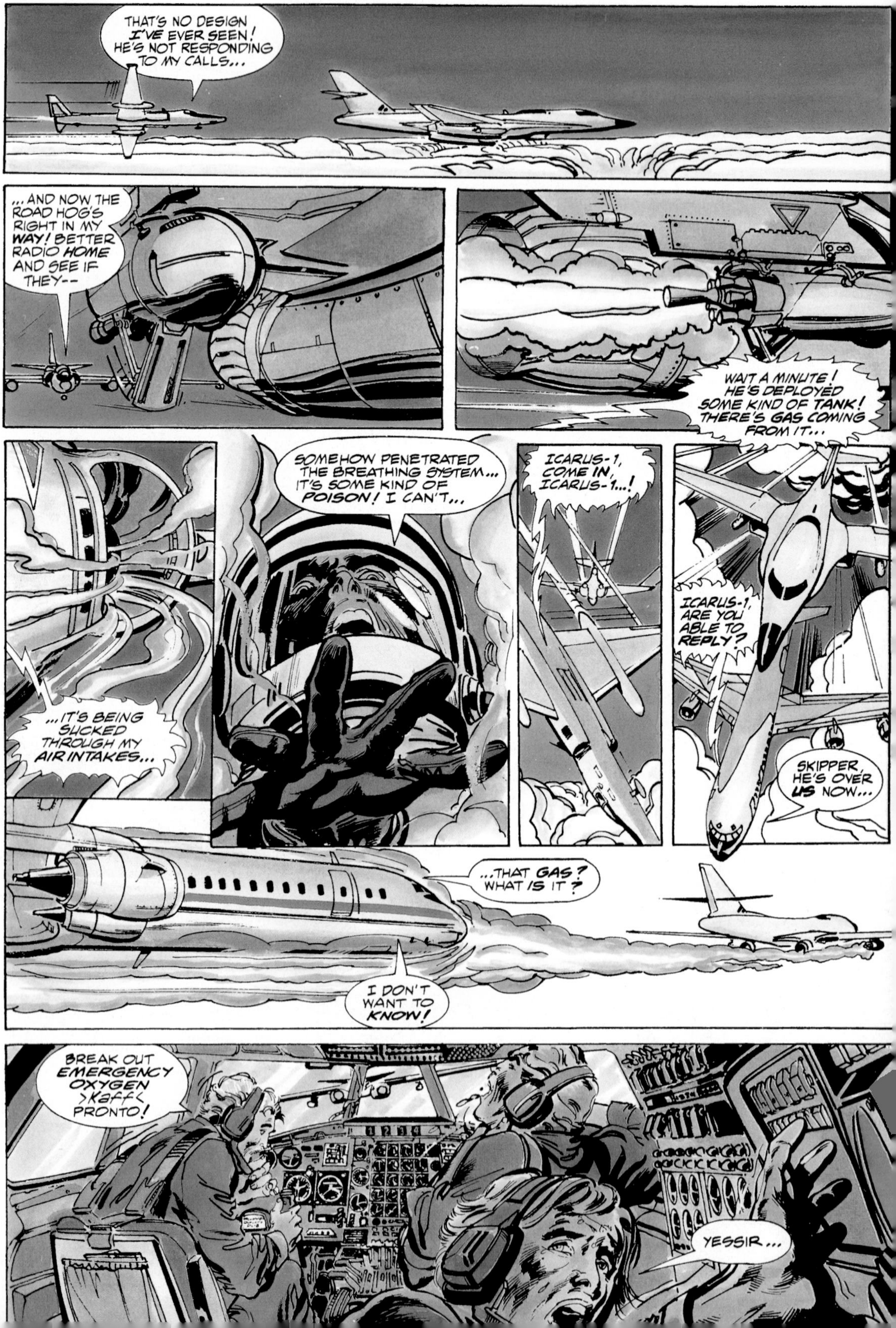
THAT'S NO DESIGN I'VE EVER SEEN! HE'S NOT RESPONDING TO MY CALLS...
...AND NOW THE ROAD HOG'S RIGHT IN MY WAY! BETTER RADIO HOME AND SEE IF THEY--
WAIT A MINUTE! HE'S DEPLOYED SOME KIND OF TANK! THERE'S GAS COMING FROM IT...
...IT'S BEING SUCKED THROUGH MY AIR INTAKES...
SOMEHOW PENETRATED THE BREATHING SYSTEM... IT'S SOME KIND OF POISON! I CAN'T...
ICARUS-1, COME IN, ICARUS-1...!
ICARUS-1, ARE YOU ABLE TO REPLY?
SKIPPER, HE'S OVER US NOW...
...THAT GAS? WHAT IS IT?
I DON'T WANT TO KNOW!
BREAK OUT EMERGENCY OXYGEN >Kaff< PRONTO!
YESSIR...

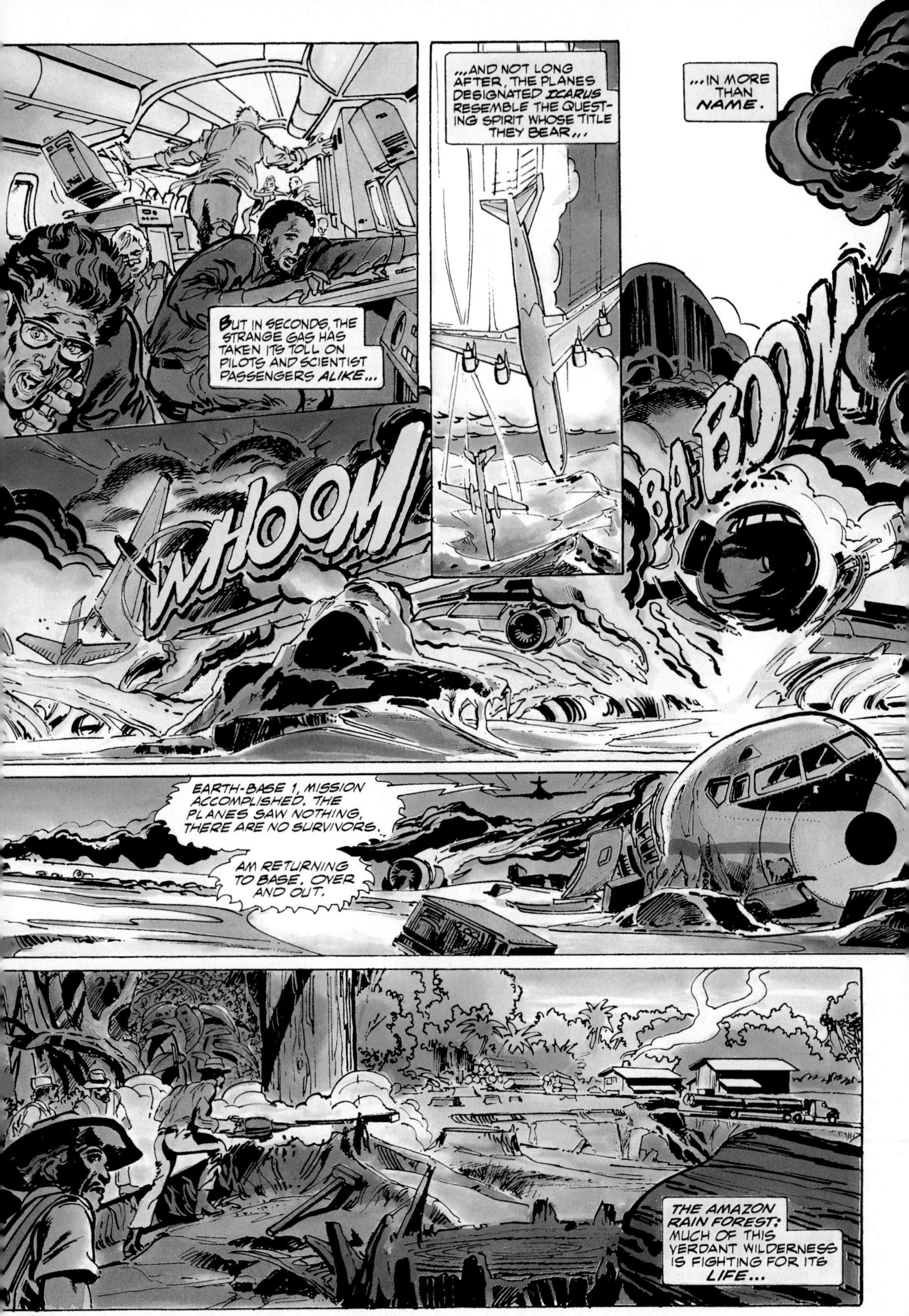
BUT IN SECONDS, THE STRANGE GAS HAS TAKEN ITS TOLL ON PILOTS AND SCIENTIST PASSENGERS ALIKE...
...AND NOT LONG AFTER, THE PLANES DESIGNATED ICARUS RESEMBLE THE QUESTING SPIRIT WHOSE TITLE THEY BEAR...
...IN MORE THAN NAME.
WHOOM
BABOOM
EARTH-BASE 1, MISSION ACCOMPLISHED. THE PLANES SAW NOTHING. THERE ARE NO SURVIVORS.
AM RETURNING TO BASE. OVER AND OUT.
THE AMAZON RAIN FOREST: MUCH OF THIS VERDANT WILDERNESS IS FIGHTING FOR ITS LIFE...

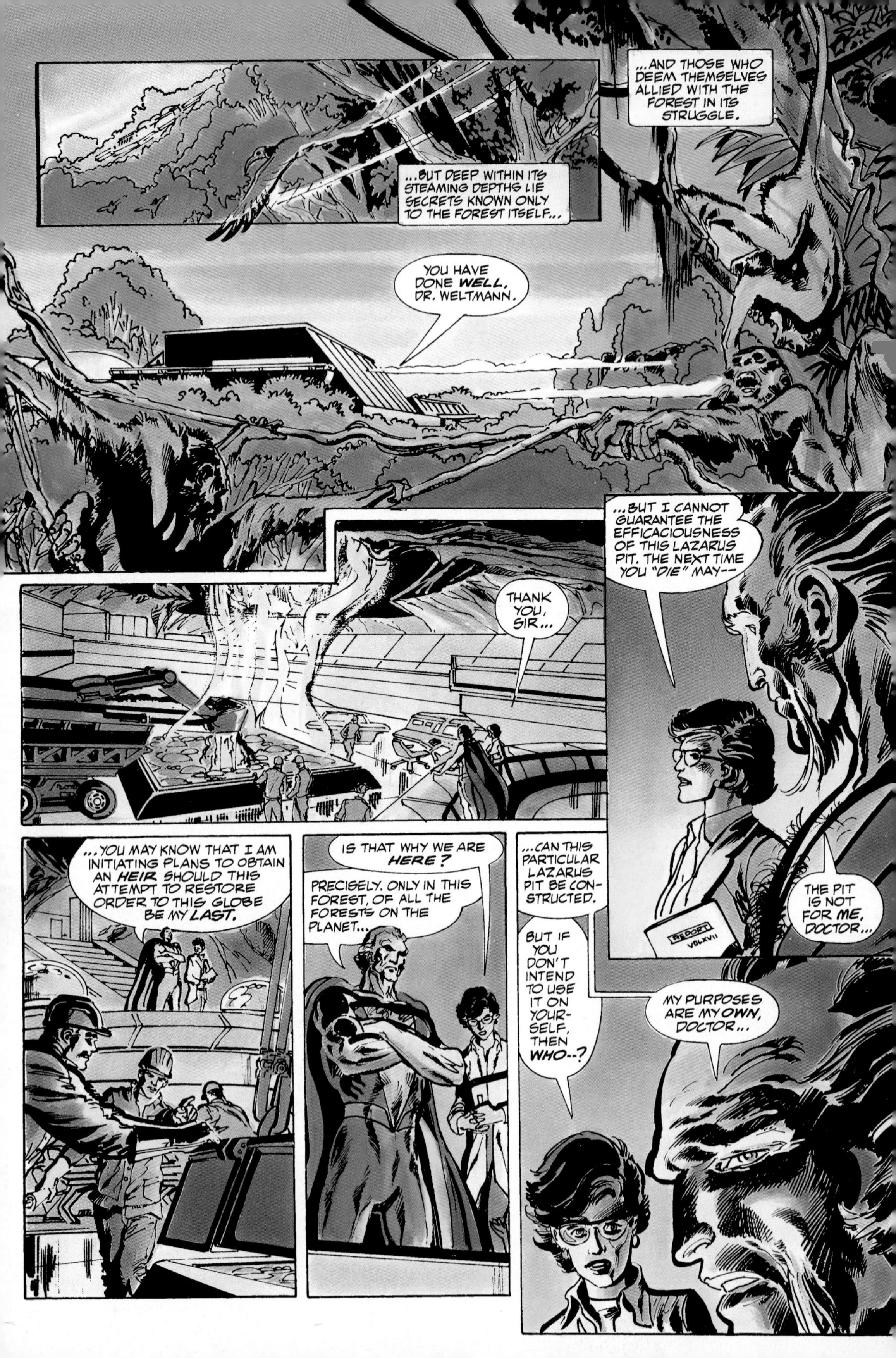
...AND THOSE WHO DEEM THEMSELVES ALLIED WITH THE FOREST IN ITS STRUGGLE.
...BUT DEEP WITHIN ITS STEAMING DEPTHS LIE SECRETS KNOWN ONLY TO THE FOREST ITSELF...
YOU HAVE DONE WELL, DR. WELTMANN.
THANK YOU, SIR...
...BUT I CANNOT GUARANTEE THE EFFICACIOUSNESS OF THIS LAZARUS PIT. THE NEXT TIME YOU "DIE" MAY--
THE PIT IS NOT FOR ME, DOCTOR...
...YOU MAY KNOW THAT I AM INITIATING PLANS TO OBTAIN AN HEIR SHOULD THIS ATTEMPT TO RESTORE ORDER TO THIS GLOBE BE MY LAST.
IS THAT WHY WE ARE HERE?
PRECISELY. ONLY IN THIS FOREST, OF ALL THE FORESTS ON THE PLANET...
...CAN THIS PARTICULAR LAZARUS PIT BE CONSTRUCTED.
BUT IF YOU DON'T INTEND TO USE IT ON YOURSELF, THEN WHO--?
MY PURPOSES ARE MY OWN, DOCTOR...
REPORT VOL XVII

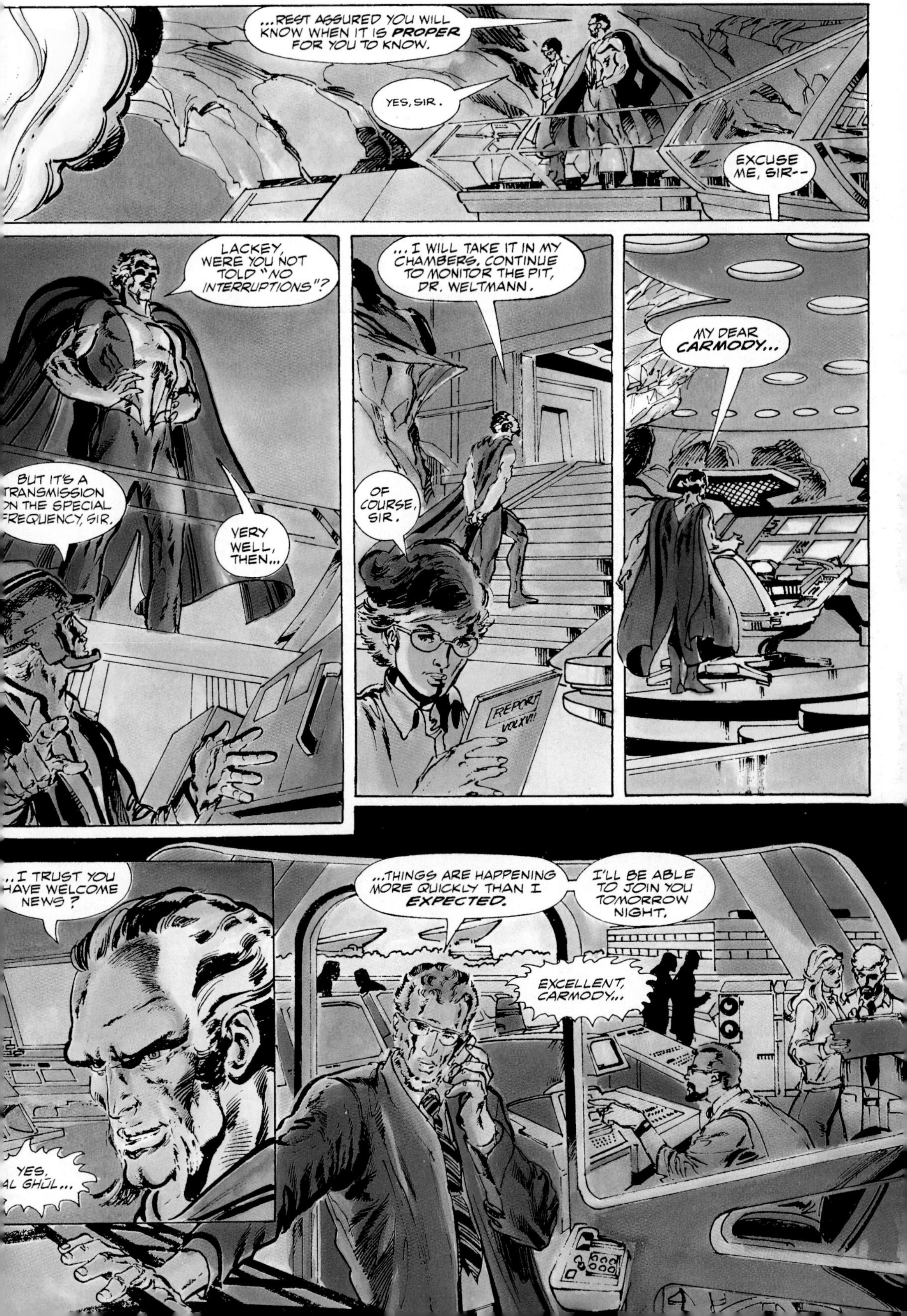
...REST ASSURED YOU WILL KNOW WHEN IT IS PROPER FOR YOU TO KNOW.
YES, SIR.
EXCUSE ME, SIR--
LACKEY, WERE YOU NOT TOLD "NO INTERRUPTIONS"?
BUT IT'S A TRANSMISSION ON THE SPECIAL FREQUENCY, SIR.
VERY WELL, THEN...
...I WILL TAKE IT IN MY CHAMBERS. CONTINUE TO MONITOR THE PIT, DR. WELTMANN.
OF COURSE, SIR.
REPORT
MY DEAR CARMODY...
...I TRUST YOU HAVE WELCOME NEWS?
YES, RA'S AL GHŪL...
...THINGS ARE HAPPENING MORE QUICKLY THAN I EXPECTED.
I'LL BE ABLE TO JOIN YOU TOMORROW NIGHT.
EXCELLENT, CARMODY...

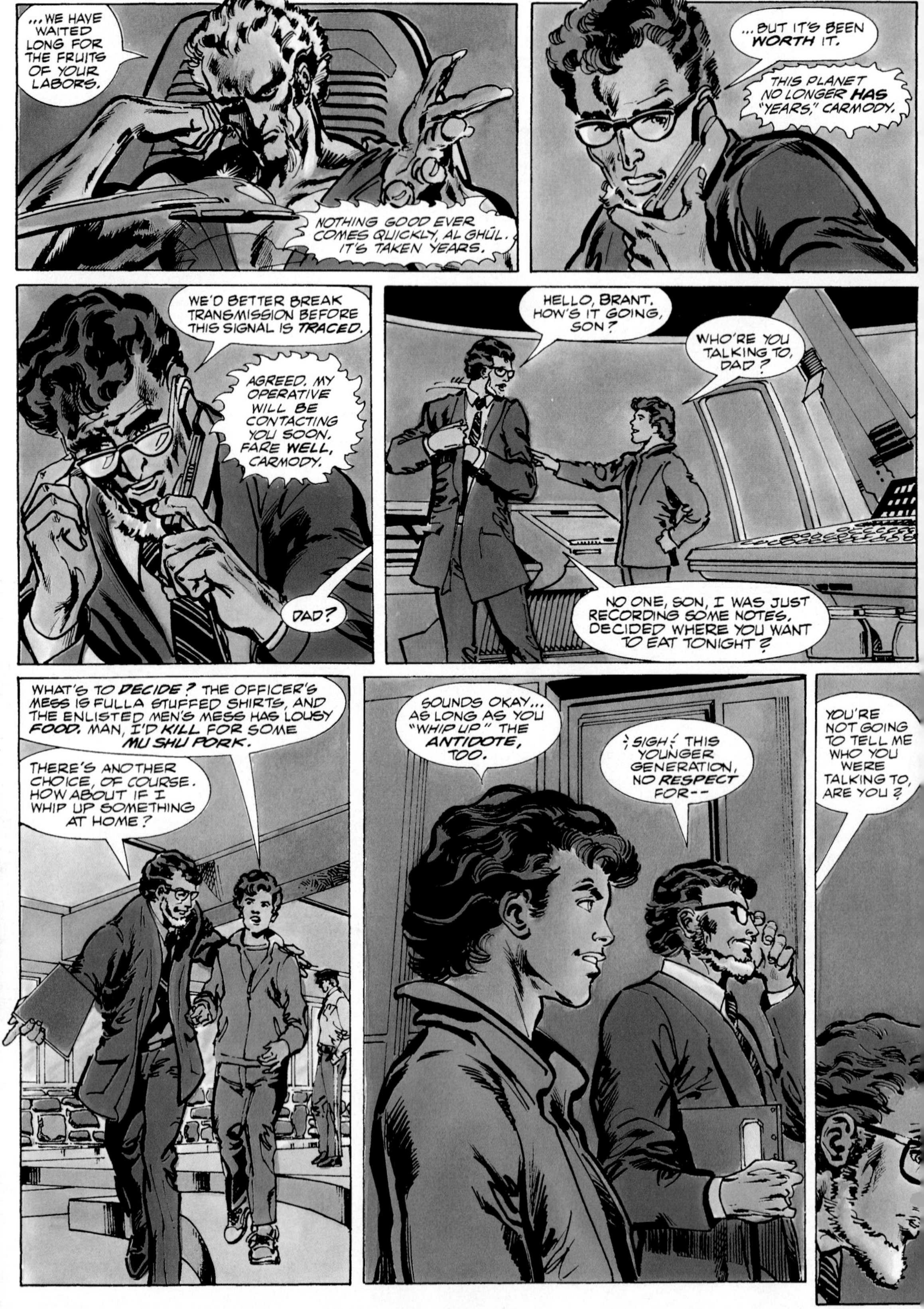

...WE HAVE WAITED LONG FOR THE FRUITS OF YOUR LABORS.
NOTHING GOOD EVER COMES QUICKLY, AL GHŪL. IT'S TAKEN YEARS.
...BUT IT'S BEEN WORTH IT.
THIS PLANET NO LONGER HAS "YEARS," CARMODY.
WE'D BETTER BREAK TRANSMISSION BEFORE THIS SIGNAL IS TRACED.
AGREED. MY OPERATIVE WILL BE CONTACTING YOU SOON. FARE WELL, CARMODY.
DAD?
HELLO, BRANT. HOW'S IT GOING, SON?
WHO'RE YOU TALKING TO, DAD?
NO ONE, SON, I WAS JUST RECORDING SOME NOTES. DECIDED WHERE YOU WANT TO EAT TONIGHT?
WHAT'S TO DECIDE? THE OFFICER'S MESS IS FULLA STUFFED SHIRTS, AND THE ENLISTED MEN'S MESS HAS LOUSY FOOD. MAN, I'D KILL FOR SOME MU SHU PORK.
THERE'S ANOTHER CHOICE, OF COURSE. HOW ABOUT IF I WHIP UP SOMETHING AT HOME?
SOUNDS OKAY... AS LONG AS YOU "WHIP UP" THE ANTIDOTE, TOO.
:SIGH: THIS YOUNGER GENERATION, NO RESPECT FOR--
YOU'RE NOT GOING TO TELL ME WHO YOU WERE TALKING TO, ARE YOU?

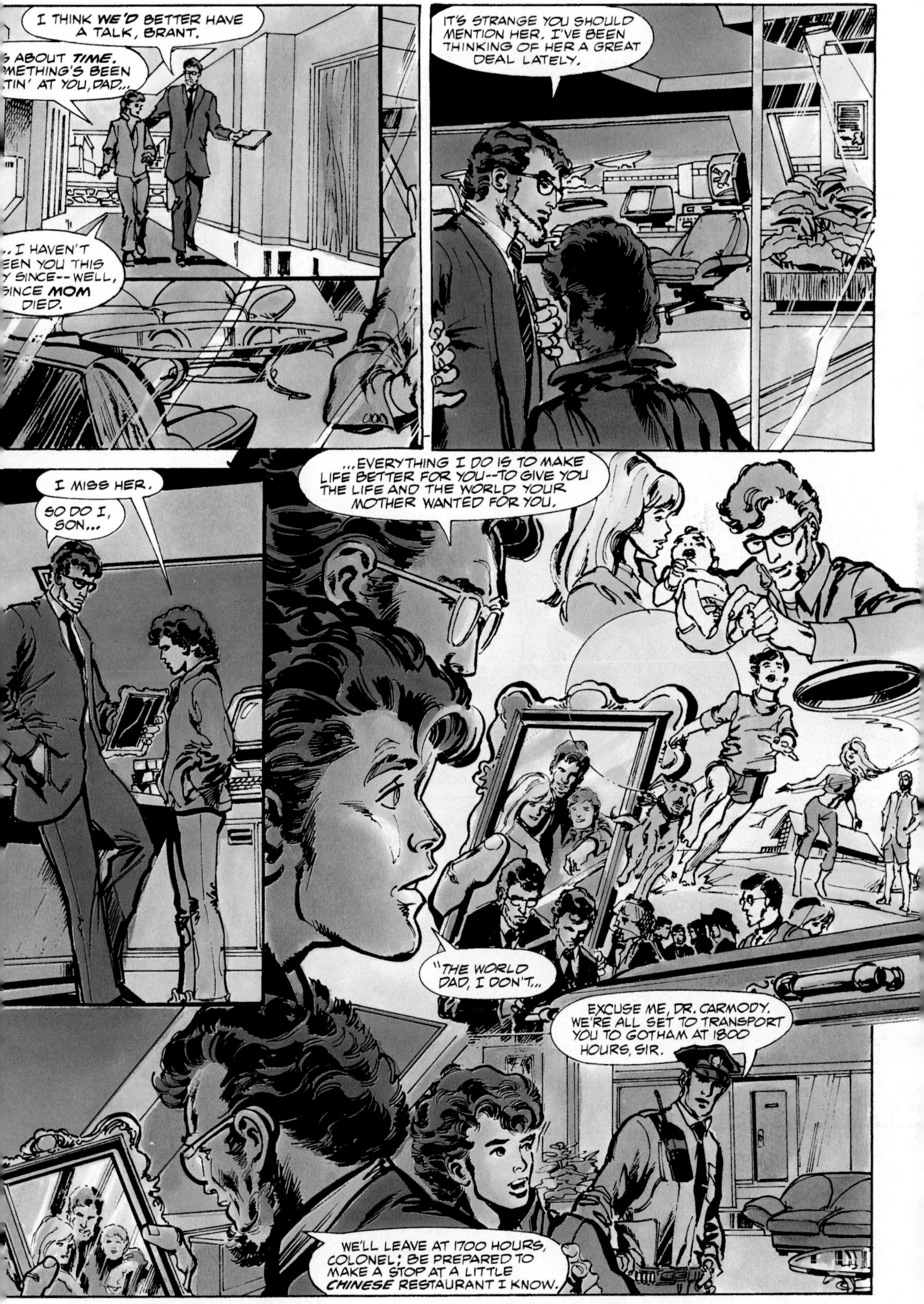
I THINK WE'D BETTER HAVE A TALK, BRANT.
...S ABOUT TIME. ...METHING'S BEEN ...TIN' AT YOU, DAD...
...I HAVEN'T ...EEN YOU THIS ...Y SINCE--WELL, ...SINCE MOM DIED.
IT'S STRANGE YOU SHOULD MENTION HER. I'VE BEEN THINKING OF HER A GREAT DEAL LATELY.
I MISS HER.
SO DO I, SON...
...EVERYTHING I DO IS TO MAKE LIFE BETTER FOR YOU--TO GIVE YOU THE LIFE AND THE WORLD YOUR MOTHER WANTED FOR YOU.
"THE WORLD" DAD, I DON'T...
EXCUSE ME, DR. CARMODY. WE'RE ALL SET TO TRANSPORT YOU TO GOTHAM AT 1800 HOURS, SIR.
WE'LL LEAVE AT 1700 HOURS, COLONEL; BE PREPARED TO MAKE A STOP AT A LITTLE CHINESE RESTAURANT I KNOW.

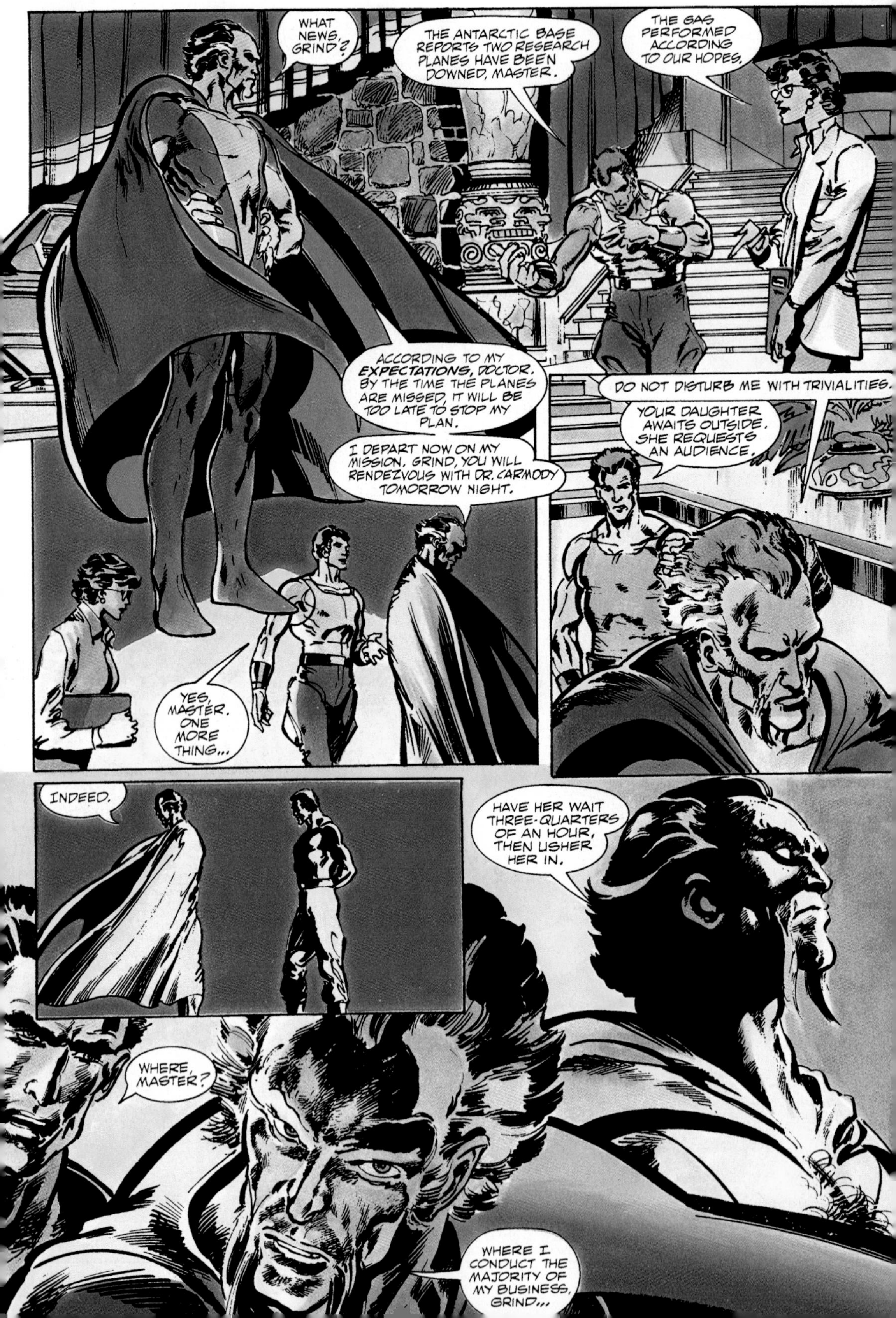
WHAT NEWS, GRIND?
THE ANTARCTIC BASE REPORTS TWO RESEARCH PLANES HAVE BEEN DOWNED, MASTER.
THE GAS PERFORMED ACCORDING TO OUR HOPES.
ACCORDING TO MY EXPECTATIONS, DOCTOR. BY THE TIME THE PLANES ARE MISSED, IT WILL BE TOO LATE TO STOP MY PLAN.
I DEPART NOW ON MY MISSION. GRIND, YOU WILL RENDEZVOUS WITH DR. CARMODY TOMORROW NIGHT.
YES, MASTER. ONE MORE THING...
YOUR DAUGHTER AWAITS OUTSIDE. SHE REQUESTS AN AUDIENCE.
DO NOT DISTURB ME WITH TRIVIALITIES.
INDEED.
HAVE HER WAIT THREE-QUARTERS OF AN HOUR, THEN USHER HER IN.
WHERE, MASTER?
WHERE I CONDUCT THE MAJORITY OF MY BUSINESS, GRIND...

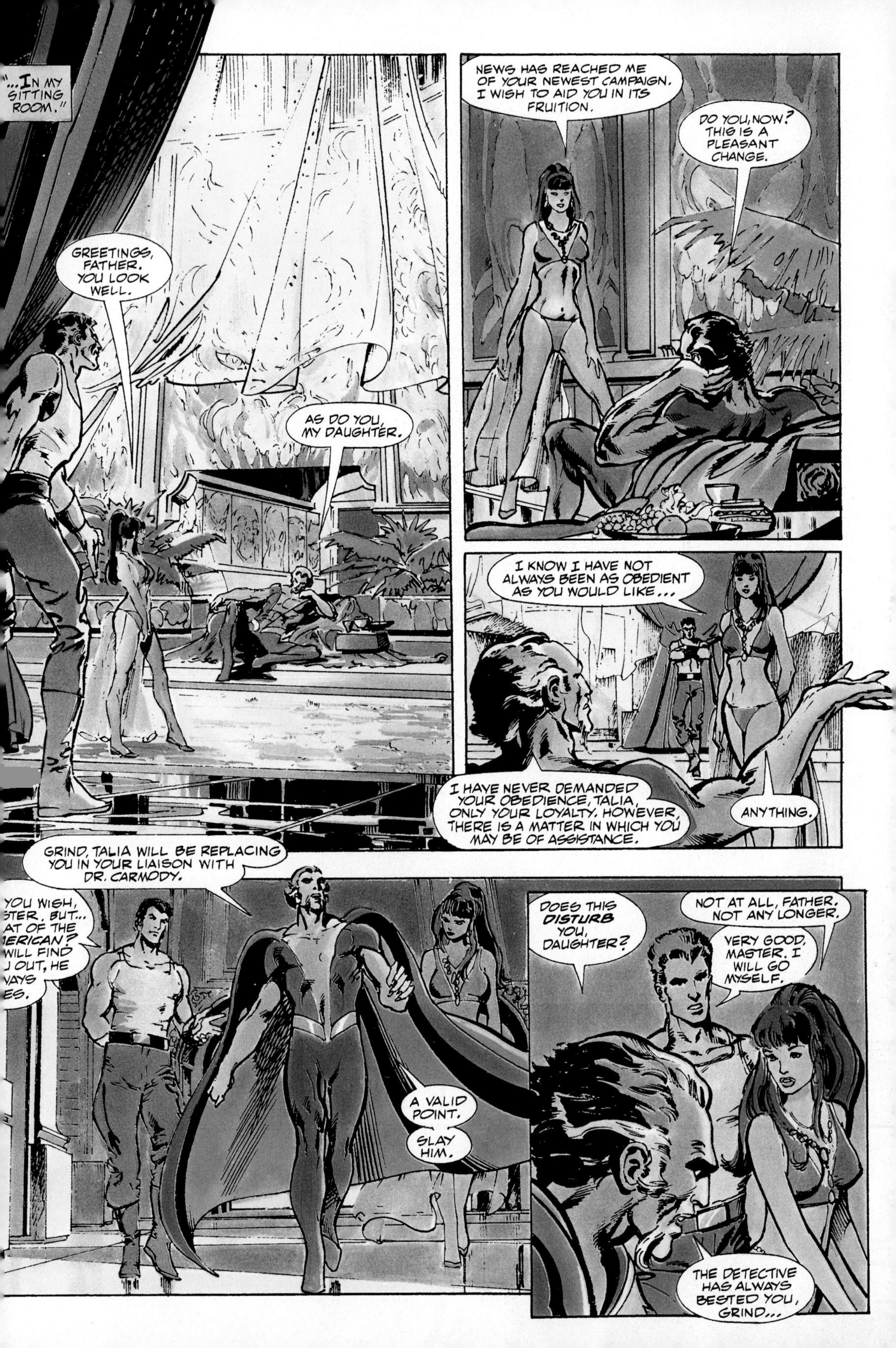
"...IN MY SITTING ROOM."
GREETINGS, FATHER. YOU LOOK WELL.
AS DO YOU, MY DAUGHTER.
NEWS HAS REACHED ME OF YOUR NEWEST CAMPAIGN. I WISH TO AID YOU IN ITS FRUITION.
DO YOU, NOW? THIS IS A PLEASANT CHANGE.
I KNOW I HAVE NOT ALWAYS BEEN AS OBEDIENT AS YOU WOULD LIKE...
I HAVE NEVER DEMANDED YOUR OBEDIENCE, TALIA, ONLY YOUR LOYALTY. HOWEVER, THERE IS A MATTER IN WHICH YOU MAY BE OF ASSISTANCE.
ANYTHING.
GRIND, TALIA WILL BE REPLACING YOU IN YOUR LIAISON WITH DR. CARMODY.
YOU WISH, STER, BUT... AT OF THE MERICAN? WILL FIND J OUT, HE WAYS ES.
A VALID POINT.
SLAY HIM.
DOES THIS DISTURB YOU, DAUGHTER?
NOT AT ALL, FATHER. NOT ANY LONGER.
VERY GOOD, MASTER. I WILL GO MYSELF.
THE DETECTIVE HAS ALWAYS BESTED YOU, GRIND...

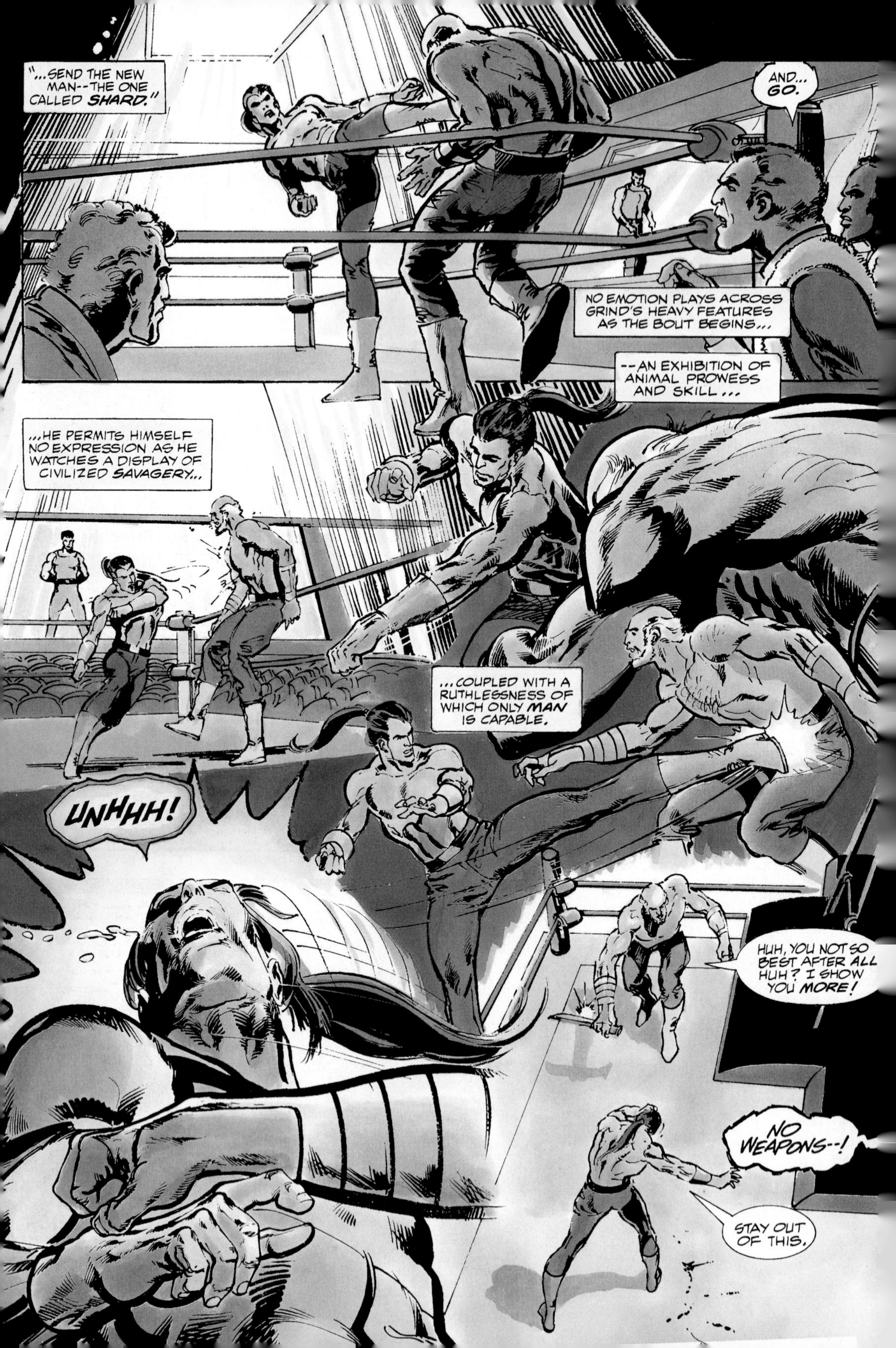
"...SEND THE NEW MAN--THE ONE CALLED SHARD."
AND... GO.
NO EMOTION PLAYS ACROSS GRIND'S HEAVY FEATURES AS THE BOUT BEGINS...
...HE PERMITS HIMSELF NO EXPRESSION AS HE WATCHES A DISPLAY OF CIVILIZED SAVAGERY...
--AN EXHIBITION OF ANIMAL PROWESS AND SKILL...
...COUPLED WITH A RUTHLESSNESS OF WHICH ONLY MAN IS CAPABLE.
UNHHH!
HUH, YOU NOT SO BEST AFTER ALL HUH? I SHOW YOU MORE!
NO WEAPONS--!
STAY OUT OF THIS.

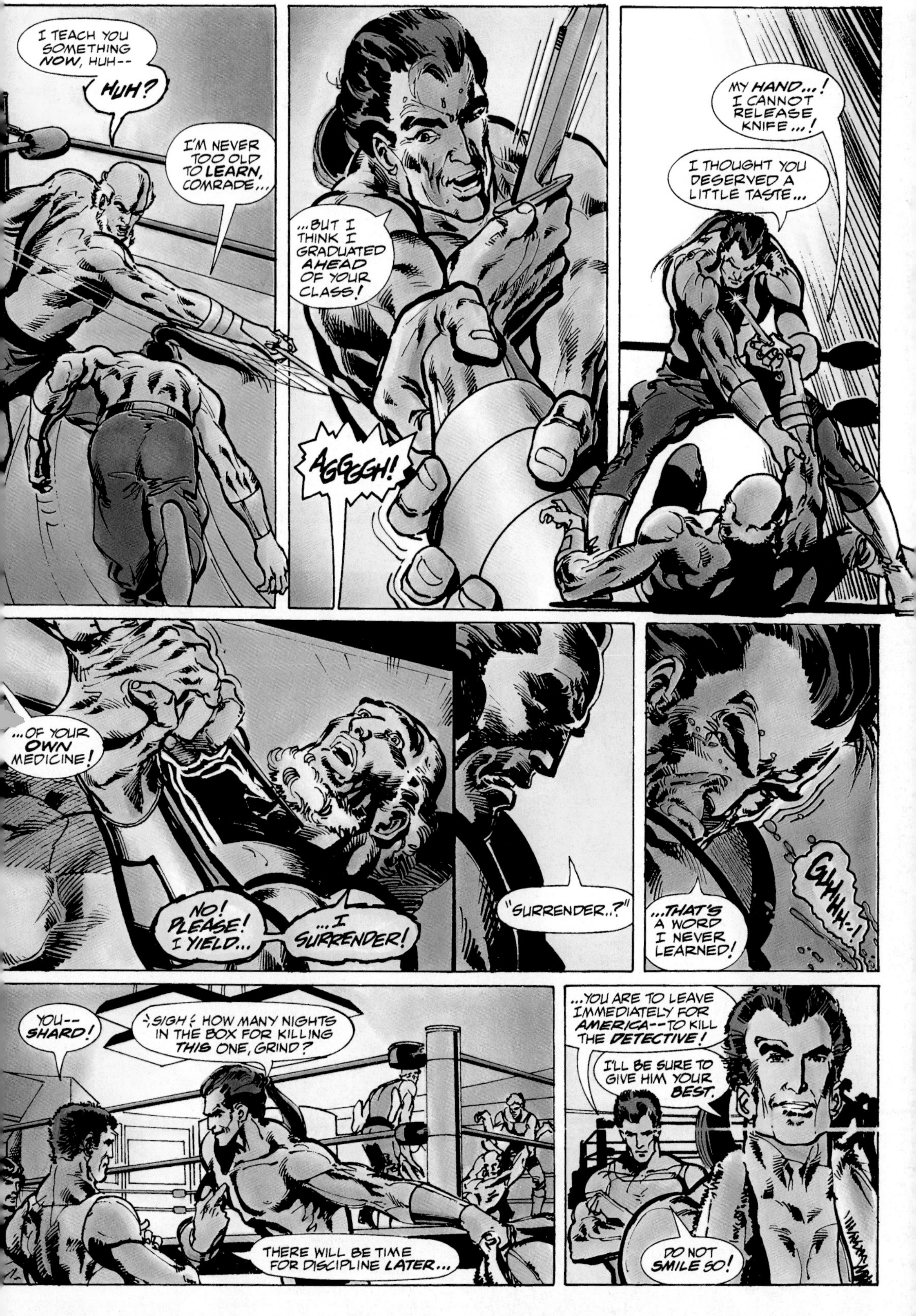
I TEACH YOU SOMETHING NOW, HUH--
HUH?
I'M NEVER TOO OLD TO LEARN, COMRADE...
...BUT I THINK I GRADUATED AHEAD OF YOUR CLASS!
AGGGGH!
MY HAND...! I CANNOT RELEASE KNIFE...!
I THOUGHT YOU DESERVED A LITTLE TASTE...
...OF YOUR OWN MEDICINE!
NO! PLEASE! I YIELD...
...I SURRENDER!
"SURRENDER..?"
...THAT'S A WORD I NEVER LEARNED!
GUHHH--!
YOU-- SHARD!
-SIGH- HOW MANY NIGHTS IN THE BOX FOR KILLING THIS ONE, GRIND?
THERE WILL BE TIME FOR DISCIPLINE LATER...
...YOU ARE TO LEAVE IMMEDIATELY FOR AMERICA--TO KILL THE DETECTIVE!
I'LL BE SURE TO GIVE HIM YOUR BEST.
DO NOT SMILE SO!

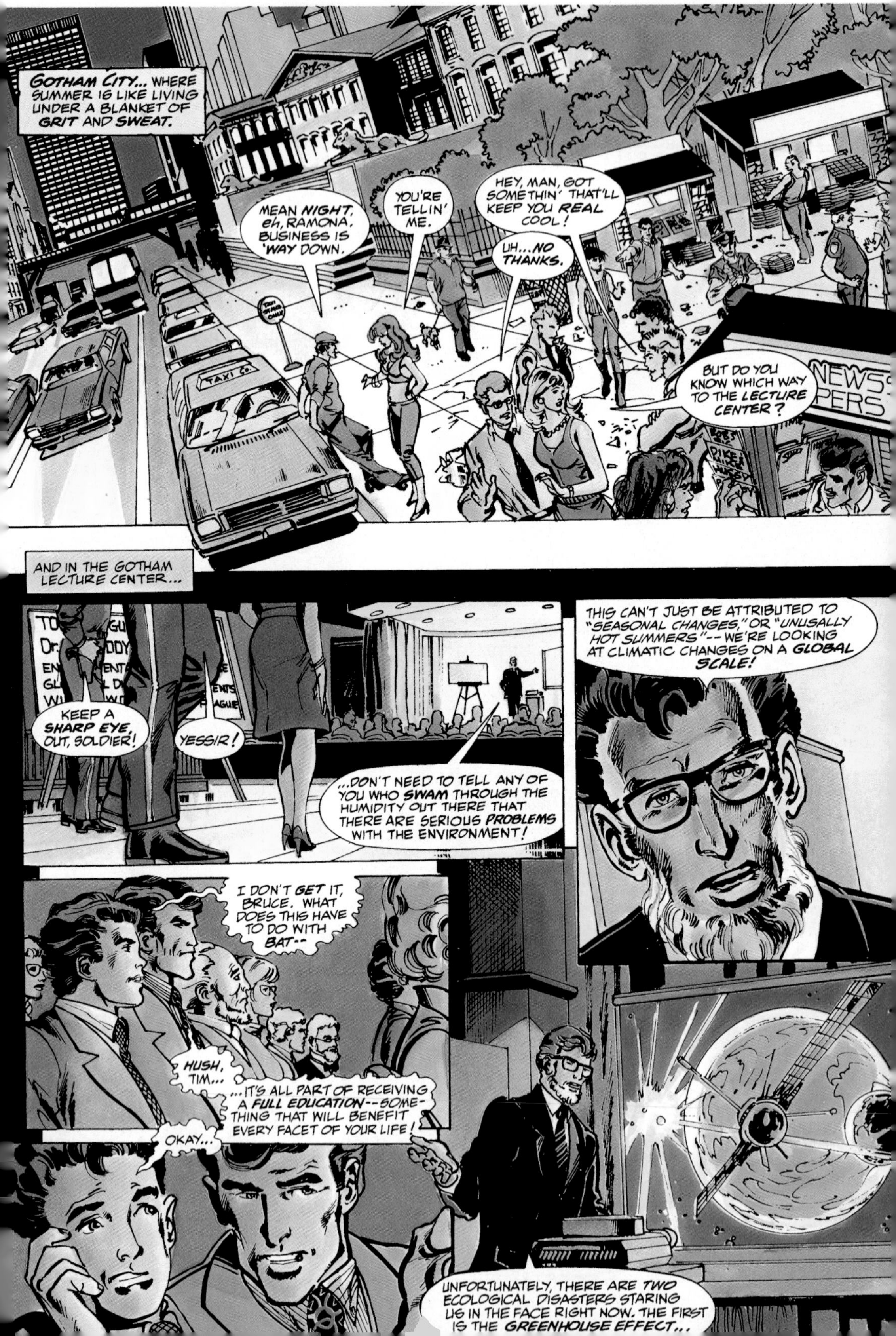
GOTHAM CITY... WHERE SUMMER IS LIKE LIVING UNDER A BLANKET OF GRIT AND SWEAT.
MEAN NIGHT, eh, RAMONA. BUSINESS IS 'WAY DOWN.
YOU'RE TELLIN' ME.
HEY, MAN, GOT SOMETHIN' THAT'LL KEEP YOU REAL COOL!
UH... NO THANKS.
BUT DO YOU KNOW WHICH WAY TO THE LECTURE CENTER?
TAXI CO.
NEWS
PERS
AND IN THE GOTHAM LECTURE CENTER...
KEEP A SHARP EYE OUT, SOLDIER!
YESSIR!
...DON'T NEED TO TELL ANY OF YOU WHO SWAM THROUGH THE HUMIDITY OUT THERE THAT THERE ARE SERIOUS PROBLEMS WITH THE ENVIRONMENT!
THIS CAN'T JUST BE ATTRIBUTED TO "SEASONAL CHANGES," OR "UNUSALLY HOT SUMMERS"-- WE'RE LOOKING AT CLIMATIC CHANGES ON A GLOBAL SCALE!
I DON'T GET IT, BRUCE. WHAT DOES THIS HAVE TO DO WITH BAT--
HUSH, TIM...
...IT'S ALL PART OF RECEIVING A FULL EDUCATION--SOMETHING THAT WILL BENEFIT EVERY FACET OF YOUR LIFE!
OKAY...
UNFORTUNATELY, THERE ARE TWO ECOLOGICAL DISASTERS STARING US IN THE FACE RIGHT NOW. THE FIRST IS THE GREENHOUSE EFFECT...

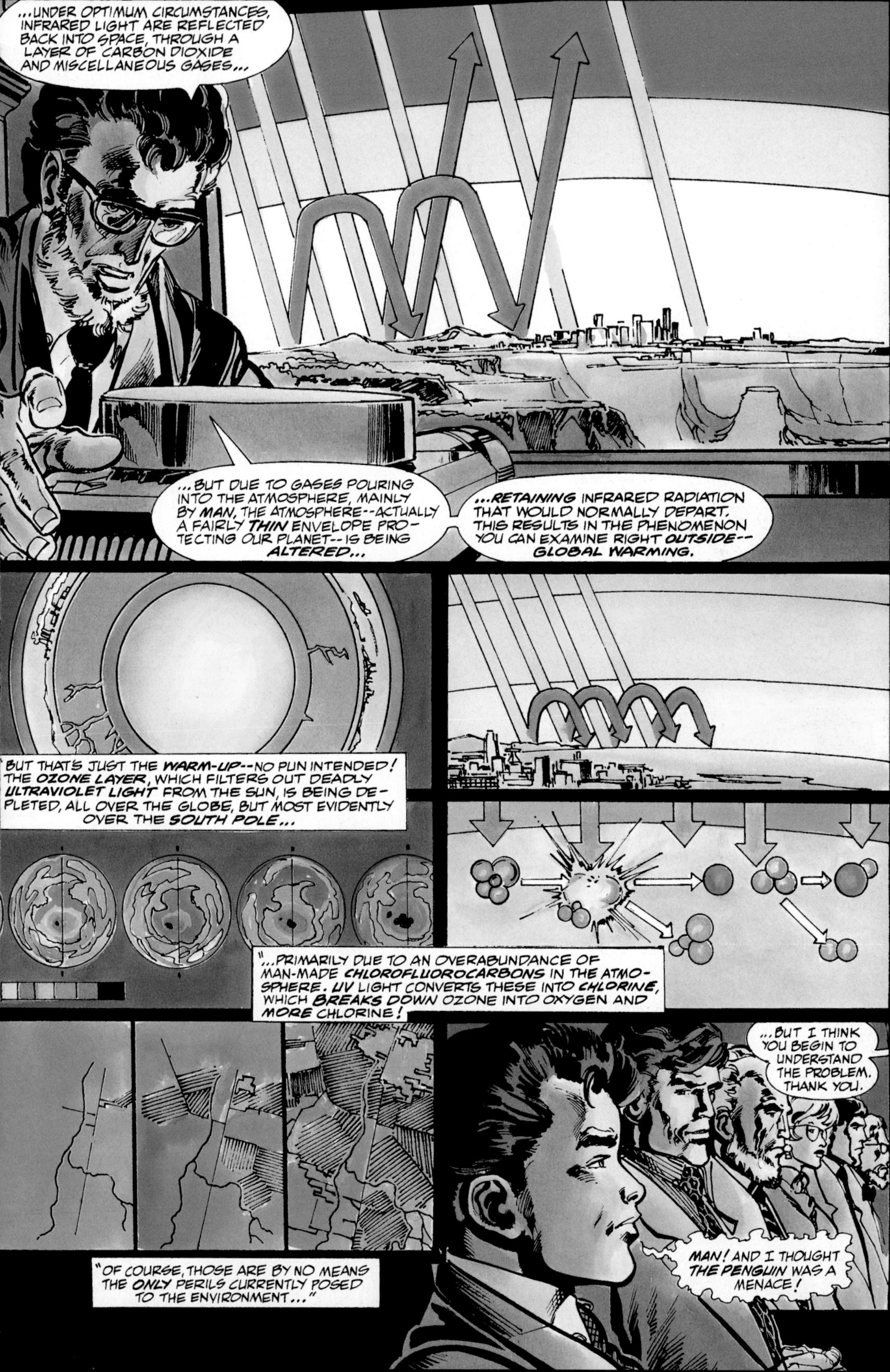
...UNDER OPTIMUM CIRCUMSTANCES, INFRARED LIGHT ARE REFLECTED BACK INTO SPACE, THROUGH A LAYER OF CARBON DIOXIDE AND MISCELLANEOUS GASES...
...BUT DUE TO GASES POURING INTO THE ATMOSPHERE, MAINLY BY MAN, THE ATMOSPHERE--ACTUALLY A FAIRLY THIN ENVELOPE PROTECTING OUR PLANET--IS BEING ALTERED...
...RETAINING INFRARED RADIATION THAT WOULD NORMALLY DEPART. THIS RESULTS IN THE PHENOMENON YOU CAN EXAMINE RIGHT OUTSIDE--GLOBAL WARMING.
BUT THAT'S JUST THE WARM-UP--NO PUN INTENDED! THE OZONE LAYER, WHICH FILTERS OUT DEADLY ULTRAVIOLET LIGHT FROM THE SUN, IS BEING DEPLETED, ALL OVER THE GLOBE, BUT MOST EVIDENTLY OVER THE SOUTH POLE...
"...PRIMARILY DUE TO AN OVERABUNDANCE OF MAN-MADE CHLOROFLUOROCARBONS IN THE ATMOSPHERE. UV LIGHT CONVERTS THESE INTO CHLORINE, WHICH BREAKS DOWN OZONE INTO OXYGEN AND MORE CHLORINE!
...BUT I THINK YOU BEGIN TO UNDERSTAND THE PROBLEM. THANK YOU.
"OF COURSE, THOSE ARE BY NO MEANS THE ONLY PERILS CURRENTLY POSED TO THE ENVIRONMENT..."
MAN! AND I THOUGHT THE PENGUIN WAS A MENACE!

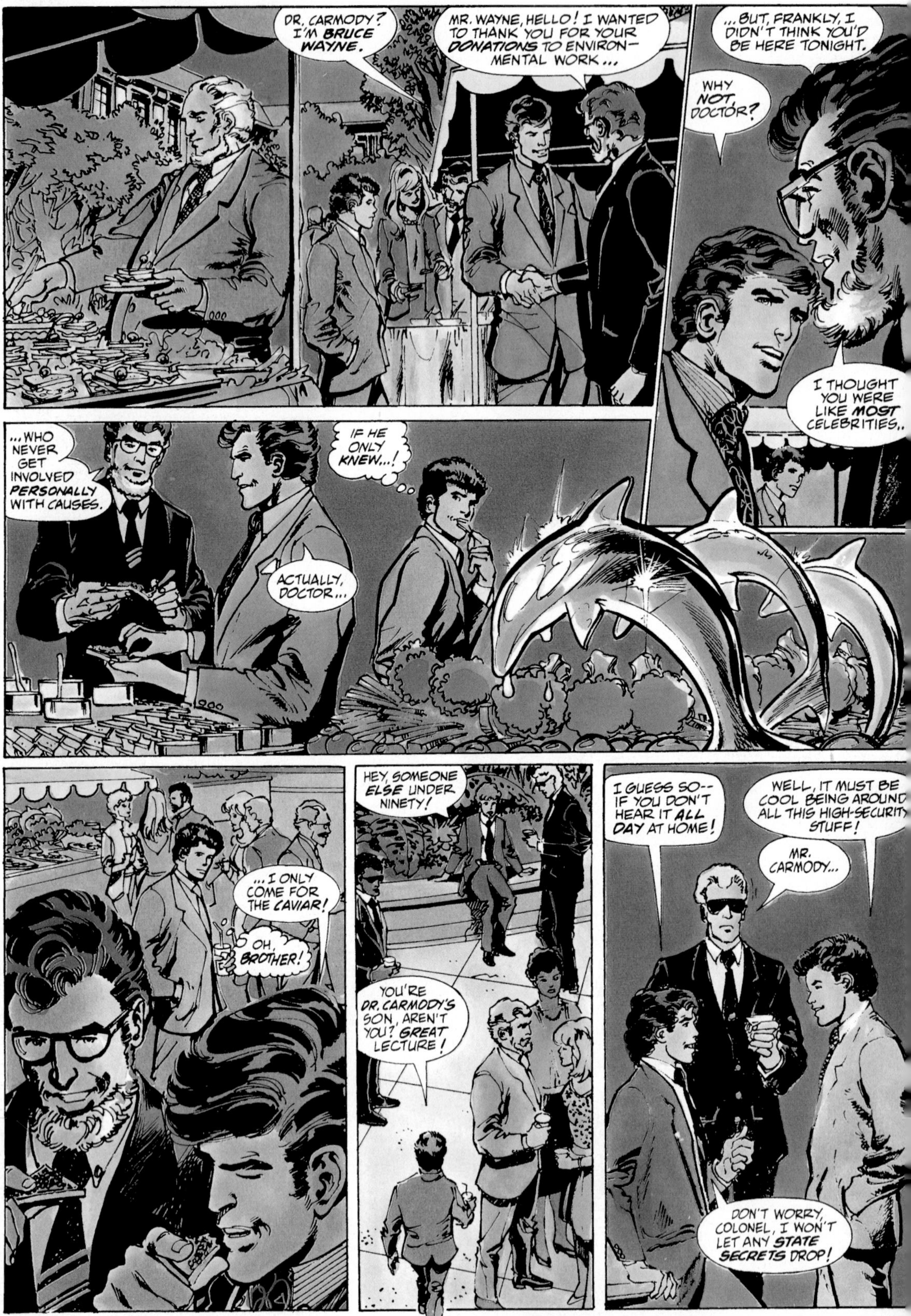

DR. CARMODY? I'M **BRUCE WAYNE.**
MR. WAYNE, HELLO! I WANTED TO THANK YOU FOR YOUR **DONATIONS** TO ENVIRON-MENTAL WORK...
...BUT, FRANKLY, I DIDN'T THINK YOU'D BE HERE TONIGHT.
WHY **NOT,** DOCTOR?
I THOUGHT YOU WERE LIKE **MOST** CELEBRITIES...
...WHO NEVER GET INVOLVED **PERSONALLY** WITH CAUSES.
IF HE ONLY **KNEW...!**
ACTUALLY, DOCTOR...
...I ONLY COME FOR THE **CAVIAR!**
OH, **BROTHER!**
HEY, SOMEONE **ELSE** UNDER NINETY!
YOU'RE **DR. CARMODY'S** SON, AREN'T YOU? **GREAT** LECTURE!
WELL, IT MUST BE COOL BEING AROUND ALL THIS HIGH-SECURITY STUFF!
I GUESS SO-- IF YOU DON'T HEAR IT **ALL DAY** AT HOME!
MR. CARMODY...
DON'T WORRY, COLONEL, I WON'T LET ANY **STATE SECRETS** DROP!

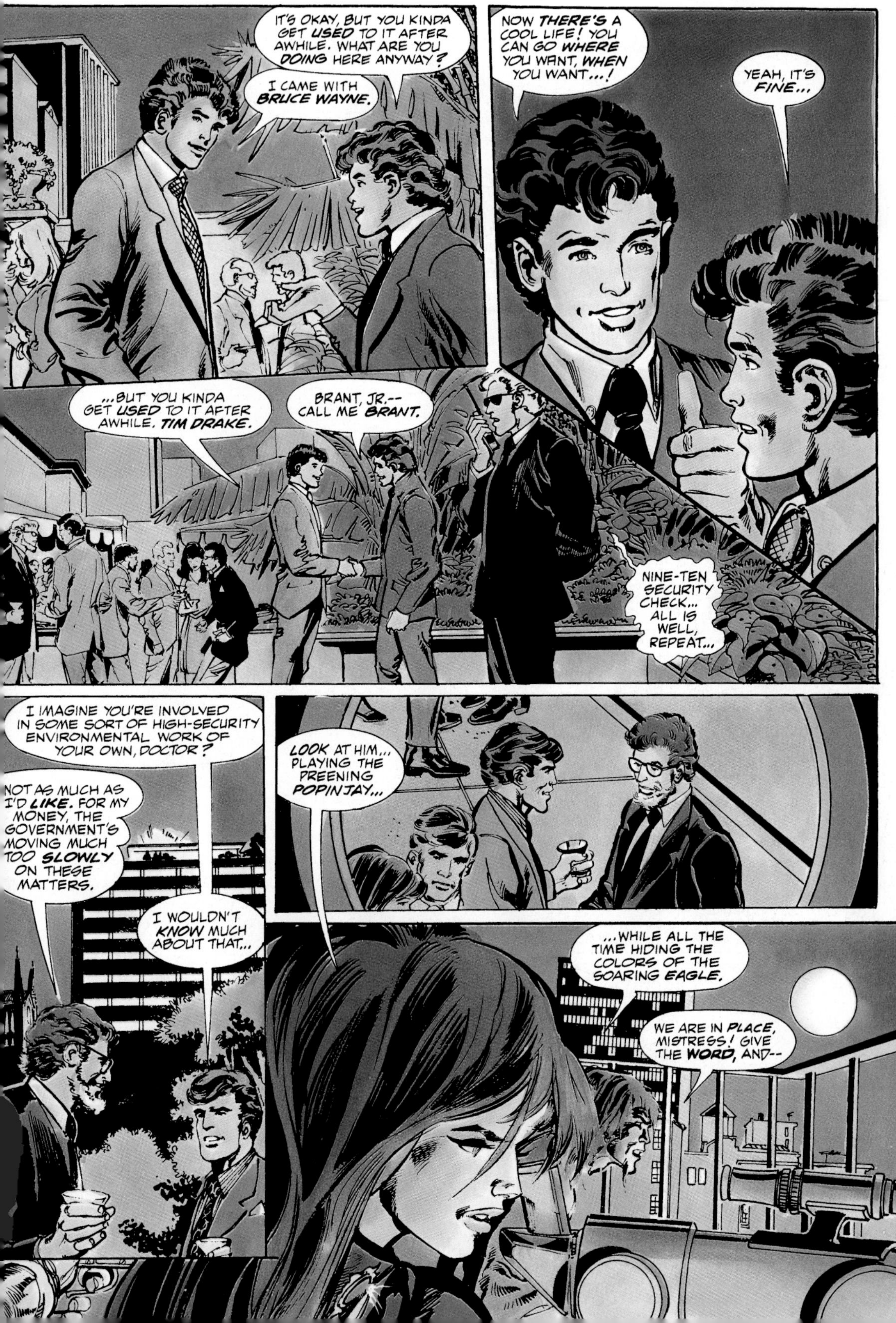
IT'S OKAY, BUT YOU KINDA GET USED TO IT AFTER AWHILE. WHAT ARE YOU DOING HERE ANYWAY?
I CAME WITH BRUCE WAYNE.
NOW THERE'S A COOL LIFE! YOU CAN GO WHERE YOU WANT, WHEN YOU WANT...!
YEAH, IT'S FINE...
...BUT YOU KINDA GET USED TO IT AFTER AWHILE. TIM DRAKE.
BRANT, JR.-- CALL ME BRANT.
NINE-TEN SECURITY CHECK... ALL IS WELL, REPEAT...
I IMAGINE YOU'RE INVOLVED IN SOME SORT OF HIGH-SECURITY ENVIRONMENTAL WORK OF YOUR OWN, DOCTOR?
NOT AS MUCH AS I'D LIKE. FOR MY MONEY, THE GOVERNMENT'S MOVING MUCH TOO SLOWLY ON THESE MATTERS.
I WOULDN'T KNOW MUCH ABOUT THAT...
LOOK AT HIM... PLAYING THE PREENING POPINJAY...
...WHILE ALL THE TIME HIDING THE COLORS OF THE SOARING EAGLE.
WE ARE IN PLACE, MISTRESS! GIVE THE WORD, AND--

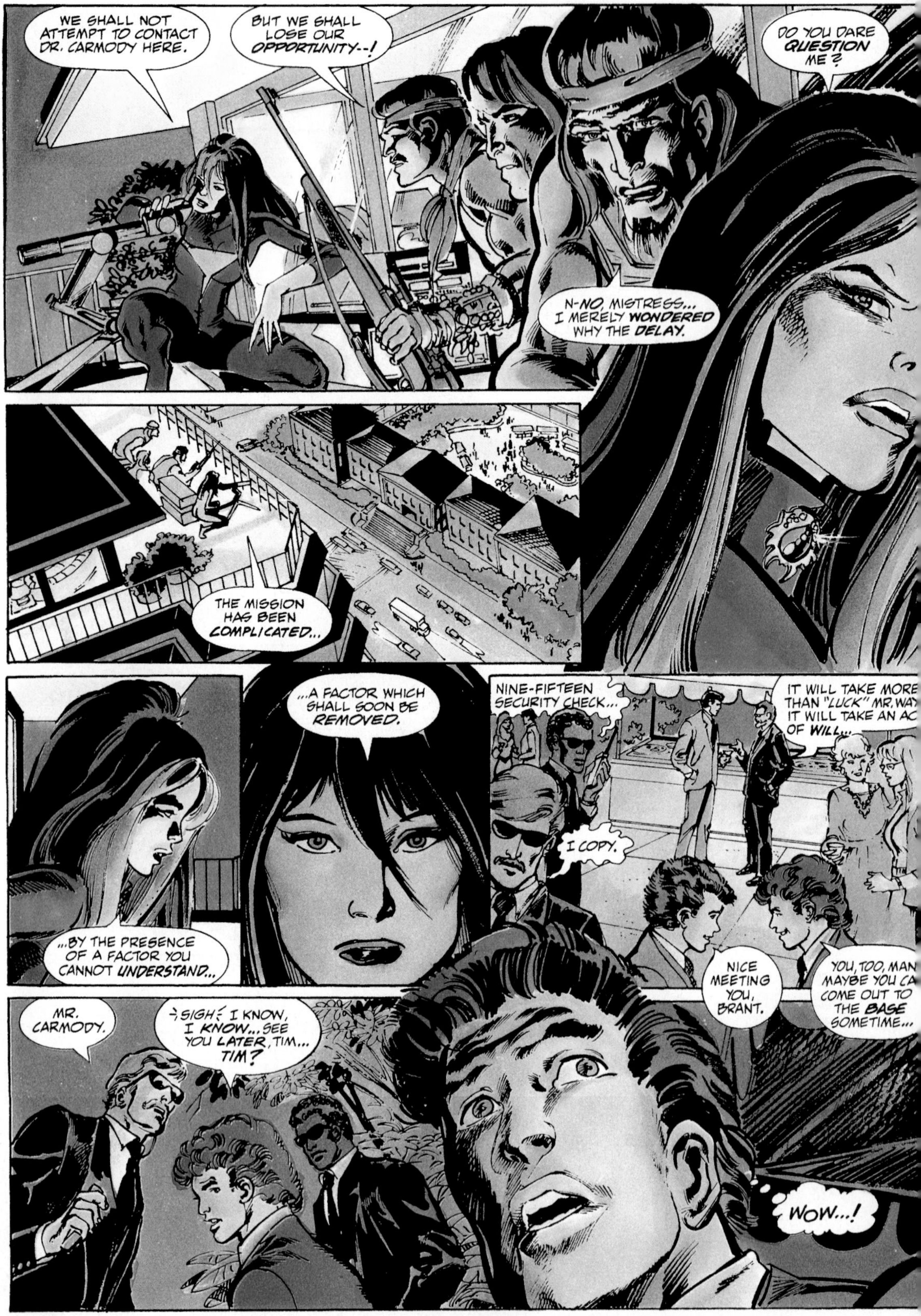
WE SHALL NOT ATTEMPT TO CONTACT DR. CARMODY HERE.
BUT WE SHALL LOSE OUR OPPORTUNITY--!
DO YOU DARE QUESTION ME?
N-NO, MISTRESS... I MERELY WONDERED WHY THE DELAY.
THE MISSION HAS BEEN COMPLICATED...
...BY THE PRESENCE OF A FACTOR YOU CANNOT UNDERSTAND...
...A FACTOR WHICH SHALL SOON BE REMOVED.
NINE-FIFTEEN SECURITY CHECK...
I COPY.
NICE MEETING YOU, BRANT.
MR. CARMODY.
-SIGH- I KNOW, I KNOW... SEE YOU LATER, TIM... TIM?
WOW...!

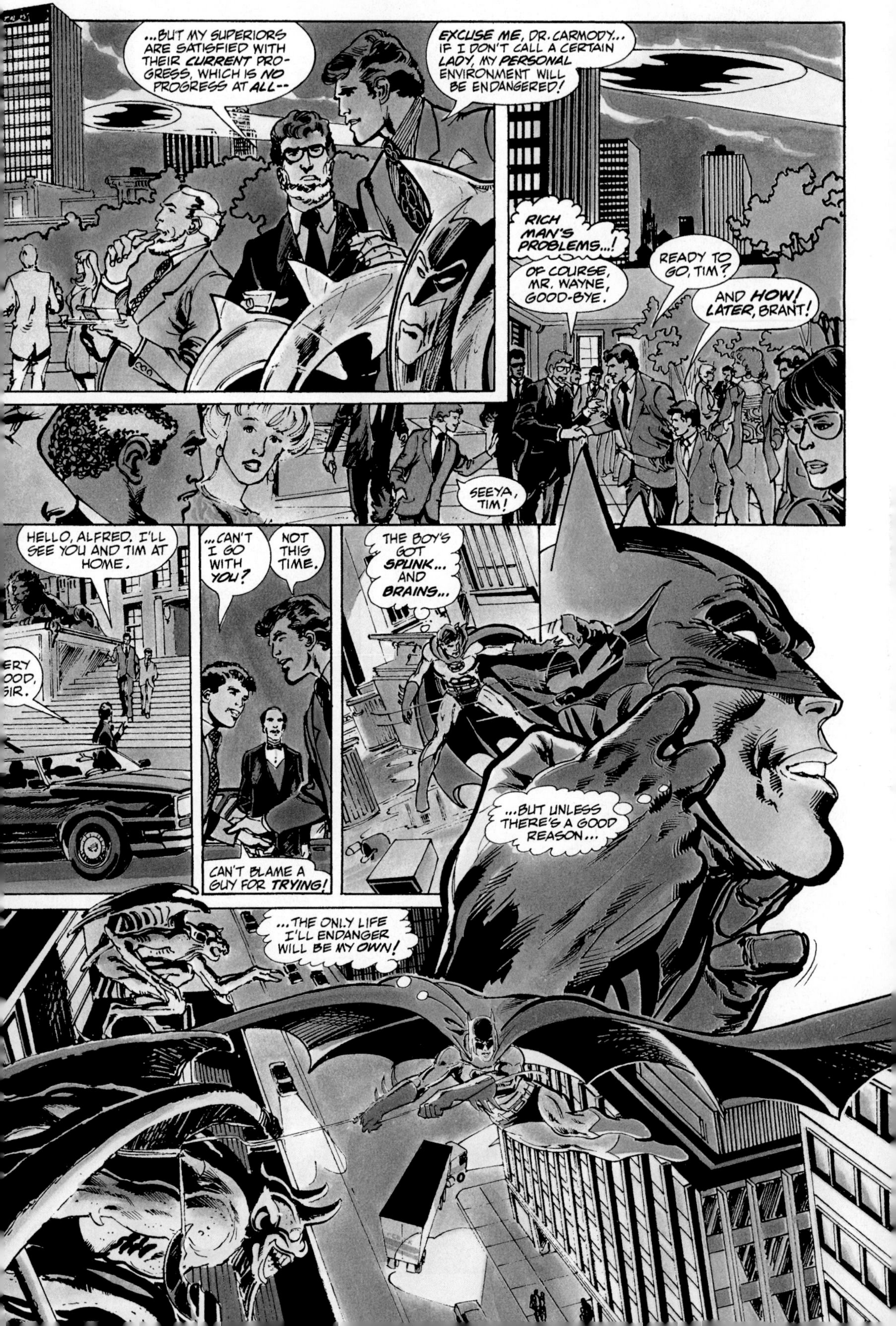
...BUT MY SUPERIORS ARE SATISFIED WITH THEIR CURRENT PROGRESS, WHICH IS NO PROGRESS AT ALL--
EXCUSE ME, DR. CARMODY... IF I DON'T CALL A CERTAIN LADY, MY PERSONAL ENVIRONMENT WILL BE ENDANGERED!
RICH MAN'S PROBLEMS...!
OF COURSE, MR. WAYNE, GOOD-BYE.
READY TO GO, TIM?
AND HOW! LATER, BRANT!
SEEYA, TIM!
HELLO, ALFRED. I'LL SEE YOU AND TIM AT HOME.
ERY OOD, SIR.
...CAN'T I GO WITH YOU?
NOT THIS TIME.
CAN'T BLAME A GUY FOR TRYING!
THE BOY'S GOT SPUNK... AND BRAINS...
...BUT UNLESS THERE'S A GOOD REASON...
...THE ONLY LIFE I'LL ENDANGER WILL BE MY OWN!

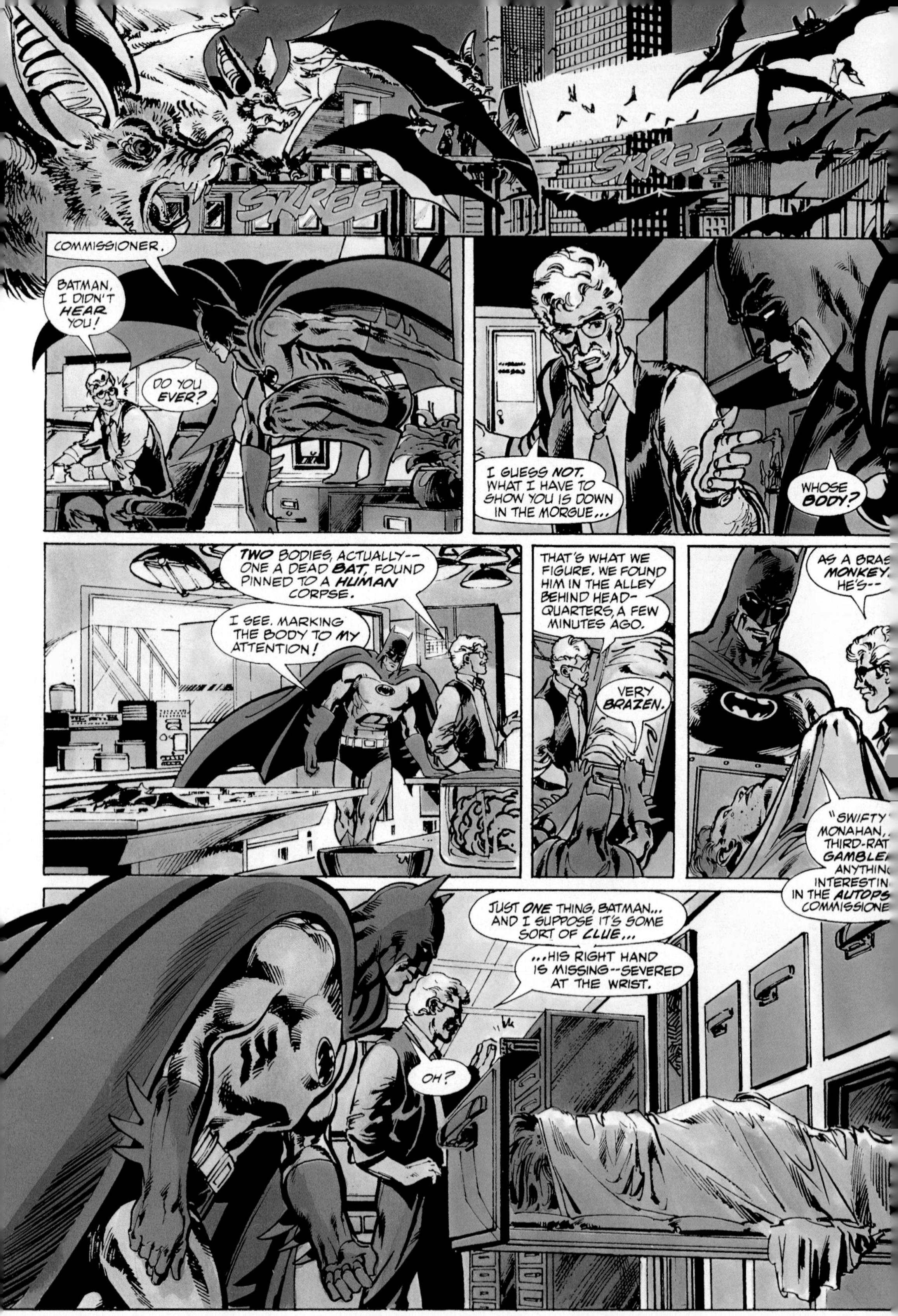

SKREE
SKREE
COMMISSIONER.
BATMAN, I DIDN'T HEAR YOU!
DO YOU EVER?
I GUESS NOT. WHAT I HAVE TO SHOW YOU IS DOWN IN THE MORGUE...
WHOSE BODY?
TWO BODIES, ACTUALLY-- ONE A DEAD BAT, FOUND PINNED TO A HUMAN CORPSE.
I SEE. MARKING THE BODY TO MY ATTENTION!
THAT'S WHAT WE FIGURE. WE FOUND HIM IN THE ALLEY BEHIND HEAD-QUARTERS, A FEW MINUTES AGO.
VERY BRAZEN.
AS A BRAS MONKEY. HE'S--
"SWIFTY" MONAHAN,.. THIRD-RAT GAMBLE ANYTHIN INTERESTIN IN THE AUTOPS COMMISSIONE
JUST ONE THING, BATMAN... AND I SUPPOSE IT'S SOME SORT OF CLUE...
...HIS RIGHT HAND IS MISSING--SEVERED AT THE WRIST.
OH?

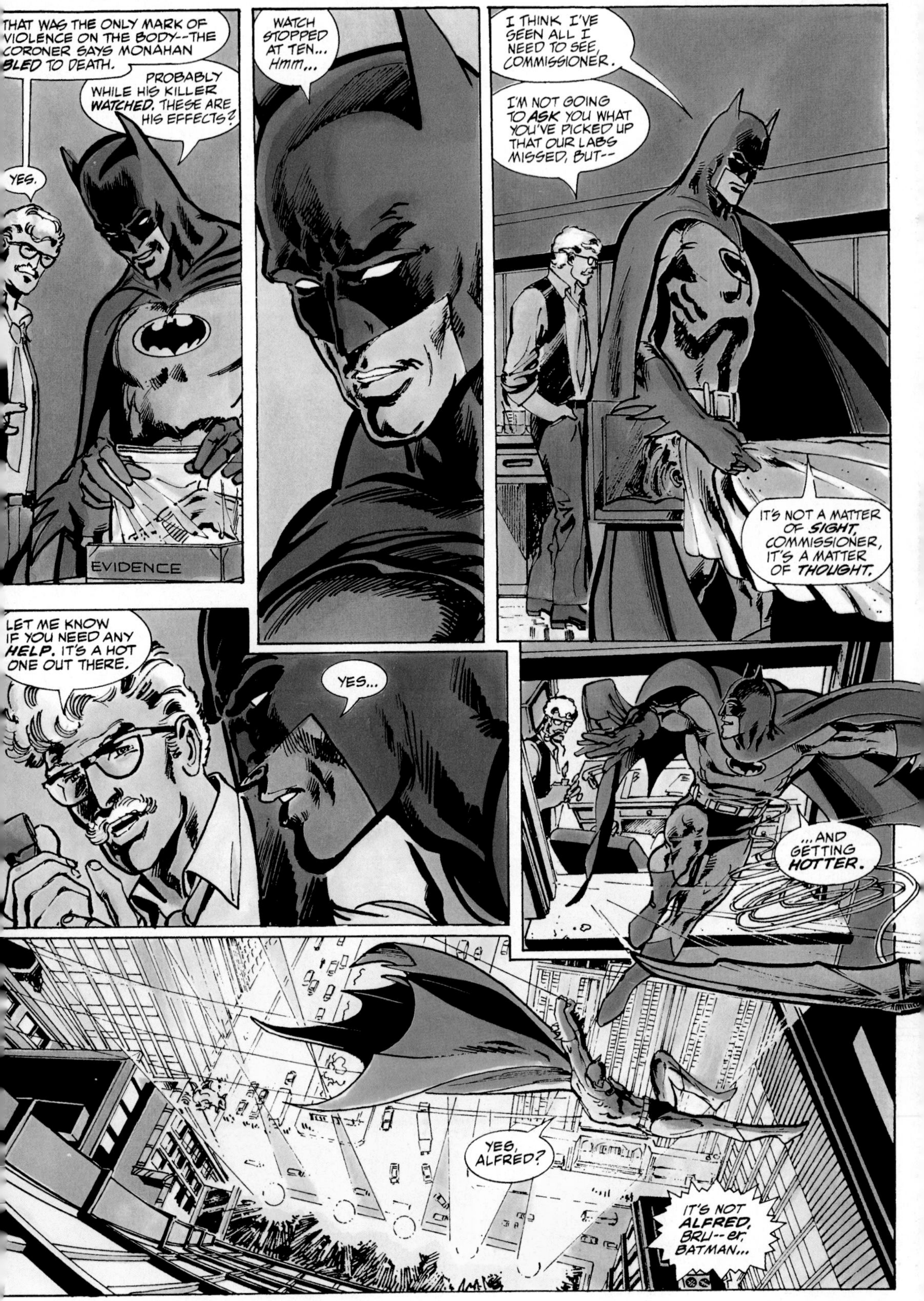
THAT WAS THE ONLY MARK OF VIOLENCE ON THE BODY--THE CORONER SAYS MONAHAN BLED TO DEATH.
PROBABLY WHILE HIS KILLER WATCHED. THESE ARE HIS EFFECTS?
YES.
EVIDENCE
WATCH STOPPED AT TEN... Hmm...
I THINK I'VE SEEN ALL I NEED TO SEE, COMMISSIONER.
I'M NOT GOING TO ASK YOU WHAT YOU'VE PICKED UP THAT OUR LABS MISSED, BUT--
IT'S NOT A MATTER OF SIGHT, COMMISSIONER, IT'S A MATTER OF THOUGHT.
LET ME KNOW IF YOU NEED ANY HELP. IT'S A HOT ONE OUT THERE.
YES...
...AND GETTING HOTTER.
YES, ALFRED?
IT'S NOT ALFRED, BRU--er, BATMAN...

IT'S *ME*. YOU *KNOW*, TIM?

WHAT DO YOU WANT?

I WAS JUST, YOU KNOW, WONDERING IF YOU NEEDED ANY *HELP!*

MASTER *TIM...!*

IT'S ALL RIGHT, *ALFRED*. TRY YOUR WITS ON *THIS* ONE:

A *GAMBLER* IS FOUND, MURDERED, ONE HAND SEVERED, HIS WATCH STOPPED AT *TEN O'CLOCK*. WHERE DOES THE KILLER WANT ME TO GO?

USE A LITTLE *THOUGHT*, AND YOU'LL *REALIZE...*

ER... I DON'T KNOW... SOME KIND OF ORGAN BANK, OR--

GOOD *GUESS* BUT THAT'S ALL IT IS.

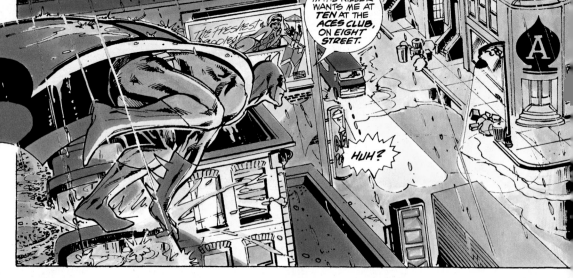

...THE KILLER WANTS ME AT *TEN* AT THE *ACES CLUB*, ON *EIGHT* STREET.

HUH?

THE *FRESHEST*

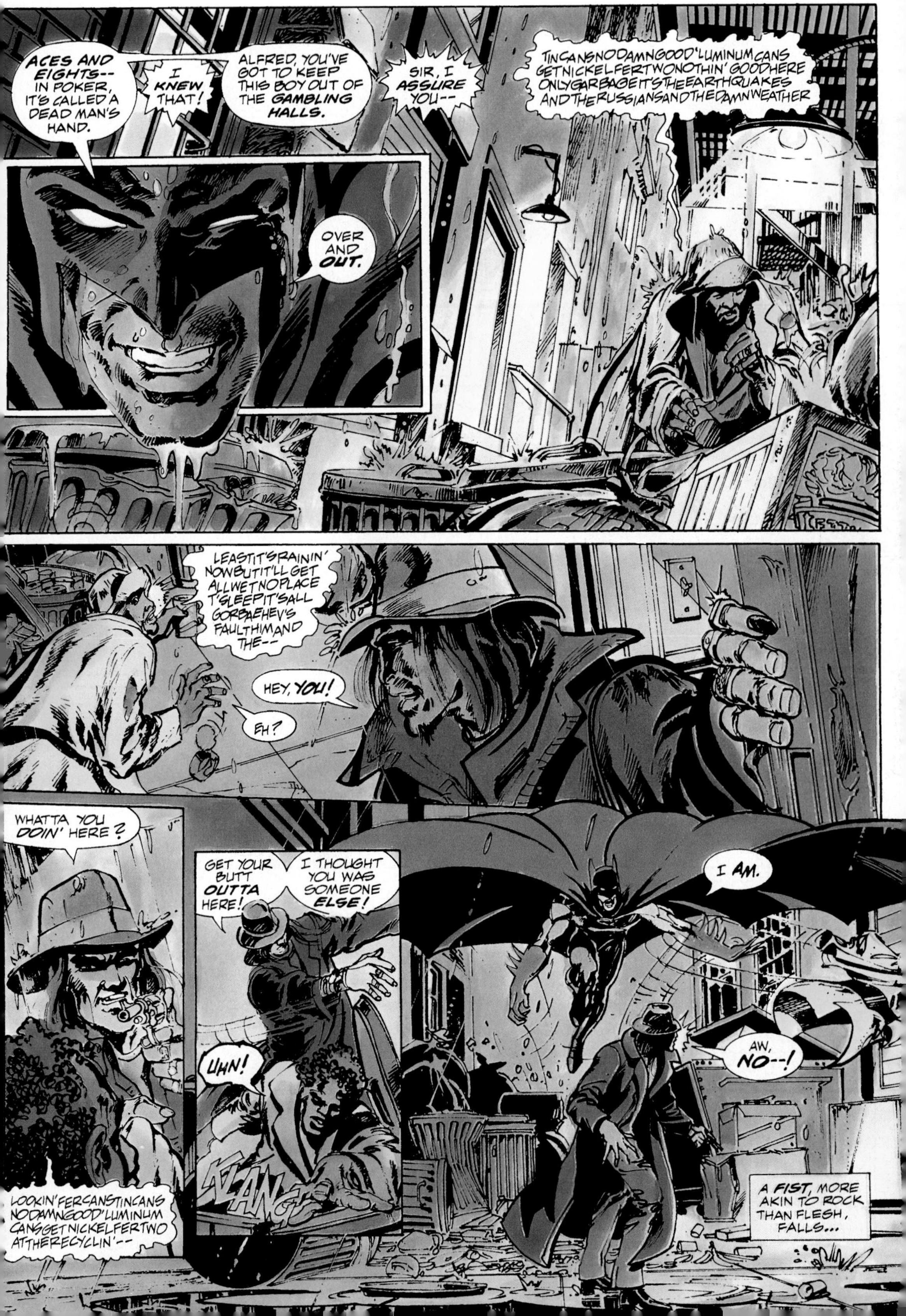

ACES AND EIGHTS-- IN POKER, IT'S CALLED A DEAD MAN'S HAND.
I KNEW THAT!
ALFRED, YOU'VE GOT TO KEEP THIS BOY OUT OF THE GAMBLING HALLS.
SIR, I ASSURE YOU--
OVER AND OUT.
TINCANSNODAMNGOOD'LUMINUMCANS GETNICKELFERTWONOTHIN'GOODHERE ONLYGARBAGEIT'STHEEARTHQUAKES ANDTHERUSSIANSANDTHEDAMNWEATHER
LEASTIT'SRAININ' NOWBUTIT'LLGET ALLWETNOPLACE T'SLEEPIT'SALL GORBAEHEV'S FAULTHIMAND THE--
HEY, YOU!
EH?
WHATTA YOU DOIN' HERE?
LOOKIN'FERCANSTINCANS NODAMNGOOD'LUMINUM CANSGETNICKELFERTWO ATTHERECYCLIN'--
GET YOUR BUTT OUTTA HERE!
I THOUGHT YOU WAS SOMEONE ELSE!
UHN!
KLANG
I AM.
AW, NO--!
A FIST, MORE AKIN TO ROCK THAN FLESH, FALLS...

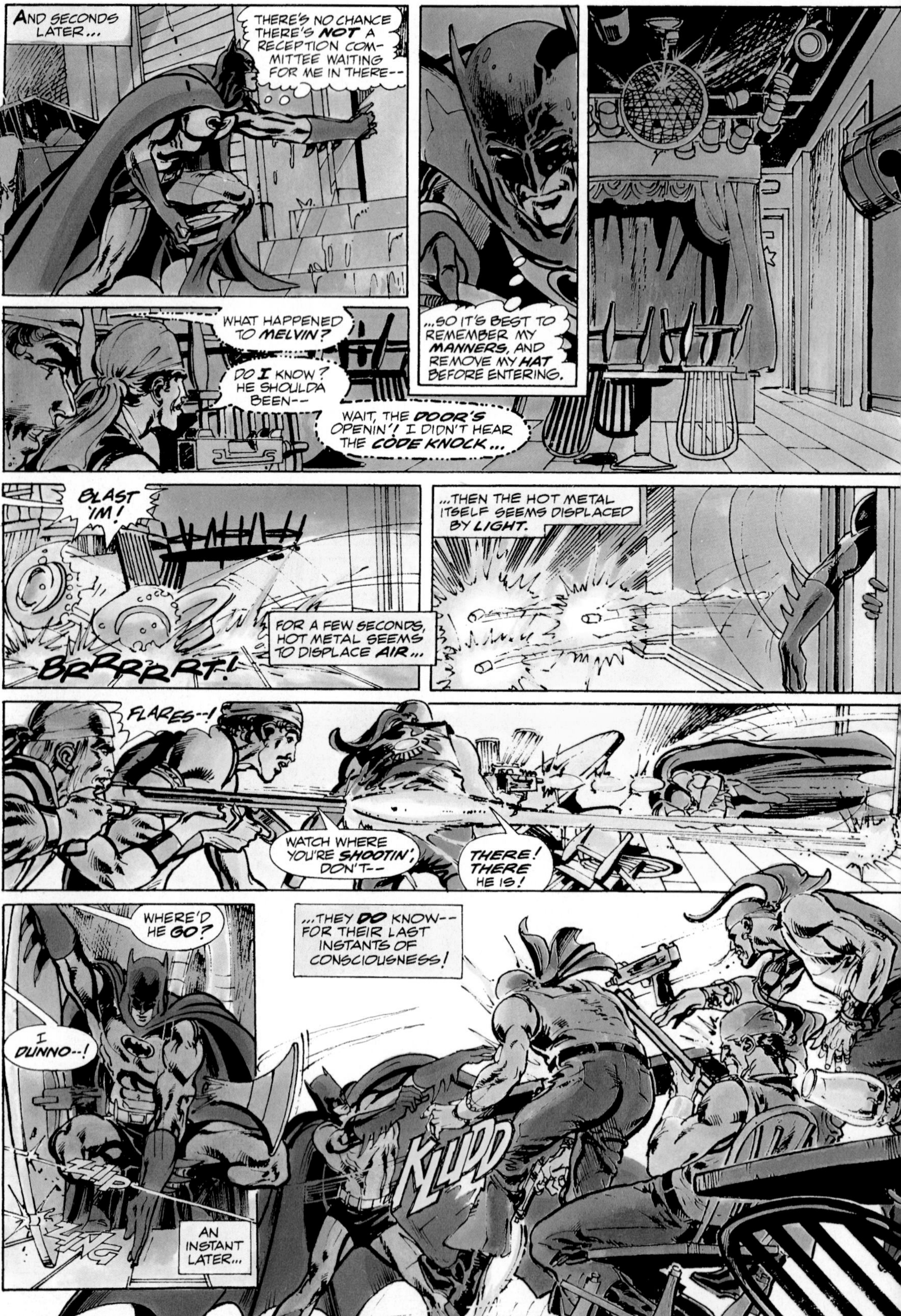

AND SECONDS LATER...
THERE'S NO CHANCE THERE'S NOT A RECEPTION COMMITTEE WAITING FOR ME IN THERE--
...SO IT'S BEST TO REMEMBER MY MANNERS, AND REMOVE MY HAT BEFORE ENTERING.
WHAT HAPPENED TO MELVIN?
DO I KNOW? HE SHOULDA BEEN--
WAIT, THE DOOR'S OPENIN'! I DIDN'T HEAR THE CODE KNOCK...
BLAST 'IM!
BRRRRRRT!
FOR A FEW SECONDS, HOT METAL SEEMS TO DISPLACE AIR...
...THEN THE HOT METAL ITSELF SEEMS DISPLACED BY LIGHT.
FLARES--!
WATCH WHERE YOU'RE SHOOTIN', DON'T--
THERE! THERE HE IS!
WHERE'D HE GO?
I DUNNO--!
...THEY DO KNOW-- FOR THEIR LAST INSTANTS OF CONSCIOUSNESS!
ZIP
KLUDD
AN INSTANT LATER...

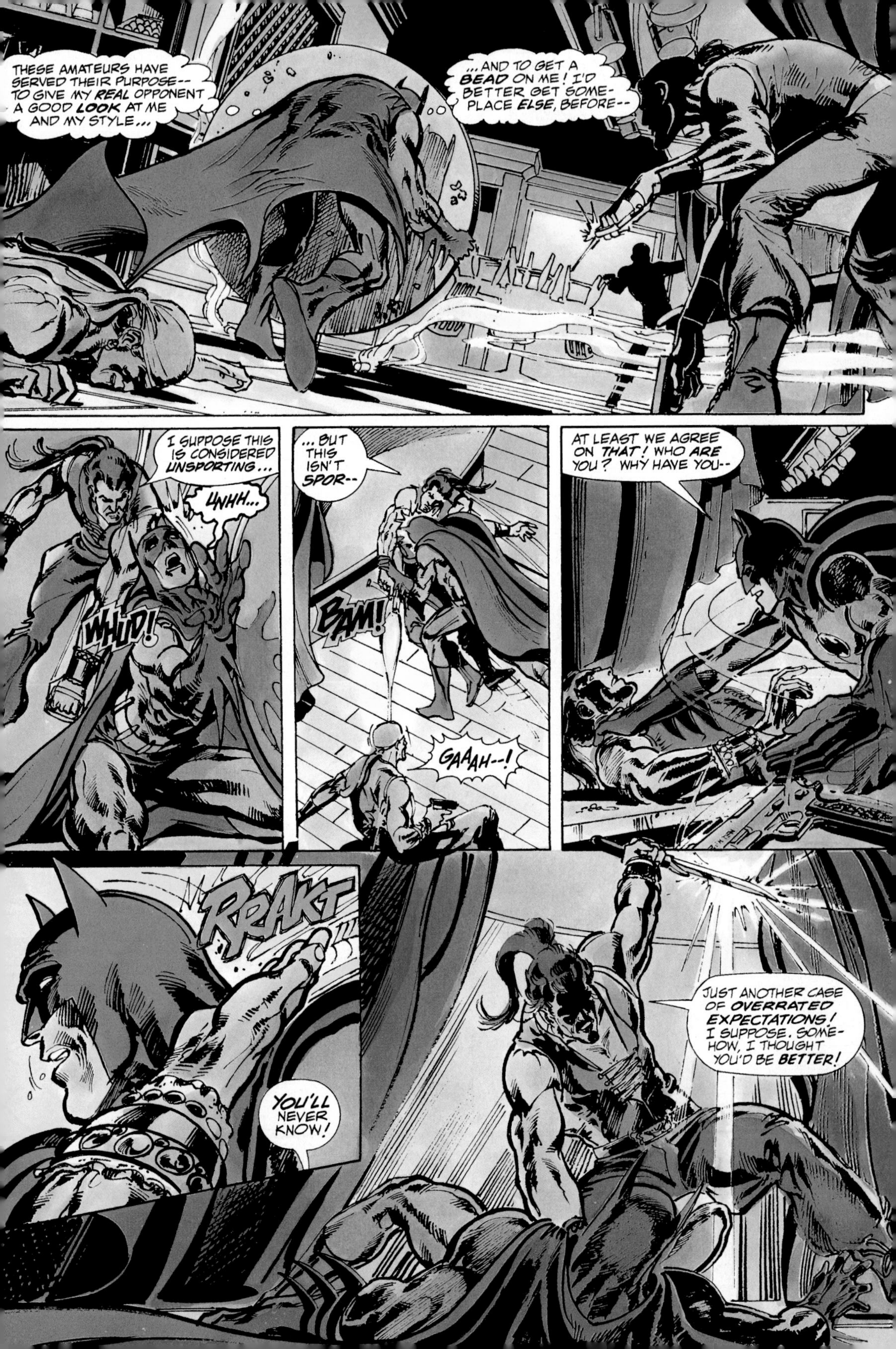
THESE AMATEURS HAVE SERVED THEIR PURPOSE-- TO GIVE MY REAL OPPONENT A GOOD LOOK AT ME AND MY STYLE...
...AND TO GET A BEAD ON ME! I'D BETTER GET SOME-PLACE ELSE, BEFORE--
I SUPPOSE THIS IS CONSIDERED UNSPORTING...
UNHH...
WHUD!
...BUT THIS ISN'T SPOR--
BAM!
GAAAH--!
AT LEAST WE AGREE ON THAT! WHO ARE YOU? WHY HAVE YOU--
RRAKT
YOU'LL NEVER KNOW!
JUST ANOTHER CASE OF OVERRATED EXPECTATIONS! I SUPPOSE. SOME-HOW, I THOUGHT YOU'D BE BETTER!

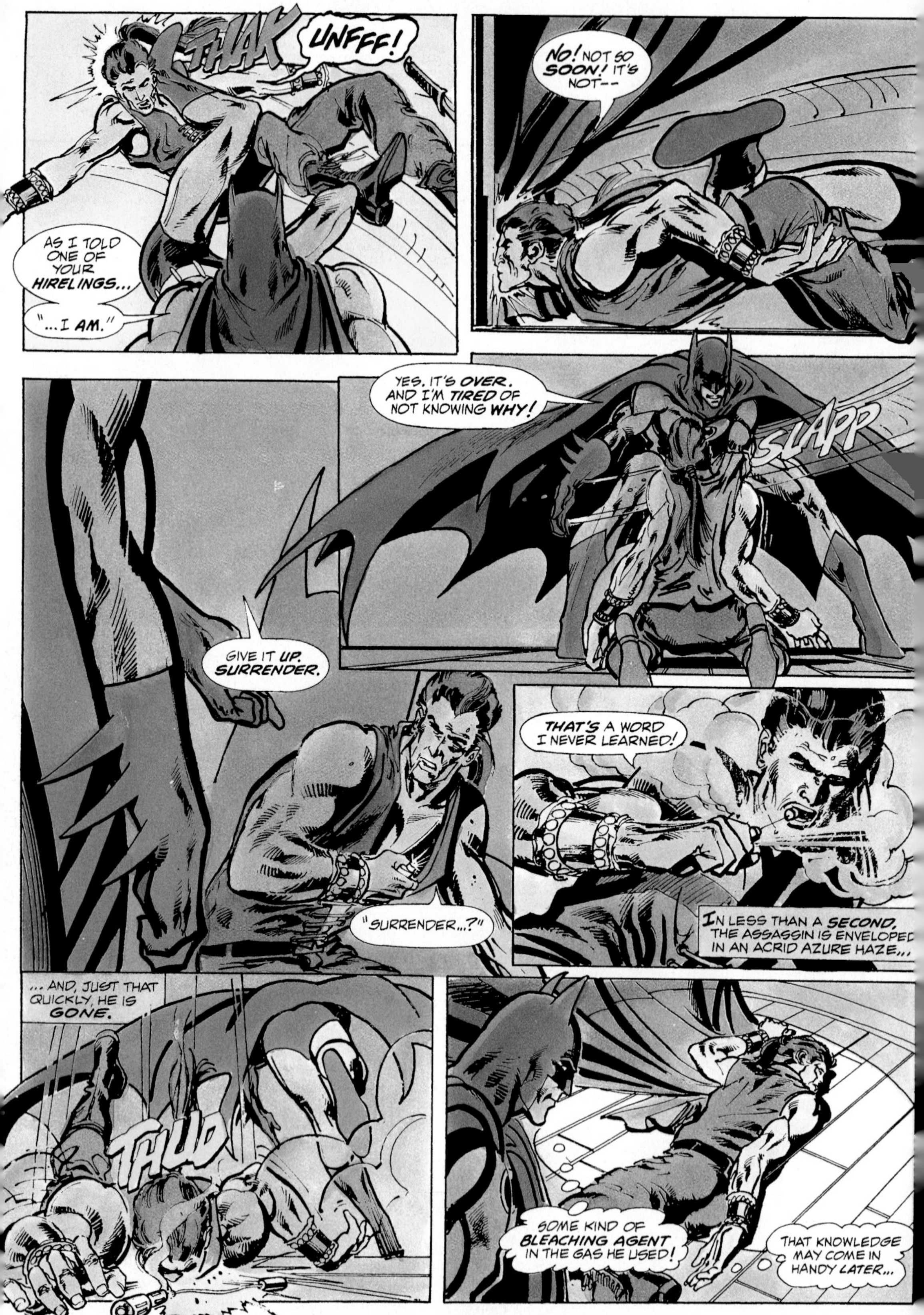
THAK
UNFFF!
AS I TOLD ONE OF YOUR HIRELINGS...
"...I AM."
NO! NOT SO SOON! IT'S NOT--
YES. IT'S OVER. AND I'M TIRED OF NOT KNOWING WHY!
SLAPP
GIVE IT UP. SURRENDER.
"SURRENDER...?"
THAT'S A WORD I NEVER LEARNED!
IN LESS THAN A SECOND, THE ASSASSIN IS ENVELOPED IN AN ACRID AZURE HAZE...
...AND, JUST THAT QUICKLY, HE IS GONE.
THUD
SOME KIND OF BLEACHING AGENT IN THE GAS HE USED!
THAT KNOWLEDGE MAY COME IN HANDY LATER...

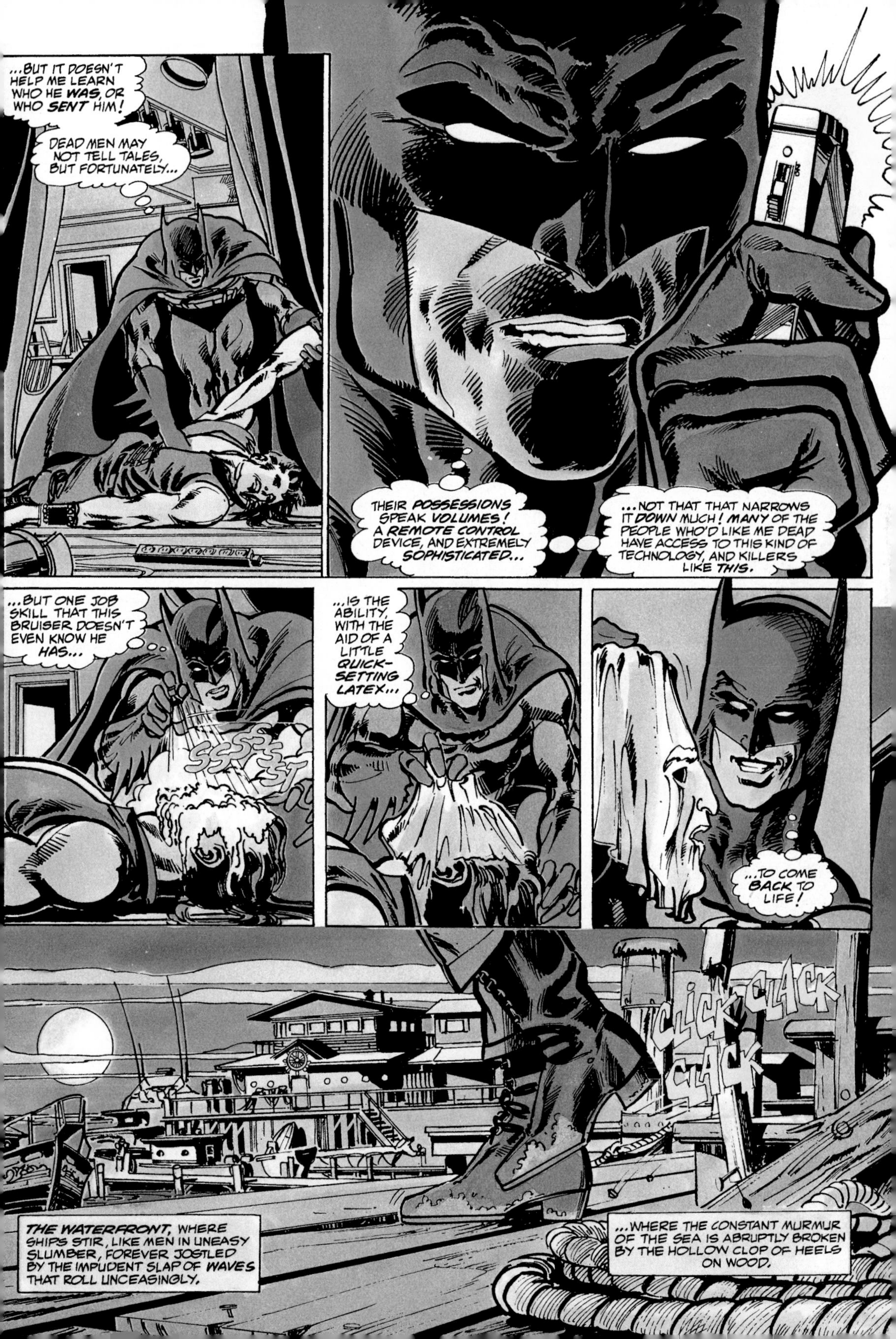
...BUT IT DOESN'T HELP ME LEARN WHO HE WAS, OR WHO SENT HIM!
DEAD MEN MAY NOT TELL TALES, BUT FORTUNATELY...
THEIR POSSESSIONS SPEAK VOLUMES! A REMOTE CONTROL DEVICE, AND EXTREMELY SOPHISTICATED...
...NOT THAT THAT NARROWS IT DOWN MUCH! MANY OF THE PEOPLE WHO'D LIKE ME DEAD HAVE ACCESS TO THIS KIND OF TECHNOLOGY, AND KILLERS LIKE THIS.
...BUT ONE JOB SKILL THAT THIS BRUISER DOESN'T EVEN KNOW HE HAS...
SSSSSSST
...IS THE ABILITY, WITH THE AID OF A LITTLE QUICK-SETTING LATEX...
...TO COME BACK TO LIFE!
THE WATERFRONT, WHERE SHIPS STIR, LIKE MEN IN UNEASY SLUMBER, FOREVER JOSTLED BY THE IMPUDENT SLAP OF WAVES THAT ROLL UNCEASINGLY.
CLICK CLACK CLACK
...WHERE THE CONSTANT MURMUR OF THE SEA IS ABRUPTLY BROKEN BY THE HOLLOW CLOP OF HEELS ON WOOD.

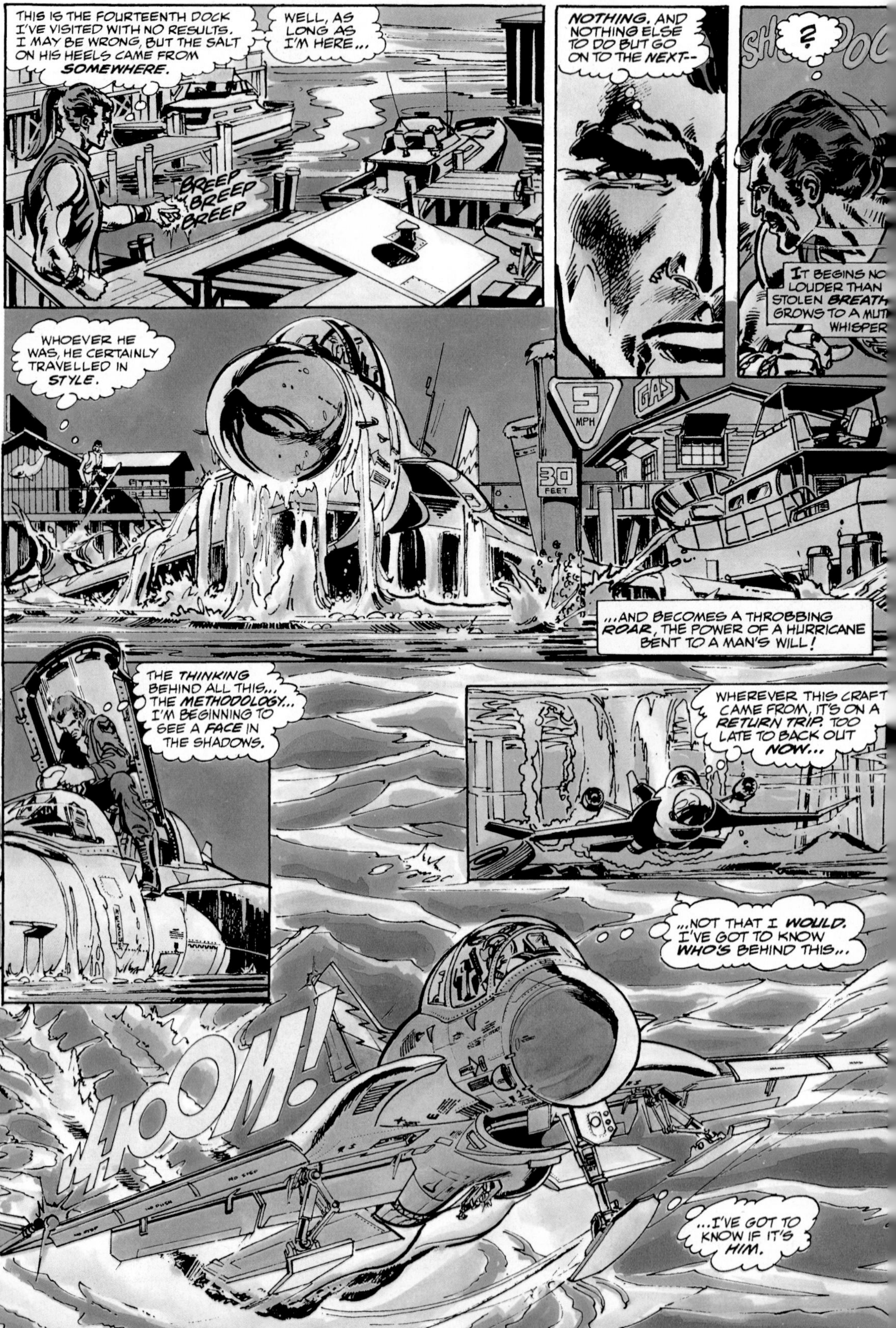

THIS IS THE FOURTEENTH DOCK I'VE VISITED WITH NO RESULTS. I MAY BE WRONG, BUT THE SALT ON HIS HEELS CAME FROM *SOMEWHERE*.
WELL, AS LONG AS I'M HERE...
BREEP BREEP BREEP
NOTHING. AND NOTHING ELSE TO DO BUT GO ON TO THE *NEXT*--
?
IT BEGINS NO LOUDER THAN STOLEN *BREATH* GROWS TO A MUT WHISPER
WHOEVER HE WAS, HE CERTAINLY TRAVELLED IN *STYLE*.
5 MPH
GAS
30 FEET
...AND BECOMES A THROBBING *ROAR*, THE POWER OF A HURRICANE BENT TO A MAN'S WILL!
THE *THINKING* BEHIND ALL THIS... THE *METHODOLOGY*... I'M BEGINNING TO SEE A *FACE* IN THE SHADOWS.
WHEREVER THIS CRAFT CAME FROM, IT'S ON A *RETURN TRIP.* TOO LATE TO BACK OUT *NOW*...
...NOT THAT I *WOULD.* I'VE GOT TO KNOW *WHO'S* BEHIND THIS...
WHOOM!
...I'VE GOT TO KNOW IF IT'S *HIM*.

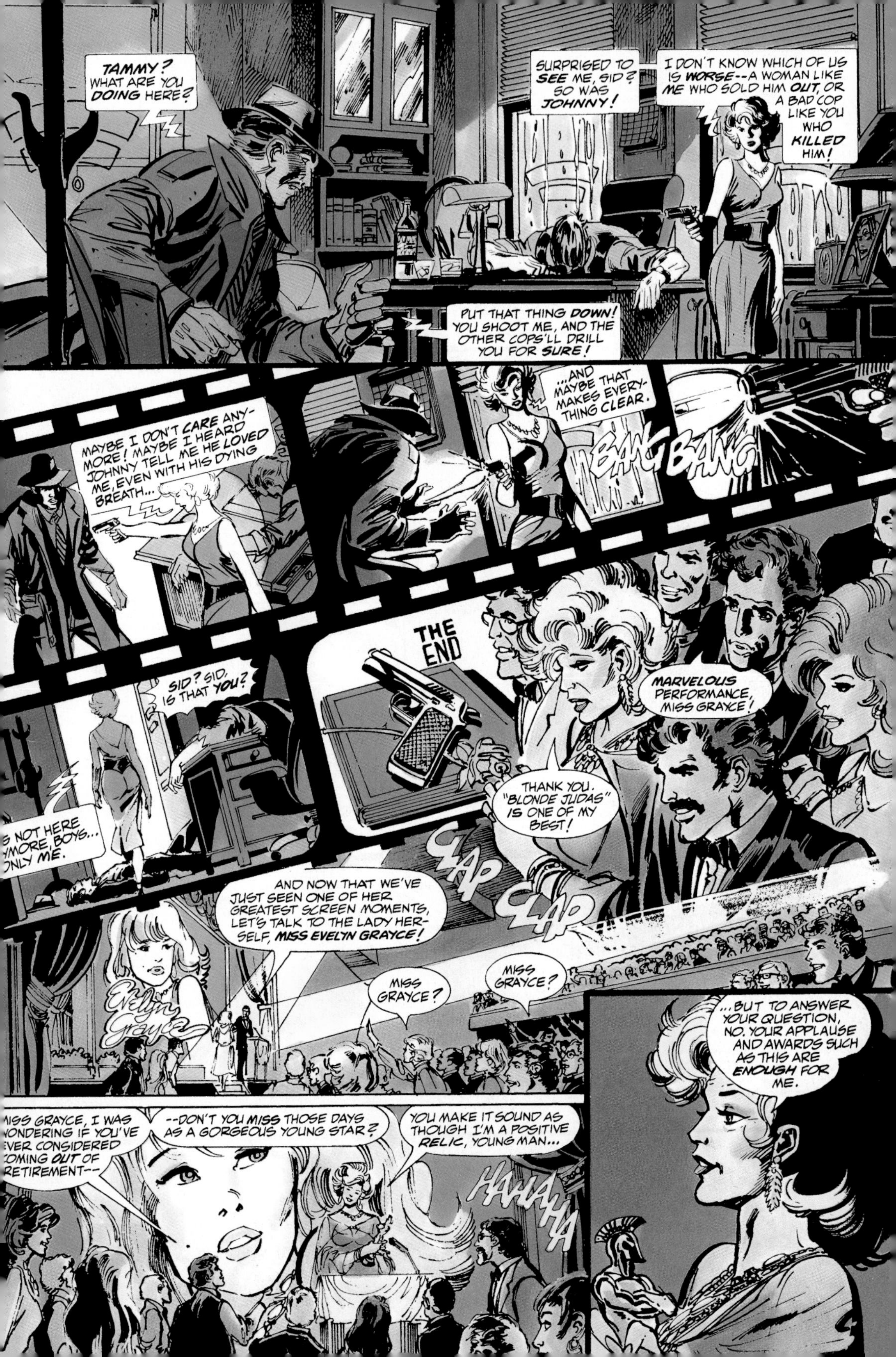
TAMMY? WHAT ARE YOU DOING HERE?
SURPRISED TO SEE ME, SID? SO WAS JOHNNY!
I DON'T KNOW WHICH OF US IS WORSE--A WOMAN LIKE ME WHO SOLD HIM OUT, OR A BAD COP LIKE YOU WHO KILLED HIM!
PUT THAT THING DOWN! YOU SHOOT ME, AND THE OTHER COPS'LL DRILL YOU FOR SURE!
MAYBE I DON'T CARE ANYMORE! MAYBE I HEARD JOHNNY TELL ME HE LOVED ME, EVEN WITH HIS DYING BREATH...
...AND MAYBE THAT MAKES EVERYTHING CLEAR.
BANG BANG
SID? SID, IS THAT YOU?
S NOT HERE YMORE, BOYS... ONLY ME.
THE END
MARVELOUS PERFORMANCE, MISS GRAYCE!
THANK YOU. "BLONDE JUDAS" IS ONE OF MY BEST!
CLAP CLAP
AND NOW THAT WE'VE JUST SEEN ONE OF HER GREATEST SCREEN MOMENTS, LET'S TALK TO THE LADY HERSELF, MISS EVELYN GRAYCE!
Evelyn Grayce
MISS GRAYCE?
MISS GRAYCE?
...BUT TO ANSWER YOUR QUESTION, NO. YOUR APPLAUSE AND AWARDS SUCH AS THIS ARE ENOUGH FOR ME.
MISS GRAYCE, I WAS WONDERING IF YOU'VE EVER CONSIDERED COMING OUT OF RETIREMENT--
--DON'T YOU MISS THOSE DAYS AS A GORGEOUS YOUNG STAR?
YOU MAKE IT SOUND AS THOUGH I'M A POSITIVE RELIC, YOUNG MAN...
HAHAHA

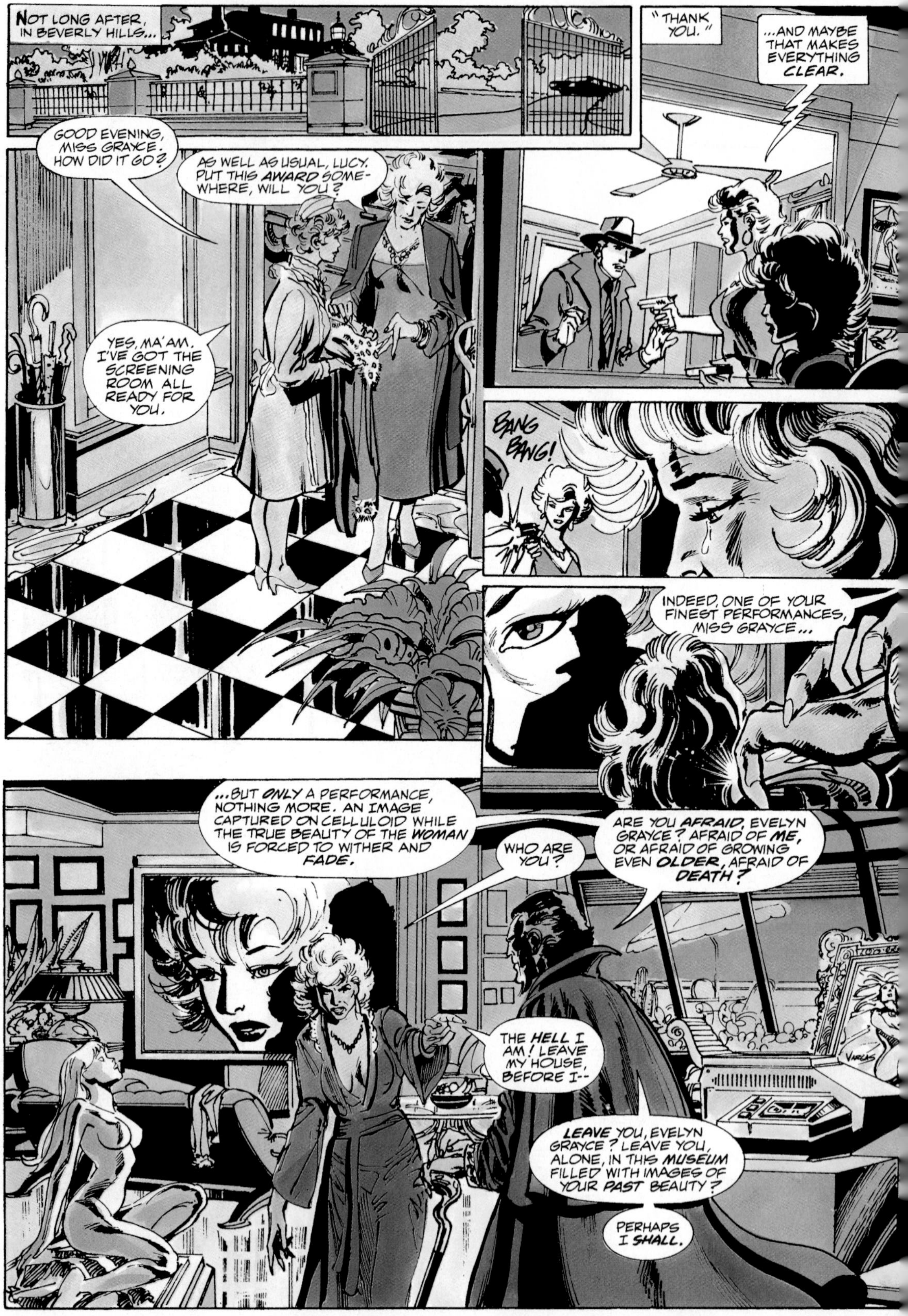
NOT LONG AFTER, IN BEVERLY HILLS...
"THANK YOU."
...AND MAYBE THAT MAKES EVERYTHING CLEAR.
GOOD EVENING, MISS GRAYCE. HOW DID IT GO?
AS WELL AS USUAL, LUCY. PUT THIS AWARD SOMEWHERE, WILL YOU?
YES, MA'AM. I'VE GOT THE SCREENING ROOM ALL READY FOR YOU.
BANG BANG!
INDEED, ONE OF YOUR FINEST PERFORMANCES, MISS GRAYCE...
...BUT ONLY A PERFORMANCE, NOTHING MORE. AN IMAGE CAPTURED ON CELLULOID WHILE THE TRUE BEAUTY OF THE WOMAN IS FORCED TO WITHER AND FADE.
WHO ARE YOU?
ARE YOU AFRAID, EVELYN GRAYCE? AFRAID OF ME, OR AFRAID OF GROWING EVEN OLDER, AFRAID OF DEATH?
THE HELL I AM! LEAVE MY HOUSE, BEFORE I--
LEAVE YOU, EVELYN GRAYCE? LEAVE YOU, ALONE, IN THIS MUSEUM FILLED WITH IMAGES OF YOUR PAST BEAUTY?
PERHAPS I SHALL.
VARGAS

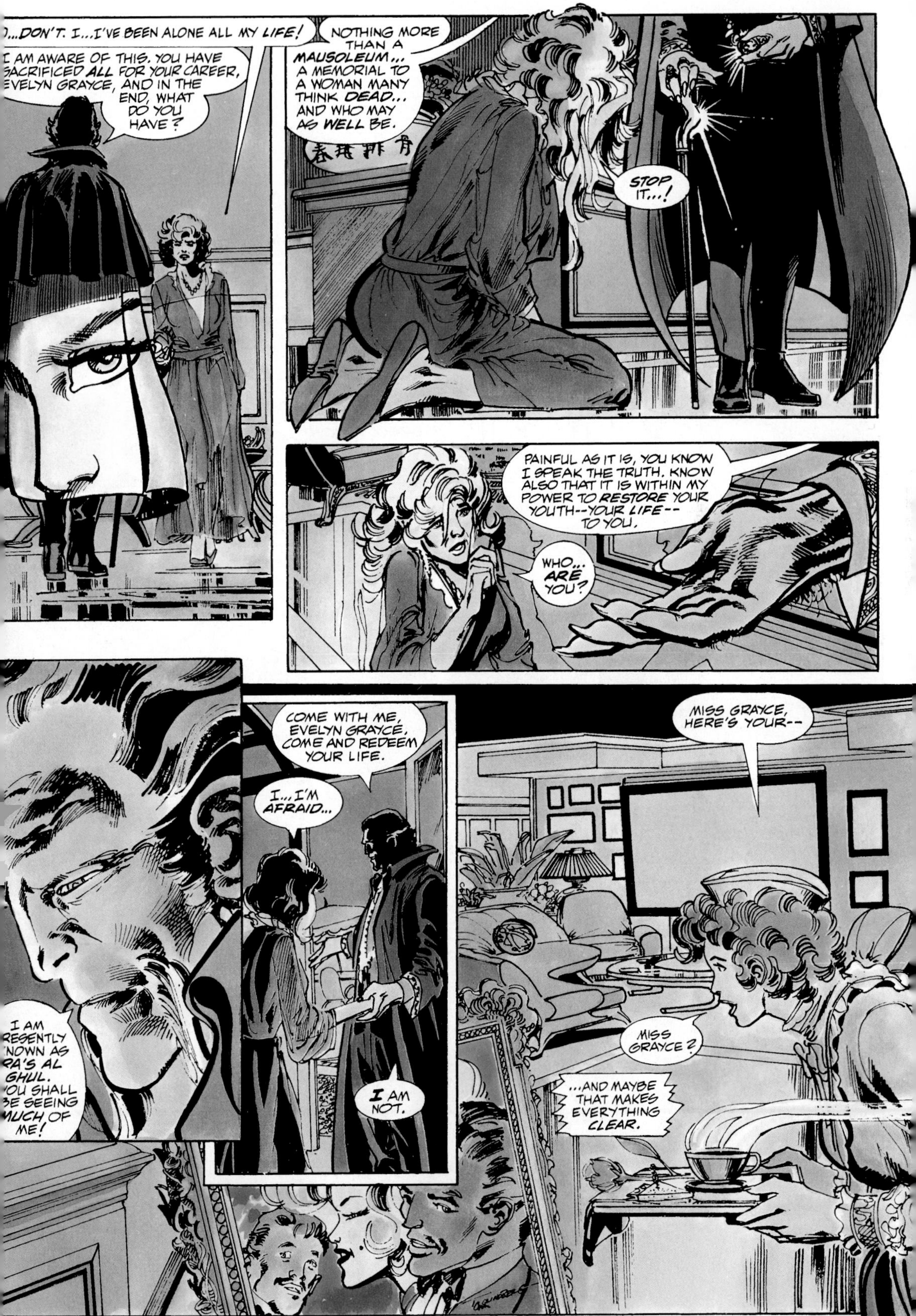

...DON'T. I...I'VE BEEN ALONE ALL MY LIFE!
I AM AWARE OF THIS. YOU HAVE SACRIFICED ALL FOR YOUR CAREER, EVELYN GRAYCE, AND IN THE END, WHAT DO YOU HAVE?
NOTHING MORE THAN A MAUSOLEUM... A MEMORIAL TO A WOMAN MANY THINK DEAD... AND WHO MAY AS WELL BE.
STOP IT...!
PAINFUL AS IT IS, YOU KNOW I SPEAK THE TRUTH. KNOW ALSO THAT IT IS WITHIN MY POWER TO RESTORE YOUR YOUTH--YOUR LIFE--TO YOU.
WHO... ARE YOU?
I AM PRESENTLY KNOWN AS RA'S AL GHUL. YOU SHALL BE SEEING MUCH OF ME!
COME WITH ME, EVELYN GRAYCE, COME AND REDEEM YOUR LIFE.
I... I'M AFRAID...
I AM NOT.
MISS GRAYCE, HERE'S YOUR--
MISS GRAYCE?
...AND MAYBE THAT MAKES EVERYTHING CLEAR.

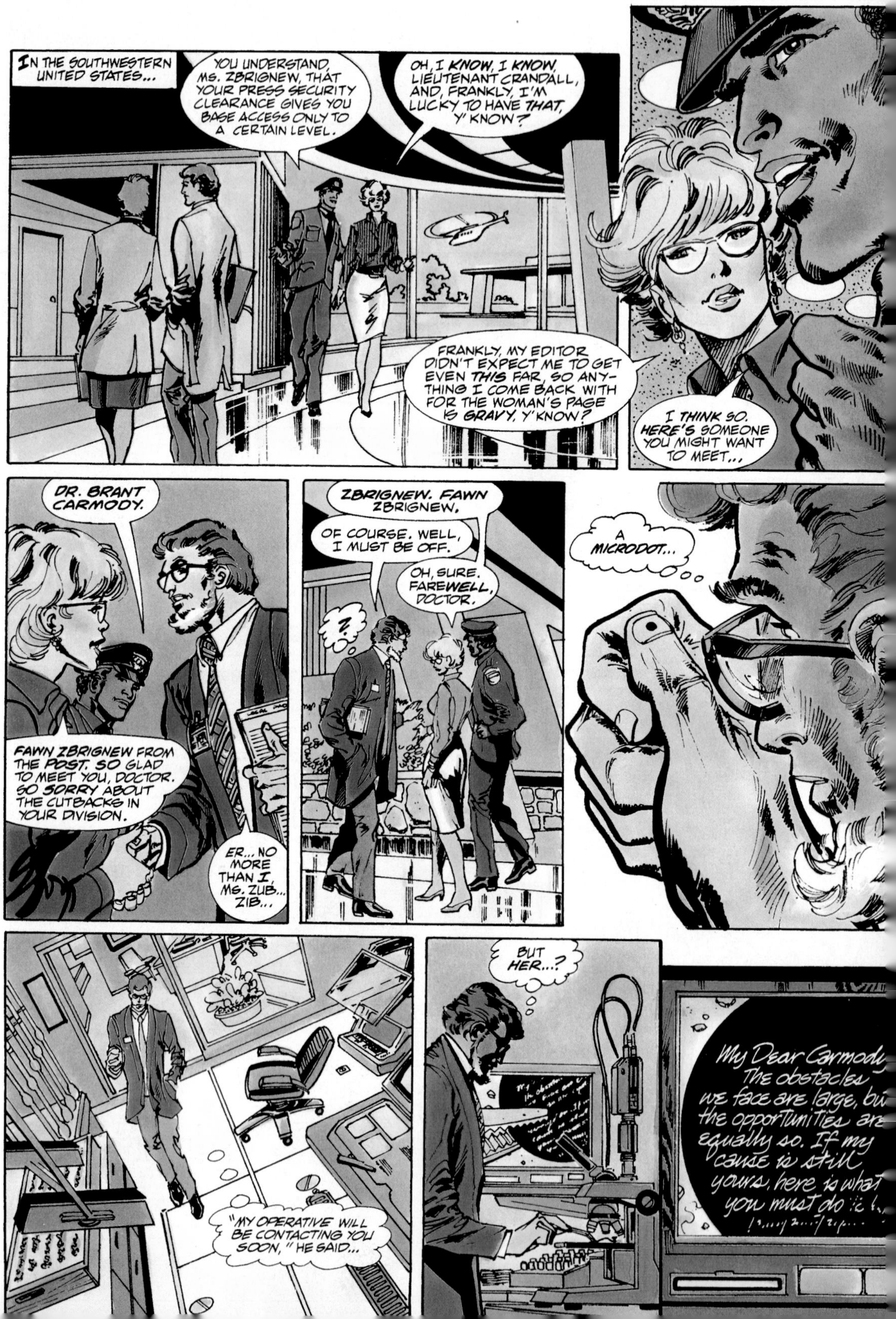
IN THE SOUTHWESTERN UNITED STATES...
YOU UNDERSTAND, MS. ZBRIGNEW, THAT YOUR PRESS SECURITY CLEARANCE GIVES YOU BASE ACCESS ONLY TO A CERTAIN LEVEL.
OH, I KNOW, I KNOW, LIEUTENANT CRANDALL, AND, FRANKLY, I'M LUCKY TO HAVE THAT, Y'KNOW?
FRANKLY, MY EDITOR DIDN'T EXPECT ME TO GET EVEN THIS FAR, SO ANY-THING I COME BACK WITH FOR THE WOMAN'S PAGE IS GRAVY, Y'KNOW?
I THINK SO. HERE'S SOMEONE YOU MIGHT WANT TO MEET...
DR. BRANT CARMODY.
FAWN ZBRIGNEW FROM THE POST. SO GLAD TO MEET YOU, DOCTOR. SO SORRY ABOUT THE CUTBACKS IN YOUR DIVISION.
ER... NO MORE THAN I, MS. ZUB... ZIB...
ZBRIGNEW. FAWN ZBRIGNEW.
OF COURSE. WELL, I MUST BE OFF.
OH, SURE. FAREWELL, DOCTOR.
?
A MICRODOT...
"MY OPERATIVE WILL BE CONTACTING YOU SOON," HE SAID...
BUT HER...?
My Dear Carmody
The obstacles
we face are large, bu
the opportunities are
equally so. If my
cause is still
yours, here is what
you must do

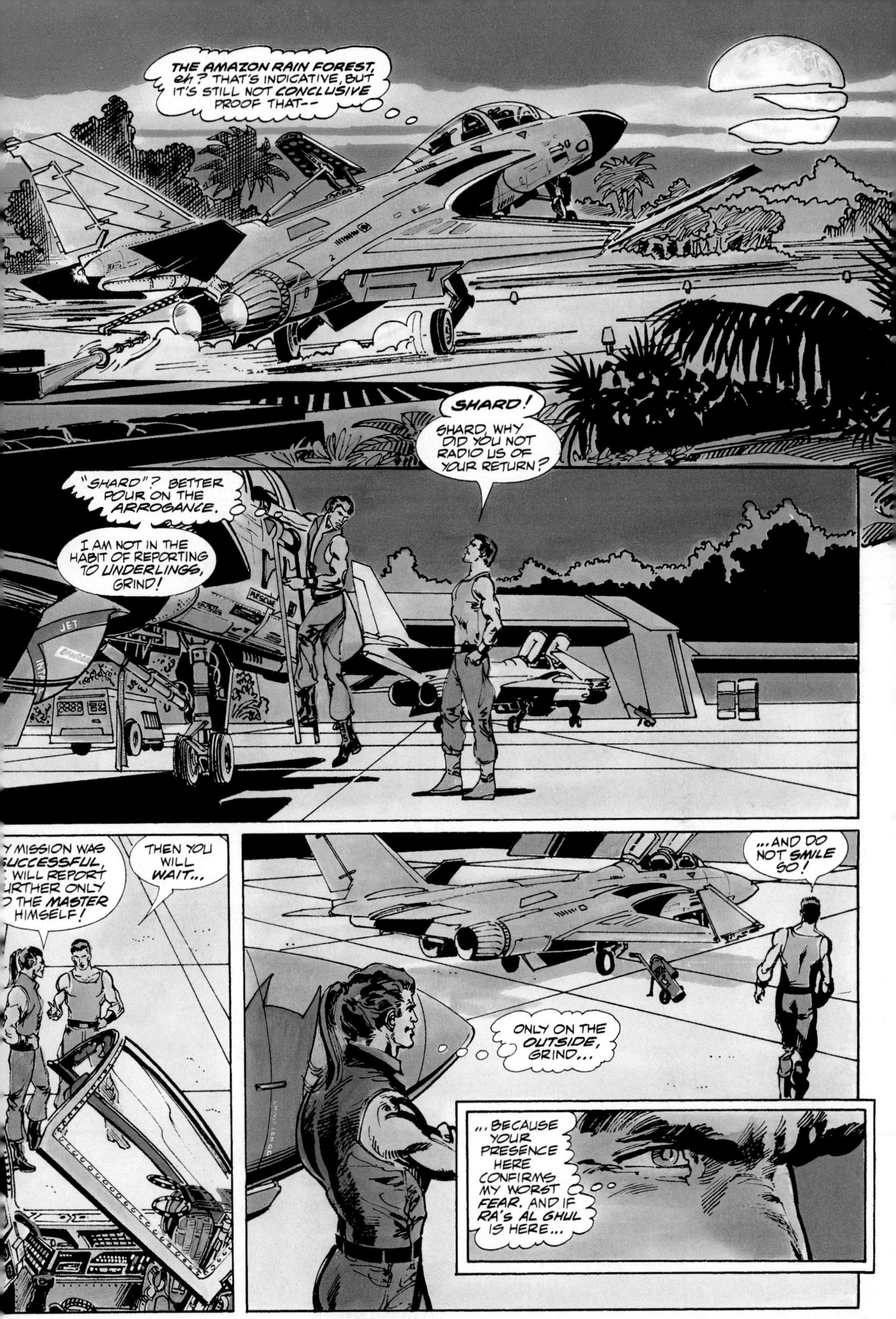
THE AMAZON RAIN FOREST, eh? THAT'S INDICATIVE, BUT IT'S STILL NOT CONCLUSIVE PROOF THAT--
SHARD!
SHARD, WHY DID YOU NOT RADIO US OF YOUR RETURN?
"SHARD"? BETTER POUR ON THE ARROGANCE.
I AM NOT IN THE HABIT OF REPORTING TO UNDERLINGS, GRIND!
RESCUE
JET
Y MISSION WAS SUCCESSFUL. WILL REPORT URTHER ONLY O THE MASTER HIMSELF!
THEN YOU WILL WAIT...
...AND DO NOT SMILE SO!
ONLY ON THE OUTSIDE, GRIND...
...BECAUSE YOUR PRESENCE HERE CONFIRMS MY WORST FEAR. AND IF RA's AL GHUL IS HERE...

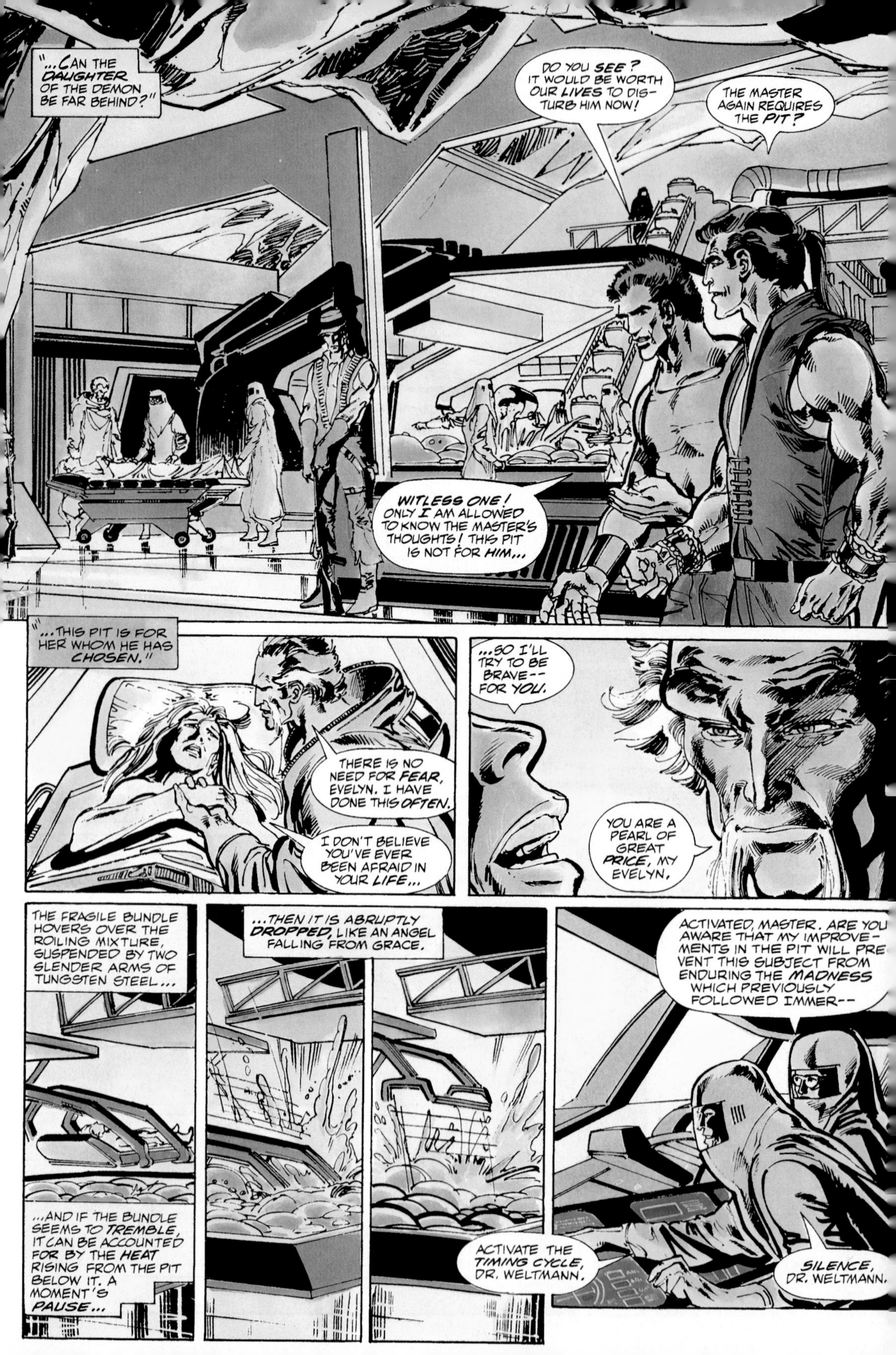

"...CAN THE DAUGHTER OF THE DEMON BE FAR BEHIND?"
THE MASTER AGAIN REQUIRES THE PIT?
DO YOU SEE? IT WOULD BE WORTH OUR LIVES TO DISTURB HIM NOW!
WITLESS ONE! ONLY I AM ALLOWED TO KNOW THE MASTER'S THOUGHTS! THIS PIT IS NOT FOR HIM...
"...THIS PIT IS FOR HER WHOM HE HAS CHOSEN."
THERE IS NO NEED FOR FEAR, EVELYN. I HAVE DONE THIS OFTEN.
I DON'T BELIEVE YOU'VE EVER BEEN AFRAID IN YOUR LIFE...
...SO I'LL TRY TO BE BRAVE--FOR YOU.
YOU ARE A PEARL OF GREAT PRICE, MY EVELYN.
THE FRAGILE BUNDLE HOVERS OVER THE ROILING MIXTURE, SUSPENDED BY TWO SLENDER ARMS OF TUNGSTEN STEEL...
...AND IF THE BUNDLE SEEMS TO TREMBLE, IT CAN BE ACCOUNTED FOR BY THE HEAT RISING FROM THE PIT BELOW IT. A MOMENT'S PAUSE...
...THEN IT IS ABRUPTLY DROPPED, LIKE AN ANGEL FALLING FROM GRACE.
ACTIVATE THE TIMING CYCLE, DR. WELTMANN.
ACTIVATED, MASTER. ARE YOU AWARE THAT MY IMPROVEMENTS IN THE PIT WILL PREVENT THIS SUBJECT FROM ENDURING THE MADNESS WHICH PREVIOUSLY FOLLOWED IMMER--
SILENCE, DR. WELTMANN.

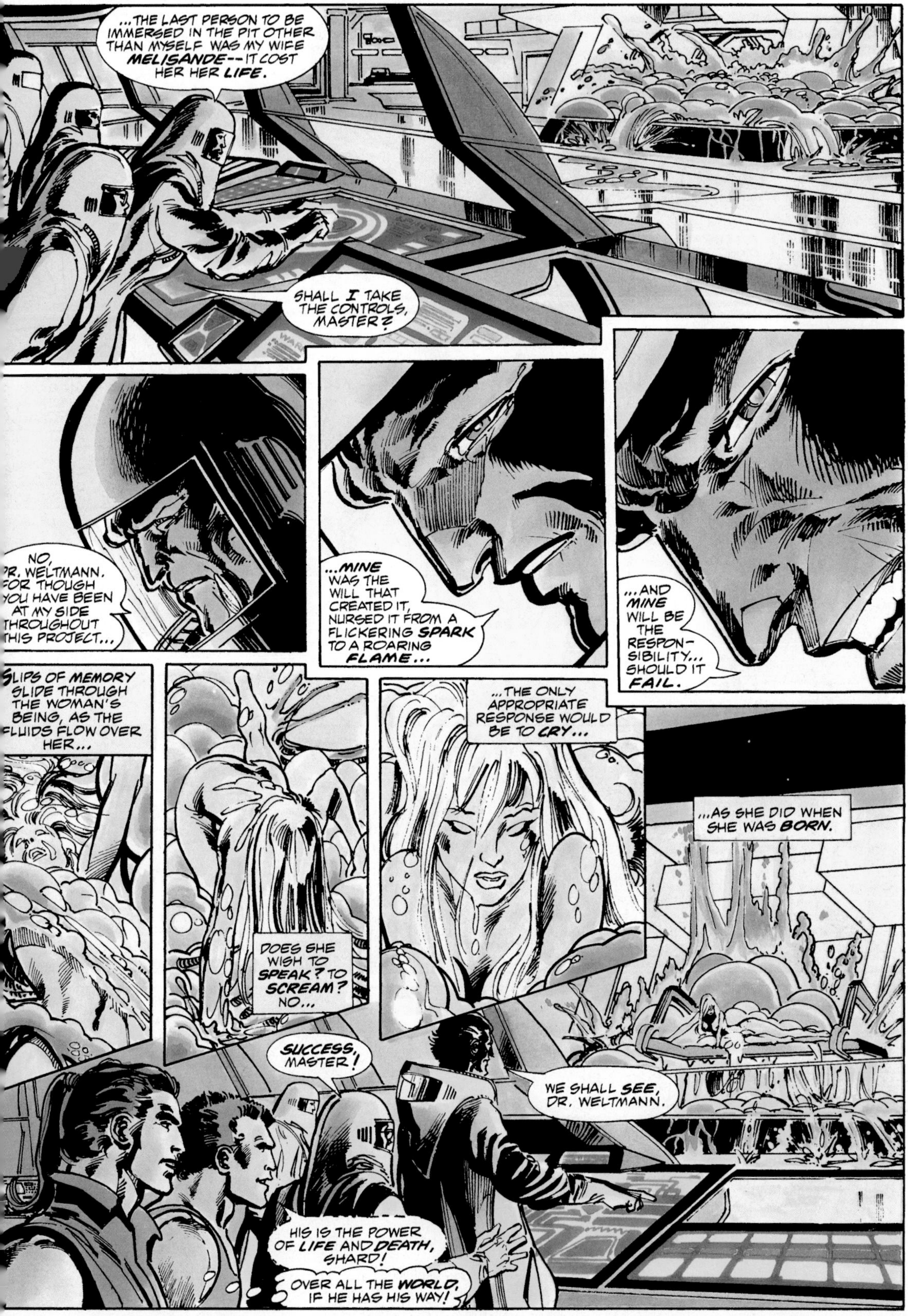
...THE LAST PERSON TO BE IMMERSED IN THE PIT OTHER THAN MYSELF WAS MY WIFE MELISANDE--IT COST HER HER LIFE.
SHALL I TAKE THE CONTROLS, MASTER?
NO, DR. WELTMANN. FOR THOUGH YOU HAVE BEEN AT MY SIDE THROUGHOUT THIS PROJECT...
...MINE WAS THE WILL THAT CREATED IT, NURSED IT FROM A FLICKERING SPARK TO A ROARING FLAME...
...AND MINE WILL BE THE RESPONSIBILITY... SHOULD IT FAIL.
SLIPS OF MEMORY SLIDE THROUGH THE WOMAN'S BEING, AS THE FLUIDS FLOW OVER HER...
DOES SHE WISH TO SPEAK? TO SCREAM? NO...
...THE ONLY APPROPRIATE RESPONSE WOULD BE TO CRY...
...AS SHE DID WHEN SHE WAS BORN.
SUCCESS, MASTER!
WE SHALL SEE, DR. WELTMANN.
HIS IS THE POWER OF LIFE AND DEATH, SHARD!
OVER ALL THE WORLD, IF HE HAS HIS WAY!

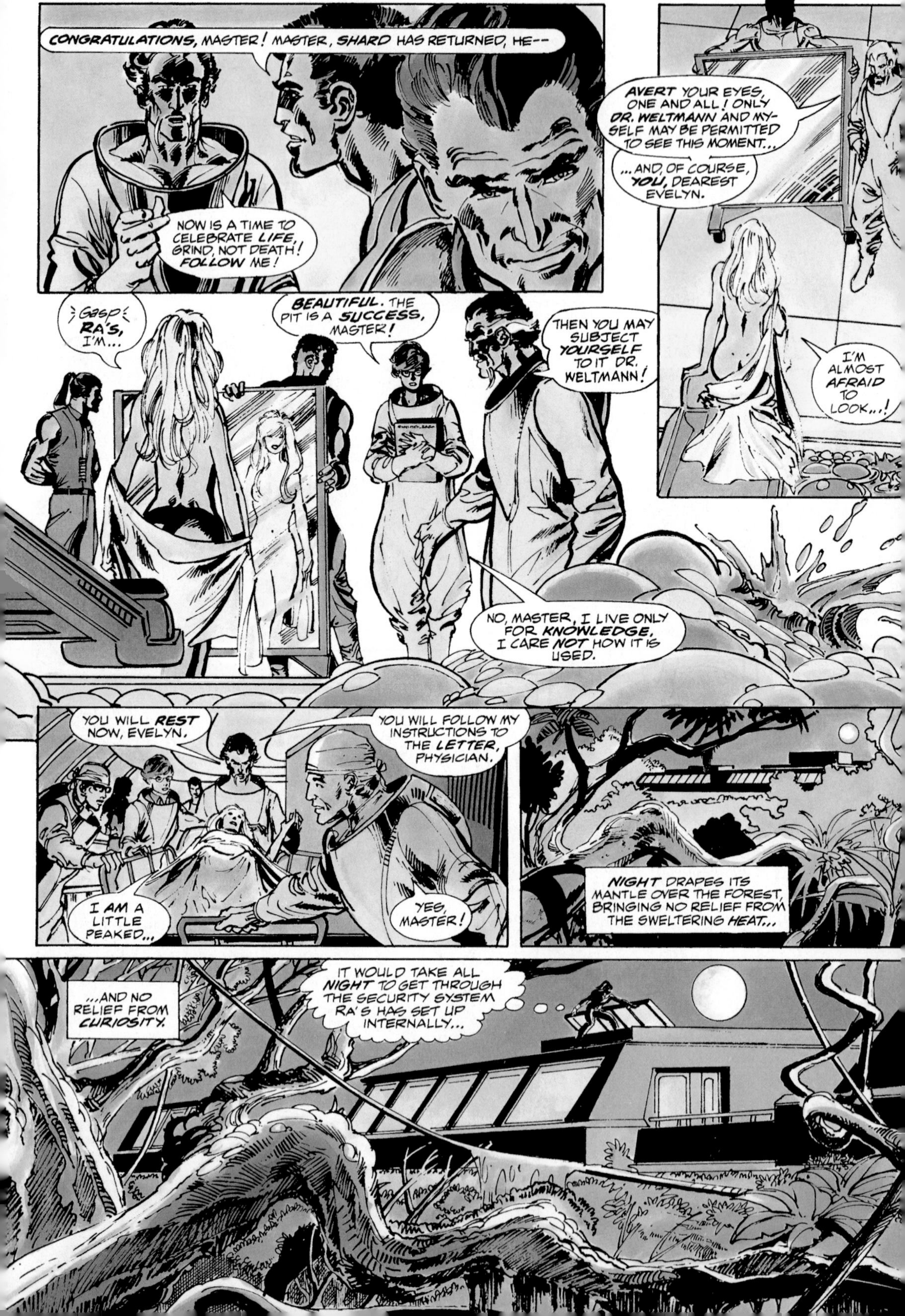
CONGRATULATIONS, MASTER! MASTER, SHARD HAS RETURNED, HE--
NOW IS A TIME TO CELEBRATE LIFE, GRIND, NOT DEATH! FOLLOW ME!
AVERT YOUR EYES, ONE AND ALL! ONLY DR. WELTMANN AND MYSELF MAY BE PERMITTED TO SEE THIS MOMENT...
...AND, OF COURSE, YOU, DEAREST EVELYN.
I'M ALMOST AFRAID TO LOOK...!
GASP RA'S, I'M...
BEAUTIFUL. THE PIT IS A SUCCESS, MASTER!
THEN YOU MAY SUBJECT YOURSELF TO IT DR. WELTMANN!
NO, MASTER, I LIVE ONLY FOR KNOWLEDGE. I CARE NOT HOW IT IS USED.
YOU WILL REST NOW, EVELYN.
YOU WILL FOLLOW MY INSTRUCTIONS TO THE LETTER, PHYSICIAN.
I AM A LITTLE PEAKED...
YES, MASTER!
NIGHT DRAPES ITS MANTLE OVER THE FOREST, BRINGING NO RELIEF FROM THE SWELTERING HEAT...
...AND NO RELIEF FROM CURIOSITY.
IT WOULD TAKE ALL NIGHT TO GET THROUGH THE SECURITY SYSTEM RA'S HAS SET UP INTERNALLY...

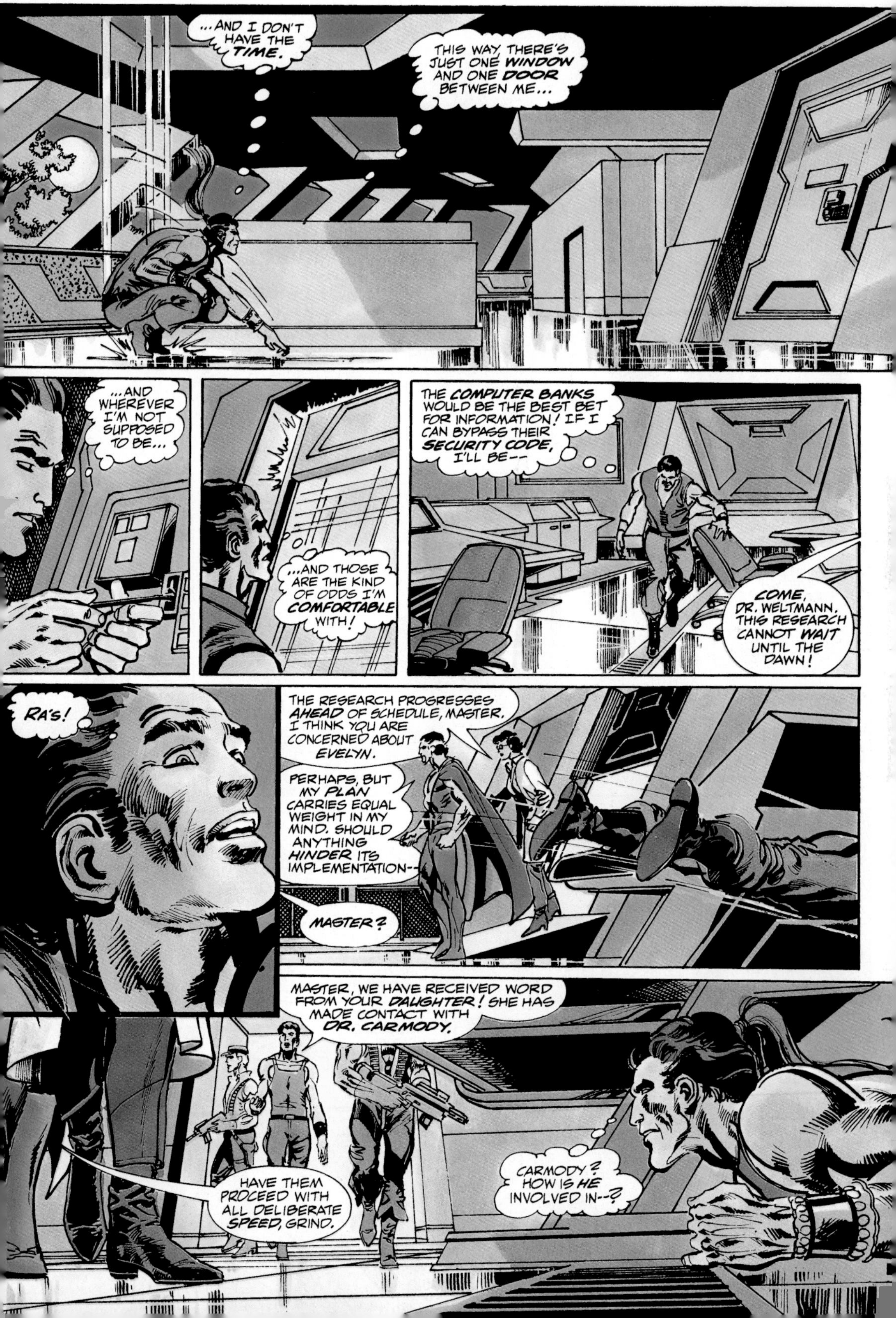
...AND I DON'T HAVE THE TIME.
THIS WAY, THERE'S JUST ONE WINDOW AND ONE DOOR BETWEEN ME...
...AND WHEREVER I'M NOT SUPPOSED TO BE...
...AND THOSE ARE THE KIND OF ODDS I'M COMFORTABLE WITH!
THE COMPUTER BANKS WOULD BE THE BEST BET FOR INFORMATION! IF I CAN BYPASS THEIR SECURITY CODE, I'LL BE--
COME, DR. WELTMANN. THIS RESEARCH CANNOT WAIT UNTIL THE DAWN!
RA'S!
THE RESEARCH PROGRESSES AHEAD OF SCHEDULE, MASTER. I THINK YOU ARE CONCERNED ABOUT EVELYN.
PERHAPS, BUT MY PLAN CARRIES EQUAL WEIGHT IN MY MIND. SHOULD ANYTHING HINDER ITS IMPLEMENTATION--
MASTER?
MASTER, WE HAVE RECEIVED WORD FROM YOUR DAUGHTER! SHE HAS MADE CONTACT WITH DR. CARMODY.
HAVE THEM PROCEED WITH ALL DELIBERATE SPEED, GRIND.
CARMODY? HOW IS HE INVOLVED IN--?

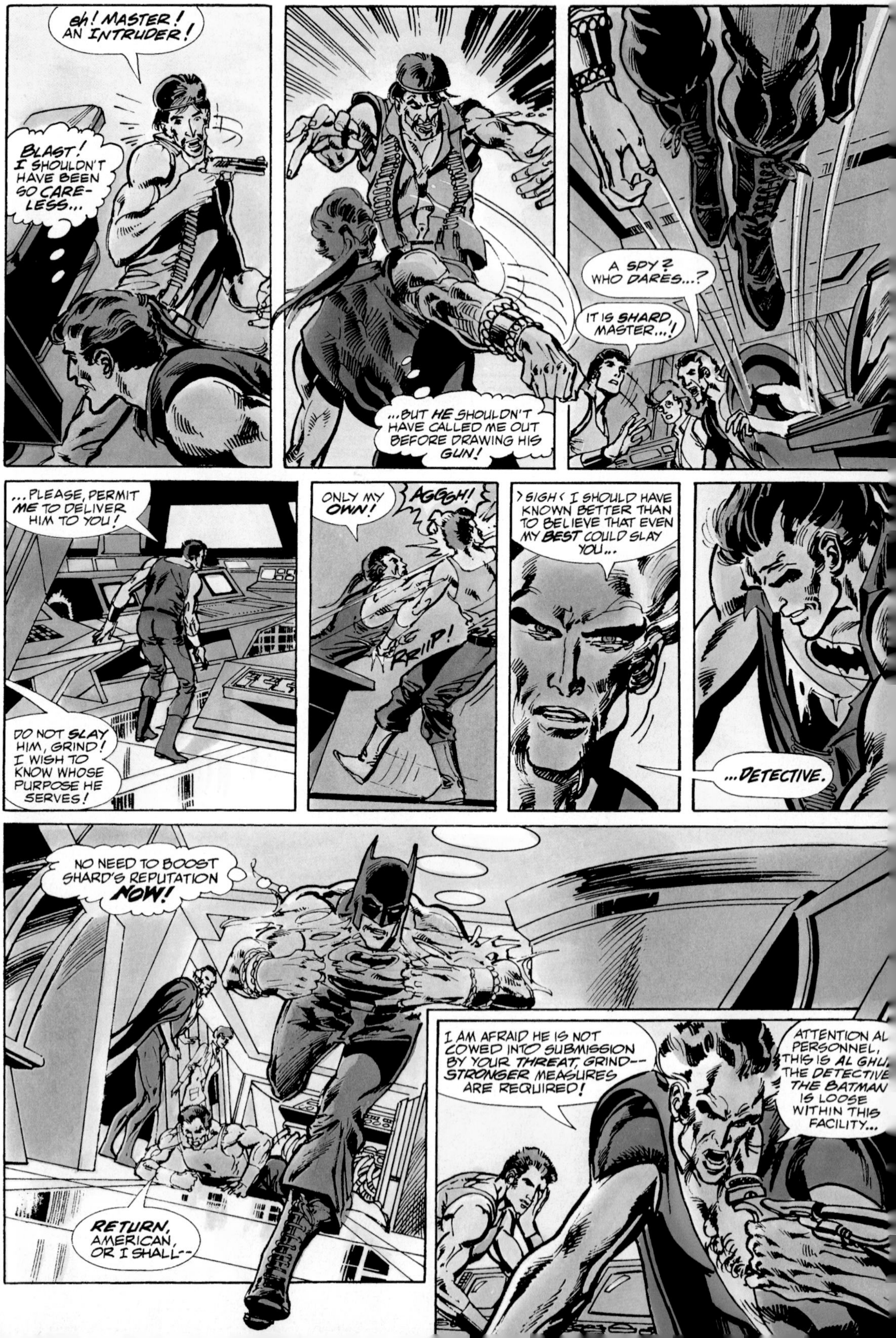

eh! MASTER! AN INTRUDER!
BLAST! I SHOULDN'T HAVE BEEN SO CARELESS...
...BUT HE SHOULDN'T HAVE CALLED ME OUT BEFORE DRAWING HIS GUN!
A SPY? WHO DARES...?
IT IS SHARD, MASTER...!
...PLEASE, PERMIT ME TO DELIVER HIM TO YOU!
DO NOT SLAY HIM, GRIND! I WISH TO KNOW WHOSE PURPOSE HE SERVES!
ONLY MY OWN!
AGGGH!
RRIIP!
>SIGH< I SHOULD HAVE KNOWN BETTER THAN TO BELIEVE THAT EVEN MY BEST COULD SLAY YOU...
...DETECTIVE.
NO NEED TO BOOST SHARD'S REPUTATION NOW!
RETURN, AMERICAN, OR I SHALL--
I AM AFRAID HE IS NOT COWED INTO SUBMISSION BY YOUR THREAT, GRIND-- STRONGER MEASURES ARE REQUIRED!
ATTENTION AL PERSONNEL, THIS IS AL GHU THE DETECTIVE THE BATMAN IS LOOSE WITHIN THIS FACILITY...

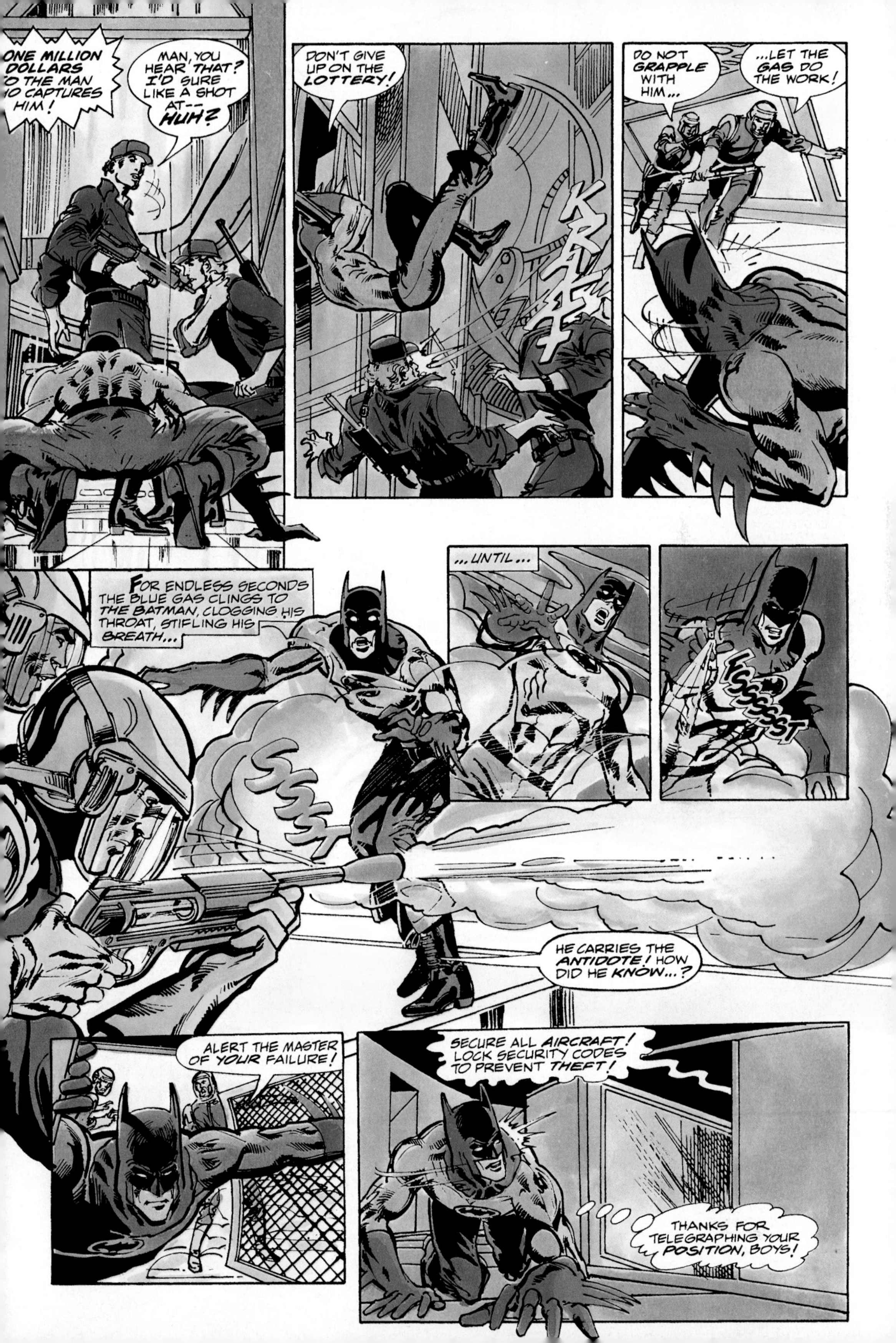
ONE MILLION DOLLARS TO THE MAN WHO CAPTURES HIM!
MAN, YOU HEAR THAT? I'D SURE LIKE A SHOT AT-- HUH?
DON'T GIVE UP ON THE LOTTERY!
KRAK
DO NOT GRAPPLE WITH HIM...
...LET THE GAS DO THE WORK!
FOR ENDLESS SECONDS THE BLUE GAS CLINGS TO THE BATMAN, CLOGGING HIS THROAT, STIFLING HIS BREATH...
SSSSST
...UNTIL...
FSSSSSST
HE CARRIES THE ANTIDOTE! HOW DID HE KNOW...?
ALERT THE MASTER OF YOUR FAILURE!
SECURE ALL AIRCRAFT! LOCK SECURITY CODES TO PREVENT THEFT!
THANKS FOR TELEGRAPHING YOUR POSITION, BOYS!

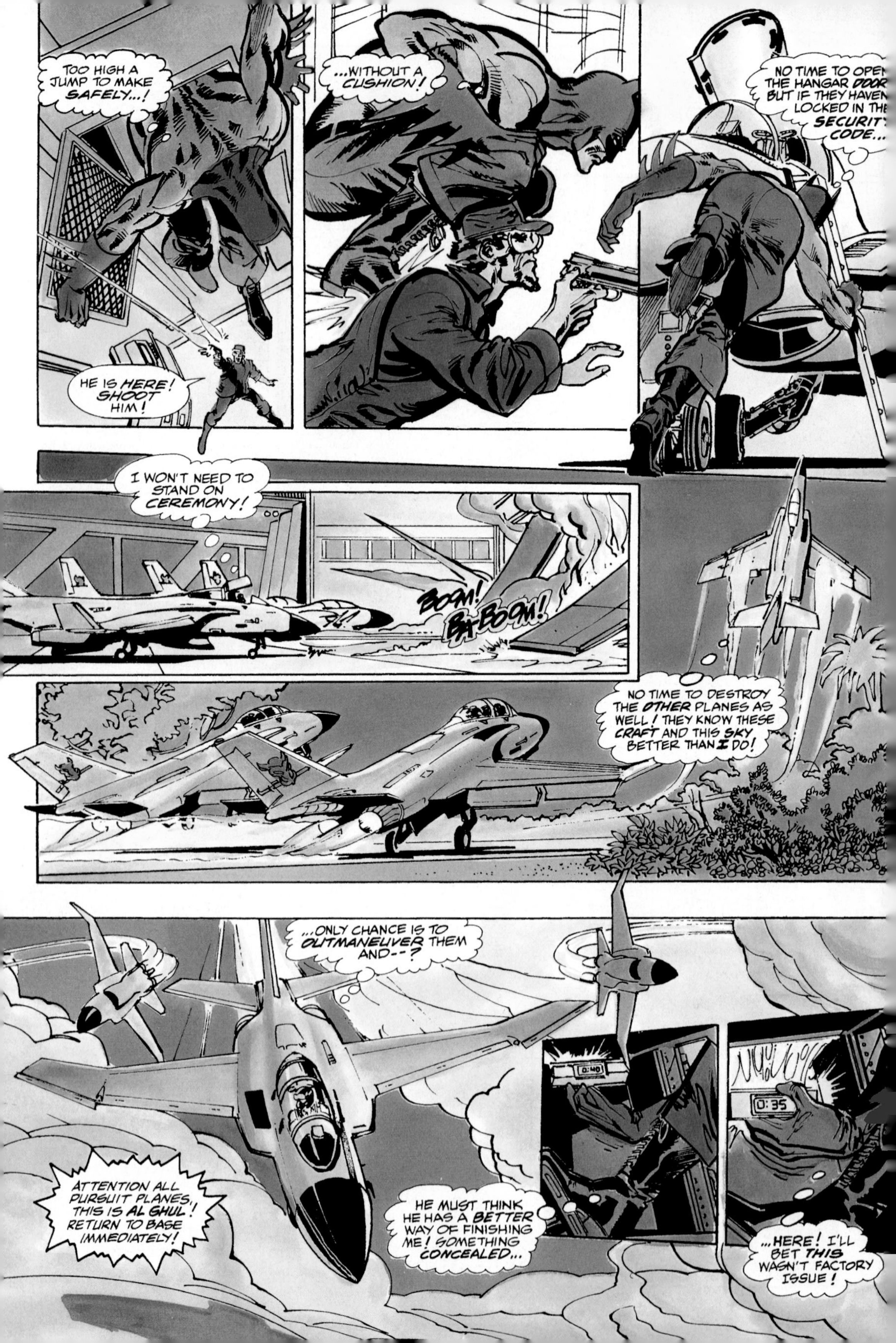
TOO HIGH A JUMP TO MAKE SAFELY...!
HE IS HERE! SHOOT HIM!
...WITHOUT A CUSHION!
NO TIME TO OPEN THE HANGAR DOORS BUT IF THEY HAVEN'T LOCKED IN THE SECURITY CODE...
I WON'T NEED TO STAND ON CEREMONY!
BOOM! BA-BOOM!
NO TIME TO DESTROY THE OTHER PLANES AS WELL! THEY KNOW THESE CRAFT AND THIS SKY BETTER THAN I DO!
...ONLY CHANCE IS TO OUTMANEUVER THEM AND--?
ATTENTION ALL PURSUIT PLANES, THIS IS AL GHUL! RETURN TO BASE IMMEDIATELY!
HE MUST THINK HE HAS A BETTER WAY OF FINISHING ME! SOMETHING CONCEALED...
0:40
0:35
...HERE! I'LL BET THIS WASN'T FACTORY ISSUE!

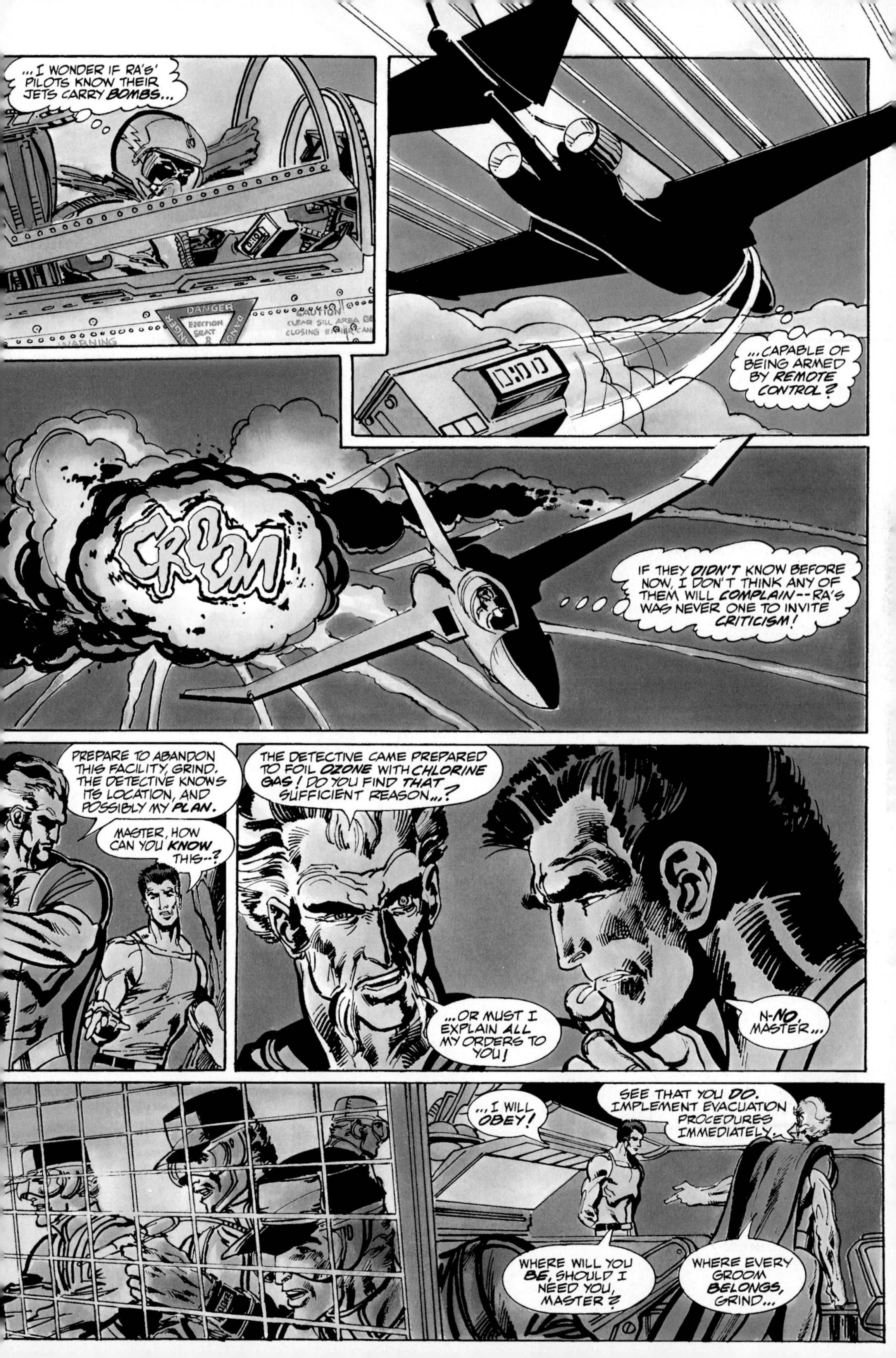
...I WONDER IF RA'S' PILOTS KNOW THEIR JETS CARRY BOMBS...
DANGER
EJECTION SEAT
CAUTION
WARNING
...CAPABLE OF BEING ARMED BY REMOTE CONTROL?
CROOM
IF THEY DIDN'T KNOW BEFORE NOW, I DON'T THINK ANY OF THEM WILL COMPLAIN--RA'S WAS NEVER ONE TO INVITE CRITICISM!
PREPARE TO ABANDON THIS FACILITY, GRIND. THE DETECTIVE KNOWS ITS LOCATION, AND POSSIBLY MY PLAN.
MASTER, HOW CAN YOU KNOW THIS--?
THE DETECTIVE CAME PREPARED TO FOIL OZONE WITH CHLORINE GAS! DO YOU FIND THAT SUFFICIENT REASON...?
...OR MUST I EXPLAIN ALL MY ORDERS TO YOU!
N-NO, MASTER...
...I WILL OBEY!
SEE THAT YOU DO. IMPLEMENT EVACUATION PROCEDURES IMMEDIATELY.
WHERE WILL YOU BE, SHOULD I NEED YOU, MASTER?
WHERE EVERY GROOM BELONGS, GRIND...

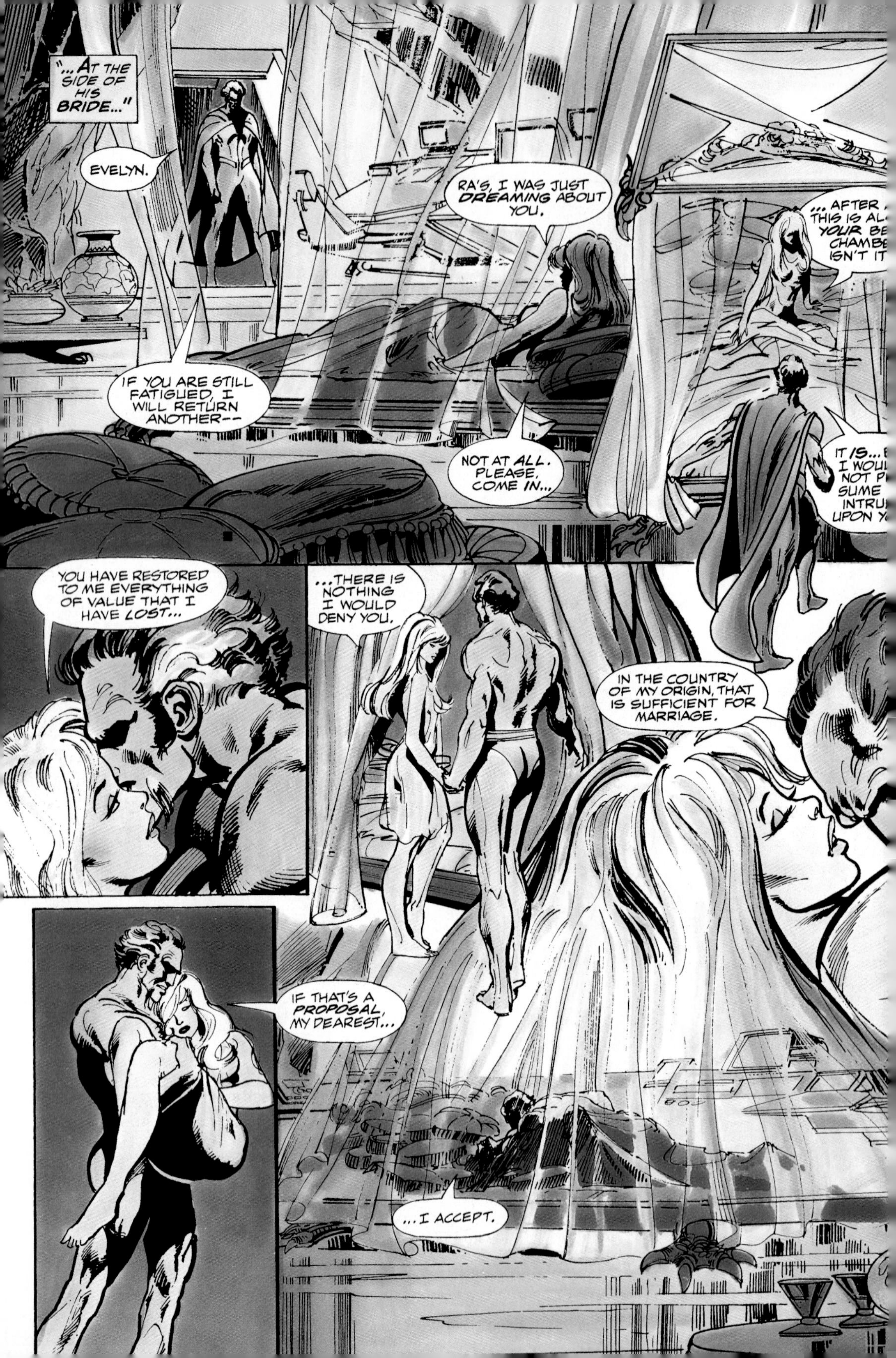
"...AT THE SIDE OF HIS BRIDE..."
EVELYN.
RA'S, I WAS JUST DREAMING ABOUT YOU.
...AFTER THIS IS AL YOUR BE CHAMBE ISN'T IT
IF YOU ARE STILL FATIGUED, I WILL RETURN ANOTHER--
NOT AT ALL. PLEASE, COME IN...
IT IS... I WOUL NOT P SUME INTRU UPON Y
YOU HAVE RESTORED TO ME EVERYTHING OF VALUE THAT I HAVE LOST...
...THERE IS NOTHING I WOULD DENY YOU.
IN THE COUNTRY OF MY ORIGIN, THAT IS SUFFICIENT FOR MARRIAGE.
IF THAT'S A PROPOSAL, MY DEAREST...
...I ACCEPT.

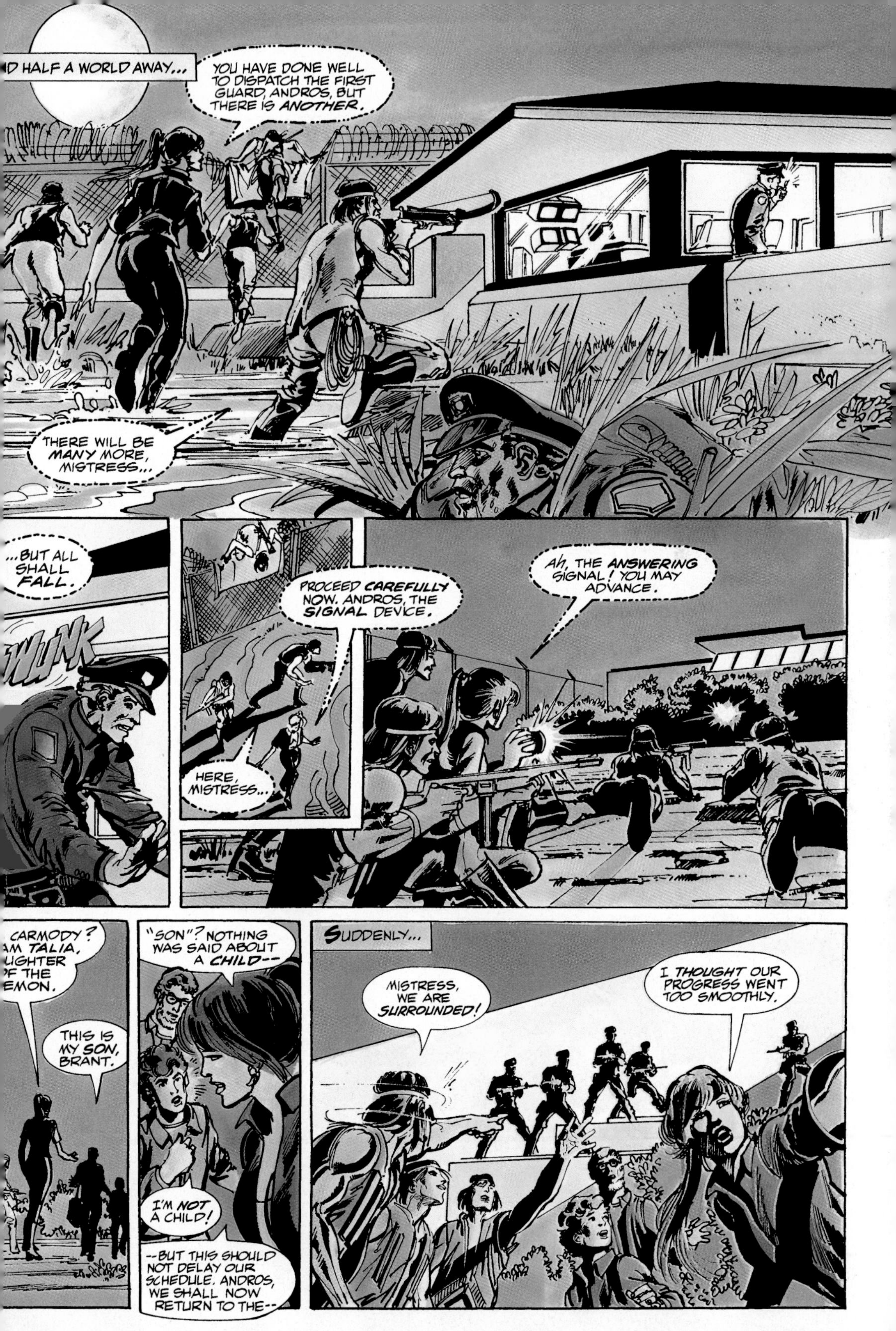
D HALF A WORLD AWAY...
YOU HAVE DONE WELL TO DISPATCH THE FIRST GUARD, ANDROS, BUT THERE IS ANOTHER.
THERE WILL BE MANY MORE, MISTRESS...
...BUT ALL SHALL FALL.
WUNK
PROCEED CAREFULLY NOW. ANDROS, THE SIGNAL DEVICE.
HERE, MISTRESS...
Ah, THE ANSWERING SIGNAL! YOU MAY ADVANCE.
CARMODY? AM TALIA, UGHTER OF THE EMON.
THIS IS MY SON, BRANT.
"SON"? NOTHING WAS SAID ABOUT A CHILD--
I'M NOT A CHILD!
--BUT THIS SHOULD NOT DELAY OUR SCHEDULE. ANDROS, WE SHALL NOW RETURN TO THE--
SUDDENLY...
MISTRESS, WE ARE SURROUNDED!
I THOUGHT OUR PROGRESS WENT TOO SMOOTHLY.

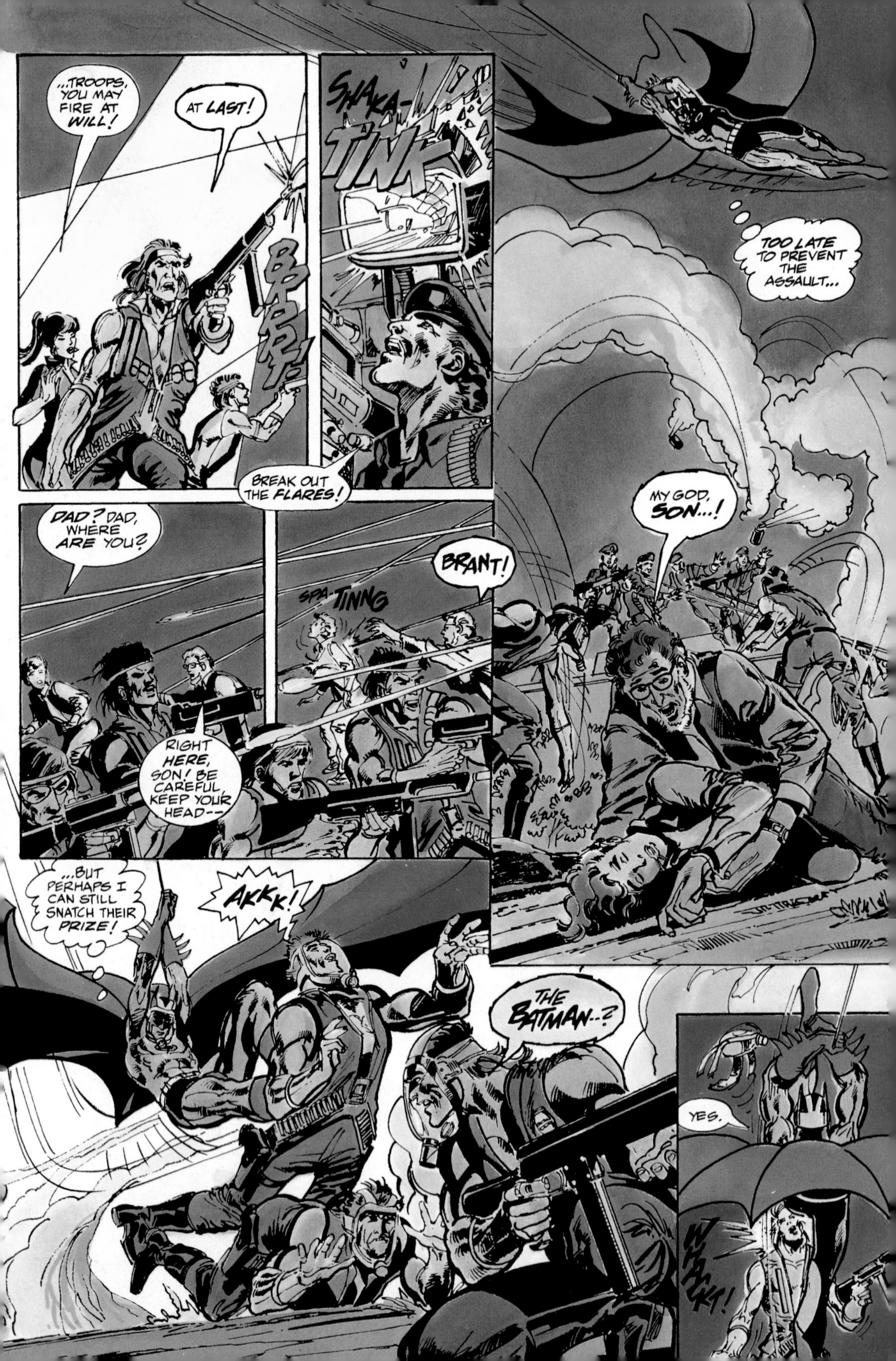

...TROOPS, YOU MAY FIRE AT WILL!
AT LAST!
BRRRT!
SHAKA-TINK
BREAK OUT THE FLARES!
TOO LATE TO PREVENT THE ASSAULT...
DAD? DAD, WHERE ARE YOU?
BRANT!
SPA-TINNG
RIGHT HERE, SON! BE CAREFUL, KEEP YOUR HEAD--
MY GOD, SON...!
...BUT PERHAPS I CAN STILL SNATCH THEIR PRIZE!
AKKK!
THE BATMAN..?
YES.
WHACK!

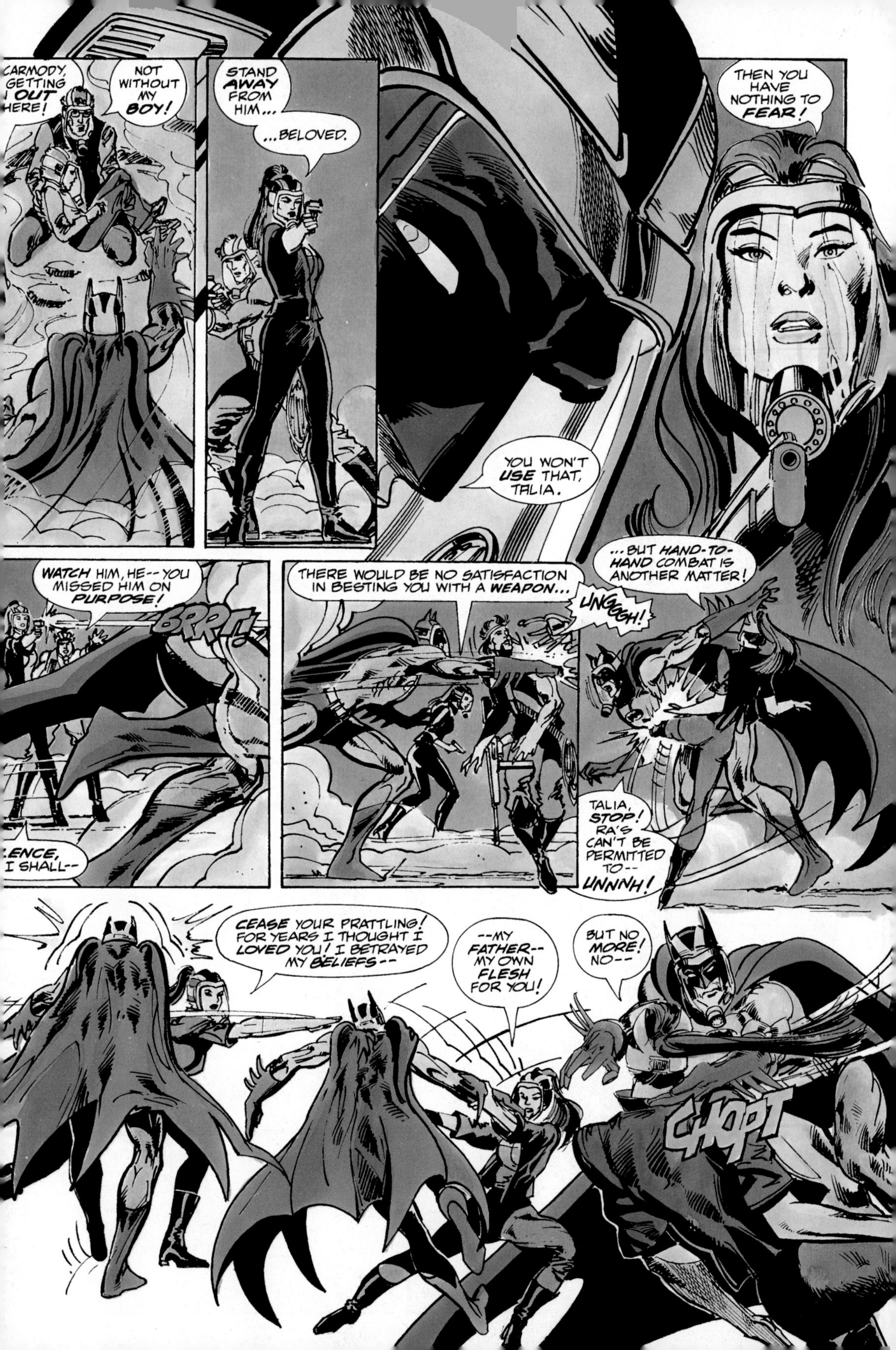

CARMODY, GETTING OUT HERE!
NOT WITHOUT MY BOY!
STAND AWAY FROM HIM...
...BELOVED.
THEN YOU HAVE NOTHING TO FEAR!
YOU WON'T USE THAT, TALIA.
WATCH HIM, HE--YOU MISSED HIM ON PURPOSE!
BRRT!
ENCE, I SHALL--
THERE WOULD BE NO SATISFACTION IN BESTING YOU WITH A WEAPON...
...BUT HAND-TO-HAND COMBAT IS ANOTHER MATTER!
UNGGGH!
TALIA, STOP! RA'S CAN'T BE PERMITTED TO--
UNNNH!
CEASE YOUR PRATTLING! FOR YEARS I THOUGHT I LOVED YOU! I BETRAYED MY BELIEFS--
--MY FATHER--MY OWN FLESH FOR YOU!
BUT NO MORE! NO--
CHOPT

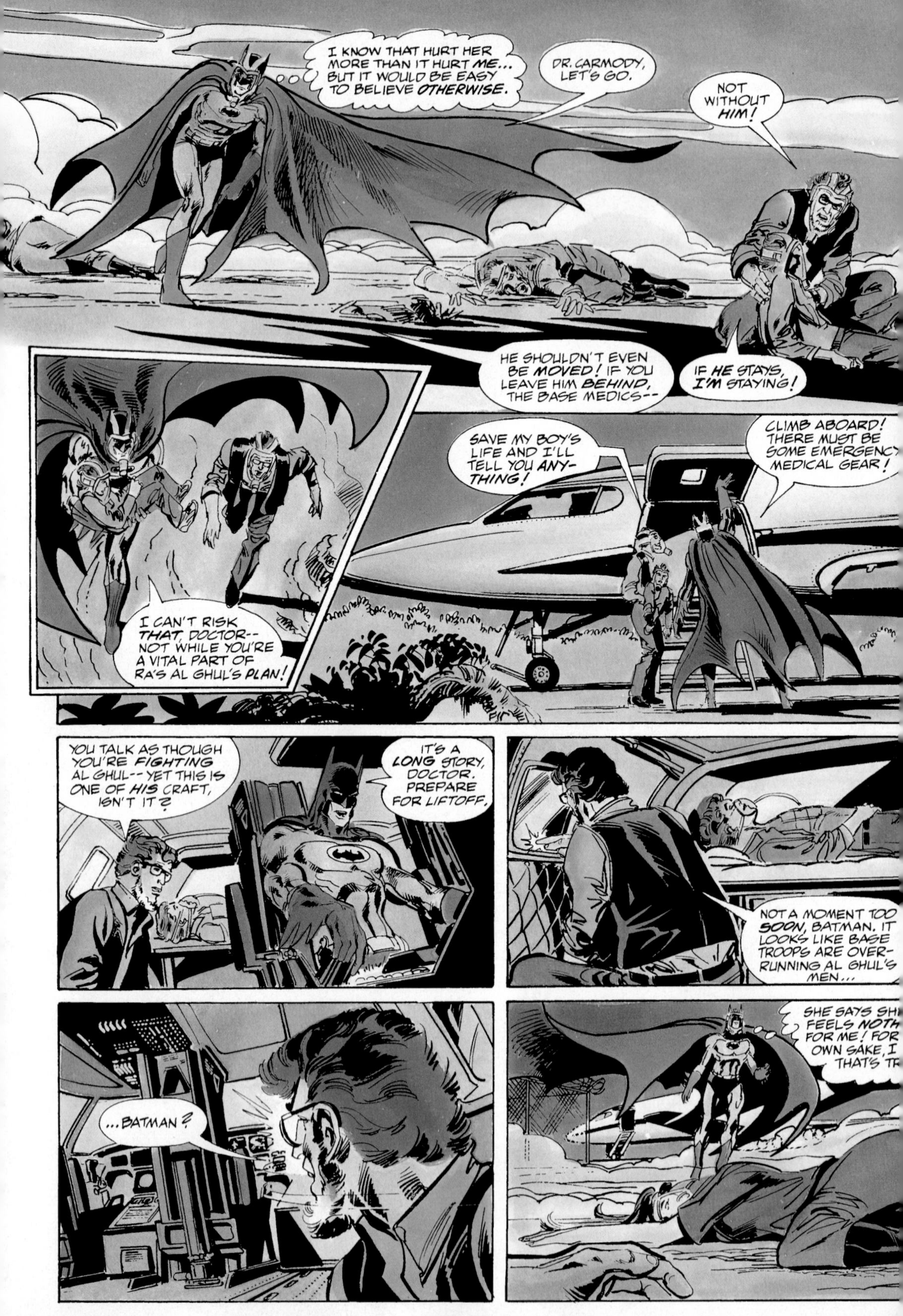

I KNOW THAT HURT HER MORE THAN IT HURT ME... BUT IT WOULD BE EASY TO BELIEVE OTHERWISE.
DR. CARMODY, LET'S GO.
NOT WITHOUT HIM!
HE SHOULDN'T EVEN BE MOVED! IF YOU LEAVE HIM BEHIND, THE BASE MEDICS--
IF HE STAYS, I'M STAYING!
I CAN'T RISK THAT, DOCTOR-- NOT WHILE YOU'RE A VITAL PART OF RA'S AL GHUL'S PLAN!
SAVE MY BOY'S LIFE AND I'LL TELL YOU ANY-THING!
CLIMB ABOARD! THERE MUST BE SOME EMERGENCY MEDICAL GEAR!
YOU TALK AS THOUGH YOU'RE FIGHTING AL GHUL-- YET THIS IS ONE OF HIS CRAFT, ISN'T IT?
IT'S A LONG STORY, DOCTOR. PREPARE FOR LIFTOFF.
NOT A MOMENT TOO SOON, BATMAN. IT LOOKS LIKE BASE TROOPS ARE OVER-RUNNING AL GHUL'S MEN...
...BATMAN?
SHE SAYS SH FEELS NOTH FOR ME! FOR OWN SAKE, I THAT'S TR

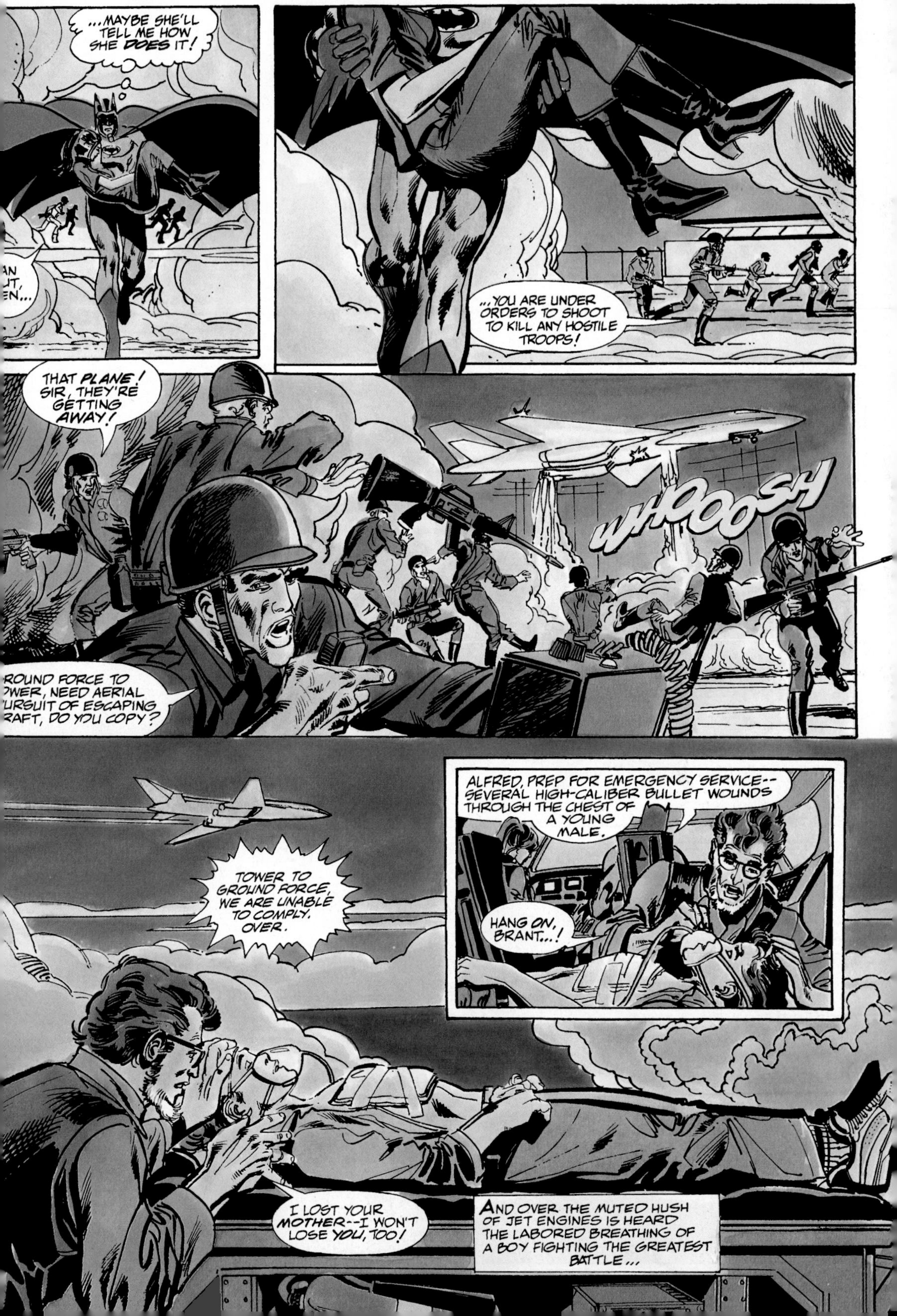
...MAYBE SHE'LL TELL ME HOW SHE DOES IT!
AN
UT,
EN...
...YOU ARE UNDER ORDERS TO SHOOT TO KILL ANY HOSTILE TROOPS!
THAT PLANE! SIR, THEY'RE GETTING AWAY!
WHOOOSH
ROUND FORCE TO
OWER, NEED AERIAL
URSUIT OF ESCAPING
RAFT, DO YOU COPY?
TOWER TO GROUND FORCE, WE ARE UNABLE TO COMPLY. OVER.
ALFRED, PREP FOR EMERGENCY SERVICE-- SEVERAL HIGH-CALIBER BULLET WOUNDS THROUGH THE CHEST OF A YOUNG MALE.
HANG ON, BRANT...!
I LOST YOUR MOTHER--I WON'T LOSE YOU, TOO!
AND OVER THE MUTED HUSH OF JET ENGINES IS HEARD THE LABORED BREATHING OF A BOY FIGHTING THE GREATEST BATTLE...

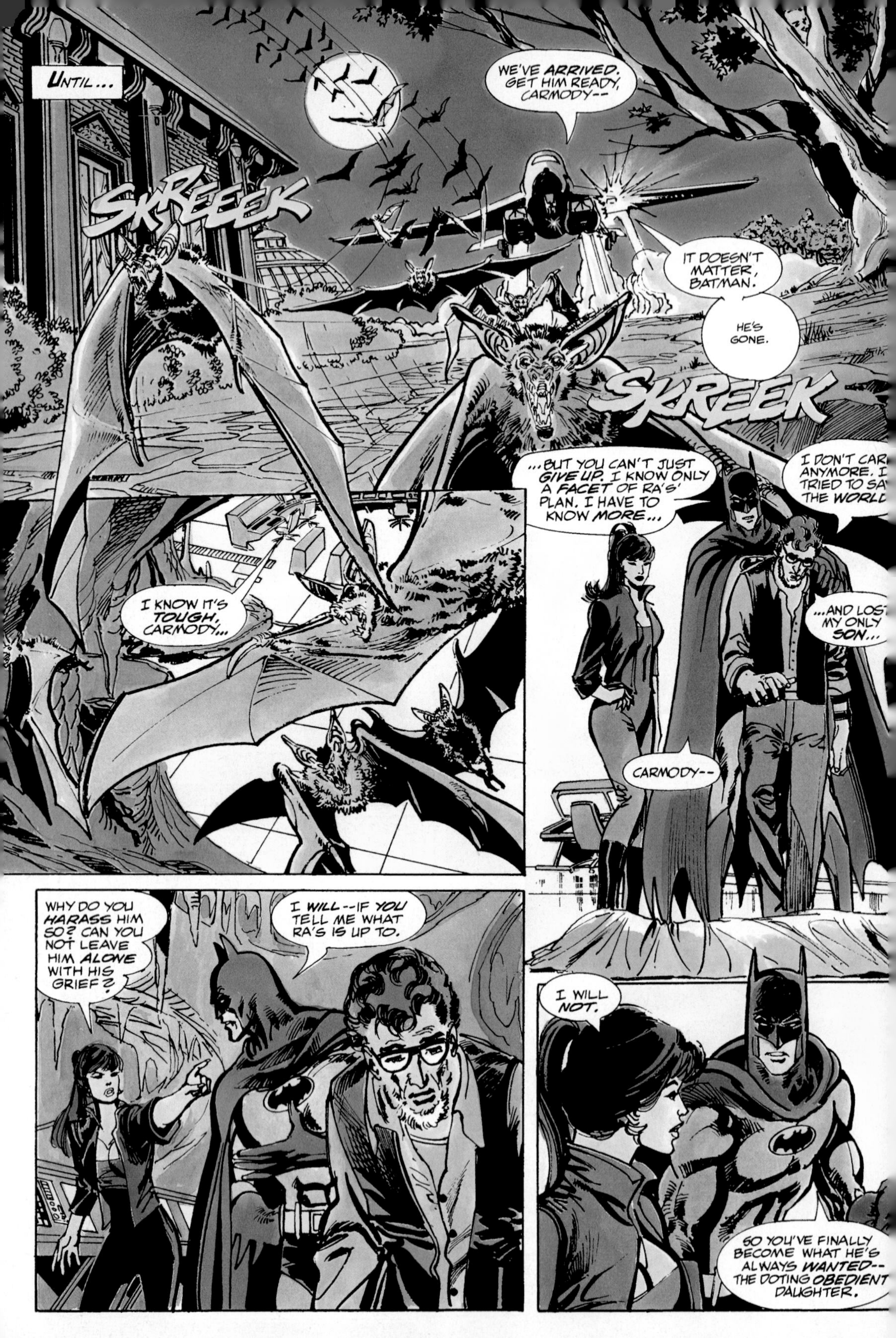
UNTIL...
WE'VE ARRIVED. GET HIM READY, CARMODY--
SKREEEK
IT DOESN'T MATTER, BATMAN.
HE'S GONE.
SKREEEK
I KNOW IT'S TOUGH, CARMODY...
...BUT YOU CAN'T JUST GIVE UP. I KNOW ONLY A FACET OF RA'S' PLAN. I HAVE TO KNOW MORE...
I DON'T CAR ANYMORE. I TRIED TO SA THE WORLD
...AND LOS MY ONLY SON...
CARMODY--
WHY DO YOU HARASS HIM SO? CAN YOU NOT LEAVE HIM ALONE WITH HIS GRIEF?
I WILL--IF YOU TELL ME WHAT RA'S IS UP TO.
I WILL NOT.
SO YOU'VE FINALLY BECOME WHAT HE'S ALWAYS WANTED-- THE DOTING OBEDIENT DAUGHTER.

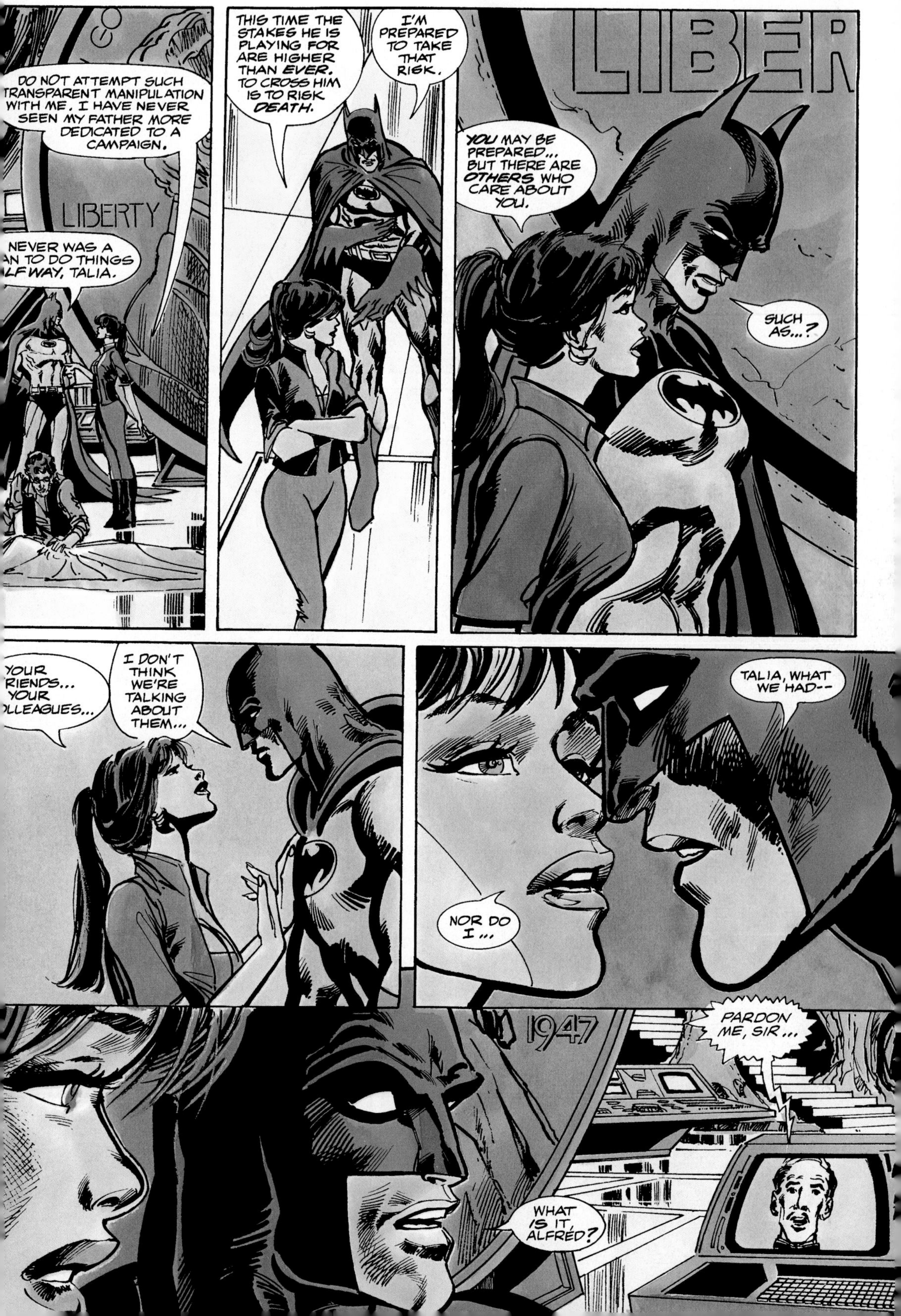
DO NOT ATTEMPT SUCH TRANSPARENT MANIPULATION WITH ME. I HAVE NEVER SEEN MY FATHER MORE DEDICATED TO A CAMPAIGN.
LIBERTY
NEVER WAS A AN TO DO THINGS LF WAY, TALIA.
THIS TIME THE STAKES HE IS PLAYING FOR ARE HIGHER THAN EVER. TO CROSS HIM IS TO RISK DEATH.
I'M PREPARED TO TAKE THAT RISK.
LIBER
YOU MAY BE PREPARED... BUT THERE ARE OTHERS WHO CARE ABOUT YOU.
SUCH AS...?
YOUR RIENDS... YOUR OLLEAGUES...
I DON'T THINK WE'RE TALKING ABOUT THEM...
TALIA, WHAT WE HAD--
NOR DO I...
1947
PARDON ME, SIR...
WHAT IS IT, ALFRED?

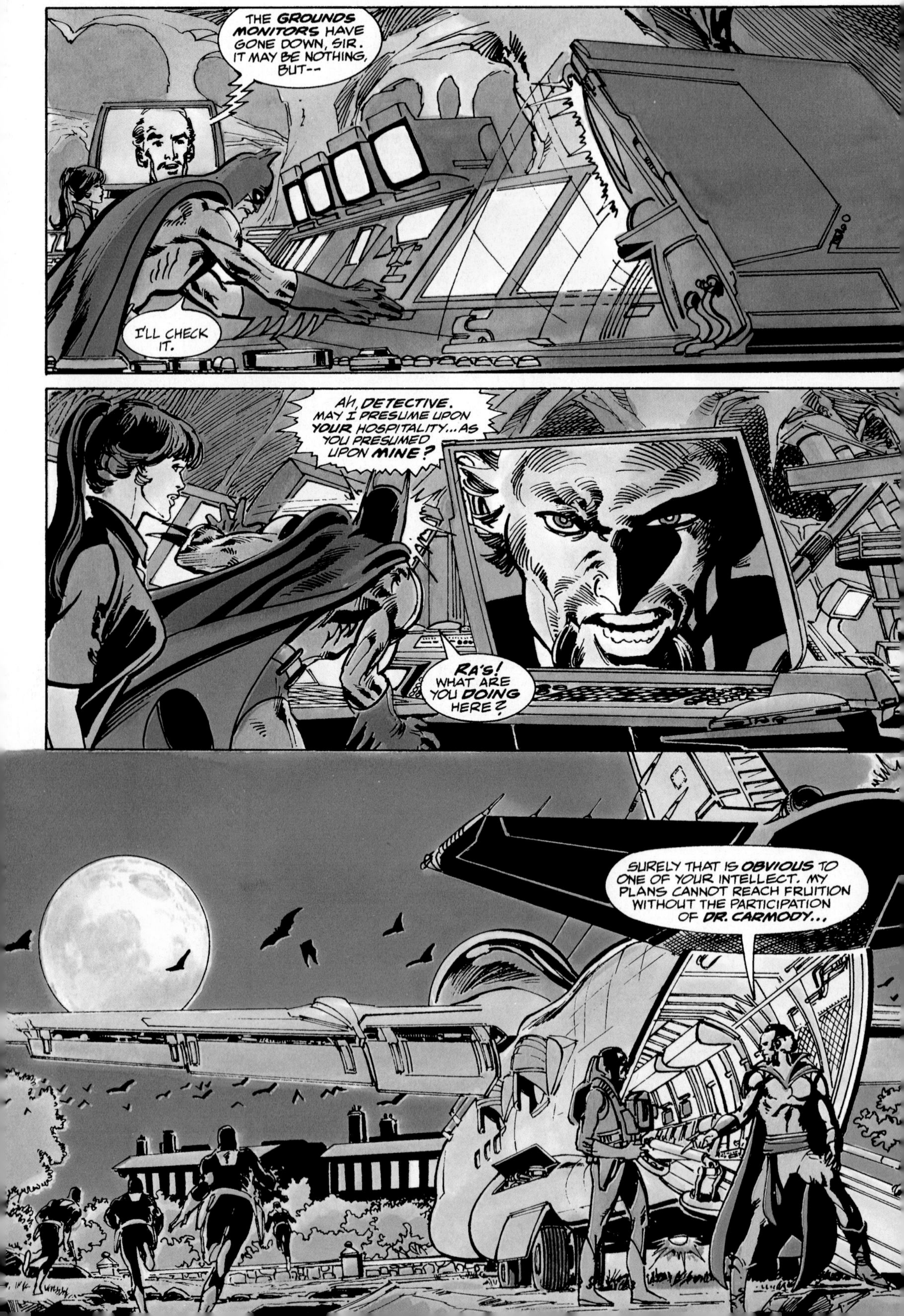
THE GROUNDS MONITORS HAVE GONE DOWN, SIR. IT MAY BE NOTHING, BUT--
I'LL CHECK IT.
AH, DETECTIVE. MAY I PRESUME UPON YOUR HOSPITALITY...AS YOU PRESUMED UPON MINE?
RA'S! WHAT ARE YOU DOING HERE?
SURELY THAT IS OBVIOUS TO ONE OF YOUR INTELLECT. MY PLANS CANNOT REACH FRUITION WITHOUT THE PARTICIPATION OF DR. CARMODY...

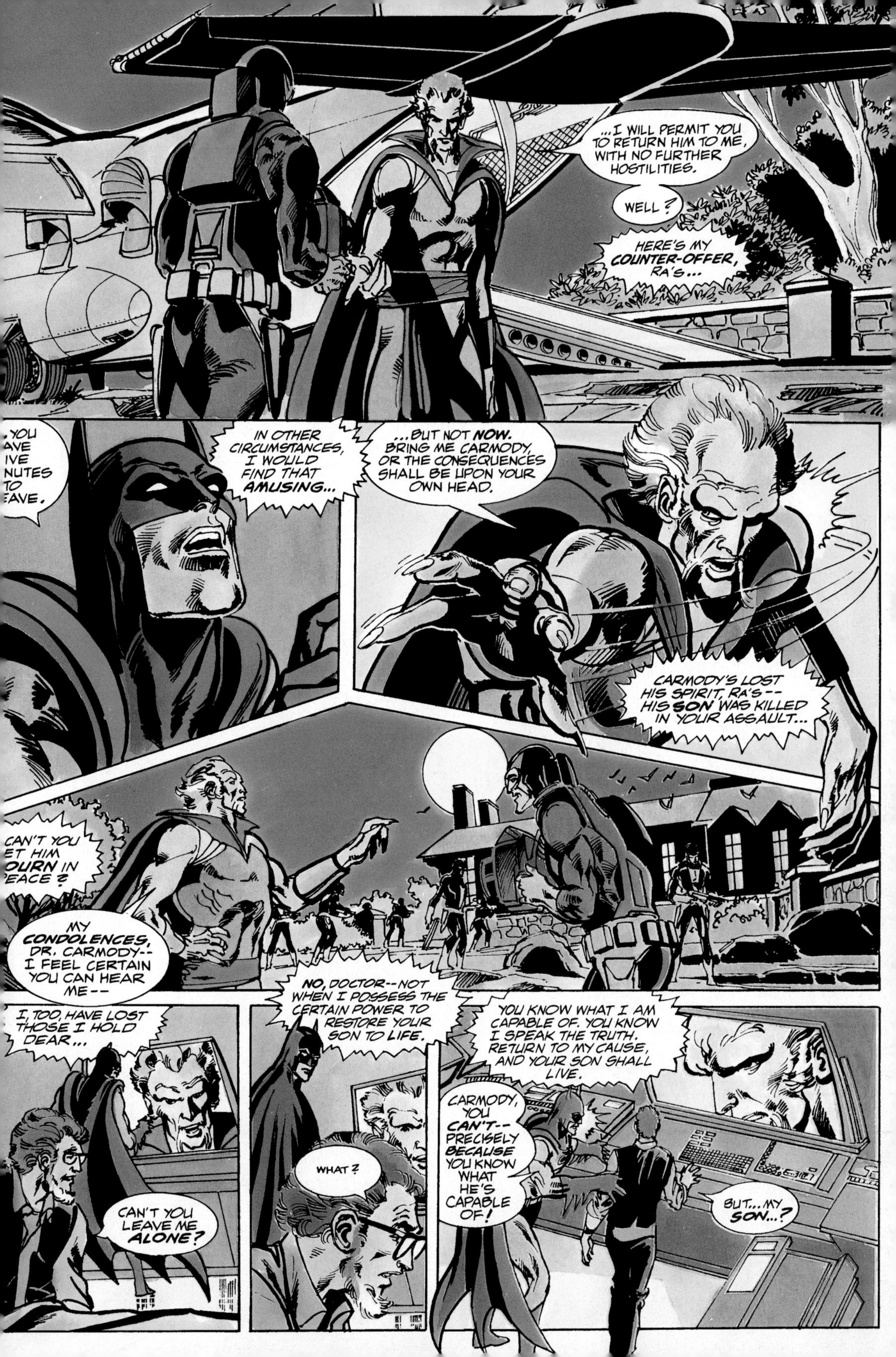
...I WILL PERMIT YOU TO RETURN HIM TO ME, WITH NO FURTHER HOSTILITIES.
WELL?
HERE'S MY COUNTER-OFFER, RA'S...
IN OTHER CIRCUMSTANCES, I WOULD FIND THAT AMUSING...
...BUT NOT NOW. BRING ME CARMODY, OR THE CONSEQUENCES SHALL BE UPON YOUR OWN HEAD.
CARMODY'S LOST HIS SPIRIT, RA'S-- HIS SON WAS KILLED IN YOUR ASSAULT...
MY CONDOLENCES, DR. CARMODY-- I FEEL CERTAIN YOU CAN HEAR ME--
I, TOO, HAVE LOST THOSE I HOLD DEAR...
CAN'T YOU LEAVE ME ALONE?
NO, DOCTOR--NOT WHEN I POSSESS THE CERTAIN POWER TO RESTORE YOUR SON TO LIFE.
WHAT?
YOU KNOW WHAT I AM CAPABLE OF. YOU KNOW I SPEAK THE TRUTH. RETURN TO MY CAUSE, AND YOUR SON SHALL LIVE.
CARMODY, YOU CAN'T-- PRECISELY BECAUSE YOU KNOW WHAT HE'S CAPABLE OF!
BUT...MY SON...?

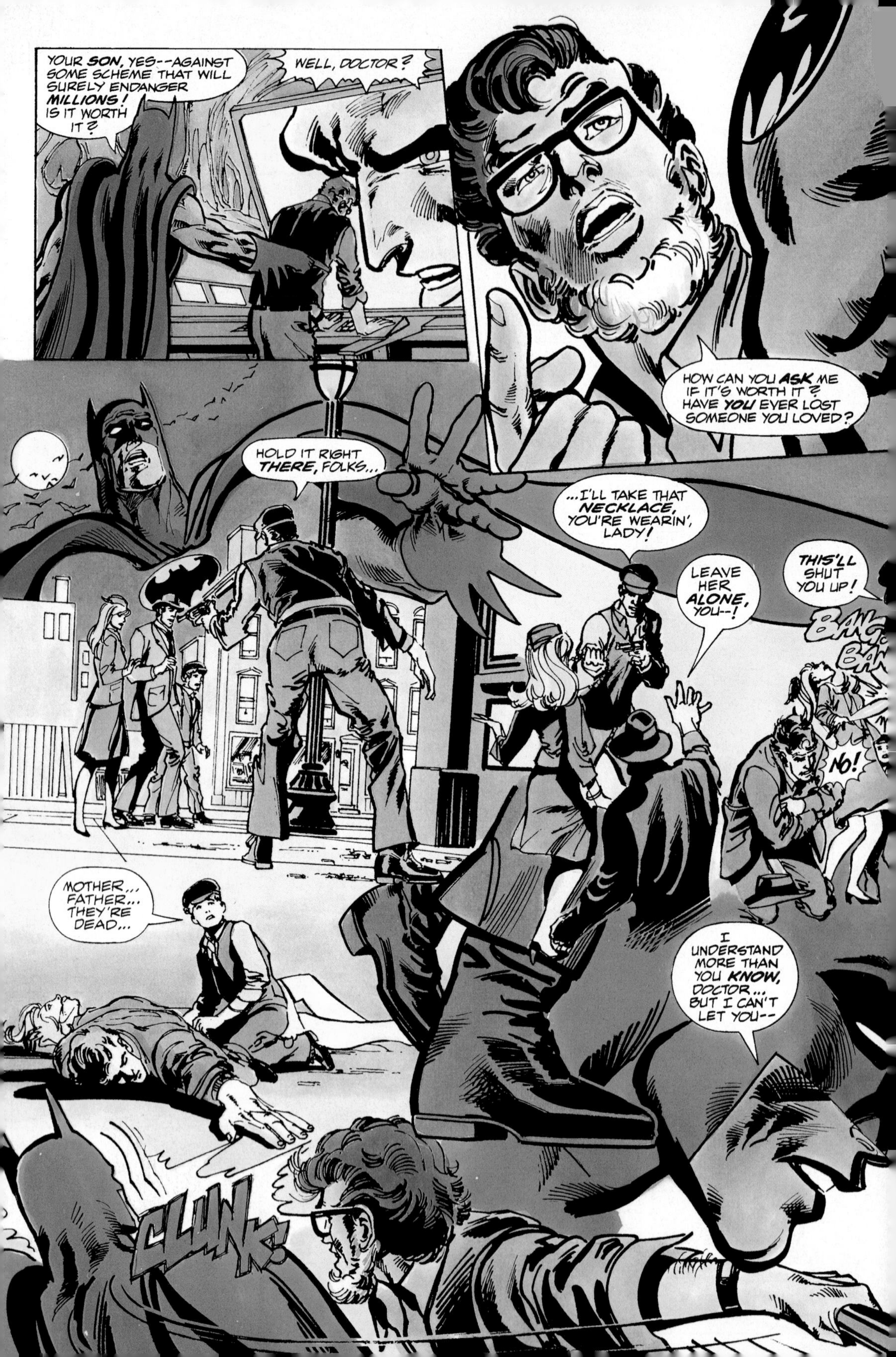

YOUR SON, YES--AGAINST SOME SCHEME THAT WILL SURELY ENDANGER MILLIONS! IS IT WORTH IT?
WELL, DOCTOR?
HOW CAN YOU ASK ME IF IT'S WORTH IT? HAVE YOU EVER LOST SOMEONE YOU LOVED?
HOLD IT RIGHT THERE, FOLKS...
...I'LL TAKE THAT NECKLACE, YOU'RE WEARIN', LADY!
LEAVE HER ALONE, YOU--!
THIS'LL SHUT YOU UP!
NO!
MOTHER... FATHER... THEY'RE DEAD...
I UNDERSTAND MORE THAN YOU KNOW, DOCTOR... BUT I CAN'T LET YOU--
CLUNK!

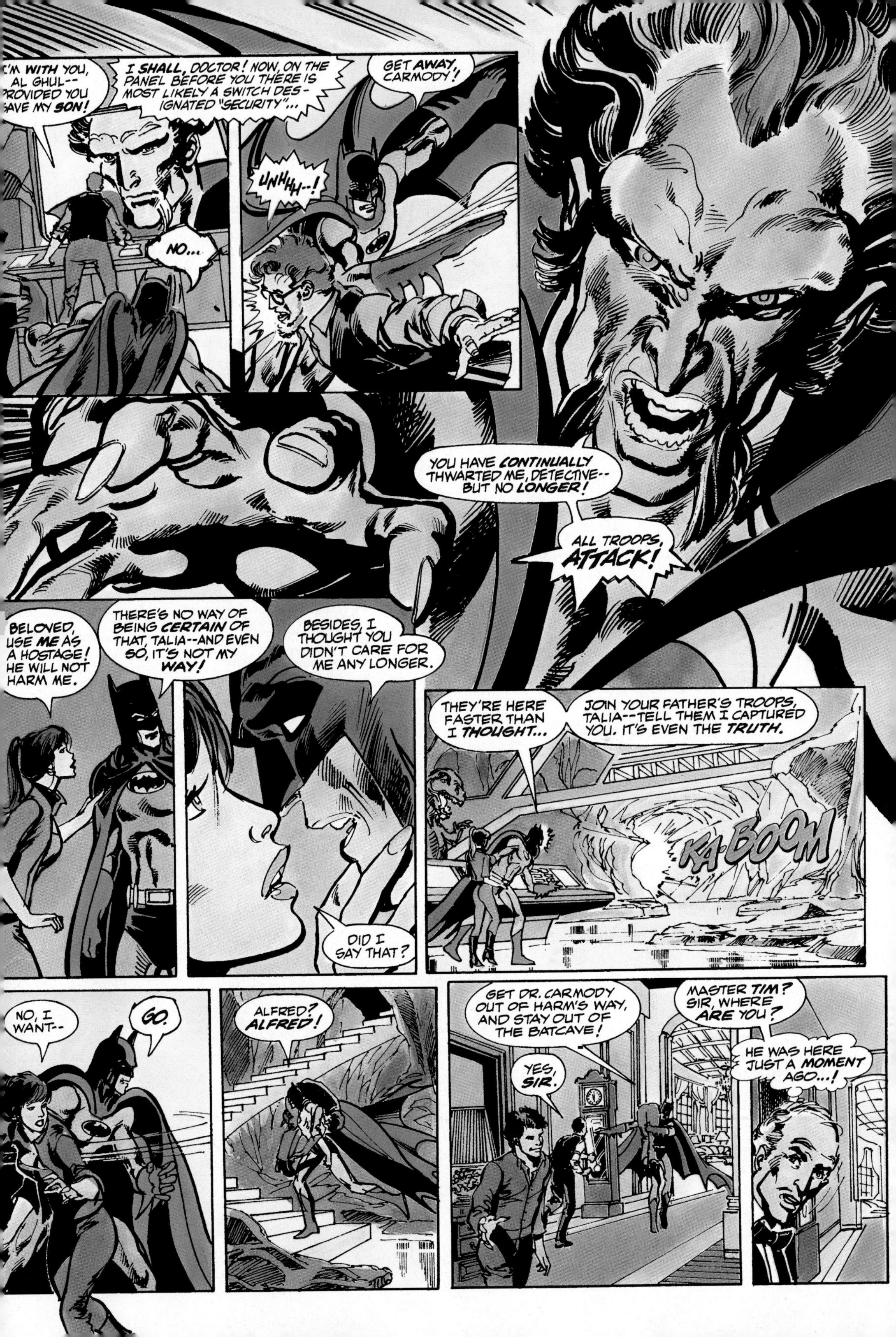
I'M WITH YOU, AL GHUL-- PROVIDED YOU SAVE MY SON!
I SHALL, DOCTOR! NOW, ON THE PANEL BEFORE YOU THERE IS MOST LIKELY A SWITCH DESIGNATED "SECURITY"...
NO...
GET AWAY, CARMODY!
UNHHH--!
YOU HAVE CONTINUALLY THWARTED ME, DETECTIVE-- BUT NO LONGER!
ALL TROOPS, ATTACK!
BELOVED, USE ME AS A HOSTAGE! HE WILL NOT HARM ME.
THERE'S NO WAY OF BEING CERTAIN OF THAT, TALIA--AND EVEN SO, IT'S NOT MY WAY!
BESIDES, I THOUGHT YOU DIDN'T CARE FOR ME ANY LONGER.
DID I SAY THAT?
THEY'RE HERE FASTER THAN I THOUGHT...
JOIN YOUR FATHER'S TROOPS, TALIA--TELL THEM I CAPTURED YOU. IT'S EVEN THE TRUTH.
KA-BOOM
NO, I WANT--
GO.
ALFRED? ALFRED!
GET DR. CARMODY OUT OF HARM'S WAY, AND STAY OUT OF THE BATCAVE!
YES, SIR.
MASTER TIM? SIR, WHERE ARE YOU?
HE WAS HERE JUST A MOMENT AGO...!

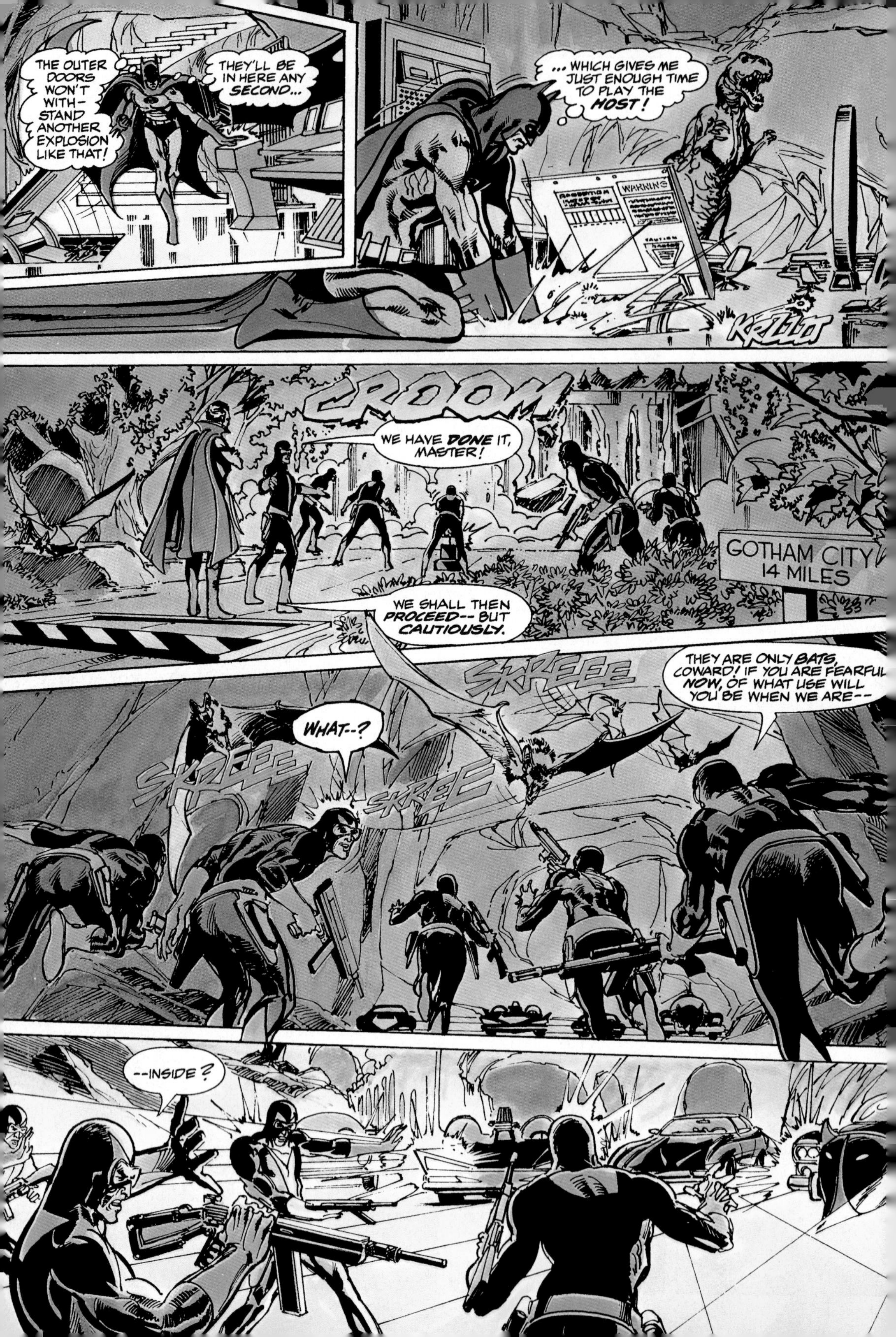
THE OUTER DOORS WON'T WITH-STAND ANOTHER EXPLOSION LIKE THAT!
THEY'LL BE IN HERE ANY SECOND...
...WHICH GIVES ME JUST ENOUGH TIME TO PLAY THE HOST!
WARNING
KRZZZT
CROOM
WE HAVE DONE IT, MASTER!
GOTHAM CITY 14 MILES
WE SHALL THEN PROCEED-- BUT CAUTIOUSLY.
SKREEE
THEY ARE ONLY BATS, COWARD! IF YOU ARE FEARFUL NOW, OF WHAT USE WILL YOU BE WHEN WE ARE--
WHAT--?
SKREEE
SKREE
--INSIDE?

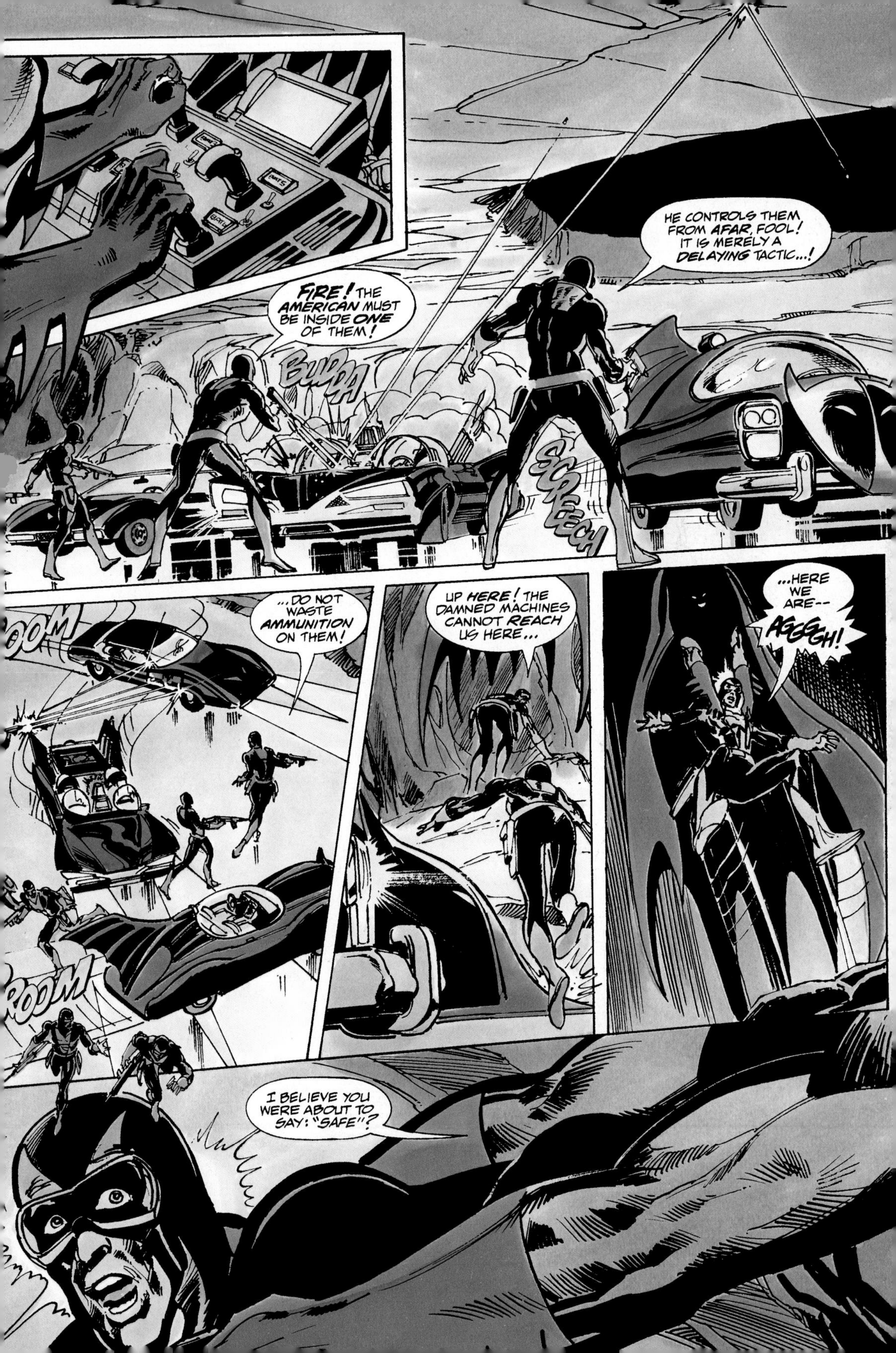
FIRE! THE AMERICAN MUST BE INSIDE ONE OF THEM!
BUDDA
HE CONTROLS THEM FROM AFAR, FOOL! IT IS MERELY A DELAYING TACTIC...!
SCREECH
...DO NOT WASTE AMMUNITION ON THEM!
ROOM
ROOM
UP HERE! THE DAMNED MACHINES CANNOT REACH US HERE...
...HERE WE ARE--
AGGGGH!
I BELIEVE YOU WERE ABOUT TO SAY: "SAFE"?

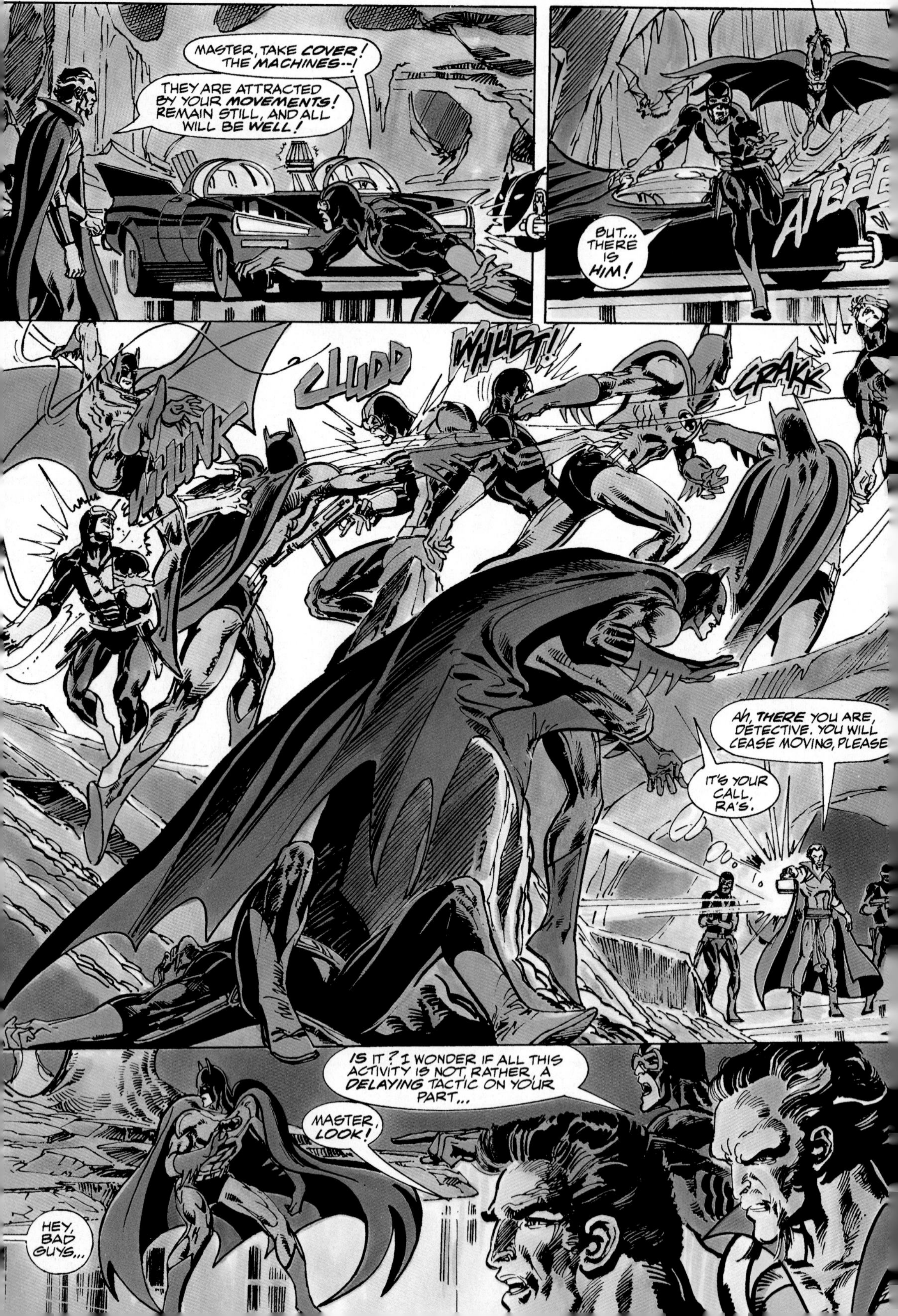
MASTER, TAKE COVER! THE MACHINES--!
THEY ARE ATTRACTED BY YOUR MOVEMENTS! REMAIN STILL, AND ALL WILL BE WELL!
BUT... THERE IS HIM!
AIEEE
WHUNK
CLUDD
WHUDT!!
CRAKK
AH, THERE YOU ARE, DETECTIVE. YOU WILL CEASE MOVING, PLEASE
IT'S YOUR CALL, RA'S.
IS IT? I WONDER IF ALL THIS ACTIVITY IS NOT, RATHER, A DELAYING TACTIC ON YOUR PART...
MASTER, LOOK!
HEY, BAD GUYS...

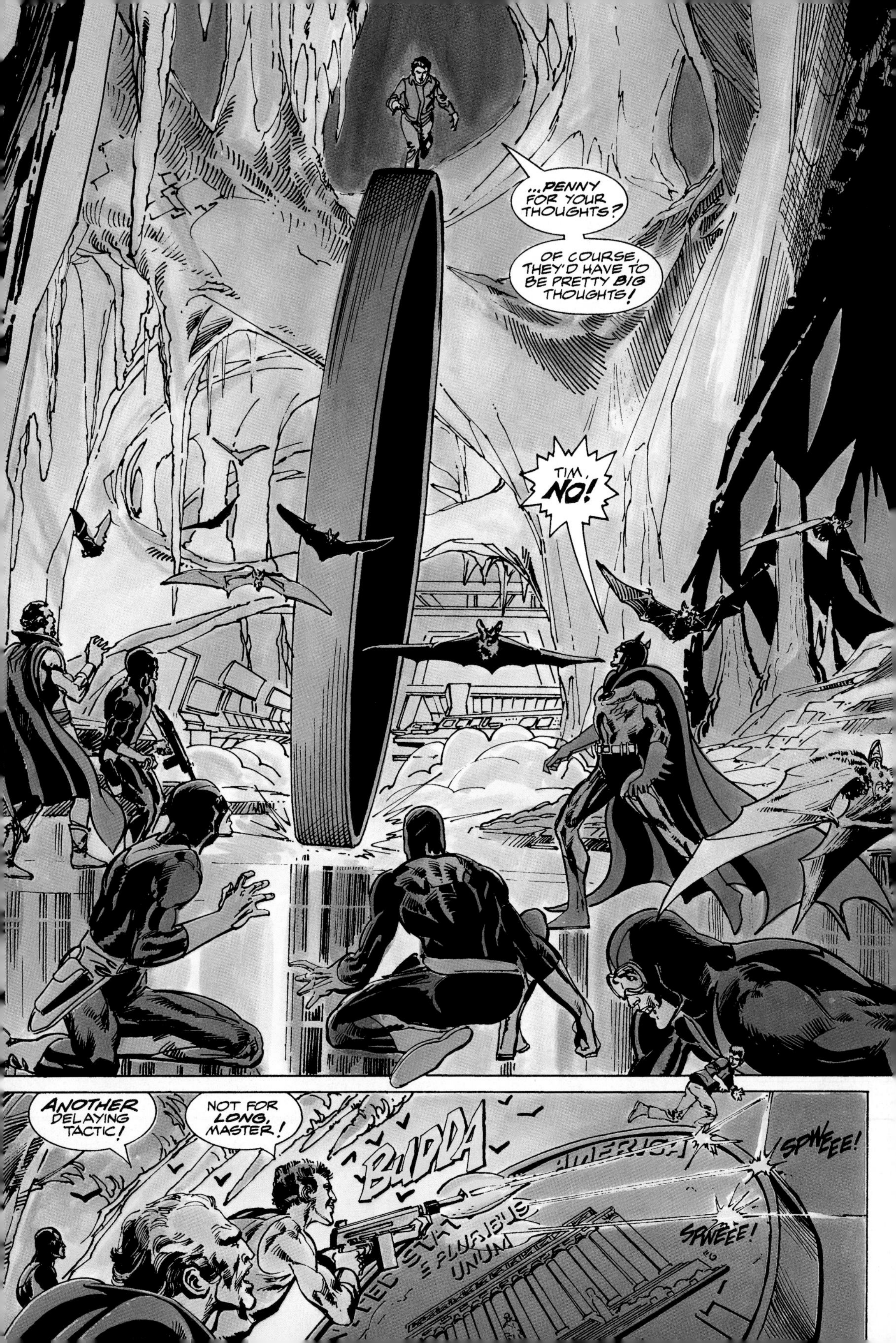

...PENNY FOR YOUR THOUGHTS?
OF COURSE, THEY'D HAVE TO BE PRETTY BIG THOUGHTS!
TIM, NO!
ANOTHER DELAYING TACTIC!
NOT FOR LONG, MASTER!
BUDDA
SPWEEE!
SPWEEE!
E PLURIBUS UNUM

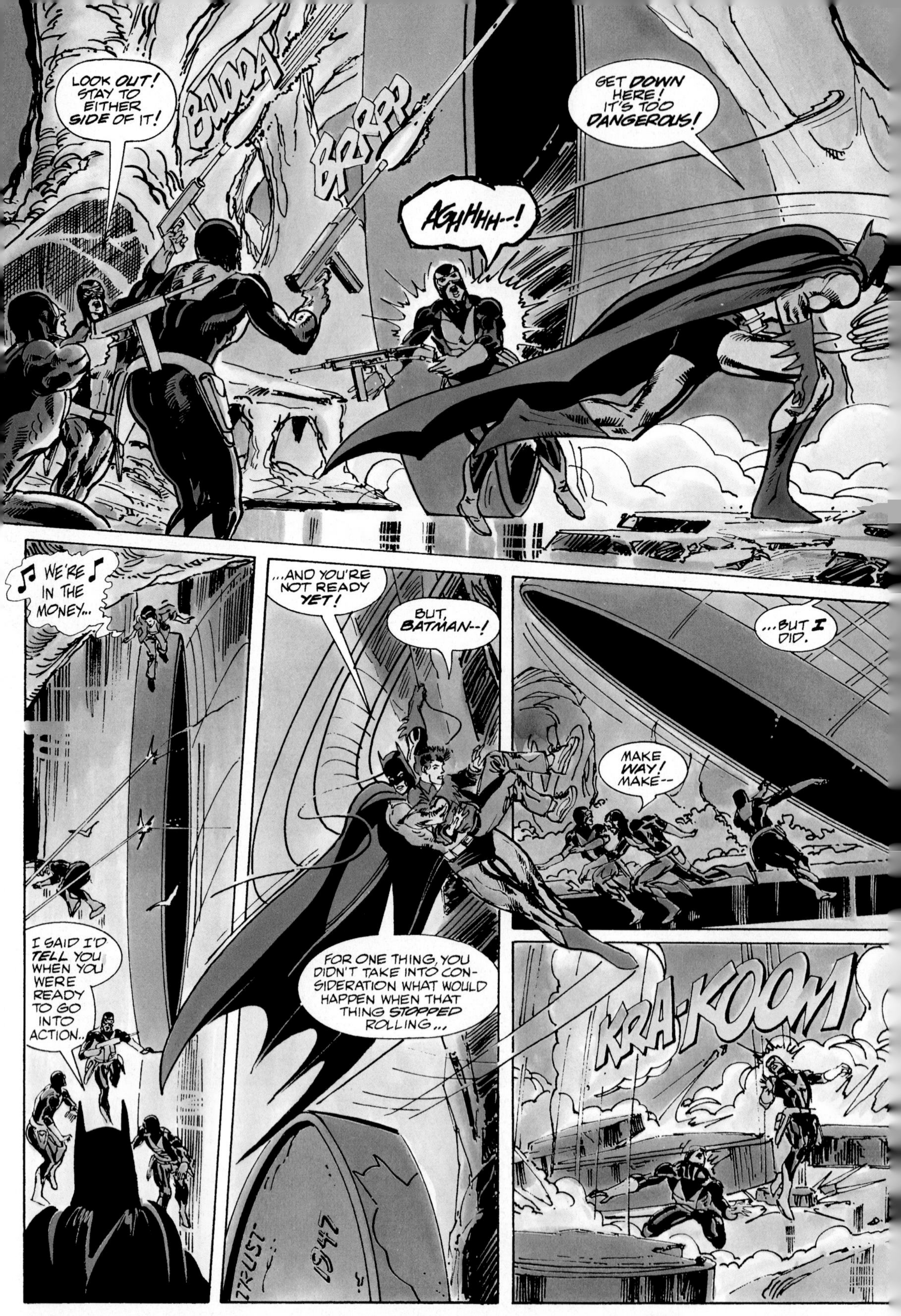

LOOK OUT! STAY TO EITHER SIDE OF IT!
BUDDA!
BRRRP.
GET DOWN HERE! IT'S TOO DANGEROUS!
AGHHHH--!
♪ WE'RE ♪ IN THE MONEY...
...AND YOU'RE NOT READY YET!
BUT, BATMAN--!
...BUT I DID.
MAKE WAY! MAKE--
I SAID I'D TELL YOU WHEN YOU WERE READY TO GO INTO ACTION...
FOR ONE THING, YOU DIDN'T TAKE INTO CONSIDERATION WHAT WOULD HAPPEN WHEN THAT THING STOPPED ROLLING...
KRA-KOOM
TRUST
1947

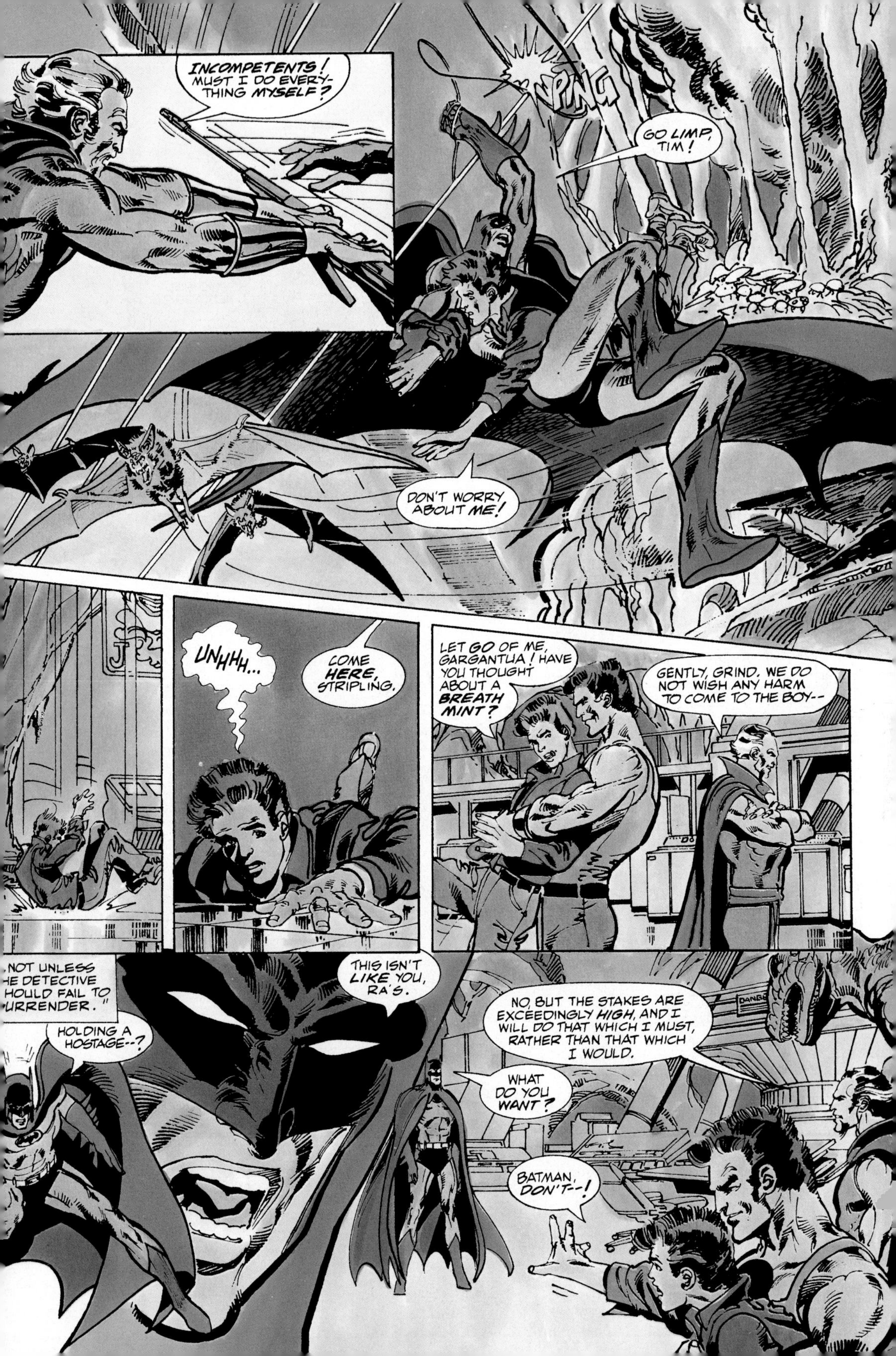
INCOMPETENTS! MUST I DO EVERYTHING MYSELF?
PING
GO LIMP, TIM!
DON'T WORRY ABOUT ME!
UNHHH...
COME HERE, STRIPLING.
LET GO OF ME, GARGANTUA! HAVE YOU THOUGHT ABOUT A BREATH MINT?
GENTLY, GRIND. WE DO NOT WISH ANY HARM TO COME TO THE BOY--
...NOT UNLESS THE DETECTIVE SHOULD FAIL TO SURRENDER."
HOLDING A HOSTAGE--?
THIS ISN'T LIKE YOU, RA'S.
NO, BUT THE STAKES ARE EXCEEDINGLY HIGH, AND I WILL DO THAT WHICH I MUST, RATHER THAN THAT WHICH I WOULD.
WHAT DO YOU WANT?
BATMAN, DON'T--!

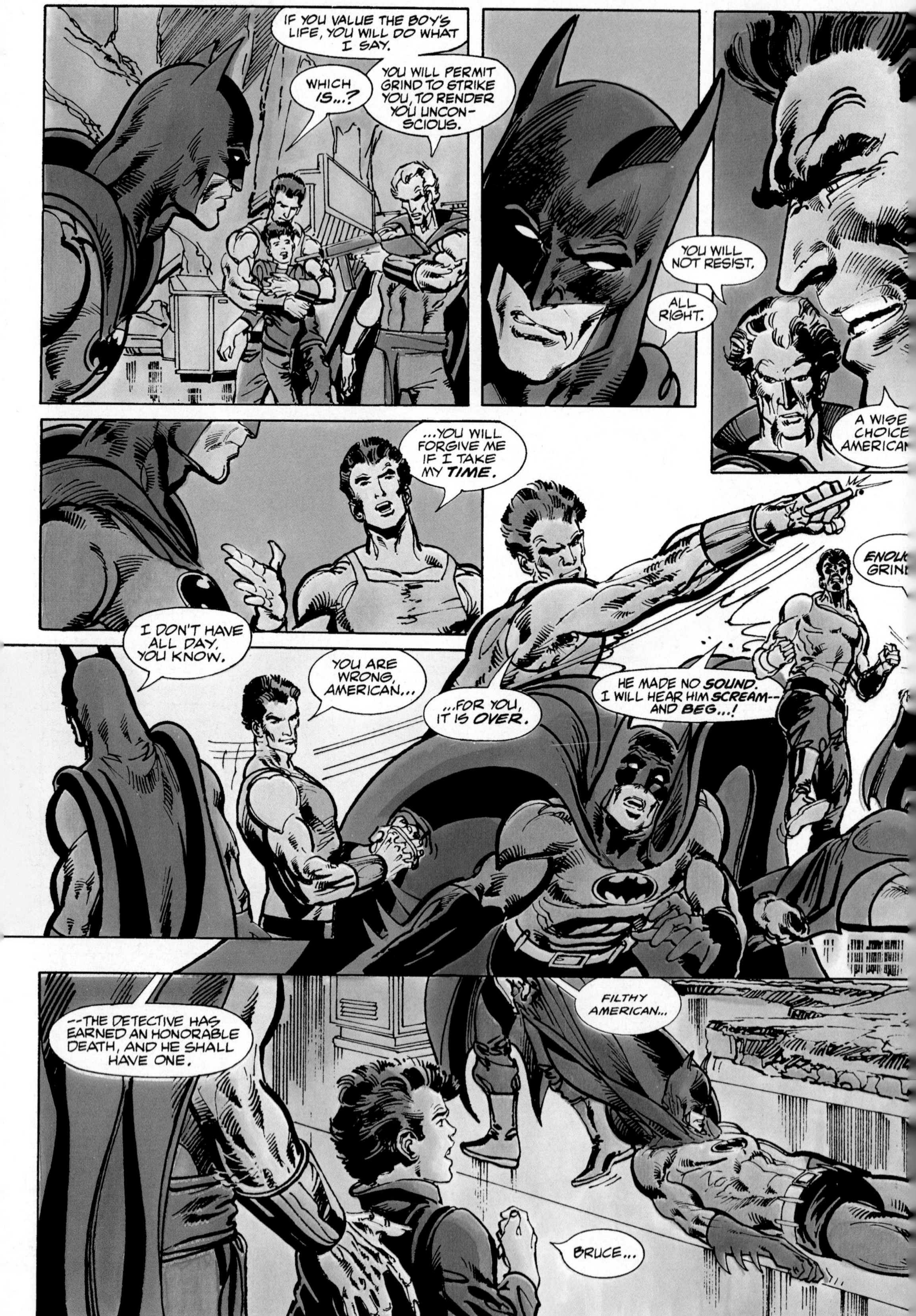

IF YOU VALUE THE BOY'S LIFE, YOU WILL DO WHAT I SAY.
WHICH IS...?
YOU WILL PERMIT GRIND TO STRIKE YOU, TO RENDER YOU UNCONSCIOUS.
YOU WILL NOT RESIST.
ALL RIGHT.
A WISE CHOICE AMERICAN
...YOU WILL FORGIVE ME IF I TAKE MY TIME.
I DON'T HAVE ALL DAY, YOU KNOW.
YOU ARE WRONG, AMERICAN...
...FOR YOU, IT IS OVER.
HE MADE NO SOUND. I WILL HEAR HIM SCREAM--AND BEG...!
FILTHY AMERICAN...
--THE DETECTIVE HAS EARNED AN HONORABLE DEATH, AND HE SHALL HAVE ONE.
BRUCE...

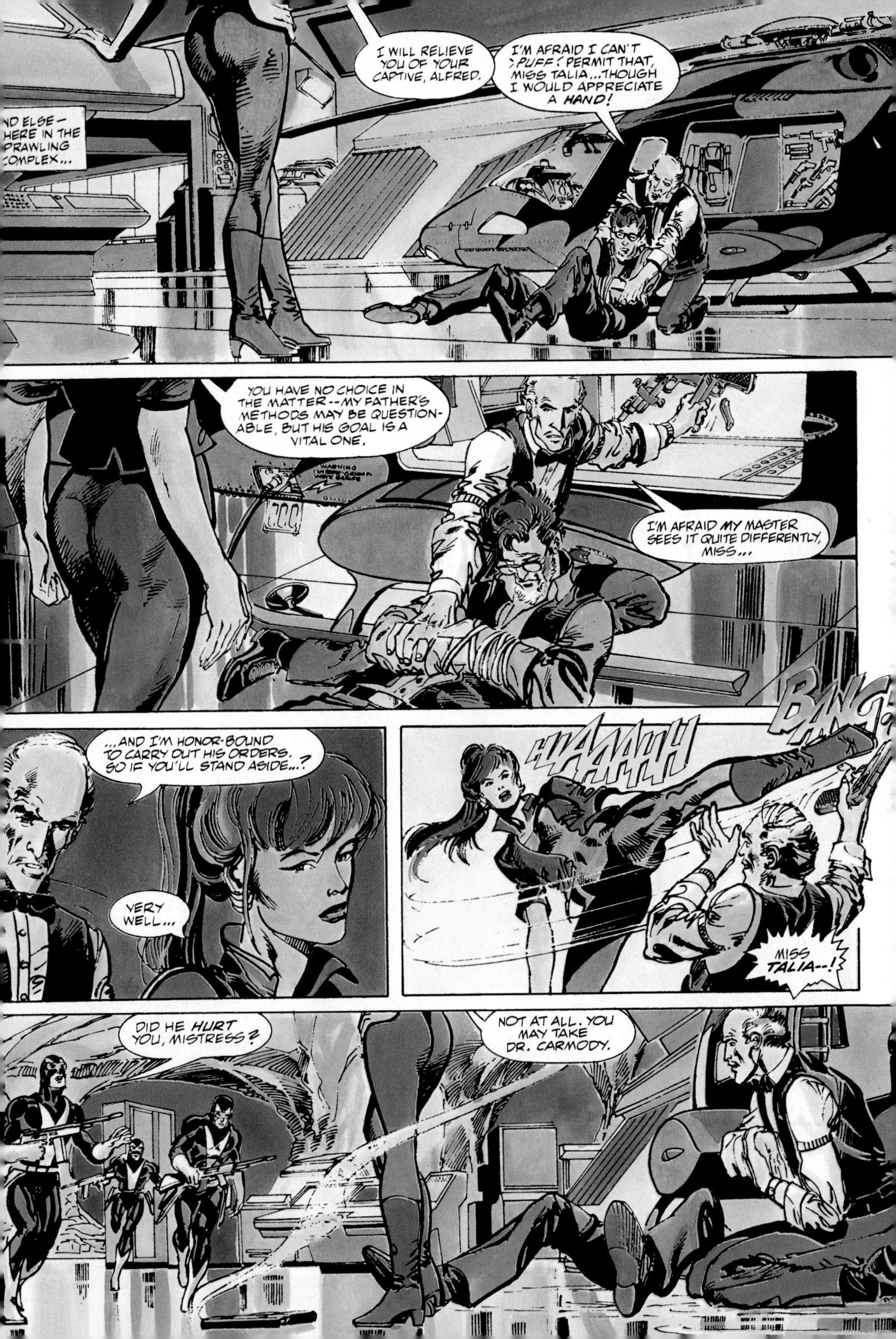
ND ELSE— HERE IN THE PRAWLING COMPLEX...
I WILL RELIEVE YOU OF YOUR CAPTIVE, ALFRED.
I'M AFRAID I CAN'T *PUFF* PERMIT THAT, MISS TALIA...THOUGH I WOULD APPRECIATE A HAND!
YOU HAVE NO CHOICE IN THE MATTER--MY FATHER'S METHODS MAY BE QUESTIONABLE, BUT HIS GOAL IS A VITAL ONE.
I'M AFRAID MY MASTER SEES IT QUITE DIFFERENTLY, MISS...
...AND I'M HONOR-BOUND TO CARRY OUT HIS ORDERS. SO IF YOU'LL STAND ASIDE...?
VERY WELL...
HWAAAAH
BANG
MISS TALIA--!
DID HE HURT YOU, MISTRESS?
NOT AT ALL. YOU MAY TAKE DR. CARMODY.

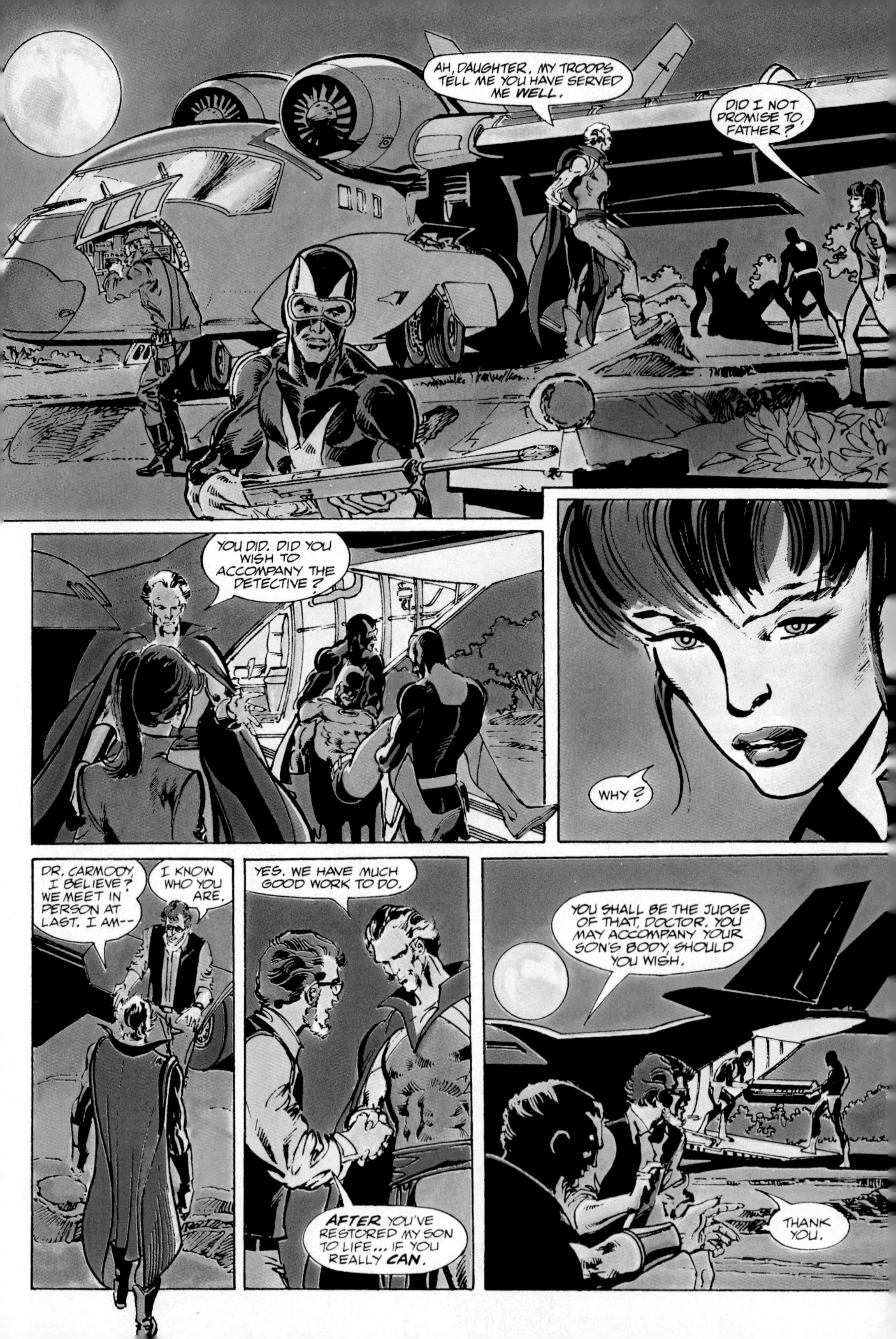

AH, DAUGHTER. MY TROOPS TELL ME YOU HAVE SERVED ME WELL.
DID I NOT PROMISE TO, FATHER?
YOU DID. DID YOU WISH TO ACCOMPANY THE DETECTIVE?
WHY?
DR. CARMODY, I BELIEVE? WE MEET IN PERSON AT LAST. I AM--
I KNOW WHO YOU ARE.
YES. WE HAVE MUCH GOOD WORK TO DO.
AFTER YOU'VE RESTORED MY SON TO LIFE... IF YOU REALLY CAN.
YOU SHALL BE THE JUDGE OF THAT, DOCTOR. YOU MAY ACCOMPANY YOUR SON'S BODY, SHOULD YOU WISH.
THANK YOU.

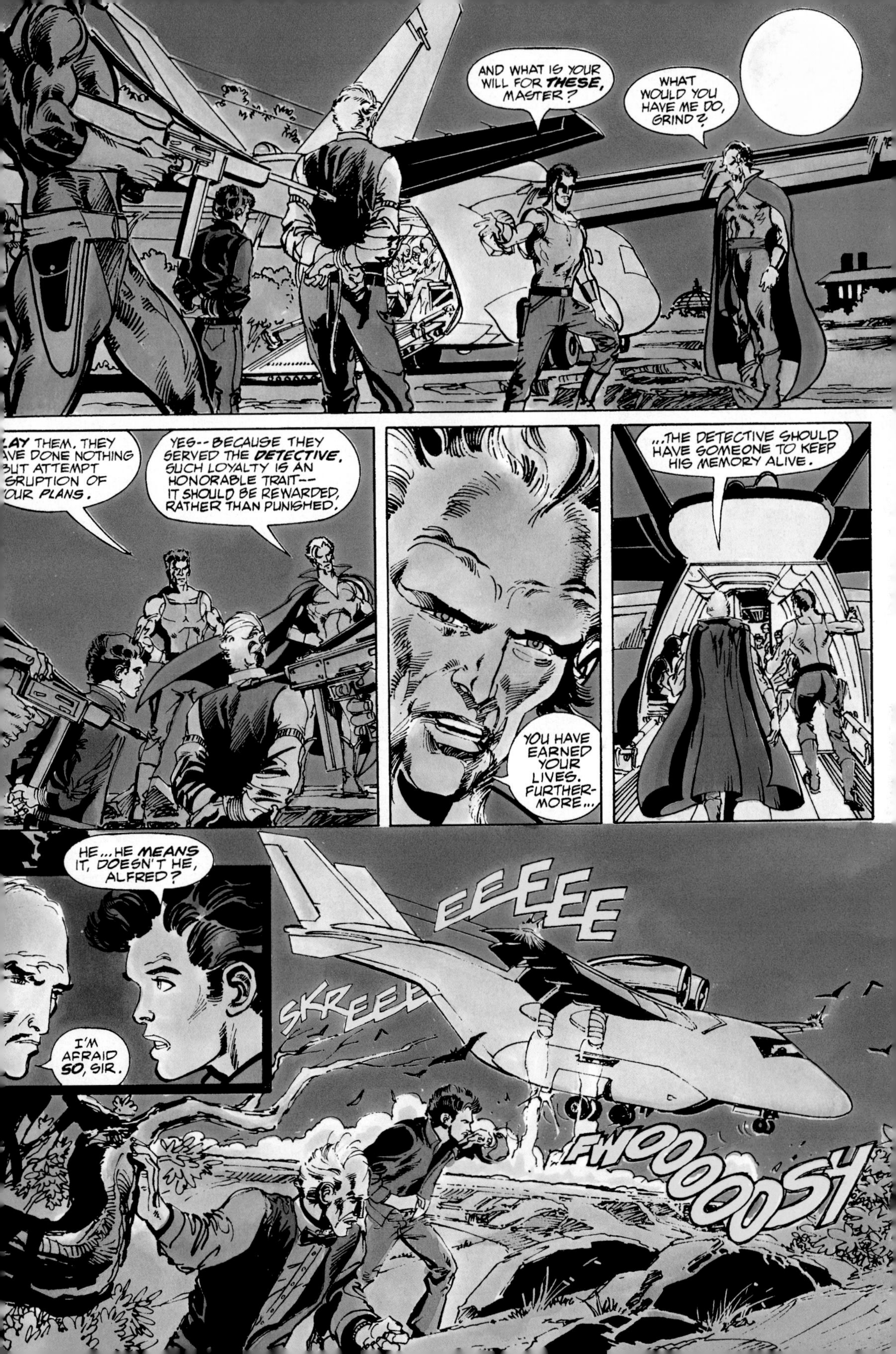
AND WHAT IS YOUR WILL FOR THESE, MASTER?
WHAT WOULD YOU HAVE ME DO, GRIND?
...LAY THEM. THEY ...AVE DONE NOTHING ...BUT ATTEMPT ...SRUPTION OF ...OUR PLANS.
YES-- BECAUSE THEY SERVED THE DETECTIVE. SUCH LOYALTY IS AN HONORABLE TRAIT-- IT SHOULD BE REWARDED, RATHER THAN PUNISHED.
YOU HAVE EARNED YOUR LIVES. FURTHER-MORE...
...THE DETECTIVE SHOULD HAVE SOMEONE TO KEEP HIS MEMORY ALIVE.
HE...HE MEANS IT, DOESN'T HE, ALFRED?
I'M AFRAID SO, SIR.
EEEEEE
SKREEEE
FWOOOOOOSH

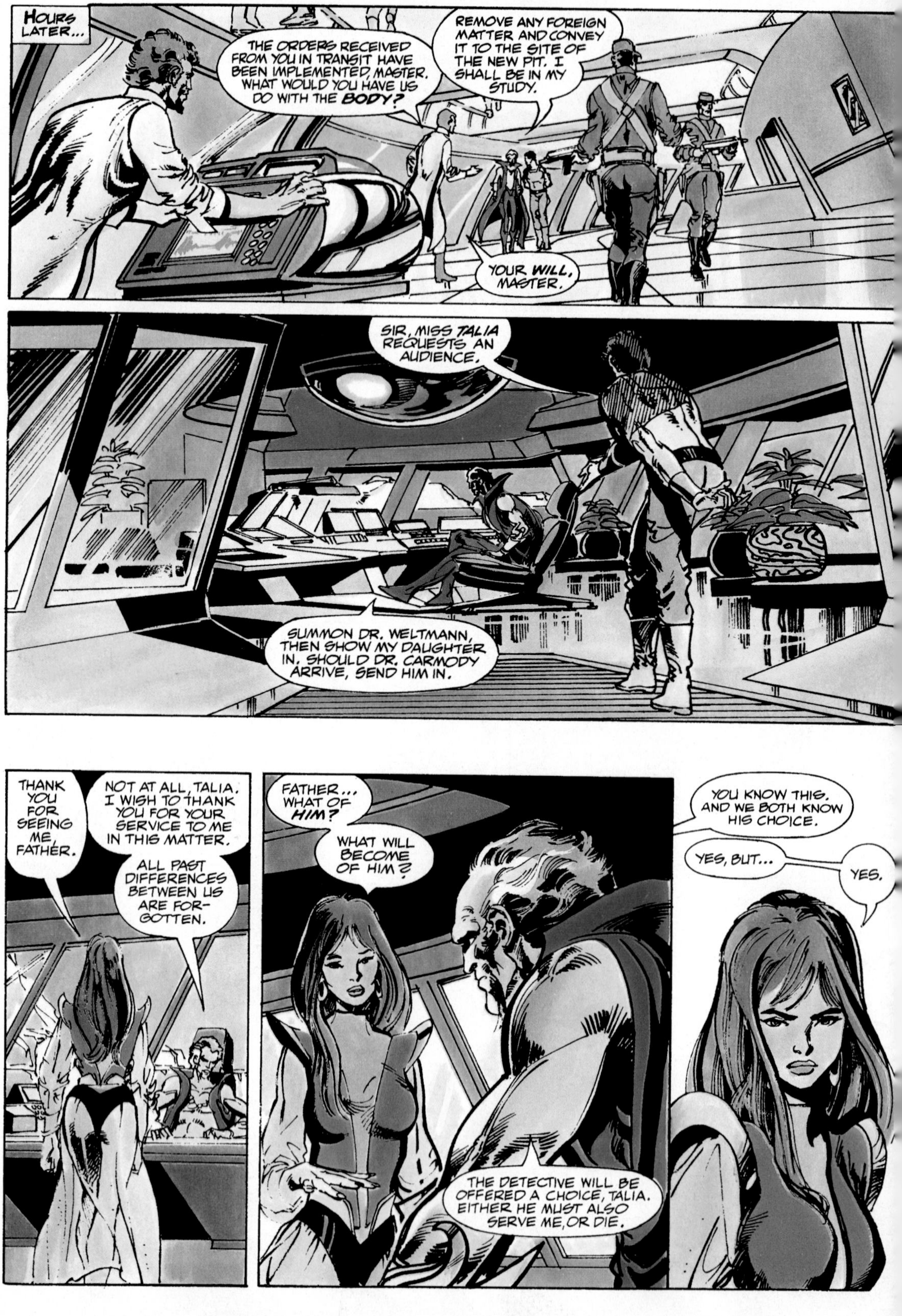
HOURS LATER...
THE ORDERS RECEIVED FROM YOU IN TRANSIT HAVE BEEN IMPLEMENTED, MASTER. WHAT WOULD YOU HAVE US DO WITH THE BODY?
REMOVE ANY FOREIGN MATTER AND CONVEY IT TO THE SITE OF THE NEW PIT. I SHALL BE IN MY STUDY.
YOUR WILL, MASTER.
SIR, MISS TALIA REQUESTS AN AUDIENCE.
SUMMON DR. WELTMANN, THEN SHOW MY DAUGHTER IN. SHOULD DR. CARMODY ARRIVE, SEND HIM IN.
THANK YOU FOR SEEING ME, FATHER.
NOT AT ALL, TALIA. I WISH TO THANK YOU FOR YOUR SERVICE TO ME IN THIS MATTER.
ALL PAST DIFFERENCES BETWEEN US ARE FORGOTTEN.
FATHER... WHAT OF HIM?
WHAT WILL BECOME OF HIM?
THE DETECTIVE WILL BE OFFERED A CHOICE, TALIA. EITHER HE MUST ALSO SERVE ME, OR DIE.
YOU KNOW THIS. AND WE BOTH KNOW HIS CHOICE.
YES, BUT...
YES.

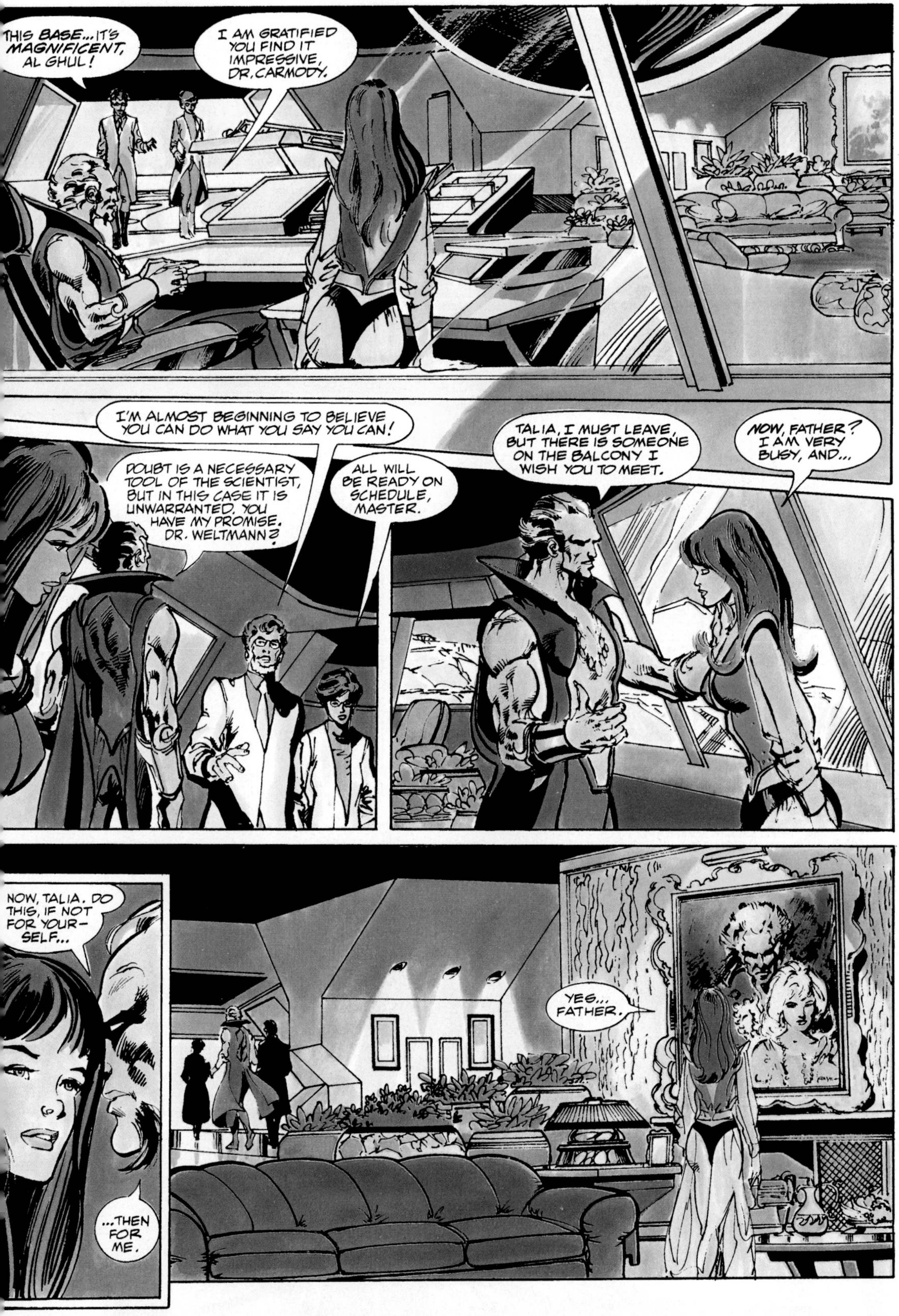

THIS BASE... IT'S MAGNIFICENT, AL GHUL!
I AM GRATIFIED YOU FIND IT IMPRESSIVE, DR. CARMODY.
I'M ALMOST BEGINNING TO BELIEVE YOU CAN DO WHAT YOU SAY YOU CAN!
DOUBT IS A NECESSARY TOOL OF THE SCIENTIST, BUT IN THIS CASE IT IS UNWARRANTED. YOU HAVE MY PROMISE. DR. WELTMANN?
ALL WILL BE READY ON SCHEDULE, MASTER.
TALIA, I MUST LEAVE, BUT THERE IS SOMEONE ON THE BALCONY I WISH YOU TO MEET.
NOW, FATHER? I AM VERY BUSY, AND...
NOW, TALIA. DO THIS, IF NOT FOR YOUR-SELF...
...THEN FOR ME.
YES... FATHER.

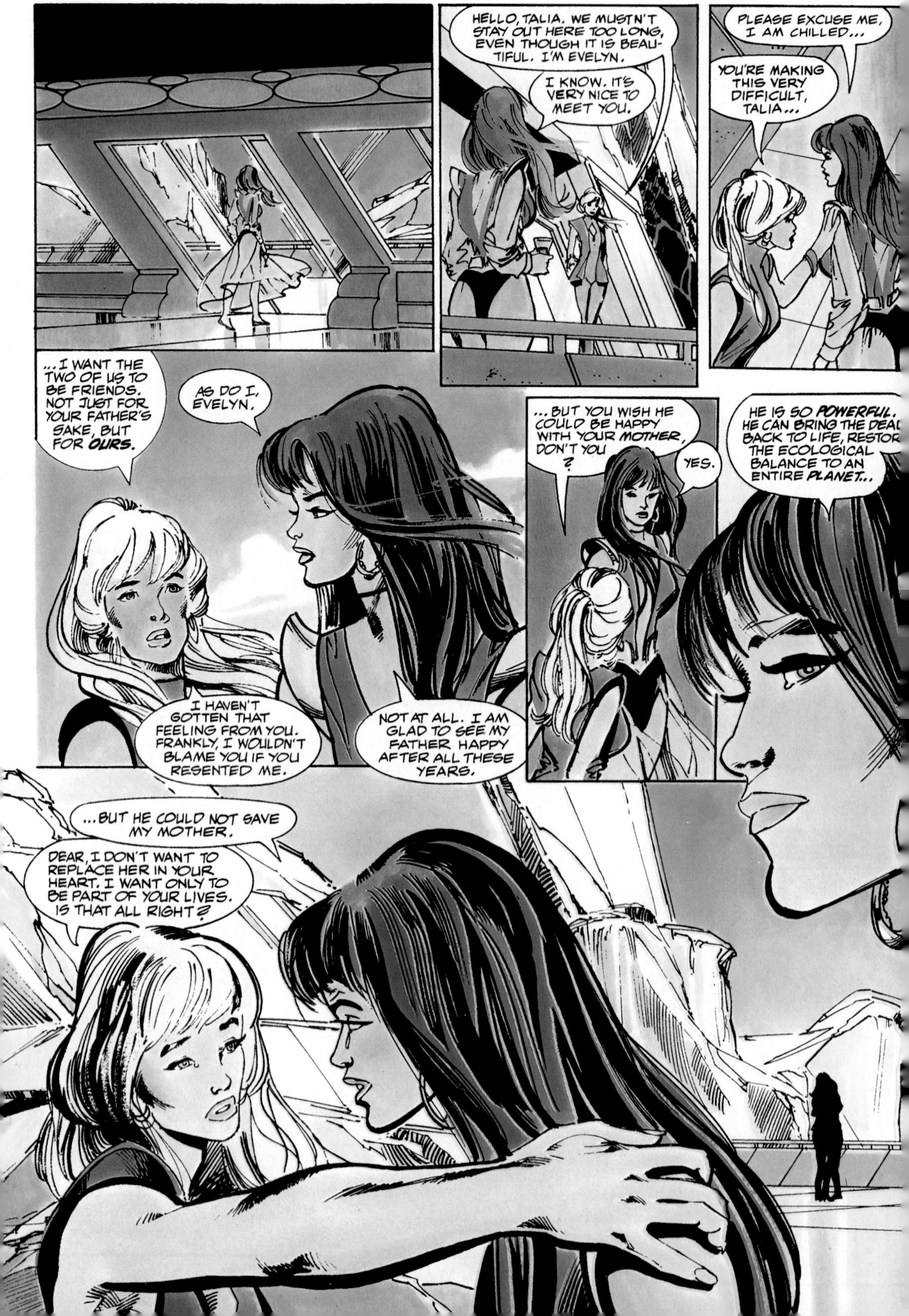
HELLO, TALIA. WE MUSTN'T STAY OUT HERE TOO LONG, EVEN THOUGH IT IS BEAUTIFUL. I'M EVELYN.
I KNOW. IT'S VERY NICE TO MEET YOU.
PLEASE EXCUSE ME, I AM CHILLED...
YOU'RE MAKING THIS VERY DIFFICULT, TALIA...
...I WANT THE TWO OF US TO BE FRIENDS. NOT JUST FOR YOUR FATHER'S SAKE, BUT FOR OURS.
AS DO I, EVELYN.
I HAVEN'T GOTTEN THAT FEELING FROM YOU. FRANKLY, I WOULDN'T BLAME YOU IF YOU RESENTED ME.
NOT AT ALL. I AM GLAD TO SEE MY FATHER HAPPY AFTER ALL THESE YEARS.
...BUT YOU WISH HE COULD BE HAPPY WITH YOUR MOTHER, DON'T YOU?
YES.
HE IS SO POWERFUL. HE CAN BRING THE DEAD BACK TO LIFE, RESTOR THE ECOLOGICAL BALANCE TO AN ENTIRE PLANET...
...BUT HE COULD NOT SAVE MY MOTHER.
DEAR, I DON'T WANT TO REPLACE HER IN YOUR HEART. I WANT ONLY TO BE PART OF YOUR LIVES. IS THAT ALL RIGHT?

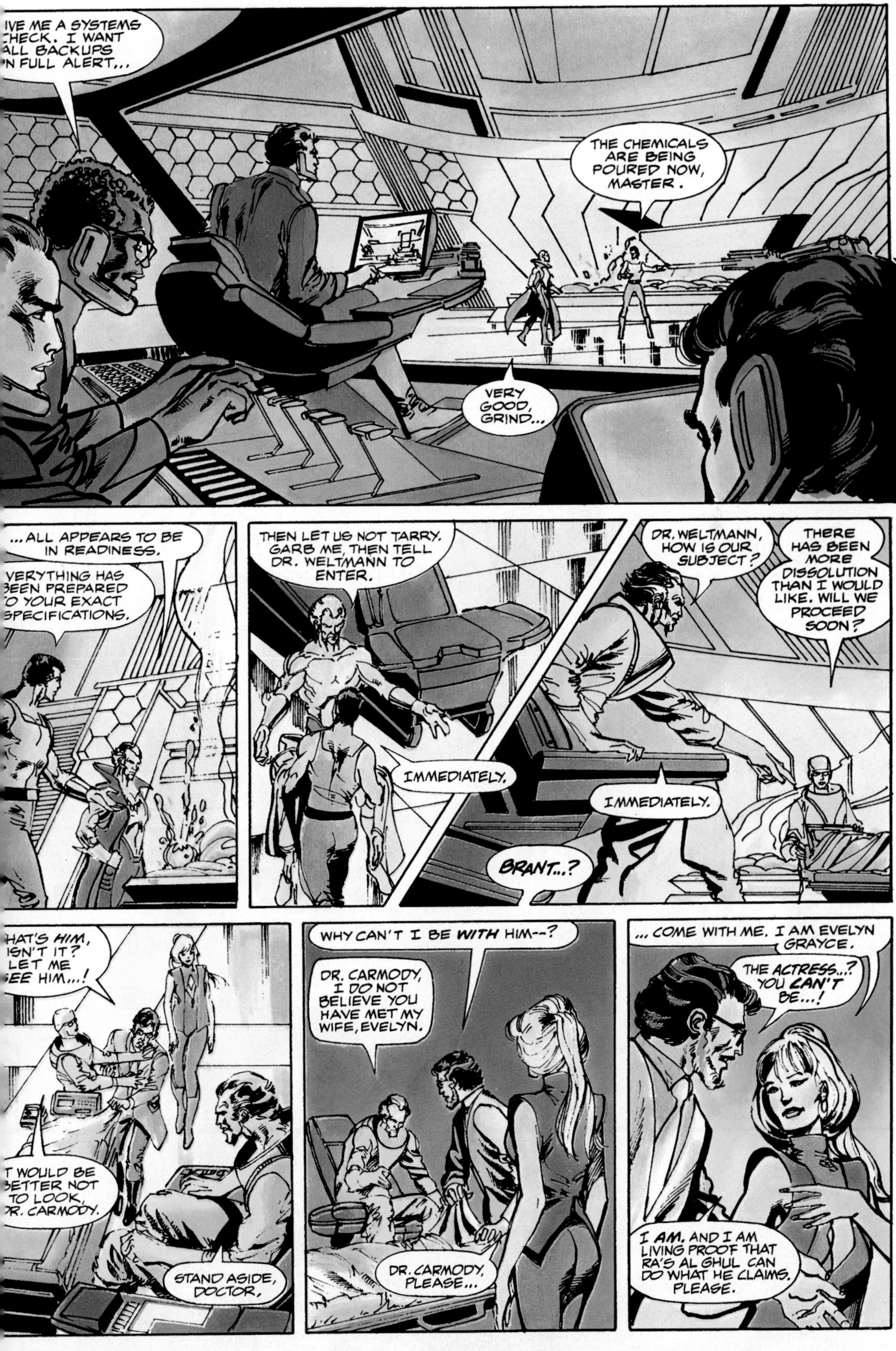
IVE ME A SYSTEMS CHECK. I WANT ALL BACKUPS ON FULL ALERT...
THE CHEMICALS ARE BEING POURED NOW, MASTER.
VERY GOOD, GRIND...
...ALL APPEARS TO BE IN READINESS.
VERYTHING HAS BEEN PREPARED TO YOUR EXACT SPECIFICATIONS.
THEN LET US NOT TARRY. GARB ME, THEN TELL DR. WELTMANN TO ENTER.
IMMEDIATELY.
DR. WELTMANN, HOW IS OUR SUBJECT?
THERE HAS BEEN MORE DISSOLUTION THAN I WOULD LIKE. WILL WE PROCEED SOON?
IMMEDIATELY.
BRANT...?
HAT'S HIM, ISN'T IT? LET ME SEE HIM...!
T WOULD BE BETTER NOT TO LOOK, R. CARMODY.
STAND ASIDE, DOCTOR,
WHY CAN'T I BE WITH HIM--?
DR. CARMODY, I DO NOT BELIEVE YOU HAVE MET MY WIFE, EVELYN.
DR. CARMODY, PLEASE...
...COME WITH ME. I AM EVELYN GRAYCE.
THE ACTRESS...? YOU CAN'T BE...!
I AM. AND I AM LIVING PROOF THAT RA'S AL GHUL CAN DO WHAT HE CLAIMS. PLEASE.

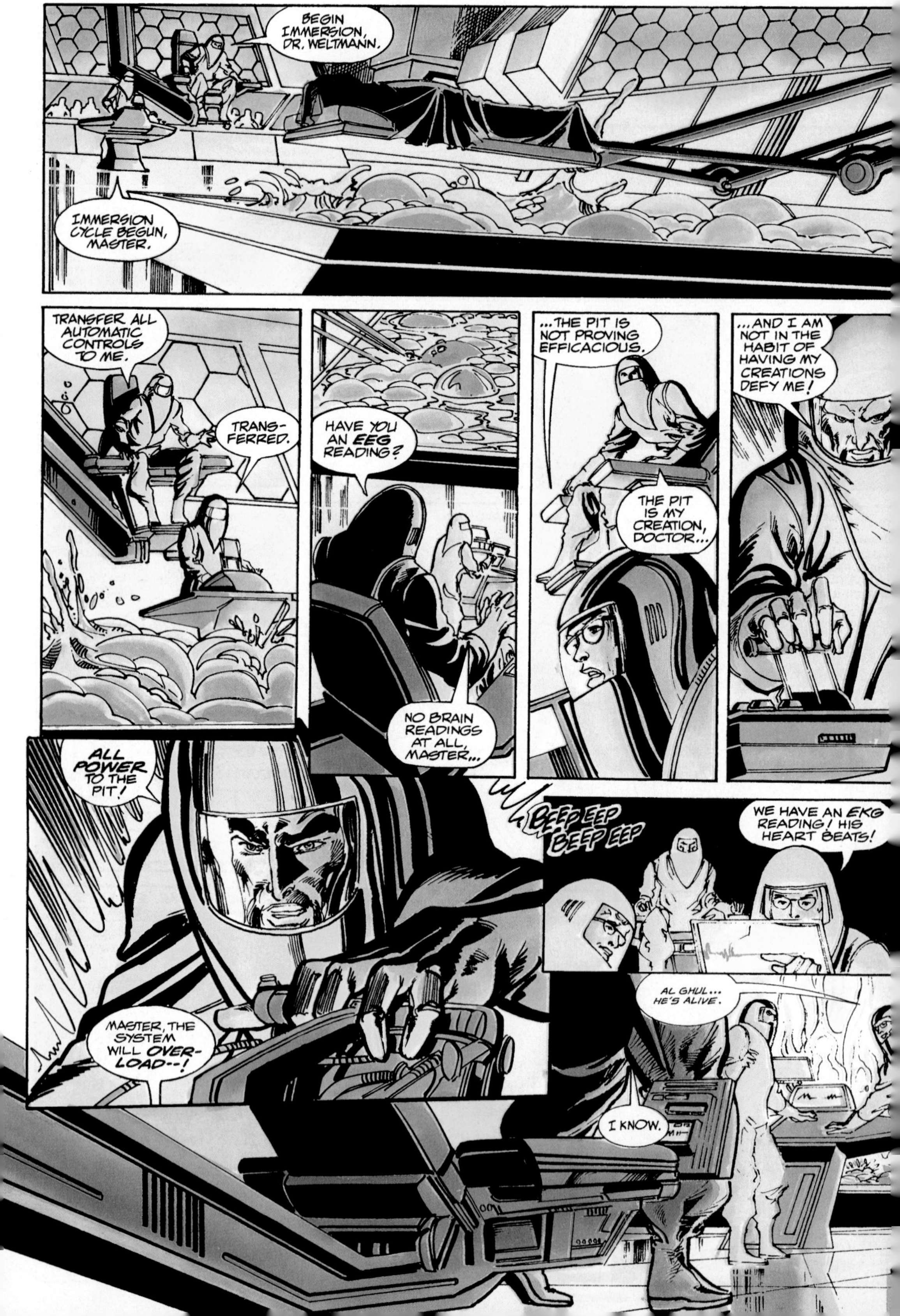
BEGIN IMMERSION, DR. WELTMANN.
IMMERSION CYCLE BEGUN, MASTER.
TRANSFER ALL AUTOMATIC CONTROLS TO ME.
TRANS-FERRED.
HAVE YOU AN EEG READING?
NO BRAIN READINGS AT ALL, MASTER...
...THE PIT IS NOT PROVING EFFICACIOUS.
THE PIT IS MY CREATION, DOCTOR...
...AND I AM NOT IN THE HABIT OF HAVING MY CREATIONS DEFY ME!
ALL POWER TO THE PIT!
MASTER, THE SYSTEM WILL OVER-LOAD--!
BEEP EEP BEEP EEP
WE HAVE AN EKG READING! HIS HEART BEATS!
AL GHUL... HE'S ALIVE.
I KNOW.

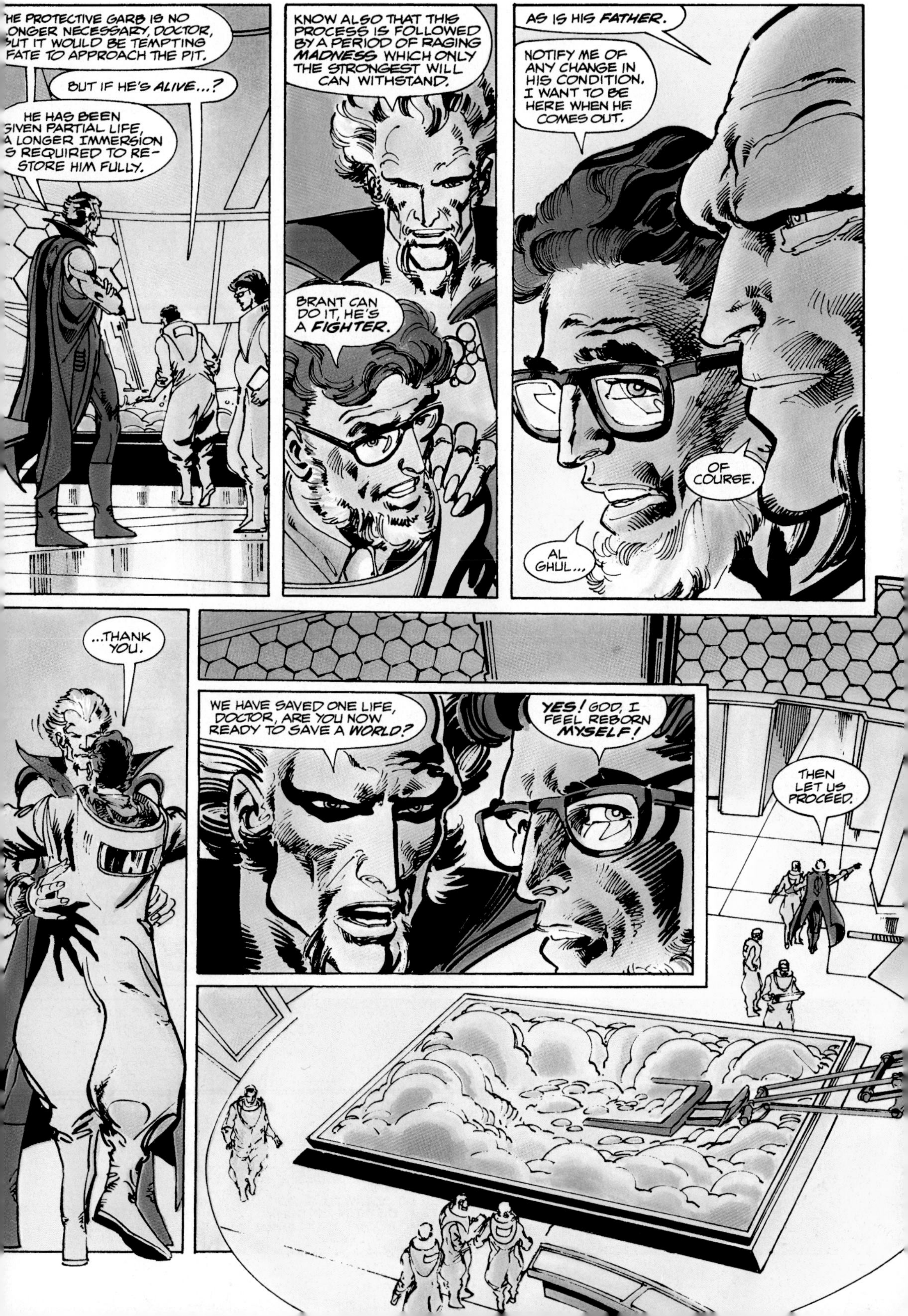
THE PROTECTIVE GARB IS NO LONGER NECESSARY, DOCTOR, BUT IT WOULD BE TEMPTING FATE TO APPROACH THE PIT.
BUT IF HE'S ALIVE...?
HE HAS BEEN GIVEN PARTIAL LIFE. A LONGER IMMERSION IS REQUIRED TO RESTORE HIM FULLY.
KNOW ALSO THAT THIS PROCESS IS FOLLOWED BY A PERIOD OF RAGING MADNESS WHICH ONLY THE STRONGEST WILL CAN WITHSTAND.
BRANT CAN DO IT, HE'S A FIGHTER.
AS IS HIS FATHER.
NOTIFY ME OF ANY CHANGE IN HIS CONDITION. I WANT TO BE HERE WHEN HE COMES OUT.
OF COURSE.
AL GHUL...
...THANK YOU.
WE HAVE SAVED ONE LIFE, DOCTOR, ARE YOU NOW READY TO SAVE A WORLD?
YES! GOD, I FEEL REBORN MYSELF!
THEN LET US PROCEED.

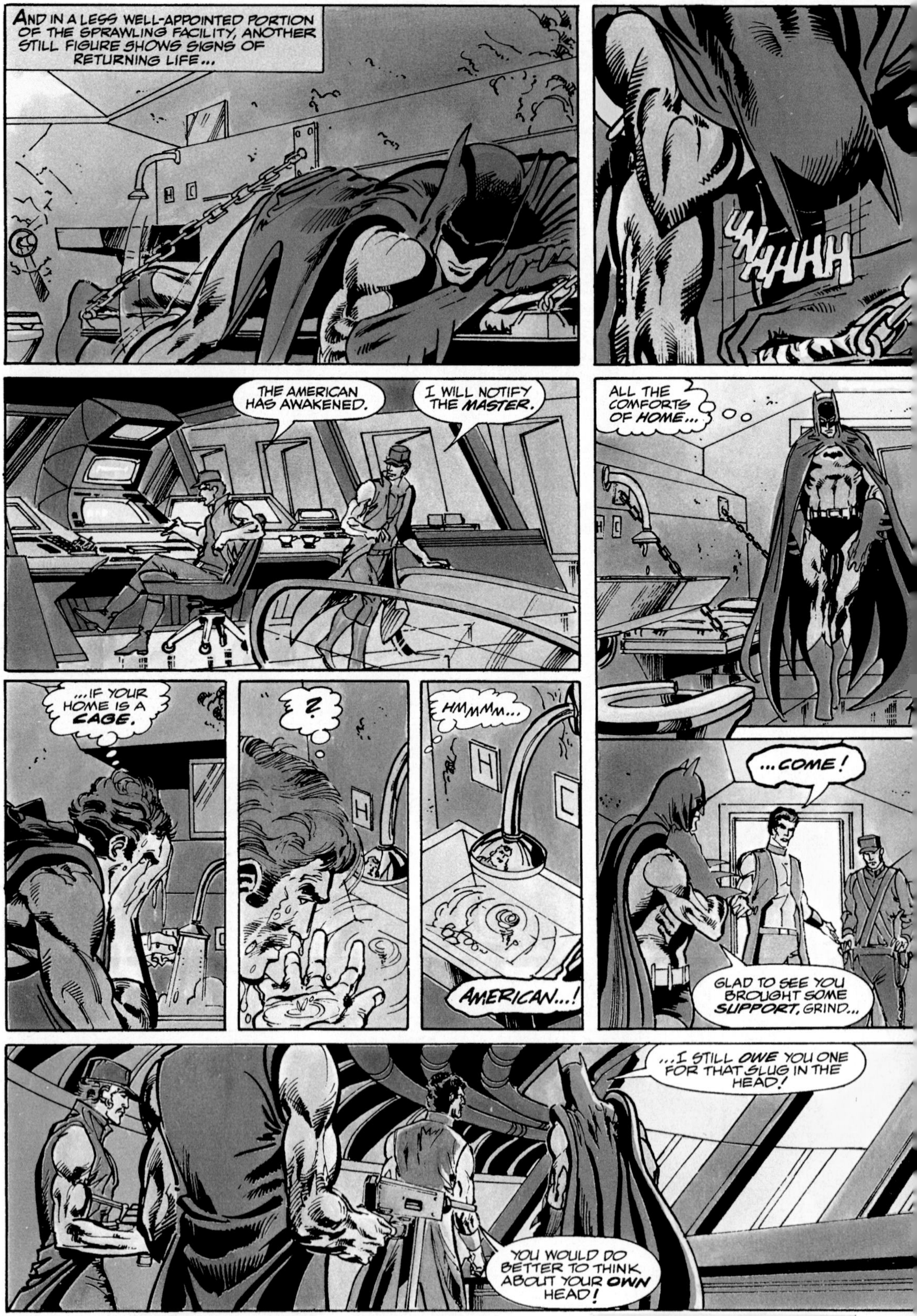
AND IN A LESS WELL-APPOINTED PORTION OF THE SPRAWLING FACILITY, ANOTHER STILL FIGURE SHOWS SIGNS OF RETURNING LIFE...
H
C
UNHHHH
THE AMERICAN HAS AWAKENED.
I WILL NOTIFY THE MASTER.
ALL THE COMFORTS OF HOME...
...IF YOUR HOME IS A CAGE.
?
HMMMM...
AMERICAN...!
...COME!
GLAD TO SEE YOU BROUGHT SOME SUPPORT, GRIND...
...I STILL OWE YOU ONE FOR THAT SLUG IN THE HEAD!
YOU WOULD DO BETTER TO THINK ABOUT YOUR OWN HEAD!

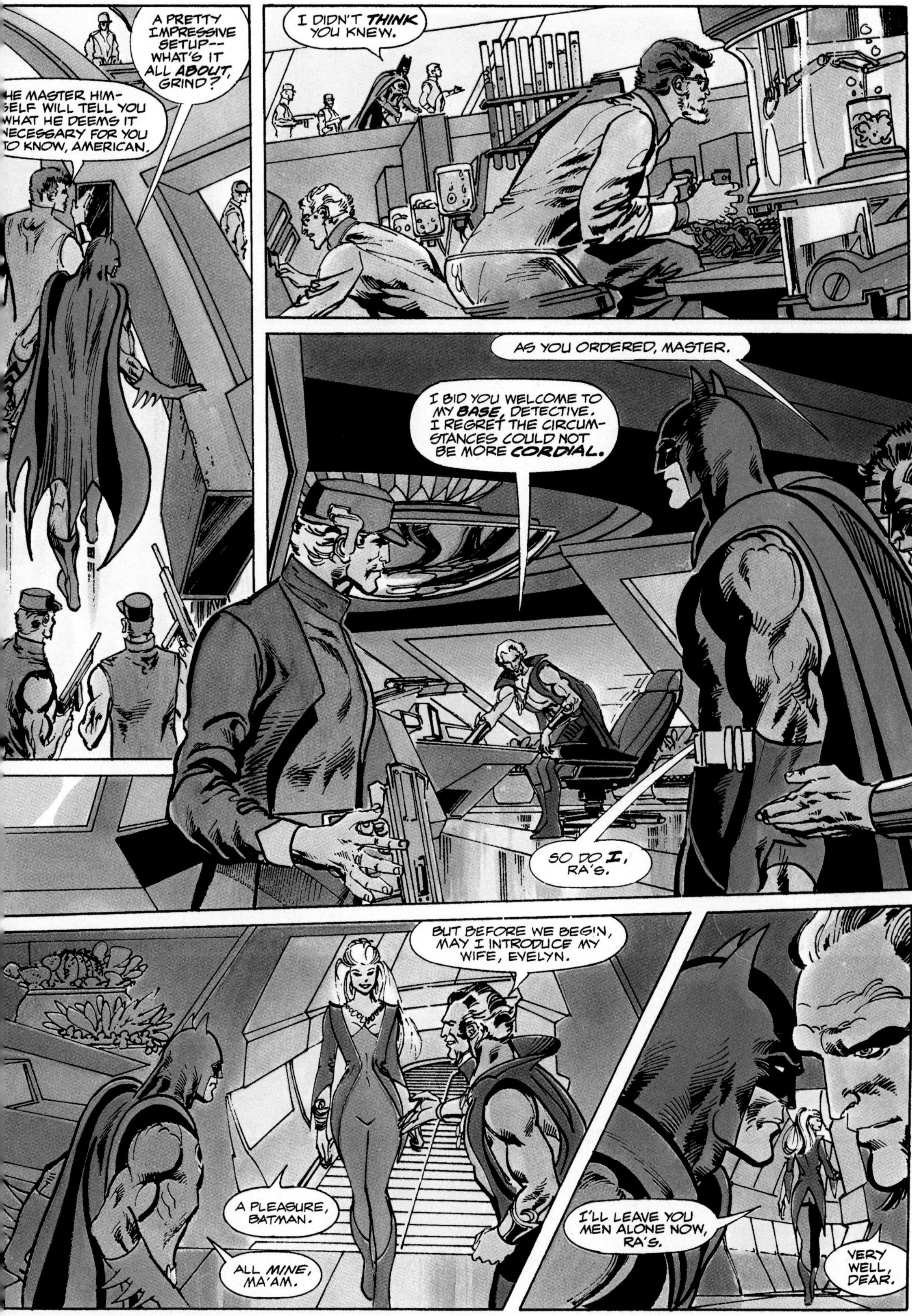
A PRETTY IMPRESSIVE SETUP-- WHAT'S IT ALL ABOUT, GRIND?
HE MASTER HIMSELF WILL TELL YOU WHAT HE DEEMS IT NECESSARY FOR YOU TO KNOW, AMERICAN.
I DIDN'T THINK YOU KNEW.
AS YOU ORDERED, MASTER.
I BID YOU WELCOME TO MY BASE, DETECTIVE. I REGRET THE CIRCUMSTANCES COULD NOT BE MORE CORDIAL.
SO DO I, RA'S.
BUT BEFORE WE BEGIN, MAY I INTRODUCE MY WIFE, EVELYN.
A PLEASURE, BATMAN.
ALL MINE, MA'AM.
I'LL LEAVE YOU MEN ALONE NOW, RA'S.
VERY WELL, DEAR.

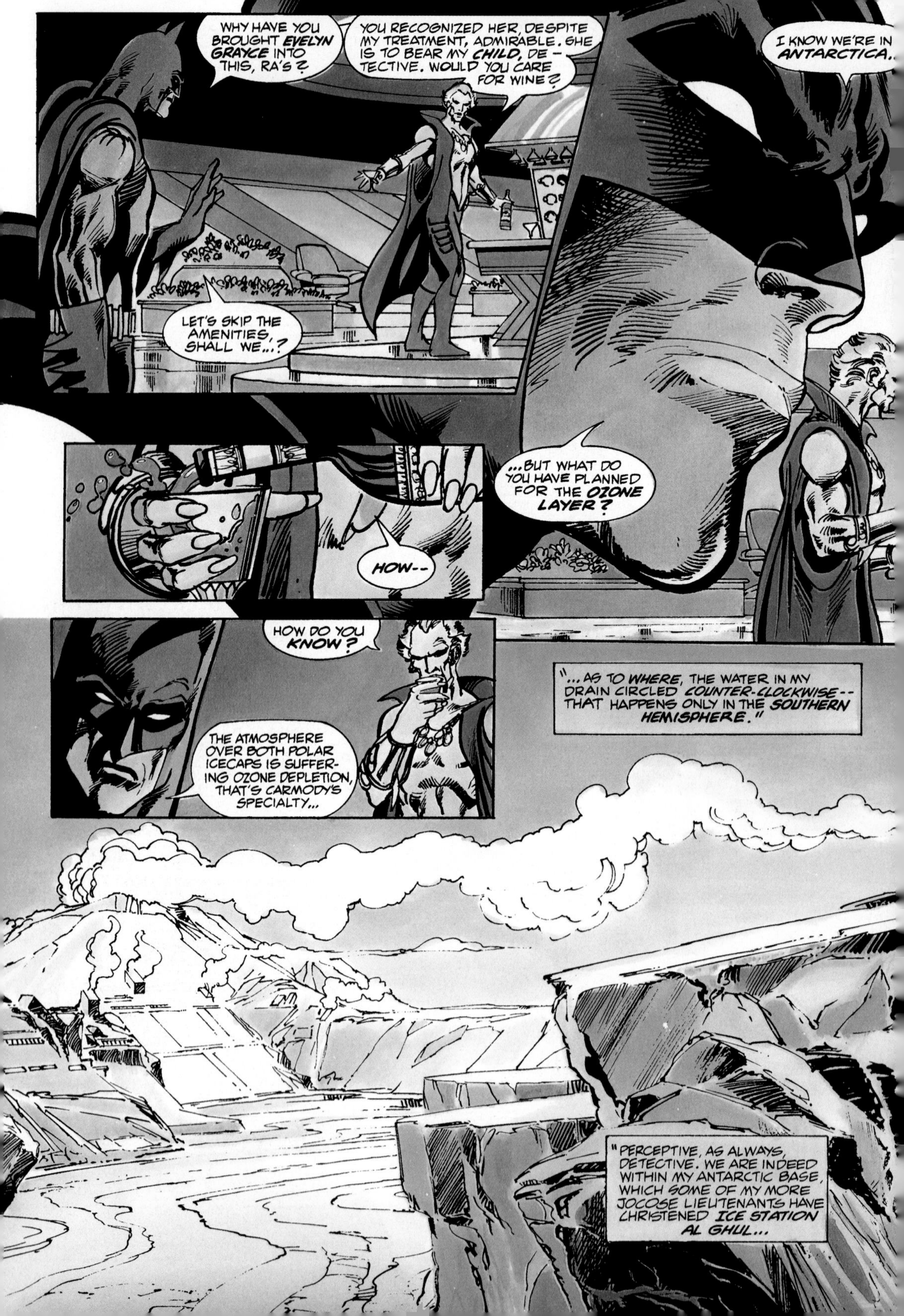
WHY HAVE YOU BROUGHT EVELYN GRAYCE INTO THIS, RA'S?
YOU RECOGNIZED HER, DESPITE MY TREATMENT, ADMIRABLE. SHE IS TO BEAR MY CHILD, DETECTIVE. WOULD YOU CARE FOR WINE?
LET'S SKIP THE AMENITIES, SHALL WE...?
I KNOW WE'RE IN ANTARCTICA...
...BUT WHAT DO YOU HAVE PLANNED FOR THE OZONE LAYER?
HOW--
HOW DO YOU KNOW?
THE ATMOSPHERE OVER BOTH POLAR ICECAPS IS SUFFERING OZONE DEPLETION, THAT'S CARMODY'S SPECIALTY...
"...AS TO WHERE, THE WATER IN MY DRAIN CIRCLED COUNTER-CLOCKWISE-- THAT HAPPENS ONLY IN THE SOUTHERN HEMISPHERE."
"PERCEPTIVE, AS ALWAYS, DETECTIVE. WE ARE INDEED WITHIN MY ANTARCTIC BASE, WHICH SOME OF MY MORE JOCOSE LIEUTENANTS HAVE CHRISTENED ICE STATION AL GHUL...

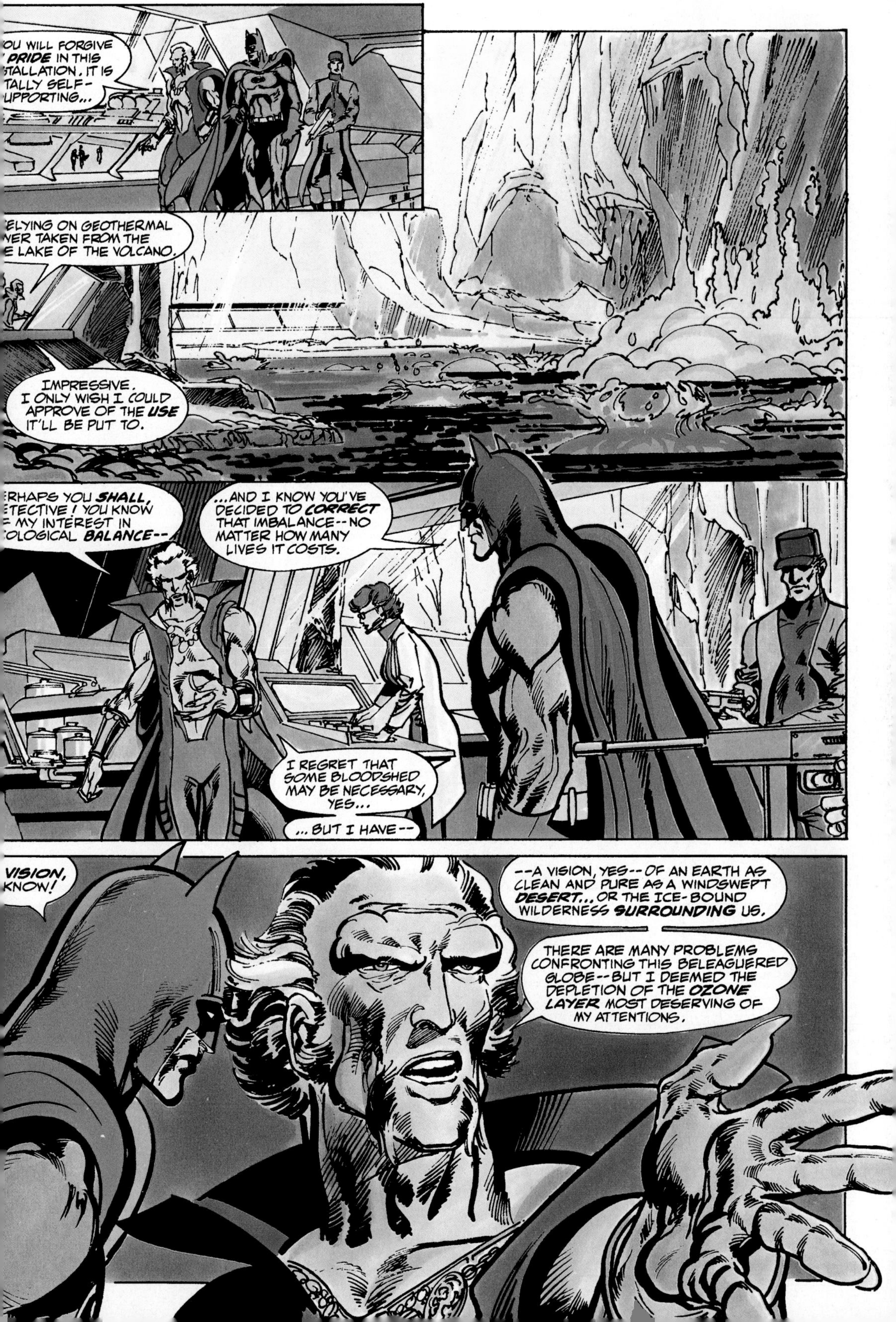

OU WILL FORGIVE
PRIDE IN THIS
STALLATION. IT IS
TALLY SELF-
UPPORTING...
ELYING ON GEOTHERMAL
WER TAKEN FROM THE
E LAKE OF THE VOLCANO.
IMPRESSIVE. I ONLY WISH I COULD APPROVE OF THE USE IT'LL BE PUT TO.
ERHAPS YOU SHALL, ETECTIVE! YOU KNOW F MY INTEREST IN COLOGICAL BALANCE--
...AND I KNOW YOU'VE DECIDED TO CORRECT THAT IMBALANCE--NO MATTER HOW MANY LIVES IT COSTS.
I REGRET THAT SOME BLOODSHED MAY BE NECESSARY, YES...
...BUT I HAVE--
VISION, KNOW!
--A VISION, YES--OF AN EARTH AS CLEAN AND PURE AS A WINDSWEPT DESERT... OR THE ICE-BOUND WILDERNESS SURROUNDING US.
THERE ARE MANY PROBLEMS CONFRONTING THIS BELEAGUERED GLOBE--BUT I DEEMED THE DEPLETION OF THE OZONE LAYER MOST DESERVING OF MY ATTENTIONS.

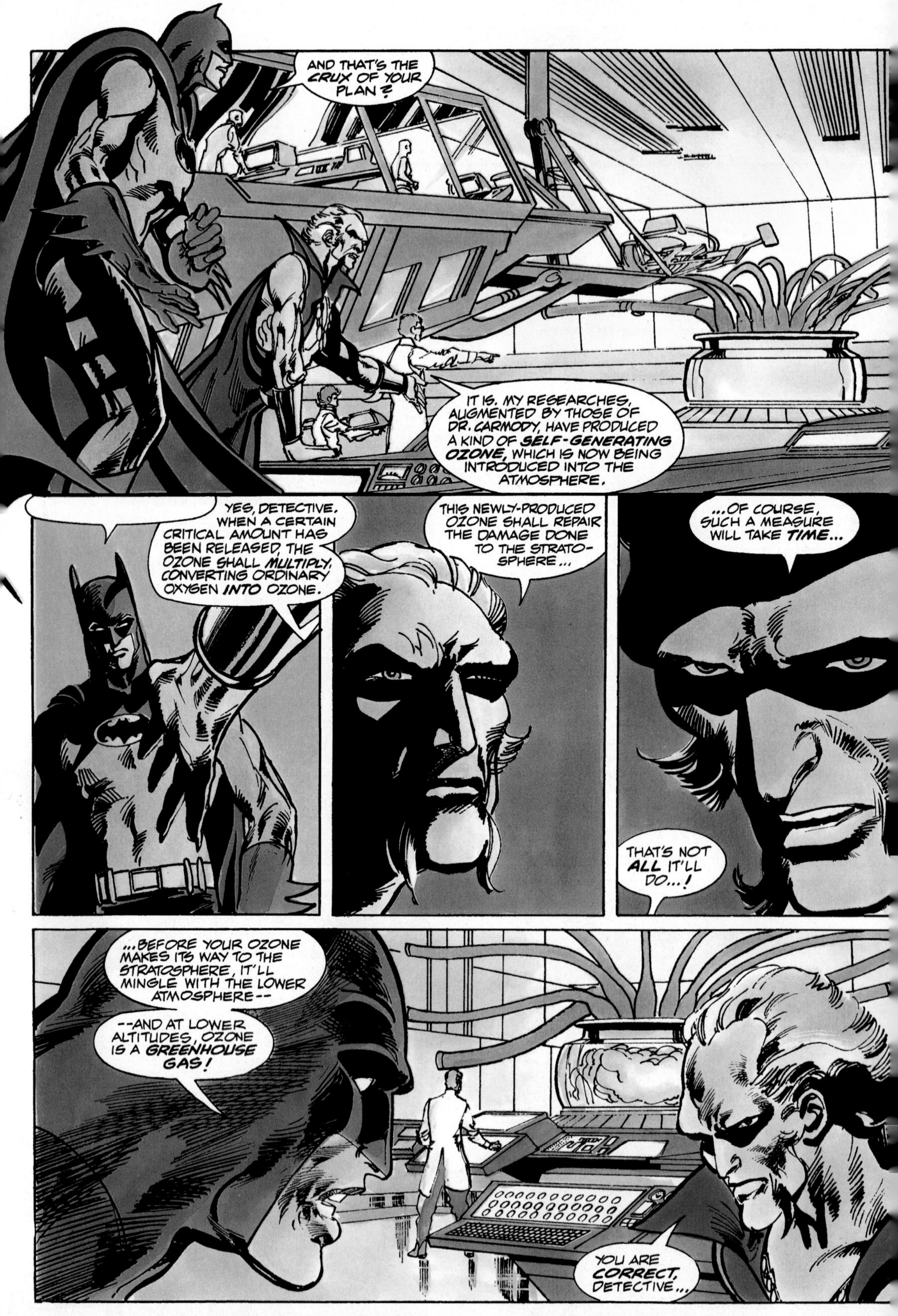
AND THAT'S THE CRUX OF YOUR PLAN?
IT IS. MY RESEARCHES, AUGMENTED BY THOSE OF DR. CARMODY, HAVE PRODUCED A KIND OF SELF-GENERATING OZONE, WHICH IS NOW BEING INTRODUCED INTO THE ATMOSPHERE.
YES, DETECTIVE. WHEN A CERTAIN CRITICAL AMOUNT HAS BEEN RELEASED, THE OZONE SHALL MULTIPLY, CONVERTING ORDINARY OXYGEN INTO OZONE.
THIS NEWLY-PRODUCED OZONE SHALL REPAIR THE DAMAGE DONE TO THE STRATOSPHERE...
...OF COURSE, SUCH A MEASURE WILL TAKE TIME...
THAT'S NOT ALL IT'LL DO...!
...BEFORE YOUR OZONE MAKES ITS WAY TO THE STRATOSPHERE, IT'LL MINGLE WITH THE LOWER ATMOSPHERE--
--AND AT LOWER ALTITUDES, OZONE IS A GREENHOUSE GAS!
YOU ARE CORRECT, DETECTIVE...

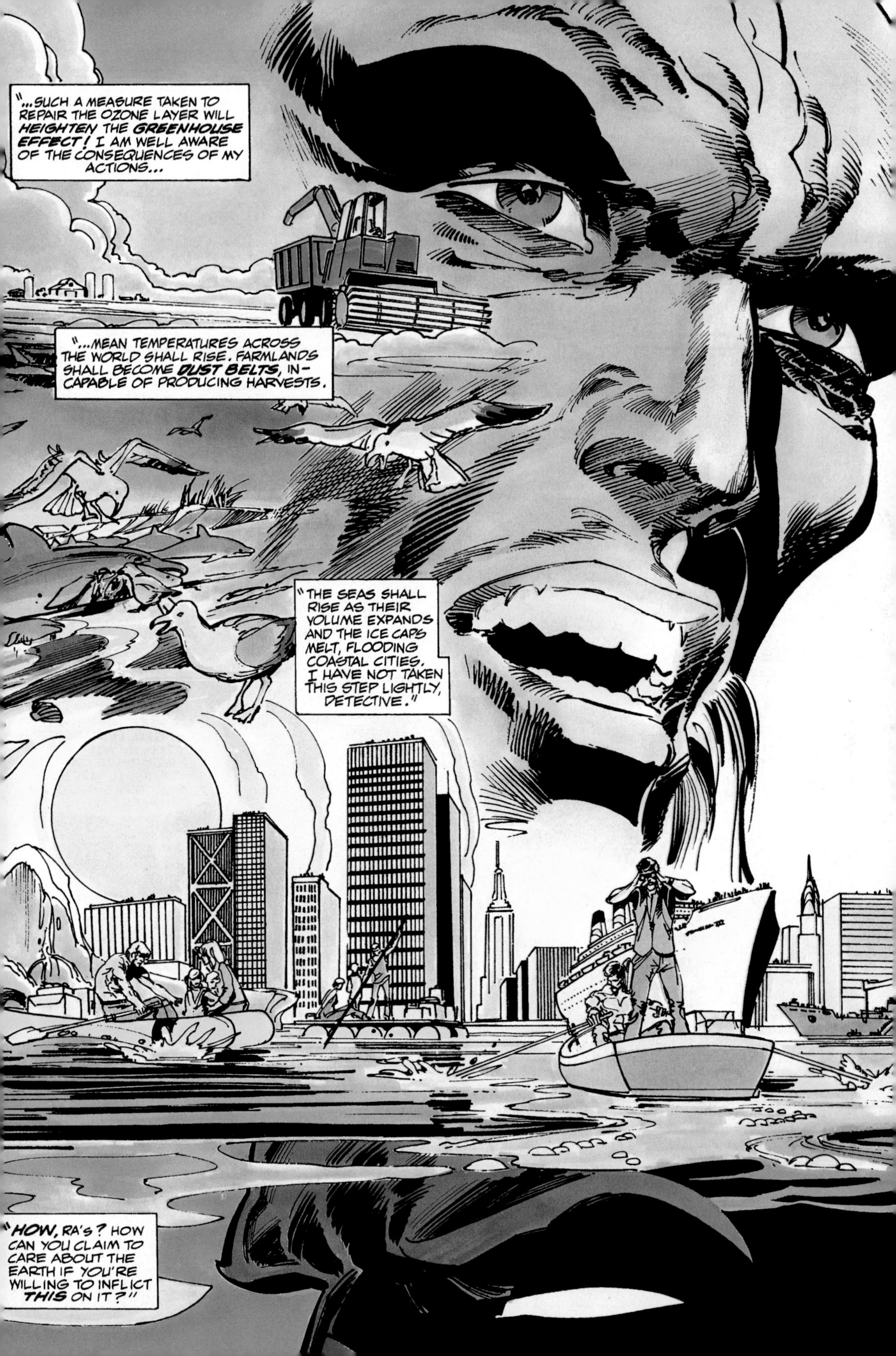
"...SUCH A MEASURE TAKEN TO REPAIR THE OZONE LAYER WILL **HEIGHTEN** THE **GREENHOUSE EFFECT!** I AM WELL AWARE OF THE CONSEQUENCES OF MY ACTIONS...
"...MEAN TEMPERATURES ACROSS THE WORLD SHALL RISE. FARMLANDS SHALL BECOME **DUST BELTS**, INCAPABLE OF PRODUCING HARVESTS.
"THE SEAS SHALL RISE AS THEIR VOLUME EXPANDS AND THE ICE CAPS MELT, FLOODING COASTAL CITIES. I HAVE NOT TAKEN THIS STEP LIGHTLY, DETECTIVE."
"**HOW**, RA'S? HOW CAN YOU CLAIM TO CARE ABOUT THE EARTH IF YOU'RE WILLING TO INFLICT **THIS** ON IT?"

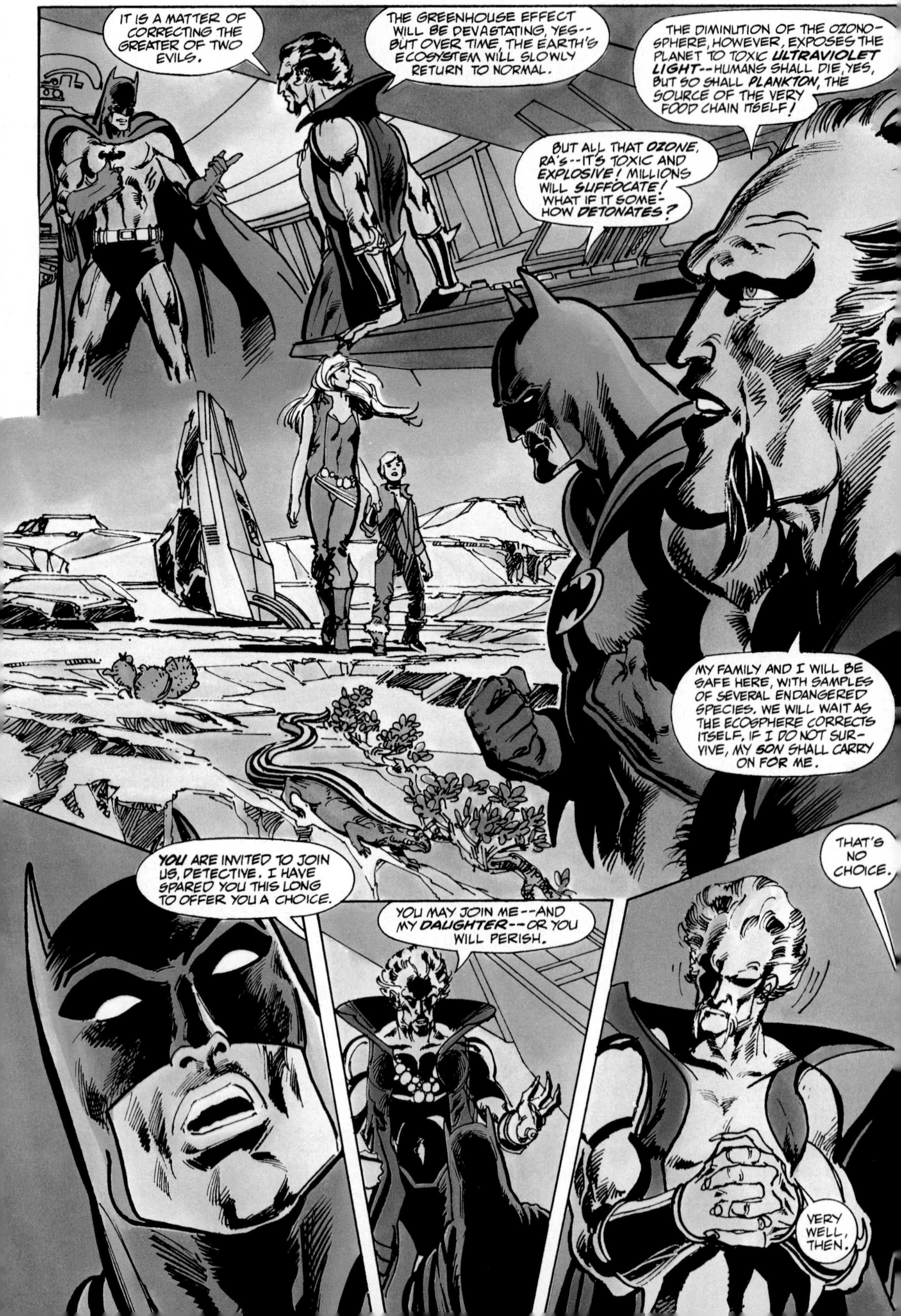
IT IS A MATTER OF CORRECTING THE GREATER OF TWO EVILS.
THE GREENHOUSE EFFECT WILL BE DEVASTATING, YES-- BUT OVER TIME, THE EARTH'S ECOSYSTEM WILL SLOWLY RETURN TO NORMAL.
THE DIMINUTION OF THE OZONOSPHERE, HOWEVER, EXPOSES THE PLANET TO TOXIC ULTRAVIOLET LIGHT--HUMANS SHALL DIE, YES, BUT SO SHALL PLANKTON, THE SOURCE OF THE VERY FOOD CHAIN ITSELF!
BUT ALL THAT OZONE, RA'S--IT'S TOXIC AND EXPLOSIVE! MILLIONS WILL SUFFOCATE! WHAT IF IT SOMEHOW DETONATES?
MY FAMILY AND I WILL BE SAFE HERE, WITH SAMPLES OF SEVERAL ENDANGERED SPECIES. WE WILL WAIT AS THE ECOSPHERE CORRECTS ITSELF. IF I DO NOT SURVIVE, MY SON SHALL CARRY ON FOR ME.
YOU ARE INVITED TO JOIN US, DETECTIVE. I HAVE SPARED YOU THIS LONG TO OFFER YOU A CHOICE.
YOU MAY JOIN ME--AND MY DAUGHTER--OR YOU WILL PERISH.
THAT'S NO CHOICE.
VERY WELL, THEN.

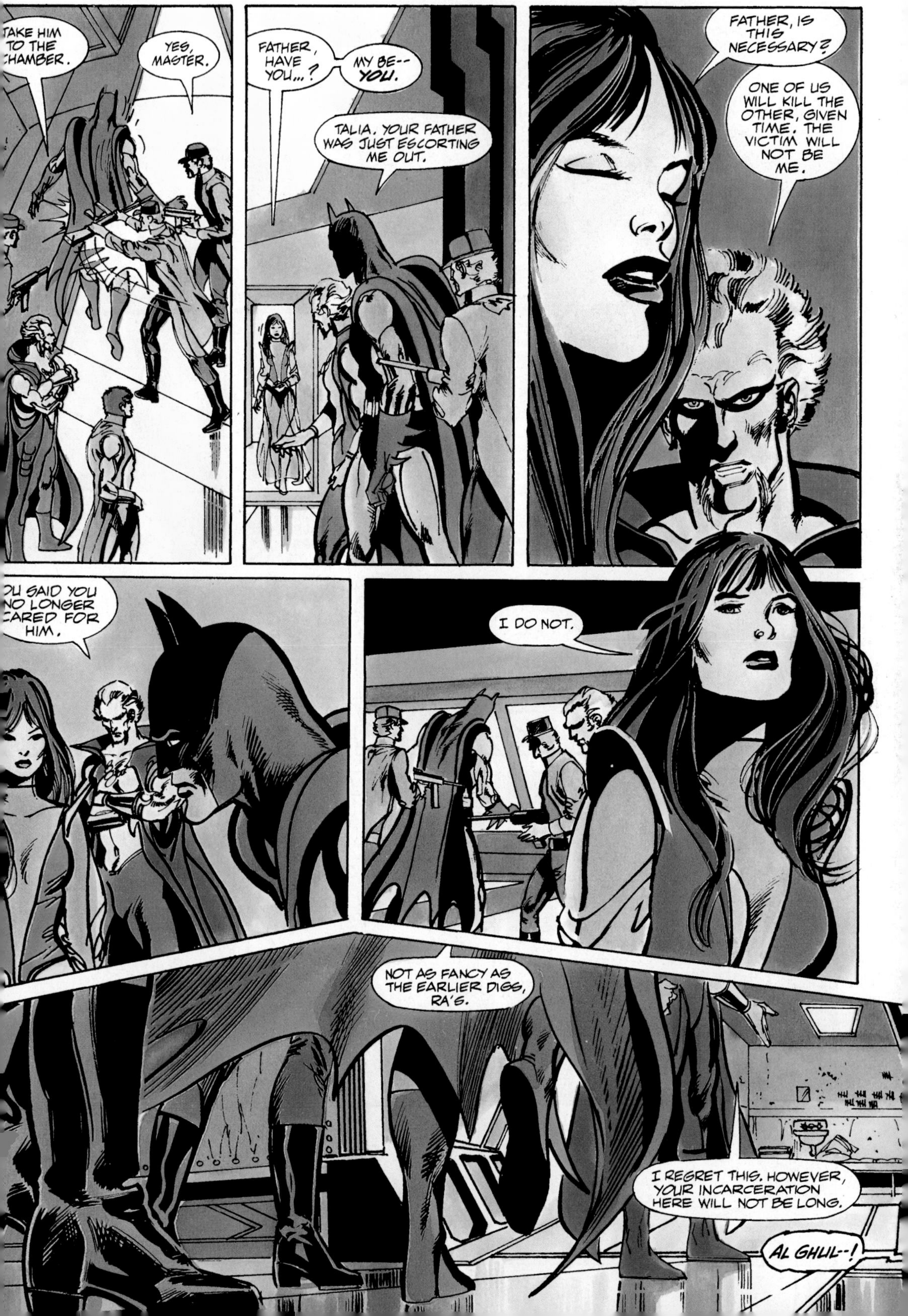
TAKE HIM TO THE CHAMBER.
YES, MASTER.
FATHER, HAVE YOU...?
MY BE-- YOU.
TALIA. YOUR FATHER WAS JUST ESCORTING ME OUT.
FATHER, IS THIS NECESSARY?
ONE OF US WILL KILL THE OTHER, GIVEN TIME. THE VICTIM WILL NOT BE ME.
YOU SAID YOU NO LONGER CARED FOR HIM.
I DO NOT.
NOT AS FANCY AS THE EARLIER DIGS, RA'S.
I REGRET THIS. HOWEVER, YOUR INCARCERATION HERE WILL NOT BE LONG.
AL GHUL--!

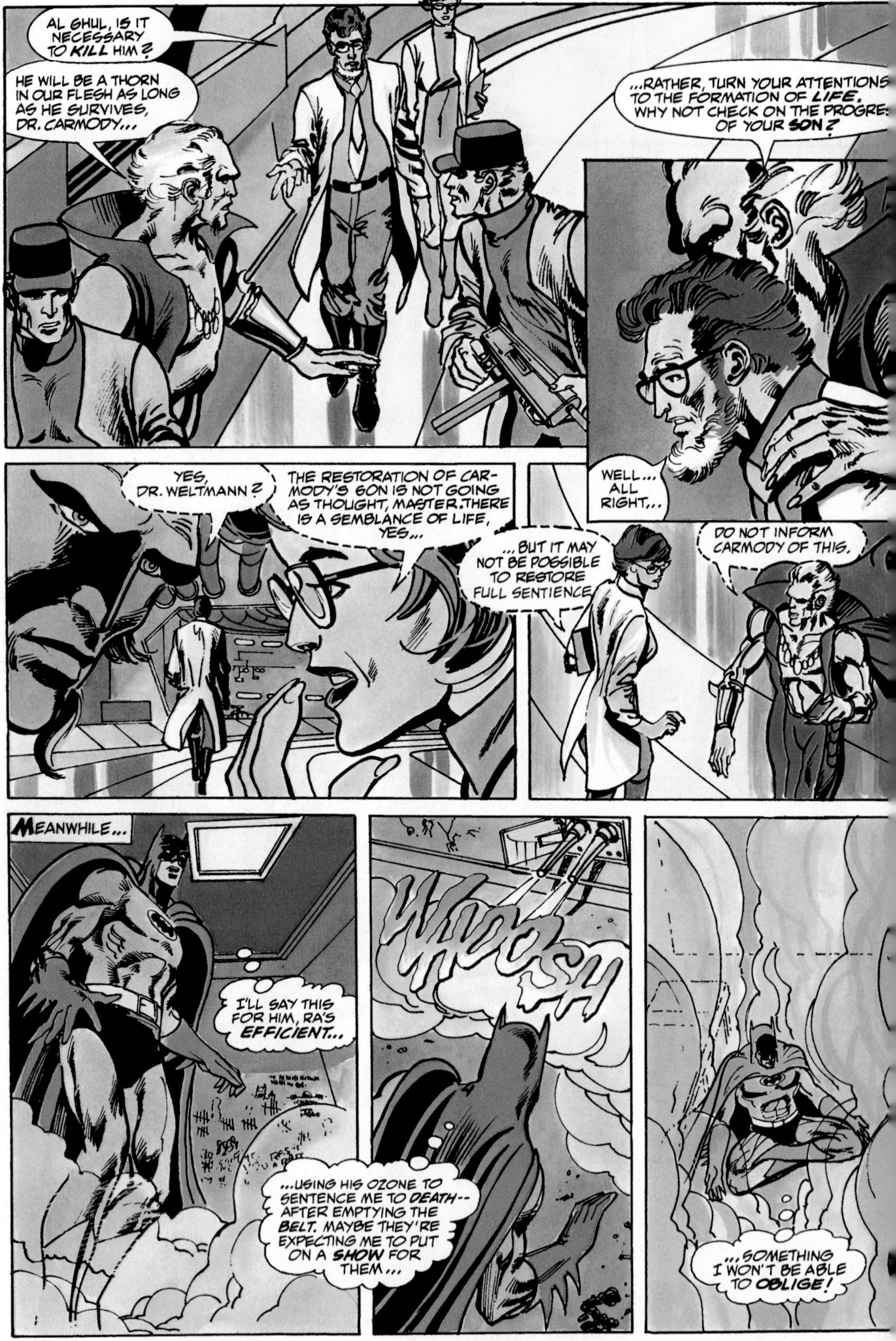
AL GHUL, IS IT NECESSARY TO KILL HIM?
HE WILL BE A THORN IN OUR FLESH AS LONG AS HE SURVIVES, DR. CARMODY...
...RATHER, TURN YOUR ATTENTIONS TO THE FORMATION OF LIFE. WHY NOT CHECK ON THE PROGRE- OF YOUR SON?
WELL... ALL RIGHT...
YES, DR. WELTMANN?
THE RESTORATION OF CAR-MODY'S SON IS NOT GOING AS THOUGHT, MASTER. THERE IS A SEMBLANCE OF LIFE, YES...
...BUT IT MAY NOT BE POSSIBLE TO RESTORE FULL SENTIENCE.
DO NOT INFORM CARMODY OF THIS.
MEANWHILE...
I'LL SAY THIS FOR HIM, RA'S EFFICIENT...
...USING HIS OZONE TO SENTENCE ME TO DEATH-- AFTER EMPTYING THE BELT. MAYBE THEY'RE EXPECTING ME TO PUT ON A SHOW FOR THEM...
WHOOSH
...SOMETHING I WON'T BE ABLE TO OBLIGE!

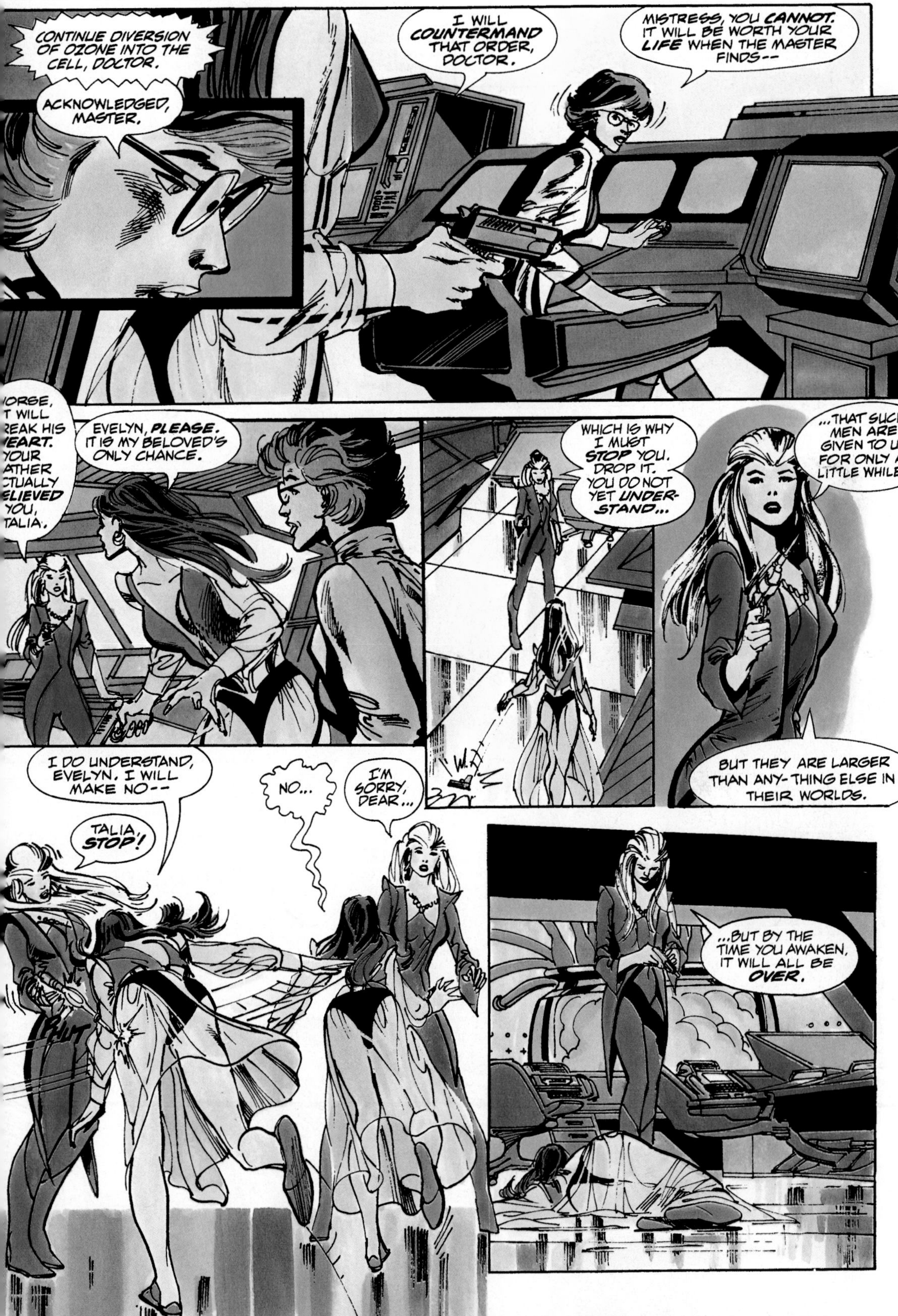
CONTINUE DIVERSION OF OZONE INTO THE CELL, DOCTOR.
ACKNOWLEDGED, MASTER.
I WILL COUNTERMAND THAT ORDER, DOCTOR.
MISTRESS, YOU CANNOT. IT WILL BE WORTH YOUR LIFE WHEN THE MASTER FINDS--
ORSE, T WILL REAK HIS EART. YOUR ATHER CTUALLY ELIEVED YOU, TALIA.
EVELYN, PLEASE. IT IS MY BELOVED'S ONLY CHANCE.
WHICH IS WHY I MUST STOP YOU. DROP IT. YOU DO NOT YET UNDERSTAND...
...THAT SUCH MEN ARE GIVEN TO US FOR ONLY A LITTLE WHILE--
BUT THEY ARE LARGER THAN ANY-THING ELSE IN THEIR WORLDS.
I DO UNDERSTAND, EVELYN. I WILL MAKE NO--
TALIA, STOP!
NO...
I'M SORRY, DEAR...
PHUT
...BUT BY THE TIME YOU AWAKEN, IT WILL ALL BE OVER.

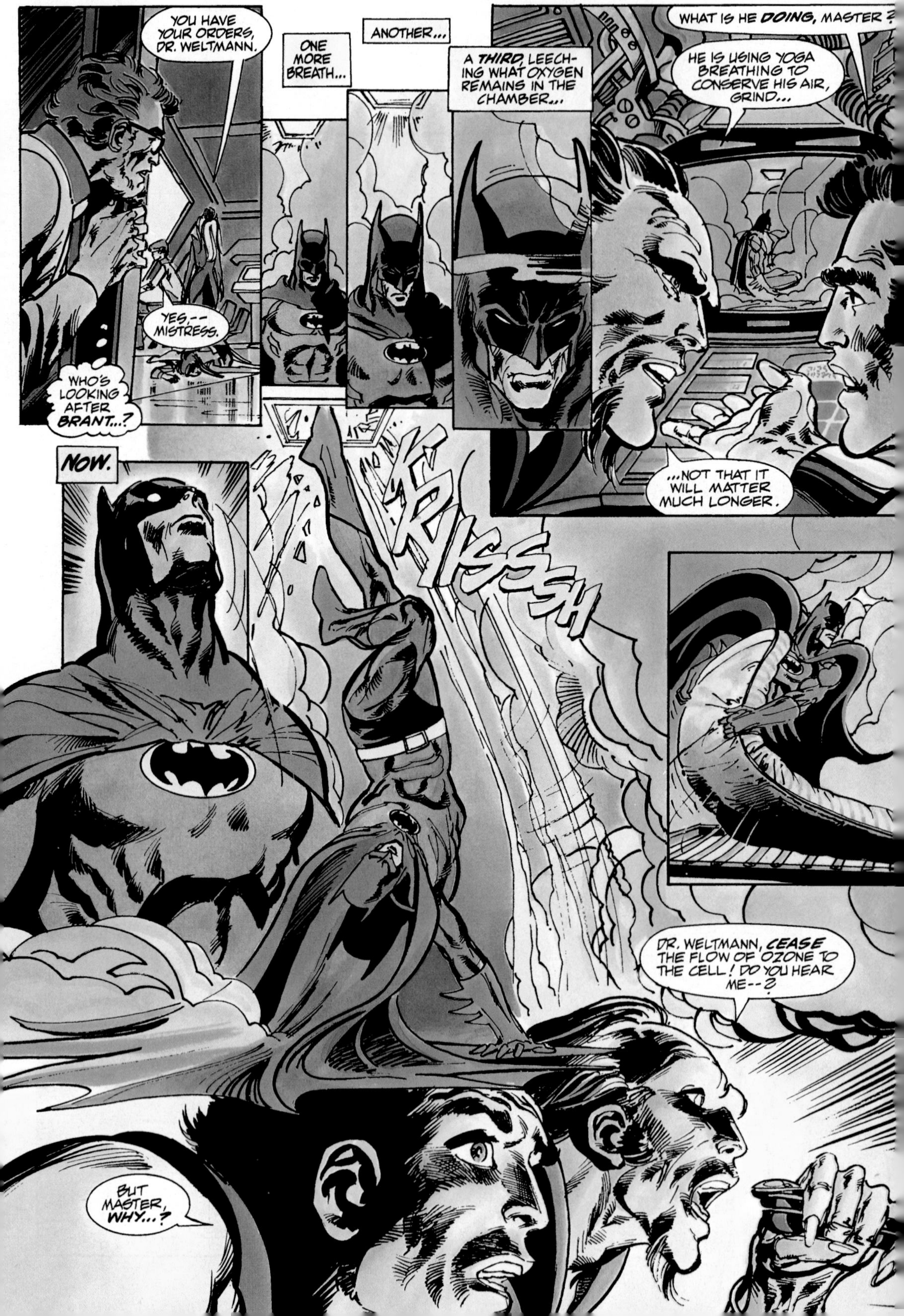

YOU HAVE YOUR ORDERS, DR. WELTMANN.
YES.-- MISTRESS.
WHO'S LOOKING AFTER BRANT...?
ONE MORE BREATH...
ANOTHER...
A THIRD, LEECHING WHAT OXYGEN REMAINS IN THE CHAMBER...
WHAT IS HE DOING, MASTER ?
HE IS USING YOGA BREATHING TO CONSERVE HIS AIR, GRIND...
...NOT THAT IT WILL MATTER MUCH LONGER.
NOW.
KRISSSH
DR. WELTMANN, CEASE THE FLOW OF OZONE TO THE CELL! DO YOU HEAR ME--?
BUT MASTER, WHY...?

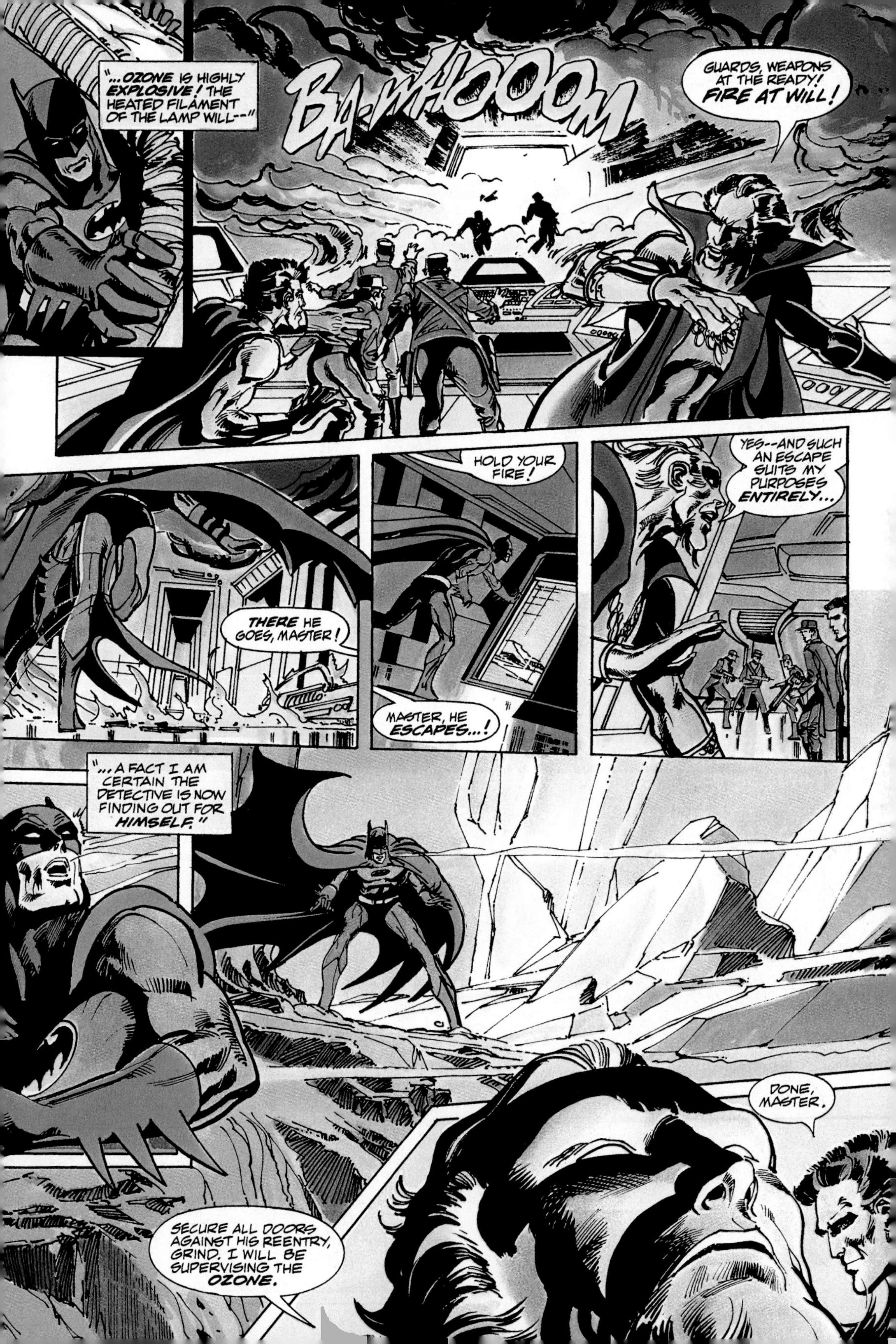
"...OZONE IS HIGHLY EXPLOSIVE! THE HEATED FILAMENT OF THE LAMP WILL--"
BA-WHOOOM
GUARDS, WEAPONS AT THE READY! FIRE AT WILL!
THERE HE GOES, MASTER!
HOLD YOUR FIRE!
MASTER, HE ESCAPES...!
YES--AND SUCH AN ESCAPE SUITS MY PURPOSES ENTIRELY...
"...A FACT I AM CERTAIN THE DETECTIVE IS NOW FINDING OUT FOR HIMSELF."
DONE, MASTER.
SECURE ALL DOORS AGAINST HIS REENTRY, GRIND. I WILL BE SUPERVISING THE OZONE.

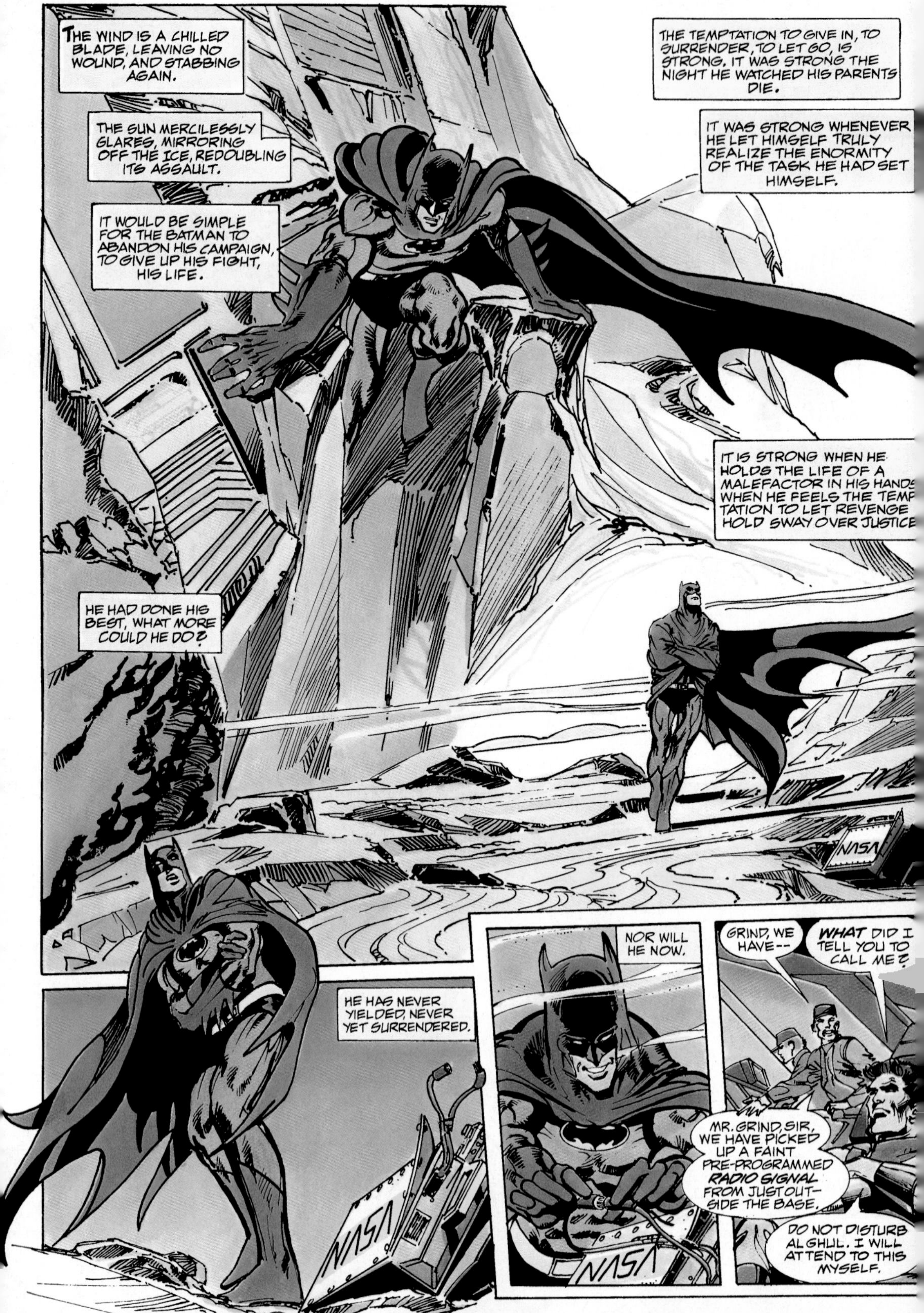
THE WIND IS A CHILLED BLADE, LEAVING NO WOUND, AND STABBING AGAIN.
THE SUN MERCILESSLY GLARES, MIRRORING OFF THE ICE, REDOUBLING ITS ASSAULT.
IT WOULD BE SIMPLE FOR THE BATMAN TO ABANDON HIS CAMPAIGN, TO GIVE UP HIS FIGHT, HIS LIFE.
THE TEMPTATION TO GIVE IN, TO SURRENDER, TO LET GO, IS STRONG. IT WAS STRONG THE NIGHT HE WATCHED HIS PARENTS DIE.
IT WAS STRONG WHENEVER HE LET HIMSELF TRULY REALIZE THE ENORMITY OF THE TASK HE HAD SET HIMSELF.
IT IS STRONG WHEN HE HOLDS THE LIFE OF A MALEFACTOR IN HIS HANDS WHEN HE FEELS THE TEMPTATION TO LET REVENGE HOLD SWAY OVER JUSTICE
HE HAD DONE HIS BEST, WHAT MORE COULD HE DO?
NASA
HE HAS NEVER YIELDED, NEVER YET SURRENDERED.
NASA
NOR WILL HE NOW.
NASA
GRIND, WE HAVE--
WHAT DID I TELL YOU TO CALL ME?
MR. GRIND, SIR, WE HAVE PICKED UP A FAINT PRE-PROGRAMMED RADIO SIGNAL FROM JUST OUTSIDE THE BASE.
DO NOT DISTURB AL GHUL. I WILL ATTEND TO THIS MYSELF.

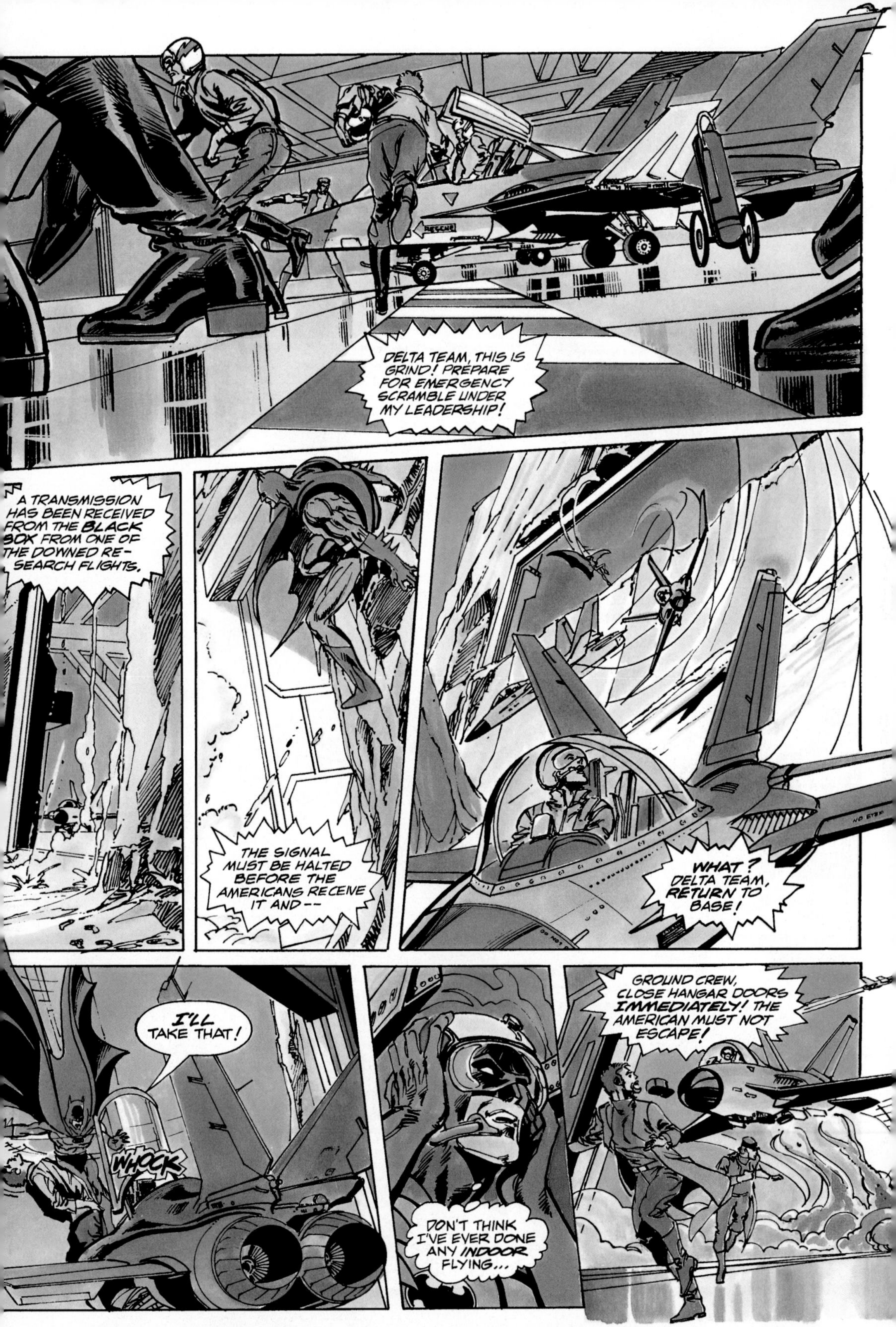
DELTA TEAM, THIS IS GRIND! PREPARE FOR EMERGENCY SCRAMBLE UNDER MY LEADERSHIP!
A TRANSMISSION HAS BEEN RECEIVED FROM THE BLACK BOX FROM ONE OF THE DOWNED RE-SEARCH FLIGHTS.
THE SIGNAL MUST BE HALTED BEFORE THE AMERICANS RECEIVE IT AND--
WHAT? DELTA TEAM, RETURN TO BASE!
I'LL TAKE THAT!
WHOCK
DON'T THINK I'VE EVER DONE ANY INDOOR FLYING...
GROUND CREW, CLOSE HANGAR DOORS IMMEDIATELY! THE AMERICAN MUST NOT ESCAPE!

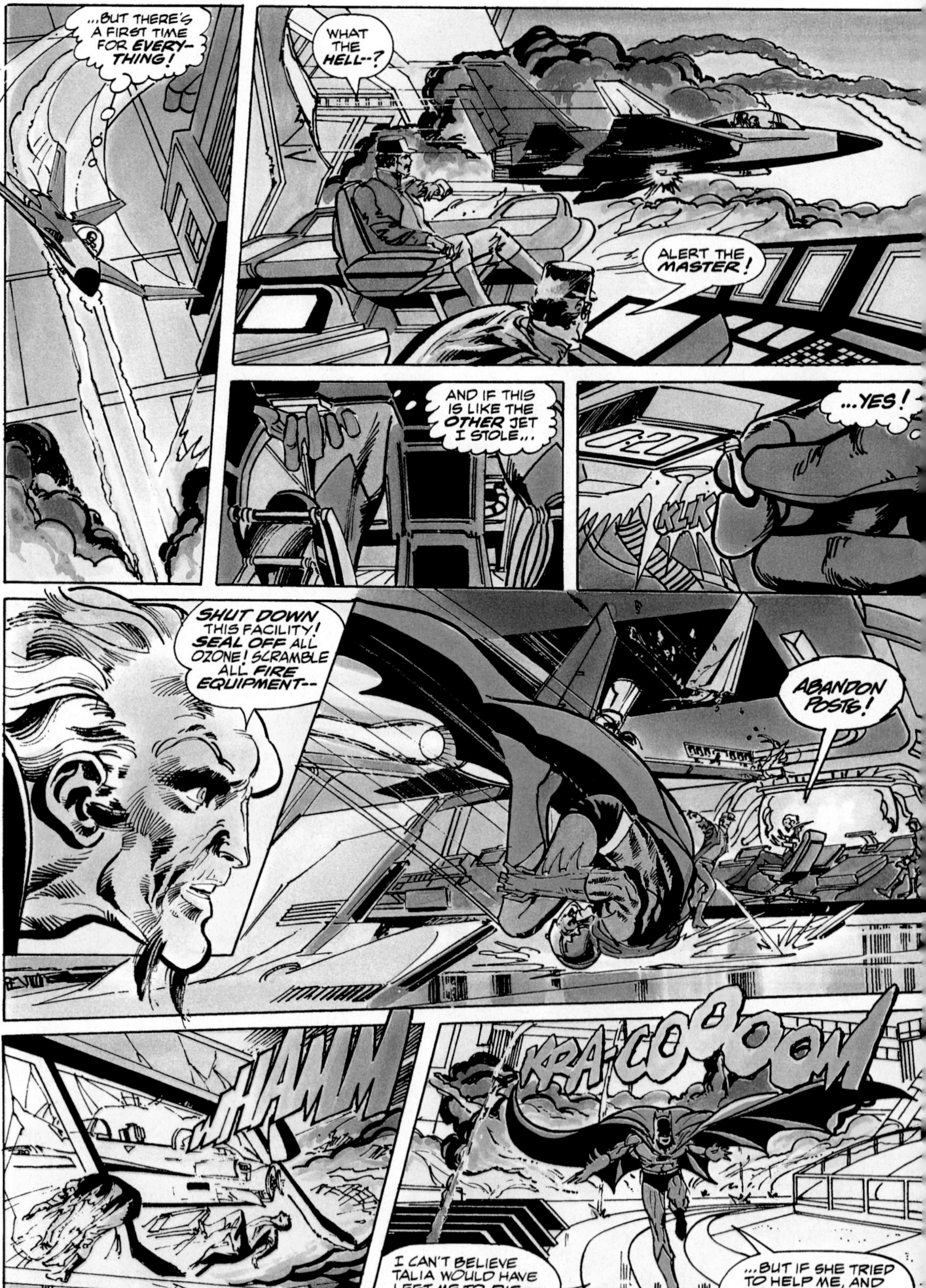
...BUT THERE'S A FIRST TIME FOR EVERYTHING!
WHAT THE HELL--?
ALERT THE MASTER!
AND IF THIS IS LIKE THE OTHER JET I STOLE...
...YES!
KLIK
SHUT DOWN THIS FACILITY! SEAL OFF ALL OZONE! SCRAMBLE ALL FIRE EQUIPMENT--
ABANDON POSTS!
KRA-COOOOOM
I CAN'T BELIEVE TALIA WOULD HAVE LEFT ME TO DIE-- OR MAYBE I JUST DON'T WANT TO...
...BUT IF SHE TRIED TO HELP ME, AND FAILED, SHE'S PROBABLY BEING HELD CAPTIVE.

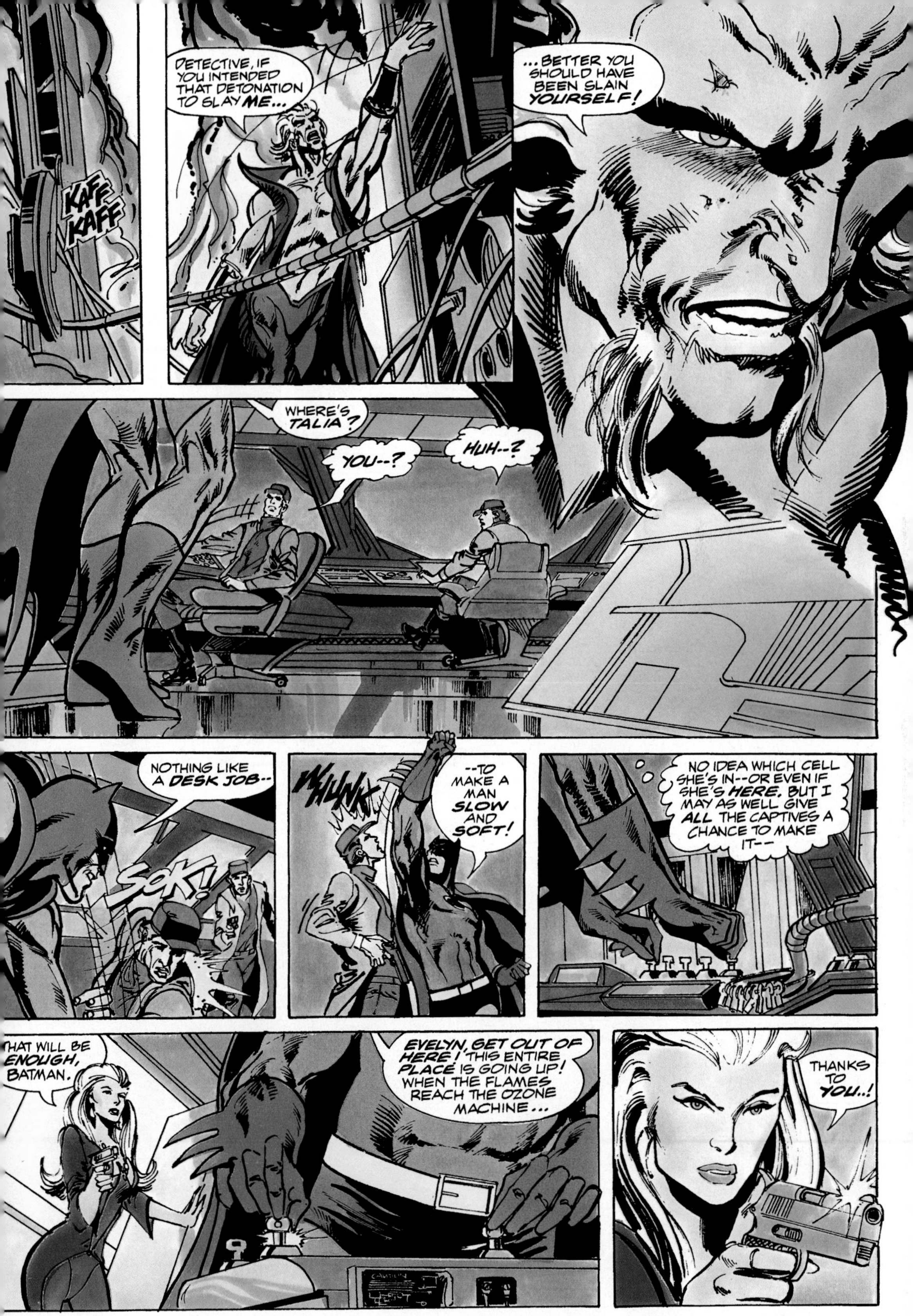
KAFF KAFF
DETECTIVE, IF YOU INTENDED THAT DETONATION TO SLAY ME...
...BETTER YOU SHOULD HAVE BEEN SLAIN YOURSELF!
WHERE'S TALIA?
YOU--?
HUH--?
NOTHING LIKE A DESK JOB--
SOK!
WHUNK
--TO MAKE A MAN SLOW AND SOFT!
NO IDEA WHICH CELL SHE'S IN--OR EVEN IF SHE'S HERE. BUT I MAY AS WELL GIVE ALL THE CAPTIVES A CHANCE TO MAKE IT--
THAT WILL BE ENOUGH, BATMAN.
EVELYN, GET OUT OF HERE! THIS ENTIRE PLACE IS GOING UP! WHEN THE FLAMES REACH THE OZONE MACHINE...
THANKS TO YOU..!

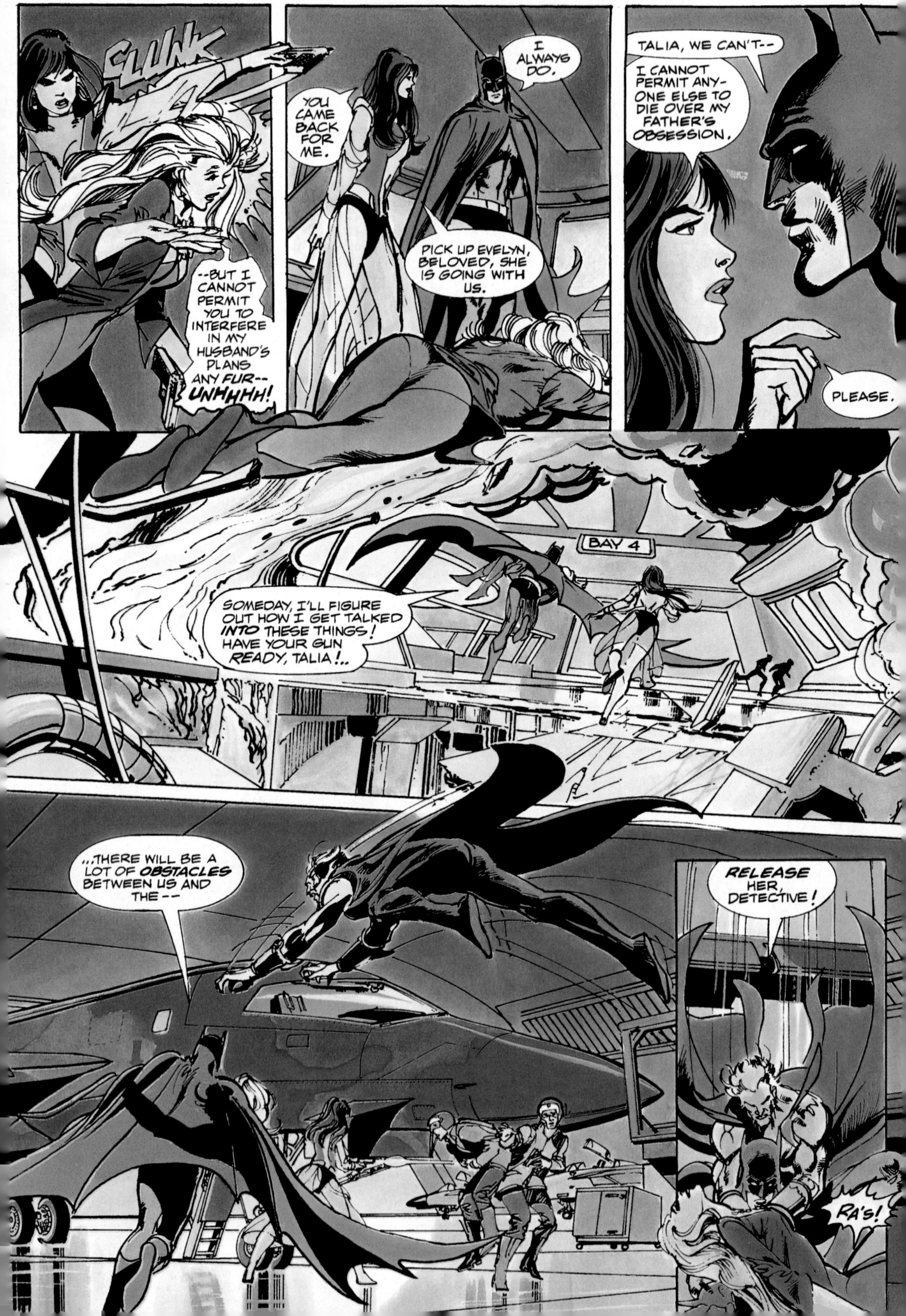

SLUNK
--BUT I CANNOT PERMIT YOU TO INTERFERE IN MY HUSBAND'S PLANS ANY FUR-- UNHHHH!
YOU CAME BACK FOR ME.
I ALWAYS DO.
PICK UP EVELYN, BELOVED, SHE IS GOING WITH US.
TALIA, WE CAN'T--
I CANNOT PERMIT ANYONE ELSE TO DIE OVER MY FATHER'S OBSESSION.
PLEASE.
BAY 4
SOMEDAY, I'LL FIGURE OUT HOW I GET TALKED INTO THESE THINGS! HAVE YOUR GUN READY, TALIA!..
...THERE WILL BE A LOT OF OBSTACLES BETWEEN US AND THE --
RELEASE HER, DETECTIVE!
RA'S!

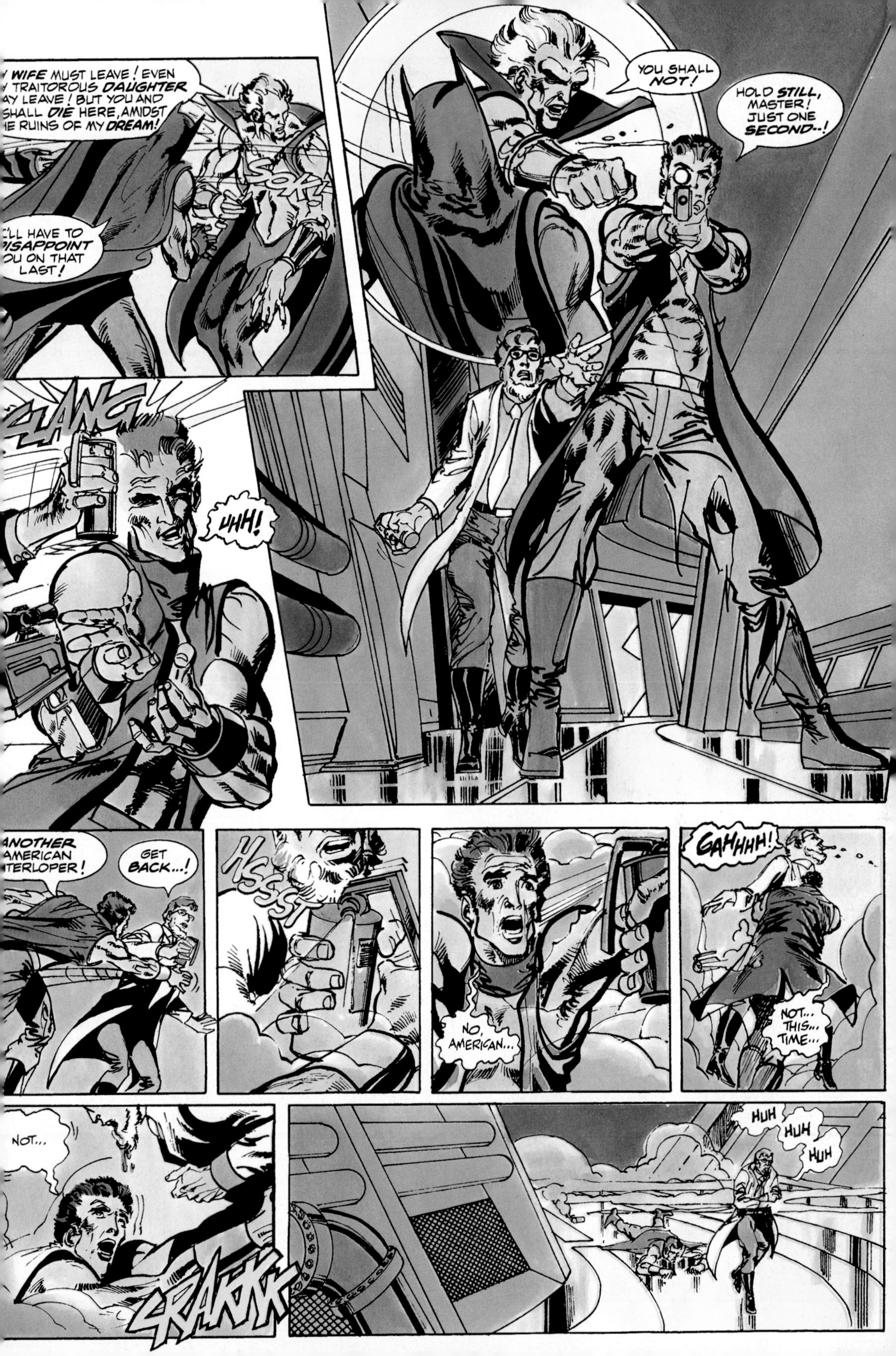

WIFE MUST LEAVE! EVEN
TRAITOROUS DAUGHTER
AY LEAVE! BUT YOU AND
SHALL DIE HERE, AMIDST
HE RUINS OF MY DREAM!
SOK!
'LL HAVE TO
ISAPPOINT
OU ON THAT
LAST!
YOU SHALL NOT!
HOLD STILL, MASTER! JUST ONE SECOND--!
LANG
UHH!
ANOTHER
AMERICAN
NTERLOPER!
GET BACK...!
HSSST
NO, AMERICAN...
GAHHHH!
NOT... THIS... TIME...
NOT...
CRAKKK
HUH
HUH
HUH

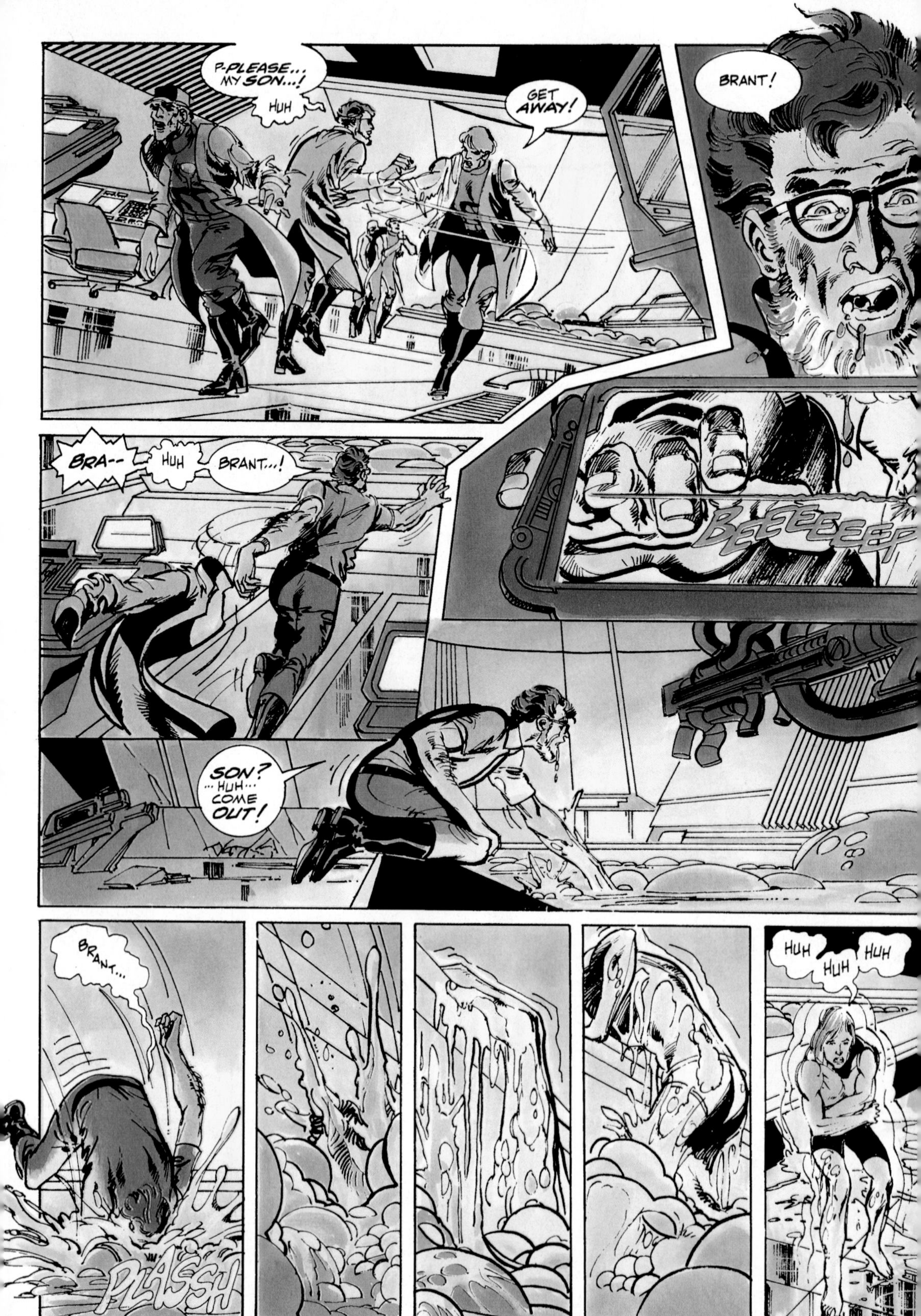

P-PLEASE... MY SON...!
HUH
GET AWAY!
BRANT!
BRA--
HUH
BRANT...!
BEEEEEEP
SON? ...HUH... COME OUT!
BRANT...
PLASSH
HUH
HUH
HUH

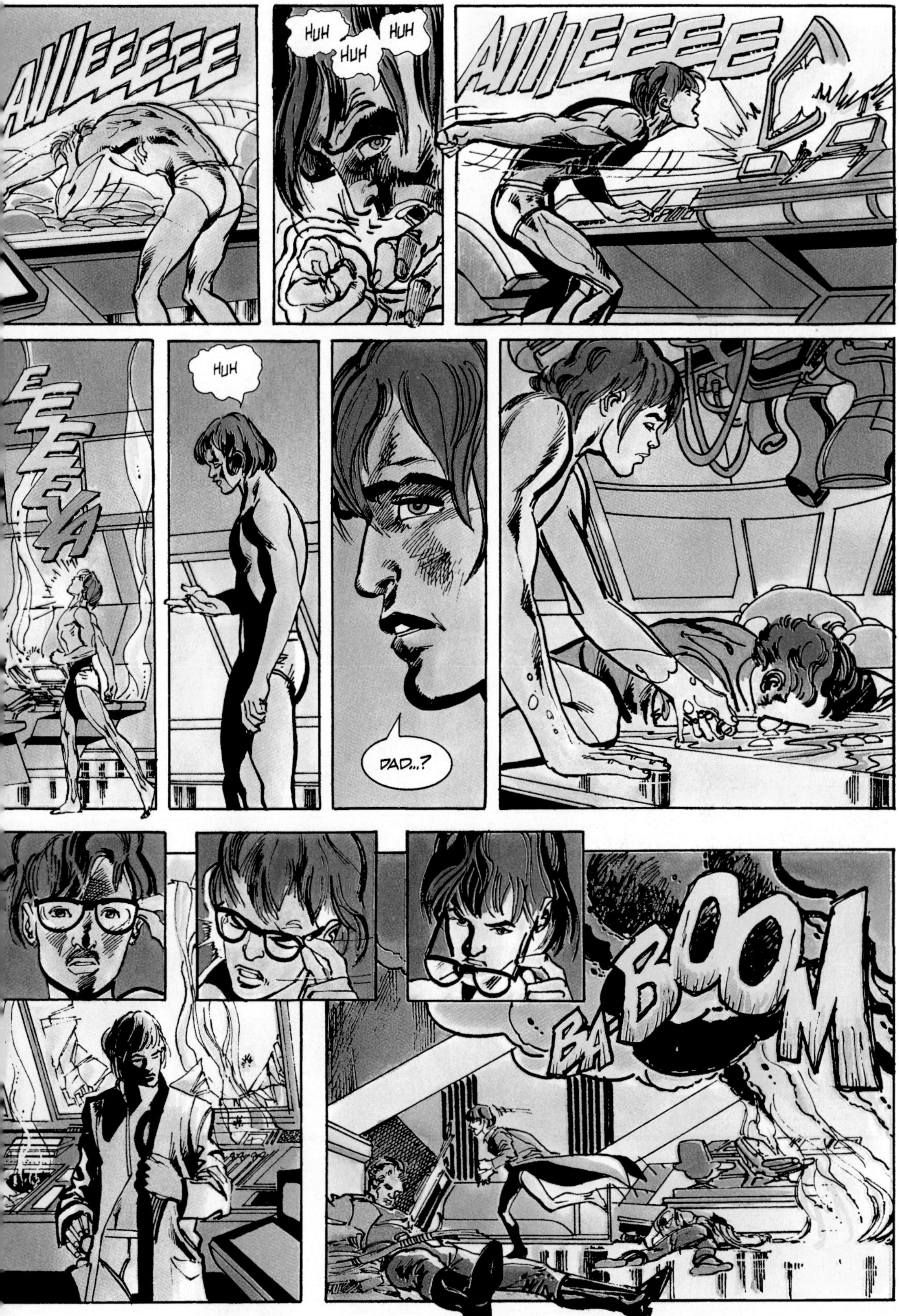

AIIIEEEEE
HUH
HUH
HUH
AIIIEEEEE
EEEEYA
HUH
DAD...?
BABOOM

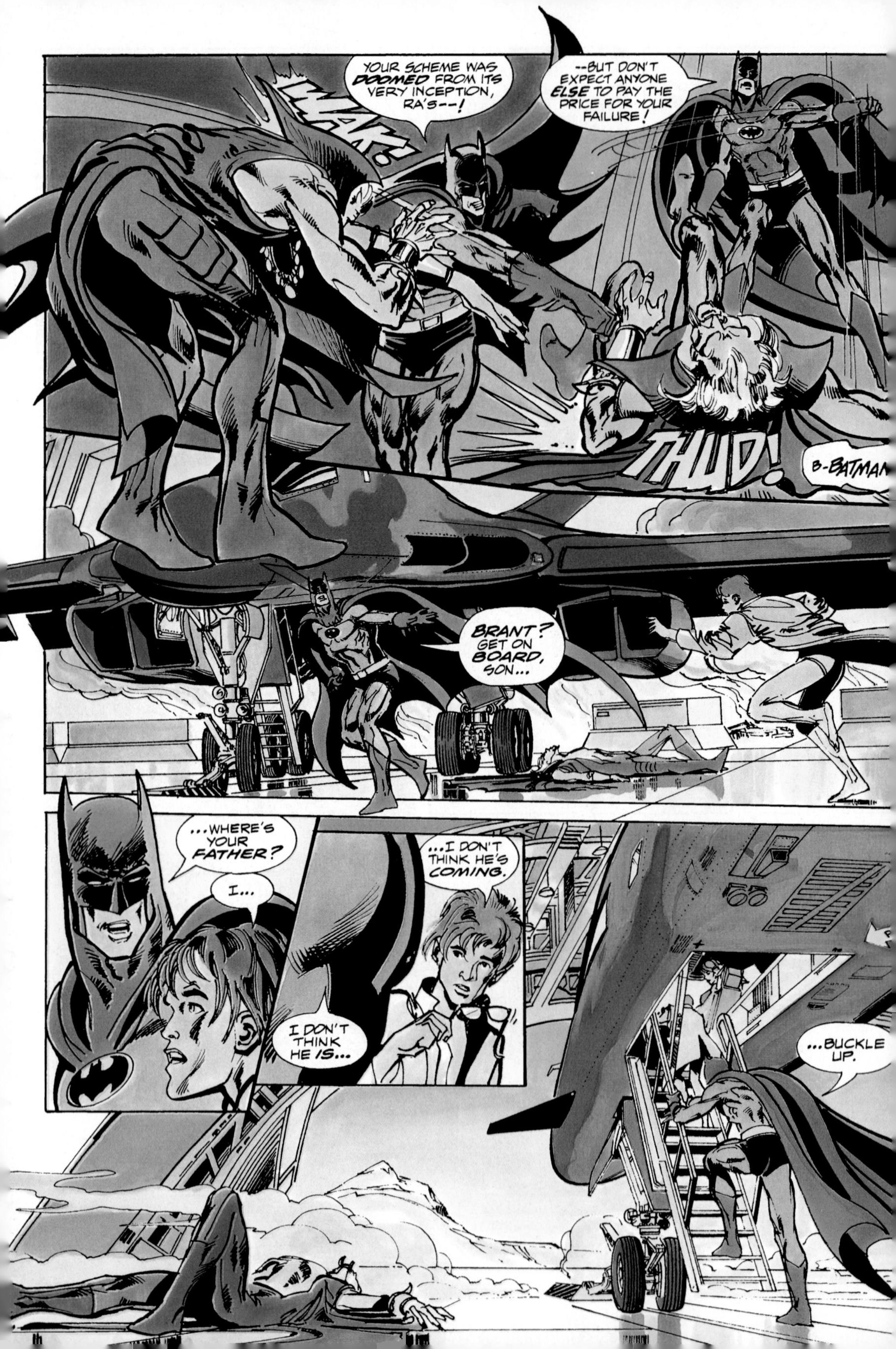
WAK!
YOUR SCHEME WAS DOOMED FROM ITS VERY INCEPTION, RA'S--!
--BUT DON'T EXPECT ANYONE ELSE TO PAY THE PRICE FOR YOUR FAILURE!
THUD!
B-BATMAN
BRANT? GET ON BOARD, SON...
...WHERE'S YOUR FATHER?
I...
...I DON'T THINK HE'S COMING.
I DON'T THINK HE IS...
...BUCKLE UP.

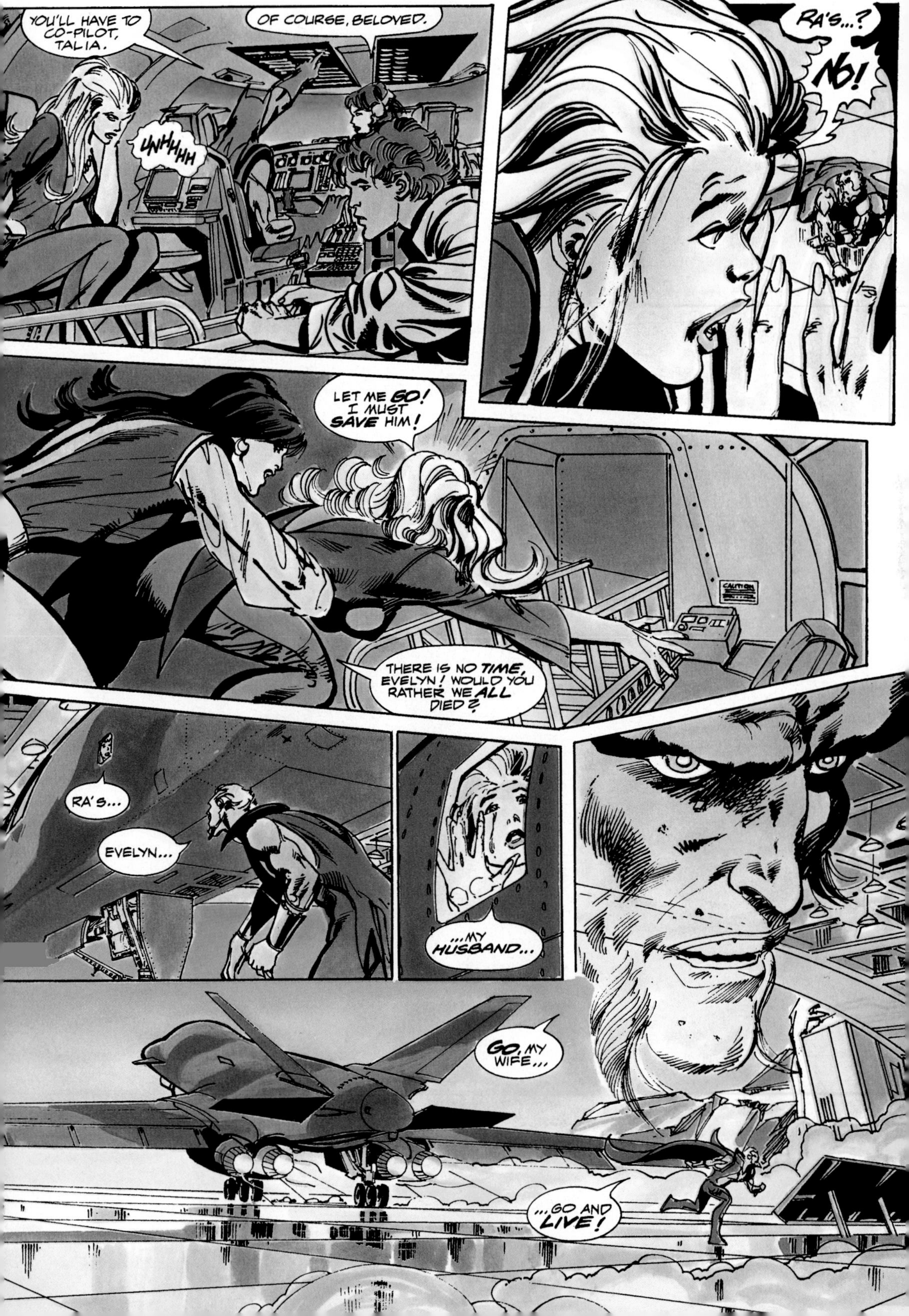
YOU'LL HAVE TO CO-PILOT, TALIA.
OF COURSE, BELOVED.
UNHHHH
RA'S...?
NO!
LET ME GO! I MUST SAVE HIM!
THERE IS NO TIME, EVELYN! WOULD YOU RATHER WE ALL DIED?
RA'S...
EVELYN...
...MY HUSBAND...
GO, MY WIFE...
...GO AND LIVE!

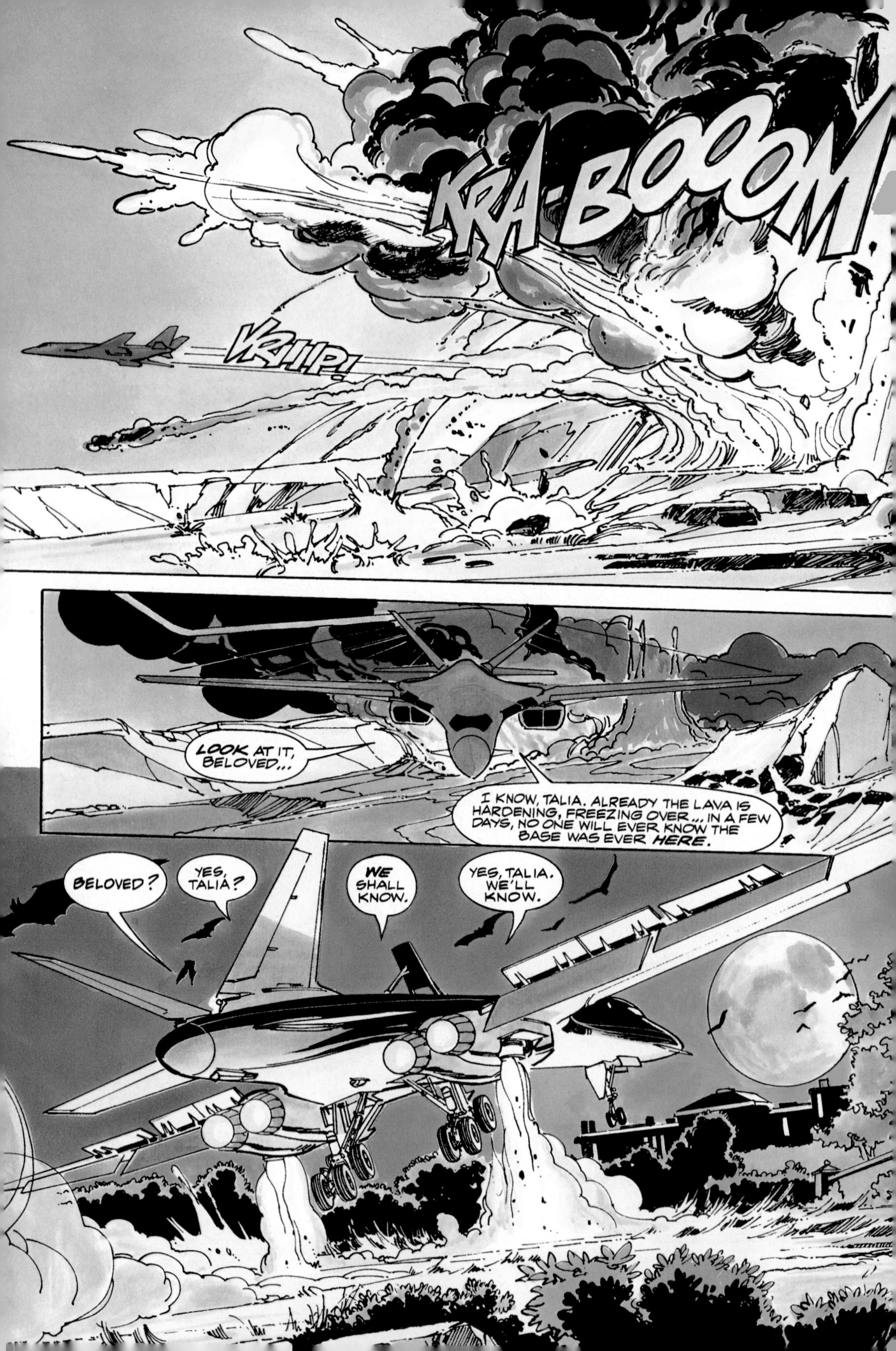
KRA-BOOOOM!
VRIIIP!
LOOK AT IT, BELOVED...
I KNOW, TALIA. ALREADY THE LAVA IS HARDENING, FREEZING OVER... IN A FEW DAYS, NO ONE WILL EVER KNOW THE BASE WAS EVER HERE.
BELOVED?
YES, TALIA?
WE SHALL KNOW.
YES, TALIA. WE'LL KNOW.

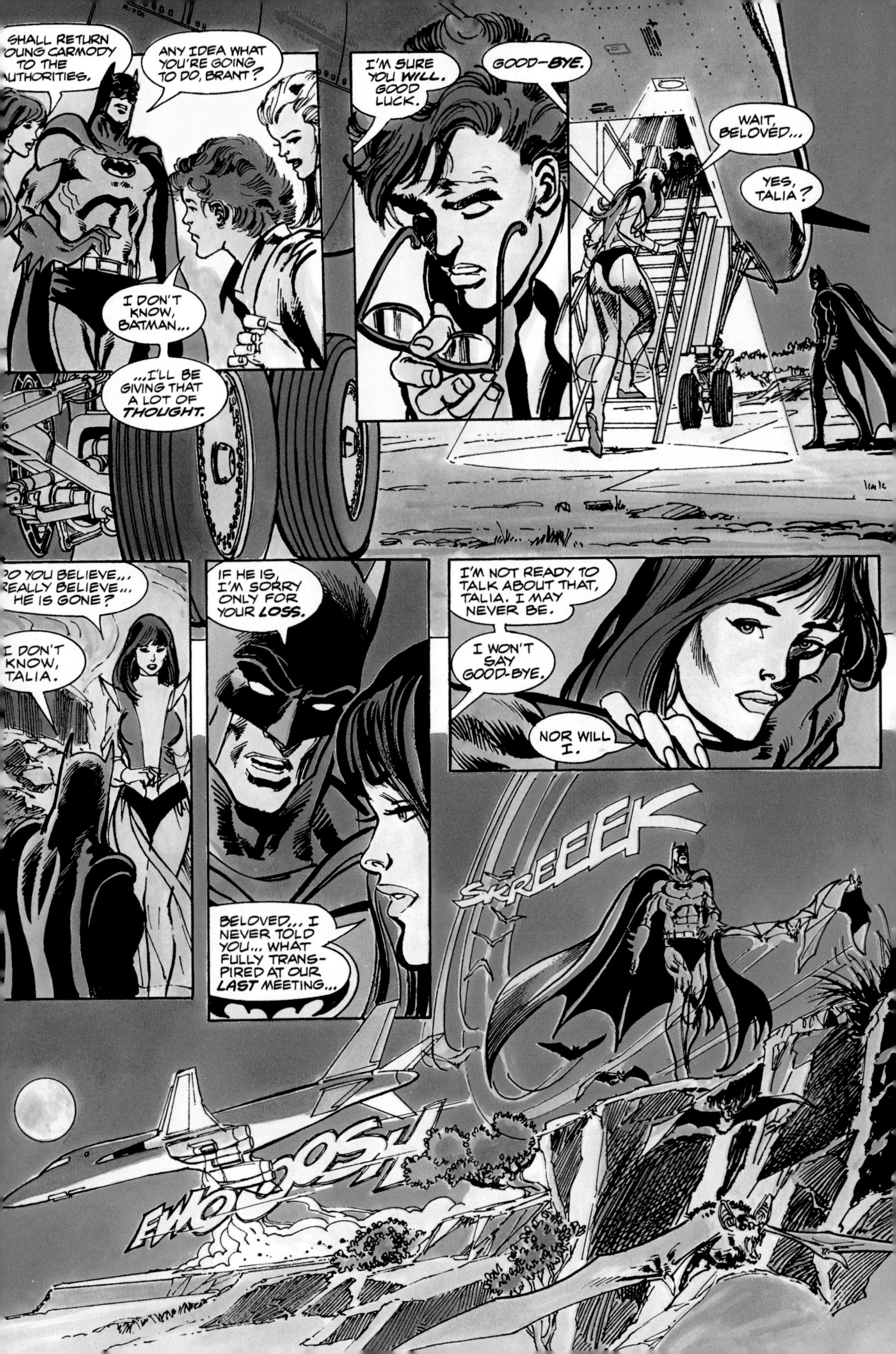
SHALL RETURN OUNG CARMODY TO THE AUTHORITIES.
ANY IDEA WHAT YOU'RE GOING TO DO, BRANT?
I DON'T KNOW, BATMAN...
...I'LL BE GIVING THAT A LOT OF THOUGHT.
I'M SURE YOU WILL. GOOD LUCK.
GOOD-BYE.
WAIT, BELOVED...
YES, TALIA?
DO YOU BELIEVE... REALLY BELIEVE... HE IS GONE?
I DON'T KNOW, TALIA.
IF HE IS, I'M SORRY ONLY FOR YOUR LOSS.
BELOVED... I NEVER TOLD YOU... WHAT FULLY TRANSPIRED AT OUR LAST MEETING...
I'M NOT READY TO TALK ABOUT THAT, TALIA. I MAY NEVER BE.
I WON'T SAY GOOD-BYE.
NOR WILL I.
SKREEEK
FWOOOSH

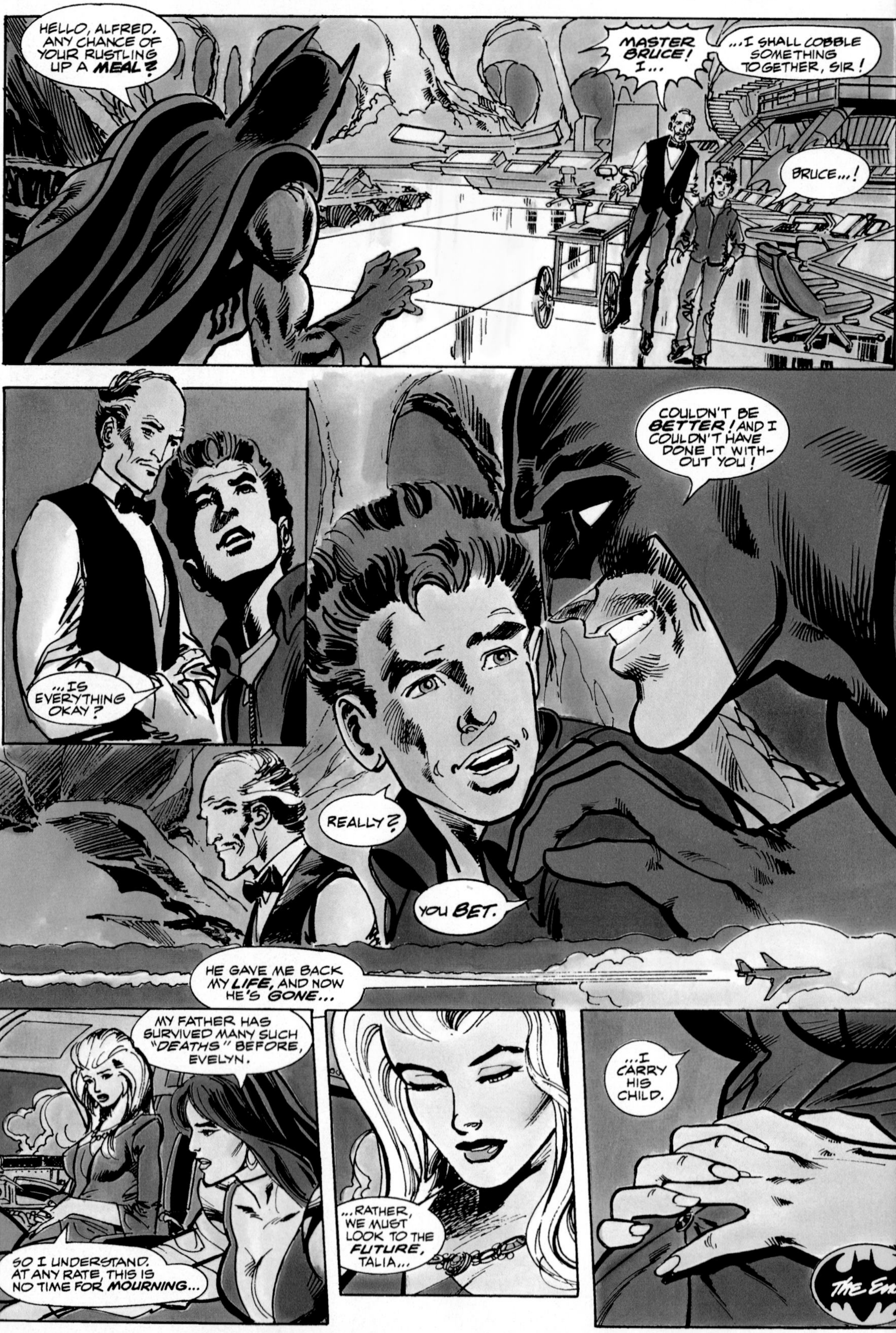
HELLO, ALFRED. ANY CHANCE OF YOUR RUSTLING UP A MEAL?
MASTER BRUCE! I...
...I SHALL COBBLE SOMETHING TOGETHER, SIR!
BRUCE...!
...IS EVERYTHING OKAY?
COULDN'T BE BETTER! AND I COULDN'T HAVE DONE IT WITH-OUT YOU!
REALLY?
YOU BET.
HE GAVE ME BACK MY LIFE, AND NOW HE'S GONE...
MY FATHER HAS SURVIVED MANY SUCH "DEATHS" BEFORE, EVELYN.
SO I UNDERSTAND. AT ANY RATE, THIS IS NO TIME FOR MOURNING...
...RATHER, WE MUST LOOK TO THE FUTURE, TALIA...
...I CARRY HIS CHILD.
The End

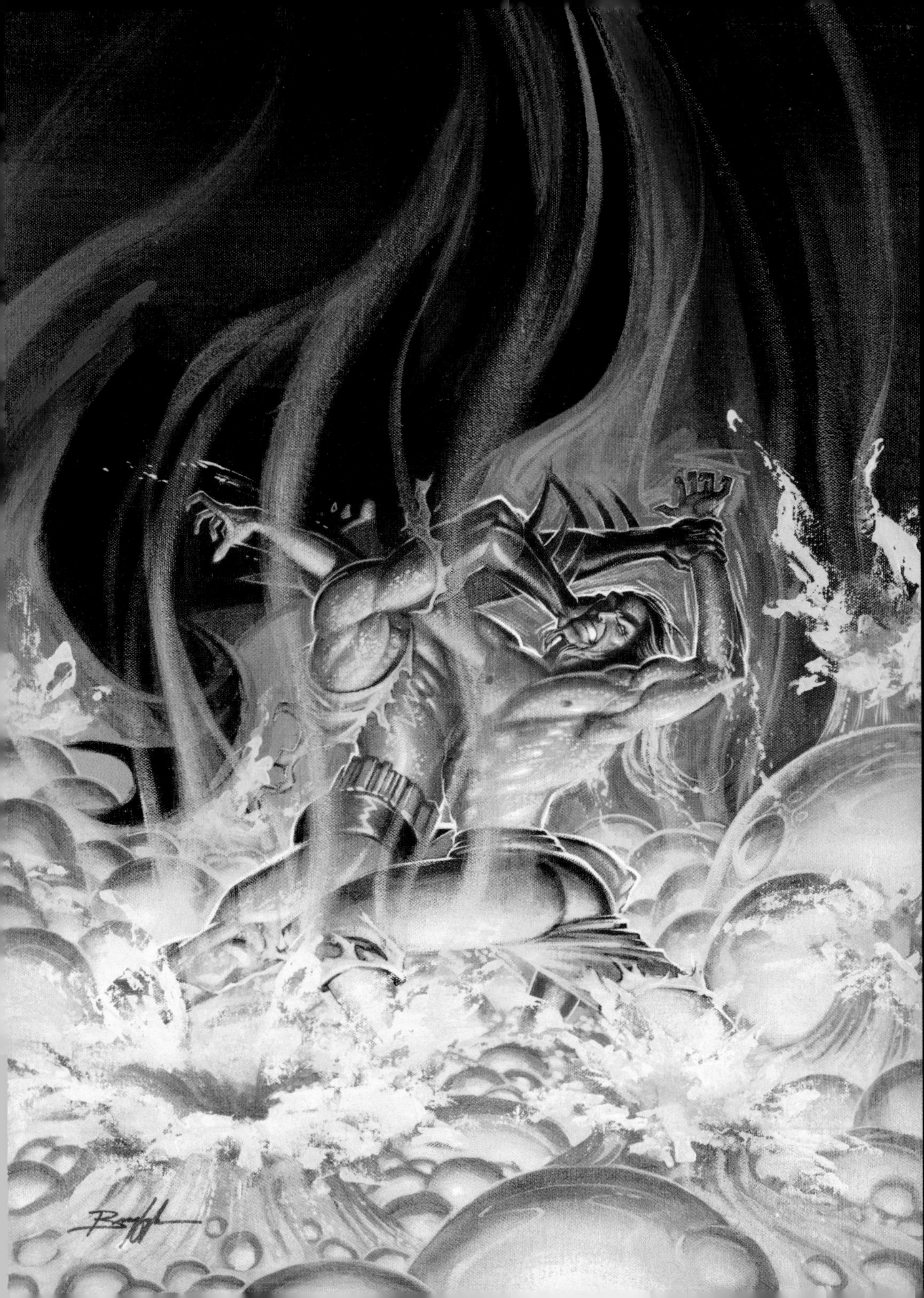

BATMAN
BIRTH OF THE DEMON

Dennis O'Neil *Writer*

Norm Breyfogle *Art, Colors & Cover*

Ken Bruzenak *Letters*

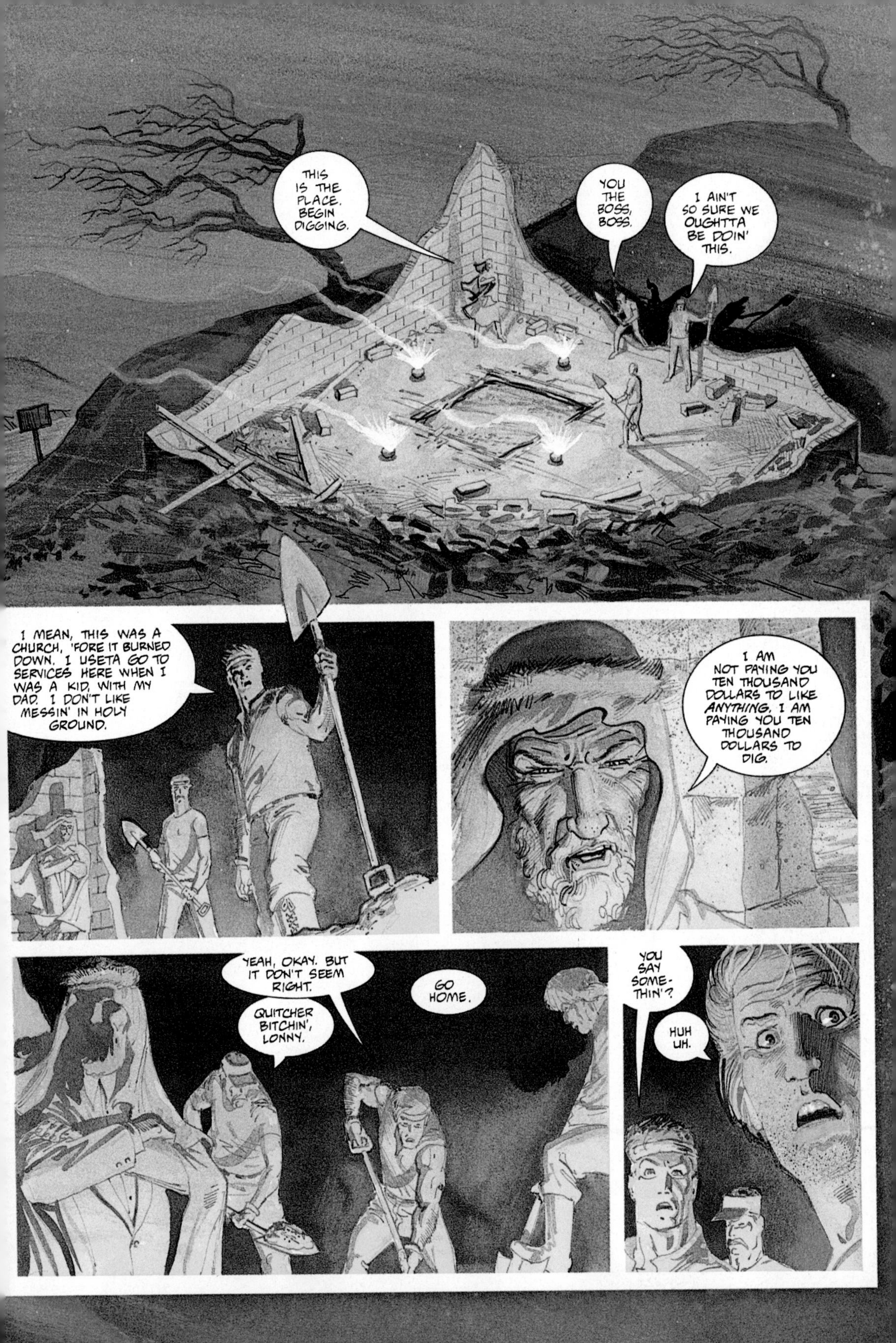
THIS IS THE PLACE. BEGIN DIGGING.
YOU THE BOSS, BOSS.
I AIN'T SO SURE WE OUGHTTA BE DOIN' THIS.
I MEAN, THIS WAS A CHURCH, 'FORE IT BURNED DOWN. I USETA GO TO SERVICES HERE WHEN I WAS A KID, WITH MY DAD. I DON'T LIKE MESSIN' IN HOLY GROUND.
I AM NOT PAYING YOU TEN THOUSAND DOLLARS TO LIKE ANYTHING. I AM PAYING YOU TEN THOUSAND DOLLARS TO DIG.
YEAH, OKAY. BUT IT DON'T SEEM RIGHT.
QUITCHER BITCHIN', LONNY.
GO HOME.
YOU SAY SOME-THIN'?
HUH UH.

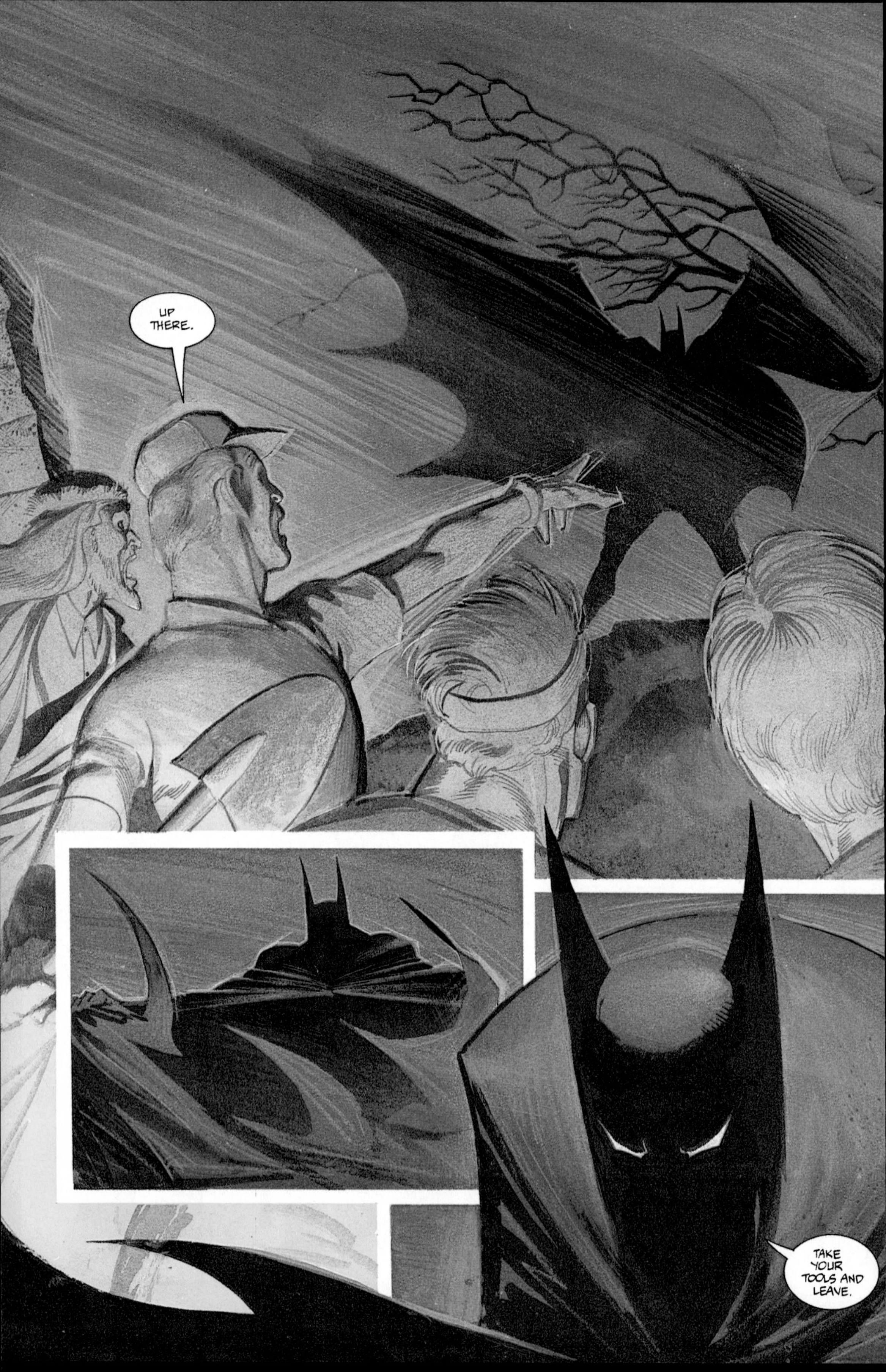
UP THERE.
TAKE YOUR TOOLS AND LEAVE.

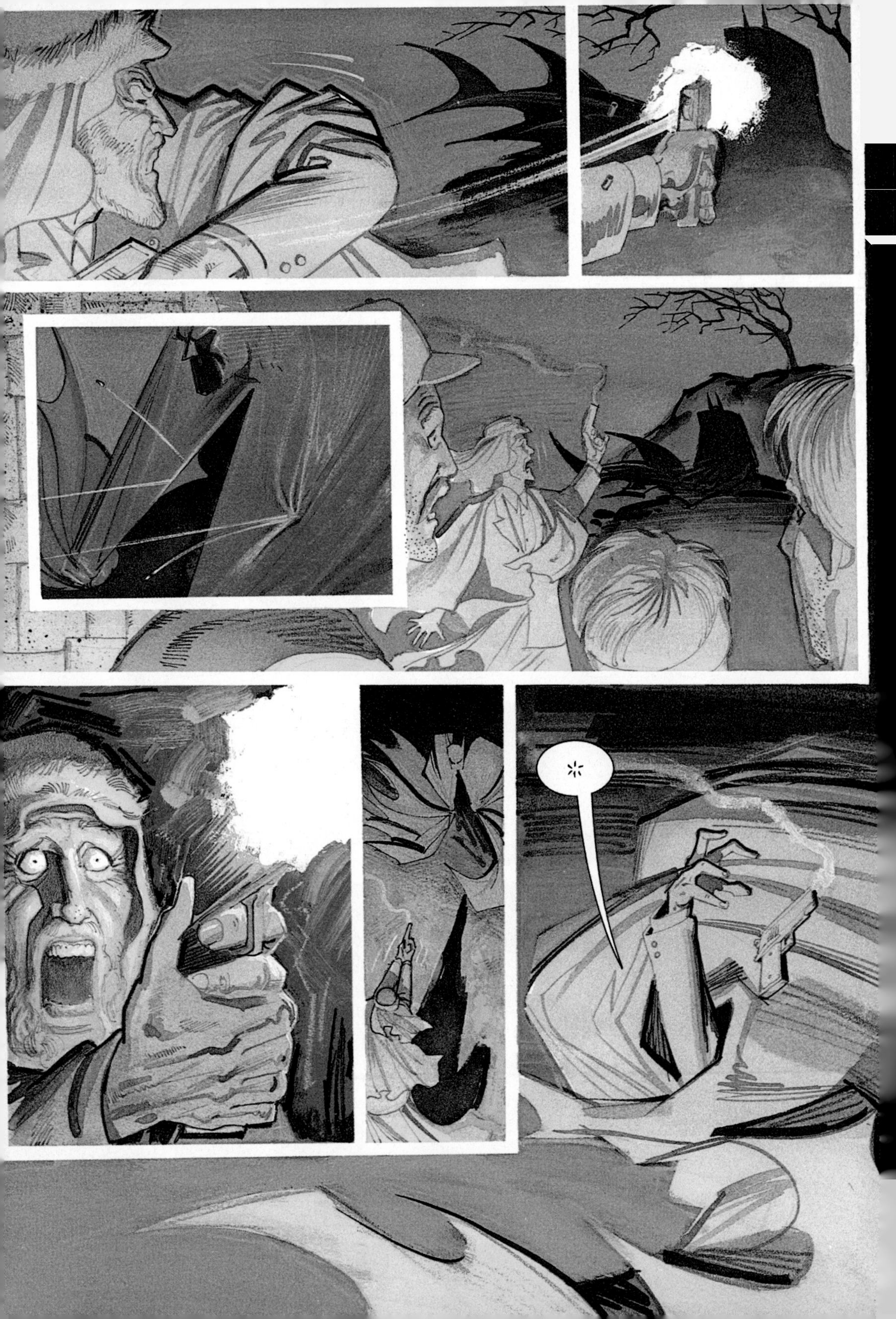

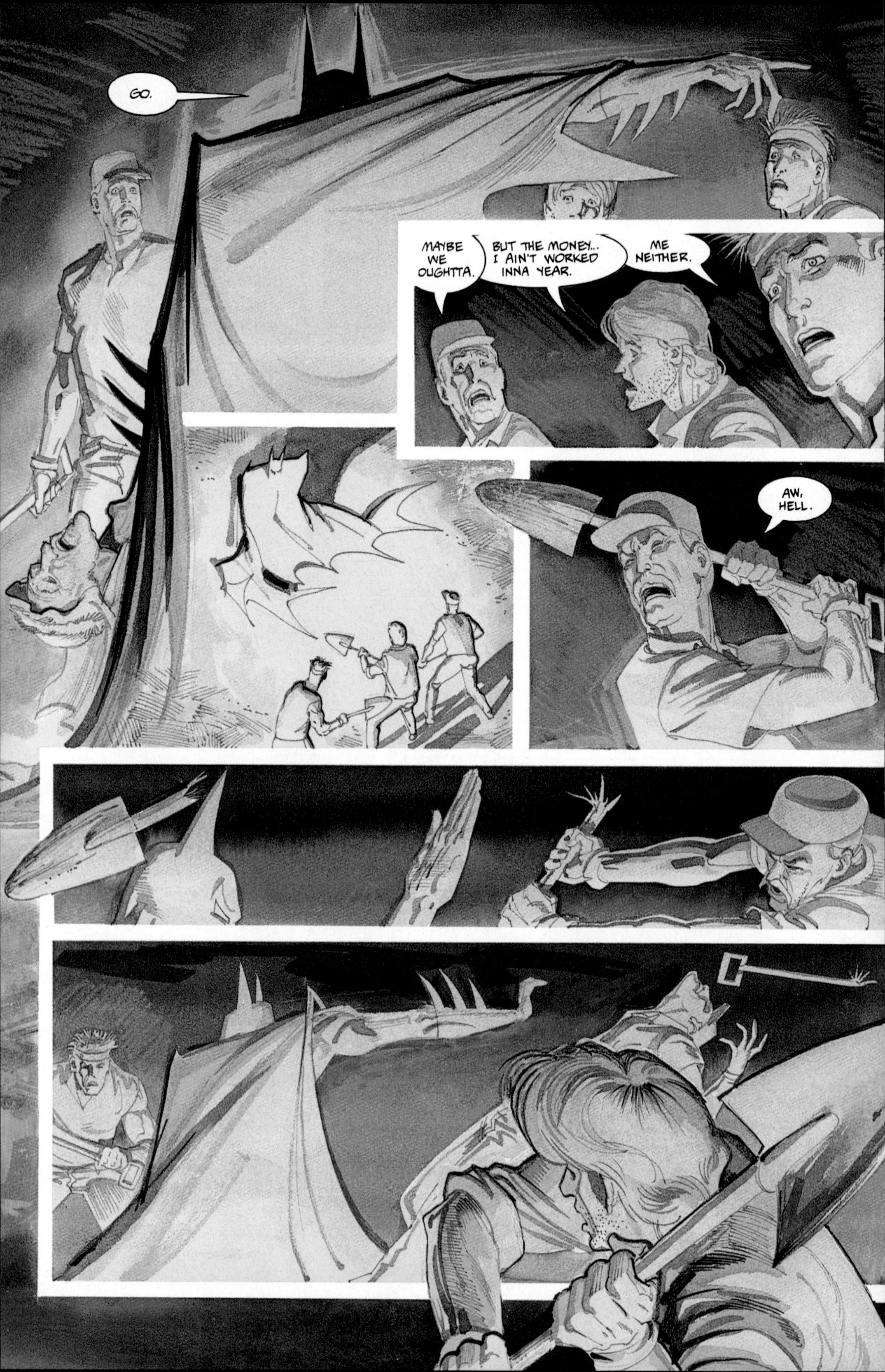
GO.
MAYBE WE OUGHTTA.
BUT THE MONEY... I AIN'T WORKED INNA YEAR.
ME NEITHER.
AW, HELL.

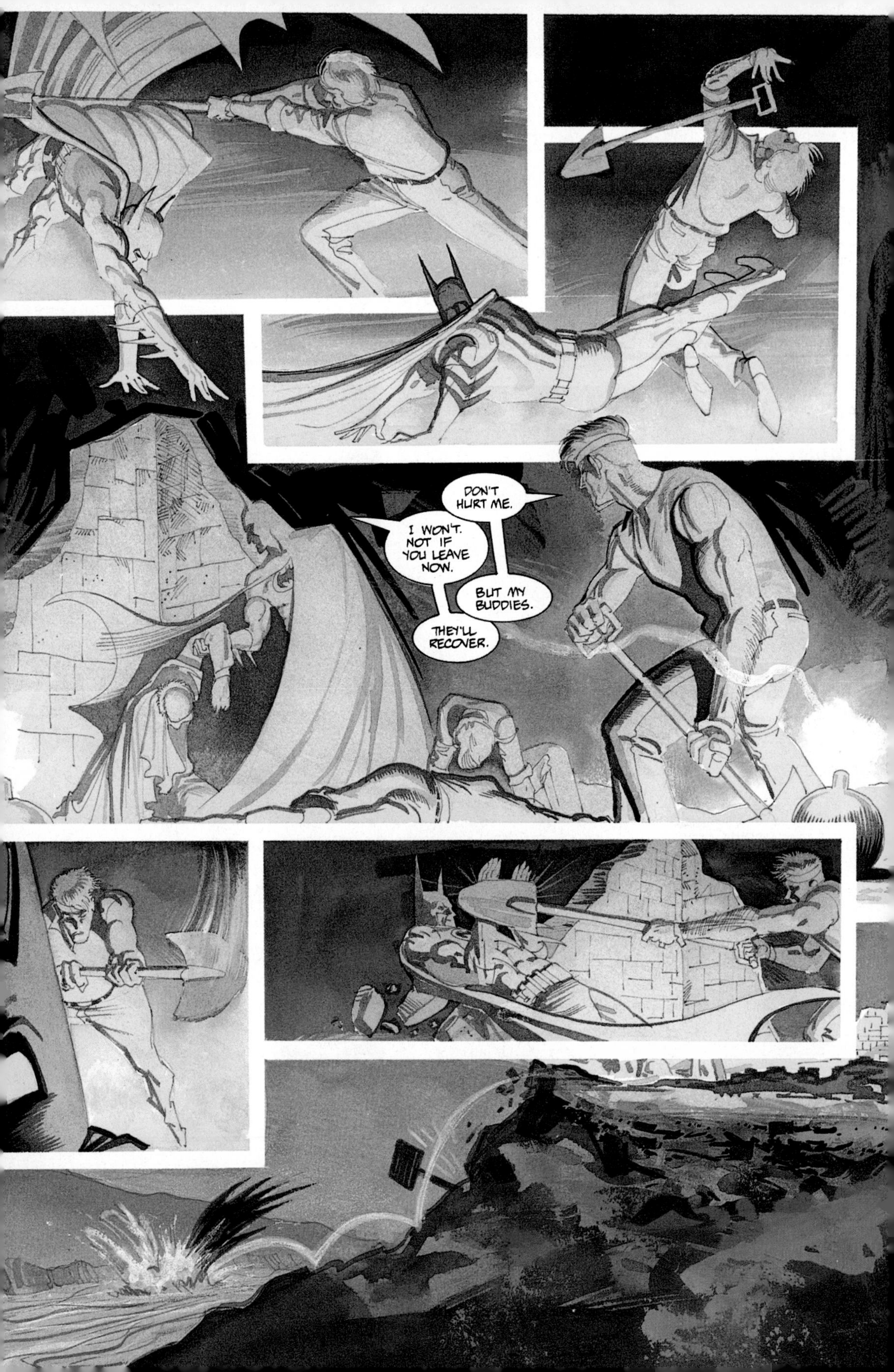
DON'T HURT ME.
I WON'T. NOT IF YOU LEAVE NOW.
BUT MY BUDDIES.
THEY'LL RECOVER.

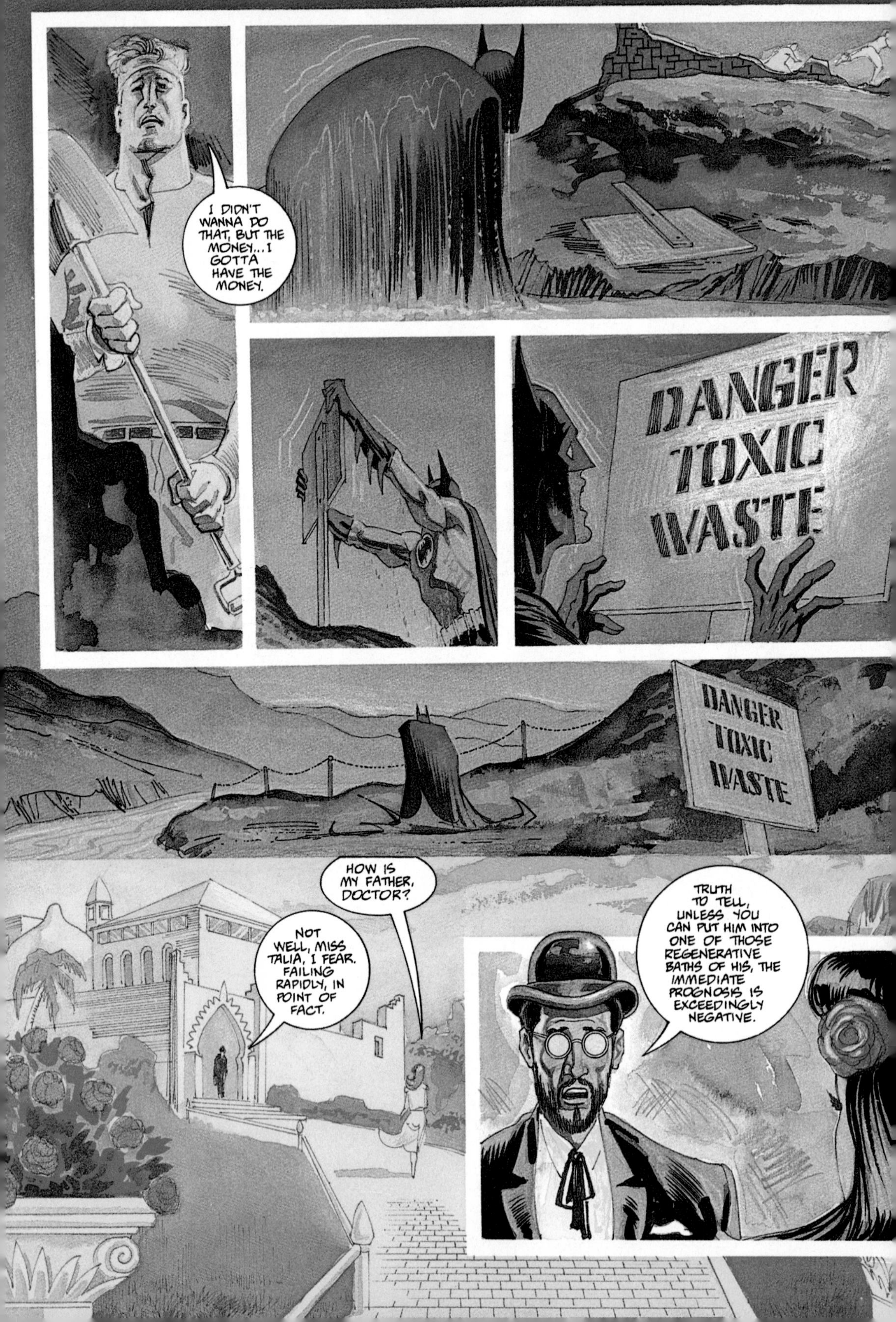
I DIDN'T WANNA DO THAT, BUT THE MONEY... I GOTTA HAVE THE MONEY.
DANGER TOXIC WASTE
DANGER TOXIC WASTE
HOW IS MY FATHER, DOCTOR?
NOT WELL, MISS TALIA, I FEAR. FAILING RAPIDLY, IN POINT OF FACT.
TRUTH TO TELL, UNLESS YOU CAN PUT HIM INTO ONE OF THOSE REGENERATIVE BATHS OF HIS, THE IMMEDIATE PROGNOSIS IS EXCEEDINGLY NEGATIVE.

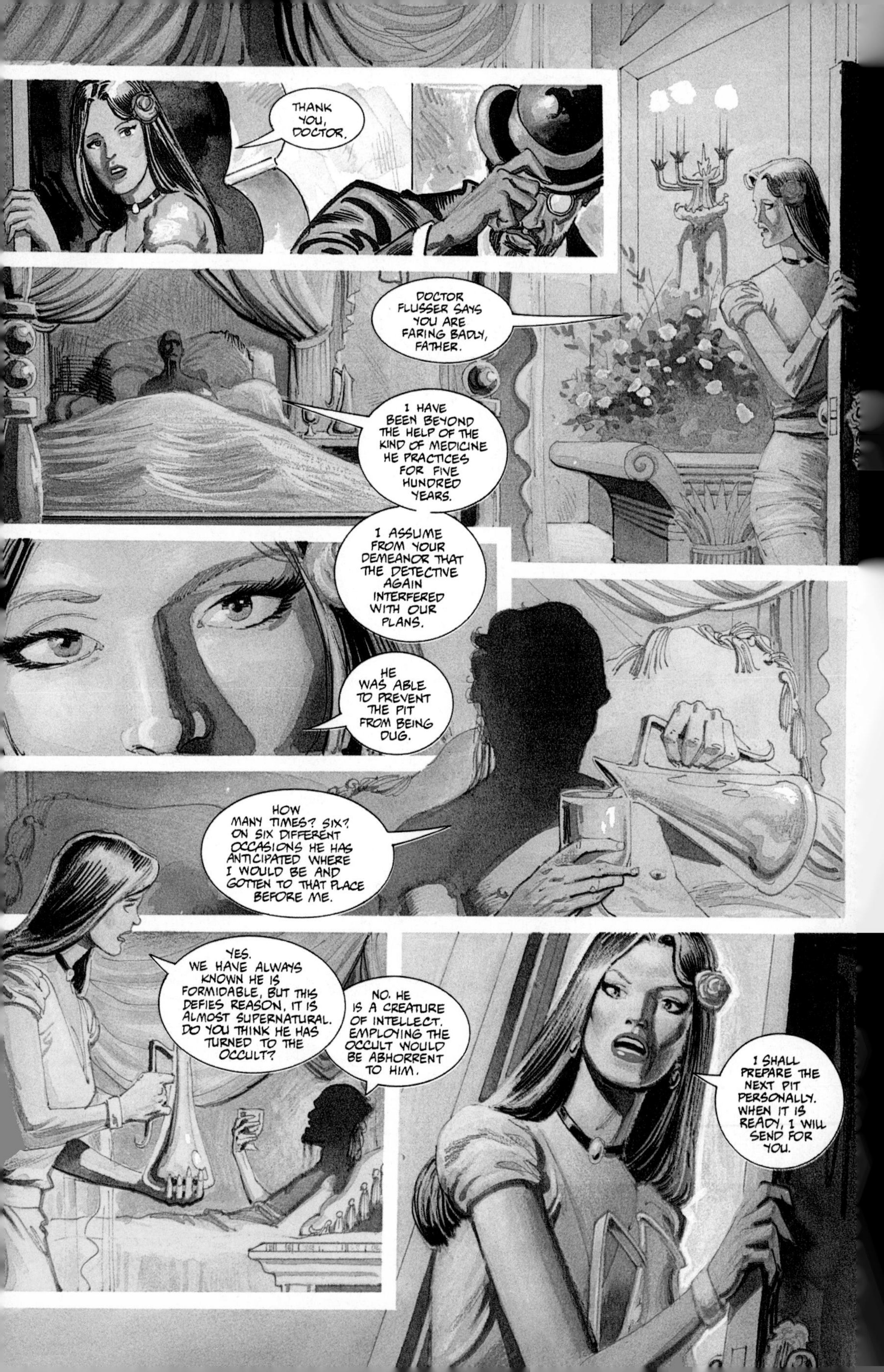
THANK YOU, DOCTOR.
DOCTOR FLUSSER SAYS YOU ARE FARING BADLY, FATHER.
I HAVE BEEN BEYOND THE HELP OF THE KIND OF MEDICINE HE PRACTICES FOR FIVE HUNDRED YEARS.
I ASSUME FROM YOUR DEMEANOR THAT THE DETECTIVE AGAIN INTERFERED WITH OUR PLANS.
HE WAS ABLE TO PREVENT THE PIT FROM BEING DUG.
HOW MANY TIMES? SIX? ON SIX DIFFERENT OCCASIONS HE HAS ANTICIPATED WHERE I WOULD BE AND GOTTEN TO THAT PLACE BEFORE ME.
YES. WE HAVE ALWAYS KNOWN HE IS FORMIDABLE, BUT THIS DEFIES REASON, IT IS ALMOST SUPERNATURAL. DO YOU THINK HE HAS TURNED TO THE OCCULT?
NO. HE IS A CREATURE OF INTELLECT. EMPLOYING THE OCCULT WOULD BE ABHORRENT TO HIM.
I SHALL PREPARE THE NEXT PIT PERSONALLY. WHEN IT IS READY, I WILL SEND FOR YOU.

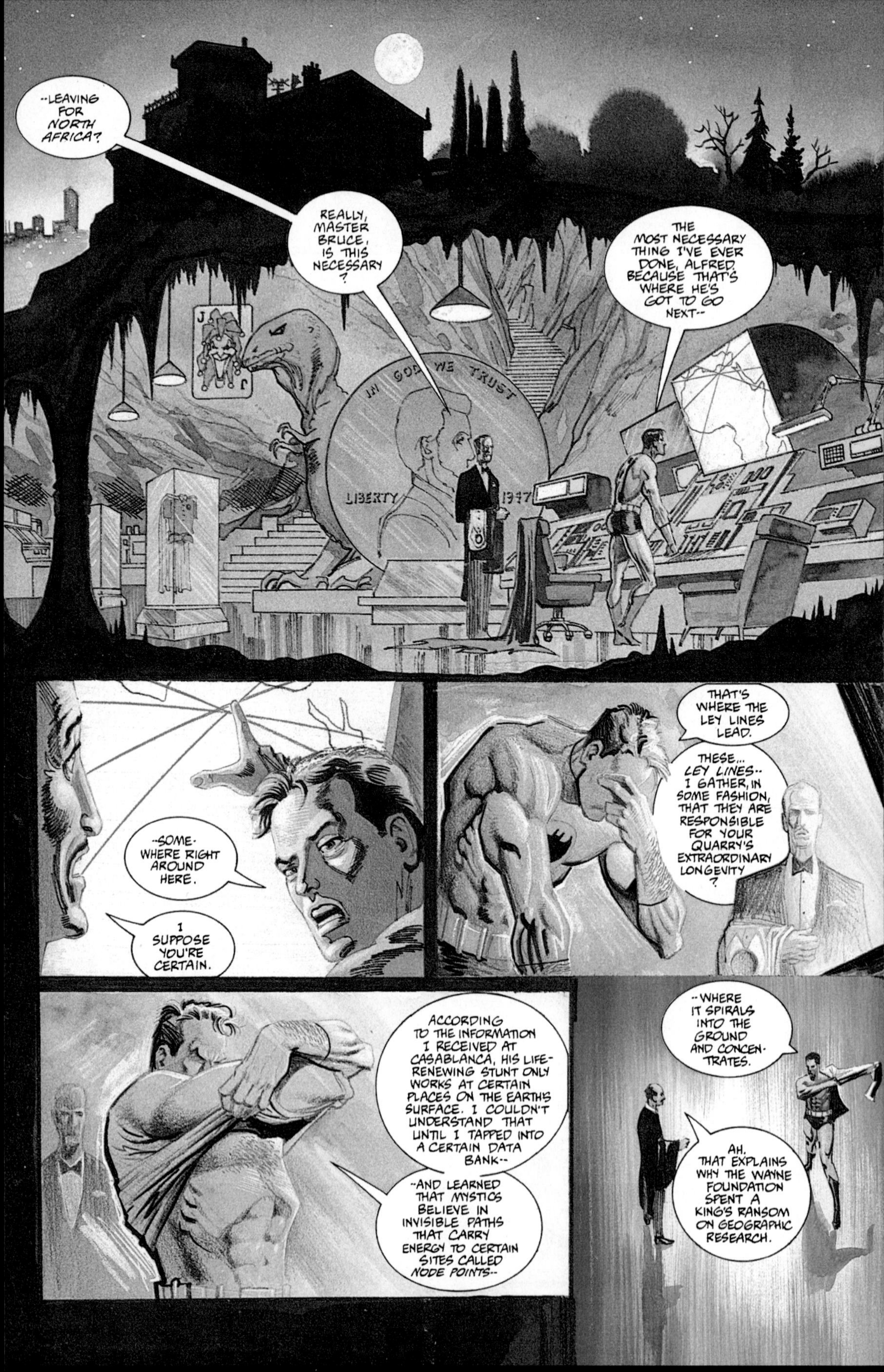
--LEAVING FOR NORTH AFRICA?
REALLY, MASTER BRUCE, IS THIS NECESSARY?
THE MOST NECESSARY THING I'VE EVER DONE, ALFRED, BECAUSE THAT'S WHERE HE'S GOT TO GO NEXT--
IN GOD WE TRUST
LIBERTY
1947
--SOME-WHERE RIGHT AROUND HERE.
I SUPPOSE YOU'RE CERTAIN.
THAT'S WHERE THE LEY LINES LEAD.
THESE... LEY LINES-- I GATHER, IN SOME FASHION, THAT THEY ARE RESPONSIBLE FOR YOUR QUARRY'S EXTRAORDINARY LONGEVITY?
ACCORDING TO THE INFORMATION I RECEIVED AT CASABLANCA, HIS LIFE-RENEWING STUNT ONLY WORKS AT CERTAIN PLACES ON THE EARTH'S SURFACE. I COULDN'T UNDERSTAND THAT UNTIL I TAPPED INTO A CERTAIN DATA BANK--
--AND LEARNED THAT MYSTICS BELIEVE IN INVISIBLE PATHS THAT CARRY ENERGY TO CERTAIN SITES CALLED NODE POINTS--
--WHERE IT SPIRALS INTO THE GROUND AND CONCEN-TRATES.
AH. THAT EXPLAINS WHY THE WAYNE FOUNDATION SPENT A KING'S RANSOM ON GEOGRAPHIC RESEARCH.

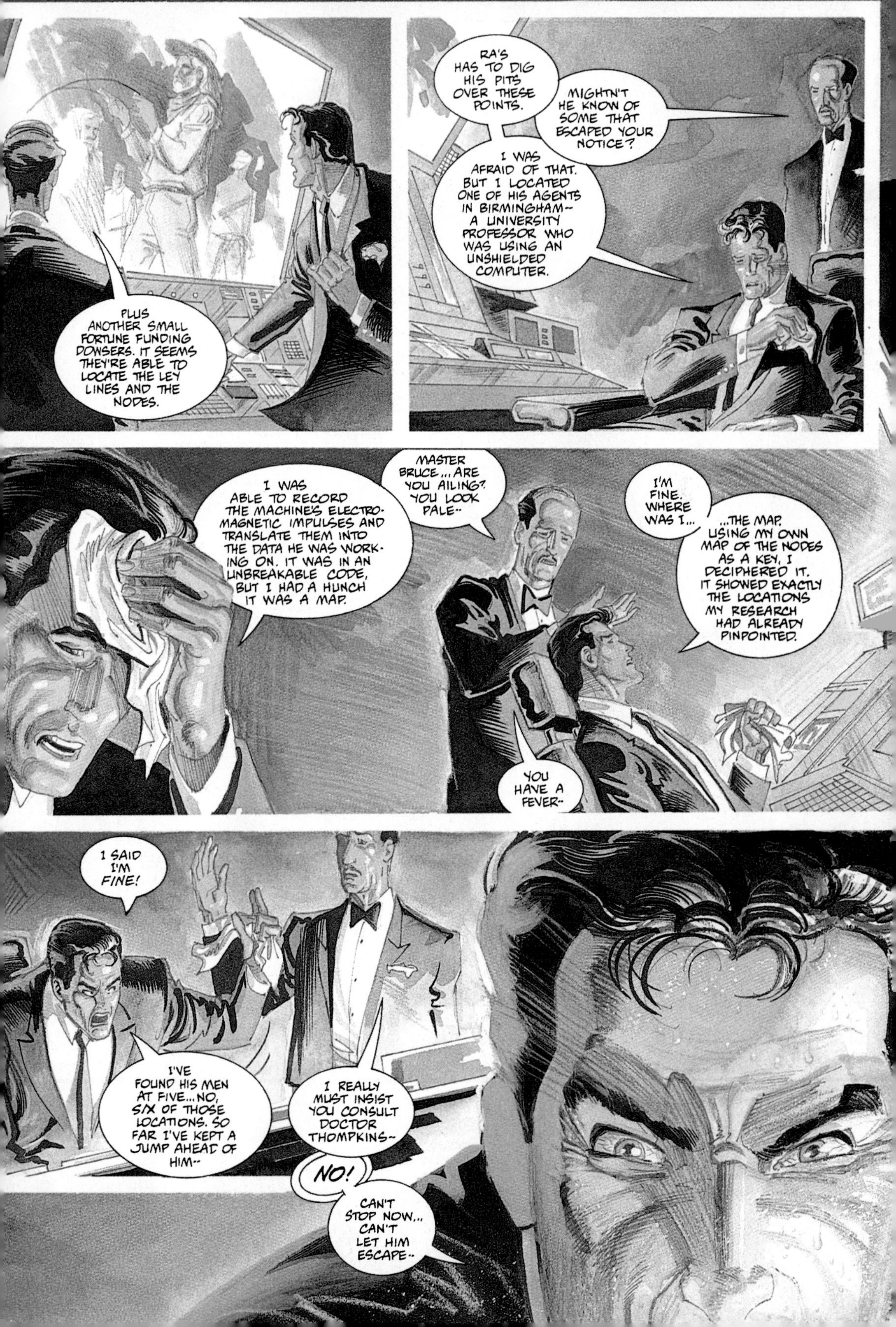
PLUS ANOTHER SMALL FORTUNE FUNDING DOWSERS. IT SEEMS THEY'RE ABLE TO LOCATE THE LEY LINES AND THE NODES.
RA'S HAS TO DIG HIS PITS OVER THESE POINTS.
MIGHTN'T HE KNOW OF SOME THAT ESCAPED YOUR NOTICE?
I WAS AFRAID OF THAT. BUT I LOCATED ONE OF HIS AGENTS IN BIRMINGHAM-- A UNIVERSITY PROFESSOR WHO WAS USING AN UNSHIELDED COMPUTER.
I WAS ABLE TO RECORD THE MACHINE'S ELECTRO-MAGNETIC IMPULSES AND TRANSLATE THEM INTO THE DATA HE WAS WORKING ON. IT WAS IN AN UNBREAKABLE CODE, BUT I HAD A HUNCH IT WAS A MAP.
MASTER BRUCE... ARE YOU AILING? YOU LOOK PALE--
I'M FINE. WHERE WAS I...
...THE MAP. USING MY OWN MAP OF THE NODES AS A KEY, I DECIPHERED IT. IT SHOWED EXACTLY THE LOCATIONS MY RESEARCH HAD ALREADY PINPOINTED.
YOU HAVE A FEVER--
I SAID I'M FINE!
I'VE FOUND HIS MEN AT FIVE... NO, SIX OF THOSE LOCATIONS. SO FAR I'VE KEPT A JUMP AHEAD OF HIM--
I REALLY MUST INSIST YOU CONSULT DOCTOR THOMPKINS--
NO!
CAN'T STOP NOW... CAN'T LET HIM ESCAPE--

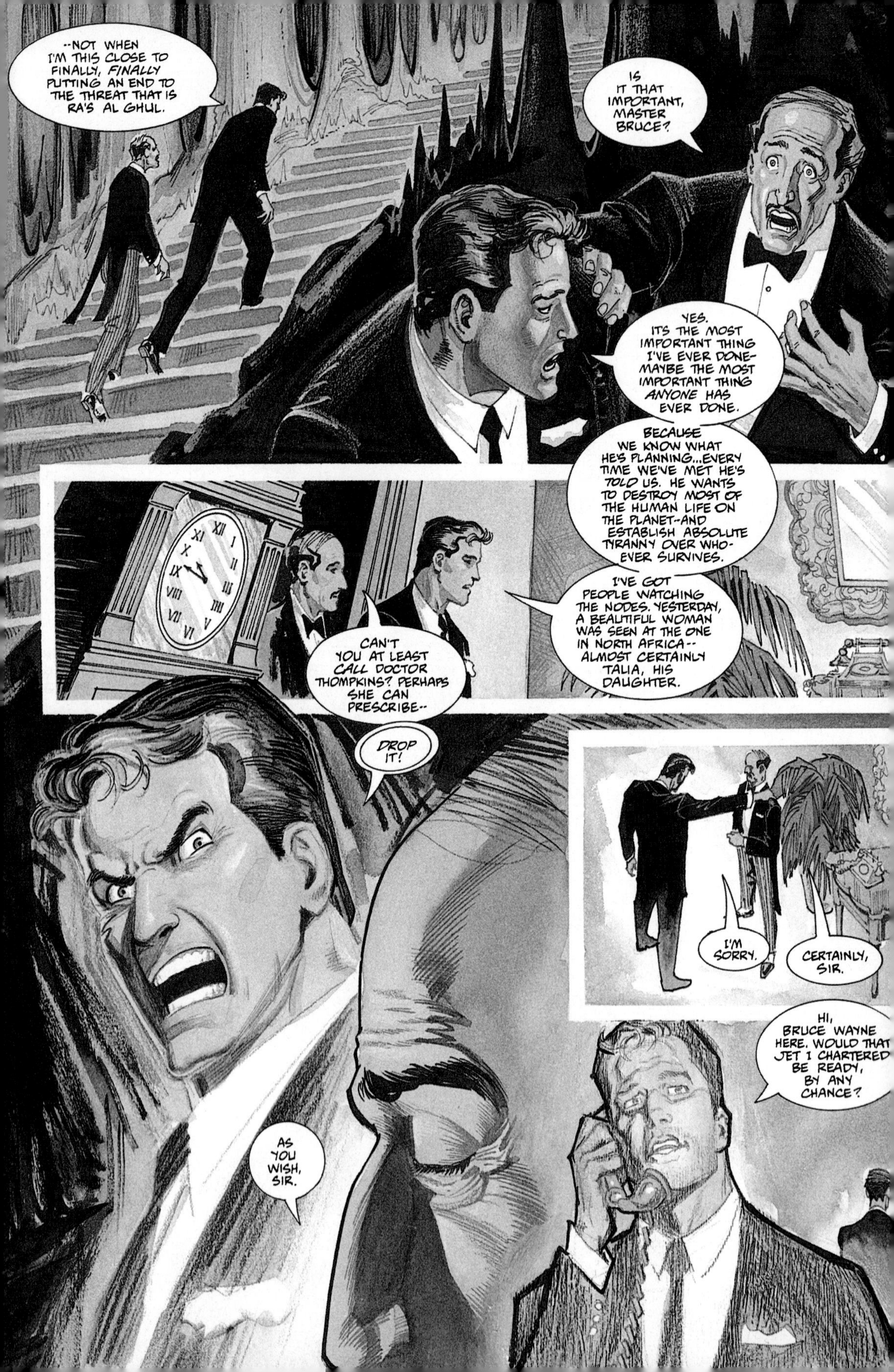
--NOT WHEN I'M THIS CLOSE TO FINALLY, *FINALLY* PUTTING AN END TO THE THREAT THAT IS RA'S AL GHUL.
IS IT THAT IMPORTANT, MASTER BRUCE?
YES. IT'S THE MOST IMPORTANT THING I'VE EVER DONE-MAYBE THE MOST IMPORTANT THING *ANYONE* HAS EVER DONE.
BECAUSE WE KNOW WHAT HE'S PLANNING...EVERY TIME WE'VE MET HE'S *TOLD* US. HE WANTS TO DESTROY MOST OF THE HUMAN LIFE ON THE PLANET--AND ESTABLISH ABSOLUTE TYRANNY OVER WHO-EVER SURVIVES.
I'VE GOT PEOPLE WATCHING THE NODES. YESTERDAY, A BEAUTIFUL WOMAN WAS SEEN AT THE ONE IN NORTH AFRICA--ALMOST CERTAINLY TALIA, HIS DAUGHTER.
CAN'T YOU AT LEAST *CALL* DOCTOR THOMPKINS? PERHAPS SHE CAN PRESCRIBE--
DROP IT!
AS YOU WISH, SIR.
I'M SORRY.
CERTAINLY, SIR.
HI, BRUCE WAYNE HERE. WOULD THAT JET I CHARTERED BE READY, BY ANY CHANCE?

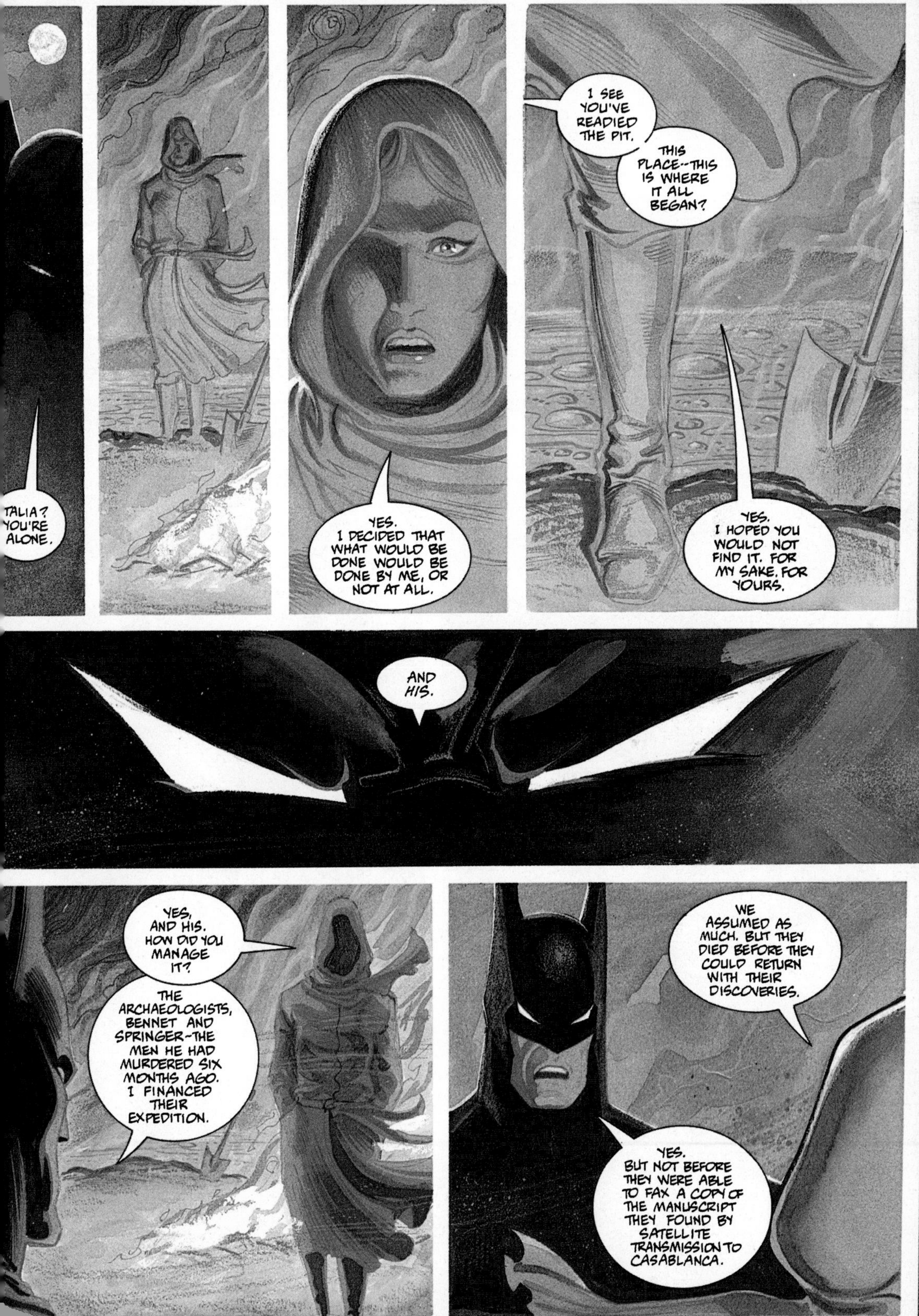
TALIA? YOU'RE ALONE.
YES. I DECIDED THAT WHAT WOULD BE DONE WOULD BE DONE BY ME, OR NOT AT ALL.
I SEE YOU'VE READIED THE PIT.
THIS PLACE--THIS IS WHERE IT ALL BEGAN?
YES. I HOPED YOU WOULD NOT FIND IT. FOR MY SAKE. FOR YOURS.
AND HIS.
YES, AND HIS. HOW DID YOU MANAGE IT?
THE ARCHAEOLOGISTS, BENNET AND SPRINGER--THE MEN HE HAD MURDERED SIX MONTHS AGO. I FINANCED THEIR EXPEDITION.
WE ASSUMED AS MUCH. BUT THEY DIED BEFORE THEY COULD RETURN WITH THEIR DISCOVERIES.
YES. BUT NOT BEFORE THEY WERE ABLE TO FAX A COPY OF THE MANUSCRIPT THEY FOUND BY SATELLITE TRANSMISSION TO CASABLANCA.

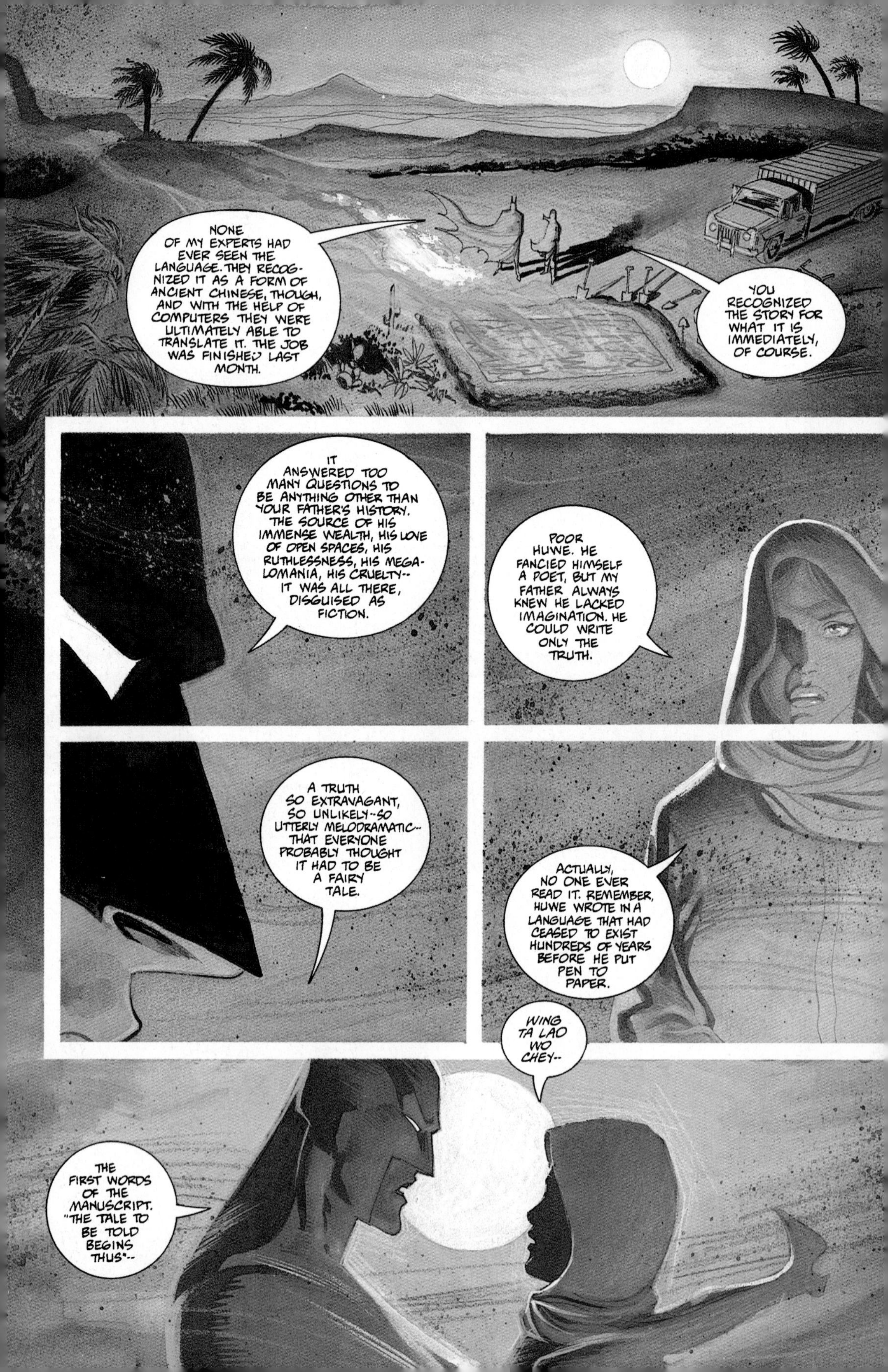
NONE OF MY EXPERTS HAD EVER SEEN THE LANGUAGE. THEY RECOGNIZED IT AS A FORM OF ANCIENT CHINESE, THOUGH, AND WITH THE HELP OF COMPUTERS THEY WERE ULTIMATELY ABLE TO TRANSLATE IT. THE JOB WAS FINISHED LAST MONTH.
YOU RECOGNIZED THE STORY FOR WHAT IT IS IMMEDIATELY, OF COURSE.
IT ANSWERED TOO MANY QUESTIONS TO BE ANYTHING OTHER THAN YOUR FATHER'S HISTORY. THE SOURCE OF HIS IMMENSE WEALTH, HIS LOVE OF OPEN SPACES, HIS RUTHLESSNESS, HIS MEGALOMANIA, HIS CRUELTY-- IT WAS ALL THERE, DISGUISED AS FICTION.
POOR HUWE. HE FANCIED HIMSELF A POET, BUT MY FATHER ALWAYS KNEW HE LACKED IMAGINATION. HE COULD WRITE ONLY THE TRUTH.
A TRUTH SO EXTRAVAGANT, SO UNLIKELY--SO UTTERLY MELODRAMATIC-- THAT EVERYONE PROBABLY THOUGHT IT HAD TO BE A FAIRY TALE.
ACTUALLY, NO ONE EVER READ IT. REMEMBER, HUWE WROTE IN A LANGUAGE THAT HAD CEASED TO EXIST HUNDREDS OF YEARS BEFORE HE PUT PEN TO PAPER.
WING TA LAO WO CHEY--
THE FIRST WORDS OF THE MANUSCRIPT. "THE TALE TO BE TOLD BEGINS THUS"--

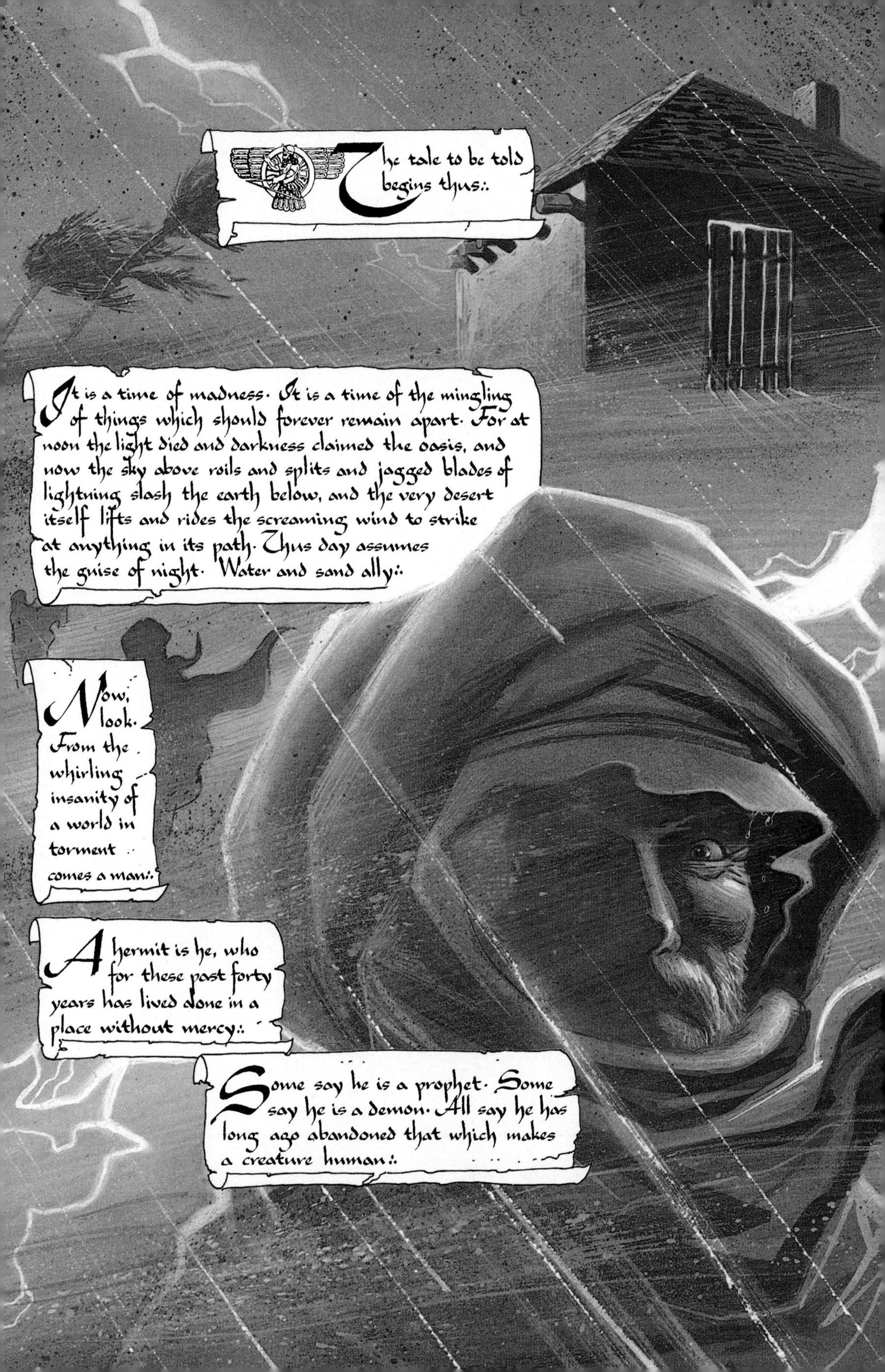
The tale to be told begins thus:.
It is a time of madness. It is a time of the mingling of things which should forever remain apart. For at noon the light died and darkness claimed the oasis, and now the sky above roils and splits and jagged blades of lightning slash the earth below, and the very desert itself lifts and rides the screaming wind to strike at anything in its path. Thus day assumes the guise of night. Water and sand ally:.
Now, look. From the whirling insanity of a world in torment comes a man:.
A hermit is he, who for these past forty years has lived alone in a place without mercy:.
Some say he is a prophet. Some say he is a demon. All say he has long ago abandoned that which makes a creature human:.

He pauses, and suddenly the storm quiets. And in the stillness can be heard the wail of a newborn infant.

GIVE HIM TO ME.

The gazes of the three women fasten on him in fascination, and they tremble as he speaks in a voice that rasps and rumbles.

TEND HIM WELL.

HIS WILL BE A LIFE LIT BY LIGHTNING. HIS YEARS WILL BE MANY, STRETCHING BEYOND THE FARTHEST DREAMS OF AGE, AND IT IS HIS DESTINY TO BE EITHER MANKIND'S SAVIOR-- OR TO DESTROY ALL THAT LIVES UPON THE EARTH.

MY TASK IS FINISHED.

As the mother looks upon her son, only minutes free from the womb, she is afrai

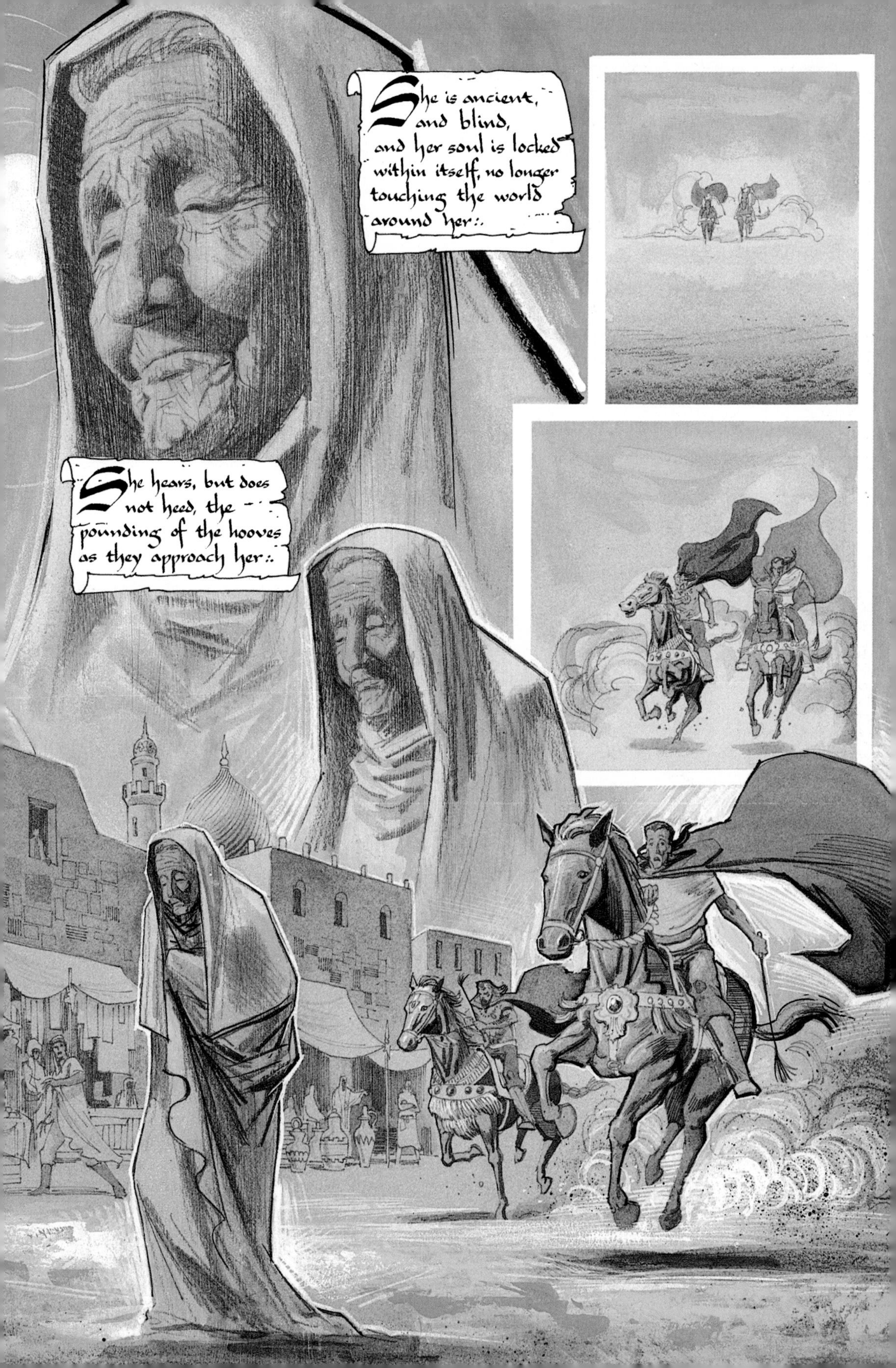
She is ancient, and blind, and her soul is locked within itself, no longer touching the world around her:.
She hears, but does not heed, the pounding of the hooves as they approach her:.

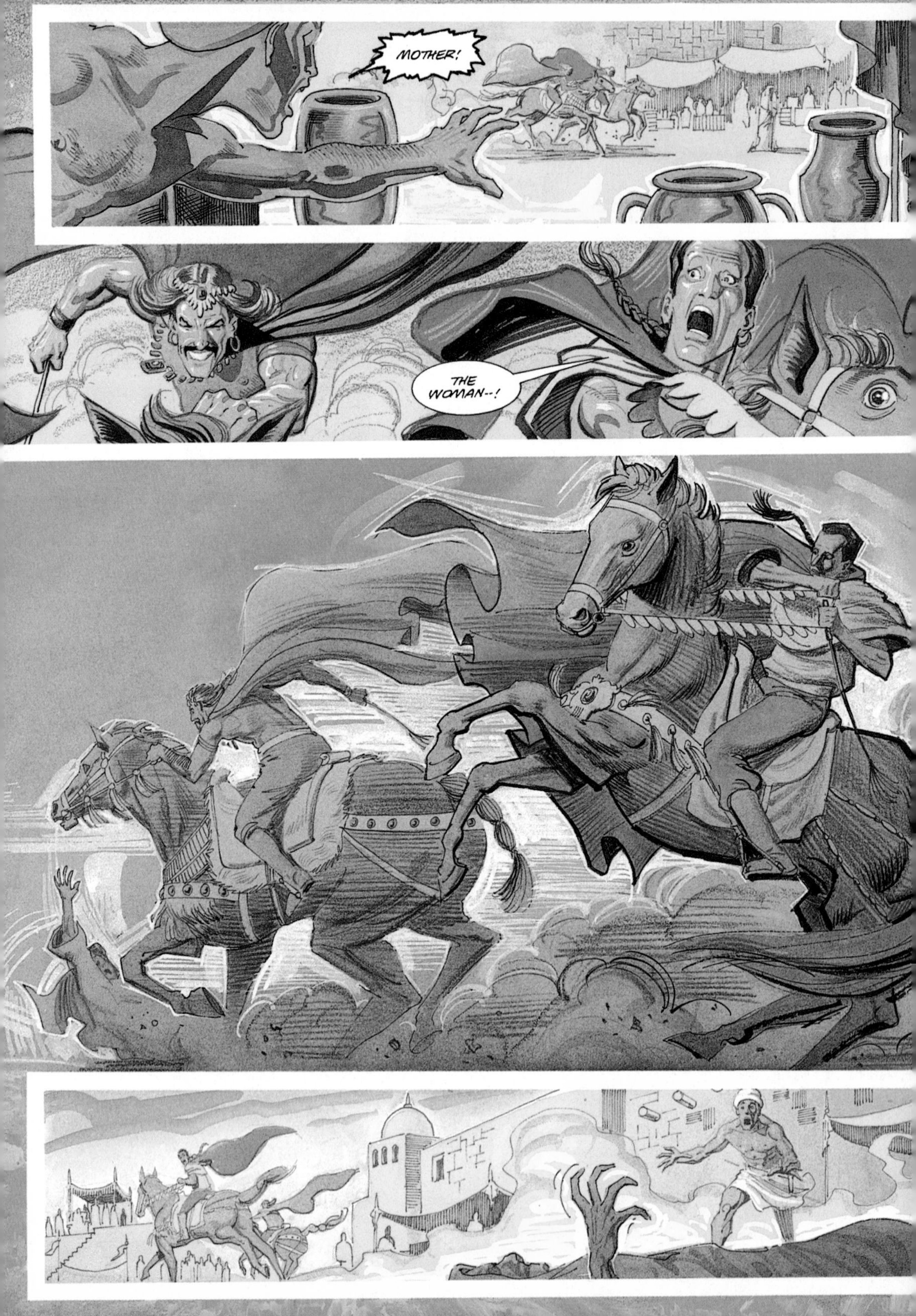
MOTHER!
THE WOMAN--!

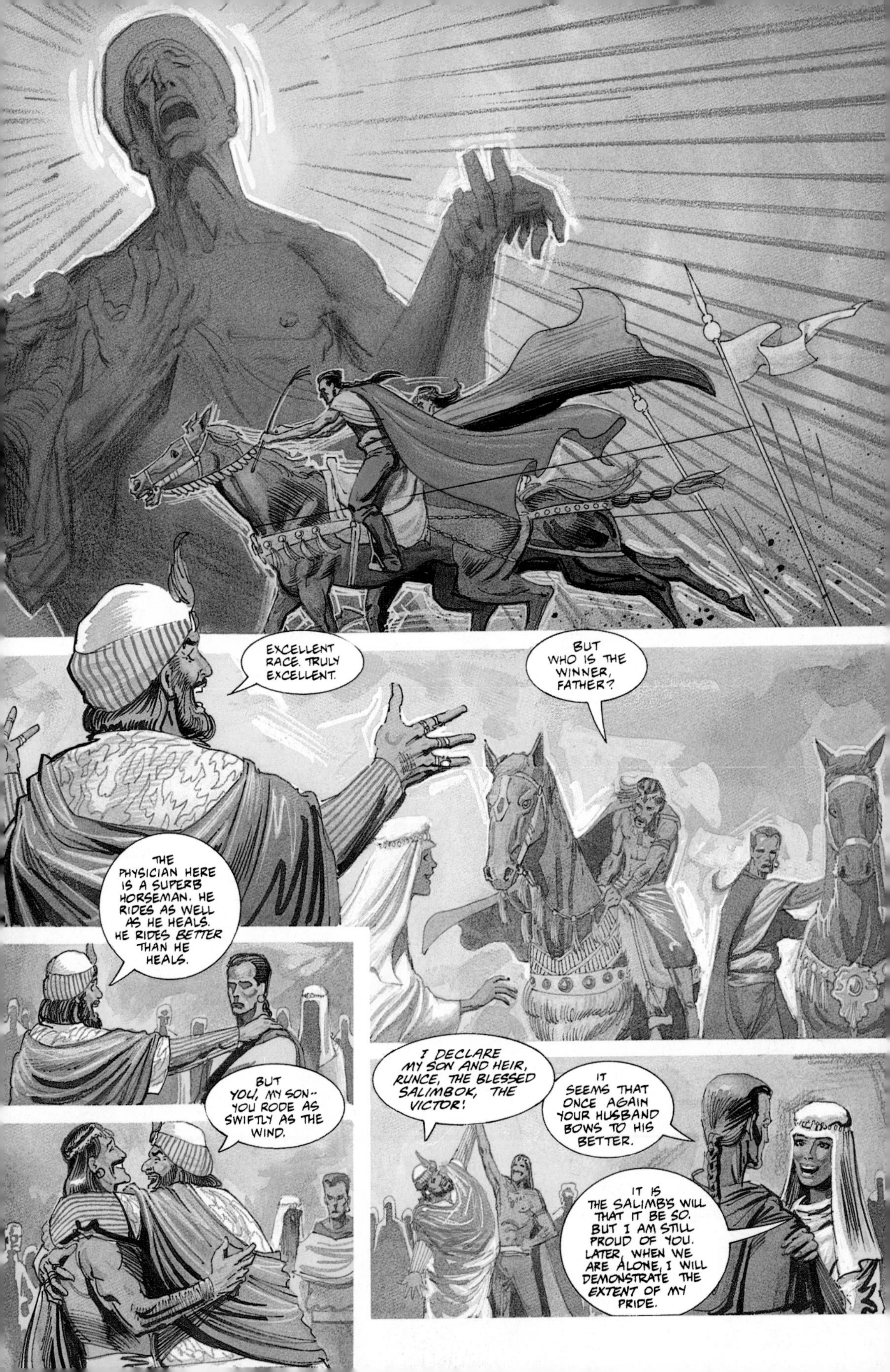
EXCELLENT RACE. TRULY EXCELLENT.
BUT WHO IS THE WINNER, FATHER?
THE PHYSICIAN HERE IS A SUPERB HORSEMAN. HE RIDES AS WELL AS HE HEALS. HE RIDES *BETTER* THAN HE HEALS.
BUT YOU, MY SON-- YOU RODE AS SWIFTLY AS THE WIND.
I DECLARE MY SON AND HEIR, RUNCE, THE BLESSED SALIMBOK, THE VICTOR!
IT SEEMS THAT ONCE AGAIN YOUR HUSBAND BOWS TO HIS BETTER.
IT IS THE SALIMB'S WILL THAT IT BE SO. BUT I AM STILL PROUD OF YOU. LATER, WHEN WE ARE ALONE, I WILL DEMONSTRATE THE *EXTENT* OF MY PRIDE.

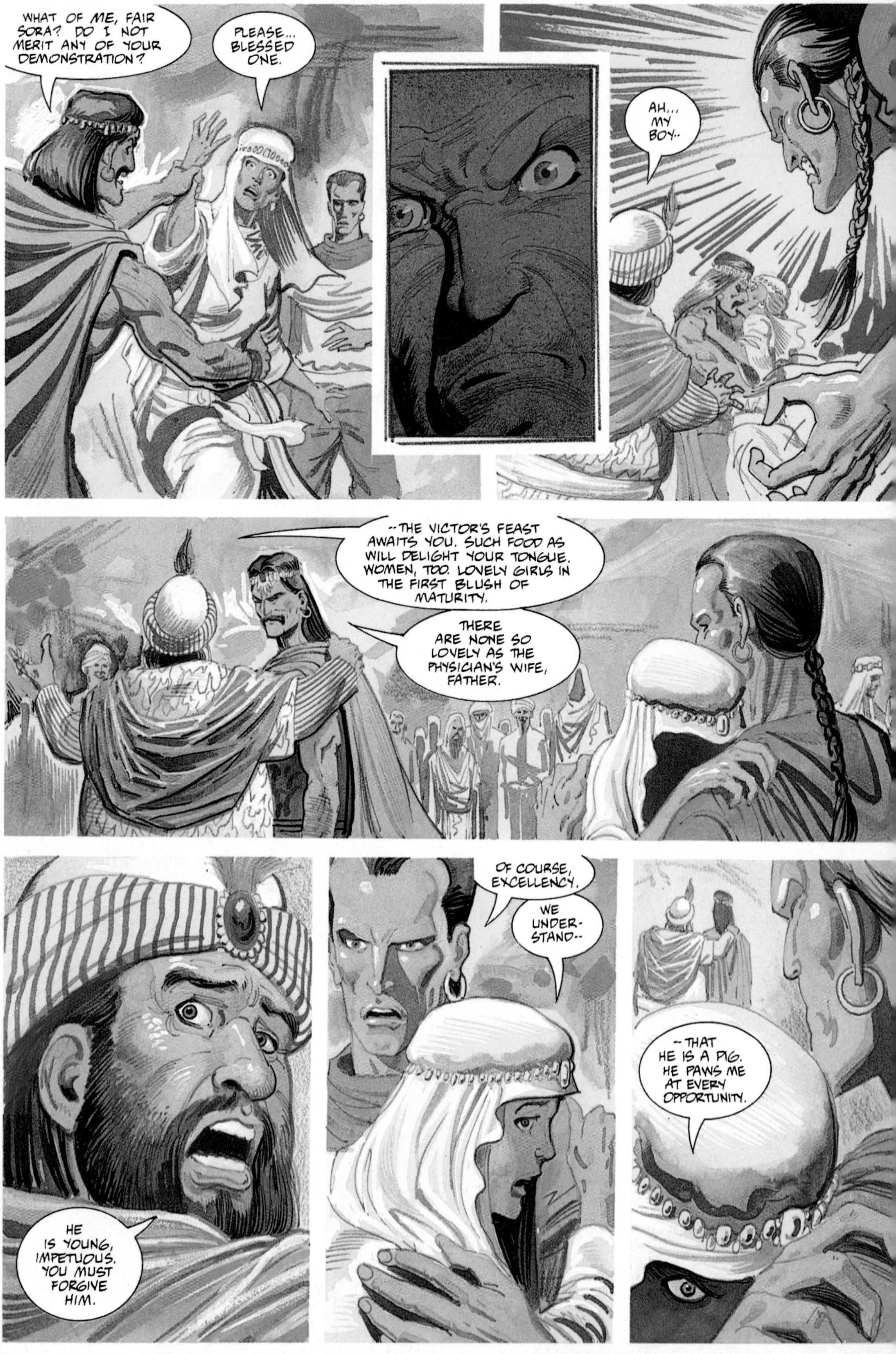
WHAT OF ME, FAIR SORA? DO I NOT MERIT ANY OF YOUR DEMONSTRATION?
PLEASE... BLESSED ONE.
AH... MY BOY..
--THE VICTOR'S FEAST AWAITS YOU. SUCH FOOD AS WILL DELIGHT YOUR TONGUE. WOMEN, TOO. LOVELY GIRLS IN THE FIRST BLUSH OF MATURITY.
THERE ARE NONE SO LOVELY AS THE PHYSICIAN'S WIFE, FATHER.
HE IS YOUNG, IMPETUOUS. YOU MUST FORGIVE HIM.
OF COURSE, EXCELLENCY.
WE UNDER-STAND--
--THAT HE IS A PIG. HE PAWS ME AT EVERY OPPORTUNITY.

AS THE SULTAN SAID, HE IS YOUNG. YEARS AND RESPONSIBILITIES WILL TEACH HIM DECORUM.

HOW DO YOU KNOW? YOU ARE NO OLDER THAN HE.

AH, BUT I HAVE READ THE WISDOM OF MEN HUNDREDS OF DECADES OLDER THAN EITHER OF US.

YOU AND YOUR READING.

I WILL MAKE YOU FORGET YOUR STUDIES.. AND THE SALIMB AND HIS SLOBBERING LOUT OF A SON..

NOT NOW, BELOVED. THERE IS SOMETHING I MUST DO.

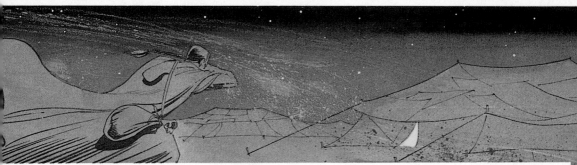

YOU! YOU ARE NOT WELCOME HERE--!

I SHALL SHOW YOU JUST HOW UNWELCOME..

I UNDERSTAND YOUR ANGER, FRIEND, AND I DO NOT BLAME YOU FOR IT. BUT BEFORE YOU SLICE ME OPEN, ALLOW ME A MOMENT WITH YOUR MOTHER.

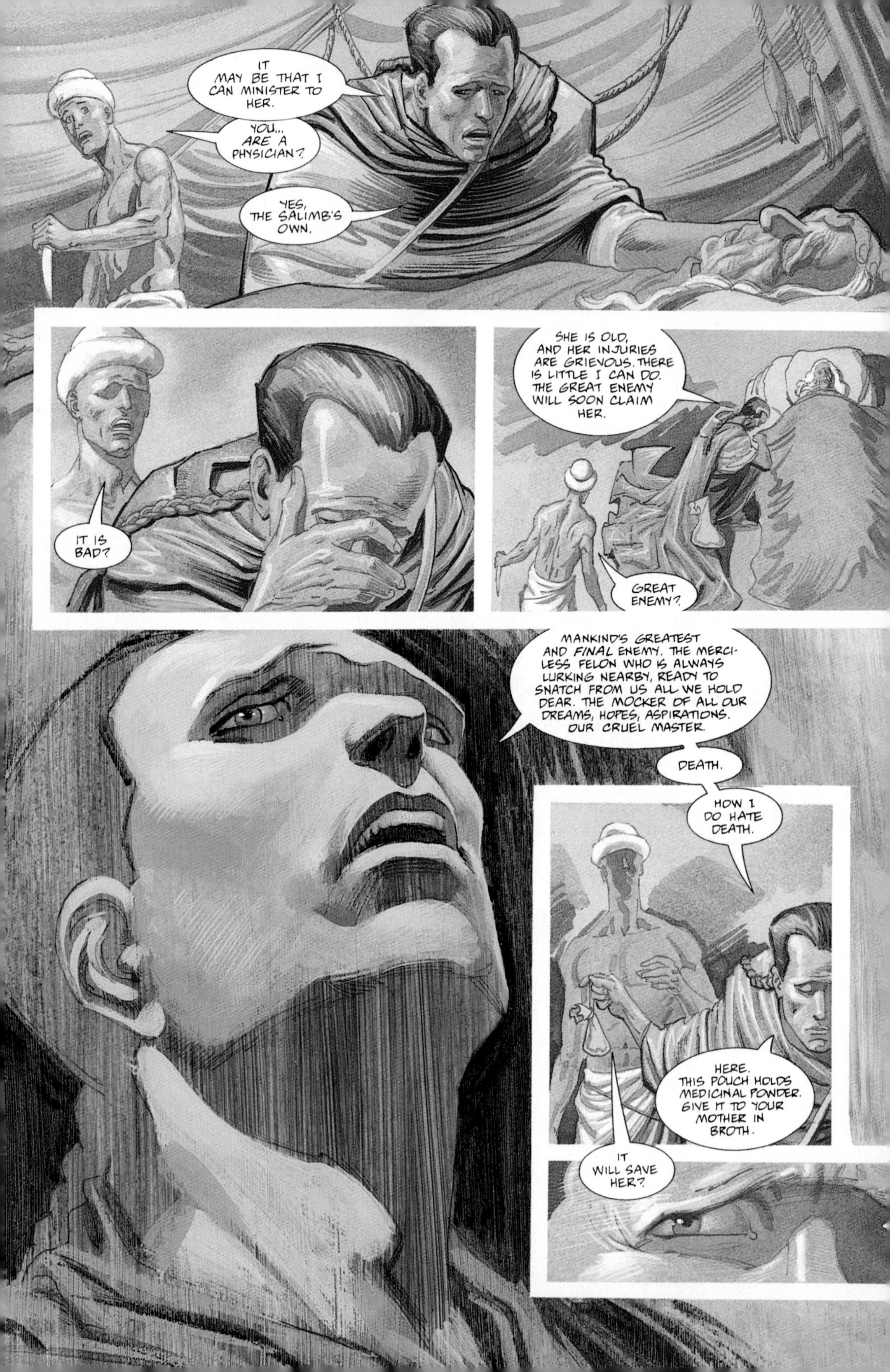

IT MAY BE THAT I CAN MINISTER TO HER.
YOU... ARE A PHYSICIAN?
YES, THE SALIMB'S OWN.
IT IS BAD?
SHE IS OLD, AND HER INJURIES ARE GRIEVOUS. THERE IS LITTLE I CAN DO. THE GREAT ENEMY WILL SOON CLAIM HER.
GREAT ENEMY?
MANKIND'S GREATEST AND FINAL ENEMY. THE MERCILESS FELON WHO IS ALWAYS LURKING NEARBY, READY TO SNATCH FROM US ALL WE HOLD DEAR. THE MOCKER OF ALL OUR DREAMS, HOPES, ASPIRATIONS. OUR CRUEL MASTER.
DEATH.
HOW I DO HATE DEATH.
HERE. THIS POUCH HOLDS MEDICINAL POWDER. GIVE IT TO YOUR MOTHER IN BROTH.
IT WILL SAVE HER?

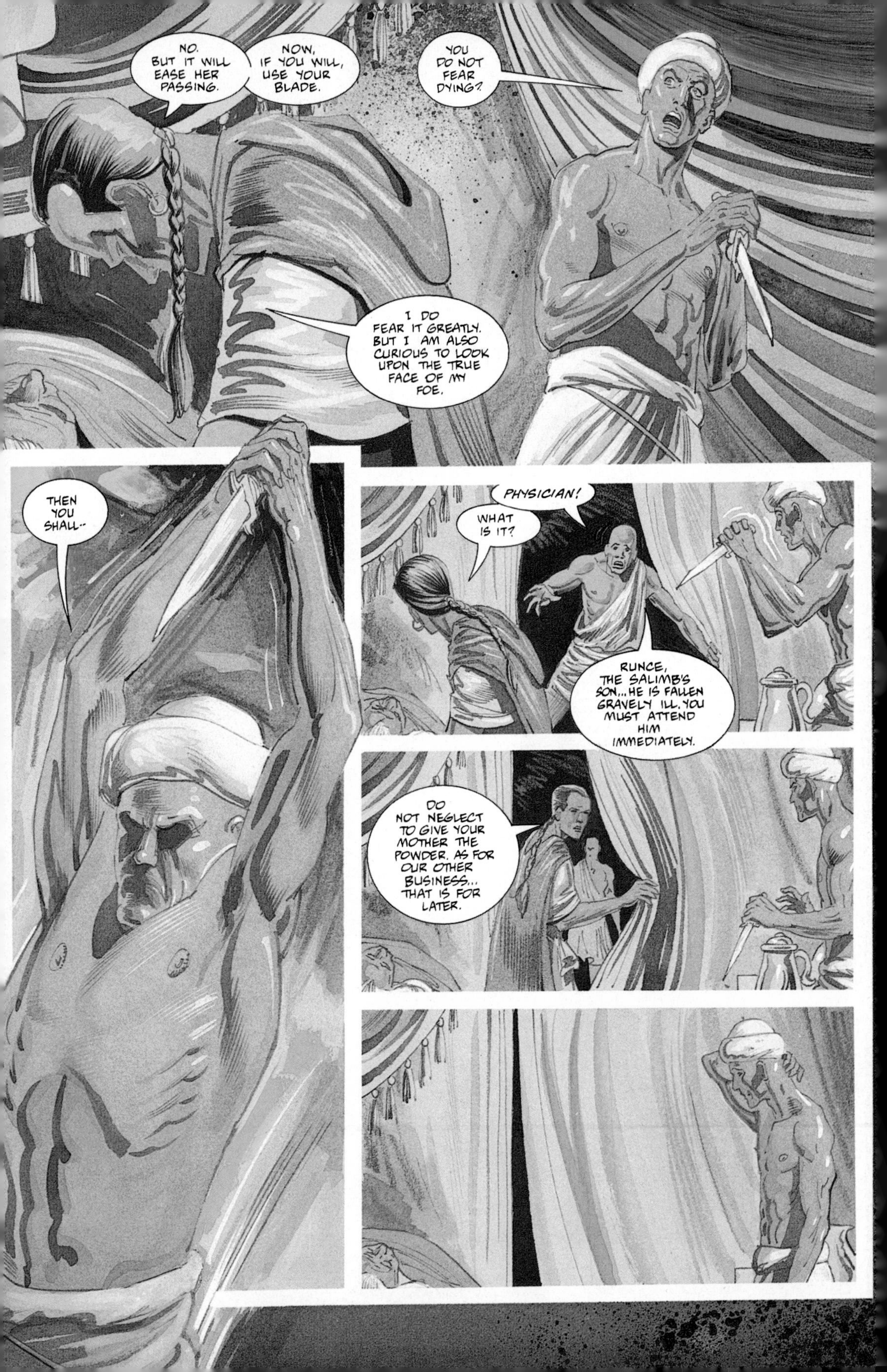
NO. BUT IT WILL EASE HER PASSING.
NOW, IF YOU WILL, USE YOUR BLADE.
YOU DO NOT FEAR DYING?
I DO FEAR IT GREATLY. BUT I AM ALSO CURIOUS TO LOOK UPON THE TRUE FACE OF MY FOE.
THEN YOU SHALL--
PHYSICIAN!
WHAT IS IT?
RUNCE, THE SALIMB'S SON... HE IS FALLEN GRAVELY ILL. YOU MUST ATTEND HIM IMMEDIATELY.
DO NOT NEGLECT TO GIVE YOUR MOTHER THE POWDER. AS FOR OUR OTHER BUSINESS... THAT IS FOR LATER.

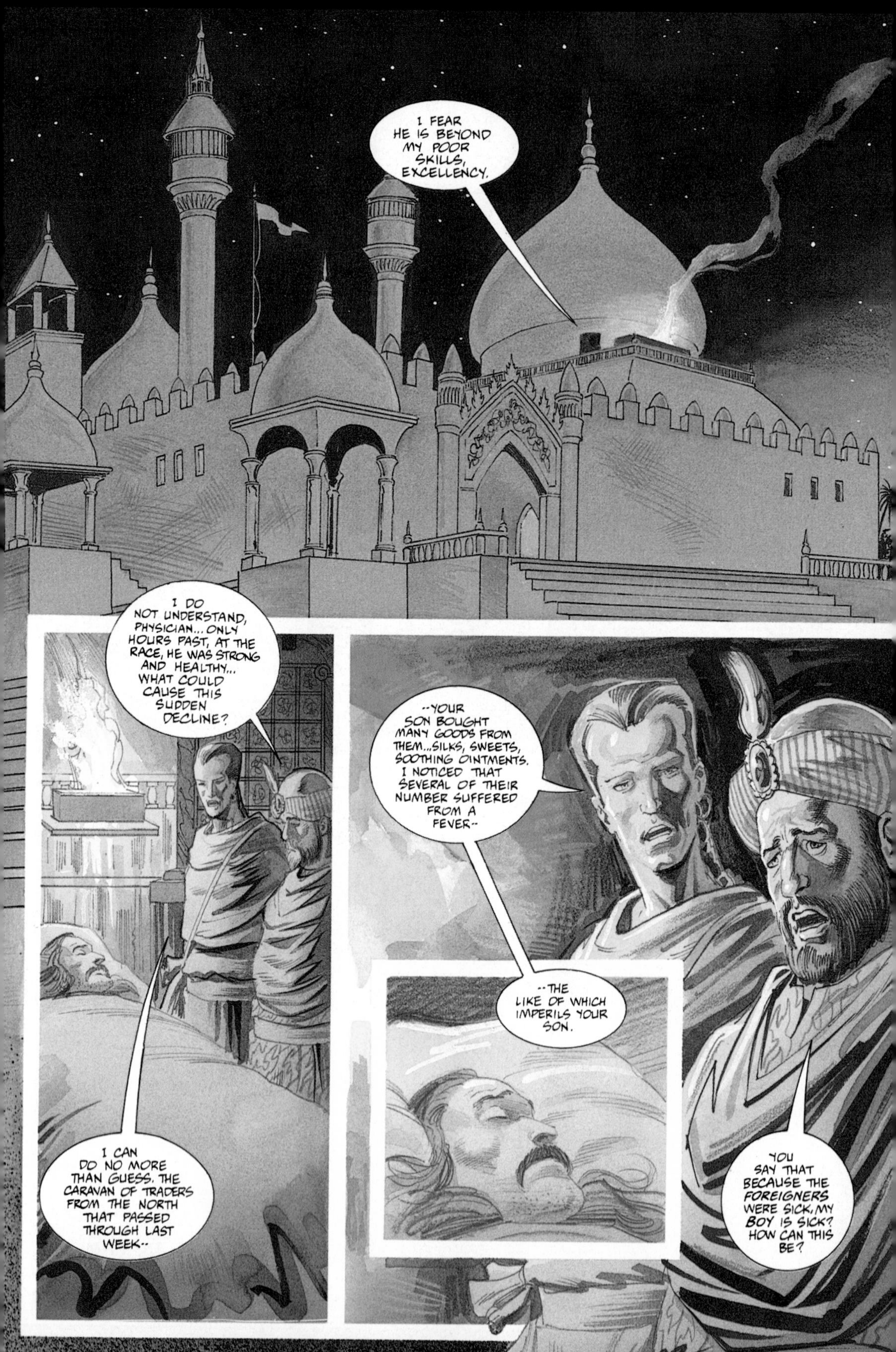
I FEAR HE IS BEYOND MY POOR SKILLS, EXCELLENCY.
I DO NOT UNDERSTAND, PHYSICIAN... ONLY HOURS PAST, AT THE RACE, HE WAS STRONG AND HEALTHY... WHAT COULD CAUSE THIS SUDDEN DECLINE?
I CAN DO NO MORE THAN GUESS. THE CARAVAN OF TRADERS FROM THE NORTH THAT PASSED THROUGH LAST WEEK--
--YOUR SON BOUGHT MANY GOODS FROM THEM...SILKS, SWEETS, SOOTHING OINTMENTS. I NOTICED THAT SEVERAL OF THEIR NUMBER SUFFERED FROM A FEVER--
--THE LIKE OF WHICH IMPERILS YOUR SON.
YOU SAY THAT BECAUSE THE FOREIGNERS WERE SICK, MY BOY IS SICK? HOW CAN THIS BE?

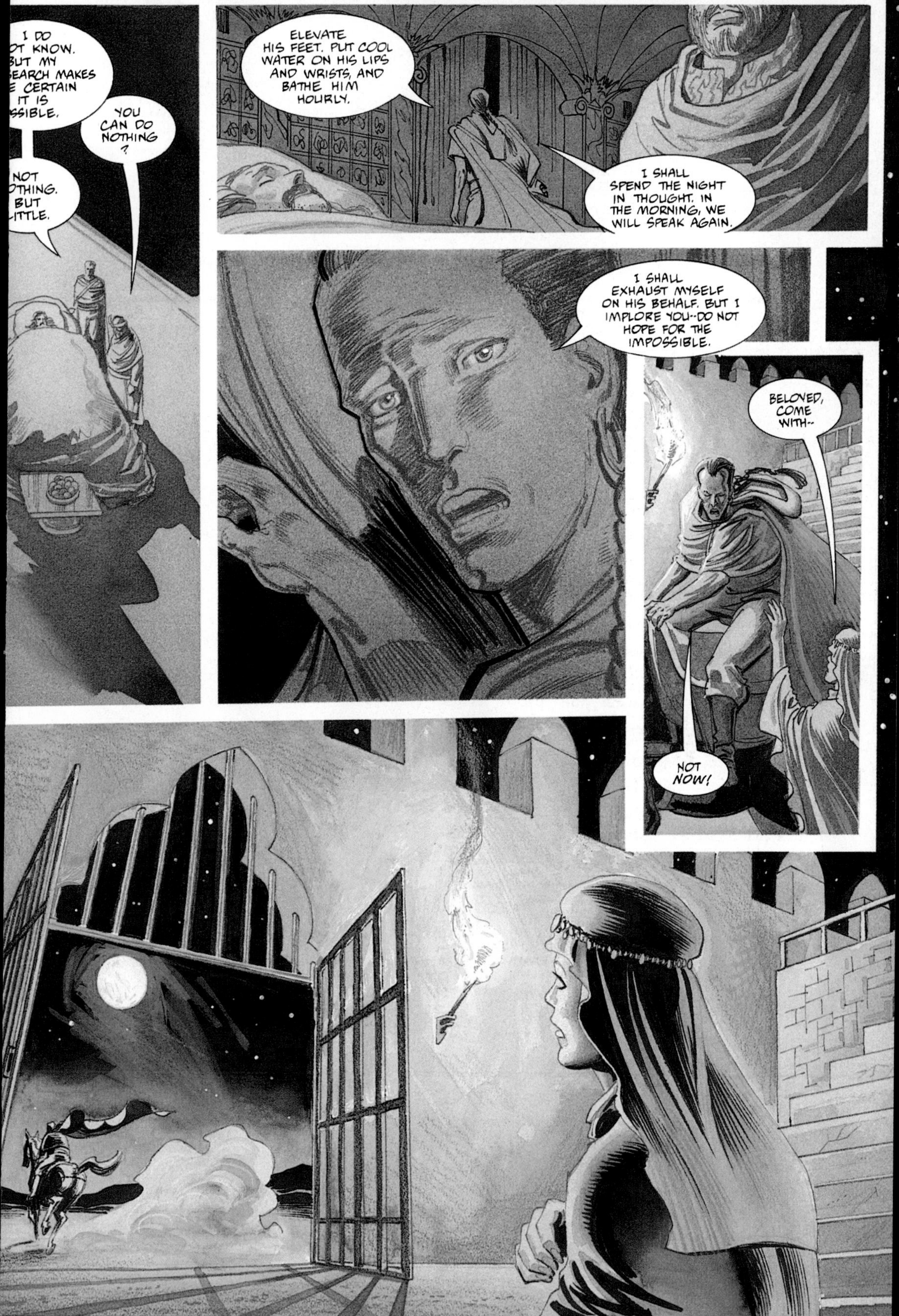

I DO OT KNOW. UT MY SEARCH MAKES E CERTAIN IT IS SSIBLE.
YOU CAN DO NOTHING?
NOT OTHING. BUT LITTLE.
ELEVATE HIS FEET. PUT COOL WATER ON HIS LIPS AND WRISTS, AND BATHE HIM HOURLY.
I SHALL SPEND THE NIGHT IN THOUGHT. IN THE MORNING, WE WILL SPEAK AGAIN.
I SHALL EXHAUST MYSELF ON HIS BEHALF. BUT I IMPLORE YOU--DO NOT HOPE FOR THE IMPOSSIBLE.
BELOVED, COME WITH--
NOT NOW!

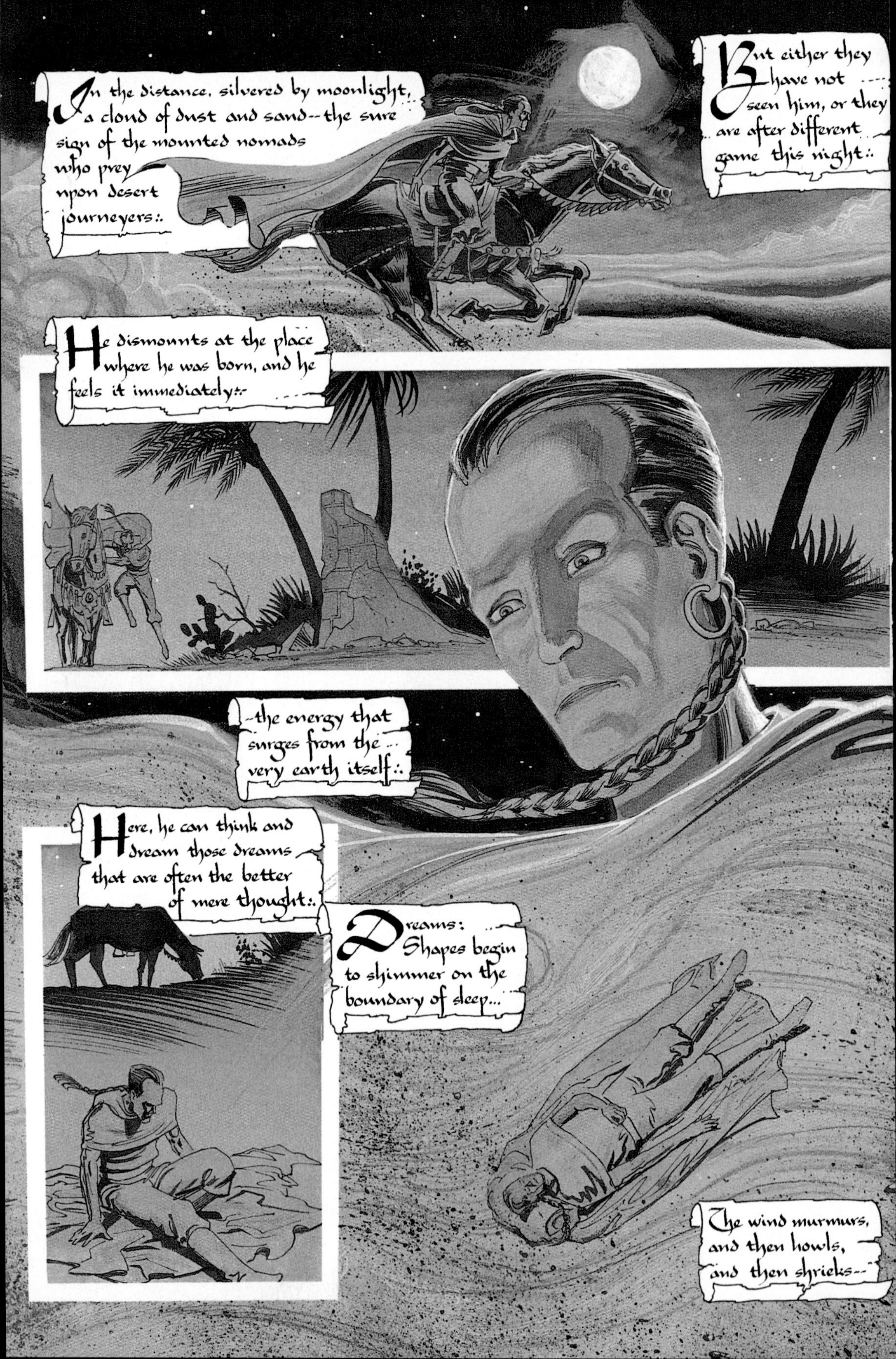
In the distance, silvered by moonlight, a cloud of dust and sand--the sure sign of the mounted nomads who prey upon desert journeyers:.
But either they have not seen him, or they are after different game this night:.
He dismounts at the place where he was born, and he feels it immediately:-
--the energy that surges from the very earth itself:.
Here, he can think and dream those dreams that are often the better of mere thought:.
Dreams: Shapes begin to shimmer on the boundary of sleep...
The wind murmurs, and then howls, and then shrieks--

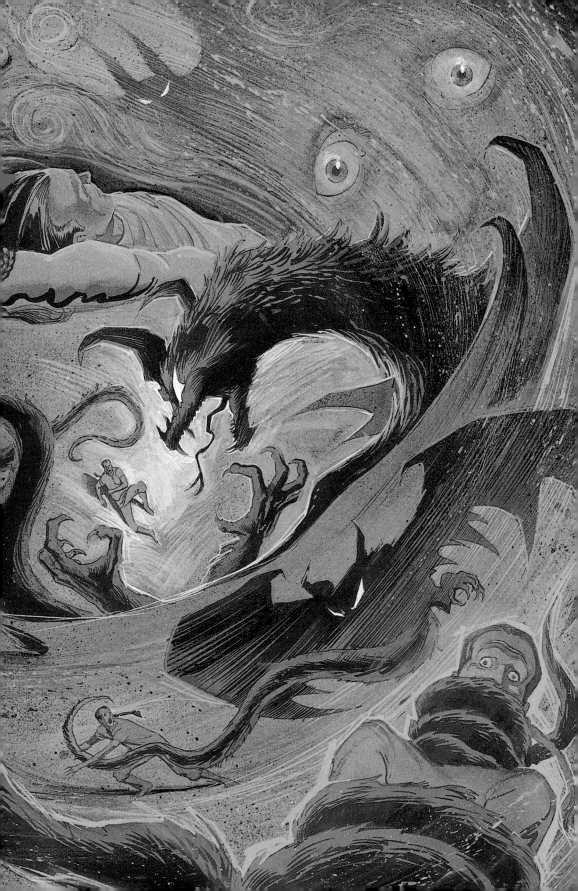

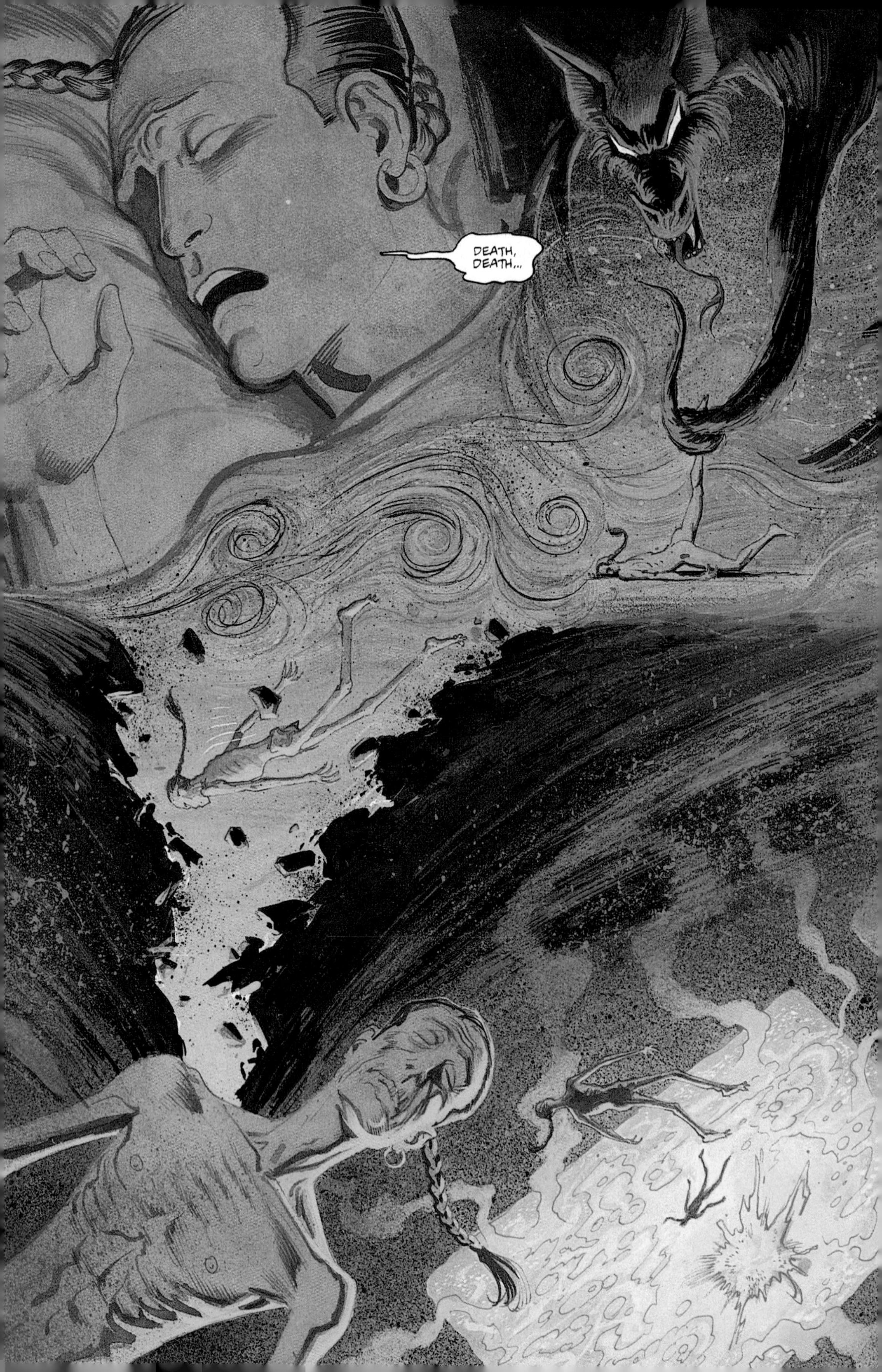
DEATH, DEATH...

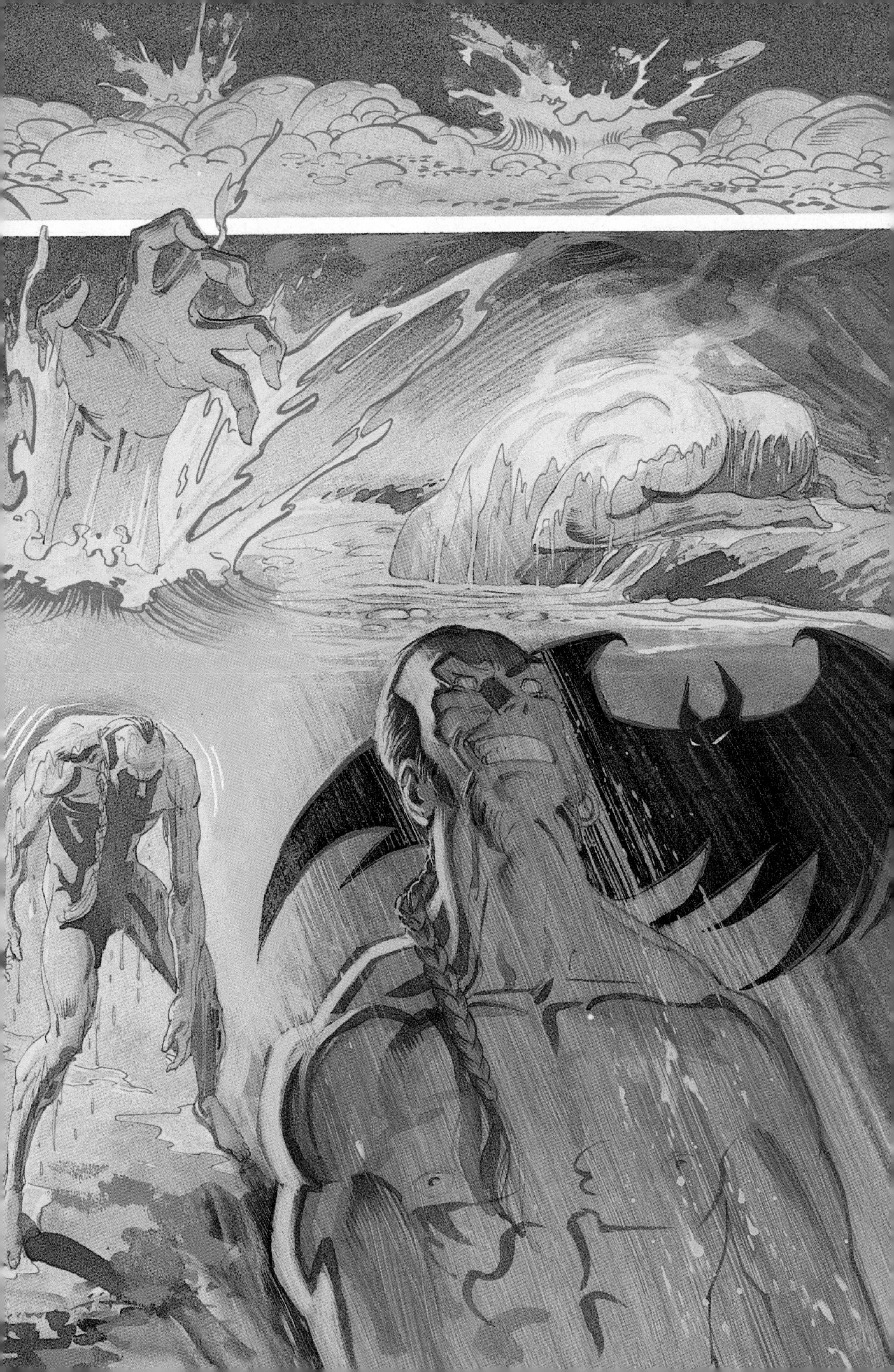

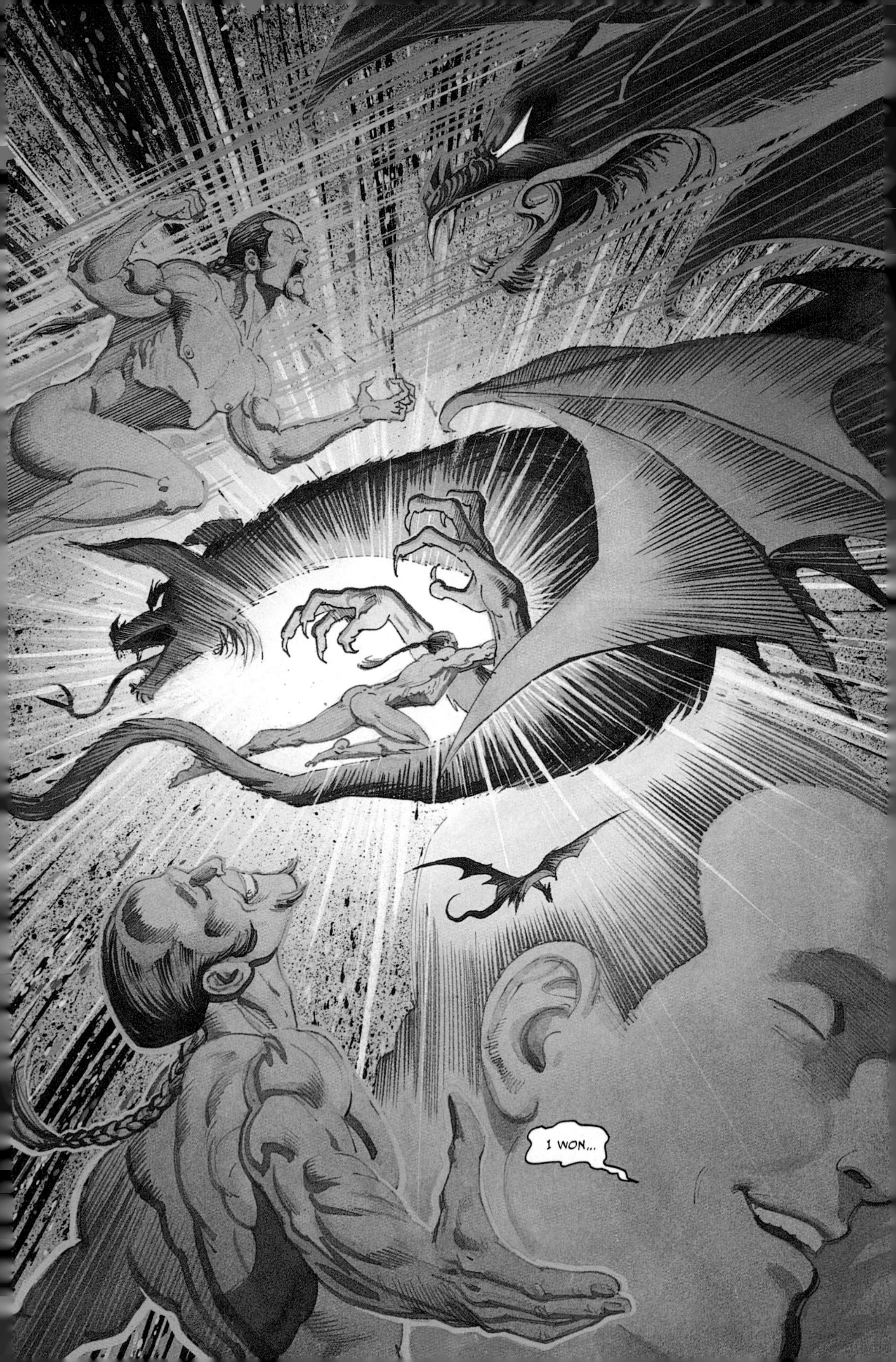
I WON...

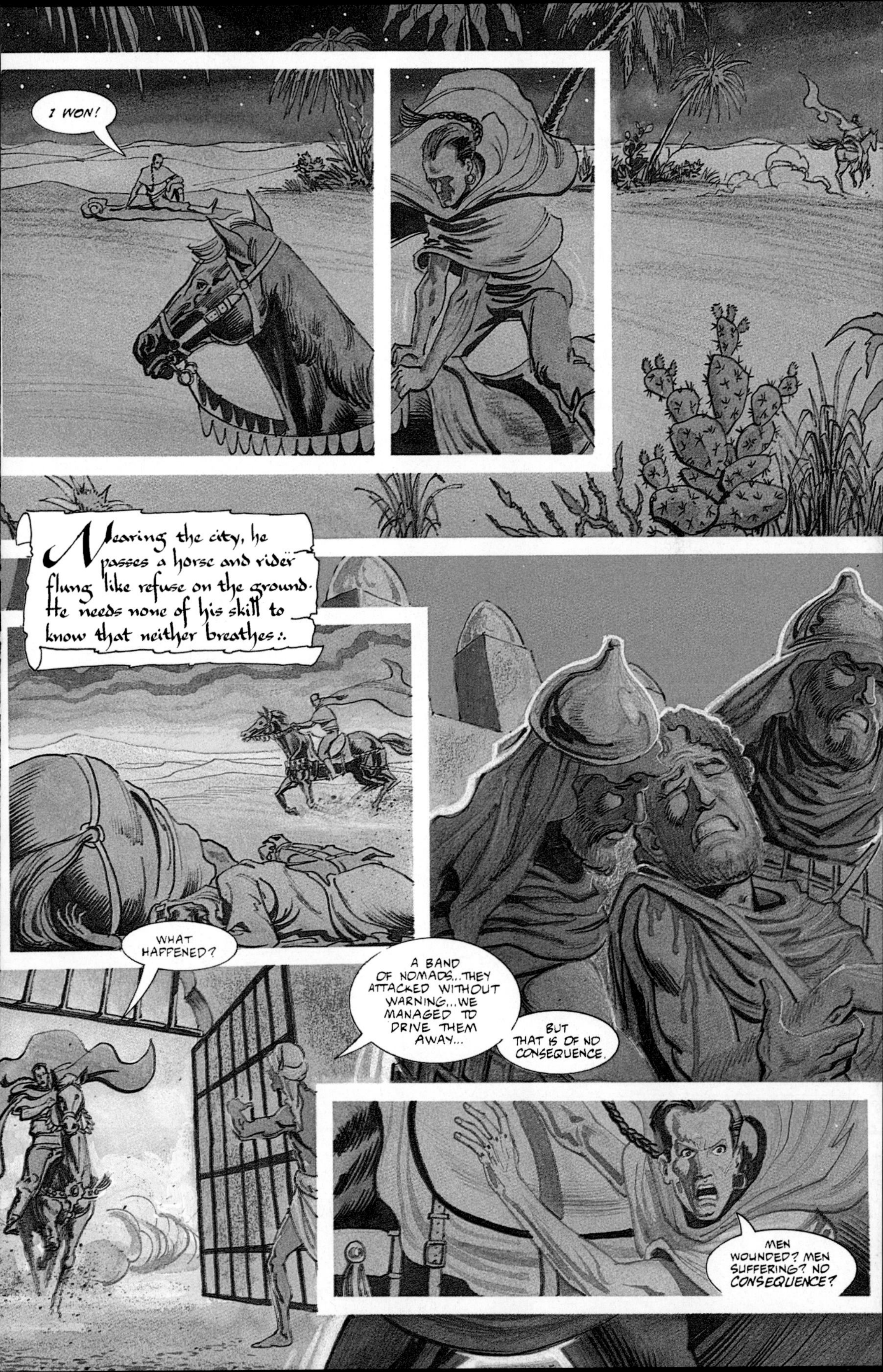
I WON!
Nearing the city, he passes a horse and rider flung like refuse on the ground. He needs none of his skill to know that neither breathes ∴
WHAT HAPPENED?
A BAND OF NOMADS... THEY ATTACKED WITHOUT WARNING... WE MANAGED TO DRIVE THEM AWAY...
BUT THAT IS OF NO CONSEQUENCE.
MEN WOUNDED? MEN SUFFERING? NO CONSEQUENCE?

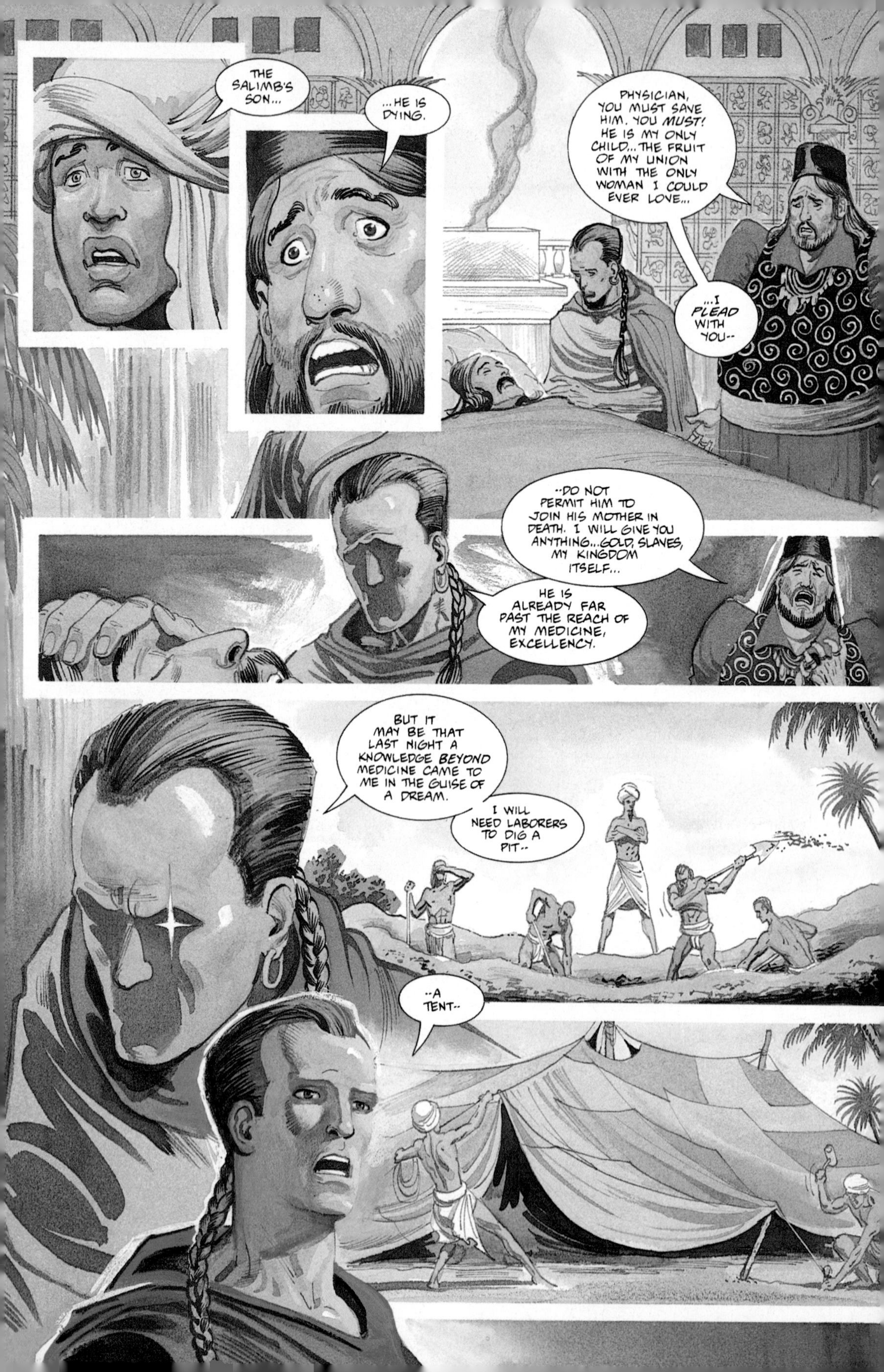
THE SALIMB'S SON...
...HE IS DYING.
PHYSICIAN, YOU MUST SAVE HIM. YOU MUST! HE IS MY ONLY CHILD... THE FRUIT OF MY UNION WITH THE ONLY WOMAN I COULD EVER LOVE...
...I PLEAD WITH YOU--
--DO NOT PERMIT HIM TO JOIN HIS MOTHER IN DEATH. I WILL GIVE YOU ANYTHING...GOLD, SLAVES, MY KINGDOM ITSELF...
HE IS ALREADY FAR PAST THE REACH OF MY MEDICINE, EXCELLENCY.
BUT IT MAY BE THAT LAST NIGHT A KNOWLEDGE BEYOND MEDICINE CAME TO ME IN THE GUISE OF A DREAM.
I WILL NEED LABORERS TO DIG A PIT--
--A TENT--

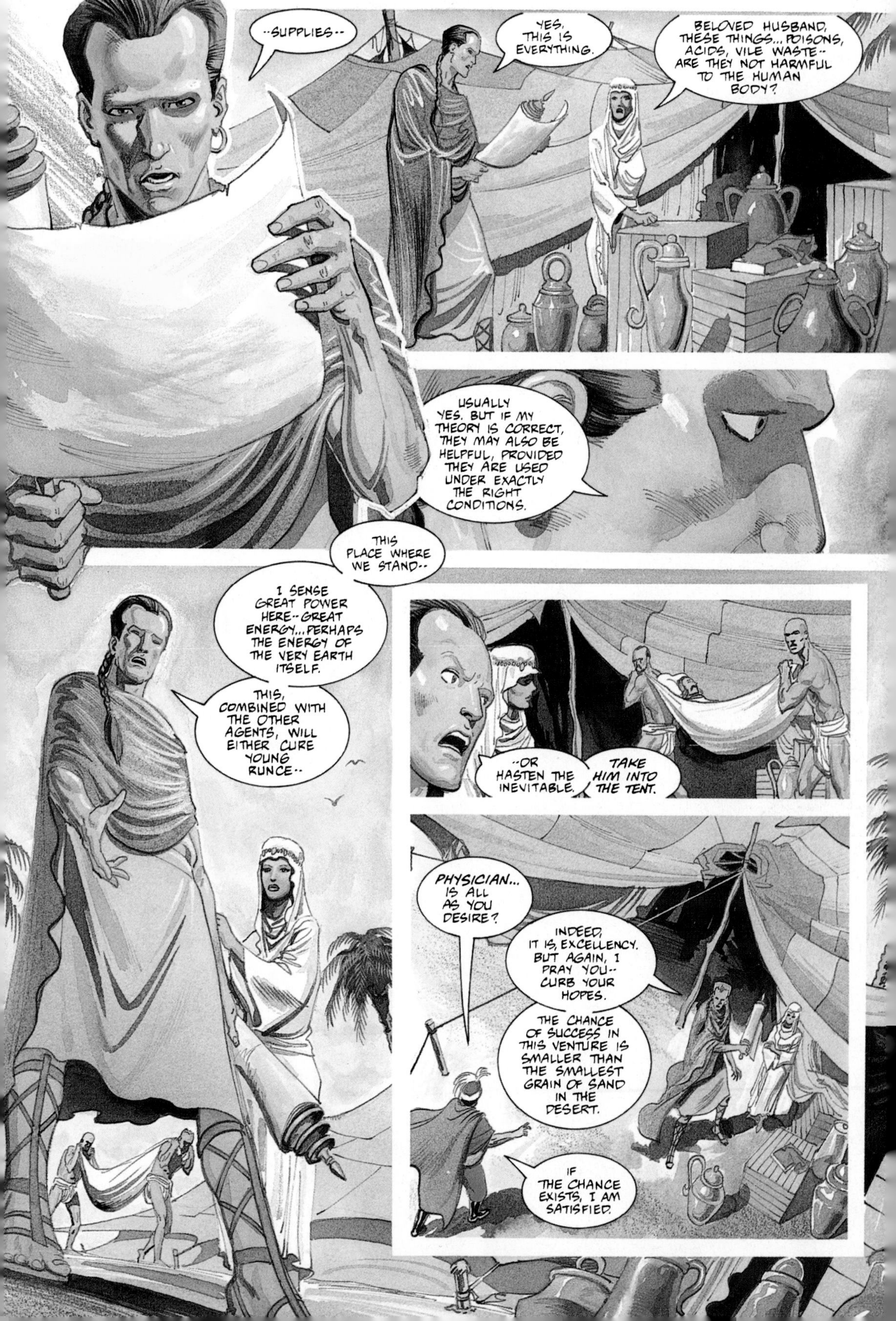
--SUPPLIES--
YES, THIS IS EVERYTHING.
BELOVED HUSBAND, THESE THINGS... POISONS, ACIDS, VILE WASTE-- ARE THEY NOT HARMFUL TO THE HUMAN BODY?
USUALLY YES. BUT IF MY THEORY IS CORRECT, THEY MAY ALSO BE HELPFUL, PROVIDED THEY ARE USED UNDER EXACTLY THE RIGHT CONDITIONS.
THIS PLACE WHERE WE STAND--
I SENSE GREAT POWER HERE--GREAT ENERGY... PERHAPS THE ENERGY OF THE VERY EARTH ITSELF.
THIS, COMBINED WITH THE OTHER AGENTS, WILL EITHER CURE YOUNG RUNCE--
--OR HASTEN THE INEVITABLE.
TAKE HIM INTO THE TENT.
PHYSICIAN... IS ALL AS YOU DESIRE?
INDEED, IT IS, EXCELLENCY. BUT AGAIN, I PRAY YOU-- CURB YOUR HOPES.
THE CHANCE OF SUCCESS IN THIS VENTURE IS SMALLER THAN THE SMALLEST GRAIN OF SAND IN THE DESERT.
IF THE CHANCE EXISTS, I AM SATISFIED.

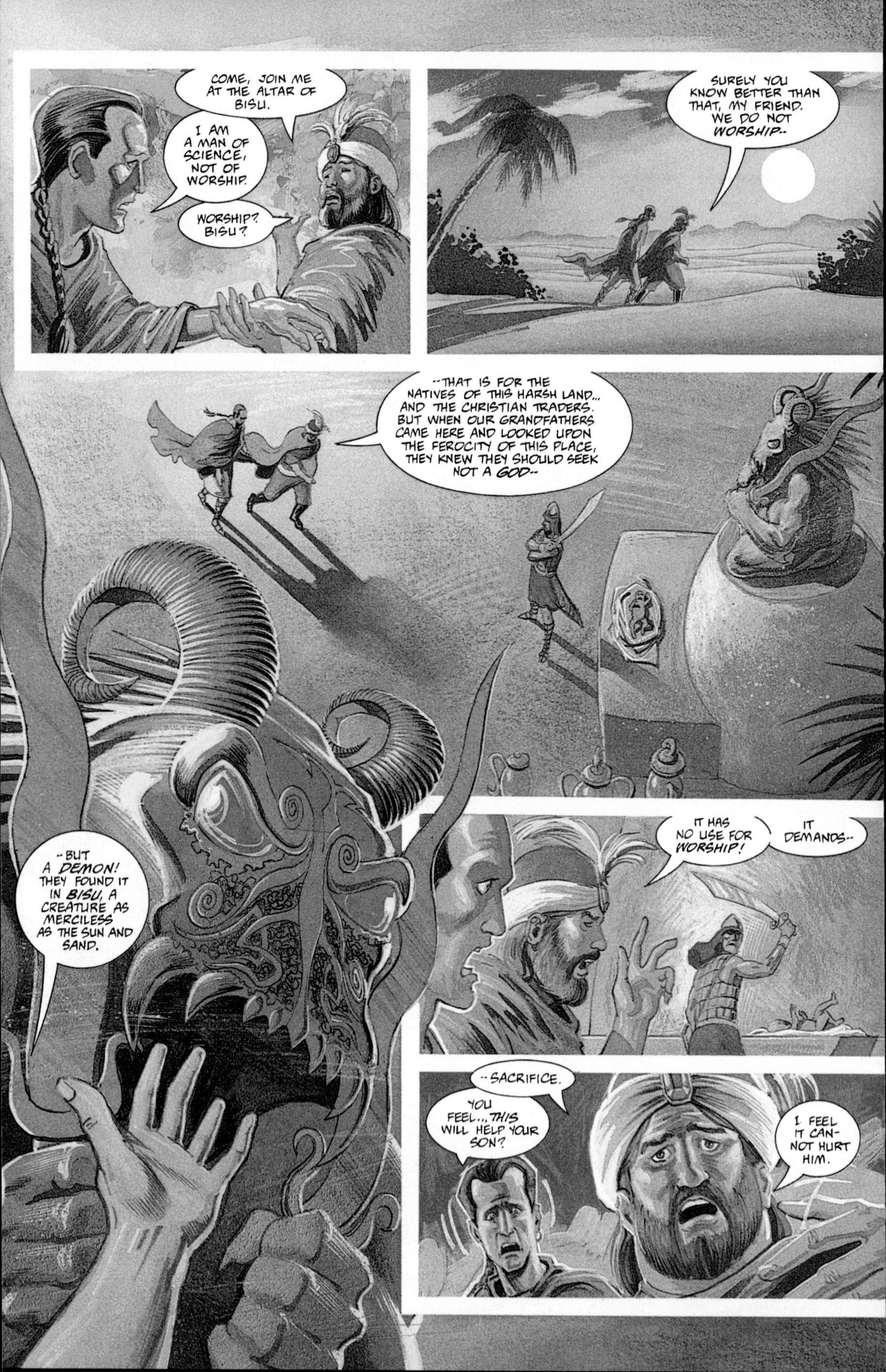
COME, JOIN ME AT THE ALTAR OF BISU.
I AM A MAN OF SCIENCE, NOT OF WORSHIP.
WORSHIP? BISU?
SURELY YOU KNOW BETTER THAN THAT, MY FRIEND. WE DO NOT WORSHIP--
--THAT IS FOR THE NATIVES OF THIS HARSH LAND... AND THE CHRISTIAN TRADERS. BUT WHEN OUR GRANDFATHERS CAME HERE AND LOOKED UPON THE FEROCITY OF THIS PLACE, THEY KNEW THEY SHOULD SEEK NOT A GOD--
--BUT A DEMON! THEY FOUND IT IN BISU, A CREATURE AS MERCILESS AS THE SUN AND SAND.
IT HAS NO USE FOR WORSHIP!
IT DEMANDS--
--SACRIFICE.
YOU FEEL... THIS WILL HELP YOUR SON?
I FEEL IT CAN-NOT HURT HIM.

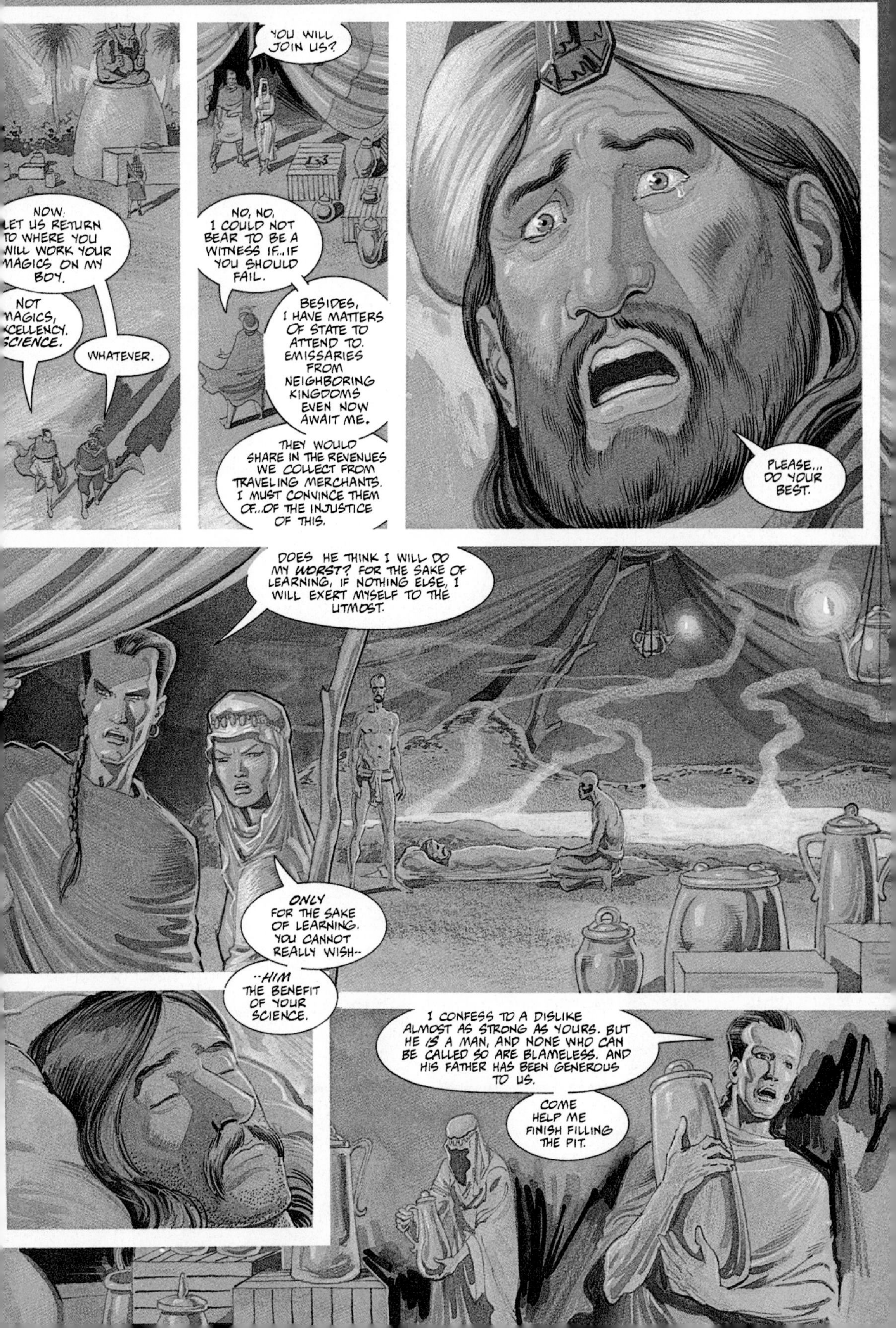

NOW. LET US RETURN TO WHERE YOU WILL WORK YOUR MAGICS ON MY BOY.
NOT MAGICS, EXCELLENCY. SCIENCE.
WHATEVER.
YOU WILL JOIN US?
NO, NO, I COULD NOT BEAR TO BE A WITNESS IF...IF YOU SHOULD FAIL.
BESIDES, I HAVE MATTERS OF STATE TO ATTEND TO. EMISSARIES FROM NEIGHBORING KINGDOMS EVEN NOW AWAIT ME.
THEY WOULD SHARE IN THE REVENUES WE COLLECT FROM TRAVELING MERCHANTS. I MUST CONVINCE THEM OF...OF THE INJUSTICE OF THIS.
PLEASE... DO YOUR BEST.
DOES HE THINK I WILL DO MY WORST? FOR THE SAKE OF LEARNING, IF NOTHING ELSE, I WILL EXERT MYSELF TO THE UTMOST.
ONLY FOR THE SAKE OF LEARNING. YOU CANNOT REALLY WISH--
--HIM THE BENEFIT OF YOUR SCIENCE.
I CONFESS TO A DISLIKE ALMOST AS STRONG AS YOURS. BUT HE IS A MAN, AND NONE WHO CAN BE CALLED SO ARE BLAMELESS. AND HIS FATHER HAS BEEN GENEROUS TO US.
COME HELP ME FINISH FILLING THE PIT.

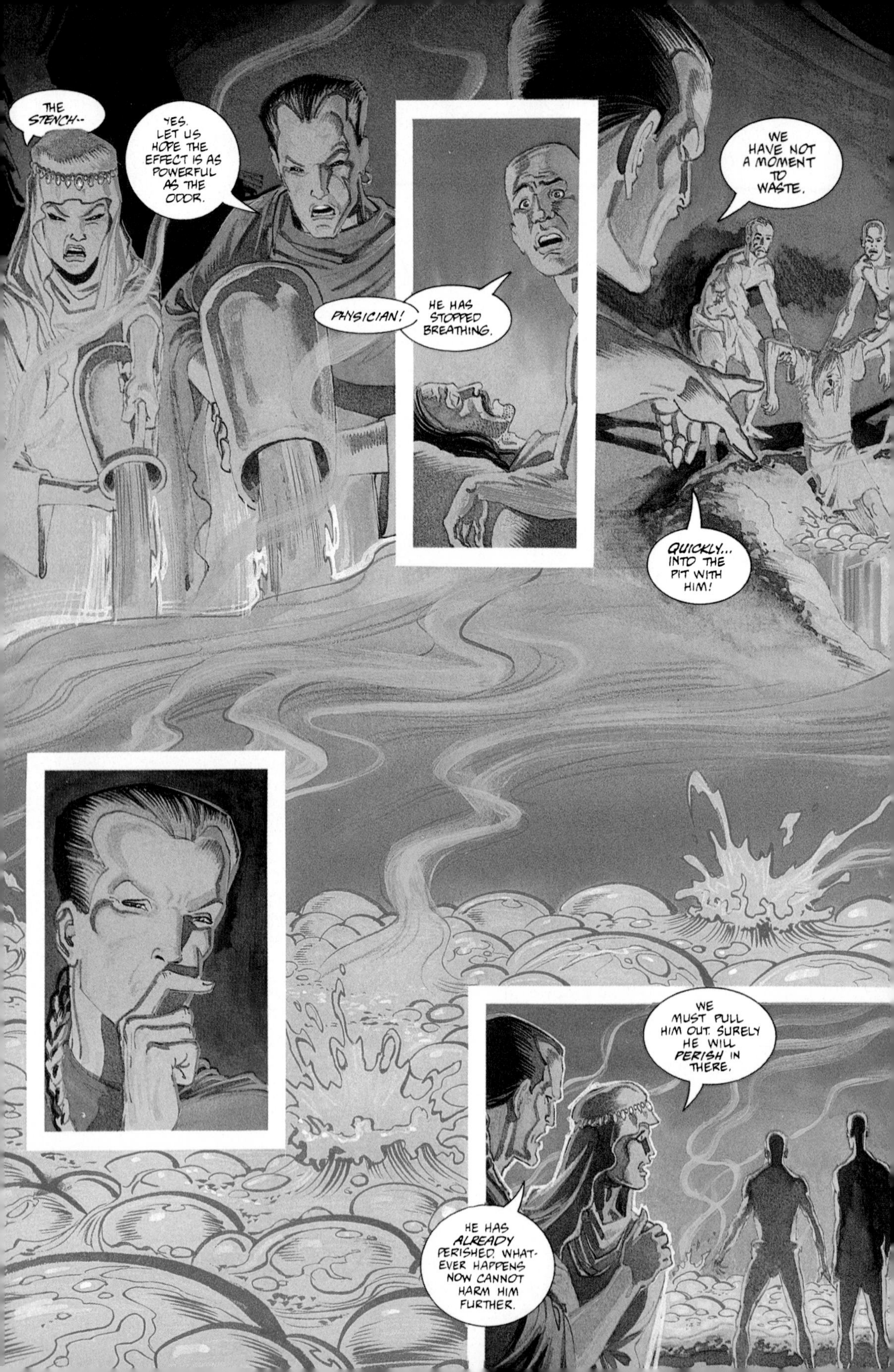
THE STENCH--
YES. LET US HOPE THE EFFECT IS AS POWERFUL AS THE ODOR.
PHYSICIAN!
HE HAS STOPPED BREATHING.
WE HAVE NOT A MOMENT TO WASTE.
QUICKLY... INTO THE PIT WITH HIM!
WE MUST PULL HIM OUT. SURELY HE WILL PERISH IN THERE.
HE HAS ALREADY PERISHED. WHATEVER HAPPENS NOW CANNOT HARM HIM FURTHER.

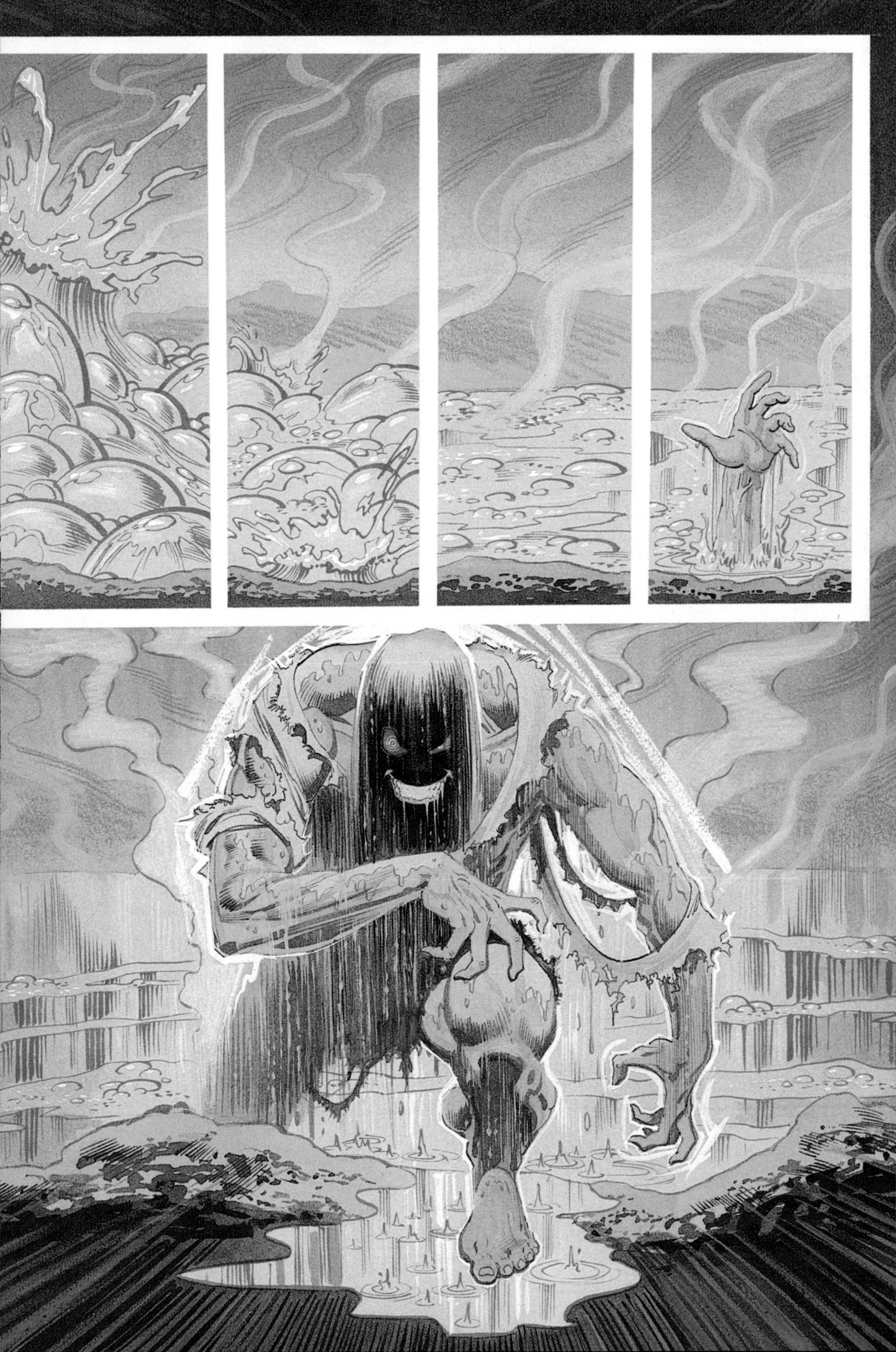

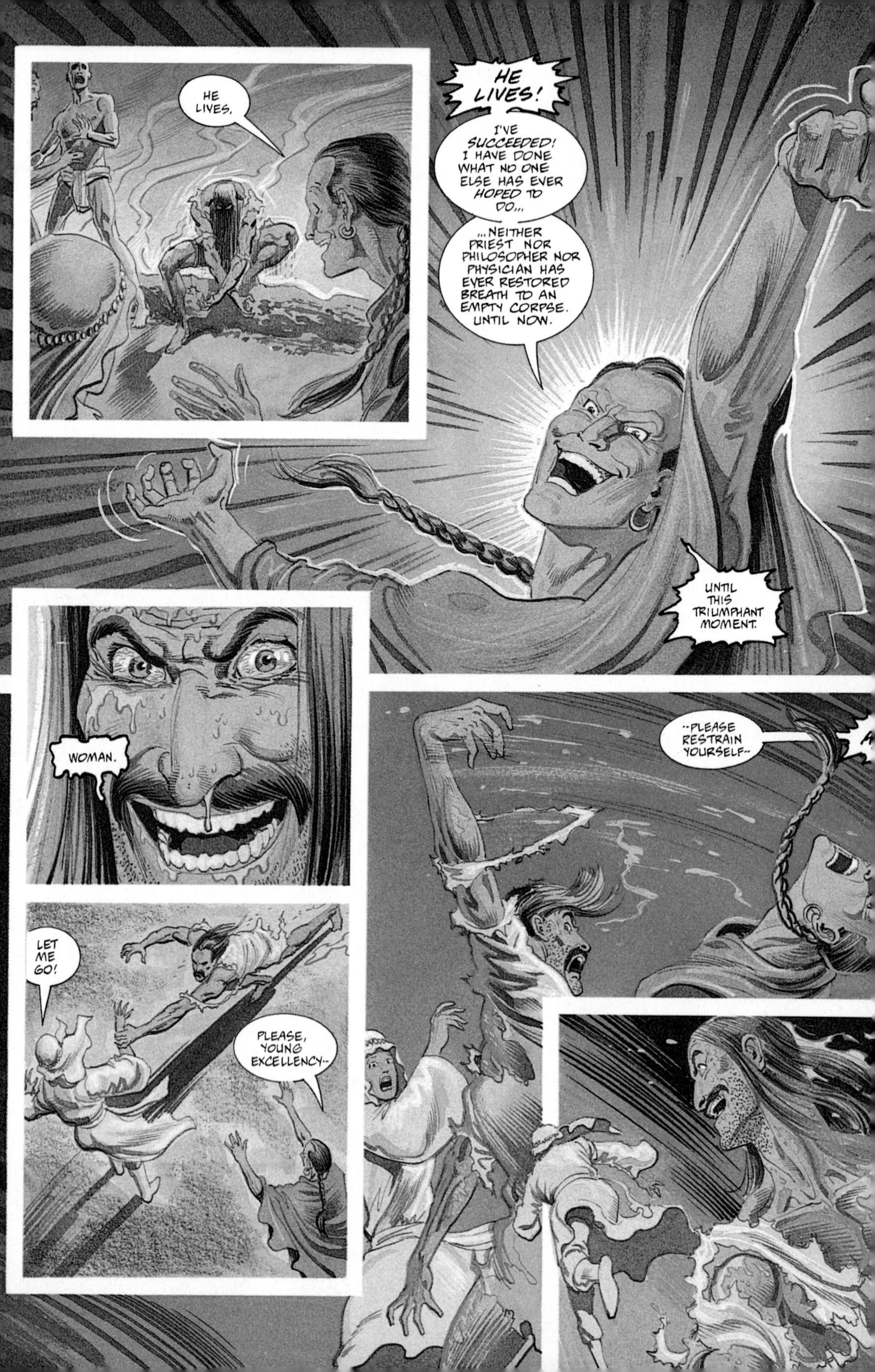

HE LIVES.
HE LIVES!
I'VE SUCCEEDED! I HAVE DONE WHAT NO ONE ELSE HAS EVER HOPED TO DO...
...NEITHER PRIEST NOR PHILOSOPHER NOR PHYSICIAN HAS EVER RESTORED BREATH TO AN EMPTY CORPSE. UNTIL NOW.
UNTIL THIS TRIUMPHANT MOMENT.
WOMAN.
--PLEASE RESTRAIN YOURSELF--
LET ME GO!
PLEASE, YOUNG EXCELLENCY--

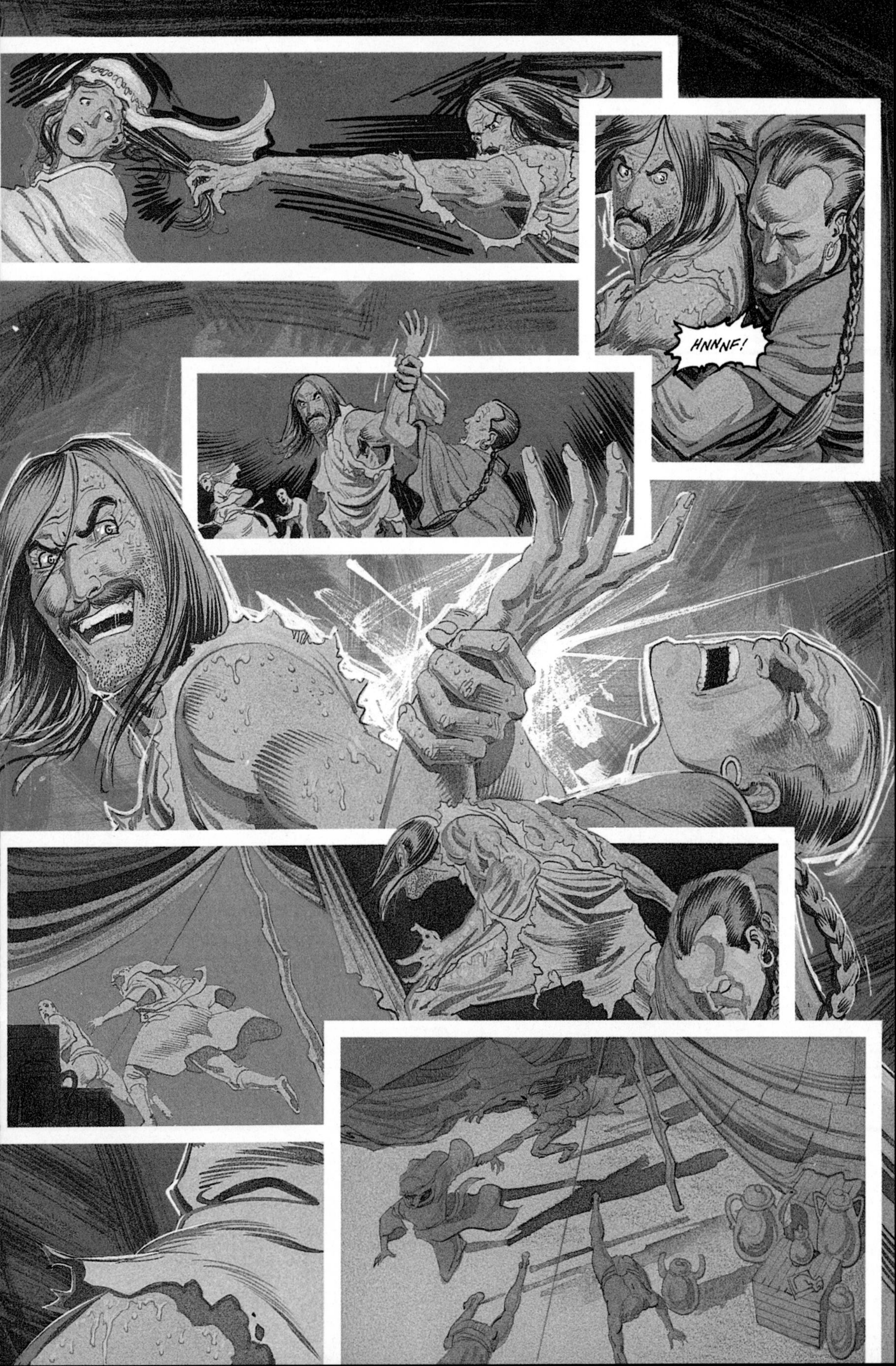
HNNNF!

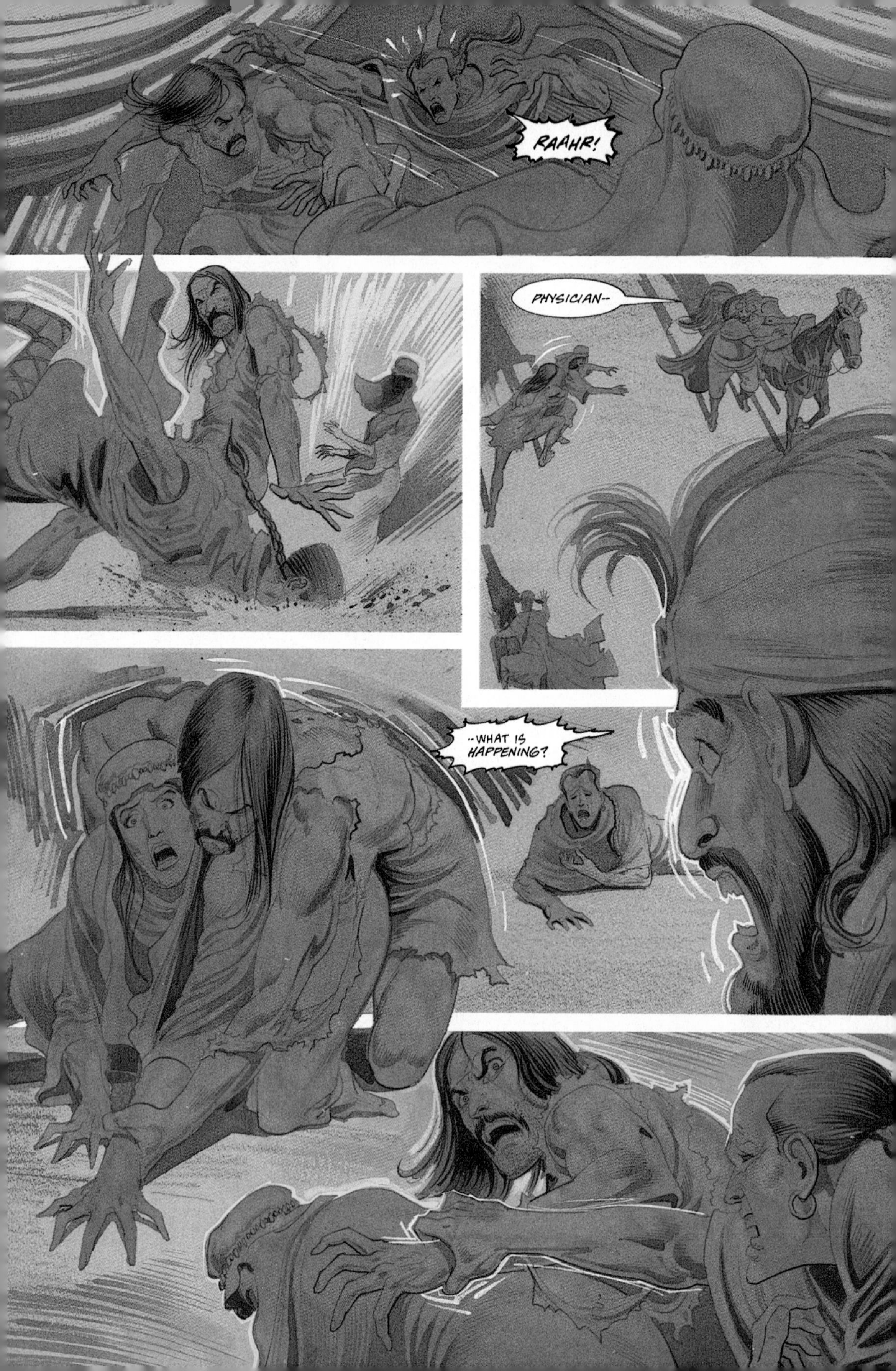
RAAHR!
PHYSICIAN--
--WHAT IS HAPPENING?

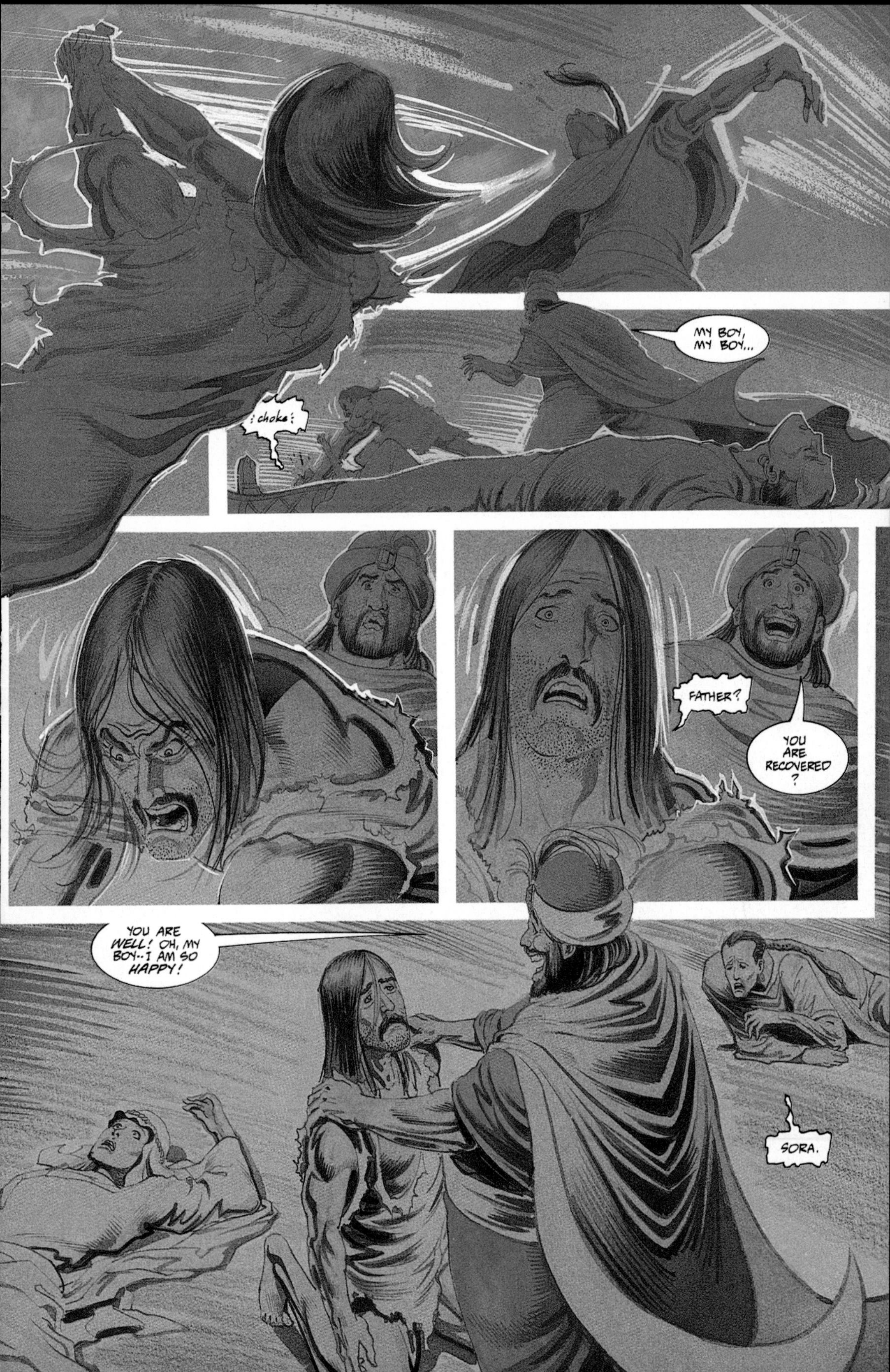
MY BOY, MY BOY...
:choke:
FATHER?
YOU ARE RECOVERED?
YOU ARE WELL! OH, MY BOY.. I AM SO HAPPY!
SORA.

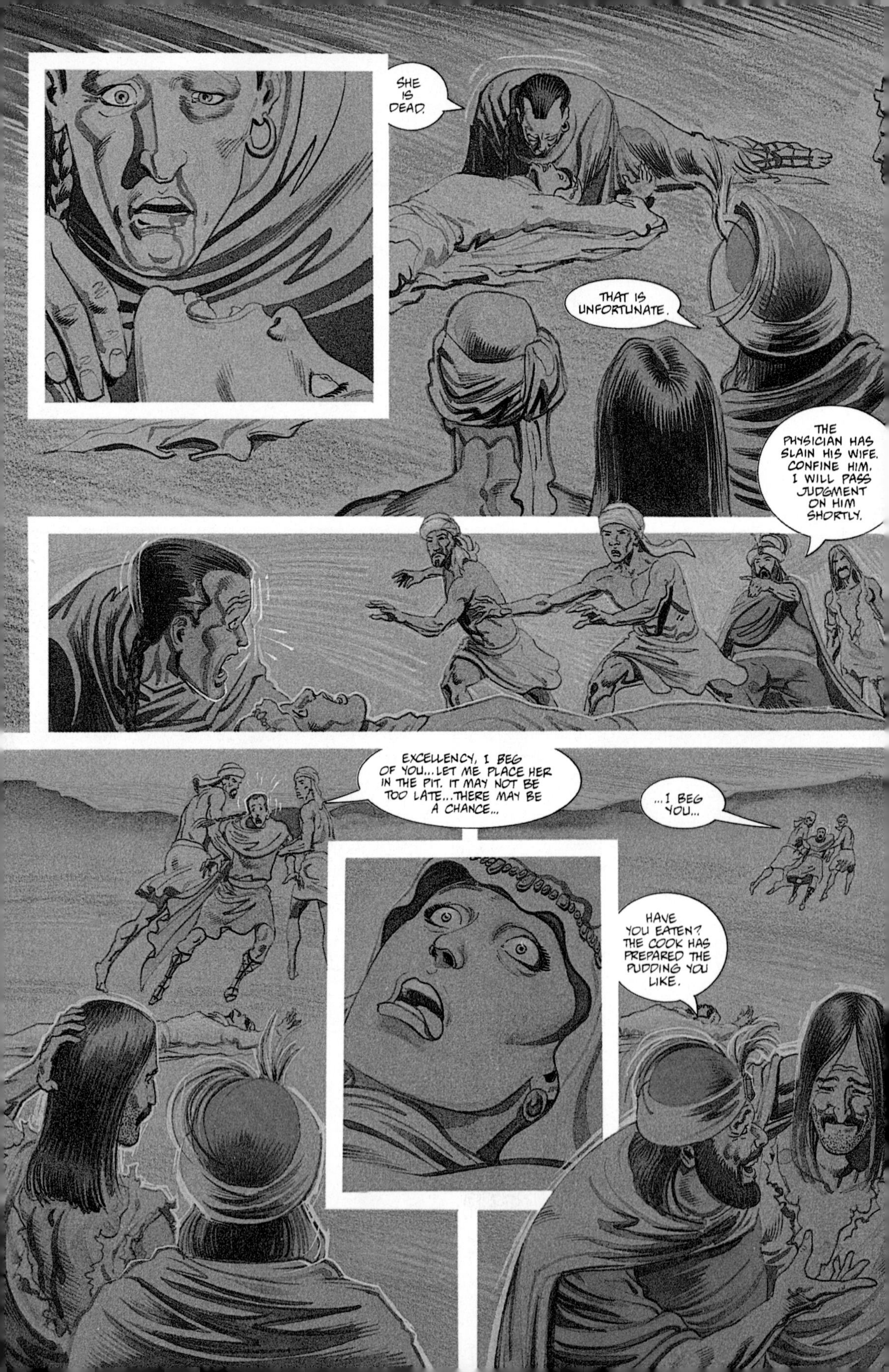
SHE IS DEAD.
THAT IS UNFORTUNATE.
THE PHYSICIAN HAS SLAIN HIS WIFE. CONFINE HIM. I WILL PASS JUDGMENT ON HIM SHORTLY.
EXCELLENCY, I BEG OF YOU... LET ME PLACE HER IN THE PIT. IT MAY NOT BE TOO LATE... THERE MAY BE A CHANCE...
...I BEG YOU...
HAVE YOU EATEN? THE COOK HAS PREPARED THE PUDDING YOU LIKE.

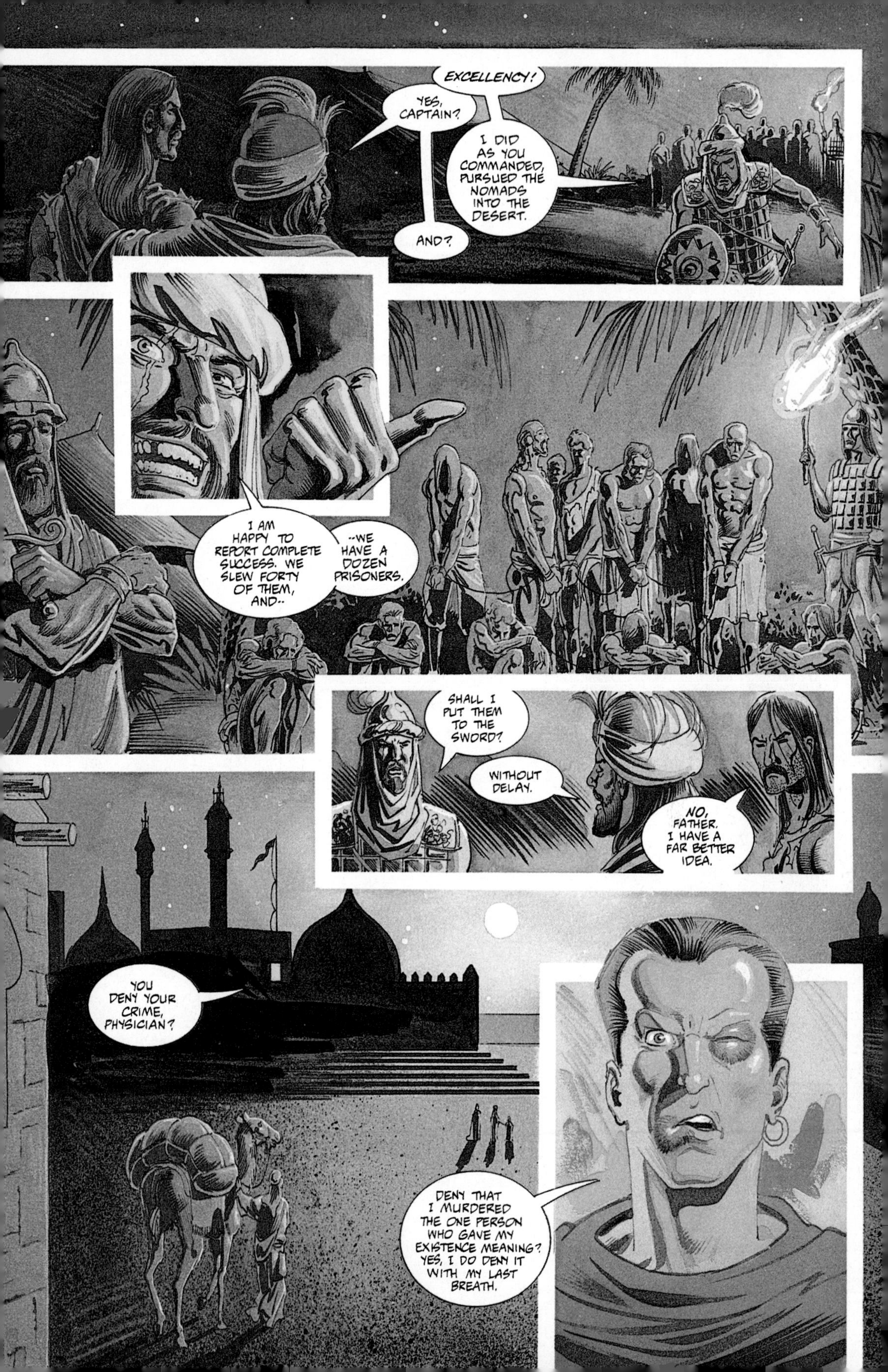

EXCELLENCY!
YES, CAPTAIN?
I DID AS YOU COMMANDED, PURSUED THE NOMADS INTO THE DESERT.
AND?
I AM HAPPY TO REPORT COMPLETE SUCCESS. WE SLEW FORTY OF THEM, AND--
--WE HAVE A DOZEN PRISONERS.
SHALL I PUT THEM TO THE SWORD?
WITHOUT DELAY.
NO, FATHER. I HAVE A FAR BETTER IDEA.
YOU DENY YOUR CRIME, PHYSICIAN?
DENY THAT I MURDERED THE ONE PERSON WHO GAVE MY EXISTENCE MEANING? YES, I DO DENY IT WITH MY LAST BREATH.

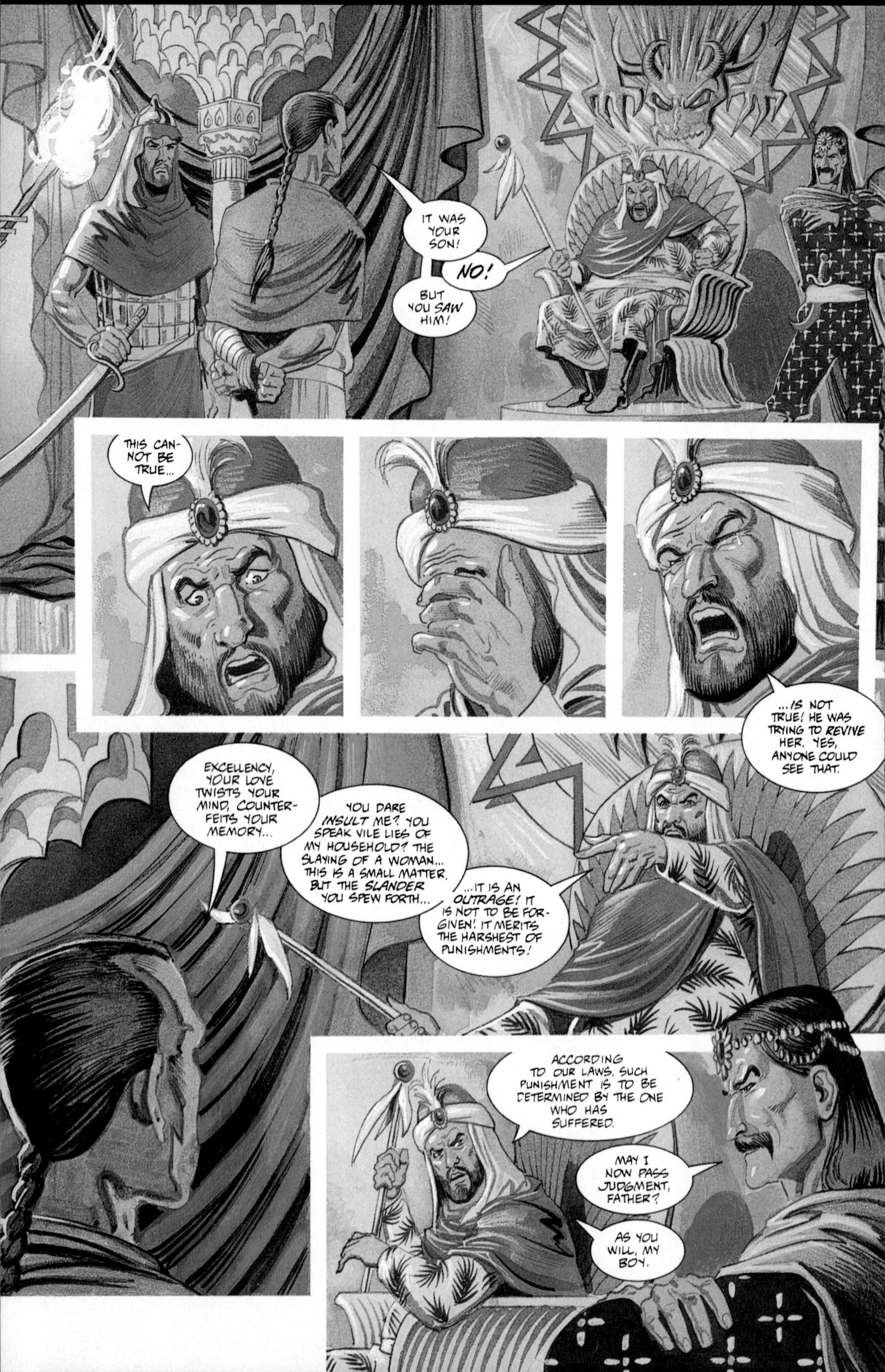
IT WAS YOUR SON!
NO!
BUT YOU SAW HIM!
THIS CAN-NOT BE TRUE...
...IS NOT TRUE! HE WAS TRYING TO REVIVE HER. YES, ANYONE COULD SEE THAT.
EXCELLENCY, YOUR LOVE TWISTS YOUR MIND, COUNTER-FEITS YOUR MEMORY...
YOU DARE INSULT ME? YOU SPEAK VILE LIES OF MY HOUSEHOLD? THE SLAYING OF A WOMAN... THIS IS A SMALL MATTER, BUT THE SLANDER YOU SPEW FORTH...
...IT IS AN OUTRAGE! IT IS NOT TO BE FOR-GIVEN! IT MERITS THE HARSHEST OF PUNISHMENTS!
ACCORDING TO OUR LAWS, SUCH PUNISHMENT IS TO BE DETERMINED BY THE ONE WHO HAS SUFFERED.
MAY I NOW PASS JUDGMENT, FATHER?
AS YOU WILL, MY BOY.

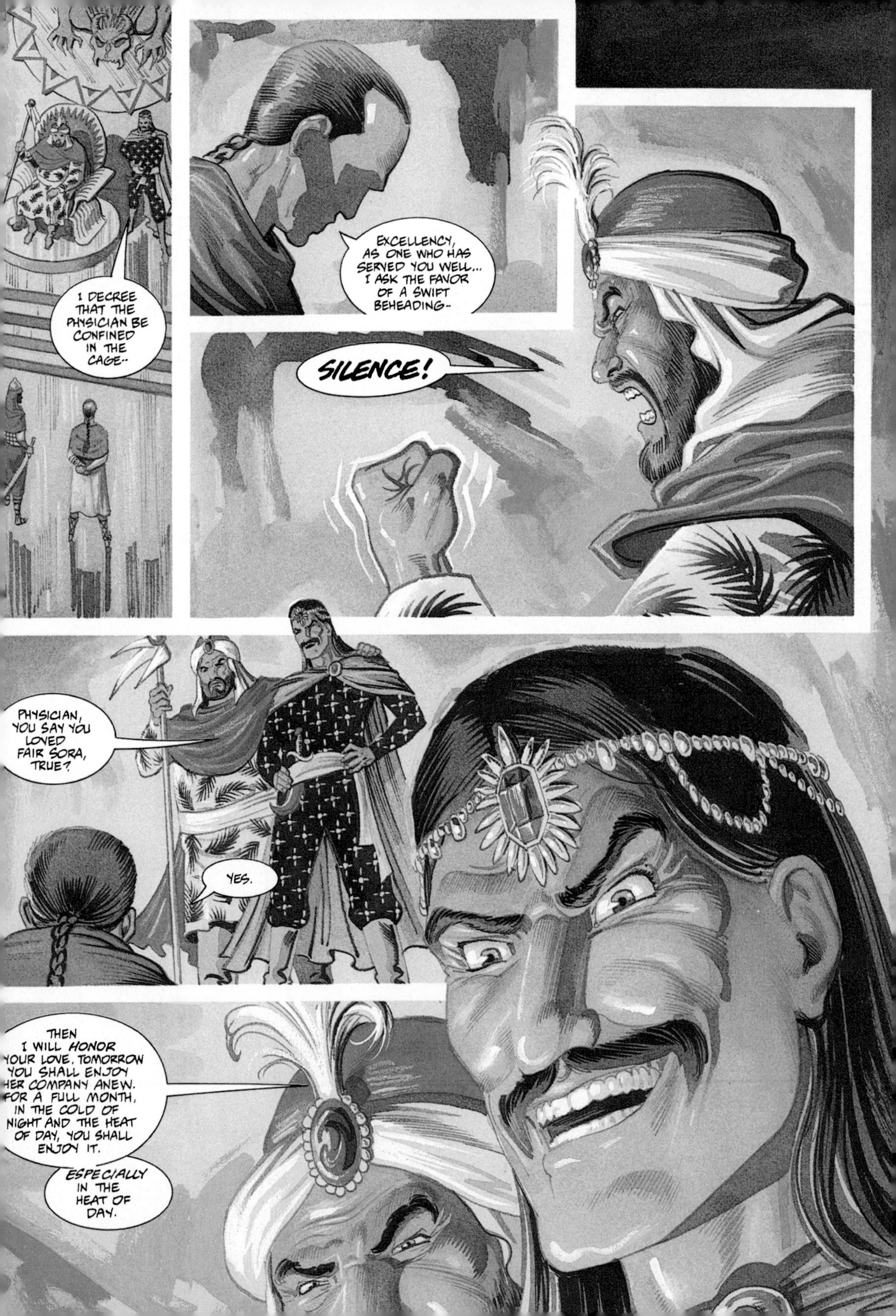

I DECREE THAT THE PHYSICIAN BE CONFINED IN THE CAGE--
EXCELLENCY, AS ONE WHO HAS SERVED YOU WELL... I ASK THE FAVOR OF A SWIFT BEHEADING--
SILENCE!
PHYSICIAN, YOU SAY YOU LOVED FAIR SORA, TRUE?
YES.
THEN I WILL HONOR YOUR LOVE. TOMORROW YOU SHALL ENJOY HER COMPANY ANEW. FOR A FULL MONTH, IN THE COLD OF NIGHT AND THE HEAT OF DAY, YOU SHALL ENJOY IT.
ESPECIALLY IN THE HEAT OF DAY.

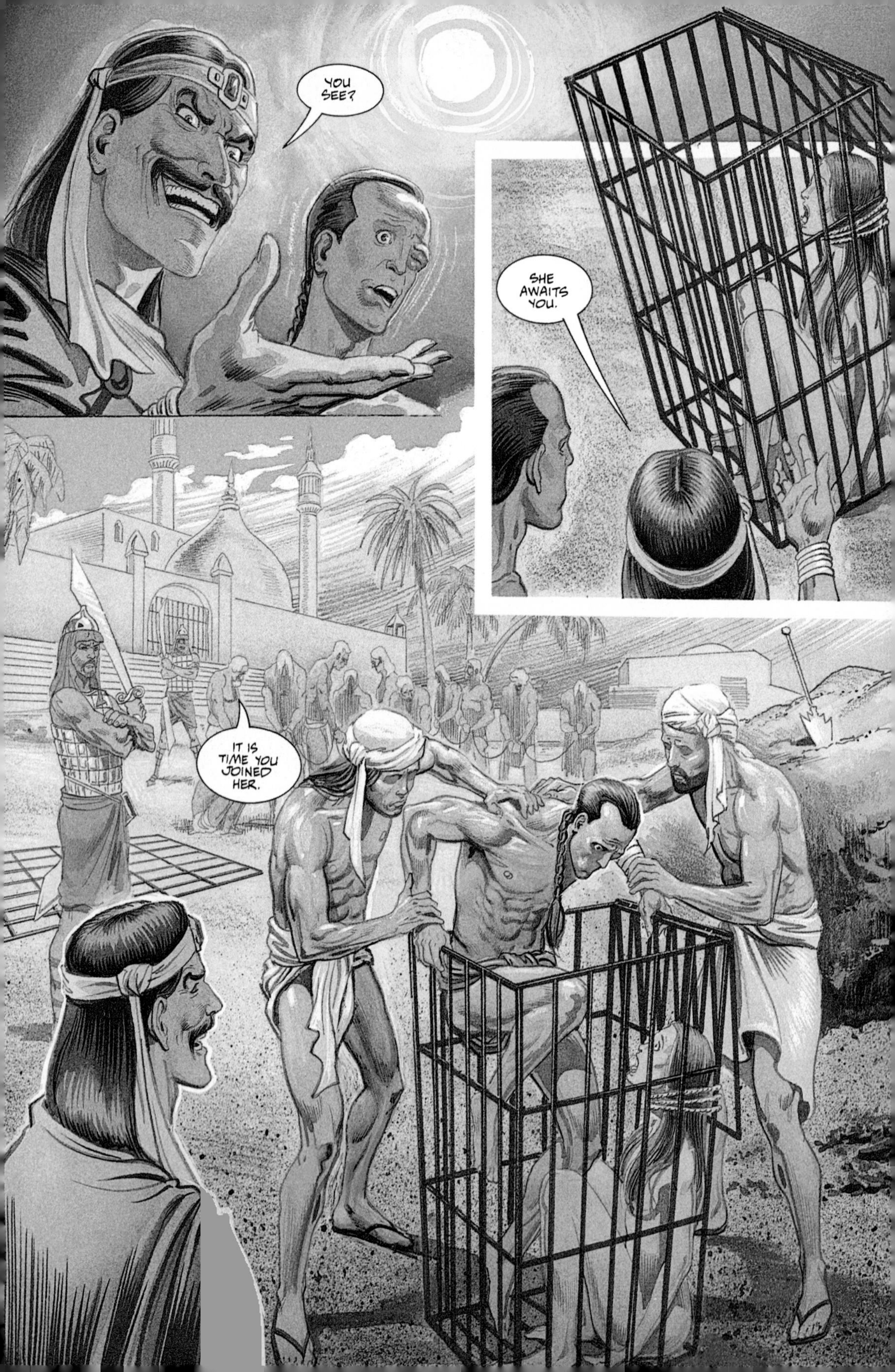
YOU SEE?
SHE AWAITS YOU.
IT IS TIME YOU JOINED HER.

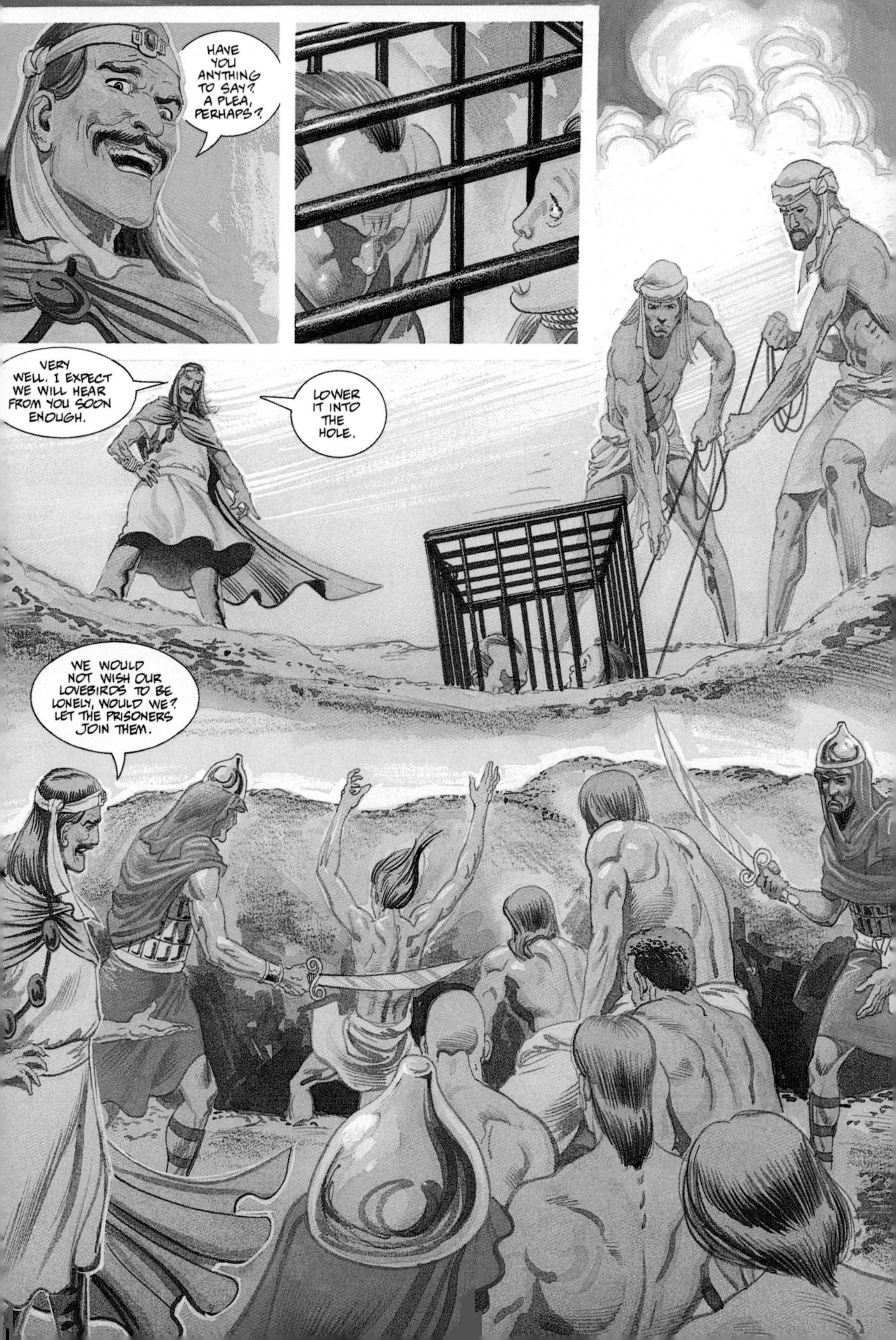
HAVE YOU ANYTHING TO SAY? A PLEA, PERHAPS?
VERY WELL. I EXPECT WE WILL HEAR FROM YOU SOON ENOUGH.
LOWER IT INTO THE HOLE.
WE WOULD NOT WISH OUR LOVEBIRDS TO BE LONELY, WOULD WE? LET THE PRISONERS JOIN THEM.

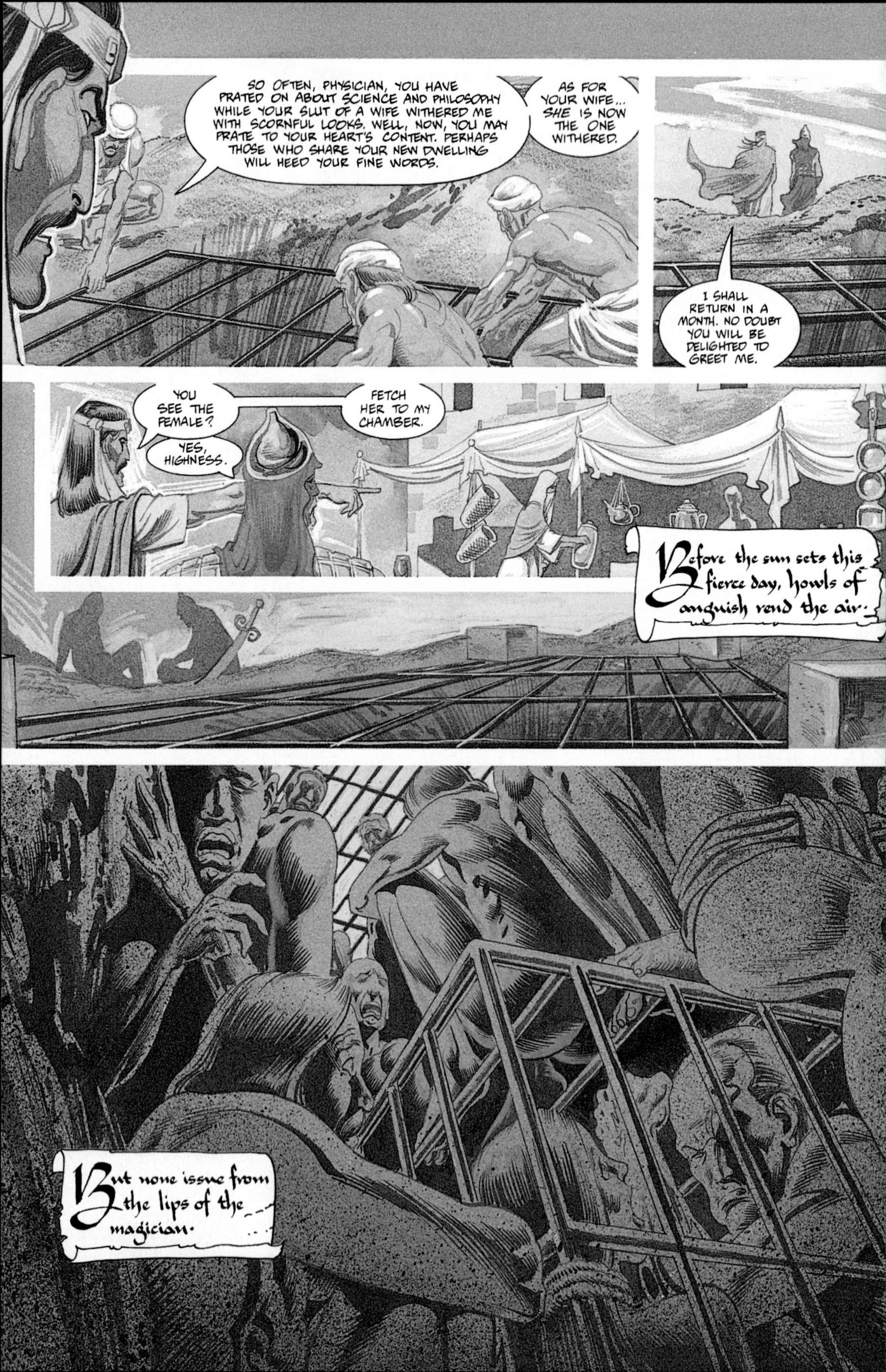
SO OFTEN, PHYSICIAN, YOU HAVE PRATED ON ABOUT SCIENCE AND PHILOSOPHY WHILE YOUR SLUT OF A WIFE WITHERED ME WITH SCORNFUL LOOKS. WELL, NOW, YOU MAY PRATE TO YOUR HEART'S CONTENT. PERHAPS THOSE WHO SHARE YOUR NEW DWELLING WILL HEED YOUR FINE WORDS.
AS FOR YOUR WIFE... SHE IS NOW THE ONE WITHERED.
I SHALL RETURN IN A MONTH. NO DOUBT YOU WILL BE DELIGHTED TO GREET ME.
YOU SEE THE FEMALE?
YES, HIGHNESS.
FETCH HER TO MY CHAMBER.
Before the sun sets this fierce day, howls of anguish rend the air.
But none issue from the lips of the magician.

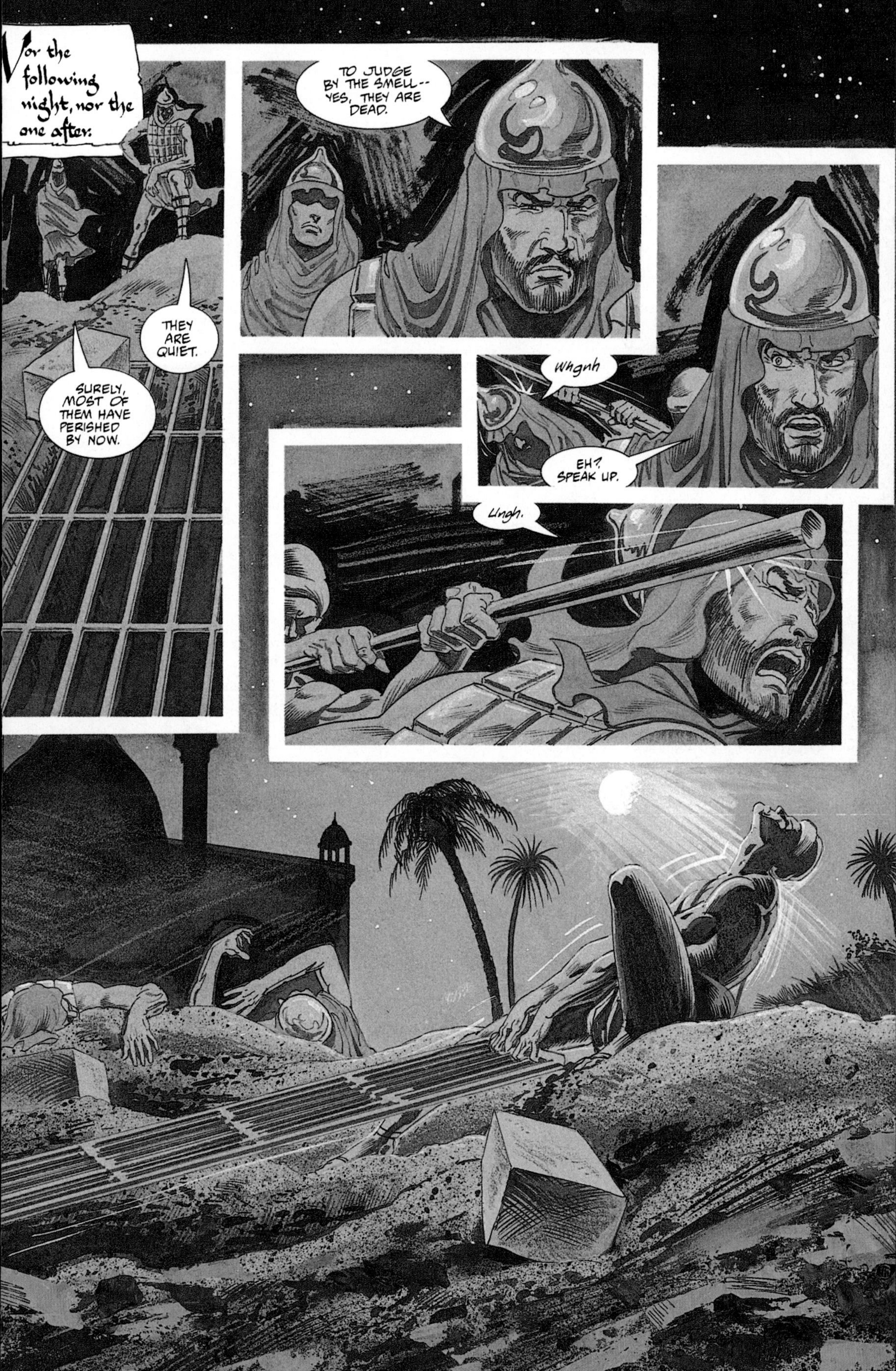
Nor the following night, nor the one after.
TO JUDGE BY THE SMELL-- YES, THEY ARE DEAD.
THEY ARE QUIET.
SURELY, MOST OF THEM HAVE PERISHED BY NOW.
Whgnh
EH? SPEAK UP.
Ungh.

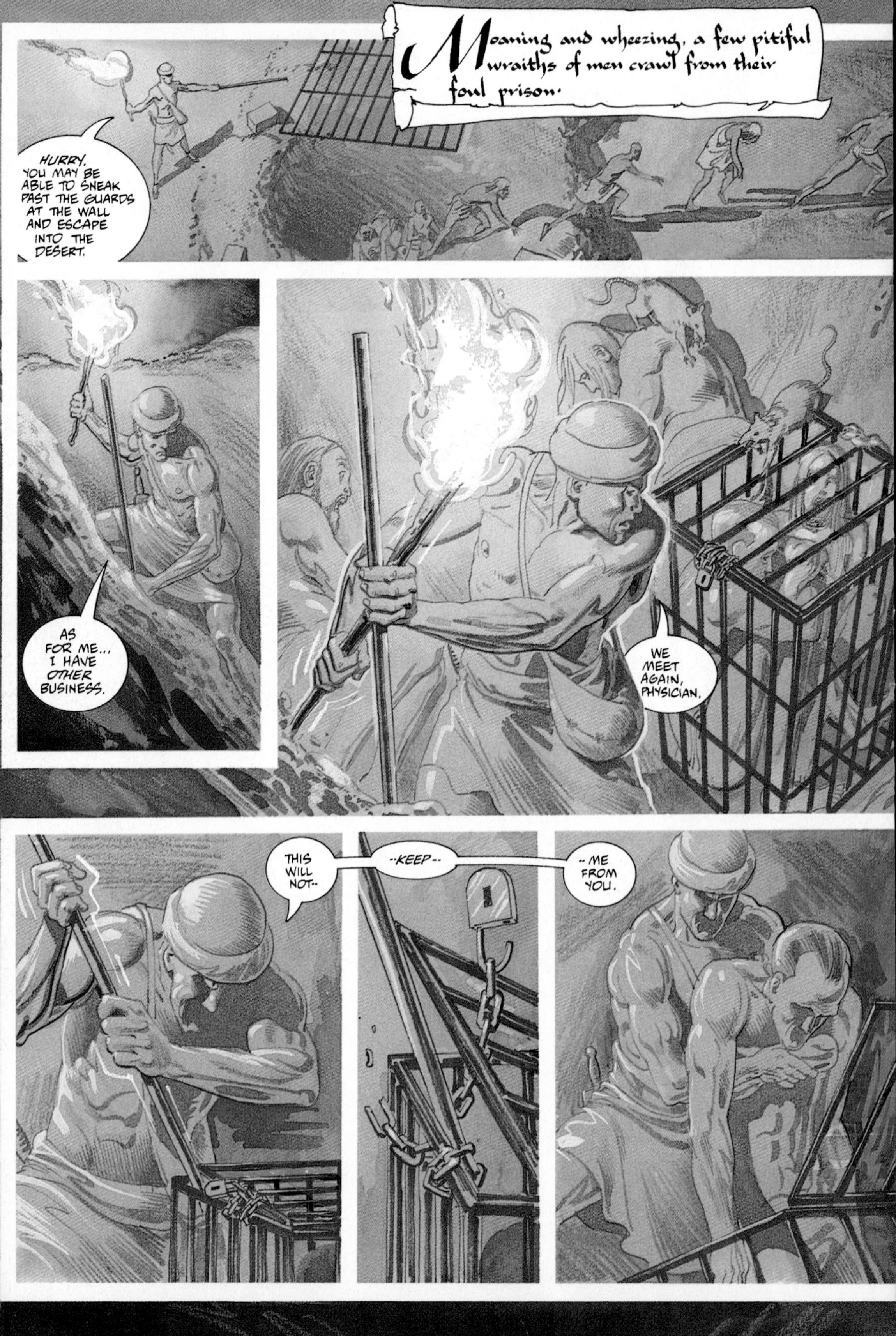
Moaning and wheezing, a few pitiful wraiths of men crawl from their foul prison.
HURRY. YOU MAY BE ABLE TO SNEAK PAST THE GUARDS AT THE WALL AND ESCAPE INTO THE DESERT.
AS FOR ME... I HAVE OTHER BUSINESS.
WE MEET AGAIN, PHYSICIAN.
THIS WILL NOT--
--KEEP--
--ME FROM YOU.

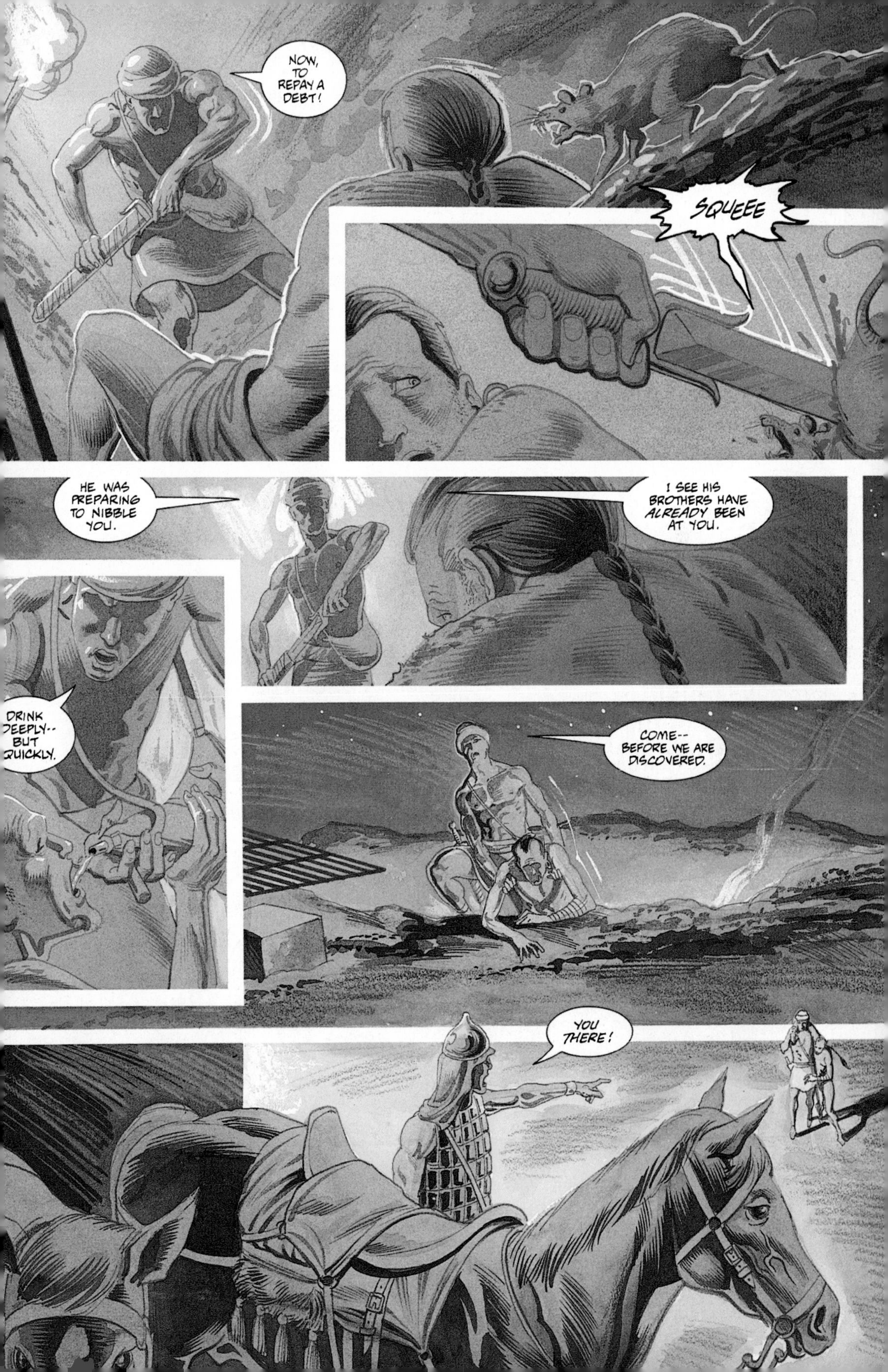
NOW, TO REPAY A DEBT!
SQUEEE
HE WAS PREPARING TO NIBBLE YOU.
I SEE HIS BROTHERS HAVE *ALREADY* BEEN AT YOU.
DRINK DEEPLY-- BUT QUICKLY.
COME-- BEFORE WE ARE DISCOVERED.
YOU THERE!

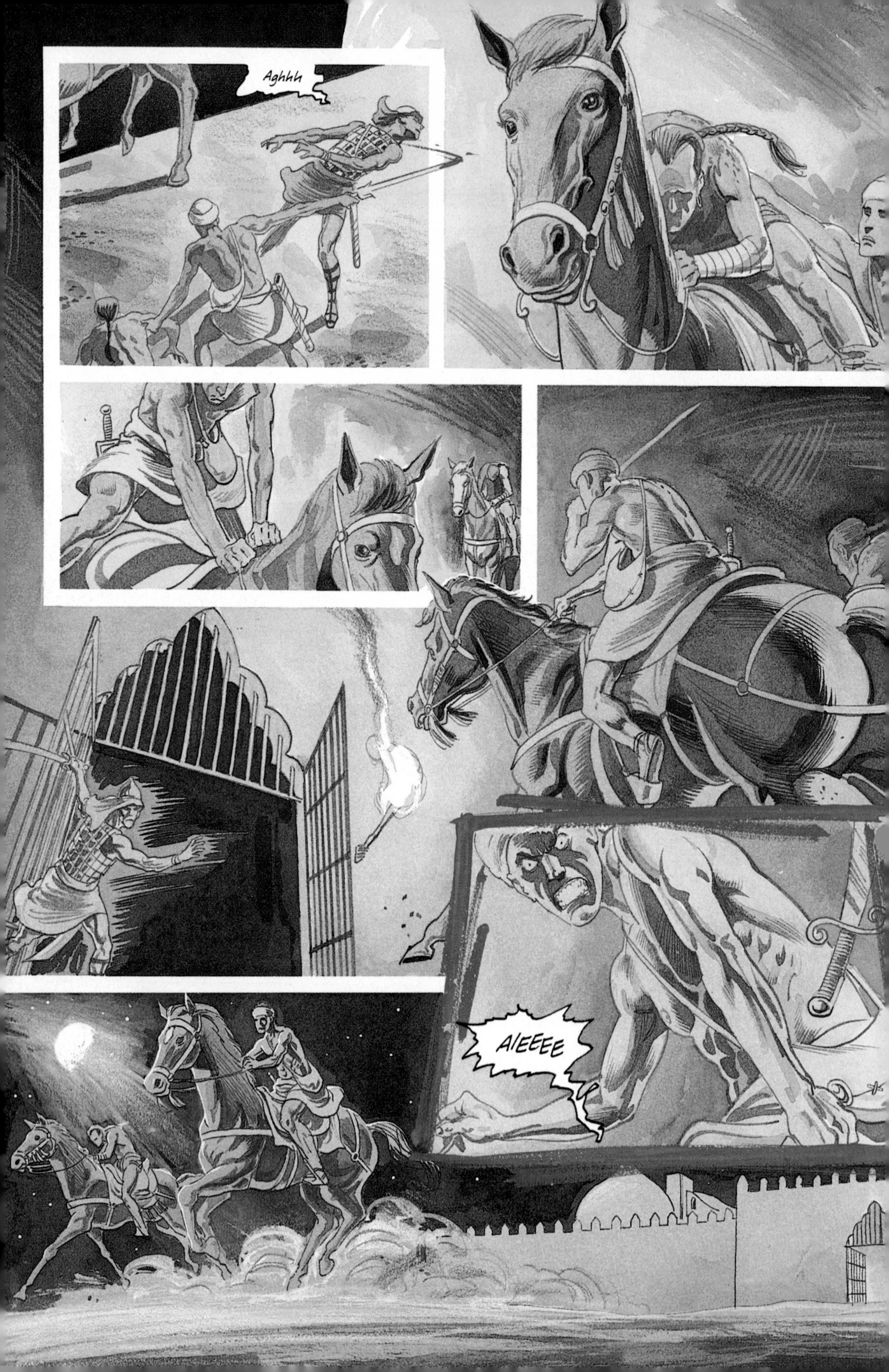
Aghhh
AIEEEE

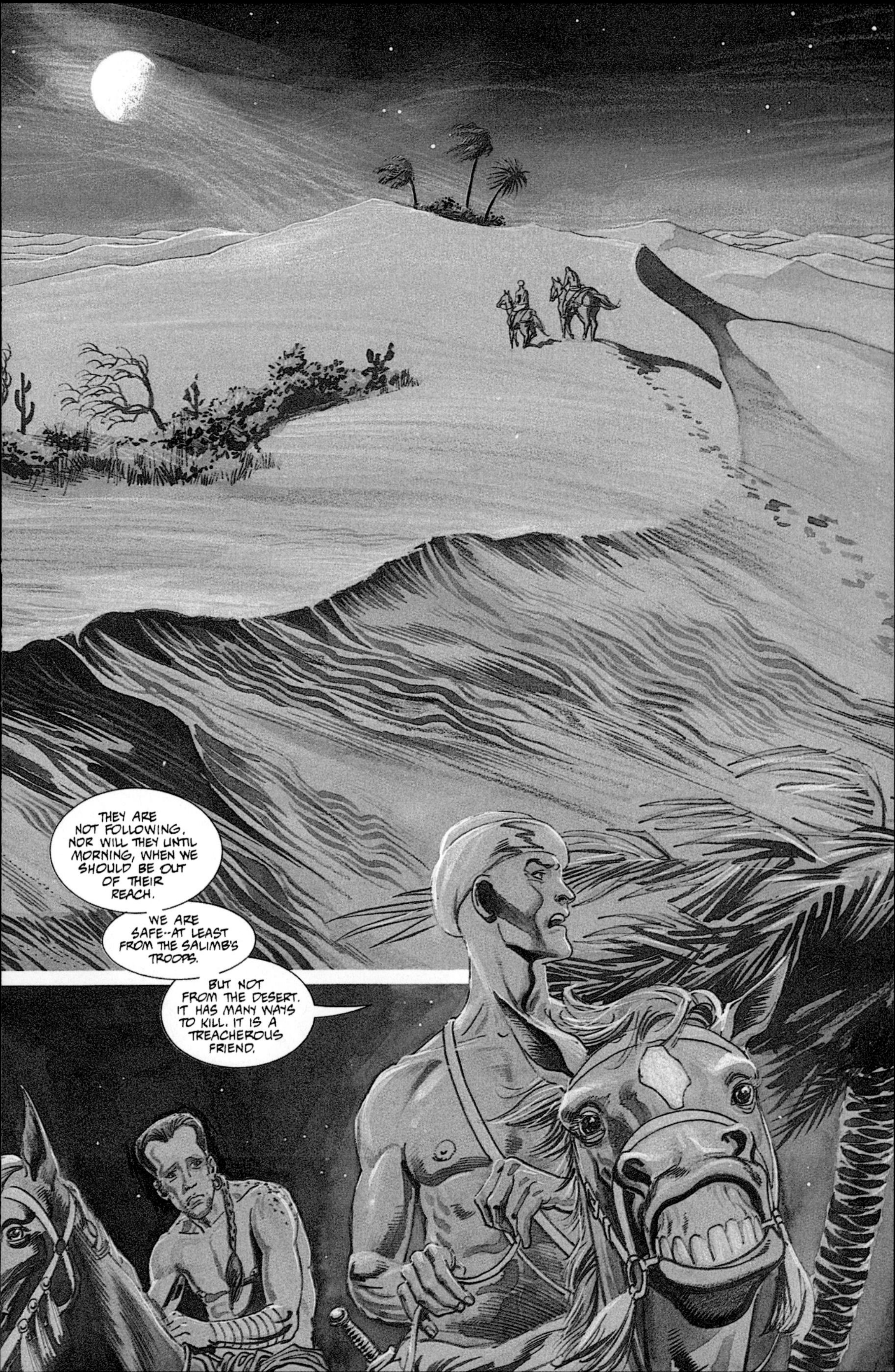
THEY ARE NOT FOLLOWING, NOR WILL THEY UNTIL MORNING, WHEN WE SHOULD BE OUT OF THEIR REACH.
WE ARE SAFE--AT LEAST FROM THE SALIMB'S TROOPS.
BUT NOT FROM THE DESERT. IT HAS MANY WAYS TO KILL. IT IS A TREACHEROUS FRIEND.

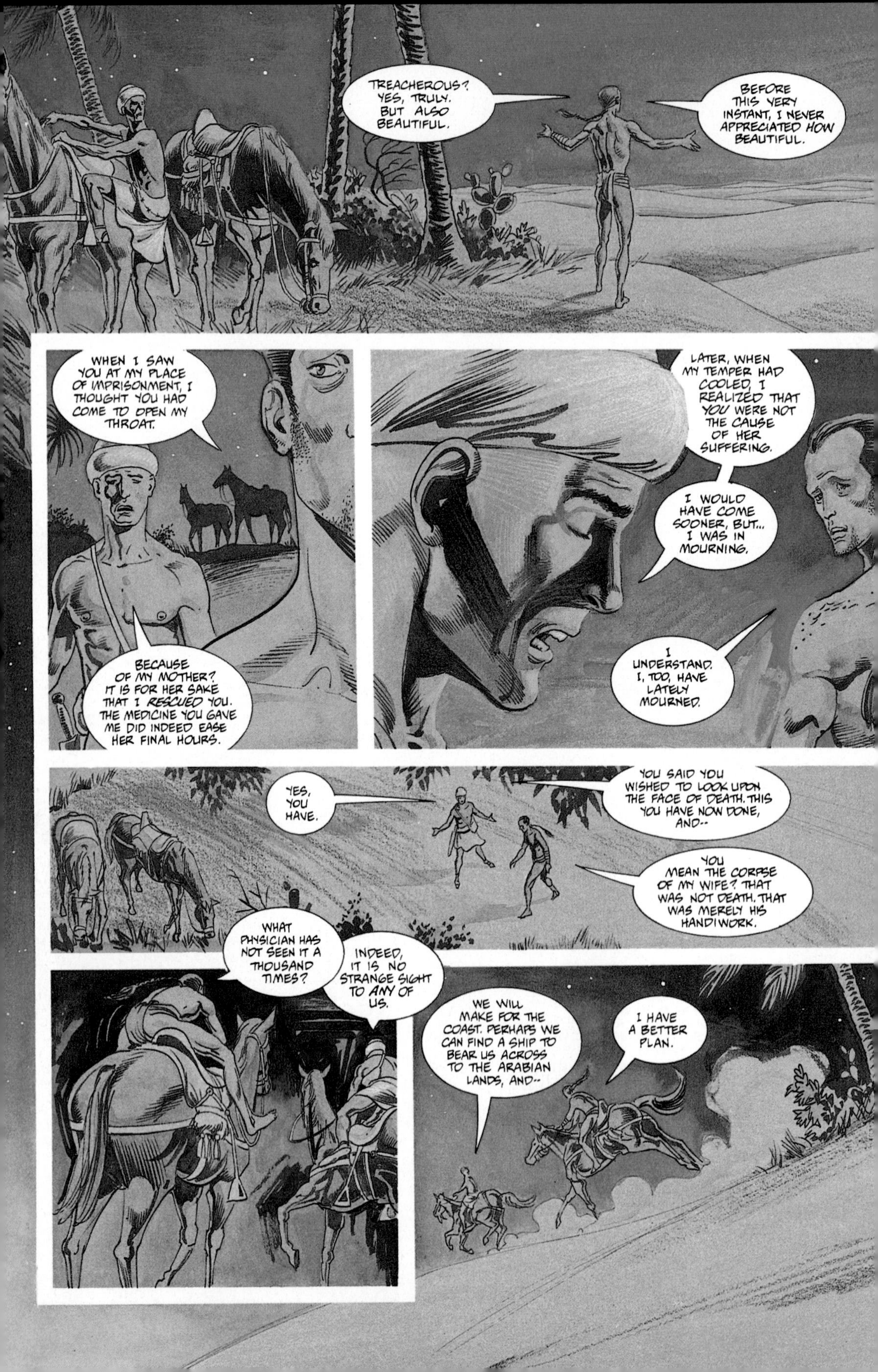

TREACHEROUS? YES, TRULY. BUT ALSO BEAUTIFUL.
BEFORE THIS VERY INSTANT, I NEVER APPRECIATED HOW BEAUTIFUL.
WHEN I SAW YOU AT MY PLACE OF IMPRISONMENT, I THOUGHT YOU HAD COME TO OPEN MY THROAT.
BECAUSE OF MY MOTHER? IT IS FOR HER SAKE THAT I RESCUED YOU. THE MEDICINE YOU GAVE ME DID INDEED EASE HER FINAL HOURS.
LATER, WHEN MY TEMPER HAD COOLED, I REALIZED THAT YOU WERE NOT THE CAUSE OF HER SUFFERING.
I WOULD HAVE COME SOONER, BUT... I WAS IN MOURNING.
I UNDERSTAND. I, TOO, HAVE LATELY MOURNED.
YES, YOU HAVE.
YOU SAID YOU WISHED TO LOOK UPON THE FACE OF DEATH. THIS YOU HAVE NOW DONE, AND--
YOU MEAN THE CORPSE OF MY WIFE? THAT WAS NOT DEATH. THAT WAS MERELY HIS HANDIWORK.
WHAT PHYSICIAN HAS NOT SEEN IT A THOUSAND TIMES?
INDEED, IT IS NO STRANGE SIGHT TO ANY OF US.
WE WILL MAKE FOR THE COAST. PERHAPS WE CAN FIND A SHIP TO BEAR US ACROSS TO THE ARABIAN LANDS, AND--
I HAVE A BETTER PLAN.

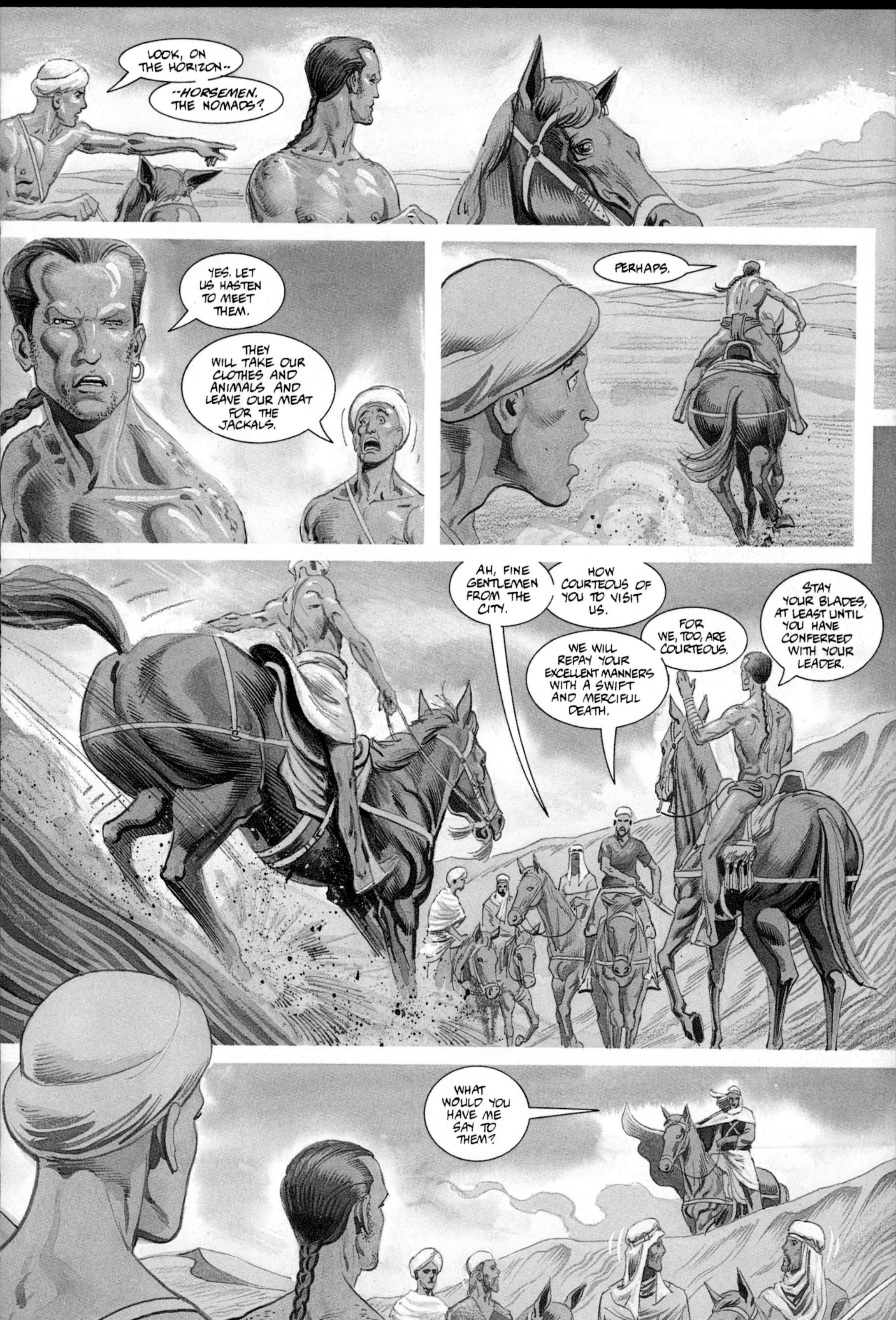
LOOK, ON THE HORIZON--
--HORSEMEN. THE NOMADS?
YES. LET US HASTEN TO MEET THEM.
THEY WILL TAKE OUR CLOTHES AND ANIMALS AND LEAVE OUR MEAT FOR THE JACKALS.
PERHAPS.
AH, FINE GENTLEMEN FROM THE CITY.
HOW COURTEOUS OF YOU TO VISIT US.
FOR WE, TOO, ARE COURTEOUS.
WE WILL REPAY YOUR EXCELLENT MANNERS WITH A SWIFT AND MERCIFUL DEATH.
STAY YOUR BLADES, AT LEAST UNTIL YOU HAVE CONFERRED WITH YOUR LEADER.
WHAT WOULD YOU HAVE ME SAY TO THEM?

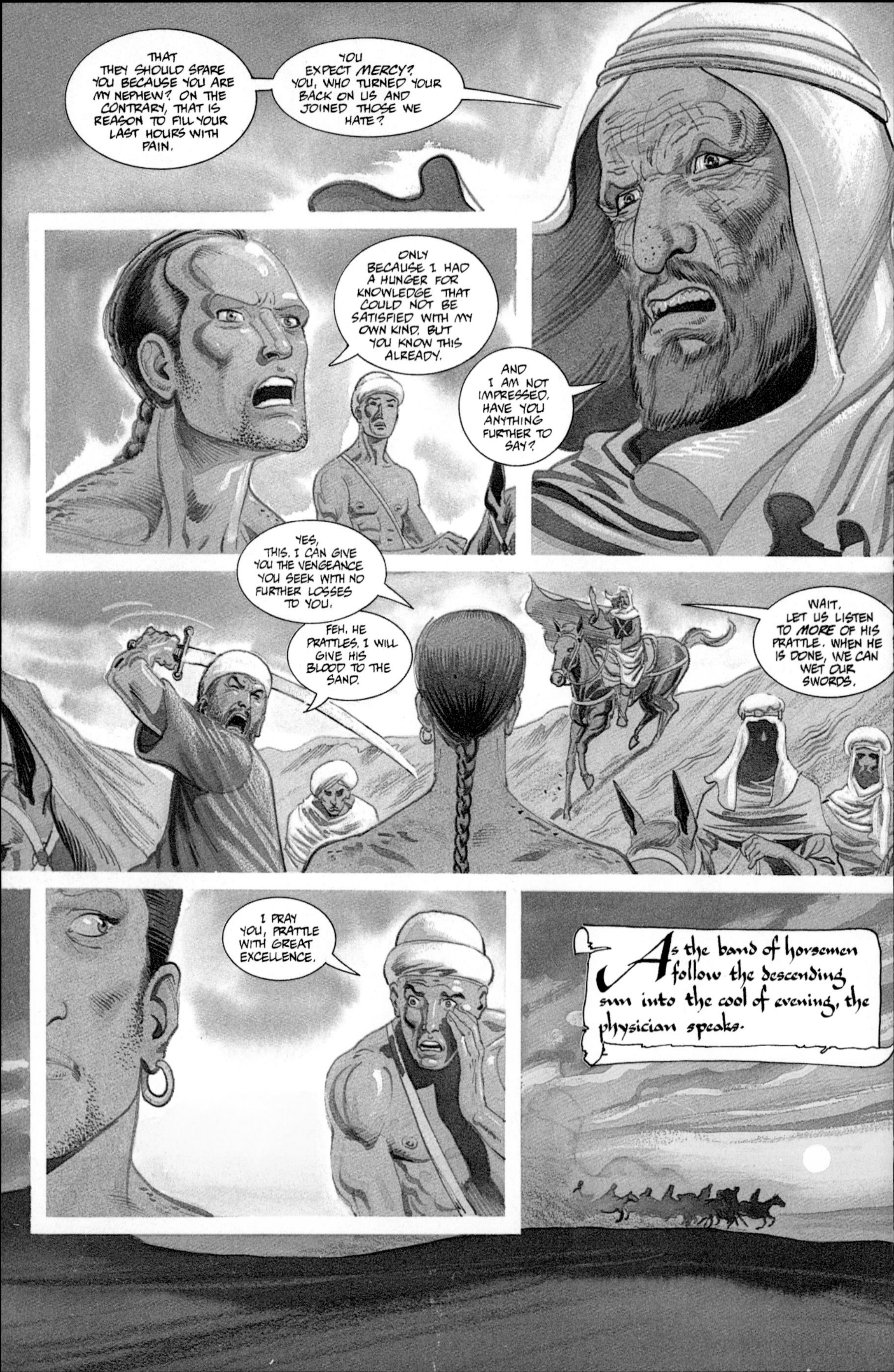
THAT THEY SHOULD SPARE YOU BECAUSE YOU ARE MY NEPHEW? ON THE CONTRARY, THAT IS REASON TO FILL YOUR LAST HOURS WITH PAIN.
YOU EXPECT MERCY? YOU, WHO TURNED YOUR BACK ON US AND JOINED THOSE WE HATE?
ONLY BECAUSE I HAD A HUNGER FOR KNOWLEDGE THAT COULD NOT BE SATISFIED WITH MY OWN KIND. BUT YOU KNOW THIS ALREADY.
AND I AM NOT IMPRESSED. HAVE YOU ANYTHING FURTHER TO SAY?
YES, THIS. I CAN GIVE YOU THE VENGEANCE YOU SEEK WITH NO FURTHER LOSSES TO YOU.
FEH. HE PRATTLES. I WILL GIVE HIS BLOOD TO THE SAND.
WAIT. LET US LISTEN TO MORE OF HIS PRATTLE. WHEN HE IS DONE, WE CAN WET OUR SWORDS.
I PRAY YOU, PRATTLE WITH GREAT EXCELLENCE.
As the band of horsemen follow the descending sun into the cool of evening, the physician speaks.

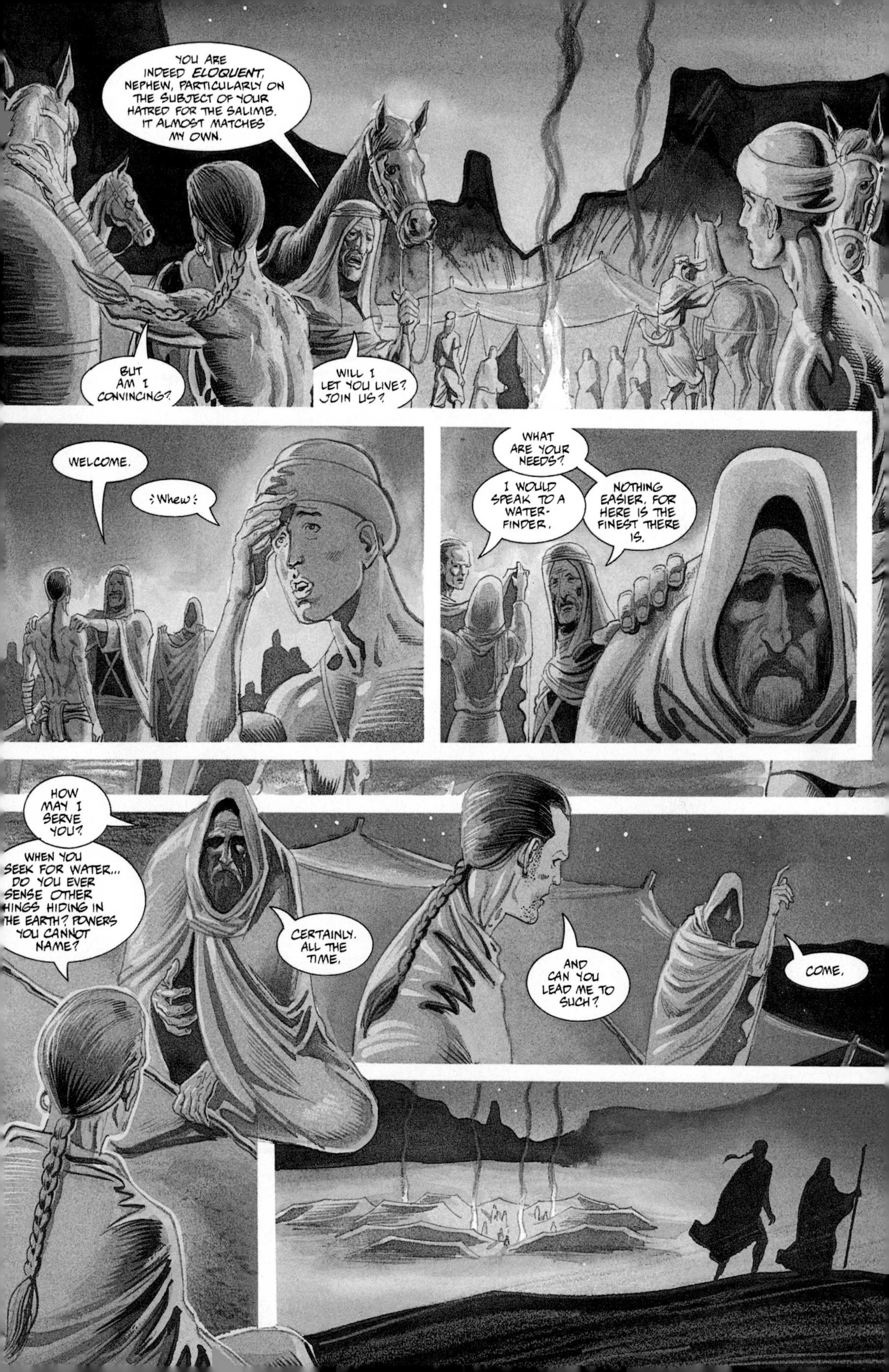
YOU ARE INDEED ELOQUENT, NEPHEW, PARTICULARLY ON THE SUBJECT OF YOUR HATRED FOR THE SALIMB. IT ALMOST MATCHES MY OWN.
BUT AM I CONVINCING?
WILL I LET YOU LIVE? JOIN US?
WELCOME.
Whew
WHAT ARE YOUR NEEDS?
I WOULD SPEAK TO A WATER-FINDER.
NOTHING EASIER, FOR HERE IS THE FINEST THERE IS.
HOW MAY I SERVE YOU?
WHEN YOU SEEK FOR WATER... DO YOU EVER SENSE OTHER THINGS HIDING IN THE EARTH? POWERS YOU CANNOT NAME?
CERTAINLY. ALL THE TIME.
AND CAN YOU LEAD ME TO SUCH?
COME.

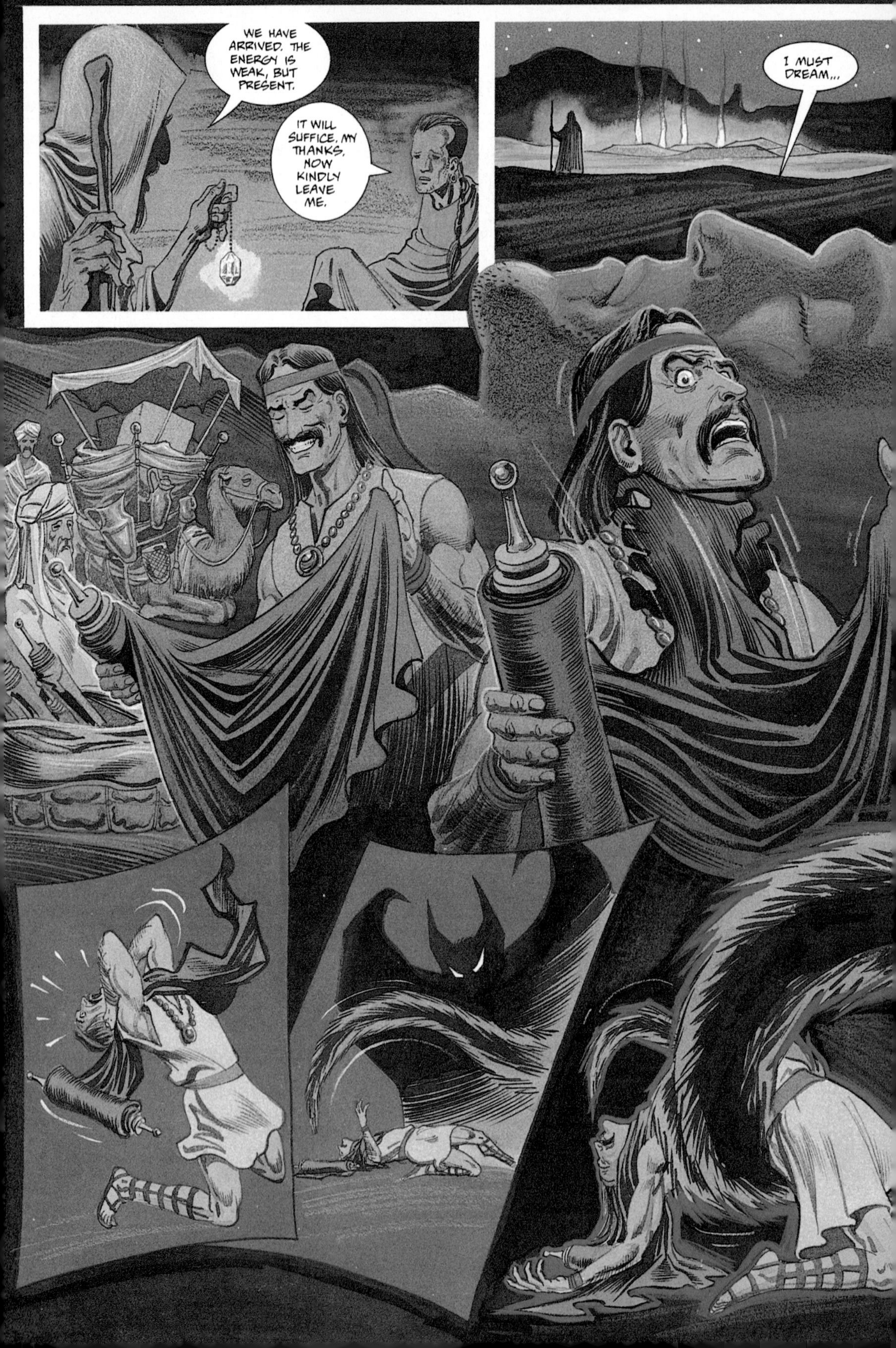
WE HAVE ARRIVED. THE ENERGY IS WEAK, BUT PRESENT.
IT WILL SUFFICE. MY THANKS. NOW KINDLY LEAVE ME.
I MUST DREAM...

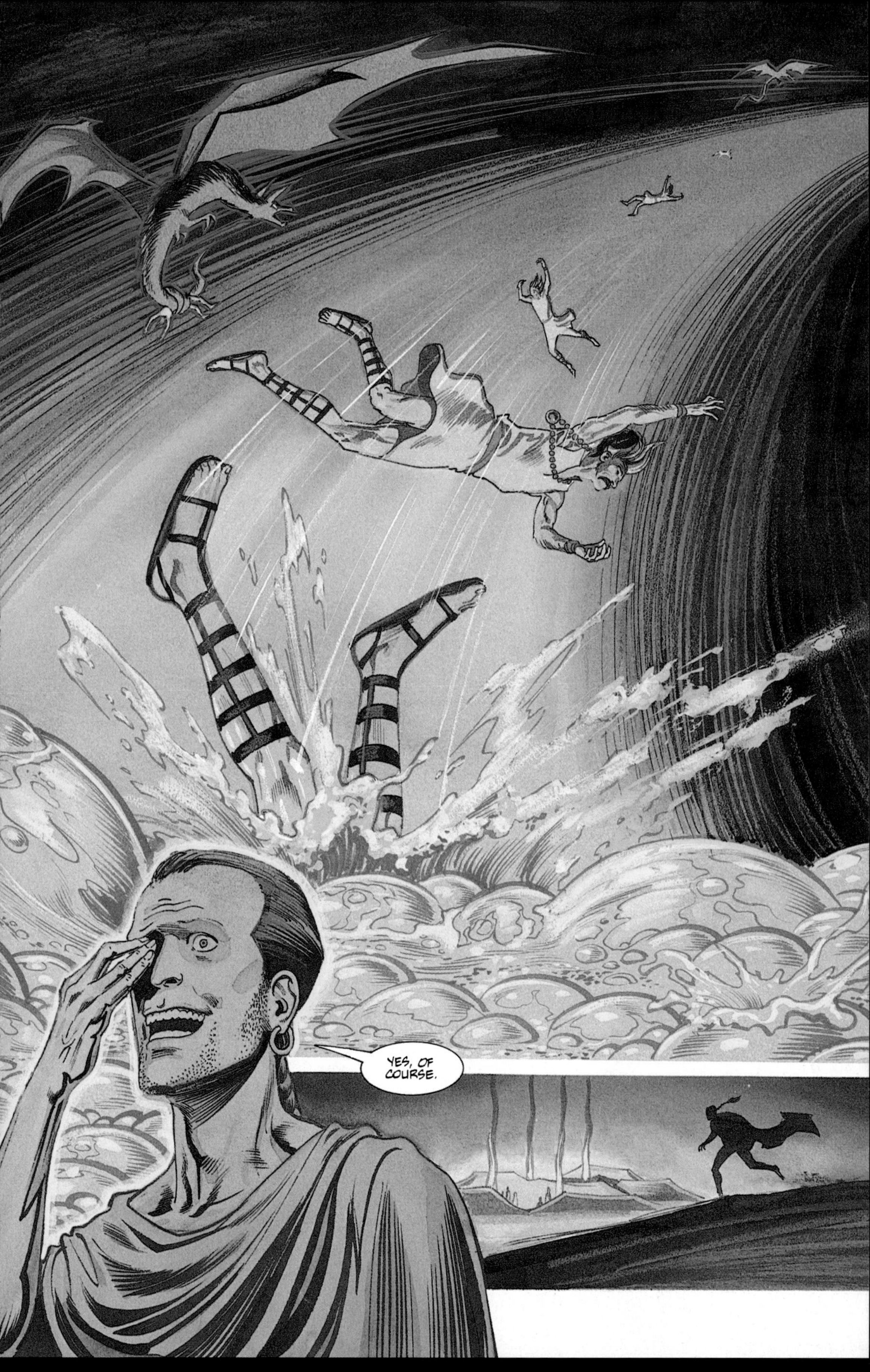
YES, OF COURSE.

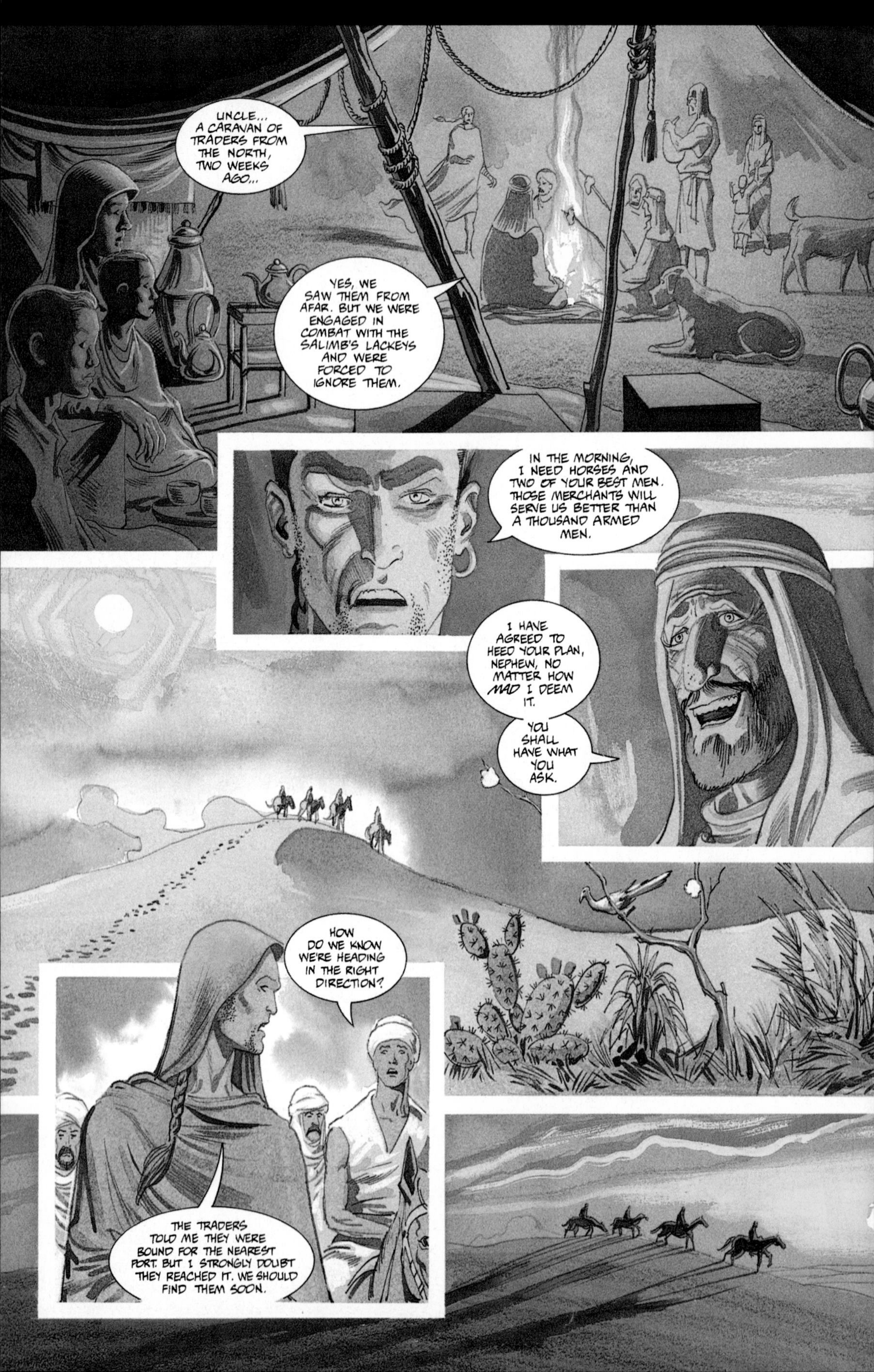
UNCLE... A CARAVAN OF TRADERS FROM THE NORTH, TWO WEEKS AGO...
YES, WE SAW THEM FROM AFAR. BUT WE WERE ENGAGED IN COMBAT WITH THE SALIMB'S LACKEYS AND WERE FORCED TO IGNORE THEM.
IN THE MORNING, I NEED HORSES AND TWO OF YOUR BEST MEN. THOSE MERCHANTS WILL SERVE US BETTER THAN A THOUSAND ARMED MEN.
I HAVE AGREED TO HEED YOUR PLAN, NEPHEW, NO MATTER HOW MAD I DEEM IT.
YOU SHALL HAVE WHAT YOU ASK.
HOW DO WE KNOW WE'RE HEADING IN THE RIGHT DIRECTION?
THE TRADERS TOLD ME THEY WERE BOUND FOR THE NEAREST PORT. BUT I STRONGLY DOUBT THEY REACHED IT. WE SHOULD FIND THEM SOON.

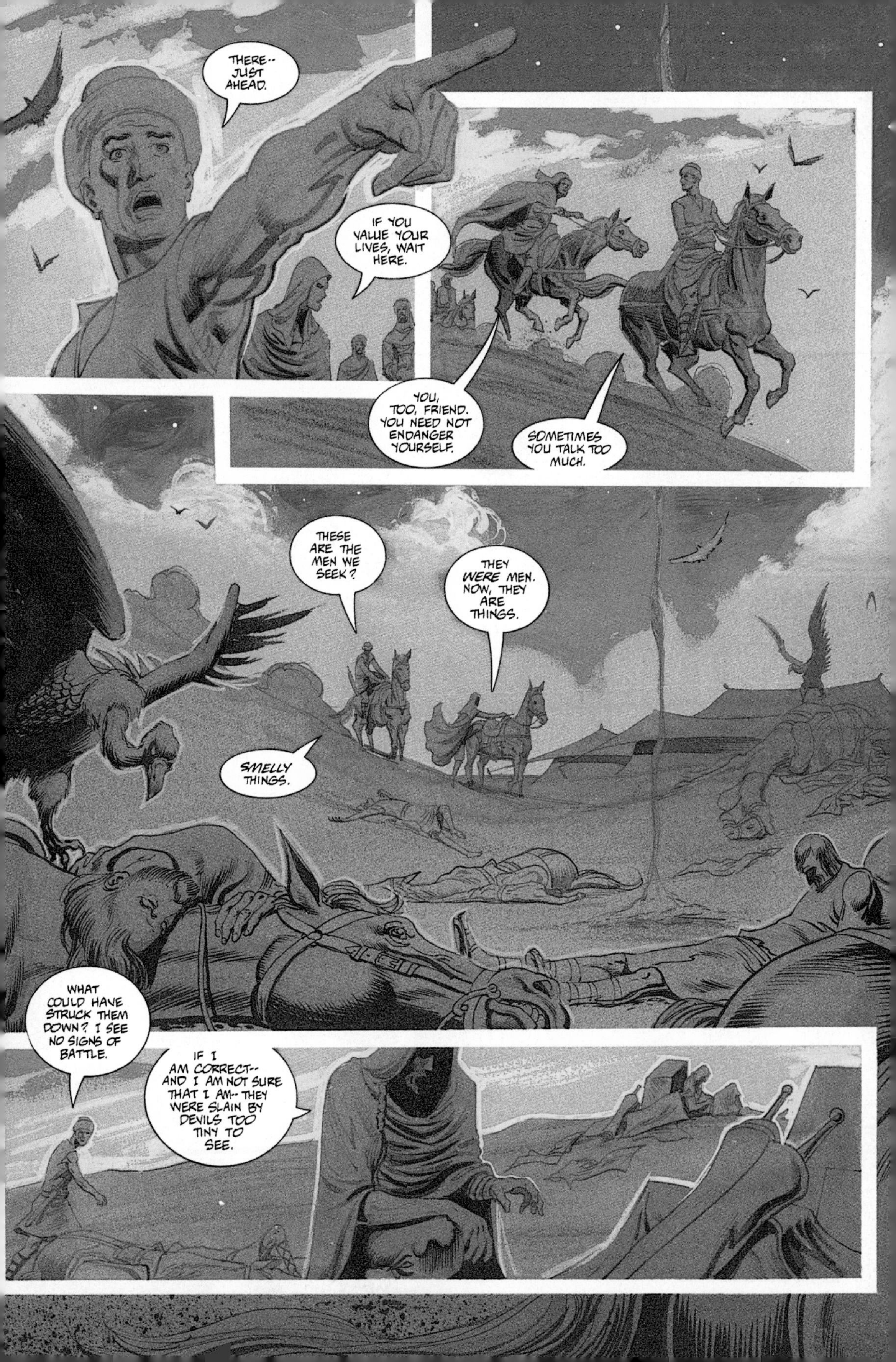
THERE-- JUST AHEAD.
IF YOU VALUE YOUR LIVES, WAIT HERE.
YOU, TOO, FRIEND. YOU NEED NOT ENDANGER YOURSELF.
SOMETIMES YOU TALK TOO MUCH.
THESE ARE THE MEN WE SEEK?
THEY *WERE* MEN. NOW, THEY ARE THINGS.
SMELLY THINGS.
WHAT COULD HAVE STRUCK THEM DOWN? I SEE NO SIGNS OF BATTLE.
IF I AM CORRECT-- AND I AM NOT SURE THAT I AM-- THEY WERE SLAIN BY DEVILS TOO TINY TO SEE.

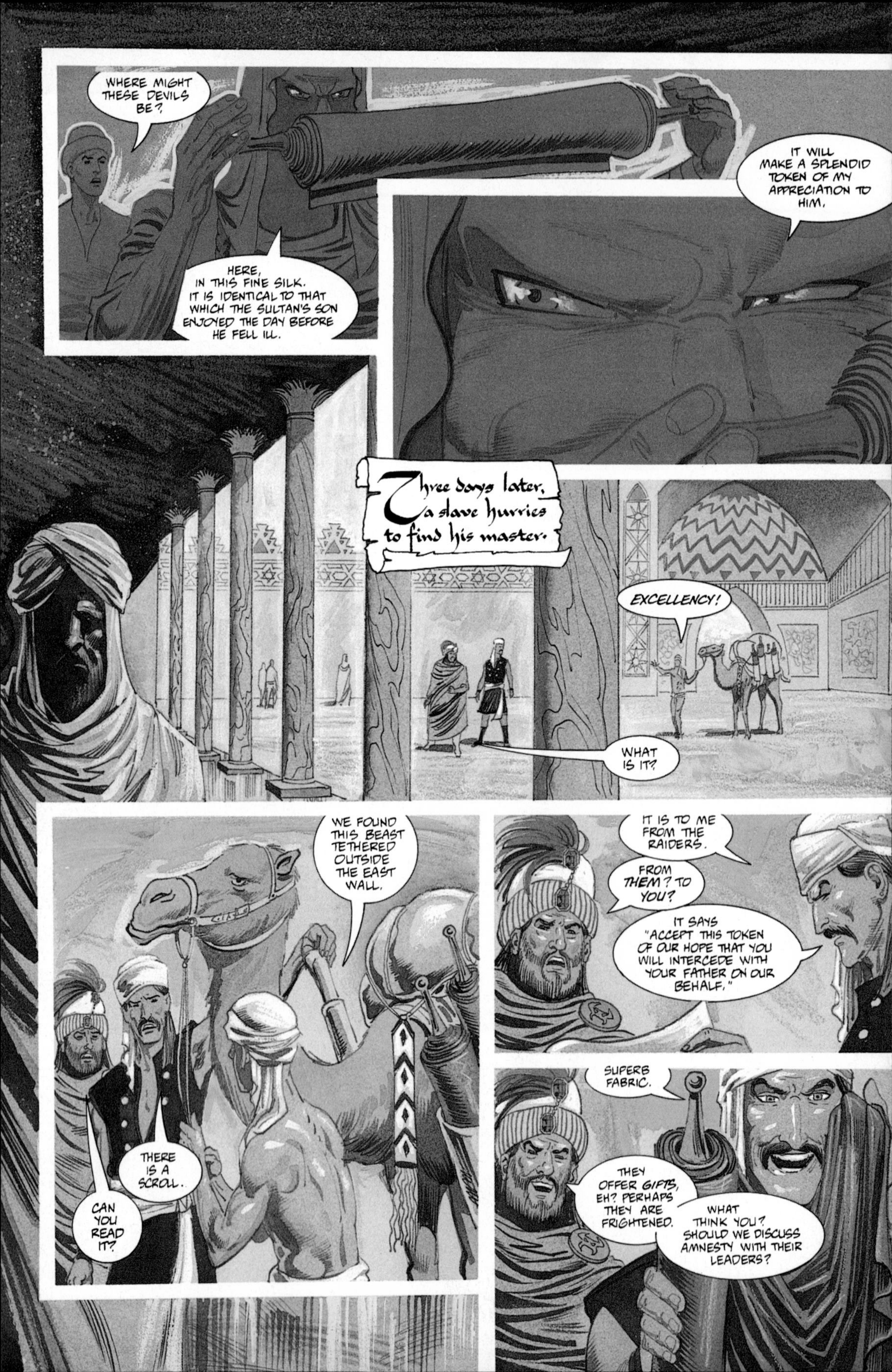

WHERE MIGHT THESE DEVILS BE?
HERE, IN THIS FINE SILK. IT IS IDENTICAL TO THAT WHICH THE SULTAN'S SON ENJOYED THE DAY BEFORE HE FELL ILL.
IT WILL MAKE A SPLENDID TOKEN OF MY APPRECIATION TO HIM.
Three days later, a slave hurries to find his master.
EXCELLENCY!
WHAT IS IT?
WE FOUND THIS BEAST TETHERED OUTSIDE THE EAST WALL.
THERE IS A SCROLL.
CAN YOU READ IT?
IT IS TO ME FROM THE RAIDERS.
FROM THEM? TO YOU?
IT SAYS "ACCEPT THIS TOKEN OF OUR HOPE THAT YOU WILL INTERCEDE WITH YOUR FATHER ON OUR BEHALF."
SUPERB FABRIC.
THEY OFFER GIFTS, EH? PERHAPS THEY ARE FRIGHTENED.
WHAT THINK YOU? SHOULD WE DISCUSS AMNESTY WITH THEIR LEADERS?

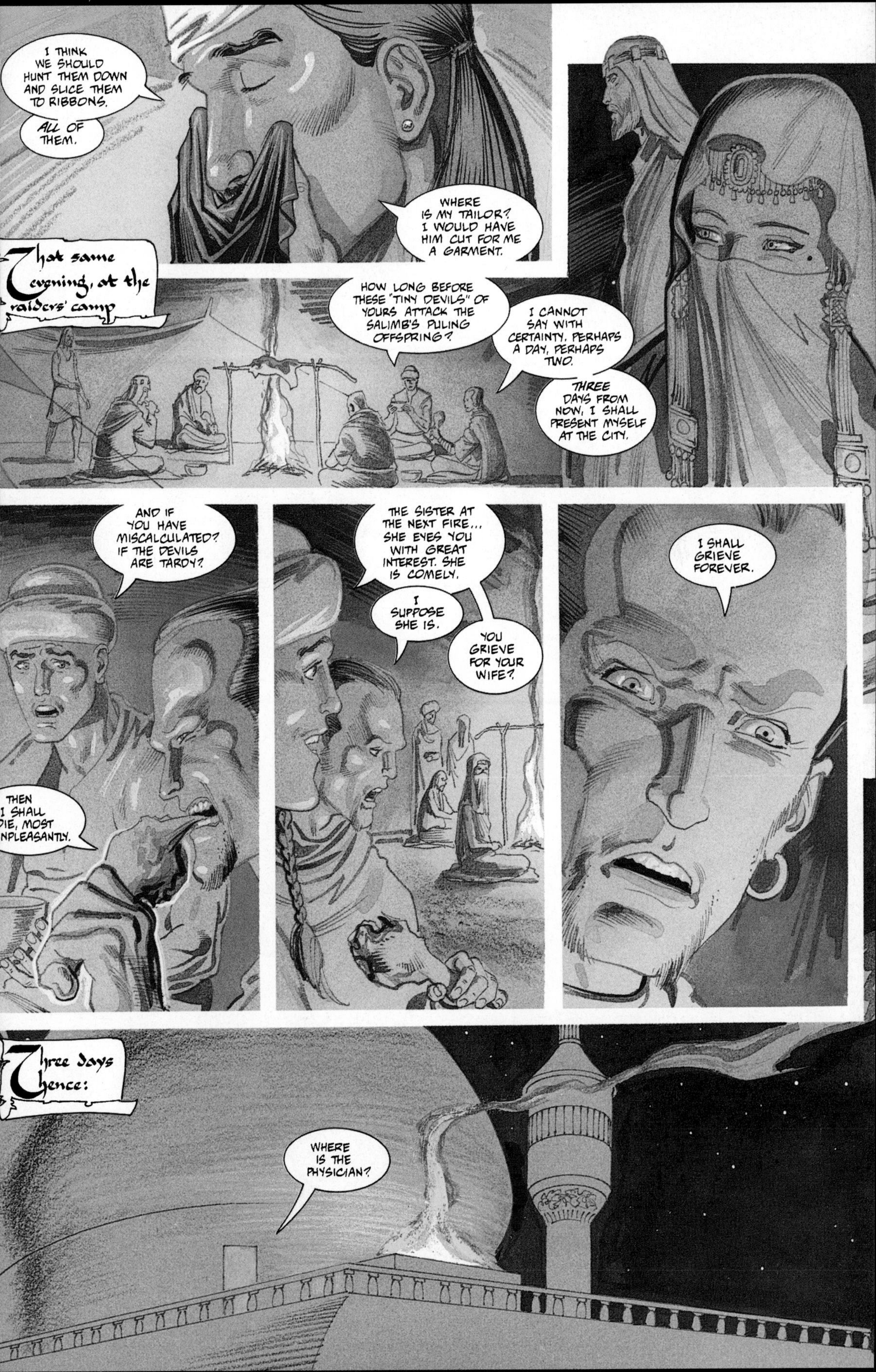
I THINK WE SHOULD HUNT THEM DOWN AND SLICE THEM TO RIBBONS.
ALL OF THEM.
WHERE IS MY TAILOR? I WOULD HAVE HIM CUT FOR ME A GARMENT.
That same evening, at the raiders' camp
HOW LONG BEFORE THESE "TINY DEVILS" OF YOURS ATTACK THE SALIMB'S PULING OFFSPRING?
I CANNOT SAY WITH CERTAINTY. PERHAPS A DAY, PERHAPS TWO.
THREE DAYS FROM NOW, I SHALL PRESENT MYSELF AT THE CITY.
AND IF YOU HAVE MISCALCULATED? IF THE DEVILS ARE TARDY?
THEN I SHALL DIE, MOST UNPLEASANTLY.
THE SISTER AT THE NEXT FIRE... SHE EYES YOU WITH GREAT INTEREST. SHE IS COMELY.
I SUPPOSE SHE IS.
YOU GRIEVE FOR YOUR WIFE?
I SHALL GRIEVE FOREVER.
Three days thence:
WHERE IS THE PHYSICIAN?

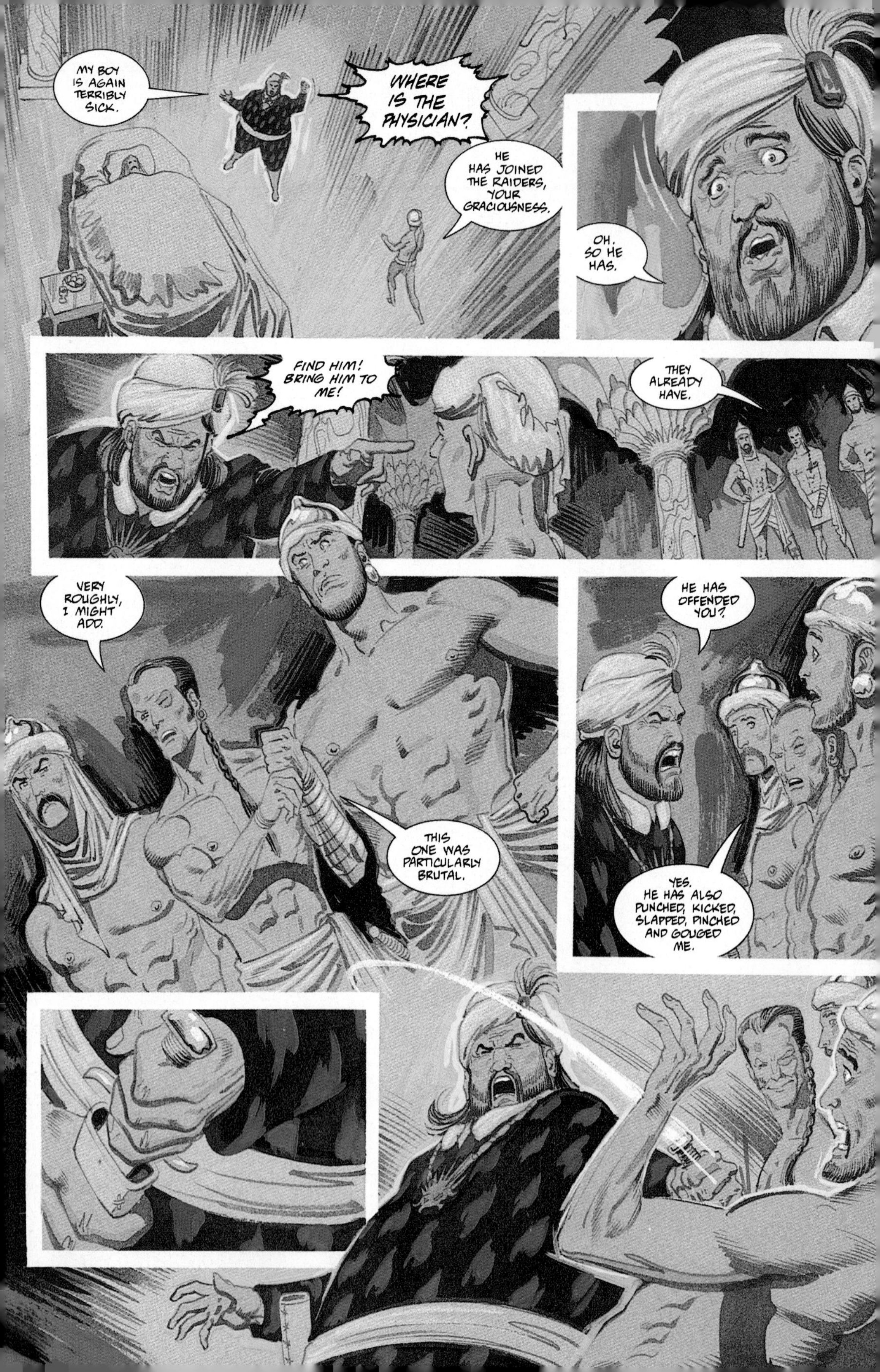
MY BOY IS AGAIN TERRIBLY SICK.
WHERE IS THE PHYSICIAN?
HE HAS JOINED THE RAIDERS, YOUR GRACIOUSNESS.
OH. SO HE HAS.
FIND HIM! BRING HIM TO ME!
THEY ALREADY HAVE.
VERY ROUGHLY, I MIGHT ADD.
THIS ONE WAS PARTICULARLY BRUTAL.
HE HAS OFFENDED YOU?
YES. HE HAS ALSO PUNCHED, KICKED, SLAPPED, PINCHED AND GOUGED ME.

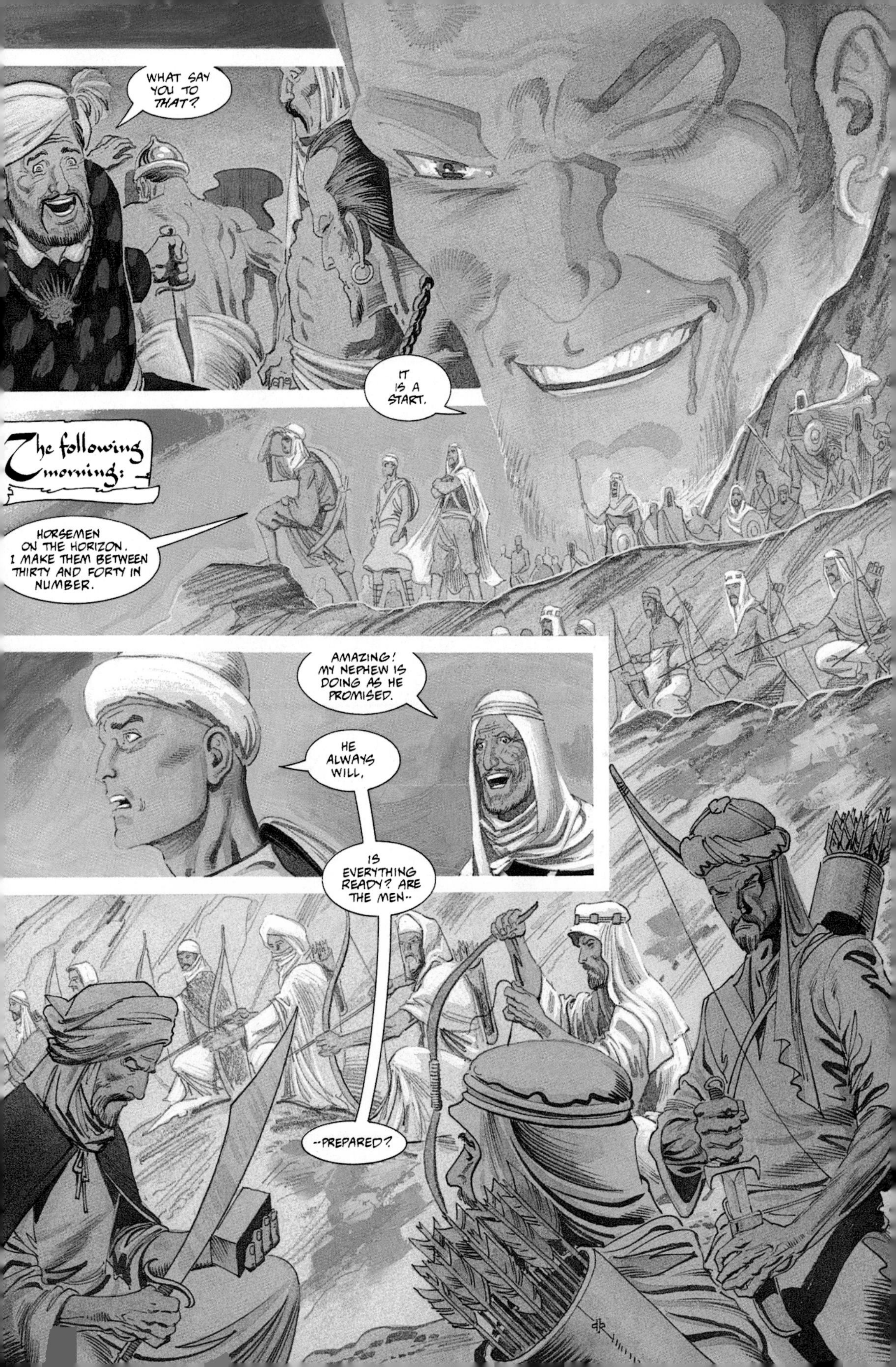
WHAT SAY YOU TO *THAT*?
IT IS A START.
The following morning:
HORSEMEN ON THE HORIZON. I MAKE THEM BETWEEN THIRTY AND FORTY IN NUMBER.
AMAZING! MY NEPHEW IS DOING AS HE PROMISED.
HE ALWAYS WILL.
IS EVERYTHING READY? ARE THE MEN--
--PREPARED?

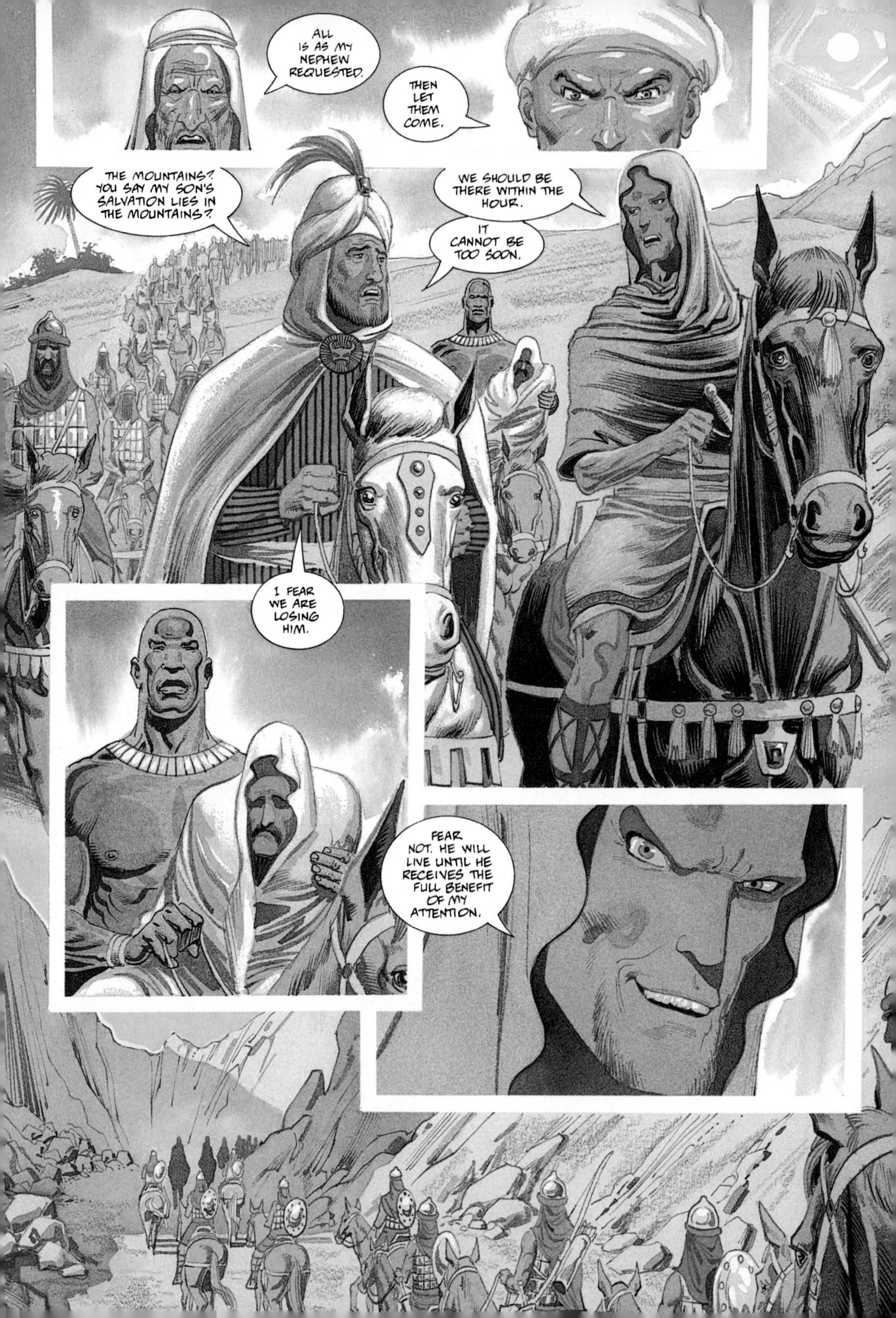
ALL IS AS MY NEPHEW REQUESTED.
THEN LET THEM COME.
THE MOUNTAINS? YOU SAY MY SON'S SALVATION LIES IN THE MOUNTAINS?
WE SHOULD BE THERE WITHIN THE HOUR.
IT CANNOT BE TOO SOON.
I FEAR WE ARE LOSING HIM.
FEAR NOT. HE WILL LIVE UNTIL HE RECEIVES THE FULL BENEFIT OF MY ATTENTION.

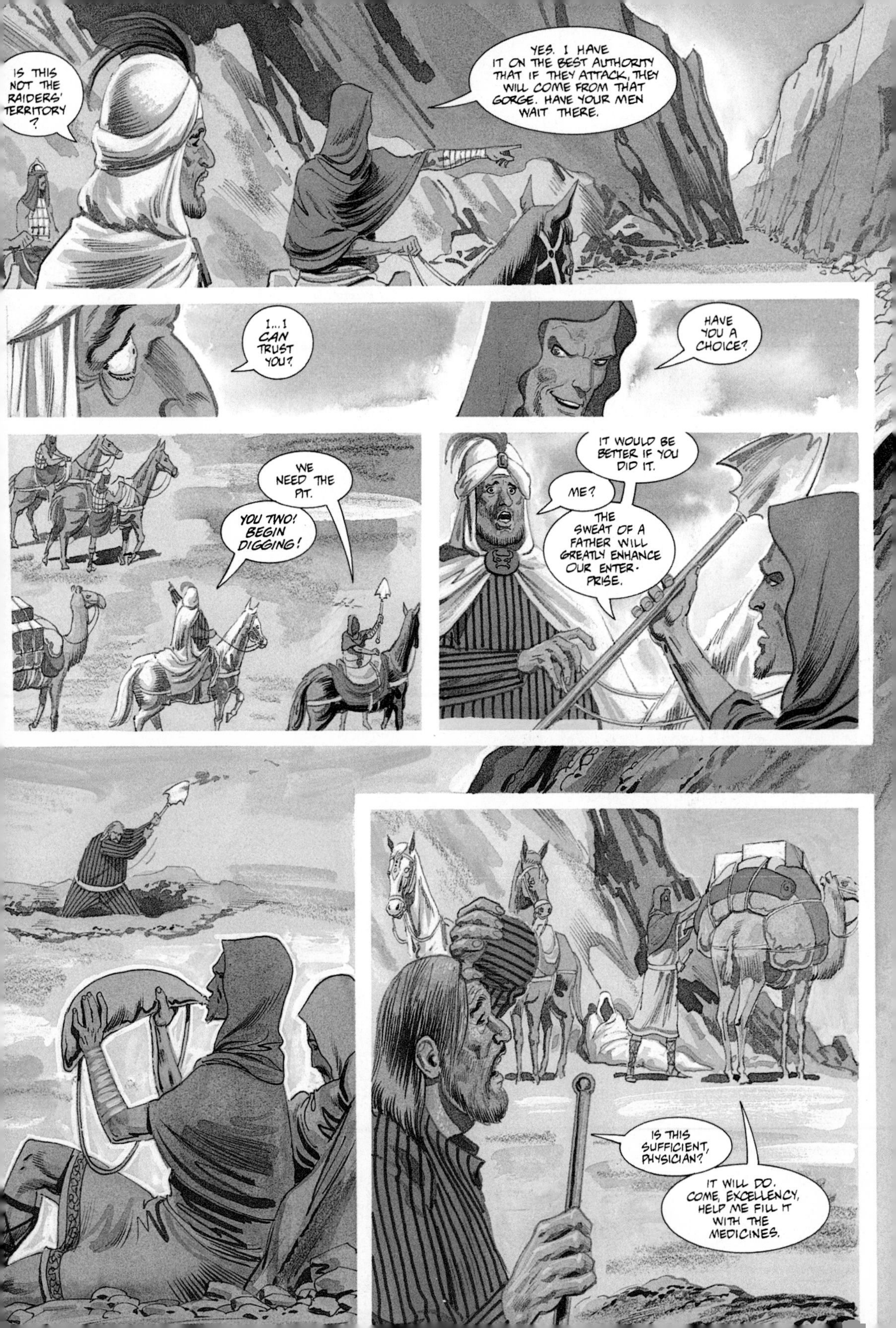
IS THIS NOT THE RAIDERS' TERRITORY?
YES. I HAVE IT ON THE BEST AUTHORITY THAT IF THEY ATTACK, THEY WILL COME FROM THAT GORGE. HAVE YOUR MEN WAIT THERE.
I...I CAN TRUST YOU?
HAVE YOU A CHOICE?
WE NEED THE PIT.
YOU TWO! BEGIN DIGGING!
IT WOULD BE BETTER IF YOU DID IT.
ME?
THE SWEAT OF A FATHER WILL GREATLY ENHANCE OUR ENTER-PRISE.
IS THIS SUFFICIENT, PHYSICIAN?
IT WILL DO. COME, EXCELLENCY, HELP ME FILL IT WITH THE MEDICINES.

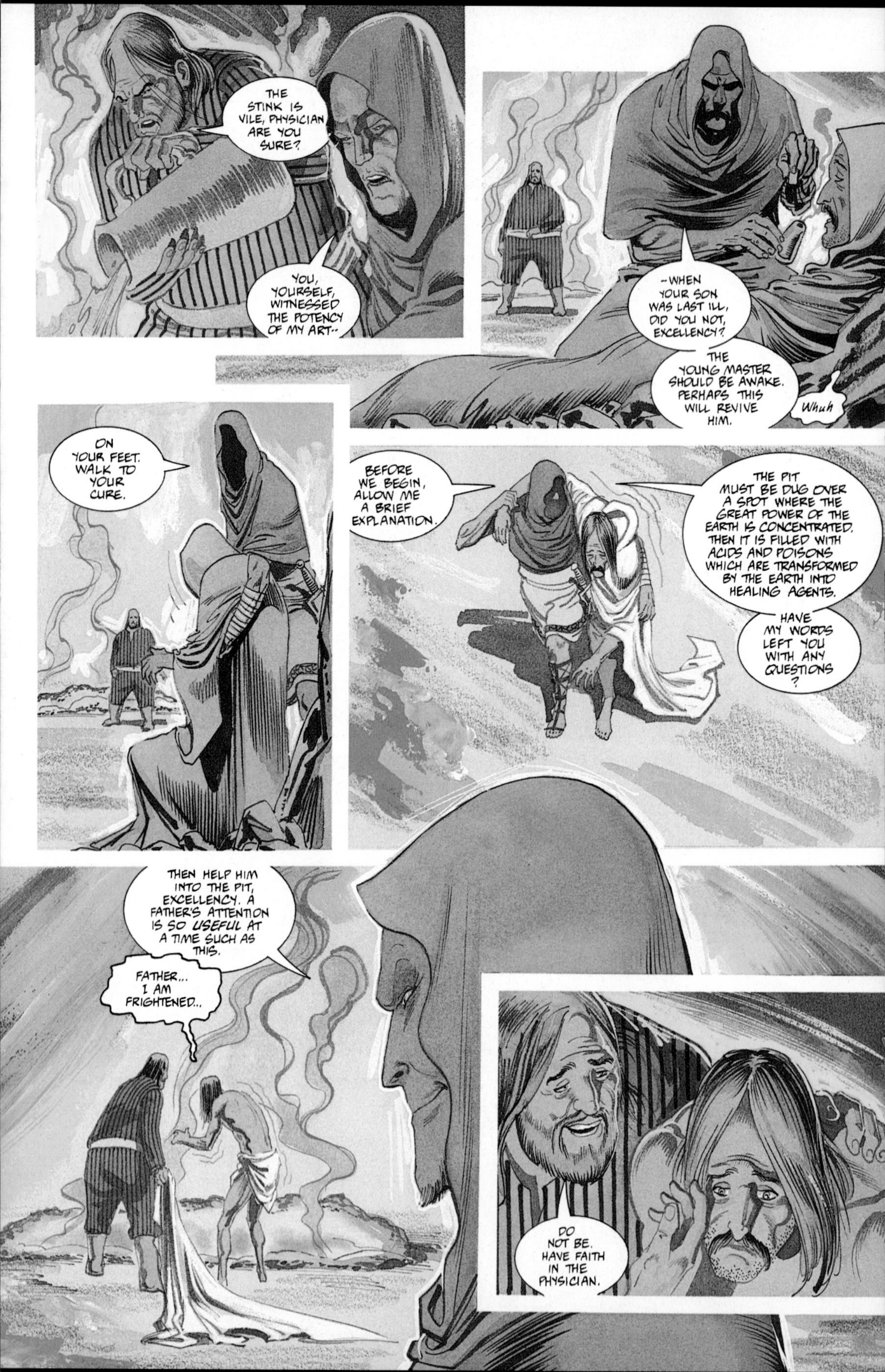
THE STINK IS VILE, PHYSICIAN ARE YOU SURE?
YOU, YOURSELF, WITNESSED THE POTENCY OF MY ART--
-WHEN YOUR SON WAS LAST ILL, DID YOU NOT, EXCELLENCY?
THE YOUNG MASTER SHOULD BE AWAKE. PERHAPS THIS WILL REVIVE HIM.
Whuh
ON YOUR FEET. WALK TO YOUR CURE.
BEFORE WE BEGIN, ALLOW ME A BRIEF EXPLANATION.
THE PIT MUST BE DUG OVER A SPOT WHERE THE GREAT POWER OF THE EARTH IS CONCENTRATED, THEN IT IS FILLED WITH ACIDS AND POISONS WHICH ARE TRANSFORMED BY THE EARTH INTO HEALING AGENTS.
HAVE MY WORDS LEFT YOU WITH ANY QUESTIONS?
THEN HELP HIM INTO THE PIT, EXCELLENCY. A FATHER'S ATTENTION IS SO *USEFUL* AT A TIME SUCH AS THIS.
FATHER... I AM FRIGHTENED...
DO NOT BE. HAVE FAITH IN THE PHYSICIAN.

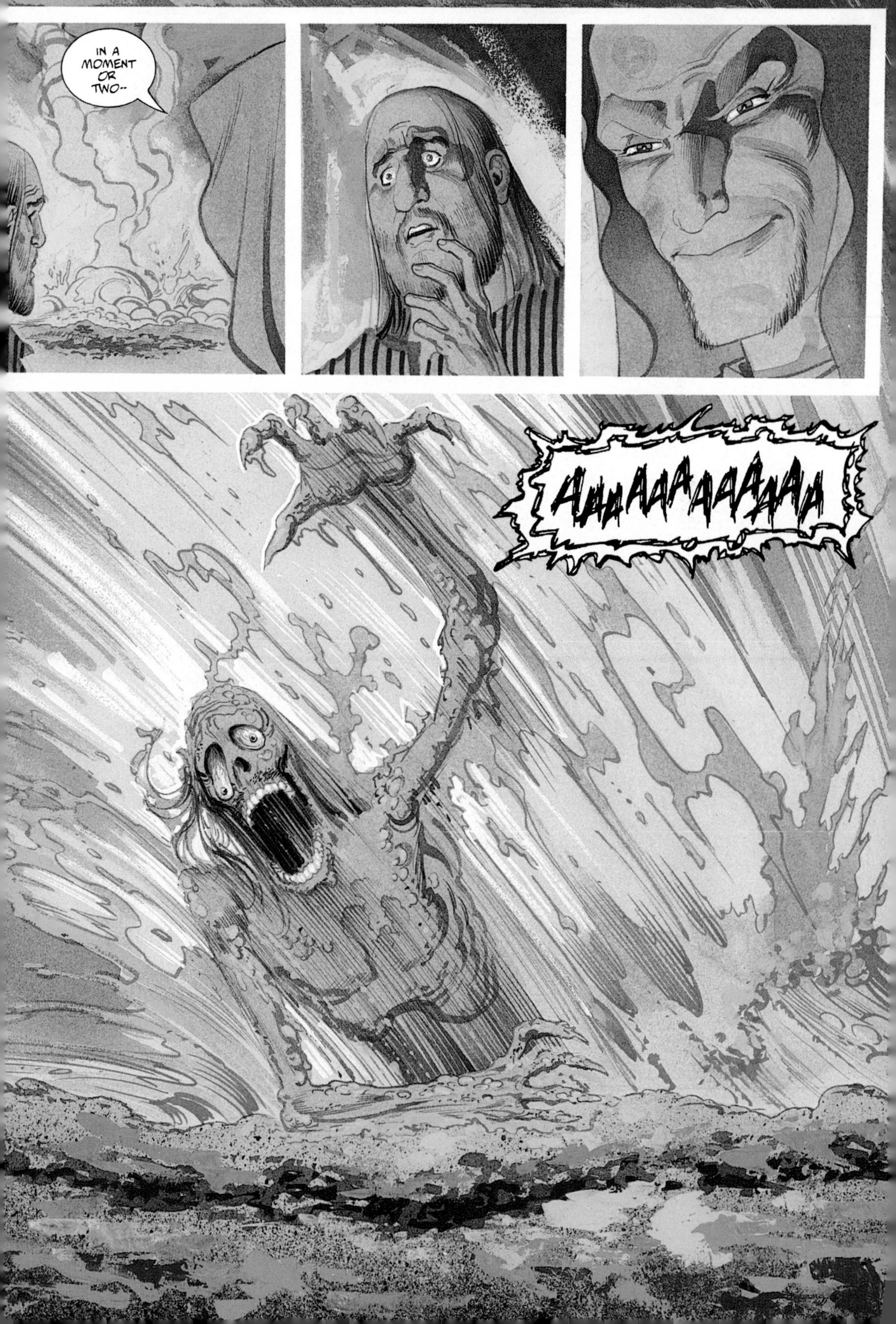
IN A MOMENT OR TWO--
AAAAAAAAAAAA

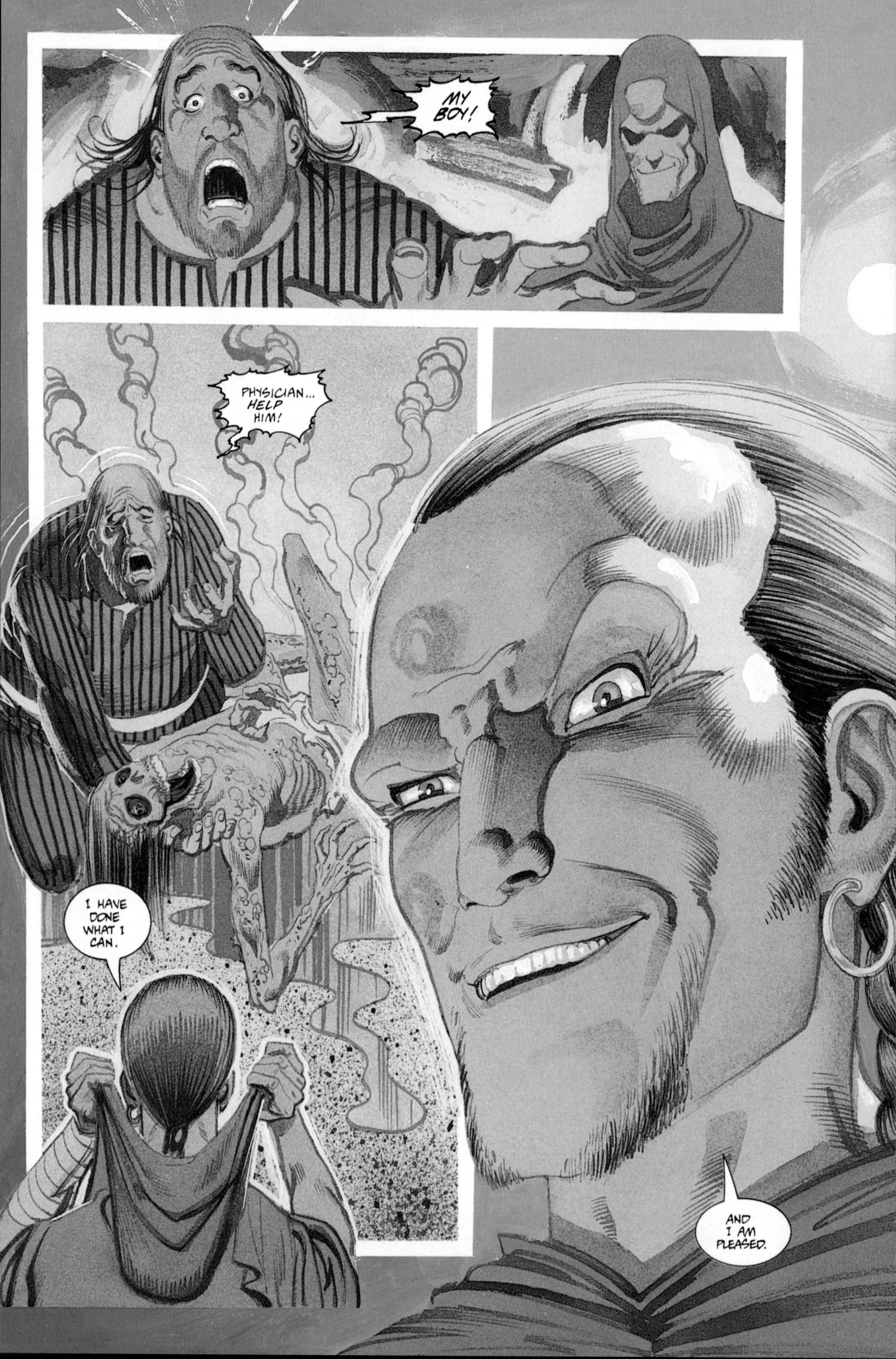
MY BOY!
PHYSICIAN... HELP HIM!
I HAVE DONE WHAT I CAN.
AND I AM PLEASED.

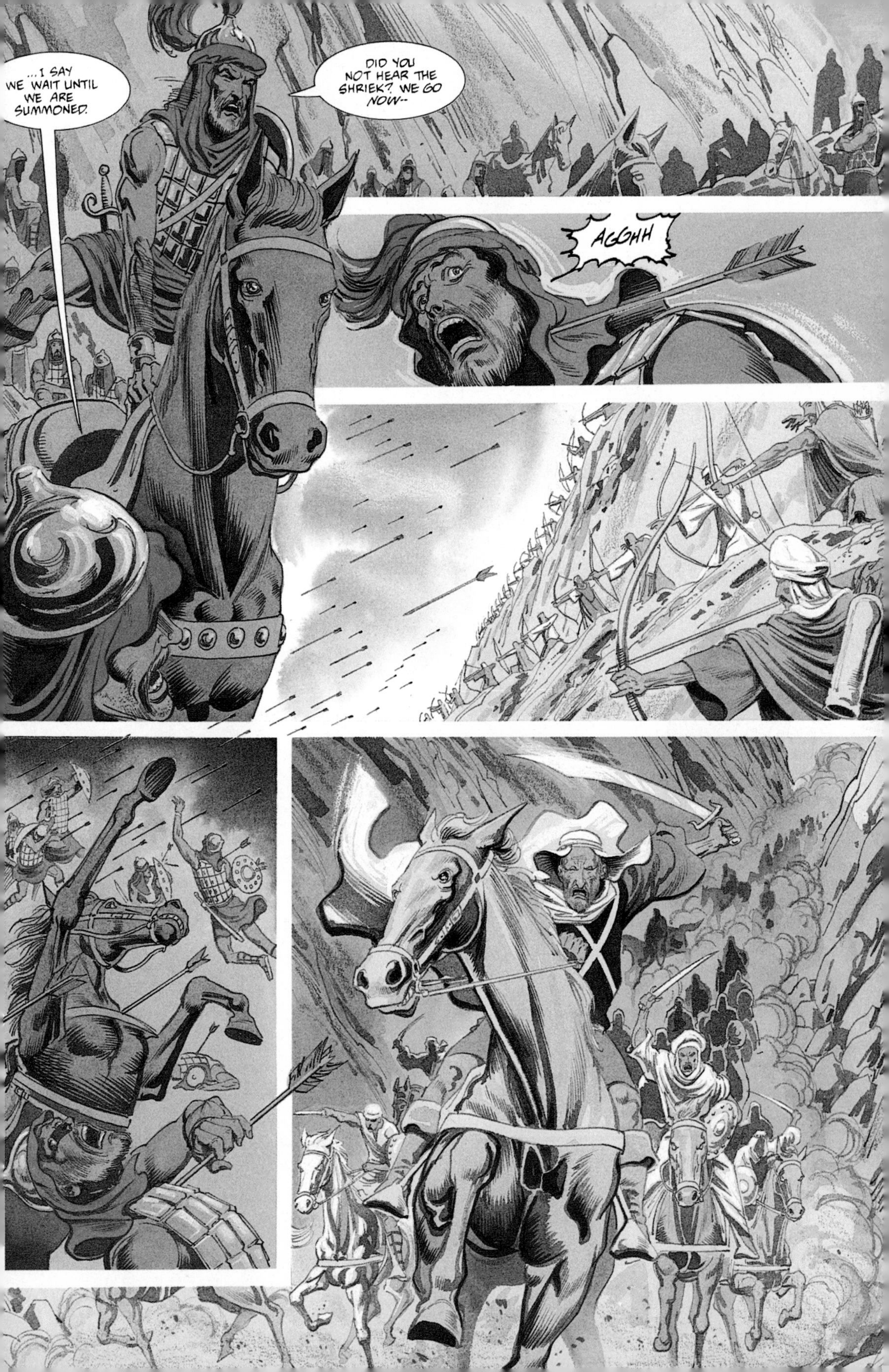
...I SAY WE WAIT UNTIL WE ARE SUMMONED.
DID YOU NOT HEAR THE SHRIEK? WE GO NOW--
AGGHH

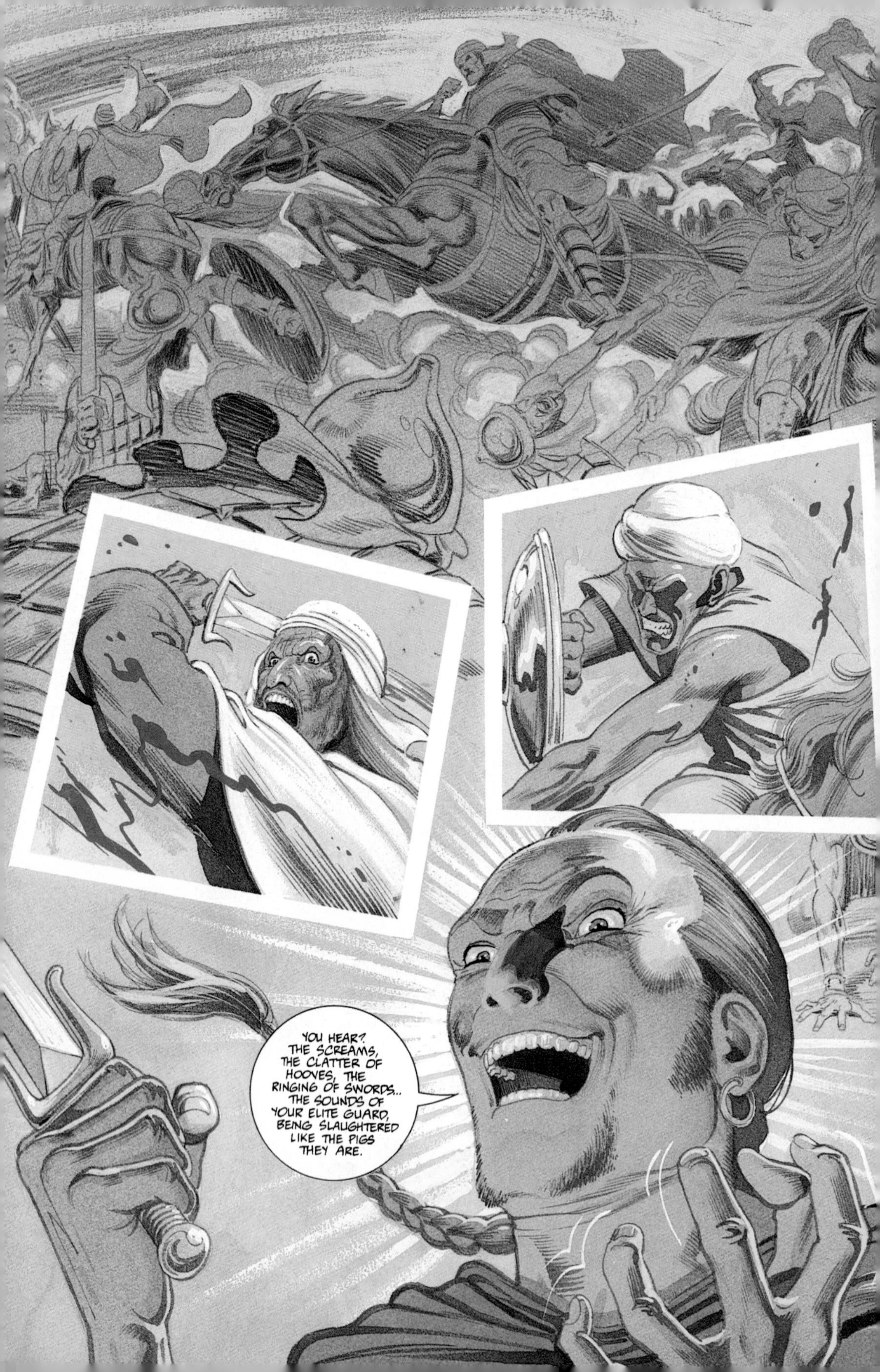
YOU HEAR? THE SCREAMS, THE CLATTER OF HOOVES, THE RINGING OF SWORDS.. THE SOUNDS OF YOUR ELITE GUARD, BEING SLAUGHTERED LIKE THE PIGS THEY ARE.

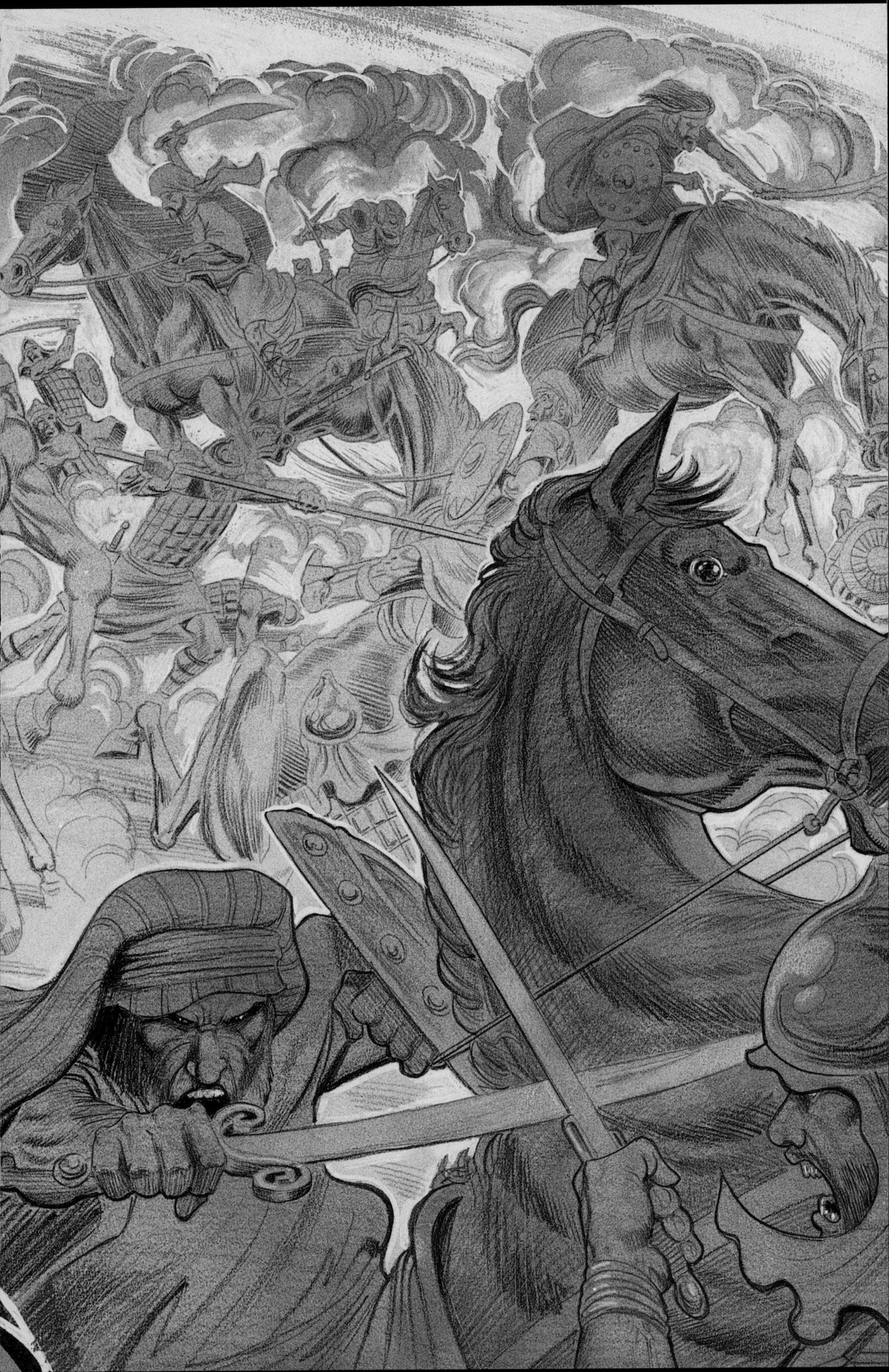

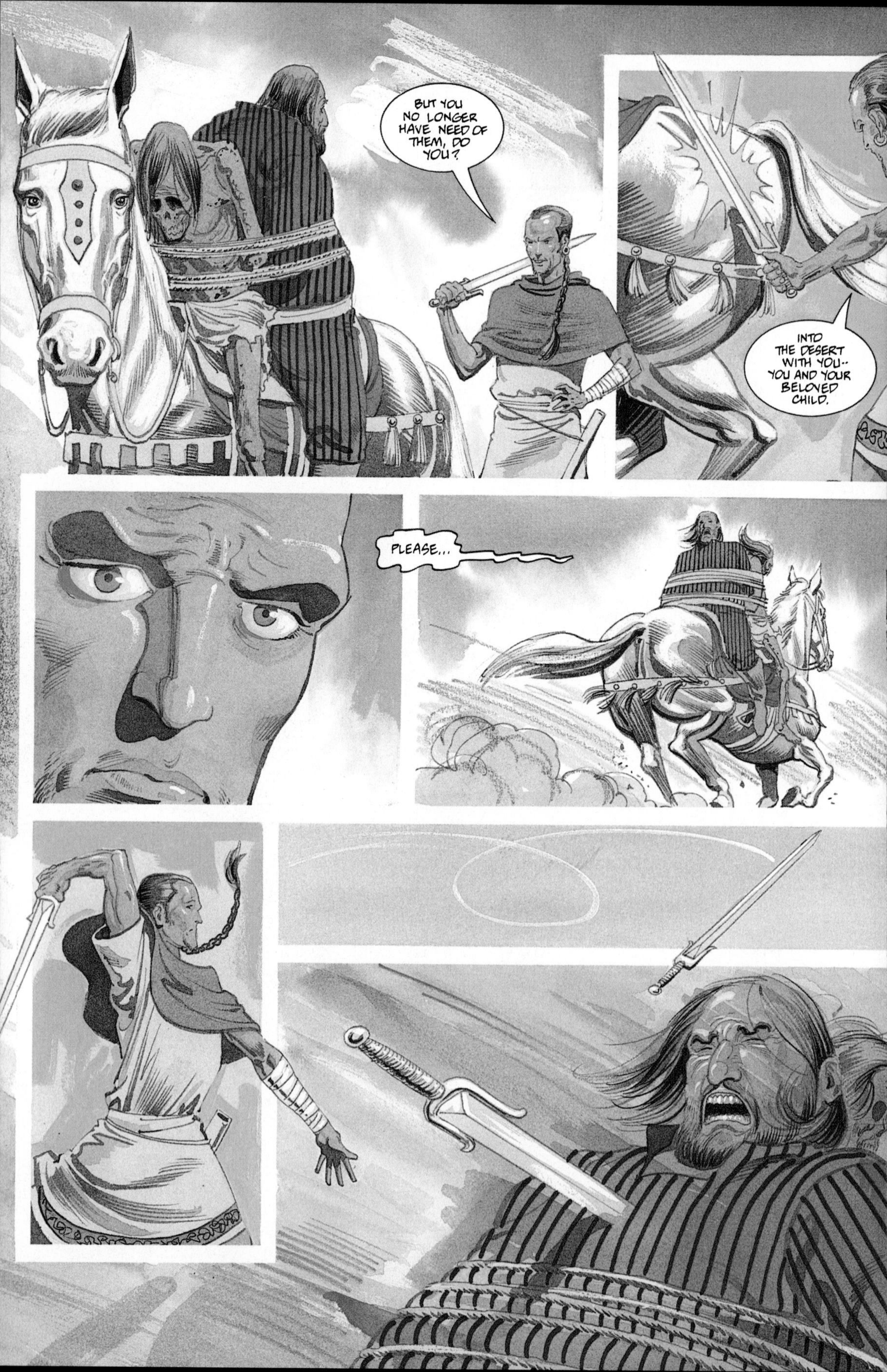
BUT YOU NO LONGER HAVE NEED OF THEM, DO YOU?
INTO THE DESERT WITH YOU.. YOU AND YOUR BELOVED CHILD.
PLEASE...

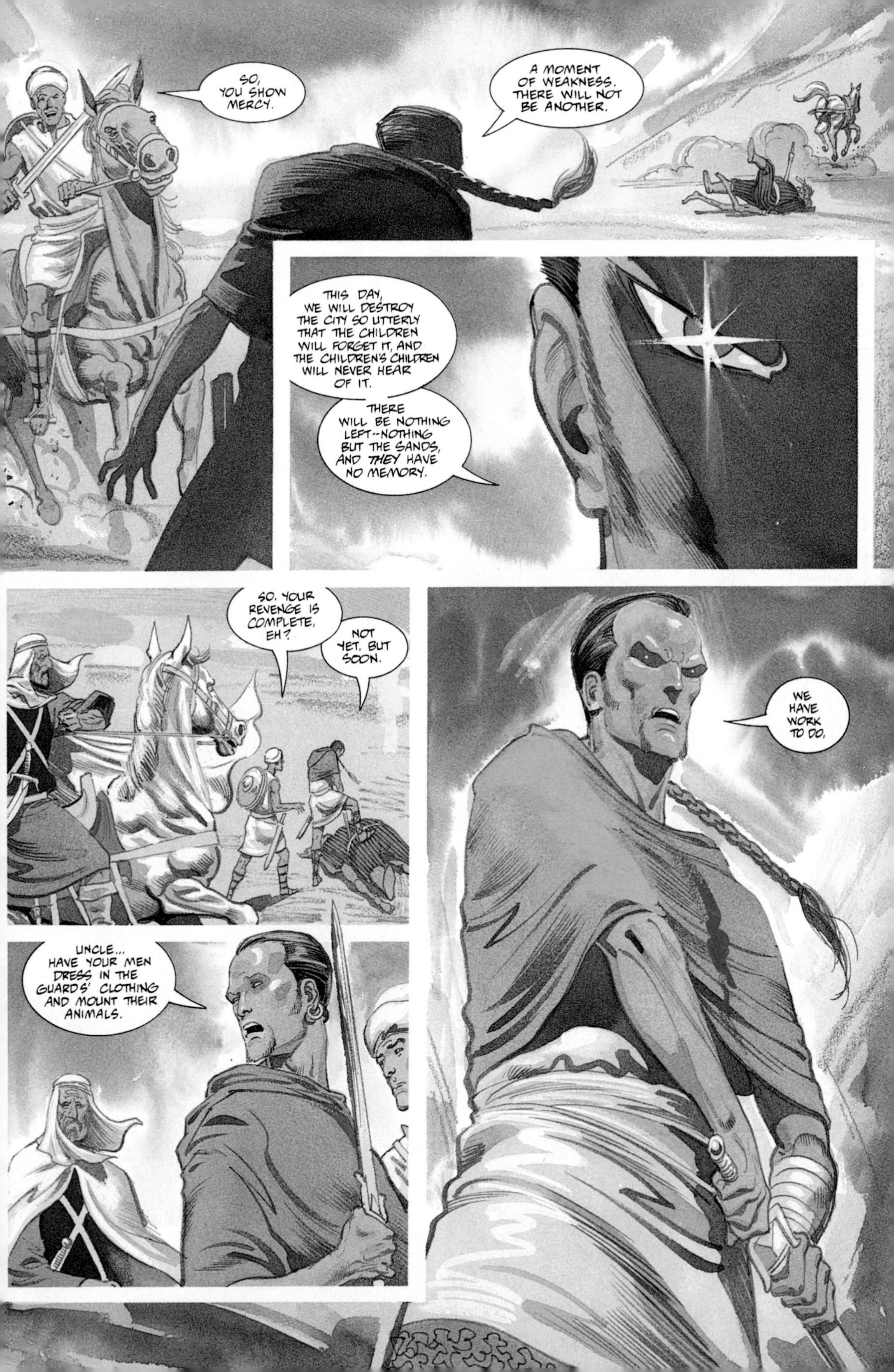
SO, YOU SHOW MERCY.
A MOMENT OF WEAKNESS. THERE WILL NOT BE ANOTHER.
THIS DAY, WE WILL DESTROY THE CITY SO UTTERLY THAT THE CHILDREN WILL FORGET IT, AND THE CHILDREN'S CHILDREN WILL NEVER HEAR OF IT.
THERE WILL BE NOTHING LEFT--NOTHING BUT THE SANDS, AND THEY HAVE NO MEMORY.
SO. YOUR REVENGE IS COMPLETE, EH?
NOT YET. BUT SOON.
UNCLE... HAVE YOUR MEN DRESS IN THE GUARDS' CLOTHING AND MOUNT THEIR ANIMALS.
WE HAVE WORK TO DO.

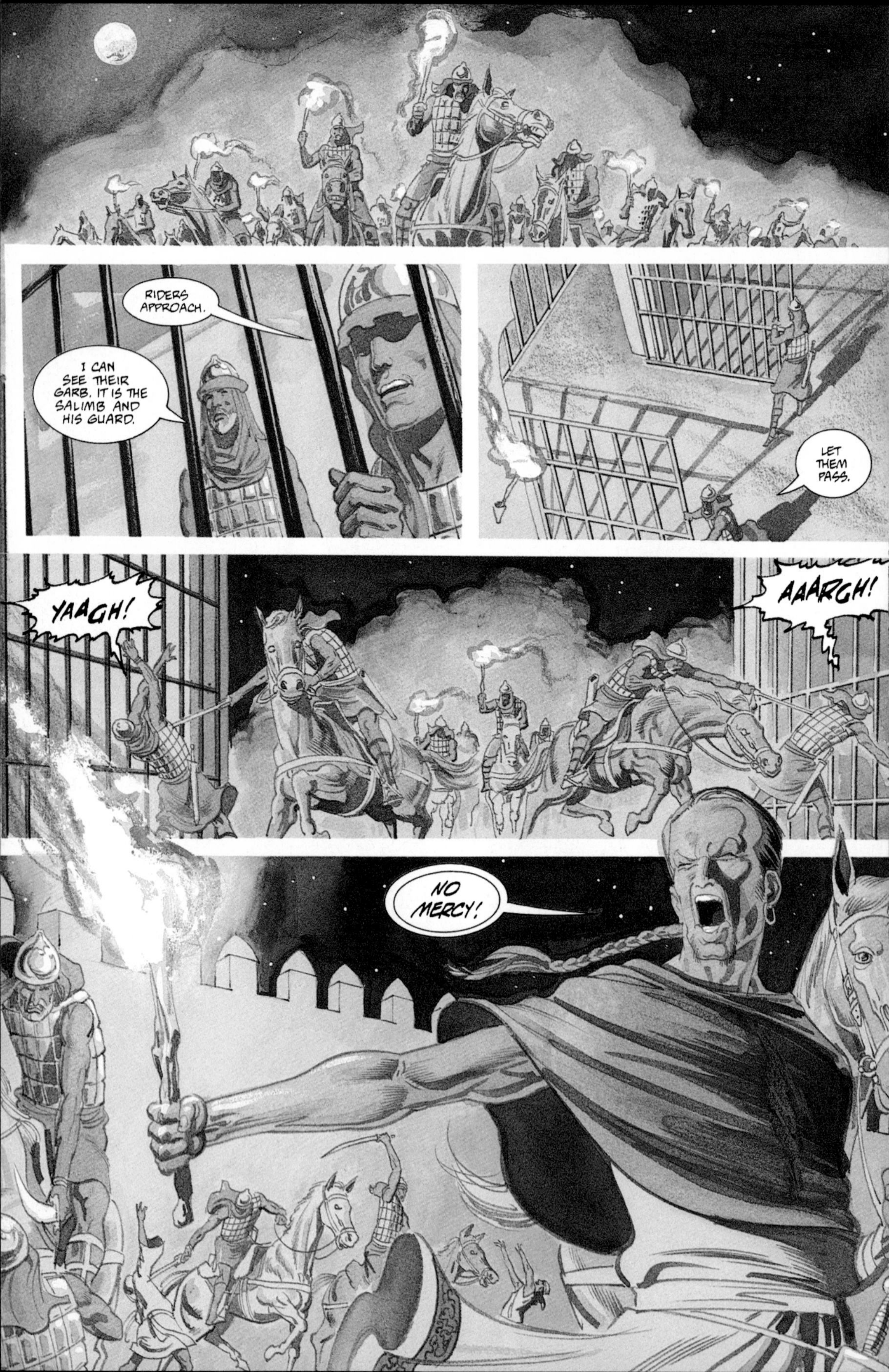
RIDERS APPROACH.
I CAN SEE THEIR GARB. IT IS THE SALIMB AND HIS GUARD.
LET THEM PASS.
YAAGH!
AAARGH!
NO MERCY!

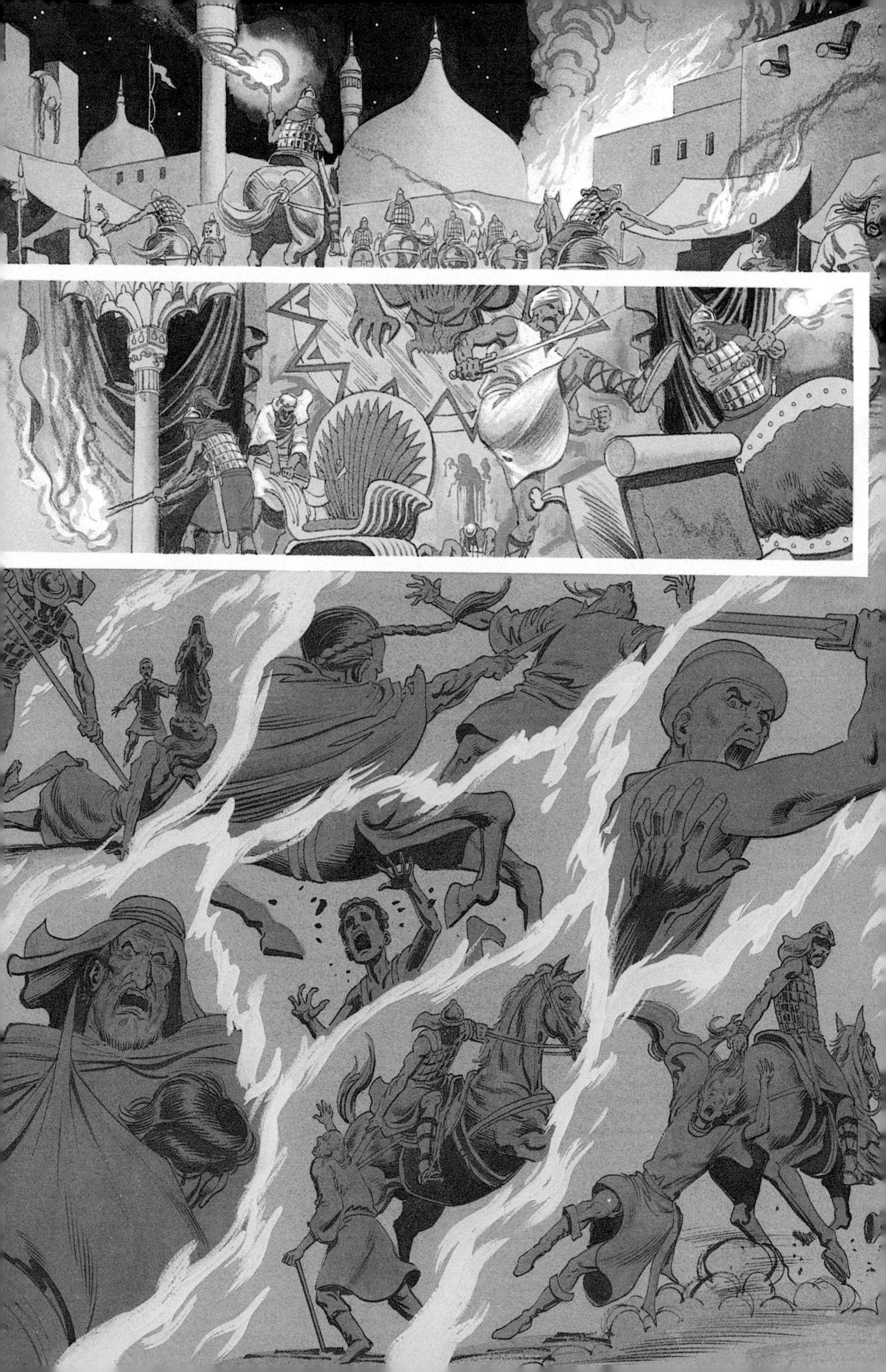

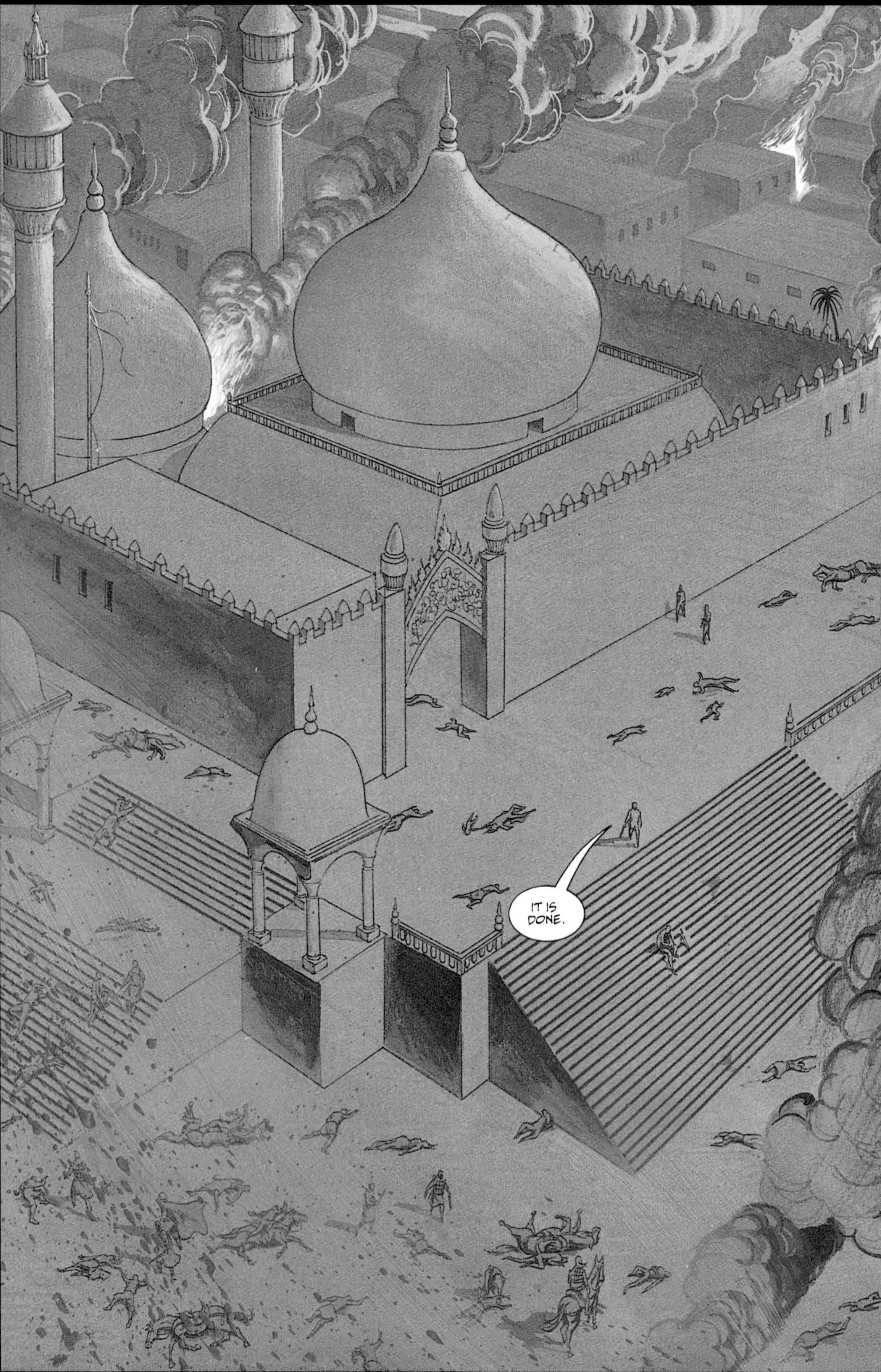
IT IS DONE.

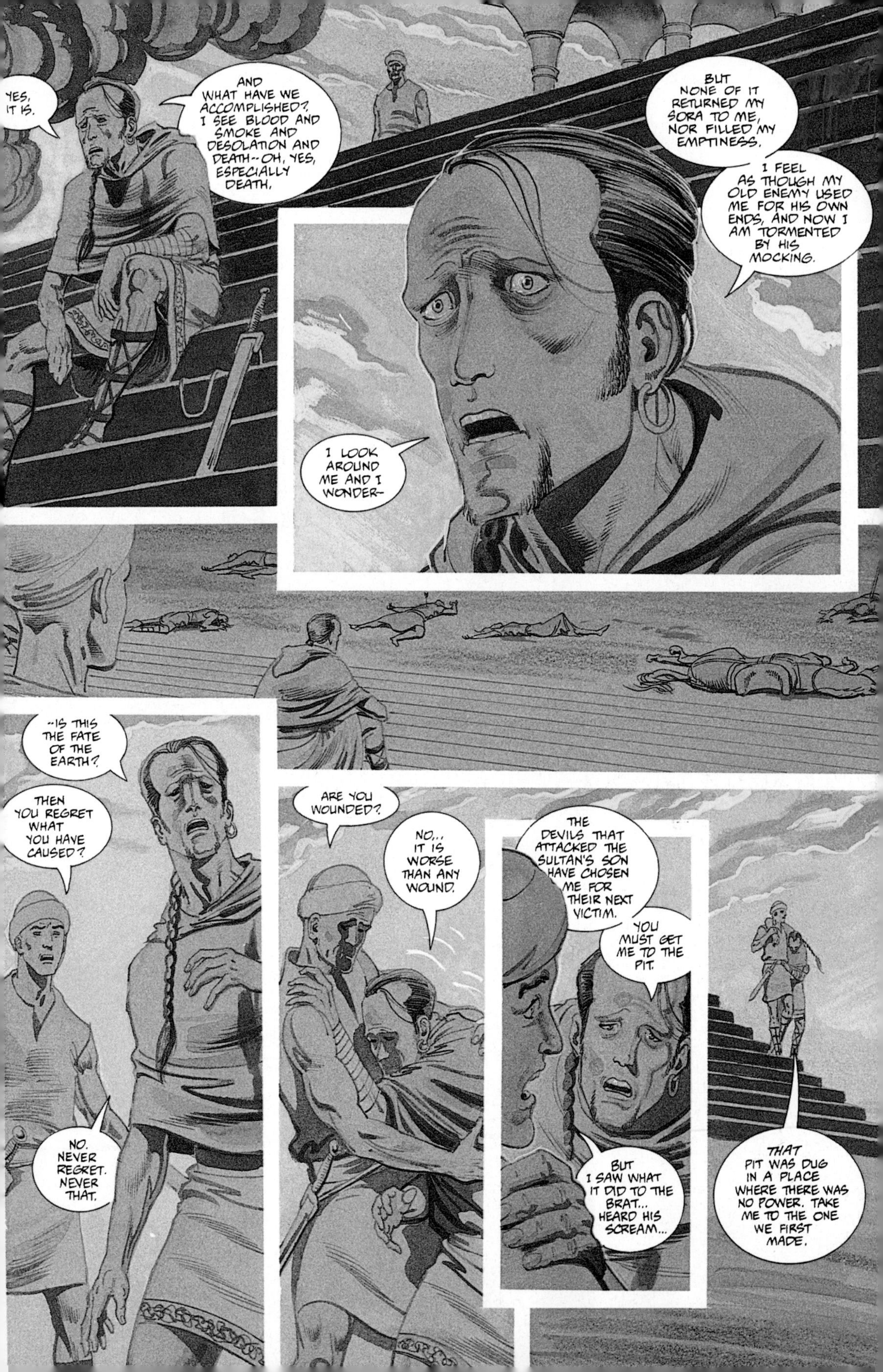
YES, IT IS.
AND WHAT HAVE WE ACCOMPLISHED? I SEE BLOOD AND SMOKE AND DESOLATION AND DEATH--OH, YES, ESPECIALLY DEATH.
BUT NONE OF IT RETURNED MY SORA TO ME, NOR FILLED MY EMPTINESS.
I FEEL AS THOUGH MY OLD ENEMY USED ME FOR HIS OWN ENDS, AND NOW I AM TORMENTED BY HIS MOCKING.
I LOOK AROUND ME AND I WONDER-
--IS THIS THE FATE OF THE EARTH?
THEN YOU REGRET WHAT YOU HAVE CAUSED?
NO. NEVER REGRET. NEVER THAT.
ARE YOU WOUNDED?
NO... IT IS WORSE THAN ANY WOUND.
THE DEVILS THAT ATTACKED THE SULTAN'S SON HAVE CHOSEN ME FOR THEIR NEXT VICTIM.
YOU MUST GET ME TO THE PIT.
BUT I SAW WHAT IT DID TO THE BRAT... HEARD HIS SCREAM...
THAT PIT WAS DUG IN A PLACE WHERE THERE WAS NO POWER. TAKE ME TO THE ONE WE FIRST MADE.

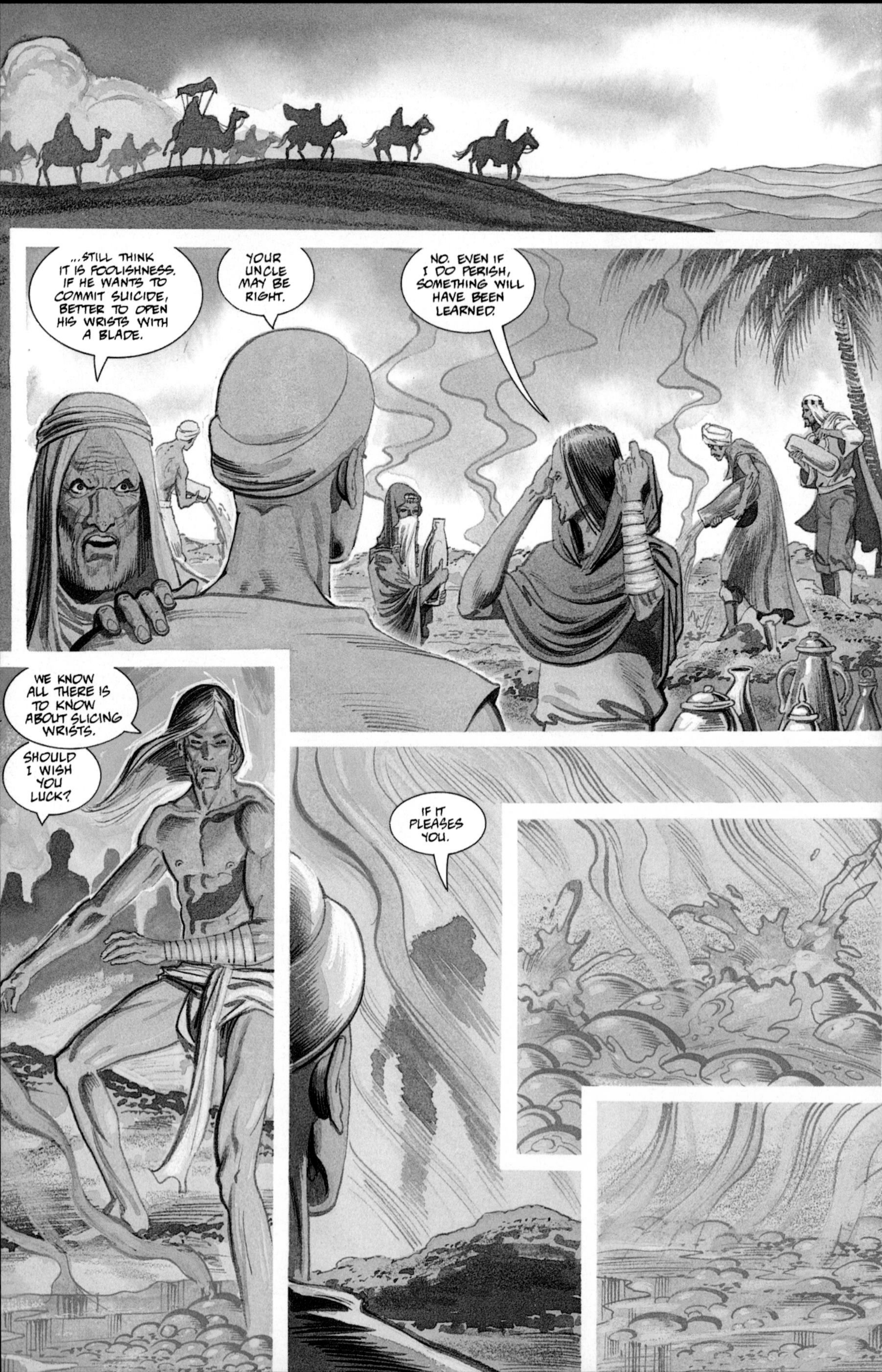
...STILL THINK IT IS FOOLISHNESS. IF HE WANTS TO COMMIT SUICIDE, BETTER TO OPEN HIS WRISTS WITH A BLADE.
YOUR UNCLE MAY BE RIGHT.
NO. EVEN IF I DO PERISH, SOMETHING WILL HAVE BEEN LEARNED.
WE KNOW ALL THERE IS TO KNOW ABOUT SLICING WRISTS.
SHOULD I WISH YOU LUCK?
IF IT PLEASES YOU.

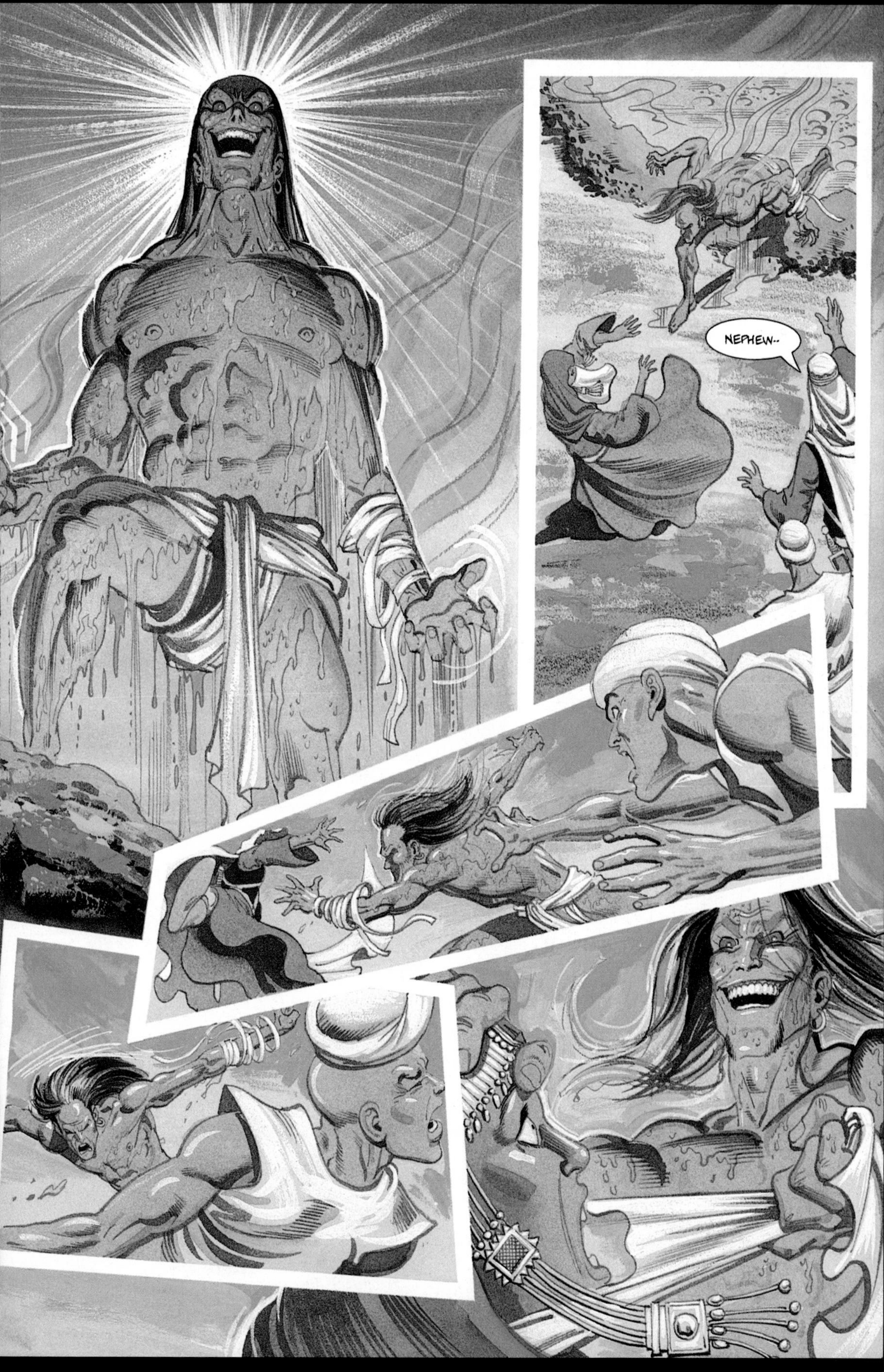
NEPHEW..

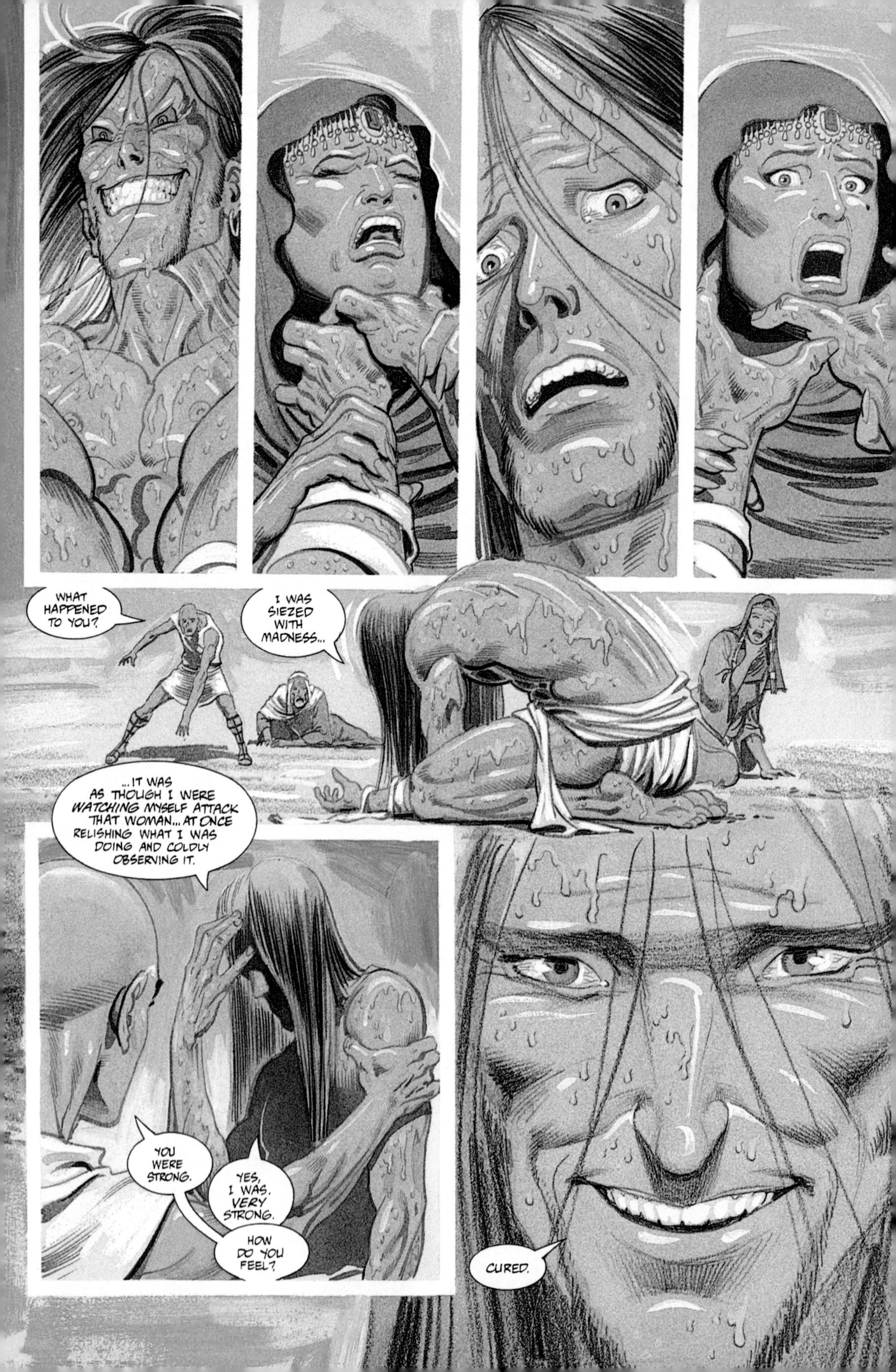
WHAT HAPPENED TO YOU?
I WAS SIEZED WITH MADNESS...
...IT WAS AS THOUGH I WERE *WATCHING* MYSELF ATTACK THAT WOMAN... AT ONCE RELISHING WHAT I WAS DOING AND COLDLY OBSERVING IT.
YOU WERE STRONG.
YES, I WAS, *VERY* STRONG.
HOW DO YOU FEEL?
CURED.

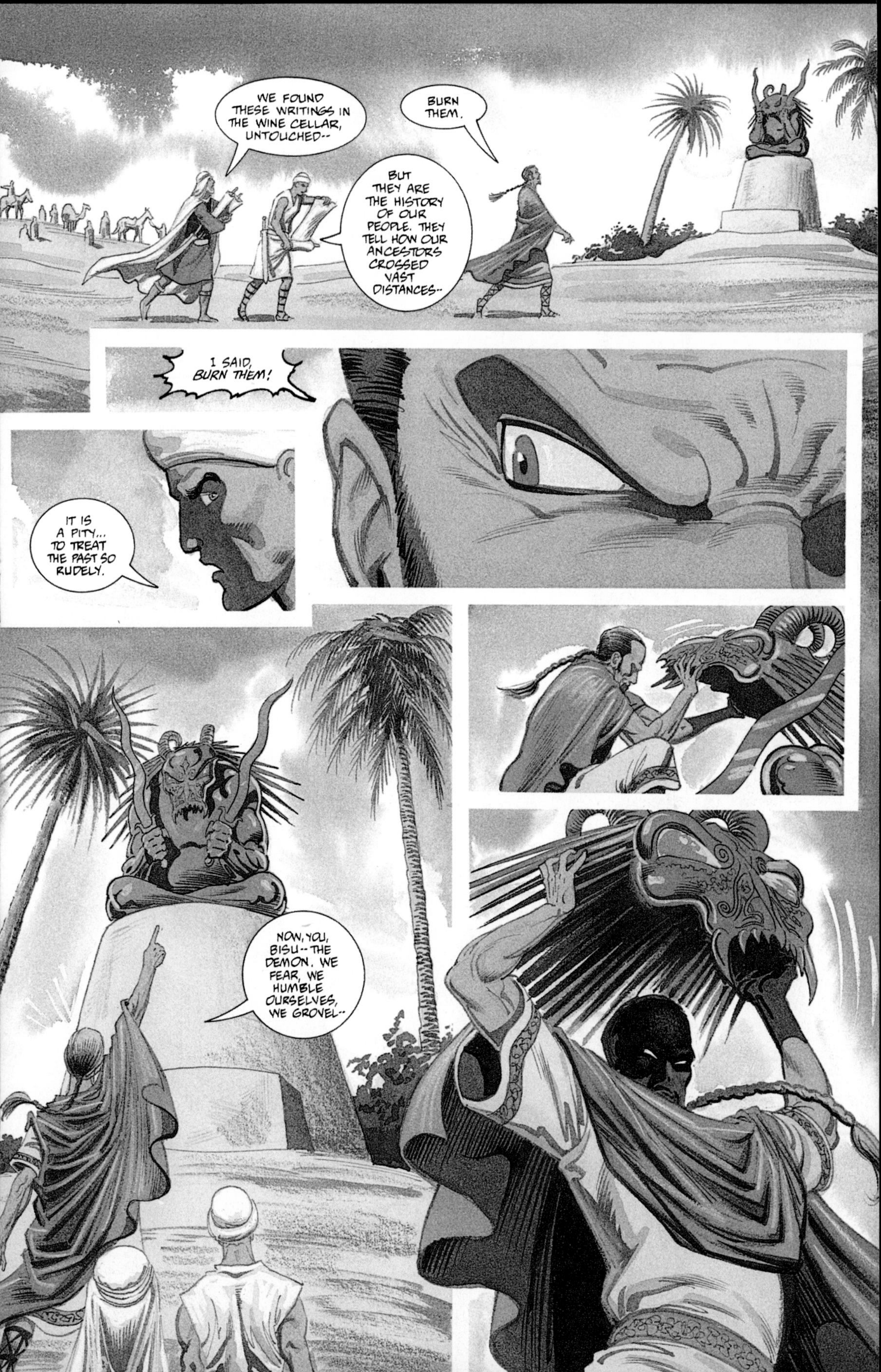

WE FOUND THESE WRITINGS IN THE WINE CELLAR, UNTOUCHED--
BURN THEM.
BUT THEY ARE THE HISTORY OF OUR PEOPLE. THEY TELL HOW OUR ANCESTORS CROSSED VAST DISTANCES--
I SAID, BURN THEM!
IT IS A PITY... TO TREAT THE PAST SO RUDELY.
NOW, YOU, BISU-- THE DEMON. WE FEAR, WE HUMBLE OURSELVES, WE GROVEL--

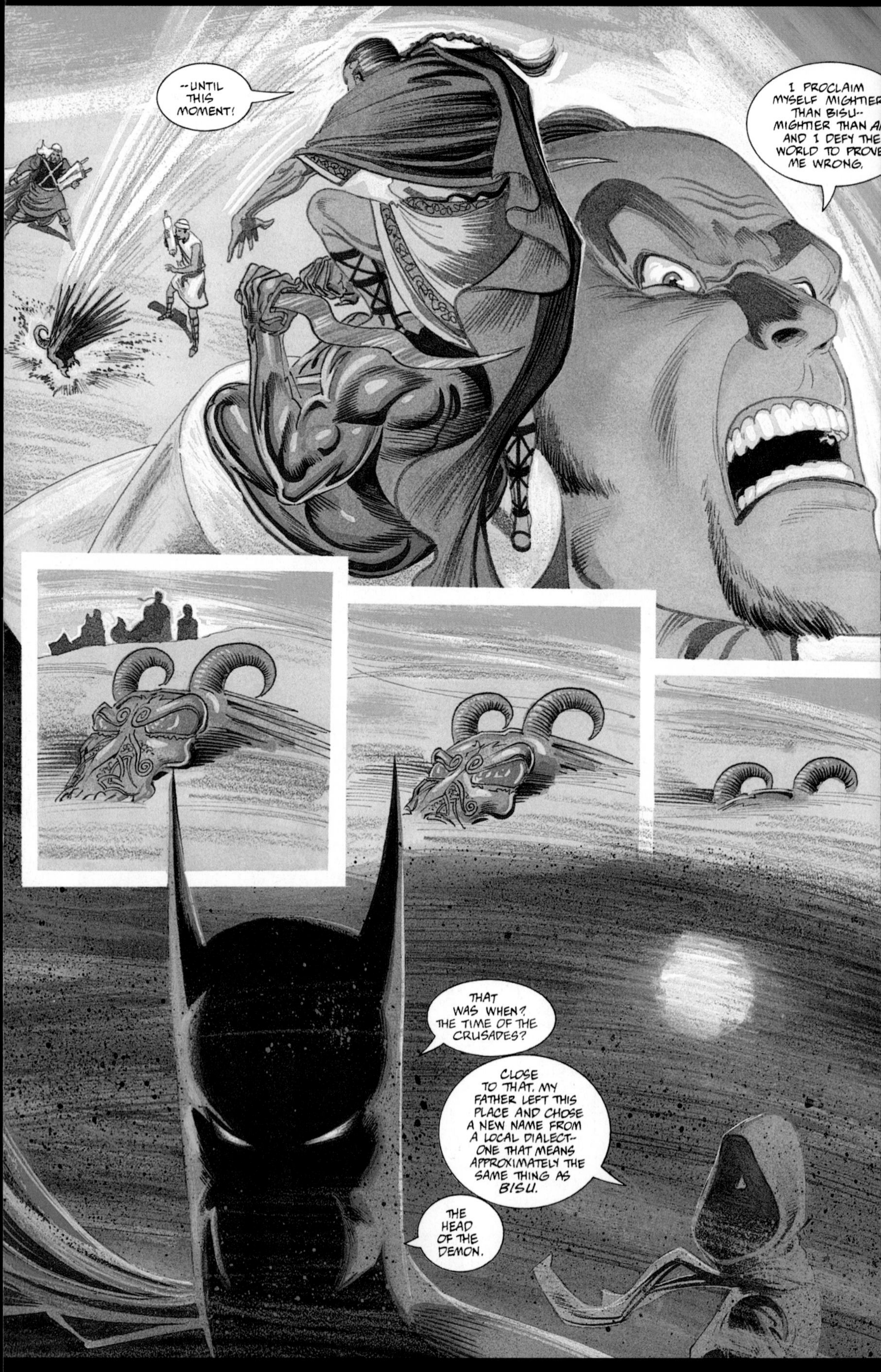

--UNTIL THIS MOMENT!
I PROCLAIM MYSELF MIGHTIER THAN BISU-- MIGHTIER THAN AL AND I DEFY THE WORLD TO PROVE ME WRONG.
THAT WAS WHEN? THE TIME OF THE CRUSADES?
CLOSE TO THAT. MY FATHER LEFT THIS PLACE AND CHOSE A NEW NAME FROM A LOCAL DIALECT-- ONE THAT MEANS APPROXIMATELY THE SAME THING AS BISU.
THE HEAD OF THE DEMON.

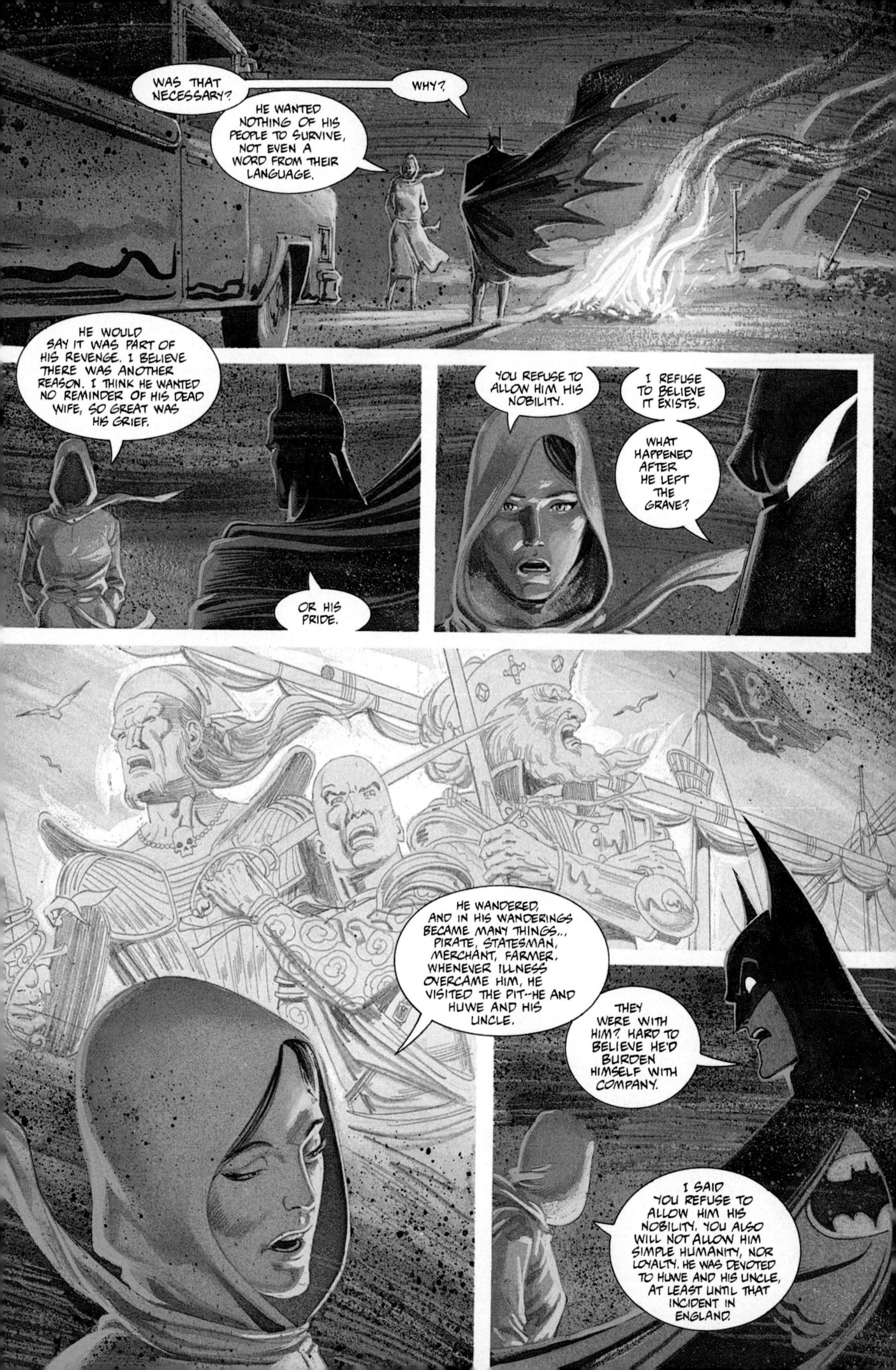

WAS THAT NECESSARY?
WHY?
HE WANTED NOTHING OF HIS PEOPLE TO SURVIVE, NOT EVEN A WORD FROM THEIR LANGUAGE.
HE WOULD SAY IT WAS PART OF HIS REVENGE. I BELIEVE THERE WAS ANOTHER REASON. I THINK HE WANTED NO REMINDER OF HIS DEAD WIFE, SO GREAT WAS HIS GRIEF.
OR HIS PRIDE.
YOU REFUSE TO ALLOW HIM HIS NOBILITY.
I REFUSE TO BELIEVE IT EXISTS.
WHAT HAPPENED AFTER HE LEFT THE GRAVE?
HE WANDERED, AND IN HIS WANDERINGS BECAME MANY THINGS... PIRATE, STATESMAN, MERCHANT, FARMER. WHENEVER ILLNESS OVERCAME HIM, HE VISITED THE PIT--HE AND HUWE AND HIS UNCLE.
THEY WERE WITH HIM? HARD TO BELIEVE HE'D BURDEN HIMSELF WITH COMPANY.
I SAID YOU REFUSE TO ALLOW HIM HIS NOBILITY. YOU ALSO WILL NOT ALLOW HIM SIMPLE HUMANITY, NOR LOYALTY. HE WAS DEVOTED TO HUWE AND HIS UNCLE, AT LEAST UNTIL THAT INCIDENT IN ENGLAND.

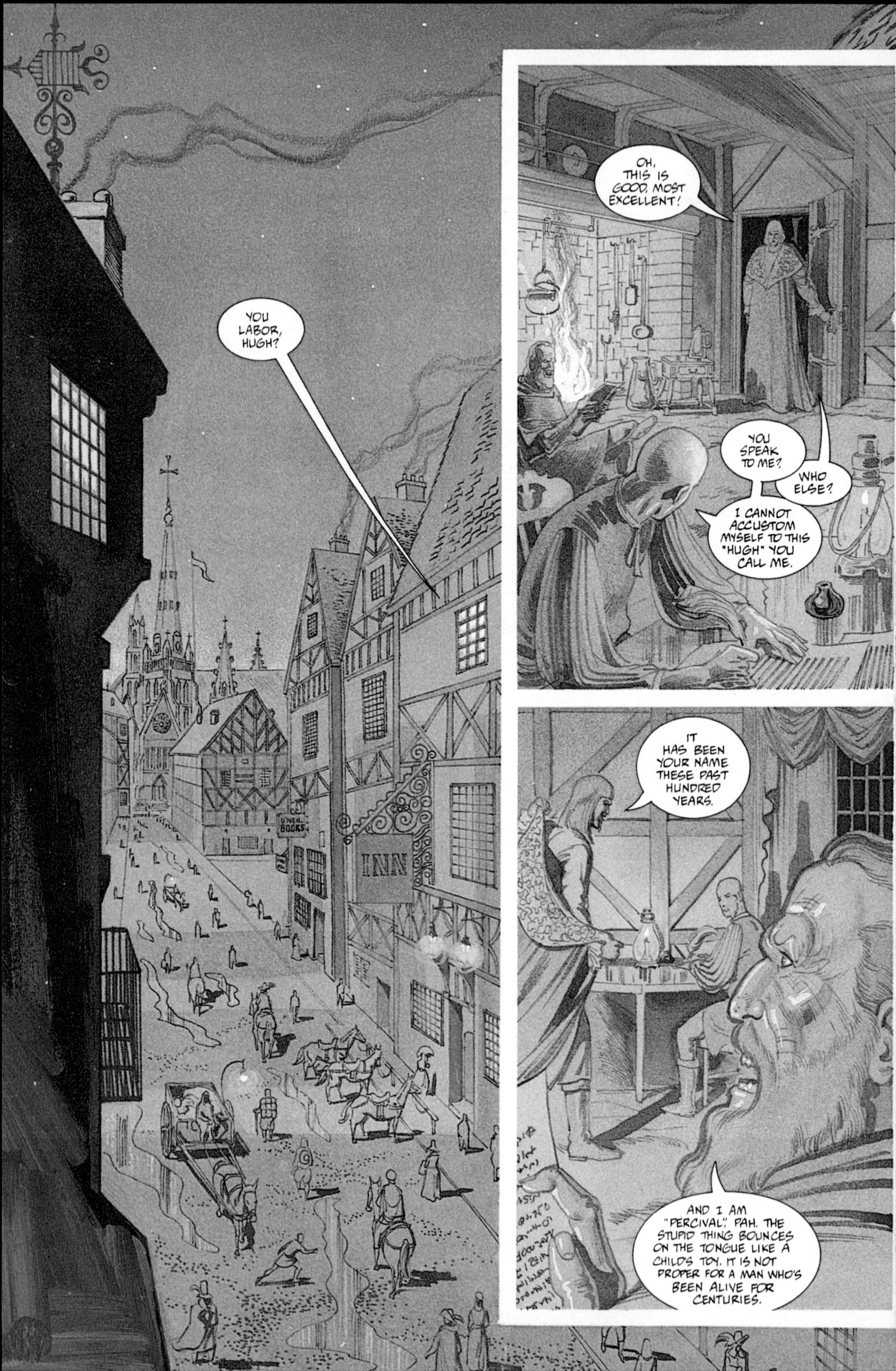
YOU LABOR, HUGH?
OH, THIS IS GOOD, MOST EXCELLENT!
YOU SPEAK TO ME?
WHO ELSE?
I CANNOT ACCUSTOM MYSELF TO THIS "HUGH" YOU CALL ME.
IT HAS BEEN YOUR NAME THESE PAST HUNDRED YEARS.
AND I AM "PERCIVAL". PAH. THE STUPID THING BOUNCES ON THE TONGUE LIKE A CHILD'S TOY. IT IS NOT PROPER FOR A MAN WHO'S BEEN ALIVE FOR CENTURIES.
INN
BOOKS

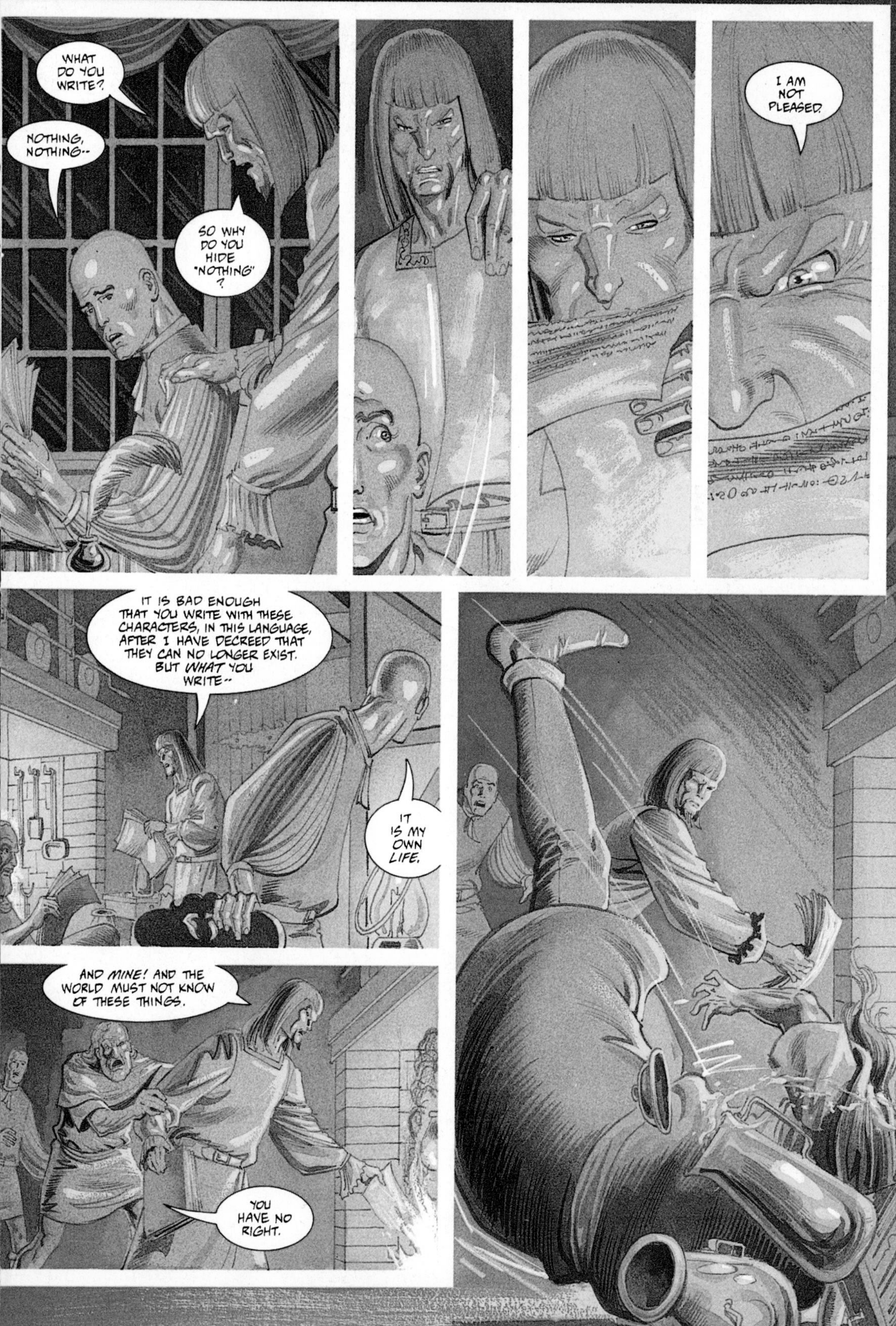
WHAT DO YOU WRITE?
NOTHING, NOTHING--
SO WHY DO YOU HIDE "NOTHING"?
I AM NOT PLEASED.
IT IS BAD ENOUGH THAT YOU WRITE WITH THESE CHARACTERS, IN THIS LANGUAGE, AFTER I HAVE DECREED THAT THEY CAN NO LONGER EXIST. BUT WHAT YOU WRITE--
IT IS MY OWN LIFE.
AND MINE! AND THE WORLD MUST NOT KNOW OF THESE THINGS.
YOU HAVE NO RIGHT.

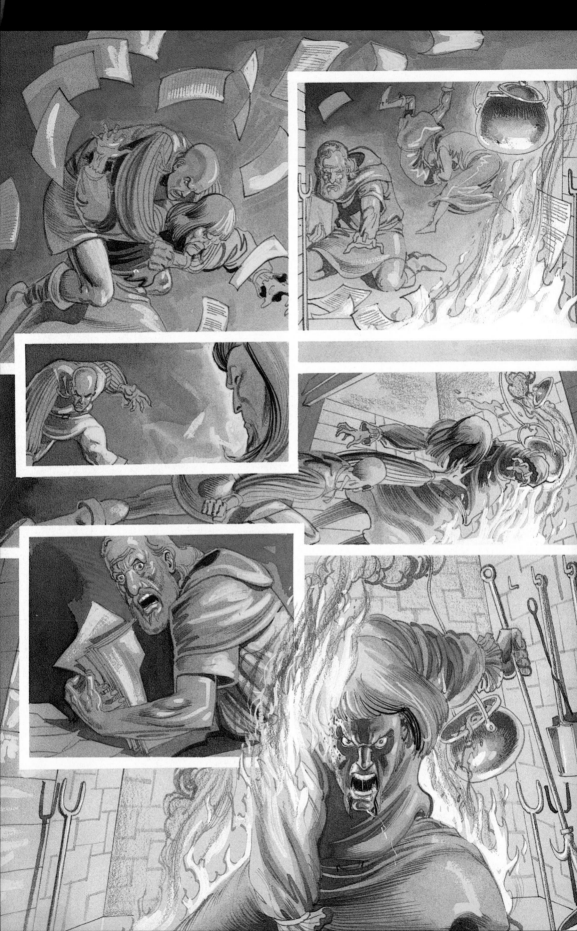

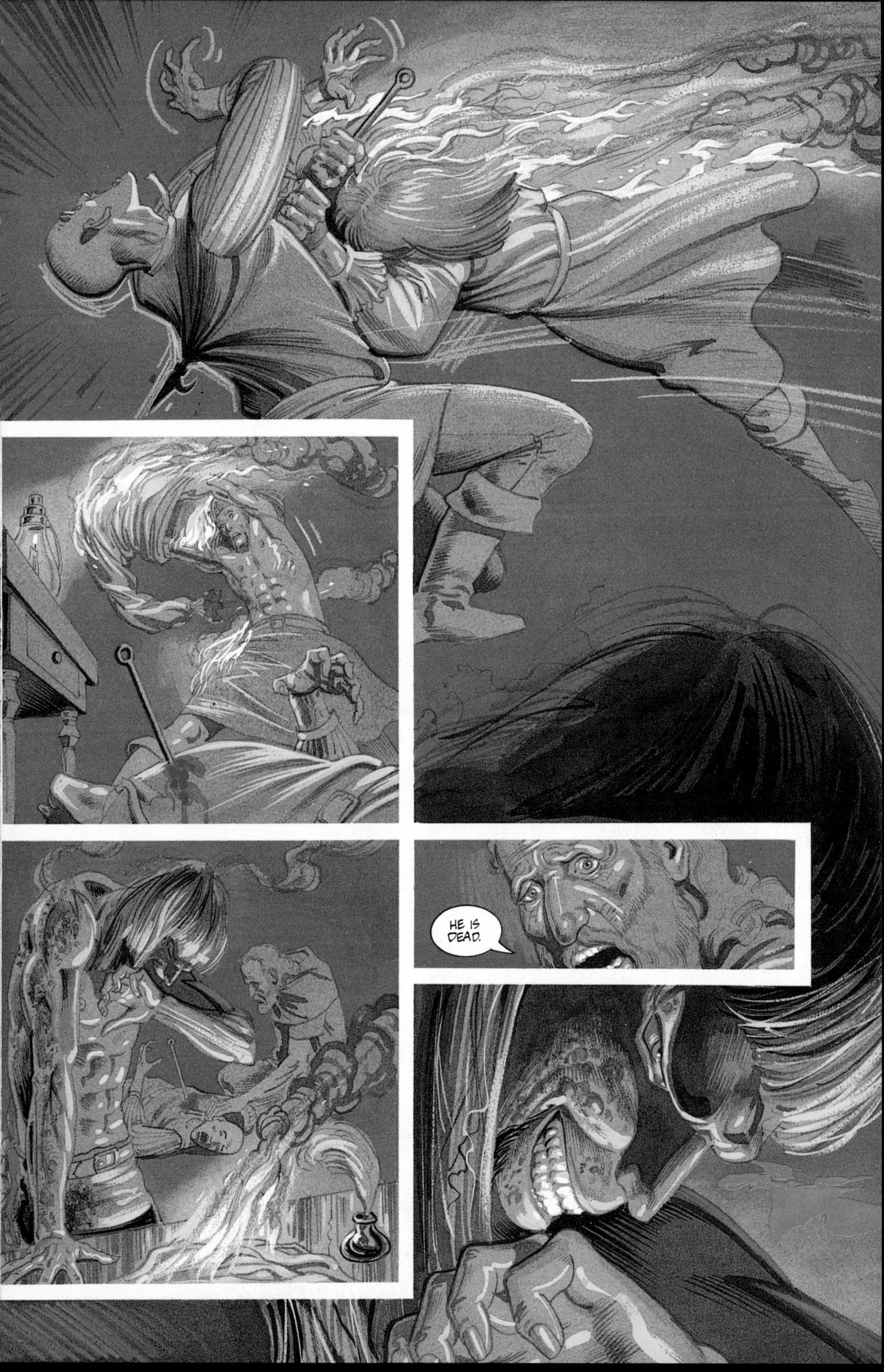
HE IS DEAD.

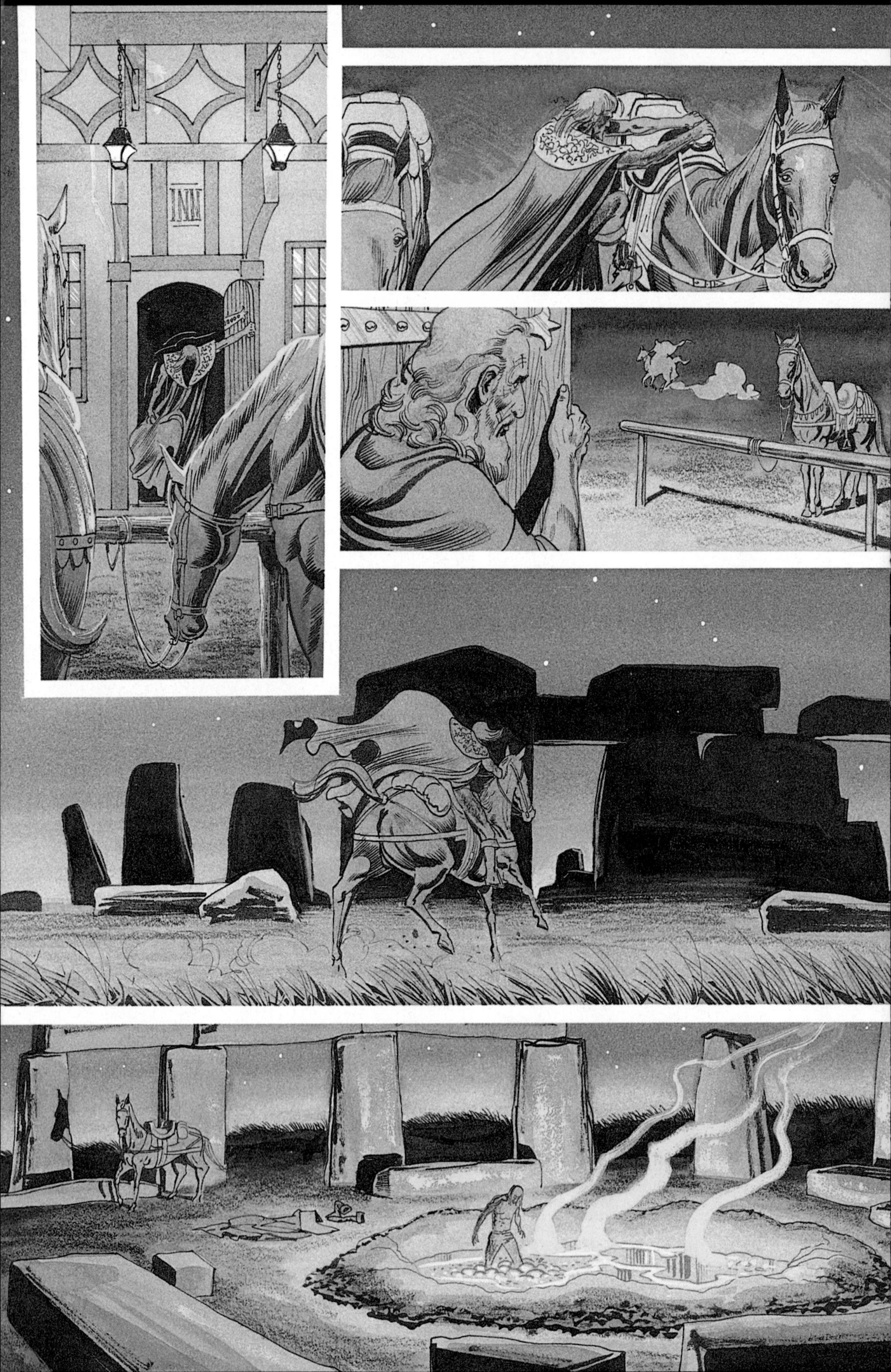
INN

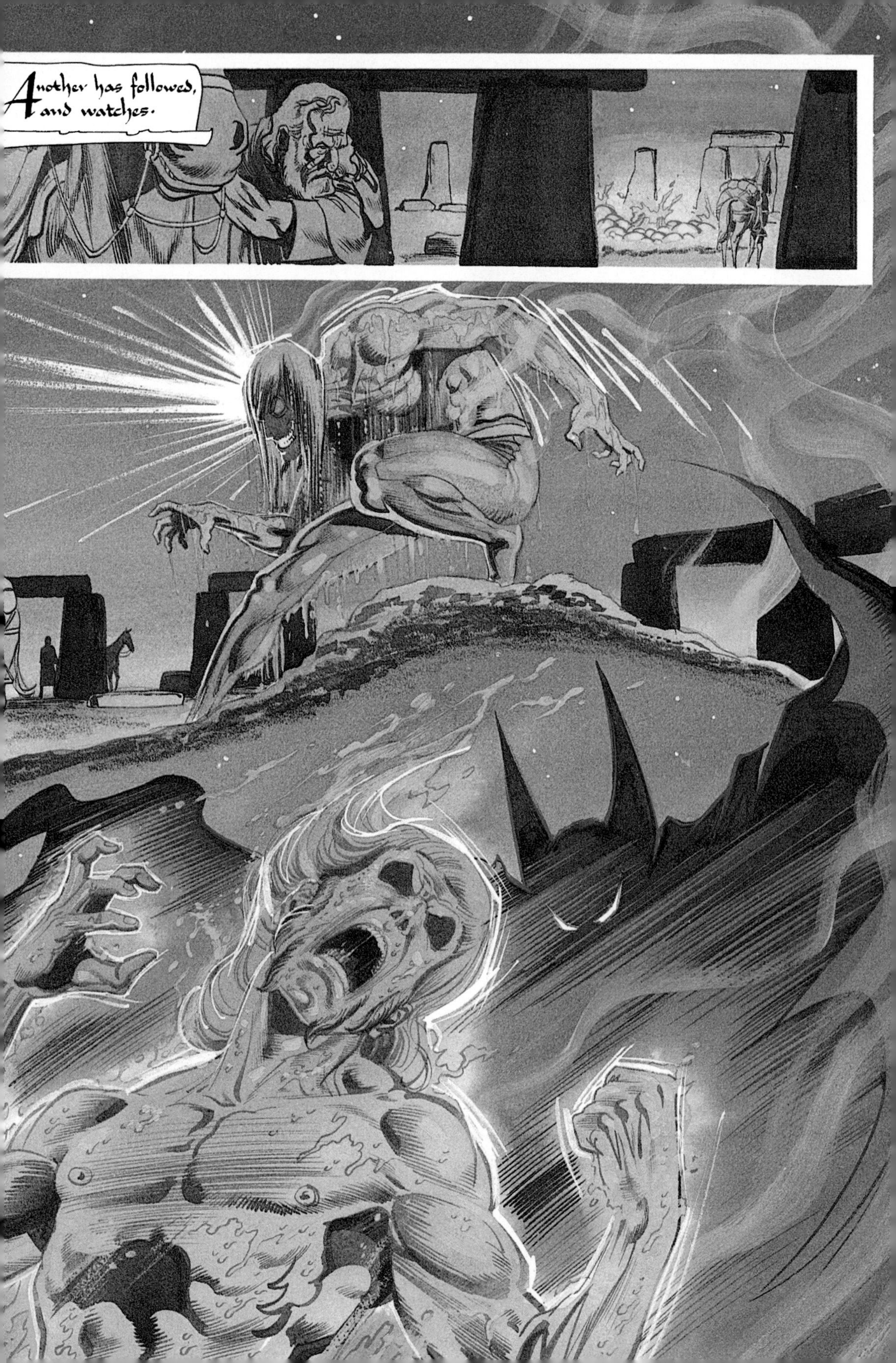
Another has followed,
and watches.

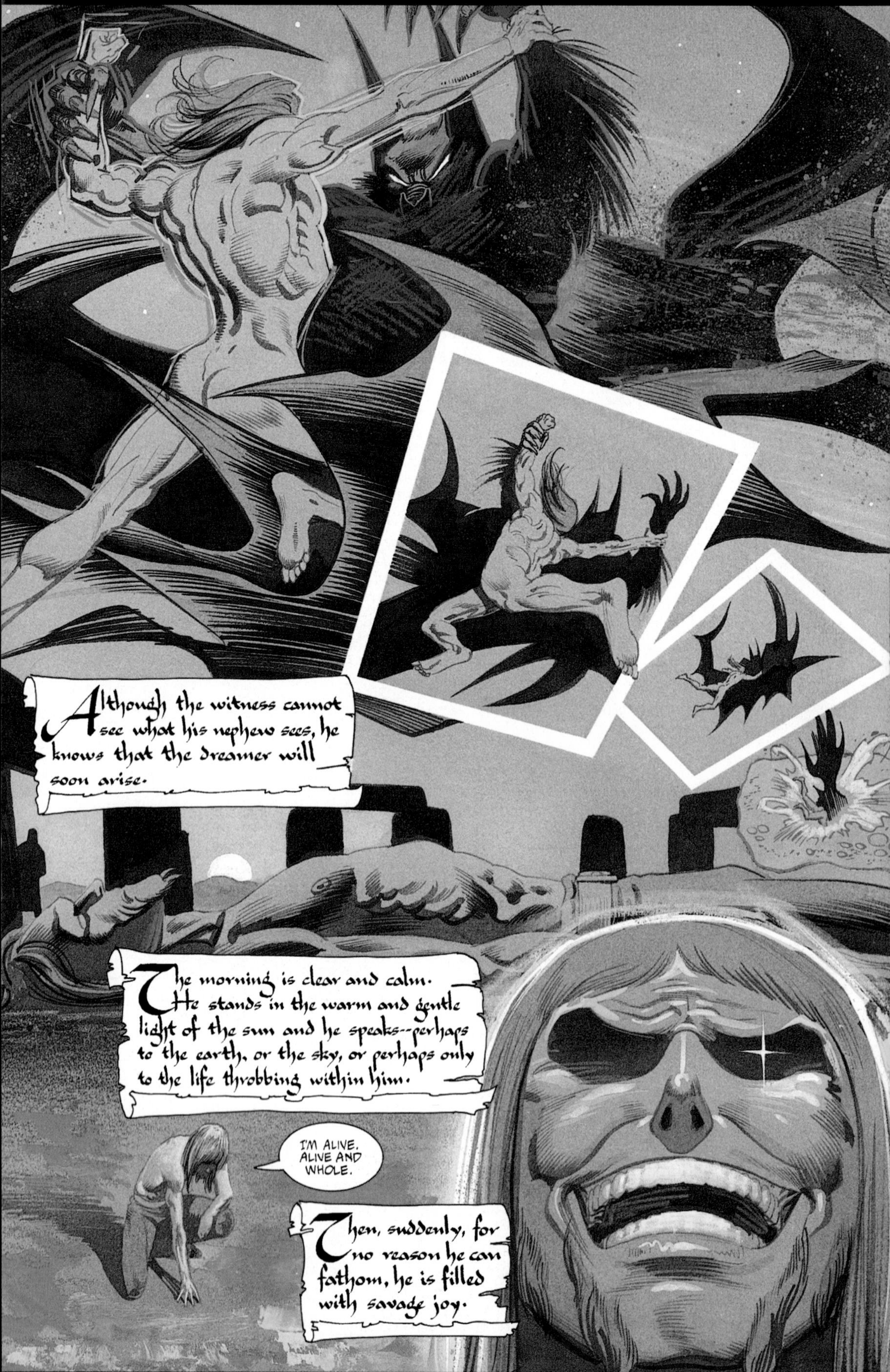
Although the witness cannot see what his nephew sees, he knows that the dreamer will soon arise.
The morning is clear and calm. He stands in the warm and gentle light of the sun and he speaks--perhaps to the earth, or the sky, or perhaps only to the life throbbing within him.
I'M ALIVE. ALIVE AND WHOLE.
Then, suddenly, for no reason he can fathom, he is filled with savage joy.

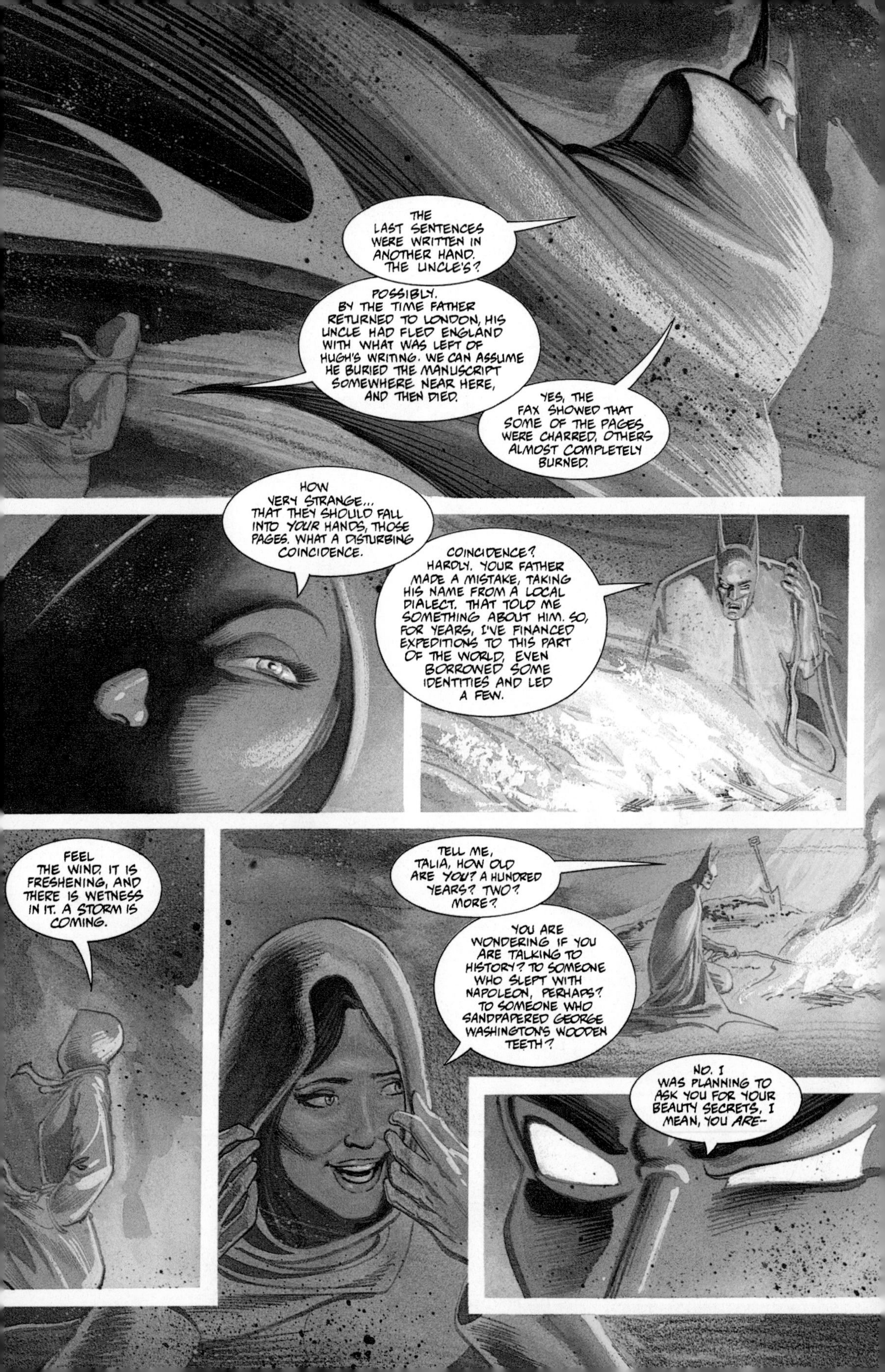
THE LAST SENTENCES WERE WRITTEN IN ANOTHER HAND. THE UNCLE'S?
POSSIBLY. BY THE TIME FATHER RETURNED TO LONDON, HIS UNCLE HAD FLED ENGLAND WITH WHAT WAS LEFT OF HUGH'S WRITING. WE CAN ASSUME HE BURIED THE MANUSCRIPT SOMEWHERE NEAR HERE, AND THEN DIED.
YES, THE FAX SHOWED THAT SOME OF THE PAGES WERE CHARRED, OTHERS ALMOST COMPLETELY BURNED.
HOW VERY STRANGE... THAT THEY SHOULD FALL INTO *YOUR* HANDS, THOSE PAGES. WHAT A DISTURBING COINCIDENCE.
COINCIDENCE? HARDLY. YOUR FATHER MADE A MISTAKE, TAKING HIS NAME FROM A LOCAL DIALECT. THAT TOLD ME SOMETHING ABOUT HIM. SO, FOR YEARS, I'VE FINANCED EXPEDITIONS TO THIS PART OF THE WORLD, EVEN BORROWED SOME IDENTITIES AND LED A FEW.
FEEL THE WIND. IT IS FRESHENING, AND THERE IS WETNESS IN IT. A STORM IS COMING.
TELL ME, TALIA, HOW OLD ARE *YOU*? A HUNDRED YEARS? TWO? MORE?
YOU ARE WONDERING IF YOU ARE TALKING TO HISTORY? TO SOMEONE WHO SLEPT WITH NAPOLEON, PERHAPS? TO SOMEONE WHO SANDPAPERED GEORGE WASHINGTON'S WOODEN TEETH?
NO. I WAS PLANNING TO ASK YOU FOR YOUR BEAUTY SECRETS, I MEAN, YOU *ARE*--

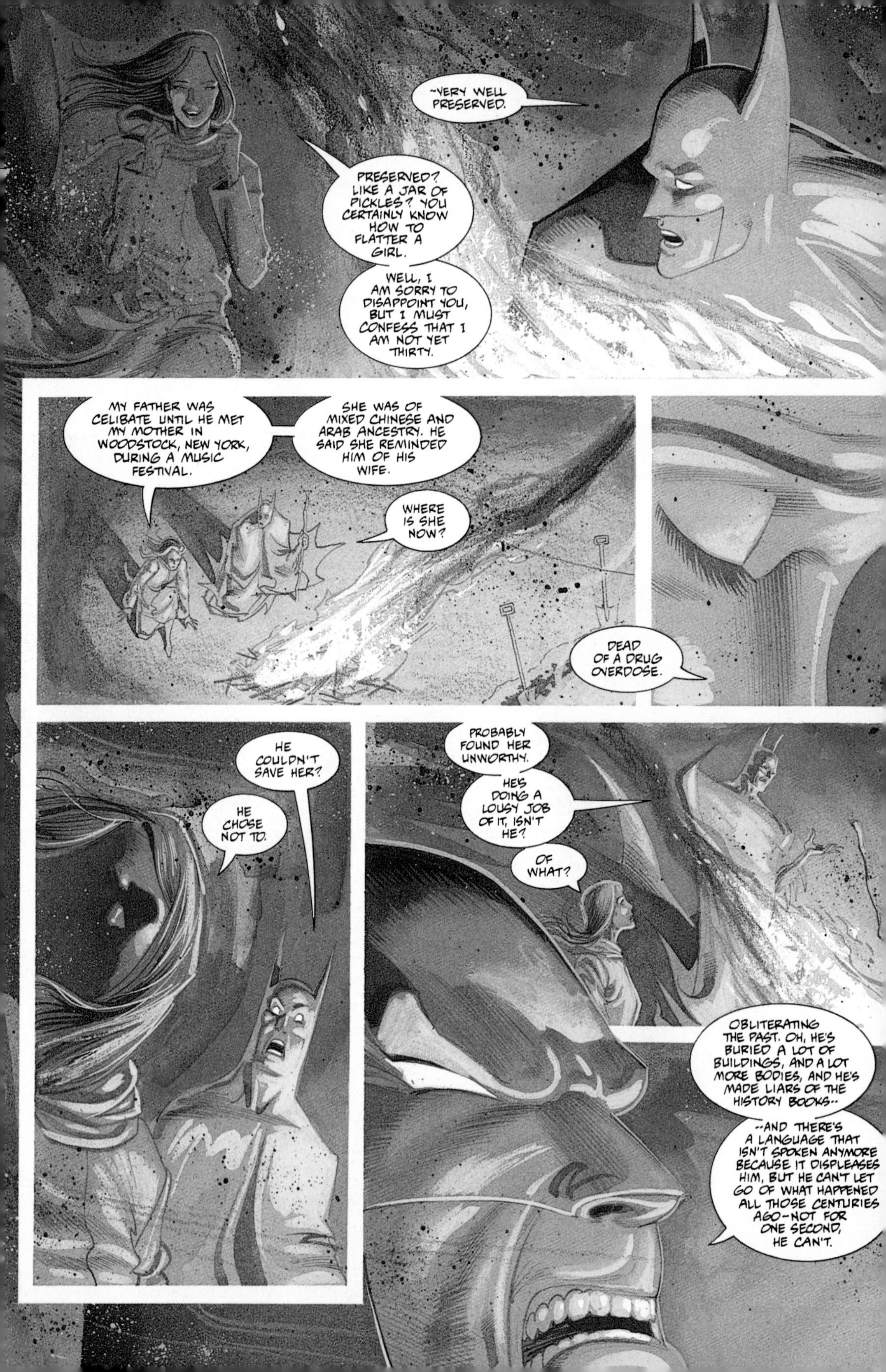

~VERY WELL PRESERVED.
PRESERVED? LIKE A JAR OF PICKLES? YOU CERTAINLY KNOW HOW TO FLATTER A GIRL.
WELL, I AM SORRY TO DISAPPOINT YOU, BUT I MUST CONFESS THAT I AM NOT YET THIRTY.
MY FATHER WAS CELIBATE UNTIL HE MET MY MOTHER IN WOODSTOCK, NEW YORK, DURING A MUSIC FESTIVAL.
SHE WAS OF MIXED CHINESE AND ARAB ANCESTRY. HE SAID SHE REMINDED HIM OF HIS WIFE.
WHERE IS SHE NOW?
DEAD OF A DRUG OVERDOSE.
HE COULDN'T SAVE HER?
HE CHOSE NOT TO.
PROBABLY FOUND HER UNWORTHY.
HE'S DOING A LOUSY JOB OF IT, ISN'T HE?
OF WHAT?
OBLITERATING THE PAST. OH, HE'S BURIED A LOT OF BUILDINGS, AND A LOT MORE BODIES, AND HE'S MADE LIARS OF THE HISTORY BOOKS--
--AND THERE'S A LANGUAGE THAT ISN'T SPOKEN ANYMORE BECAUSE IT DISPLEASES HIM, BUT HE CAN'T LET GO OF WHAT HAPPENED ALL THOSE CENTURIES AGO--NOT FOR ONE SECOND, HE CAN'T.

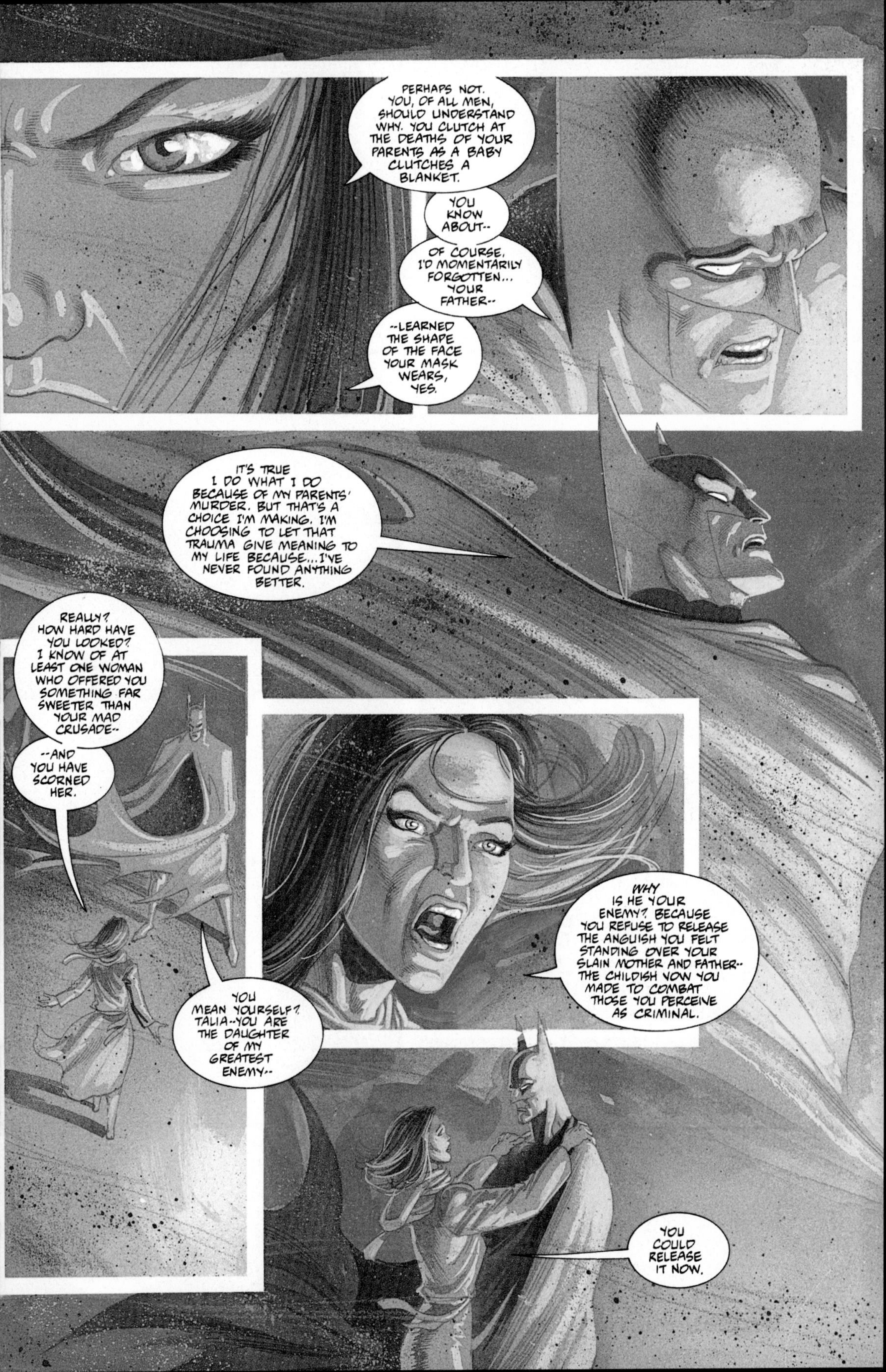
PERHAPS NOT. YOU, OF ALL MEN, SHOULD UNDERSTAND WHY. YOU CLUTCH AT THE DEATHS OF YOUR PARENTS AS A BABY CLUTCHES A BLANKET.
YOU KNOW ABOUT--
OF COURSE. I'D MOMENTARILY FORGOTTEN... YOUR FATHER--
--LEARNED THE SHAPE OF THE FACE YOUR MASK WEARS, YES.
IT'S TRUE I DO WHAT I DO BECAUSE OF MY PARENTS' MURDER. BUT THAT'S A CHOICE I'M MAKING. I'M CHOOSING TO LET THAT TRAUMA GIVE MEANING TO MY LIFE BECAUSE... I'VE NEVER FOUND ANYTHING BETTER.
REALLY? HOW HARD HAVE YOU LOOKED? I KNOW OF AT LEAST ONE WOMAN WHO OFFERED YOU SOMETHING FAR SWEETER THAN YOUR MAD CRUSADE--
--AND YOU HAVE SCORNED HER.
YOU MEAN YOURSELF? TALIA--YOU ARE THE DAUGHTER OF MY GREATEST ENEMY--
WHY IS HE YOUR ENEMY? BECAUSE YOU REFUSE TO RELEASE THE ANGUISH YOU FELT STANDING OVER YOUR SLAIN MOTHER AND FATHER-- THE CHILDISH VOW YOU MADE TO COMBAT THOSE YOU PERCEIVE AS CRIMINAL.
YOU COULD RELEASE IT NOW.

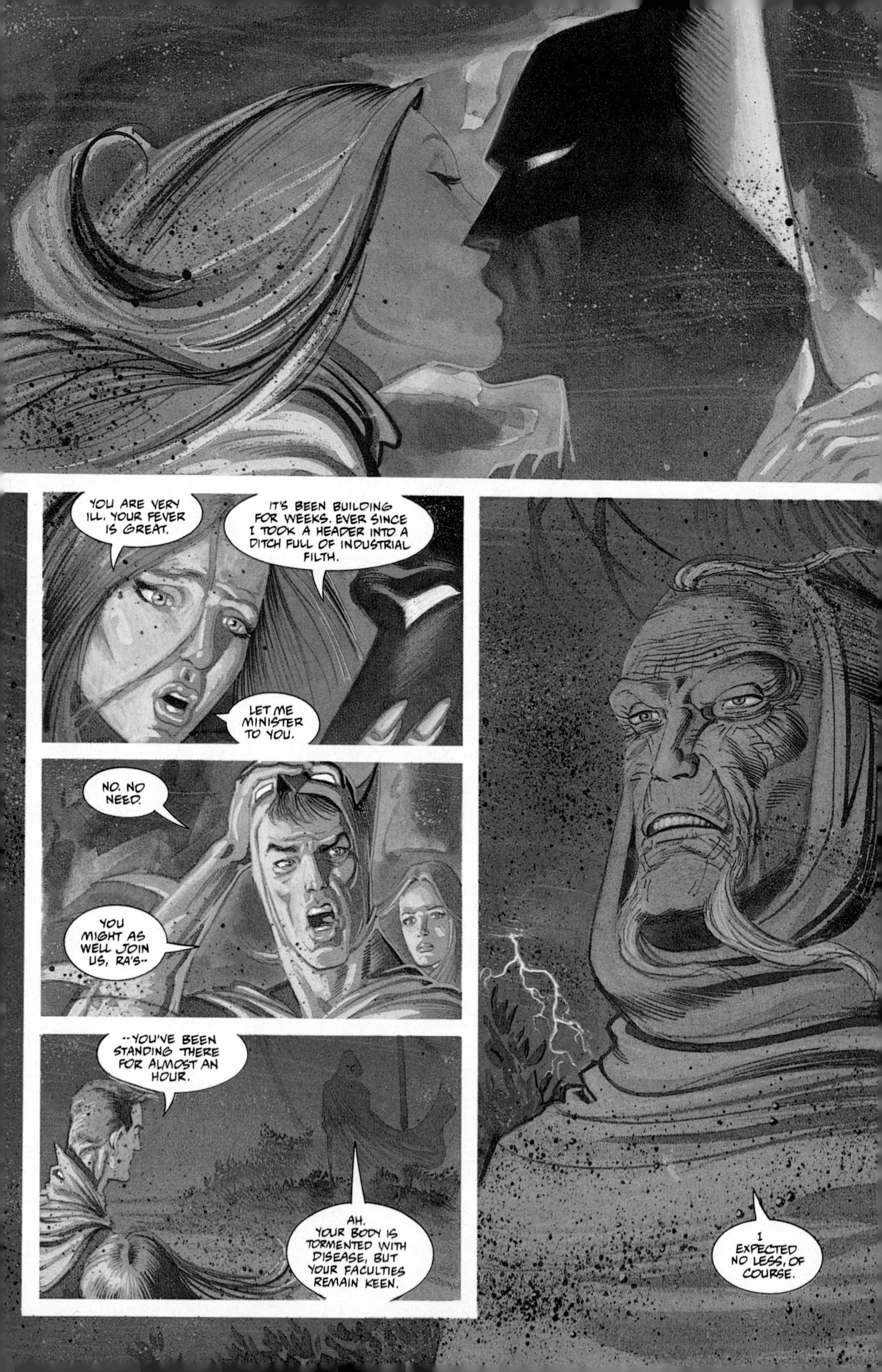
YOU ARE VERY ILL. YOUR FEVER IS GREAT.
IT'S BEEN BUILDING FOR WEEKS. EVER SINCE I TOOK A HEADER INTO A DITCH FULL OF INDUSTRIAL FILTH.
LET ME MINISTER TO YOU.
NO. NO NEED.
YOU MIGHT AS WELL JOIN US, RA'S--
--YOU'VE BEEN STANDING THERE FOR ALMOST AN HOUR.
AH. YOUR BODY IS TORMENTED WITH DISEASE, BUT YOUR FACULTIES REMAIN KEEN.
I EXPECTED NO LESS, OF COURSE.

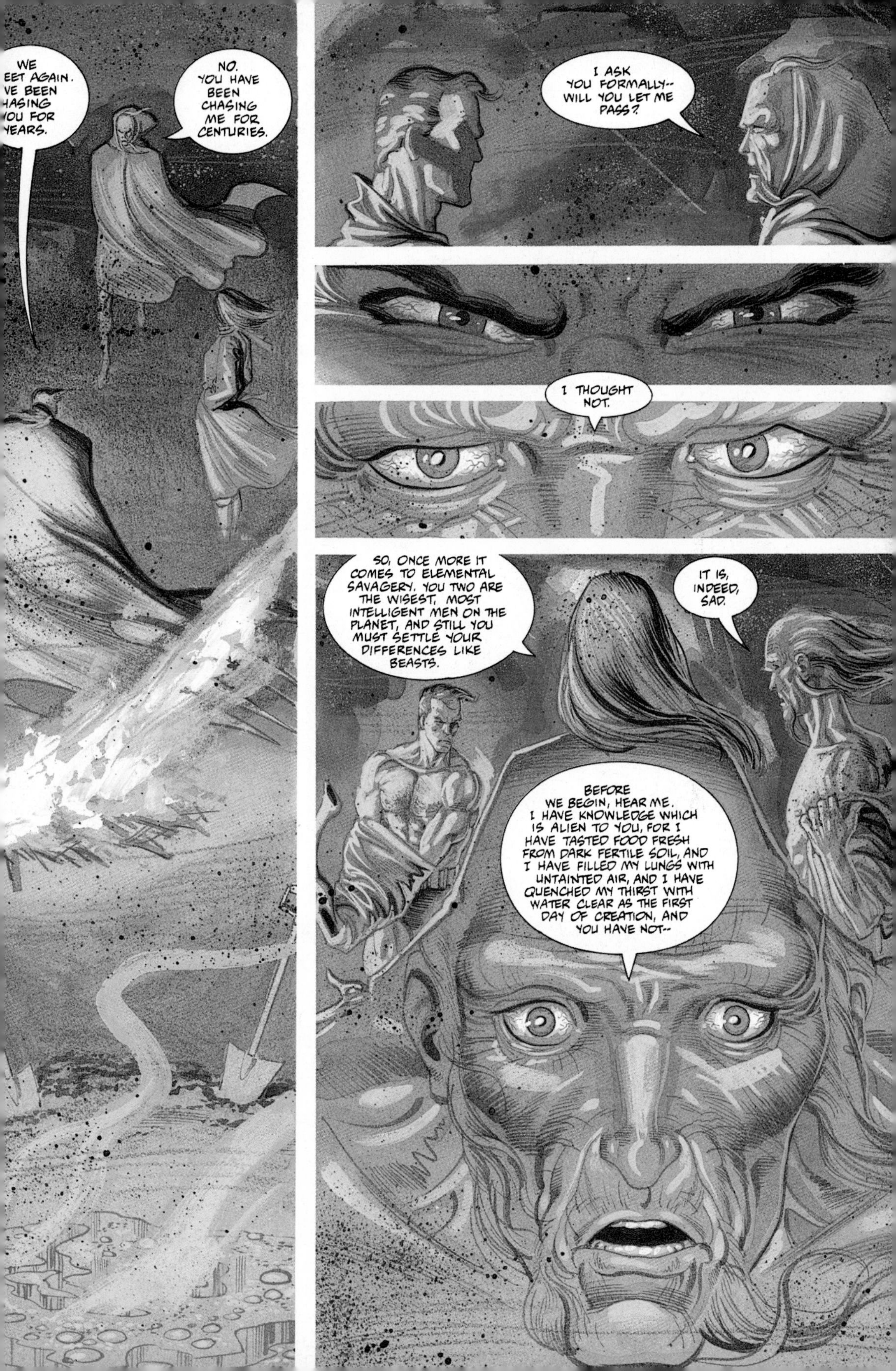

WE EET AGAIN. VE BEEN HASING OU FOR YEARS.
NO. YOU HAVE BEEN CHASING ME FOR CENTURIES.
I ASK YOU FORMALLY-- WILL YOU LET ME PASS?
I THOUGHT NOT.
SO, ONCE MORE IT COMES TO ELEMENTAL SAVAGERY. YOU TWO ARE THE WISEST, MOST INTELLIGENT MEN ON THE PLANET, AND STILL YOU MUST SETTLE YOUR DIFFERENCES LIKE BEASTS.
IT IS, INDEED, SAD.
BEFORE WE BEGIN, HEAR ME. I HAVE KNOWLEDGE WHICH IS ALIEN TO YOU, FOR I HAVE TASTED FOOD FRESH FROM DARK FERTILE SOIL, AND I HAVE FILLED MY LUNGS WITH UNTAINTED AIR, AND I HAVE QUENCHED MY THIRST WITH WATER CLEAR AS THE FIRST DAY OF CREATION, AND YOU HAVE NOT--

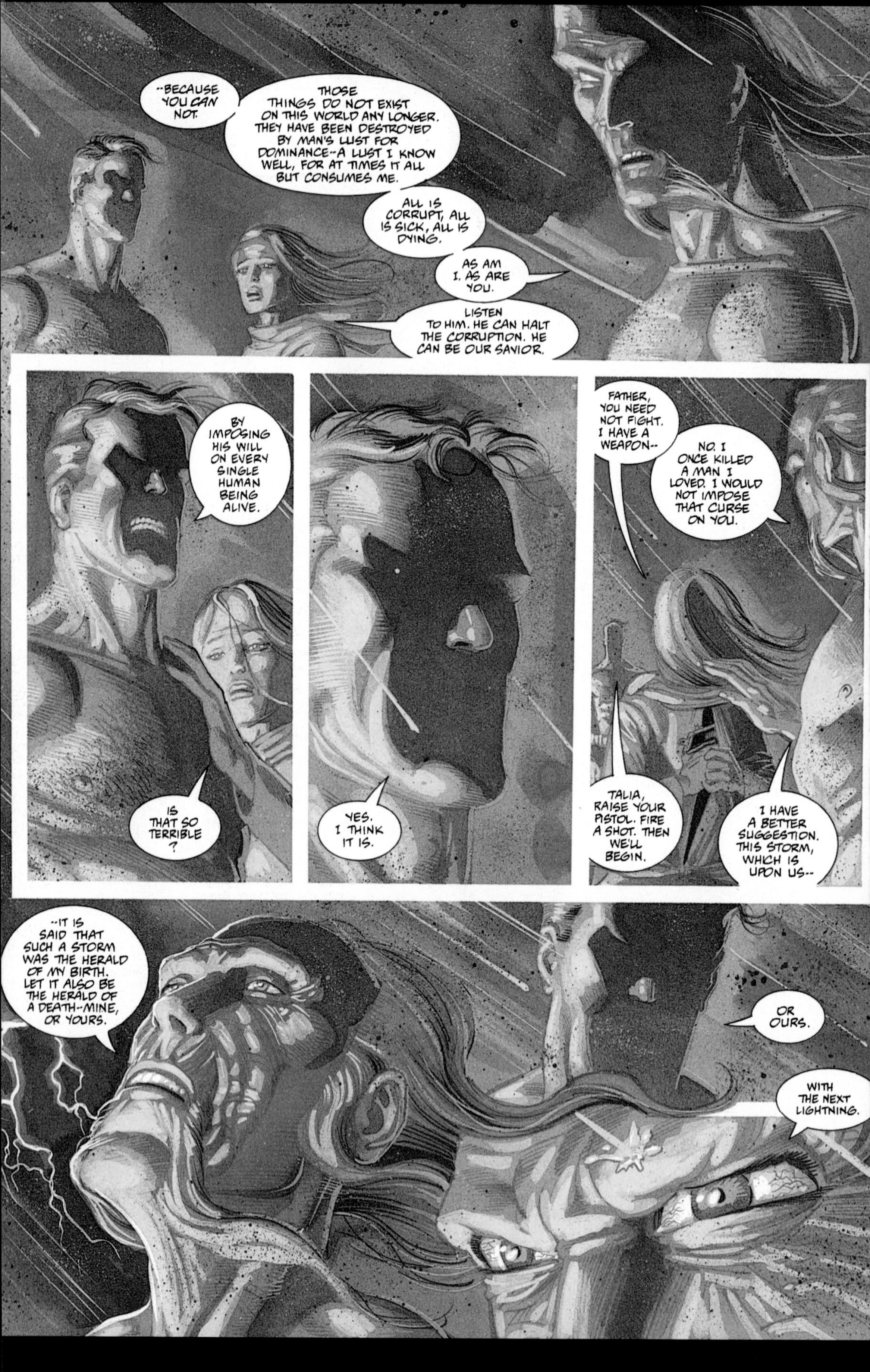

--BECAUSE YOU CAN NOT.
THOSE THINGS DO NOT EXIST ON THIS WORLD ANY LONGER. THEY HAVE BEEN DESTROYED BY MAN'S LUST FOR DOMINANCE--A LUST I KNOW WELL, FOR AT TIMES IT ALL BUT CONSUMES ME.
ALL IS CORRUPT, ALL IS SICK, ALL IS DYING.
AS AM I. AS ARE YOU.
LISTEN TO HIM. HE CAN HALT THE CORRUPTION. HE CAN BE OUR SAVIOR.
BY IMPOSING HIS WILL ON EVERY SINGLE HUMAN BEING ALIVE.
IS THAT SO TERRIBLE?
YES. I THINK IT IS.
FATHER, YOU NEED NOT FIGHT. I HAVE A WEAPON--
NO. I ONCE KILLED A MAN I LOVED. I WOULD NOT IMPOSE THAT CURSE ON YOU.
TALIA, RAISE YOUR PISTOL. FIRE A SHOT. THEN WE'LL BEGIN.
I HAVE A BETTER SUGGESTION. THIS STORM, WHICH IS UPON US--
--IT IS SAID THAT SUCH A STORM WAS THE HERALD OF MY BIRTH. LET IT ALSO BE THE HERALD OF A DEATH--MINE, OR YOURS.
OR OURS.
WITH THE NEXT LIGHTNING.

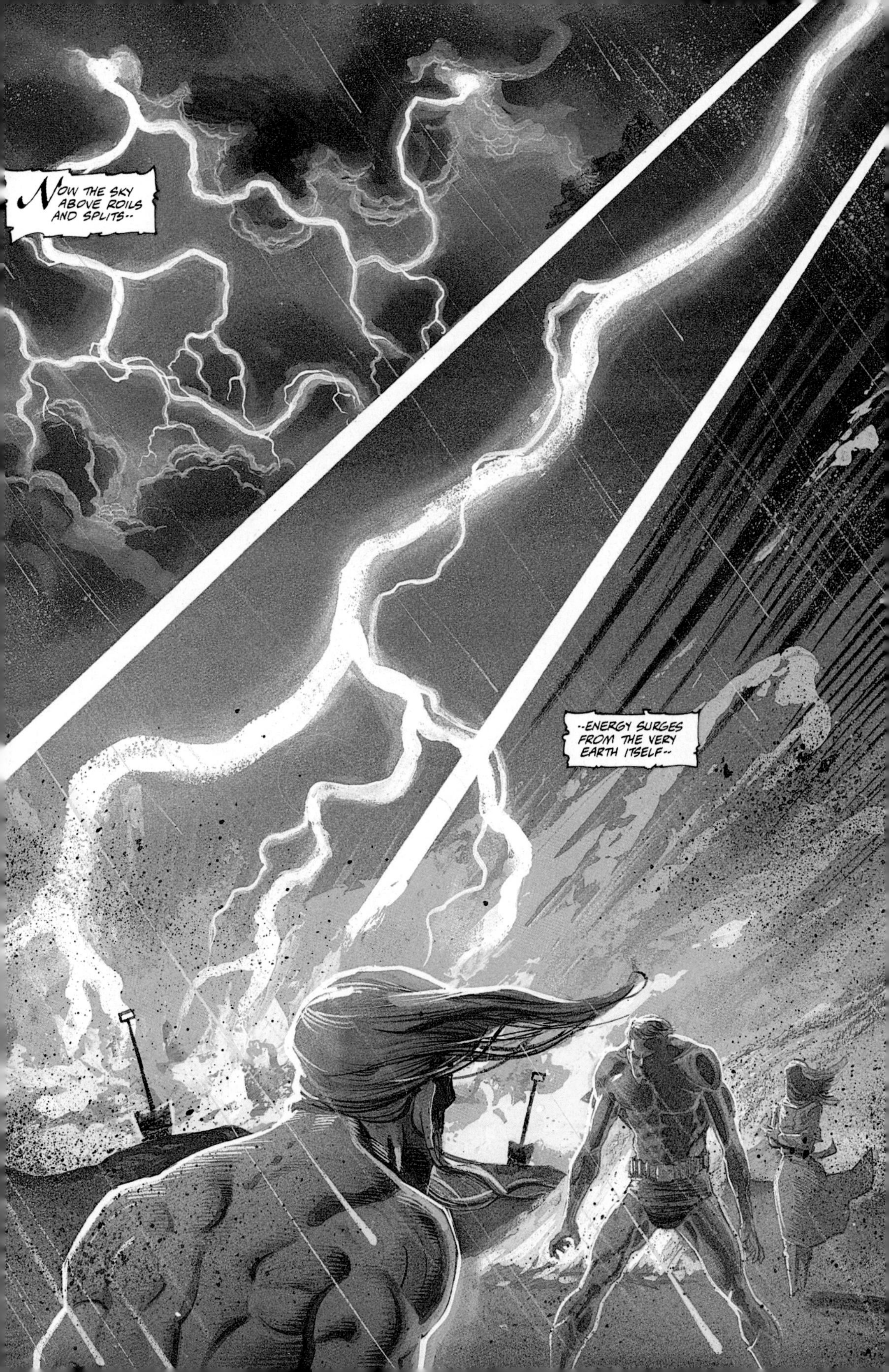
Now the sky above roils and splits--
--Energy surges from the very earth itself--

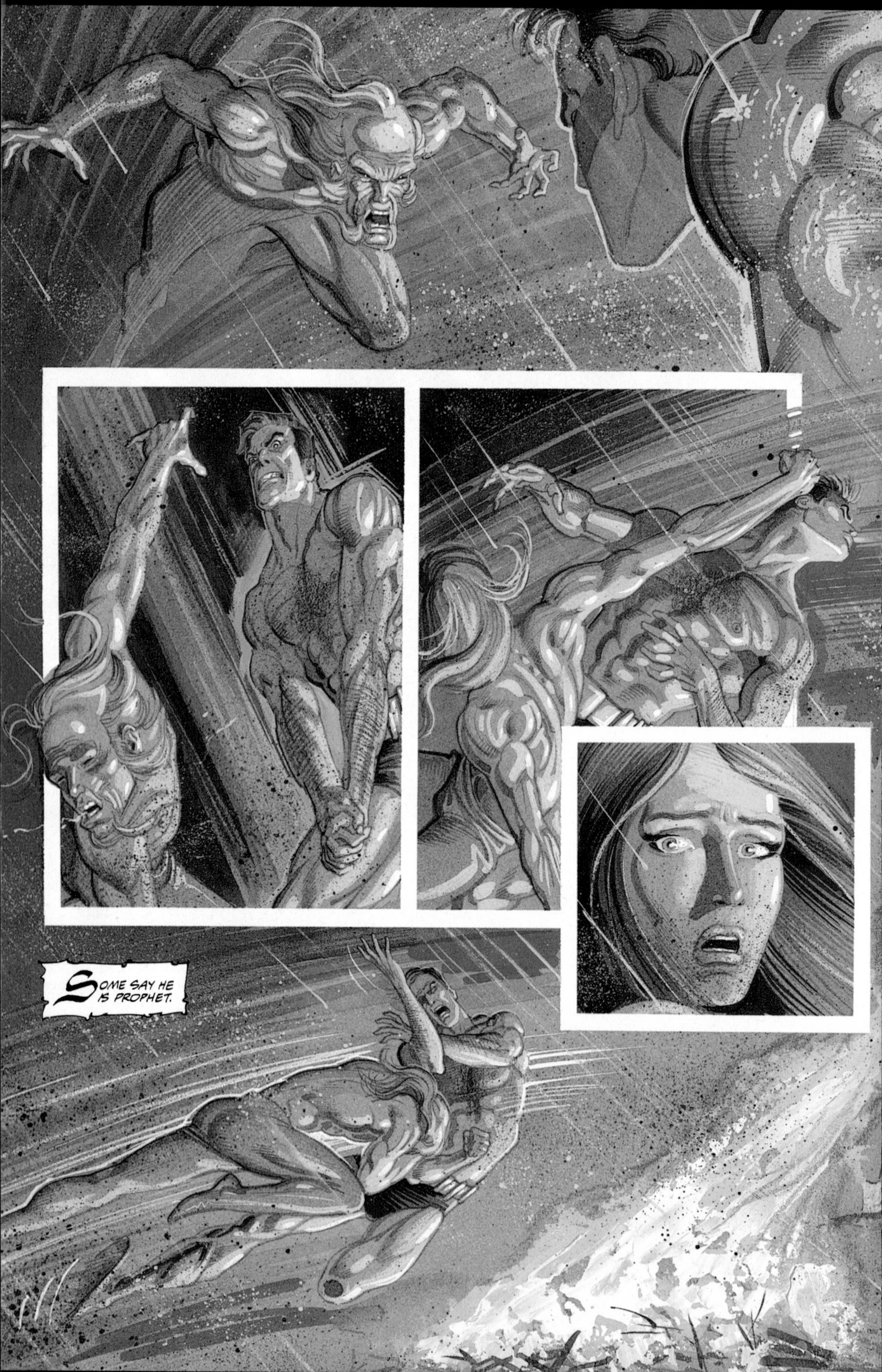
SOME SAY HE IS PROPHET.

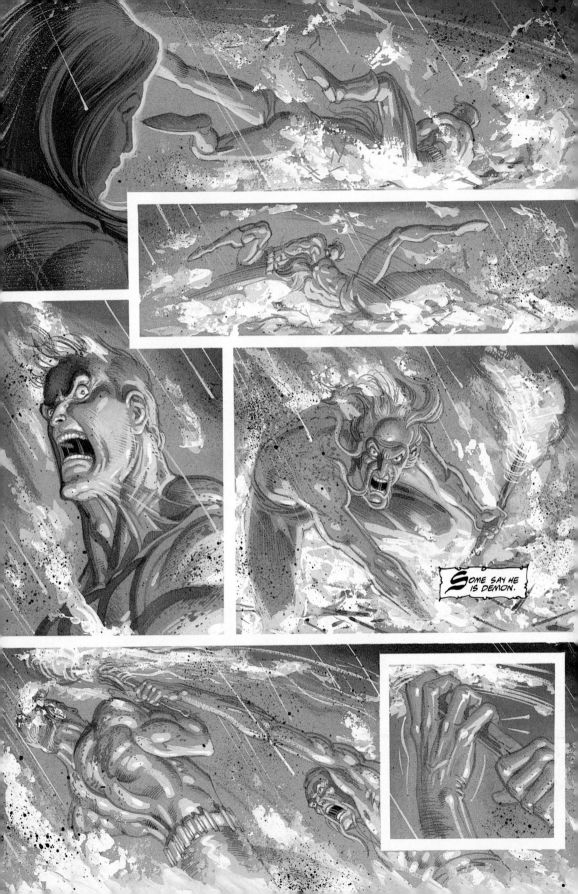

SOME SAY HE IS DEMON.

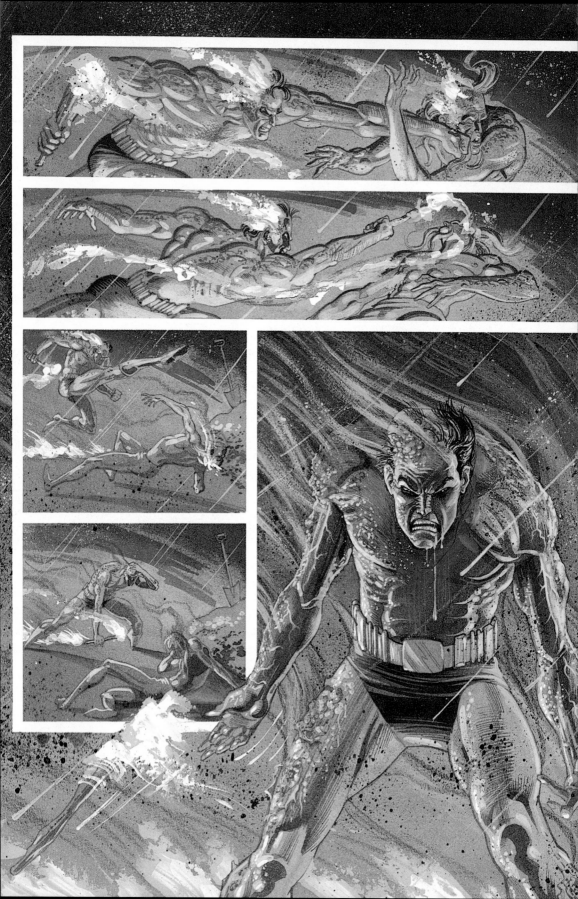

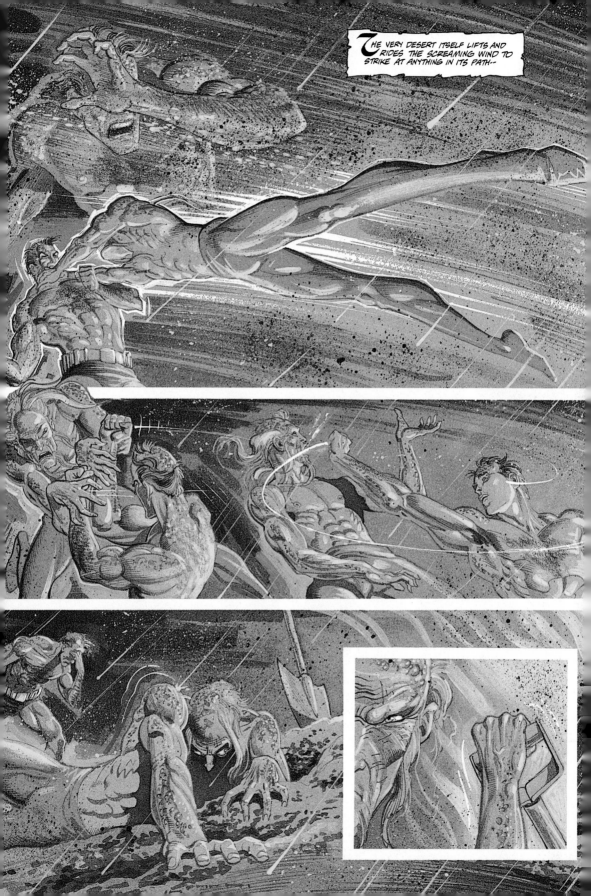

THE VERY DESERT ITSELF LIFTS AND RIDES THE SCREAMING WIND TO STRIKE AT ANYTHING IN ITS PATH--

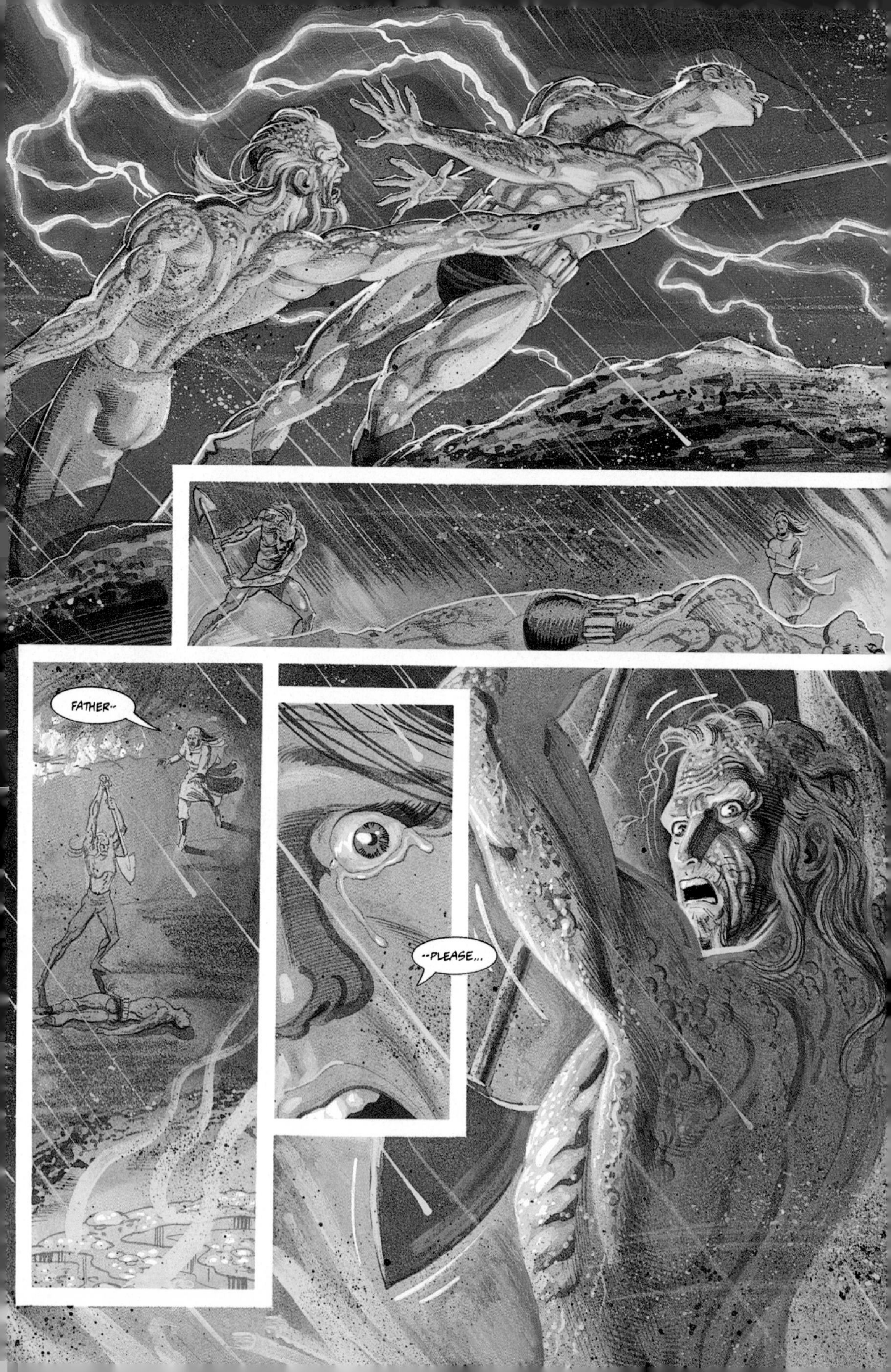
FATHER--
--PLEASE...

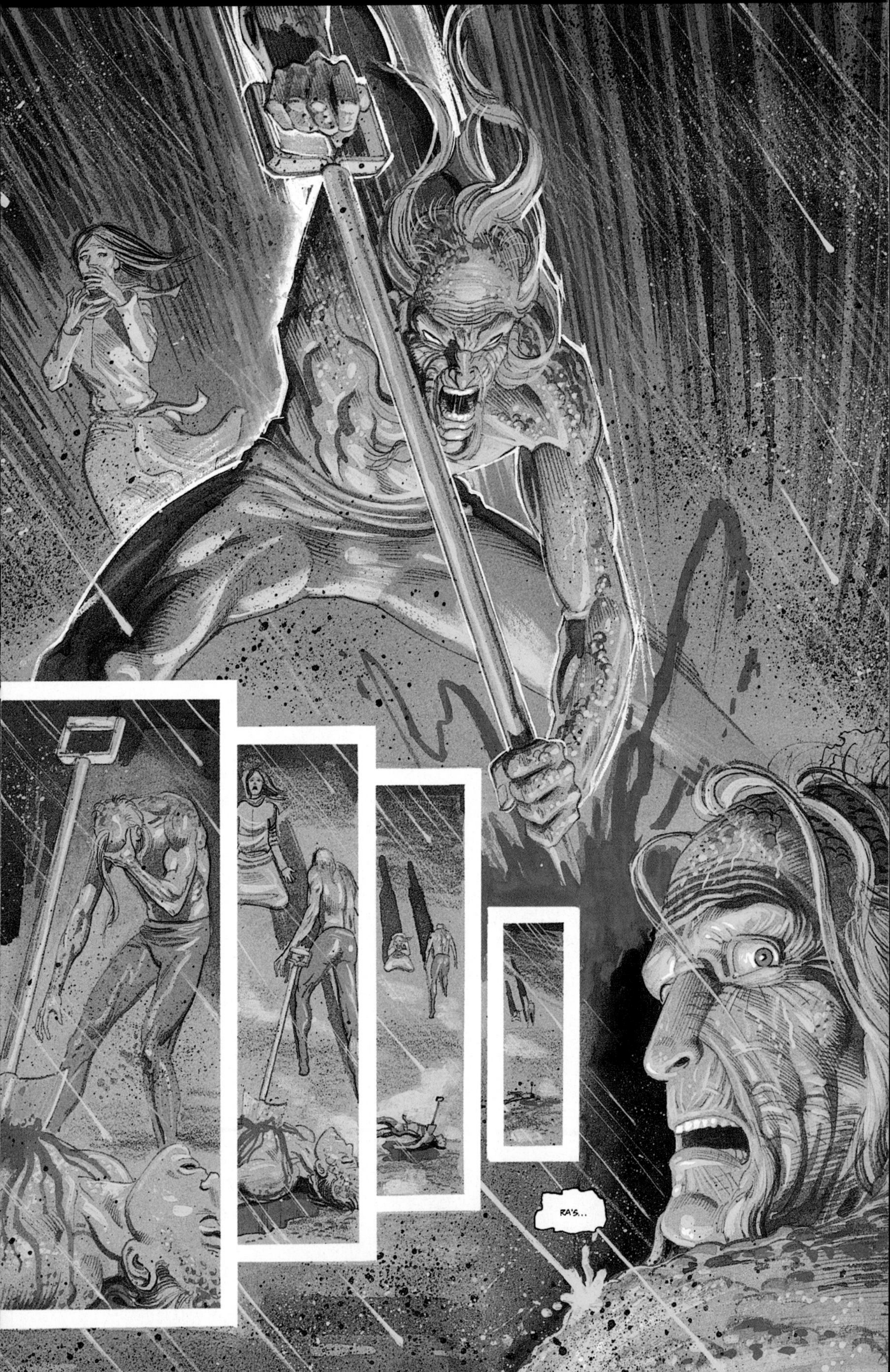
RA'S...

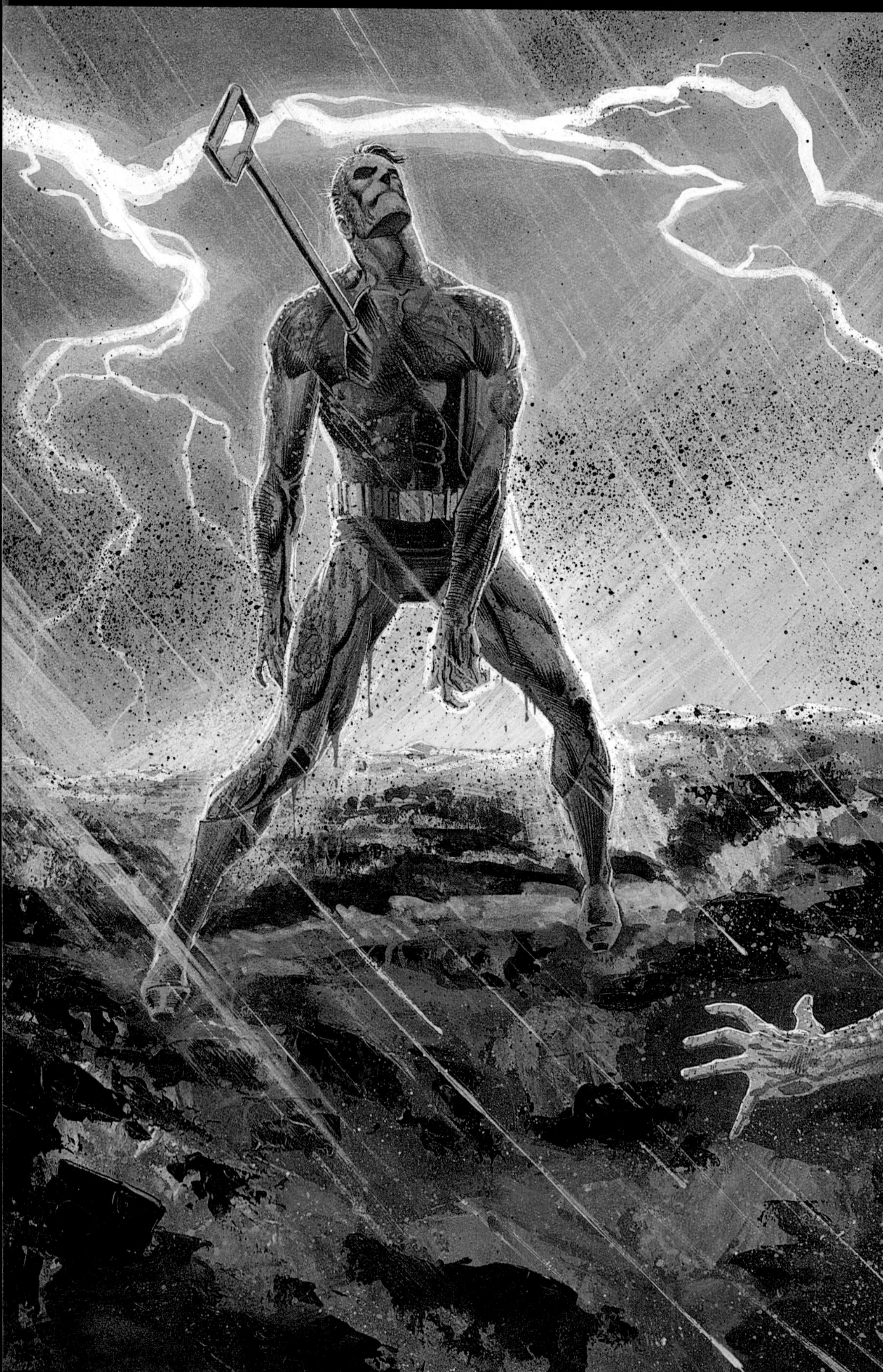

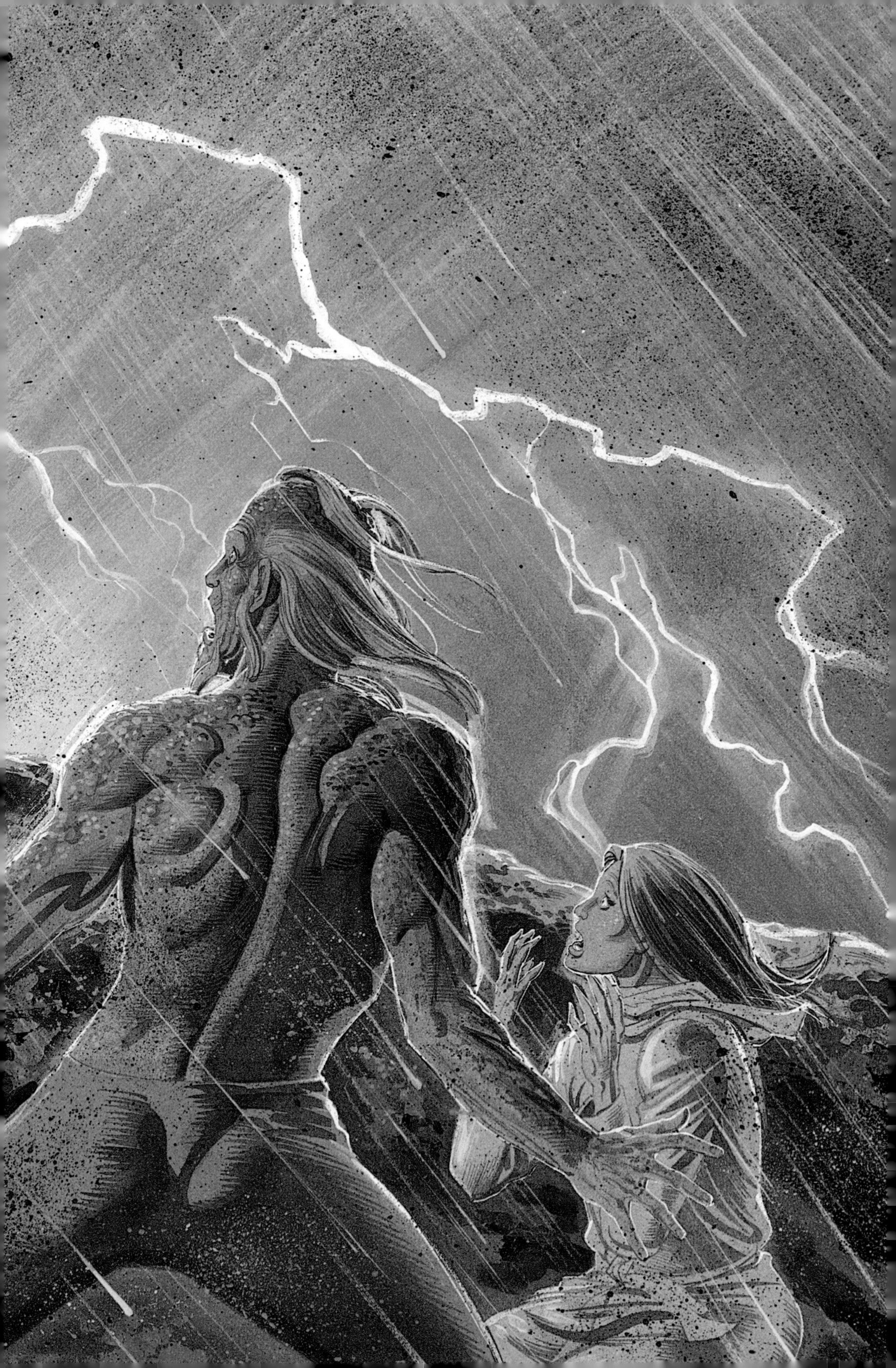

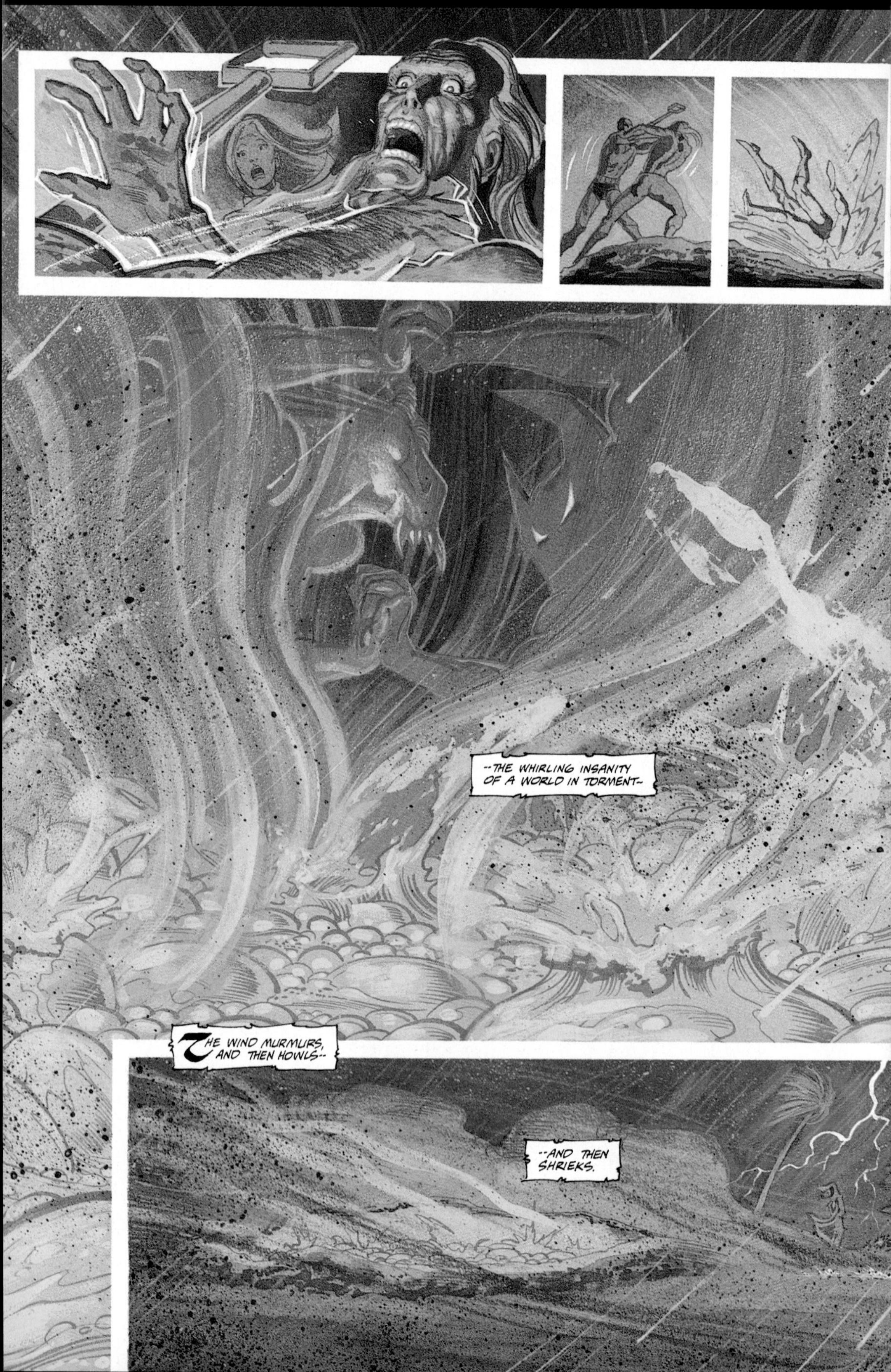
--THE WHIRLING INSANITY OF A WORLD IN TORMENT--
THE WIND MURMURS, AND THEN HOWLS--
--AND THEN SHRIEKS.

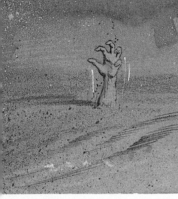

THE MORNING IS CLEAR AND CALM. HE STANDS IN THE WARM AND GENTLE LIGHT OF THE SUN AND HE SPEAKS, THOUGH THERE IS NO ONE TO HEAR.

I'M ALIVE. ALIVE AND WHOLE. I GUESS THAT'S A MIRACLE.

AND YOU, MY ENEMY? ARE YOU LYING SOMEWHERE NEARBY, TWISTED AND LIFELESS?

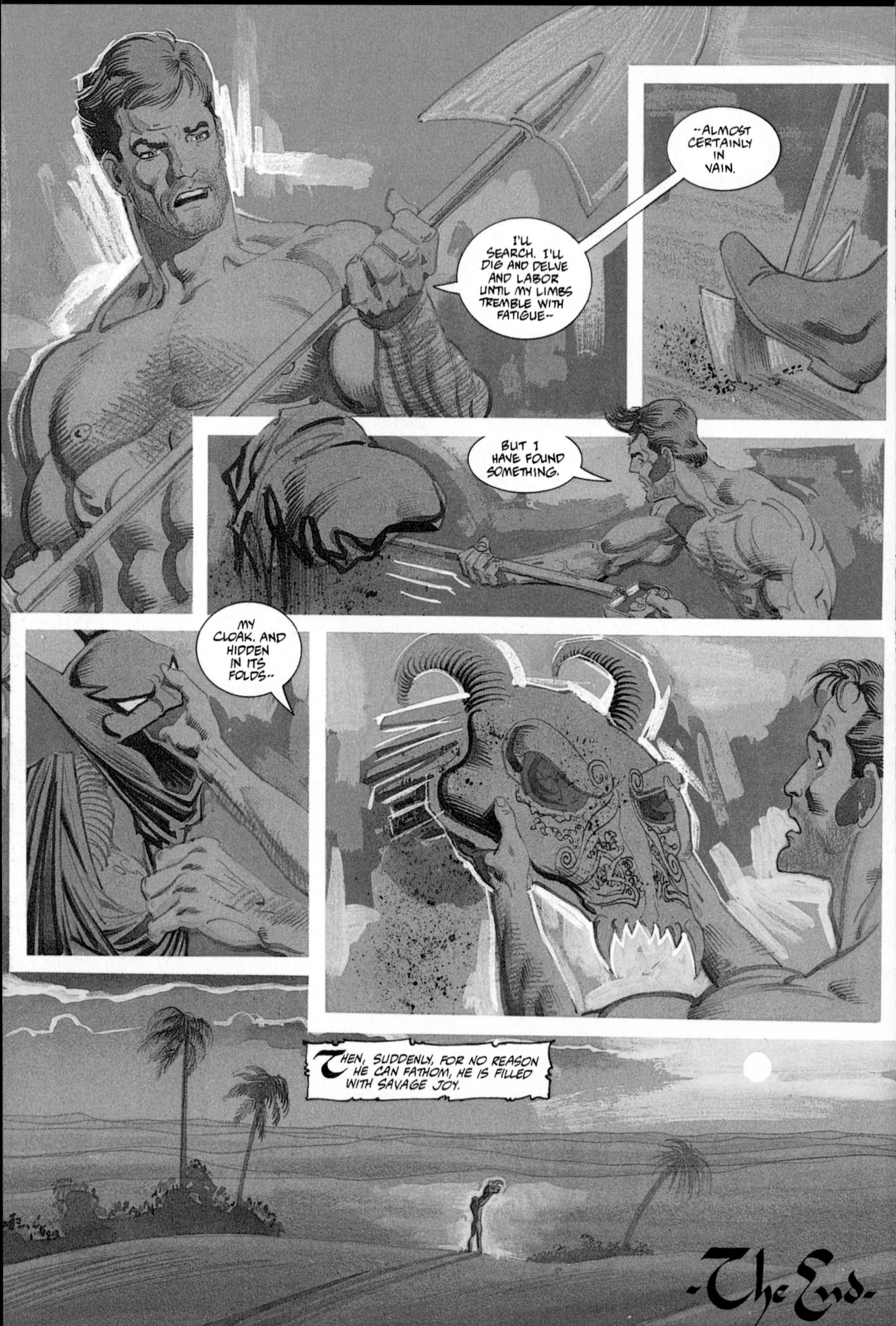
I'LL SEARCH. I'LL DIG AND DELVE AND LABOR UNTIL MY LIMBS TREMBLE WITH FATIGUE--
--ALMOST CERTAINLY IN VAIN.
BUT I HAVE FOUND SOMETHING.
MY CLOAK, AND HIDDEN IN ITS FOLDS--
THEN, SUDDENLY, FOR NO REASON HE CAN FATHOM, HE IS FILLED WITH SAVAGE JOY.
-The End-

BATMAN: SON OF THE DEMON reissue cover by Andy Kubert

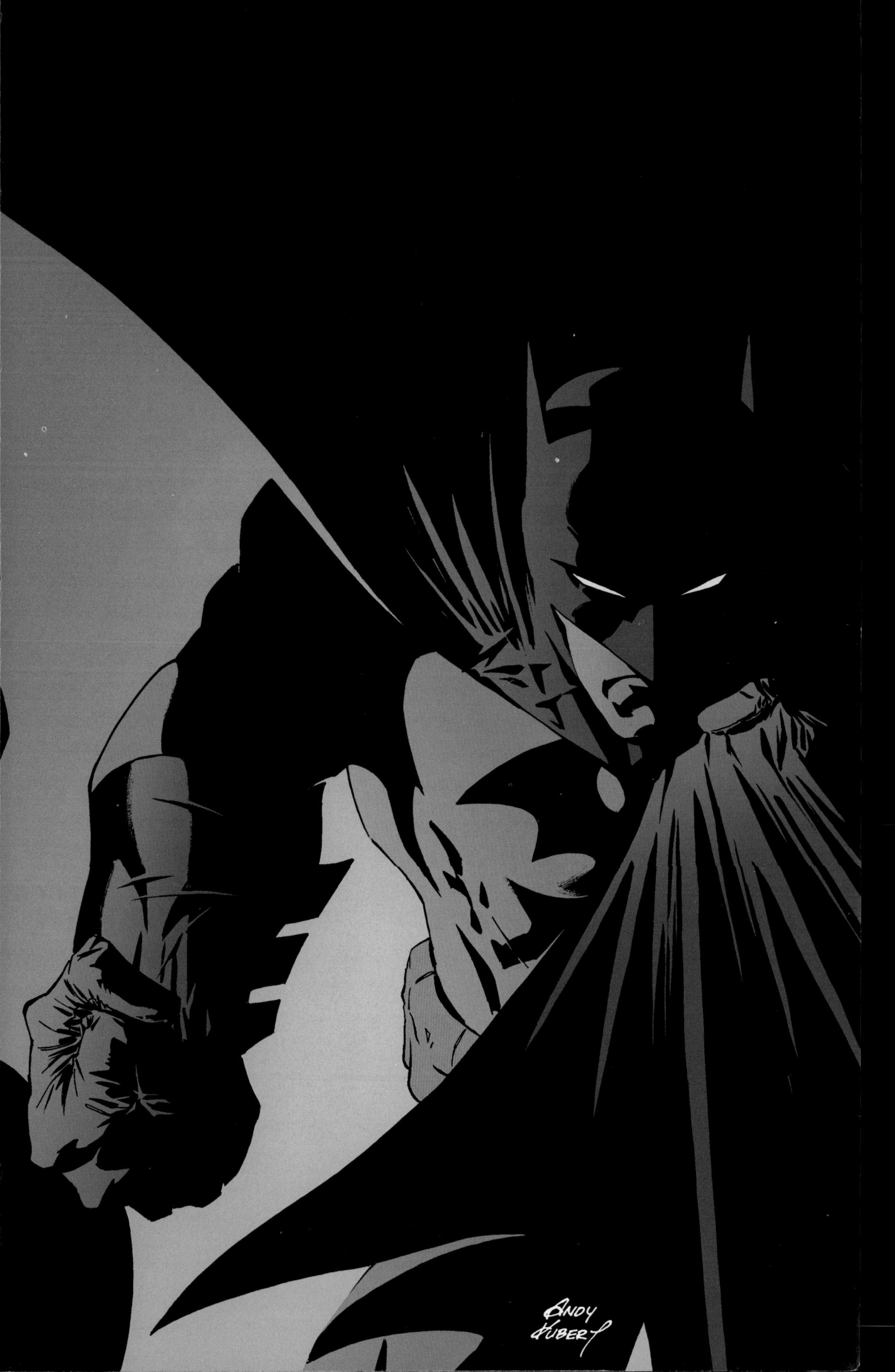
ANDY
KUBERT

BATMAN: SON OF THE DEMON paperback collection cover by Jerry Bingham

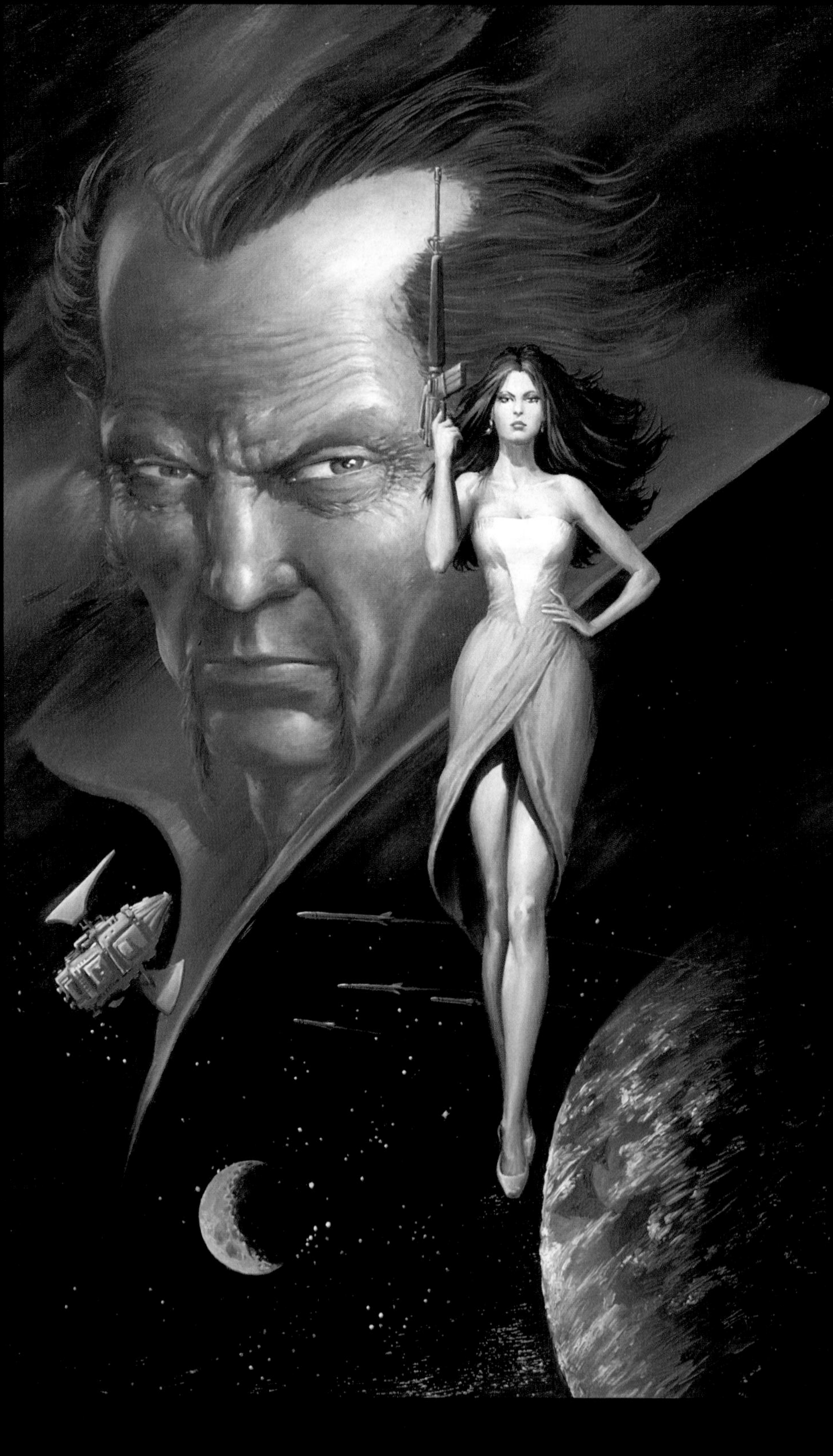

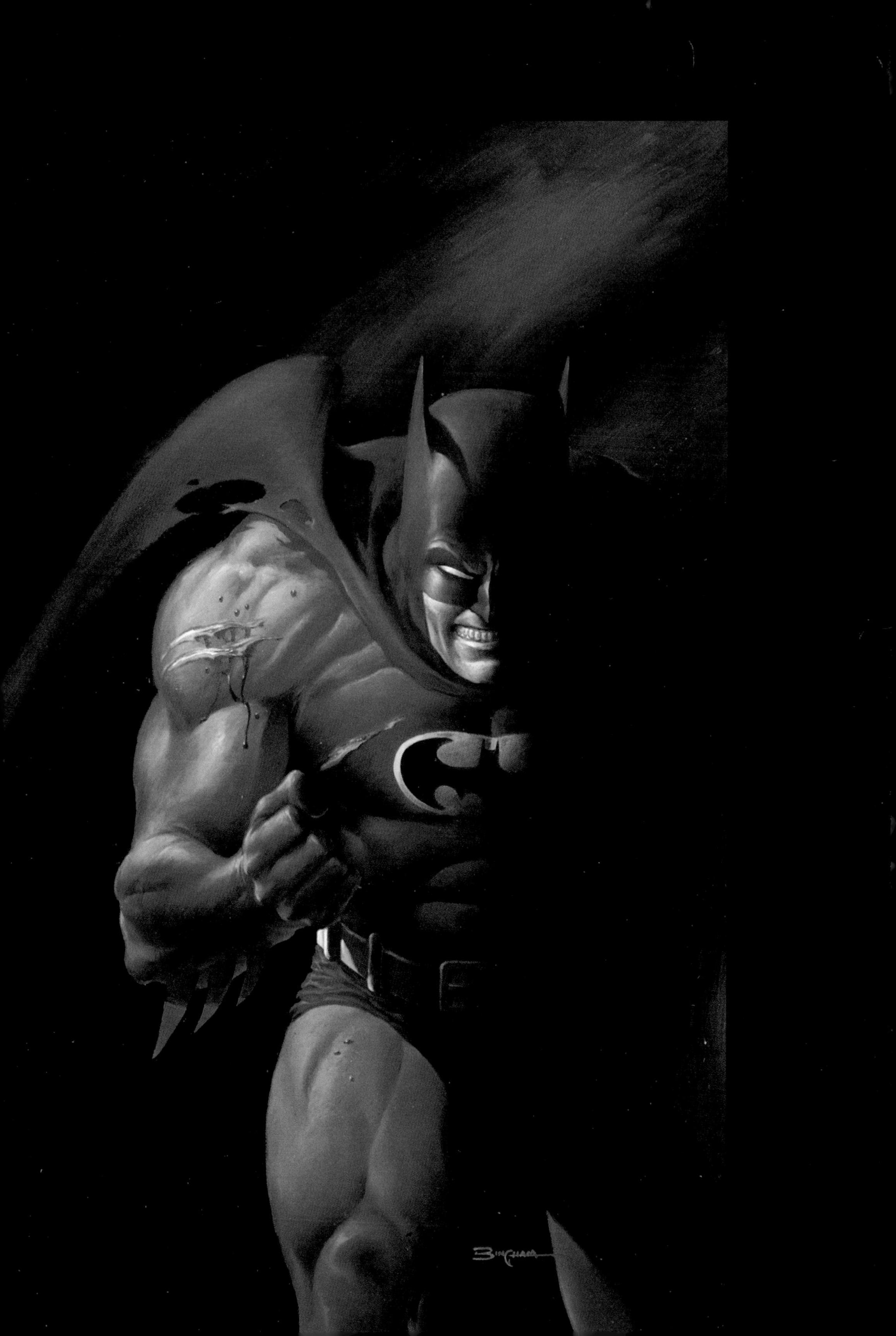

BATMAN: BIRTH OF THE DEMON hardcover collection cover by Norm Breyfogle

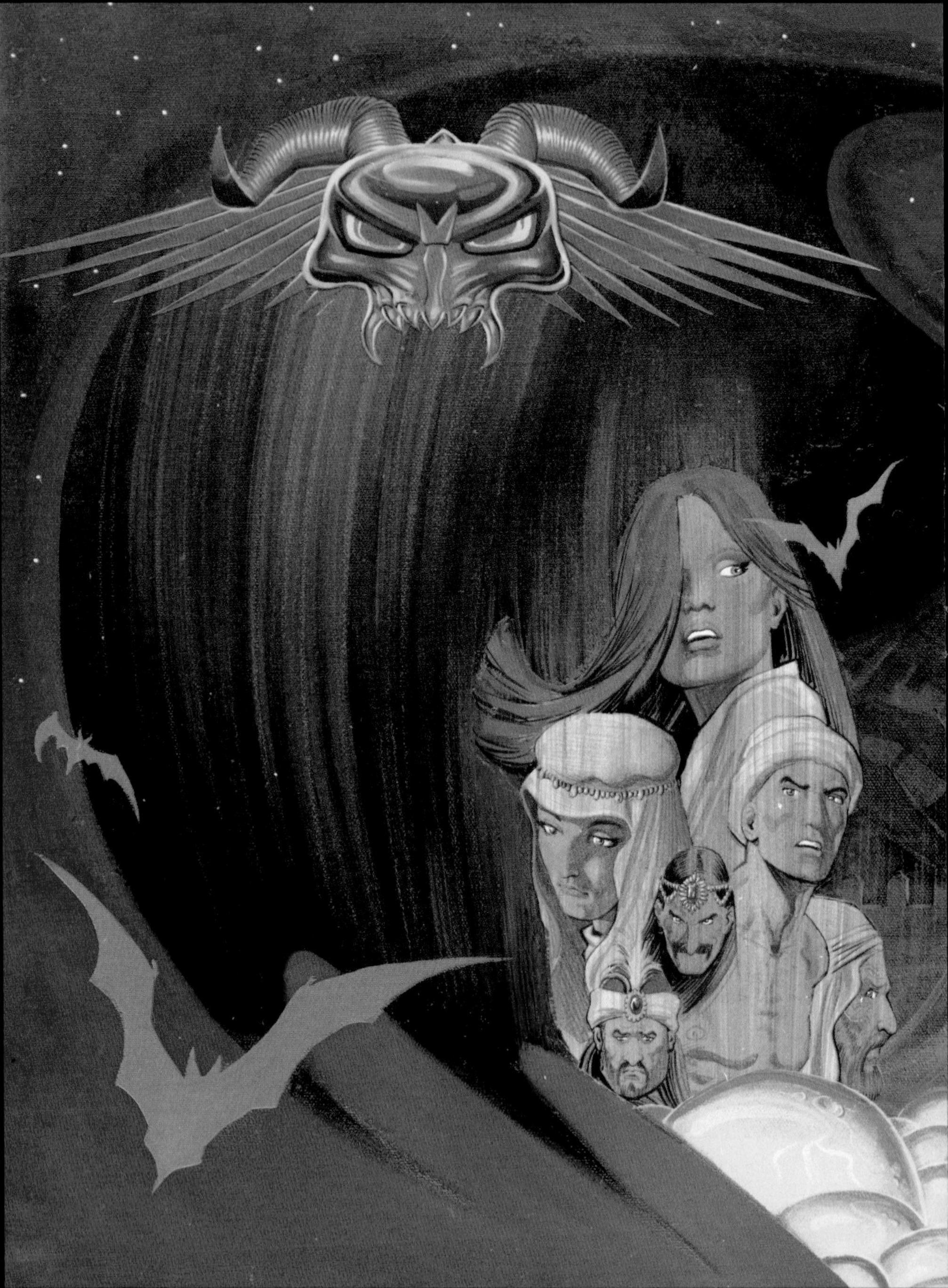

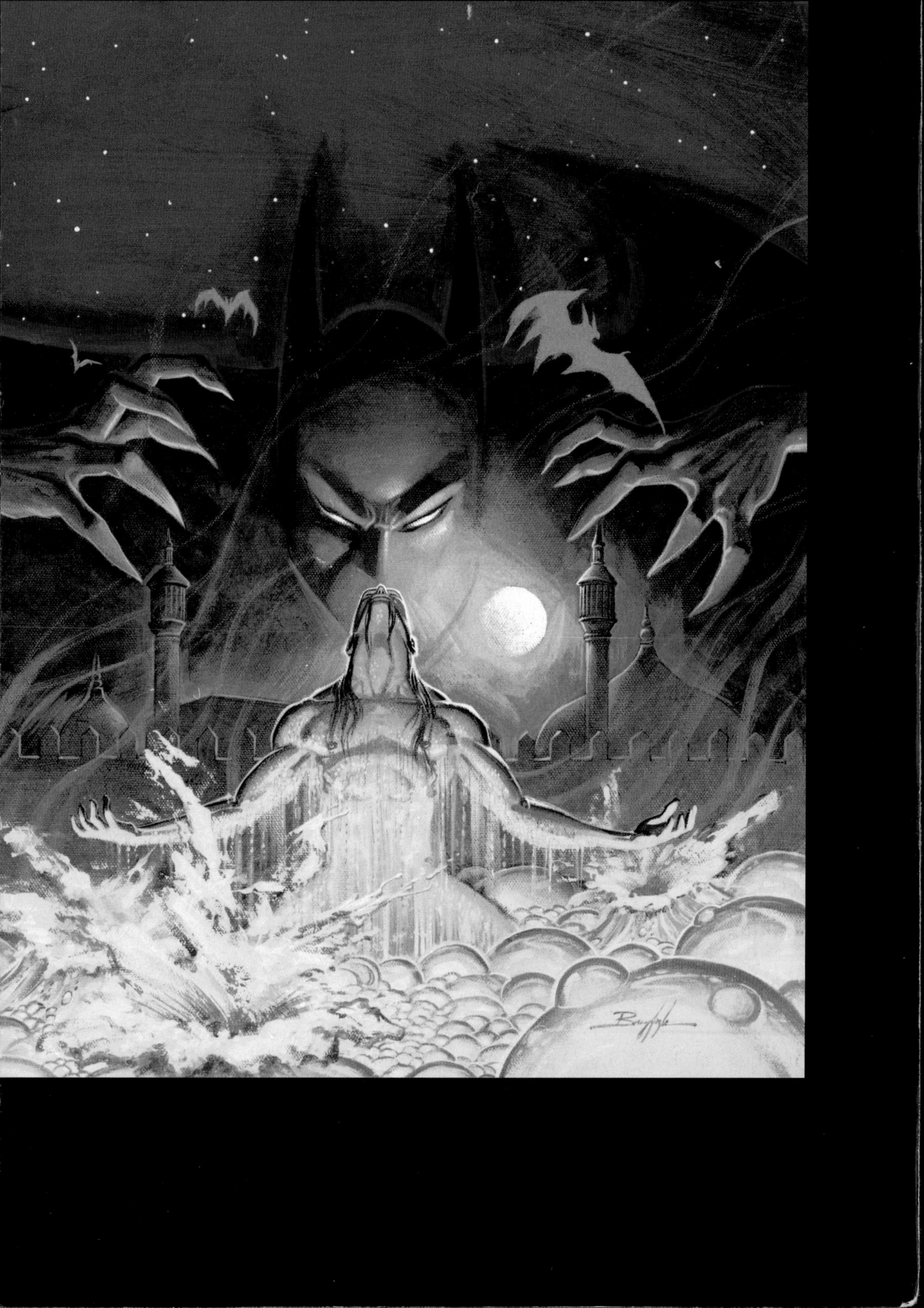

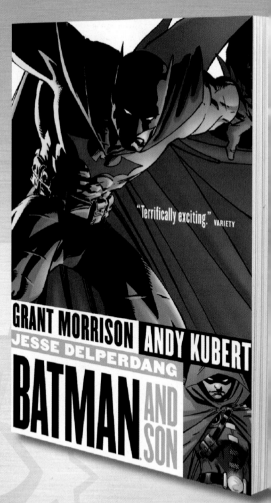